PRINCIPLES OF ECONOMICS AND THE CANADIAN ECONOMY

FOURTH EDITION

PRINCIPLES OF ECONOMICS
AND THE CANADIAN ECONOMY

FOURTH EDITION

Professor Ruben C. Bellan
Dean of Studies
St. John's College
University of Manitoba

McGRAW-HILL RYERSON LIMITED

Toronto   Montreal   New York   London   Sydney
Johannesburg   Mexico   Panama
Düsseldorf   Singapore   Rio De Janeiro   Kuala Lumpur   New Delhi

PRINCIPLES OF ECONOMICS AND THE CANADIAN ECONOMY
FOURTH EDITION

Library of Congress Catalog Card Number: 71-38532

ISBN 0-07-092925-4

2 3 4 5 6 7 8 9 10 D-72 1 0 9 8 7 6 5 4 3 2

Printed and bound in Canada

PREFACE TO THE FOURTH EDITION

Three basic convictions prompted the author to write this book: that the basic principles of Economics can readily be explained to any intelligent person; that Canadian students taking an introductory course in the subject should have a Canadian textbook; that a proper appreciation of modern economic institutions requires knowledge of their historical background.

Economic principles are developed rigorously, but by a watchful step-by-step procedure and in terms readily intelligible to a layman. The reader should be able to understand every portion of the book, without being dependent on an instructor for clarification. The teacher who uses the book as a text should not find it necessary to devote class time to "explaining" it. Rather, he should be free to spend his time on the elaboration of particular themes, on more advanced discussions of aspects in which he has a particular interest, and perhaps on the challenging of views here expressed.

Every student taking his first course in economic principles really ought to have a text book which has been written with particular reference to his own country. As a matter of course, the first instruction of Canadian students in the subject should include descriptions of the distinctive features of the Canadian economy, and of the economic programmes and economic policies of Canadian governments. The author feels that simply as a matter of national pride, examples adduced to illustrate theoretical principles should be drawn from Canadian experience; even though, in the matter dealt with, Canadian experience may be no different from that of other countries. Accordingly, the book contains descriptions of Canada's money supply, its banking system, its national income, its pattern of international trade, its trade union organizations, and the business cycles which it has experienced; Canadian government policy is described in respect to agricultural price supports, the restraint of monopoly, tariffs, trade union privileges, international assistance, and economic stabilization. Canadian students should be acquainted with some of the economic institutions and economic programmes of other countries, particularly those which, through their example or their operations, have a powerful influence on the Canadian economy. Accordingly, the book includes descriptions of British and American trade union legislation, of the U.S. banking system, and of U.S. legislation in respect to price supports and the control of monopoly.

The book contains rather more historical matter than is found in most text books on principles. The description of each current policy and existing institution is prefaced by a narrative relating how it originated, and how it came to attain its present state of development. The author feels that such historical background renders the subject much more interesting—dullness is no particular virtue in a text book—and contributes indispensably to real understanding: the roots of a problem or policy, and the foundations of an institution are of key importance. No student can properly appreciate why particular policies are in effect, and why particular institutions operate the way they do, without knowledge of the situations from which they emerged, and the events which shaped the course of their development.

The sequence in which the different topics are presented reflects the author's mild preference. So far as he is concerned, no topic has an overriding claim to prior treatment. The fact is that all branches of economics are so interrelated and interdependent that they should all be learned simultaneously. In beginning the course with any branch of the subject, the teacher is bound to be hampered by the fact that students are unacquainted with other branches. Since everything cannot be learned at once, it is necessary to settle for a sequence of topics which cannot be absolutely satisfactory. The author has presented the topics in the present order only because he feels somewhat less dissatisfied with this sequence than with the alternatives. Other teachers may prefer to present the topics in a different order; the book lends itself readily to alternative sequences.

The customary exonerations are in order. In the preparations of this edition, as with the three previous editions, the author benefited greatly from suggestions proffered by others; however, he alone must bear the responsibility for errors and deficiencies.

RUBEN C. BELLAN

To my Mother and Father

CONTENTS

PART ONE: INTRODUCTION

1

The Subject Matter
of Economics

WHAT IS ECONOMIC ACTIVITY?

Economic activity is simply the daily work of mankind, performed to acquire what mankind needs and wants. The 3,000 million human beings who inhabit the earth all need food, clothing and shelter to sustain life, and typically desire a host of extras in order to live comfortably and agreeably. By utilizing the earth's resources they are able to fulfil these needs and wants. The earth nourishes animals whose flesh can be eaten, and whose hides can be used for clothing. It yields up edible fruits, vegetables and grains, and plants which can be fashioned into clothing; it harbours minerals and supports forests which can be fabricated into buildings for man's shelter, and into an infinite diversity of other things for his use as well. This bounty of nature does not exist in convenient places, and in forms ready made to fit human needs and wants; it is raw, unformed, hidden in the bowels of the earth, in the depths of the seas; the profuse resources of nature must be laboriously drawn from where they occur, and painstakingly fabricated into forms suitable for use. Man's economic activity consists of the application of brains and energy to the raw possibilities offered by nature in order to obtain his needs and desires.

Every generation of mankind has necessarily engaged in economic activity, with the character of that activity reflecting the degree and quality of the prevailing civilization. The economic activity of primitive man was of the crudest and simplest sort; lacking the capacity to reason and to plan, he employed his brute energy in the most direct fashion to snatch from the earth's profusion the wherewithal of survival. Economic activity today is, by contrast, exceedingly complex. We follow highly intricate procedures to satisfy a vast and ever-widening array of desires. We have devised not only huge and complicated machines to do our bidding, but, in addition, complex agencies and institutions which contribute usefully toward the fulfilment of wants. We have organizations such as banks, insurance companies, mortgage companies, brokerage firms and supermarkets, each having been established because it renders economic efforts somehow more effective. In a modern country, few men apply themselves directly to nature as did our primitive forbears; instead, we apply our

3

efforts primarily to the machines and organizations which human ingenuity has devised. Thanks to their effectiveness, our productivity is enormously enhanced.

Two Definitions of Economics

As one famous definition states, ". . . Economics is a study of mankind in the ordinary business of life; it examines that part of individual and social action which is most closely connected with the attainment and with the use of the material requisites of well being."[1] Another widely quoted definition stresses the significance of the fact that the means of satisfying human wants are available only in limited quantities, so that when these means are employed to achieve some objectives, other objectives must necessarily be relinquished, i.e. we have the means to achieve some of our desires, but not all. Accordingly, Economics is considered to be in effect a study of the logic whereby we choose between alternative possible objectives. "Economics is the science which studies human behaviour as a relationship between ends and scarce means which have alternative uses."[2]

Economic Systems

To achieve the best possible results, any country must carry on its economic activities systematically. The efforts of millions of people must be effectively coordinated so that they produce the largest possible output. Care must be taken to ensure that goods are produced in the right proportions: even the richest country in the world possesses only limited quantities of human energy, natural resources, and capital equipment; if it devotes too much of its productive capacity to some things, inevitably it will have to produce less of other things than would have been desirable. When goods have been produced they must be divided up among the people in accordance with acceptable principles.

Different economic systems may be employed. A socialistic system involves complete control of production by government officials. They decide what is to be produced, by what means and in what quantities; they decide, too, how the product is to be distributed. A free enterprise system such as our own involves the control of production primarily by private firms and individuals. Private persons, each controlling some part of the country's productive power, decide what to produce and by what means; the product is distributed in accordance with private wealth and income.

We are not concerned here with the question of which system is "better".[3] Each has its strong and weak points; each has its advocates and opponents. Neither system exists in absolutely pure form: a limited degree of private enterprise exists

---

[1]Alfred Marshall, *Principles of Economics*, 8th ed. (London: 1930), p. 1.
[2]Lionel Robbins, *An Essay on the Nature and Significance of Economic Science.* (London, 1935), p. 16.
[3]For a comparison of economic systems, see chapter 31.

in socialistic countries; a substantial amount of production is socialistically controlled in free enterprise countries. Whichever system is employed, it may be operated poorly, yielding disappointing results. For lack of proper coordination, many people in a country may be idle or may work at cross purposes, so that total output is less than it might have been. Because of errors in judgment on the part of the people in charge, too much may be produced of some things and too little of others. The country's output may be unfairly distributed, with some people getting too much and others too little.

The Role of the Economist

The responsibility of the economist is to learn how the economic system of his country is supposed to operate, and to advise the authorities so that they may administer it most effectively. If problems and difficulties arise, the economist should suggest solutions. His role is analogous to that of the doctor who advises people what they must do to keep healthy and, if they fall sick, tells them what to do in order to get well again. To be able to give such advice the doctor must possess several types of knowledge: he must know the normal operation of the human body; he must be familiar with possible remedies for different ailments; he must be aware of the effects produced by each remedy. In the same way the economist must understand the normal operation of his country's economic system; he must be familiar with remedies for problems which may arise; he must know the various consequences likely to be produced by remedial measures.

How does the economist acquire the necessary knowledge of the characteristics and limitations of an economic society, and consequently of the principles according to which economic activity ought to be directed? Such knowledge is acquired by observation and logical deduction based upon that observation. The economist observes men's economic activities and the reactions of the environment upon which these actions are performed. Through repeated observations, he becomes aware of regular tendencies, of typical behaviour and reaction patterns. Mere observation of phenomena is not enough, however; through observation we may learn what events have occurred, but not *why* they occurred. No event shouts out to us the reason for its occurrence. But the knowledge of *why* events take place is absolutely indispensable to a proper understanding of them, and to the useful employment of that understanding. Knowing cause-effect relationships enables us to forestall the occurrence of any event which is unfavourable, or to arrange its recurrence if it is favourable. Such knowledge is truly power, and the economist seeks to acquire it.

Economics Contrasted with the Physical Sciences

How does the economist derive explanations for the phenomena which he observes? The task would be easy if each type of event had a single cause, and if this cause always occurred in isolation, each time being followed by the same result. Cause-effect relationships would be absolutely clear-cut; each time an event occurred, its cause would be obvious and unmistakable. Unfortunately, the causation of many economic phenomena is rarely clear and unambiguous. More often, an event occurs after a great many preceding developments; of these, one alone is perhaps the cause, while the others merely happened at the same time, with their occurrence being in no way responsible for the following event. In such a case, how can it be established which occurrence was the cause and which were merely coincidental?

If, for instance, an economic recession develops in Canada and we seek its cause, we might find half a dozen possible causes. In examining the general situation out of which the recession emerged, we might find that just before the recession developed, exports had fallen, that the nation's banks had tightened up on credit, that business men had shown signs of pessimism, that consumers had reduced their purchases, that the government had reduced its spending, that population had begun to decline, and that attractive investment opportunities had become fewer. How can the economist ascertain which one (or more) of these factors was the responsible cause of the recession, and which factors, while occurring at the same time, were not of material significance?

In dealing with problems of this sort, the economist labours under severe handicaps; physical scientists, such as chemists and physicists, are much more fortunate. They deal with relatively simple phenomena, many of which can be artificially induced and analyzed in a laboratory under controlled conditions. The economist is quite unable to carry out controlled experiments comparable to those upon which research in the physical sciences so heavily depends. The phenomena which the economist studies are the activities of millions of human beings carried out in an infinitely complex environment. The assured uniformities of the physical sciences are totally absent. While one batch of a chemical may be relied upon to be absolutely identical with another batch, and one piece of rock may have exactly the same composition as another piece of rock, each human being is different from every other human being. Each has a unique physical and mental endowment; each has a particular reaction pattern, a particular set of motivations and scale of values. Substantial similarities are evident among the members of large groups of individuals, but there are never the absolute uniformities which characterize the objects of research in the physical sciences.

The activities of these millions of multi-faceted individuals are carried on within an infinitely complicated, ever-changing environment. The earth, from which man obtains the means of satisfying his needs and wants, is a creation of infinite variety and mood; the institutions which man has contrived, and through which he channels his efforts, are hardly less varied, while ever-new forms and varieties are being evolved. The situations which the economist studies are characterized by a veritable infinity of elements; the cause of each phenomenon which he studies must be sought from among an infinite number of possible causes. This boundless complexity rules out the possibility of employing the experimental method of the physical scientist, in which one element is varied while all others are kept constant. An infinite number of elements cannot be controlled; furthermore, the human beings in the situation would not willingly, and in any case could not, remain absolutely constant in all respects, while the scientist varied one element in a situation at a time in order to ascertain definitively the effect of each variation.

The Derivation of Economic Theories

To derive explanations for the infinitely complicated phenomena which he studies, the economist adopts a strategem. He devises in his mind a highly simplified *model* of the situation which he desires to analyze. While the actual situation has an infinity of elements, the economist's observations will have indicated to him that they are not all of equal importance or relevance. The economist abstracts only the most important elements, and fabricates his model from them alone. His model represents reality in the same way that the map of a country represents its main outlines, without including features and details which are of secondary significance. There is this difference however; a map exists on paper, while the economist's model of a real situation exists only in his mind.

Employing a methodology analogous to that of the physical scientist in a controlled experiment, the economist proceeds to analyze the behaviour of his model. Since the model is structurally simple, constructed from only a few elements, he is capable of envisioning it clearly and fully in his mind. Keeping all others constant, he varies one of its elements; drawing on experience, acquired knowledge and logical deduction, he visualizes how the model would react to this specific variation of this particular element. He varies the element in all possible ways, always keeping the others rigorously constant, and visualizing the specific effect of each such variation. He varies each element in turn, each time keeping all others constant, and each time visualizing how the model would react. From such a series of experiments, conducted entirely in his mind, he learns how the model reacts to all possible variations in each of its constituent elements. He learns what cause-effect relationships are present in the model, or, in other words, he determines the principles according to which the model operates.

The model has been closely patterned after a real situation, having been constructed from the leading elements of that situation. It may be reasonably inferred, therefore, that the working principles which have been ascertained in the model closely resemble the working principles of the real situation after which it is patterned, and that any discrepancies will be minor, since the model differs from reality only in matters of detail. These working principles which the economist has derived from his analysis of the model constitute a hypothesis or *theory* which he now offers as an explanation for the real situation. His method in deriving this theory is roughly analogous to that of the ship-builder who constructs a scale model of any new vessel he proposes to build and, in a testing pool, subjects this model to scale replicas of the storms and tides the real vessel is likely to encounter; the reactions of the model suggest to him how the real vessel will perform under actual operating conditions.

In attempting to apply to the real world the theory he has derived from his analysis of the model, the economist may suffer a setback. It may become perfectly obvious that the theory is wrong, in the sense that it fails to provide a credible explanation for the real phenomenon. The reason for this failure may be two-fold. The model-builder may have failed to include in the model highly important characteristics of the real world; and for this reason it may operate differently from the reality which it is supposed to represent, just as a map may be misleading in that it fails to represent highly important features of a country's terrain. Secondly, while the model may adequately correspond to reality, the analysis performed upon it by the economist may be faulty. He reached his conclusions through logical deduction and the application of ideas derived from experience; but his logic may have been faulty, his experiences may have been misleading. Because his model has been improperly constructed, or because he has wrongly interpreted it, the theory which he derives from his analysis of the model may fail to provide a credible explanation of reality.

Such a failure is a reverse but not a disaster. Once he has ascertained that his theory is unsatisfactory, the true scientist proceeds to devise another one, by examining the possibilities that his model may operate differently from what he had first supposed, or by constructing a different model. The indefatigable scientist will continue to vary his model and ascertain all possible interpretations of each model until finally he attains a theory which, when applied to the real world, provides a demonstrably valid explanation. With this achievement he has attained his objective—the explanation of why in the real world a particular event or set of events tends to occur.

Procedures such as the foregoing are indispensable if we are to derive explanations for the economic phenomena that we observe in the world. If we are to learn why certain types of events occur, we must suggest possible explanations, testing the validity of each one suggested, until finally one of the hypotheses satisfies all our tests and consequently is recognized as the valid explanation. It should be emphasized that a theory must be considered only as a *possible* explanation, until it is proven or disproven by testing. All too often, unfortunately, individuals advance theories to explain phenomena and, without adequate testing, claim that these theories constitute valid explanations. When subsequently these theories prove to be wrong, many people express doubts about the usefulness of all theorizing. It is not the use but the misuse of the theoretical method which has produced this result. If we are to increase our knowledge of the world, we *must* derive theories; if we do not devise theories and test them, then we do not have even the possibility of achieving an explanation. The fact that some of the suggested explanations (theories) prove to be wrong, should not deter us from devising and testing fresh ones. So long as we keep doing this, we have the possibility of achieving an explanation for the phenomenon we are studying; once we stop theorizing, then we do not have even the possibility of achieving the explanation we seek.

The Principles of Economics

The phrase "Principles of Economics" refers to an aggregation of theories, each being put forward as an explanation of some aspect of economic activity. Thus, there have been developed theories of how prices are determined, of how banking systems operate, of why international trade takes place. Each theory has been developed by the method previously described: the economist devised in his mind a model of the real world activity which he wished to explain, and through logical deduction ascertained the working principles of that model. The theory which he advanced to explain the real world activity was essentially his interpretation of how the model worked. In regard to some economic phenomena, different theories are believed by different economists today; the divergence springs from the fact that they do not construct their models in the same way, or do not uniformly interpret the same model. Very likely such differences will always exist. There is no absolutely conclusive test whereby to assess the validity of economic theories; adherents to one theory may continue to dispute conflicting theories advanced by others. For a great many aspects of economic activity, however, a single theory has come to be accepted generally as *the* explanation. The theoretical principles presented in this text are mostly in this category, being essentially the same as those contained in a score of textbooks used on this continent.

These theories have evolved from nearly two centuries of observation and logical deduction carried on by successive generations of economists. Scotland's Adam Smith published the first modern type of treatise on economics in 1776; since that time there has been an unbroken succession of economists, in other countries as well as in Great Britain, who, like Adam Smith, studied the economic phenomena of their time and advanced explanatory hypotheses. The aggregate of economic theories has been continuously enlarged by fresh contributions; many theories have been revised or altogether discarded in the course of time as a later generation of economists, possessing a larger fund of knowledge and experience, realized the inadequacy or error of views held by their forbears. The sweeping changes which have occurred in the character of economic activity during the past two centuries have made necessary explanations for new phenomena and new problems.

It is a reasonable presumption that the economic theories held today will not prove to be final for all time; very likely they will be modified by future generations which will have the benefit of further economic development as well as additional knowledge and experience. However, although the body of economic ideas handed down over the past two centuries has been repeatedly revised and enlarged, a substantial portion has remained intact through time; some theories which were first propounded long ago are still demonstrably true. And so, just as it may be taken for granted that the textbooks of a generation hence will differ substantially from those presently in use, it may be presumed that in a good many respects they will be similar as well.

SCOPE OF THE BOOK

Each of the eight parts into which this book is divided deals with a major area of economic inquiry. The relevant economic principles are explained; the main features of the institutions which are involved are described. A good deal of historical background is provided, and special reference is made to the Canadian economy.

Part I describes the various forms which business establishments may take in a modern society.

Part II deals with the forces which determine the prices of individual goods and the various ways in which governments interfere with these forces.

Part III analyzes the logic according to which an individual firm makes its decisions in respect to selling price and output. The problem of monopoly is described, together with the measures adopted by the governments of Canada and the United States to deal with it.

Part IV examines the principles which determine the incomes different people earn, be they worker, business man, capitalist, or landlord. A brief history is given of the trade union movement in Great Britain, the United States, and Canada. The functioning of modern trade unions is described.

Part V shows why international trade is desirable, explains how it is financed, and describes the deliberately erected barriers which hinder trade.

Part VI deals with the expenditures and revenues of governments, with special reference to public finance in Canada.

Par VII describes the nature of money, the implication of changes in the money supply, and explains how the operations of our banking system affect the money supply.

Part VIII describes the factors which determine the size of a nation's total output in any year, and thus the real income of its people. The reasons for cyclical fluctuation are examined, along with measures that may be applied to prevent fluctuation. Consideration is given to the factors which determine the geographical location of a nation's enterprises. The sources of economic progress are reviewed and the prospects of future progress are considered. The final chapter describes how the communist system came to be introduced in Russia, how it operates, and how it compares with capitalism.

SUMMARY

Economic activity consists of the daily work of mankind, performed in order to acquire the means of satisfying human wants and needs. This work must be performed, since these means of satisfying wants are not freely available to men, without effort on their part.

The character of economic activity at any time reflects the current state of men's knowledge and the character of their wants.

The task of the economist is to ascertain how people decide what economic goals to strive for, and how they organize their activities to attain these goals. The economist seeks to discern cause-effect relationships in phenomena of an economic character; employing that knowledge, he can suggest how men ought to organize their economic efforts in order to achieve a maximum of the output which they desire.

To discover why things happen the way they do, the economist constructs "models" of the phenomena he wishes to explain; he carries out, in his mind, controlled experiments wherein he ascertains the working principles of these models. He suggests that the principles which he has ascertained for a model apply also to the real world situation upon which the model was patterned.

A text on principles of economics includes a number of theories relating to various aspects of man's economic activity. Each theory has been formulated to explain a particular type of phenomenon.

A modern text represents the current state of a stream of thought which is two centuries old and which has been continuously modified and enlarged by successive generations of economists.

FOR REVIEW AND DISCUSSION

1. The character of economic activity changes through time; its basic objectives do not. Explain.
2. If all goods were always available in unlimited quantity and without any effort on man's part, there would be no need for economics or economists. Why?
3. The hard-headed individual who says "Give me facts, not theories," is somewhat thick-headed as well. Do you agree?
4. Training in economic analysis should be helpful in fields beyond the purely economic. Why?
5. Distinguish between the work of the engineer and that of the economist.
6. Define: capitalism, communism, socialism.

2

The Organization
of Business
Enterprise

THE DAILY MIRACLE

Regularly Canada's millions of housewives proceed to the nation's stores to buy food and clothing for their families. Each day their children attend the nation's public schools. Each night families relax and rest in the privacy of their homes. What miracle provides the food and clothing they buy, the schools their children attend, the homes they live in? By what miracle does it come about, to take two specific instances, that loaves of bread are piled on grocery shelves each day and shirts are heaped on haberdashers' counters, awaiting customers' purchases?

By no miracle at all really; those goods are there, available for housewives to buy, because a great many people in Canada previously applied a wide variety of efforts. The bread is there because farmers grew grain, because railways carried the grain to flour mills, because flour mills ground the grain into flour, because bakeries baked the flour into bread. The shirts are on haberdashers' counters because importers brought raw cotton into Canada, because textile mills spun the cotton into yarn and wove the yarn into cloth, because factories converted the cloth into shirts. Everything else which the people of Canada buy and use is produced through a similar combination of efforts, with a great variety of concerns each contributing some necessary function.

Private Initiative

Each of these business organizations consists of people, working in some kind of plant, using machinery and materials, under the direction of a manager. Who created these different organizations, each to perform its indispensable services, so that the people of Canada could have their food, their clothing, their homes, their education, their entertainment? Who provided the money required to purchase the plant, equipment and materials which these organizations required? Who selected their managers? How were their workers recruited, by what inducements or compulsions?

In Canada, these productive organizations are established primarily through private effort and initiative. Ordinary citizens furnish the funds needed to acquire the plant, equipment and materials necessary for most enterprises; those who supply

12

the funds generally exercise the control. Other people supply their labour, without any compulsion exercised upon them to do so. The motive of all is the same, to receive monetary reward. Those who supply property or money receive rent, interest or dividends; those who are in charge receive profits; those who supply labour receive wages or salaries. Where private initiative fails to provide some necessary service, the government steps in and establishes an organization which will provide it.

Anyone in the country who earns income receives it as reward for his particular contribution to production. He must have worked for, or directed, or supplied capital to, some private or public enterprise. That enterprise would contribute, in one way or another, to the production of the multitude of goods and services which the Canadian people need and want. The income which the individual receives for his efforts enables him to purchase his share of the total of goods and services produced.

In this chapter we shall examine the various ways in which productive establishments may be organized. We shall be concerned most particularly with these key aspects of their organization: from whom and upon what conditions they *obtain their capital*; who *exercises control* and upon what terms. Our description is of practice in Canada, but it would not be materially different for any other country with a free enterprise economy similar to our own.

THE PROPRIETORSHIP

The Enterprise of One Individual

A single individual may establish and direct his own business organization to produce some commodity, or to provide some service. In law, his establishment would be referred to as a *proprietorship*. He needs no one's permission;[1] if he sees the opportunity of gaining a reward for himself by setting up his own business concern, he is perfectly free to do so. Out of his own savings and borrowings he himself provides the money needed to launch the enterprise. He is in full charge; he decides what, where, how to produce, and where, how, at what price to sell. He receives as personal income whatever profit the enterprise yields. But he carries full responsibility. Whatever losses the enterprise suffers he must make good: he can be required to hand over, to satisfy creditors, even property which he owns outside of his business venture.

Limitations

The proprietorship form of business organization has its limitations, and its advantages. Its capital is likely to be small: only the savings and borrowings of a single

[1]This statement must be qualified. Some industries are considered to be of special public concern and are therefore subject to special controls by governments. Any one who wishes to set up a business concern in such an industry accordingly requires specific government authorization e.g., special licences are required to establish breweries or distilleries, and to operate taverns, cocktail bars and cabarets. This authorization is required no matter what *form* a business organization has, i.e. whether it is a proprietorship, partnership, corporation or cooperative.

person have been invested. If the individual is a Rockefeller, of course, the fact that he is the sole source of capital is not a serious limitation. But Rockefellers are few and the overwhelming majority of proprietorships are small concerns. Being generally confined to small scale operations, proprietorships cannot usually operate in those fields where efficient and profitable production can be achieved only with the use of large staffs and massive and costly equipment. In a good many cases a proprietorship is too small even to employ paid help; the owner is obliged to perform a variety of jobs himself. For some of these he may be ill-suited, and the whole enterprise suffers accordingly. A small enterprise may also require the owner's continuous presence. Prolonged absence on his part, such as might be caused by illness, may prove to be disastrous.

Financial Risks

Severe financial hazards beset the proprietorship. The owner, as we have seen, is fully responsible for all its losses, and may therefore lose property over and above what he actually invested in the business. If he should decide to leave the business, he may find it impossible to recover his investment. He must find someone who can raise the capital involved, and possesses as well the willingness and ability to perform the various jobs which the owner must handle himself. Persons who possess all these qualities in combination may be extremely rare. If he does materialize, such a person may drive a hard bargain. Knowing that the owner who wishes to give up his business cannot sell out on better terms to any one else, he may offer a good deal less than it is worth to him. If the owner dies, his heirs may encounter the same problem. They may find it impossible to realize the full value of their heritage, if it consists of a business establishment which depended for its success upon the personality and ability of one particular man.

Merits

The proprietorship has its place. Where the total market for a product is small, large scale methods of production are out of the question and the little business establishment is not at all handicapped because of its size. The small, independent firm competes well, too, in industries whose operations are non-routine in character so that judgment must constantly be exercised. The owner of a firm must make the judgments himself or closely supervise hired employees who make them. The firm cannot normally be very large because one person is capable of making only a limited number of well considered judgments in a given space of time or can effectively supervise only a limited number of employees who are making judgments. The work of farmers and professional people is of this non-routine character; so is repair work of any kind and the manufacture of style goods. In such industries the success of the individual firm will depend primarily on the personality, judgment and ability of the person in charge, the amount of capital available being of secondary significance; here the proprietorship is likely to be the dominant form of business organization.[2]

THE PARTNERSHIP

Various Forms

As has been the case since time immemorial, two or more persons may join together to establish and administer a single enterprise. The terms of their partnership will be laid down in an oral or written agreement. This agreement will specify what capital is to be subscribed by each partner, what authority each is to exercise in the enterprise, what share of its profit each is to receive. There is no standard formula; every partnership makes its own arrangements. In some cases partners share equally in the profits, in others unequally. A partner may subscribe capital but not participate in the management,[3] or he may participate in the management but not subscribe to the capital. During the Middle Ages partnerships became common particularly in operations which maintained branches in different localities. For example, mercantile and banking houses which did business in several cities would have a partner in charge of each branch; oftentimes the partners would be members of the same family. In a good many cases a family partnership would come into being when a father who had built up a large firm, passed it on to his several children, to be managed jointly by them.

Advantages

As compared to the proprietorship, the partnership has important advantages. Because it has raised funds from more than one person, its capital is likely to be larger; it is likely, therefore, to be able to undertake operations on a larger scale. Each of the partners may be able to handle very well one aspect of the firm's operations. The enterprise is therefore more efficiently conducted than it would be if one person handled everything, including those matters for which he was poorly qualified. Decisions reached through a conference of partners may be a good deal wiser than decisions made by a single individual. Finally, each member of a partnership enjoys an important measure of security: if ever he is temporarily incapacitated, the enterprise will still continue, managed by the other partners. When he recovers, he can

---

[2]The progress of technology may of course bring reversals. Improvements in the quality and effectiveness of machinery and equipment may weight the scales in favour of large scale operations which extensively employ machinery and equipment. Such a development appears to be under way in agriculture, where large farms are becoming fairly common, and in the practice of medicine, where large clinics are growing in number. On the other hand technological advance may favour small scale firms, e.g., the development of the electric motor and the gas engine enabled small firms to operate power equipment; previously, when engines were driven by steam they could be used only in large plants, for only large plants could maintain the required steam-generating capacity.

[3]In this case he would be called a "sleeping" or "silent" partner.

return to a still flourishing concern. In a proprietorship, on the other hand, a temporary absence of the owner may result in permanent and perhaps fatal harm to the enterprise.

Disadvantages

In important respects, a partnership is inferior to the one-man concern. It is bedevilled by unique managerial problems. The partners may not be able to agree; with each enjoying equal authority, disagreement among them may render it impossible to carry out any policy at all. Any one partner is empowered to act on behalf of the full partnership; the other partners may find themselves obligated by a commitment into which he entered without their knowledge or consent.[4]

The member of a partnership is exposed to even greater financial hazard than is the owner of a proprietorship. Each member of a partnership is legally liable for the debts of the entire enterprise.[5] One partner may find himself obligated to make good, out of his own personal property, the losses sustained by the partnership as a whole.[6] Furthermore, a partner who would like to withdraw his investment is dependent on the goodwill of his partners. He can sell his interest only to them or to some outside party who is acceptable to them. He must either accept their terms, or find someone who combines the qualities of being able to raise the necessary sum to buy him out, being willing to pay it, and being acceptable to the other partners.

Finally, some of the weaknesses of the proprietorship beset the partnership as well. Its capital has been subscribed by only a very small number of people.[7] While probably larger than it would be if just one person were involved, its capital is still likely therefore to be relatively small, inadequate to permit really large scale operations. Because it is composed of specified persons, a partnership is automatically dissolved when one member departs or dies. Being therefore liable to abrupt termina-

---

[4]A partner cannot, however, commit his fellows to an undertaking which lies beyond the purposes for which the partnership was formed. e.g. If three men form a partnership to manufacture shoes, any one can commit the firm in regard to the purchase of leather from a tannery; no one partner can however commit the firm, without consent of the others, to the purchase of a movie theatre.

[5]Under Canadian law a person who contributes capital to a partnership but does not participate in its management, may have the status of "limited partner". In such case he cannot be held liable for the debts of the partnership and can, at most, lose the capital he has subscribed. The terms of a limited partnership agreement must be recorded in a written agreement which is filed in a public office.

[6]Sir Walter Scott, the great nineteenth century poet and novelist, suffered such a fate as a result of becoming a partner in an Edinburgh publishing house. The firm failed in 1825, owing its creditors a total of £130,000. The other partners declared themselves unable to pay, leaving the entire sum as Scott's personal liability. For the rest of his life he wrote prodigiously to earn money with which to pay off this gigantic debt, and did manage to pay nearly £40,000 over to the creditors before he died.

[7]In some provinces the number of partners in any enterprise is limited by statute. Thus in Newfoundland no firm may have more than 10 partners; in Saskatchewan and Alberta no more than 20.

tion at any time, it is an unsuitable organization for carrying on any enterprise which requires the acquisition of extensive and durable buildings and equipment. A dissolution of the partnership, which could occur at any time, might render it necessary to dispose quickly of its property, possibly at considerable loss.

THE CORPORATION

Origins—The Early Joint Stock Companies

The limitations of the proprietorship and the partnership made necessary, as early as the 16th century, the development of a new form of business organization. Economic activity had quickened in Western Europe following the Renaissance, the discovery of America and the discovery of all-water routes to the Far East. A host of new economic opportunities had appeared, and ambitious men reached for them eagerly. But many of the dazzling opportunities could be exploited only by very large-scale undertakings, and the risk involved was great. Trading voyages to distant lands, ventures into mining, banking, manufacturing, insurance, all offered the possibility of huge returns on investment, together with the possibility of no returns whatsoever and investments entirely lost. It was difficult to raise from among just a few people the capital required for such undertakings. A few individuals could not provide the immense sum needed to establish a bank or insurance company or to build a turnpike. Even if they could, they would be exposing themselves to very great risk; each man would be commiting a very large sum to a single, uncertain venture.

Enterprising promoters accordingly organized joint-stock companies to carry out large-scale, risky undertakings, and invited the public to subscribe to the capital through the purchase of *stock*, with stockholders receiving returns according to the success of the enterprise. Each stock was of relatively small value and a person could buy as many as he liked, investing as much as he cared to in any particular company. Because stocks could be sold to a great many people, a huge capital could be accumulated. Because each individual investor was able to invest only a small sum if he wished, he could avoid the hazard of a large investment in a single risky enterprise.

Early Stock Market Crashes

The handsome returns yielded by some of the early joint-stock companies induced great enthusiasm. Promoters organized joint-stock companies to carry on enterprises of practically every description, selling the stock readily to a receptive public. Thousands of persons who possessed some capital but were unable or disinclined to establish therewith a business of their own, eagerly bought stock in the new ventures. Stocks were readily transferable; a purchaser could rely on getting his money back if he wished, by selling his stock to some other eager investor. Quickening public interest and demand caused the prices of stocks to rise; rising prices brought on feverish speculations which culminated in precipitous crashes in both France and England in the year 1720.[8] Stock values collapsed, bringing severe losses to thousands of unfortunate investors.

Restrictive Legislation

The British government passed the Bubble Act in 1720, which required the would-be promoters of any joint-stock venture to obtain a charter, the charter to be granted only by Parliament in response to a petition. The procedure laid down to obtain a charter was costly, tedious and liable to mishap on political grounds; so long as this legislation was in effect, the number of joint-stock companies grew only slowly. In France, similar legislation was introduced, with similar effect.

Incorporation Made Easy

During the course of the nineteenth century, however, governments everywhere eased their restrictions on the formation of joint-stock companies. General incorporation laws were introduced which authorized public officials to issue charters, eliminating the cost and hazard of petitions to Parliament. In Canada today the promoters of a joint-stock company simply apply for a charter to a government department.[9] With their application they file a statement which describes the purpose for which the company is being established, how it will be financed, how control over it will be exercised, and other relevant data. Government officials examine this statement and, if its proposals do not contravene the law in any way, will issue the desired charter. Once they have the charter, the promoters can proceed to sell stock to the public.

Legal Privileges of Corporations

A chartered company has a legal personality; it has all the legal rights, privileges and responsibilities of an adult human being. It can hold property in its own name, enter into contracts, sue and be sued in a court of law. Officers of the company act as its agents in these matters; through their agency the company is able to exercise its rights and can be obliged to fulfil its responsibilities.

[8]The South Sea Bubble in England, and the Mississippi Land Bubble in France.

[9]In Canada, if the promoters expect their company to operate in only one province, they will obtain a provincial charter from the Provincial Secretary. If they expect the firm to operate in more than one province they will likely obtain a federal charter from the Secretary of State for Canada. Such a charter authorizes them to carry on business anywhere in the country. In the United States, where the federal government issues no charters, a nation-wide corporation can obtain its charter in whatever state it pleases. Since the issue of charters can be a lucrative source of revenue, there has been keen competition among states to attract national concerns. To induce firms to take out their particular charters, some states deliberately liberalized their laws, so as to impose a minimum of restraint upon locally chartered corporations. New Jersey went furthest of all in this regard, which is why so many of the leading corporations in the U.S. have taken out their charters in this state.

The law confers *limited liability* upon the shareholders of a corporation. In their early days, joint-stock companies were considered to be merely a form of partnership with a multitude of partners. Creditors attempted to collect from stockholders on debts owed by the company in which they held stock. Such attempts were generally futile, and in the course of the nineteenth century most countries recognized in law a situation which existed in fact. Legislation was introduced which specifically exempted persons from liability for the debts of companies in which they owned stocks. Thus they gained legal protection against a danger to which a single proprietor or a member of a partnership is exposed, the danger of losing more than the amount actually invested.

Modern Securities—Three Main Types

During the course of time, various types of corporation security were devised. All were designed to be sold to investors, with the proceeds being used to finance the company's operations; but each type carried its own provisions in regard to how the investor was to be repaid, how he would share in the company's earnings, and what voice he would have in its control. The three basic types of security issued nowadays are the *common share*, the *preferred share*, and the *bond*.

The Common Share. The purchaser of a common share acquires two key privileges: the right to a share in the company's profits, and the right to a vote in the administration of its affairs. His share in profits and his voting power will be proportionate to his share holding. For example, if he owns five shares out of 1,000,000 issued, he will receive $5/_{1,000,000}$ of the profit distributed, and will have five votes out of a million which could be cast.[10] He is not assured of any particular rate of return, nor even that he will get his investment back. Instead he is merely promised that, out of profit earned and distributed by the company, he will receive his proportionate share, and that if the company is liquidated and its property sold, he will receive his share of the proceeds after all prior obligations have been met. If he wishes to recover his investment at any time he can do so only by selling his share to someone else, for whatever price that person is prepared to pay.

The Preferred Share. A preferred share differs from a common share in three major respects: its holder is promised a specific sum of money each year as dividend on his investment; the dividend must be paid before dividends can be paid to common shareholders; a preferred share does not usually carry the right to vote.[11] A preferred share resembles a common share in that its owner is not promised the return of his investment at any particular time. If he wishes to get his money back he can do so only by selling his share to some other person. (In some cases the company reserves the right to redeem preferred shares at some stipulated price.)

[10]Some firms issue two types of common shares, Class A and Class B, with both being entitled to share equally in profits, but only Class B shares having voting rights.

[11]In a good many cases it is provided that preferred shareholders be accorded voting rights if they have not received their dividends as promised.

Many preferred shares are cumulative: if the company fails to pay the promised dividend in any particular year, then in a later year when profits are sufficiently large, it must pay to the preferred shareholders not only the dividends currently due, but the ones which had been due but were not paid in the earlier year.

The Bond. The buyer of a company bond is not, as is a shareholder, a part owner of the company. His status is that of a money lender, the bond being a certificate in which the company acknowledges its debt to him. Since he has made a loan, he must be repaid; accordingly, a bond provides that the holder be repaid on some specified date,[12] and that until then, he be paid a specified sum each year as interest. Not being a part owner, he has no vote. However, the terms of most bonds confer very considerable powers upon bondholders in the event of their not receiving the interest or principal which is due to them.

Why the Variety?

The foregoing description of shares and bonds, it should be emphasized, has dealt with their usual features only. Every company may, within limits, specify just what rights and privileges are acquired by the purchasers of its securities. Also, the same company may issue different groups of securities within the same general type; e.g. several classes of preferred shares may be issued, with each class carrying its own particular rights and privileges.

A corporation must issue common shares: these are the securities which represent ownership and control. It is not obligated however to issue preferred shares or bonds; presumably it will do so only if this appears to be advantageous to the common shareholders. For example, if a company which was highly profitable required additional capital, it would prefer to obtain the needed money by selling bonds upon which only a relatively low interest need be paid. If it raised the extra capital by selling more shares, the new shareholders would participate equally in the firm's profits, leaving a good deal less for the original shareholders than would be the case if new contributors of capital were merely paid interest. On the other hand, if the firm's prospects were uncertain, new investors might be prepared to advance money only upon the very strong security of bonds.[13]

Priority of Payments

The interest or dividends due annually to the different classes of investors in a company are paid out in accordance with a rigid priority schedule. Out of the company's earnings bondholders must receive their interest first; next, preferred shareholders

---

[12]The company is not obliged to pay off the bondholder before this date. If he wishes to recover his money earlier, he can do so only by selling his bond to some other person for whatever price he can get. This price could be more or less than the redemption price which the company must pay on the date when the bond falls due.

[13]A company which raises capital by selling bonds may realize a tax advantage. Interest paid to bondholders is legally considered to be an expense which reduces the firm's taxable income; dividends paid to shareholders are not similarly deductible for tax purposes.

receive their promised dividends; common shareholders receive what is left. Thus in a year of low earnings, common shareholders, and perhaps even preferred shareholders, might receive nothing; in a year of very large earnings, on the other hand, common shareholders would receive a great deal, while the others would get only their usual return.

For example, suppose that Company X raised its capital of $16 million by selling:

1,000,000 common shares @ $1	=	$ 1,000,000
50,000 10% preferred shares @ $100	=	5,000,000
100,000 8% bonds @ $100	=	10,000,000

The first charge each year on the company's earnings would be $8 per bond, or $800,000 to the bondholders. The second charge would be $10 per preferred share, or $500,000 to the preferred shareholders. Common shareholders would divide up among themselves whatever was left out of earnings, after $1,300,000 had been paid out to the bondholders and preferred shareholders. If the Company's earnings were precisely $1,300,000, they would get nothing.[14] If earnings were $2,000,000 they would divide up $700,000 for a dividend of 70 cents per share. If earnings were $5 million, they would divide up $3,700,000, for a dividend of $3.70 per share.

Undistributed Profit

The common shareholders will not necessarily receive in dividends the full sum remaining out of earnings, after bond interest and dividends on preferred shares have been paid. The directors may decide to retain some portion in the company, possibly to build up cash reserves, or to acquire additional assets, or to pay off debts. The effect is to increase shareholders' equity in the company—the difference between the amount of its assets and the amount of its obligations. Shareholders do not lose that portion of profits which is not distributed; instead of receiving it in cash they receive it in the form of an increase in the amount of their ownership rights in the company.

Stock Exchanges

Company shares and bonds have for centuries been articles of commerce. The buyers are people who have money to invest and the sellers are either company promoters who are offering brand new securities for sale in order to raise funds for new enterprises, or people who previously bought securities and now wish to have their money instead. Markets came into being where those who wished to buy securities could meet those who wished to sell. A class of dealer emerged, contemptuously referred to in 17th century England as "stock jobbers", who specialized in the purchase and sale

---

[14]If earnings were only $800,000, even the preferred shareholders would get nothing. If they were less than $800,000 so that even the bondholders could not be paid, the bondholders might be empowered to take action against the company.

of stocks on behalf of clients. In London these early stock brokers came together chiefly in Jonathan's Coffee House and on the street outside; only in 1802 did they erect a building of their own. In New York the first stock brokers met to do business under the shade of an old button-wood tree on present day Wall Street.

Large stock exchanges exist today in most of the major cities of the Western World, each serving the basic function of bringing together the buyers and sellers of securities. All transactions in these exchanges are carried out by dealers who buy and sell on behalf of clients, being paid on a commission basis. Hundreds of different securities are traded regularly on each of the major exchanges, with thousands of orders coming in daily to buy and to sell. With an enormous number of persons and firms buying and selling, anyone who wishes to sell a particular security can always find a buyer, and anyone who wishes to buy can always find a seller. Painstaking and elaborate procedures are employed to ensure that would-be buyers achieve their purchases, and would-be sellers their sales, in a minimum of time and at the most favourable price possible.

Control of a Corporation

The common shareholders, the legal owners of a corporation, are its ultimate authority. Their number is generally too large, however, to permit them actually to administer the firm. (The American Telephone and Telegraph Company has more than three million shareholders.) Provision is made accordingly for an annual shareholders' meeting, at which a Board of Directors is elected from among the shareholders. In this election each shareholder may cast one vote per share held. Shareholders who are unable to attend have the right to transfer their voting power to someone who will be present, by signing a *proxy* form to that effect.

The Board of Directors, which has been elected by the majority of votes cast at the shareholders' meeting, is responsible for guiding the affairs of the company during the following year. It will not manage the firm on a day to day basis; that is done by a full-time hired manager. It will meet regularly, perhaps once a month, to consider the affairs of the company, making decisions on major issues, and giving guidance to the managerial staff. At the next shareholders' meeting the Board will present a set of financial statements (described in the Appendix to this chapter), and render an accounting of its stewardship.

The Corporation—A Social Boon

The corporate form of business organization has played an indispensable role in the development of modern economic society. It has made possible the accumulation of a huge amount of capital for a single undertaking, thereby making possible large scale enterprise under private auspices. In addition, the corporate form of organization has furnished a procedure whereby the ownership and control of an establishment can be smoothly transferred, without disturbing its working in any way. Without the device of incorporation, we probably could not have our mighty and productive private organizations, comprised of vast physical properties and staffs of thousands, which carry on permanently, unaffected by the departure or death of any individual.

A Boon to Private Investors

Corporate organization has provided superior opportunity to the individual investor. The person who has savings is able to invest them without setting up a business of his own; he can purchase a share in an enterprise which someone else will manage. He is not obliged to hazard a very large sum in a single enterprise; he can purchase the securities of many different firms, avoiding the risk of crippling loss as a result of the failure of a single concern. The various classes of investor are all able to satisfy their requirements: the cautious ones can purchase securities which offer low but certain returns; the daring ones can invest in speculative stocks which offer the possibility of very great returns (coupled with the possibility of very great loss). The limited liability features guarantees to all investors that they cannot lose more than they have invested. Finally, the individual can withdraw his investment from a firm at any time he chooses. Unlike the member of a partnership he can sell his investment to whomever he pleases and, thanks to the existence of highly organized stock exchanges, he can rely on finding, at any time, a buyer who will pay a price determined by market conditions.

Private Companies

A good many firms which are entirely owned by one person or by a small group of persons, may nevertheless be organized as corporations, being known as "private companies". Ownership and control over such a company would be vested as usual in its common shares, but these would all be held by one person, or by a small number of persons.[15]

When a private company is prohibited by law from selling its shares or bonds to the general public, and therefore cannot raise capital from the public at large, the owners may, nevertheless, derive substantial benefit from corporate organization. They gain thereby the privilege of limited liability, together with the possibility of financial advantage in respect both to income taxes and succession duties. Corporate organization may furthermore prove to be highly convenient even when the number of owners is very small. With each of the owners holding a specific number of shares, the firm's profits, and control over its affairs, can be divided up with great precision. A transfer of ownership, when it becomes necessary, can be carried out quite simply, by means of a transfer of shares; in a partnership, on the other hand, it may prove awkward to effect such a transfer.

[15]In Canada the number of shareholders in a private company may not exceed fifty.

A Danger—Fraudulent Promotion

The strength of the corporation is its weakness. Because it gathers together the savings of a very large number of people, it can amass a huge amount of capital for a single enterprise. However, because the number of investors is very large, they are liable to exploitation by unscrupulous promoters and managers. With each investor contributing only a small sum, he is unlikely to investigate carefully the promoter's claims. With their total number large, investors are unlikely to be able to organize themselves effectively.

Through the past three centuries fraudulent promoters have organized companies which had no earthly chance of success, and sold their worthless stocks to gullible investors. Most of the proceeds went into their pockets. "Stock-watering" has been an all too frequent practice: dealers have sold the stocks of already existing companies at prices grossly in excess of the value of their actual property. The amount of money lost by investors has been stupendous. It is estimated, for instance, that of the $50 billions of securities issued in the United States in the decade after World War I, fully one half proved to be worthless.[16] Increasingly stringent legislation has curtailed abuses, but we still read in the daily press of shady promoters who either break the law outright or find loopholes in it, to their gain and investors' loss.

Another Danger—Control by Selfish Interests

The shareholders of even a soundly established corporation may get less than is their due. The Board of Directors which administers the firm may favour the interests of the group which elected it, to the disadvantage of other shareholders. The Board may not even represent a majority of the share holdings. The fact is that most share owners, having only a small interest in any company, do not bother to attend the annual shareholders' meeting. It becomes possible therefore for a small group, holding considerably less than one-half the outstanding shares, to constitute a majority interest at shareholders' meetings and so to decide who gets elected to the Board. In the case of a few giant American corporations, control is exercised by a group which possesses less than ten per cent of the shares outstanding.

Management Control

In a great many corporations effective control is exercised by the management, the chief executives who run the firm on a day-to-day basis. By virtue of two considerations they are able to dominate annual shareholders' meetings: firstly they hold a substantial, concentrated block of shares; secondly, having mailed out proxy forms to each shareholder, in which they invited the transfer of the shareholder's vote to themselves, they have in addition the voting power of all those shareholders who

[16]H. L. Purdy, M. L. Lindahl, W. A. Carter, *Corporate Concentration and Public Policy*, (New York, 1942), p. 134.

signed and returned the proxies. While nominally they are responsible to the board, in fact they are able to name themselves to the board, together with other persons of their choosing. A recent survey indicated that of the 200 largest non-financial corporations in the United States, approximately one-third were management controlled.

Where a small group of insiders is able to dominate a corporation they may use their power for personal gain, and to the general stockholders' detriment. They may reward themselves with huge salaries and bonuses.[17] Because their own tax obligations are thereby reduced, the directors of a company may hold back a large portion of its earnings as undistributed profit, even though most shareholders would prefer to have the earnings immediately paid out to them as dividends. The managerial group may knowingly adopt policies which are harmful to the Company's interests. They may embark on programmes of expansion which are not warranted, but serve only to swell the power and importance of managers through enlarging the property under their control. Directors may arrange that a corporation buy some of its needs, at excessive prices, from some other concern which they own or in which they have large interests.

The fact that control over a great corporation is concentrated in a few hands, poses problems and dangers for society as a whole. Through its control over corporation policy in regard to the procurement of supplies, employment, the establishment of branch plants, the pricing of products, a small group may affect the lives of many thousands of people. Unwise, irresponsible or selfish decisions made by one or two highly placed individuals can cause widespread harm. Furthermore, once it is ensconced, the controlling group may be virtually impossible to dislodge; herculean efforts may be needed to gather together the superior voting power required to unseat them.[18]

Corporation Manners Improving

The history of corporate enterprise supplies numerous instances of malpractice. Just how extensive they are today, it is impossible to estimate. There are reasonable grounds for supposing, however, that abuses are a good deal less frequent and less glaring than was the case in the past. Where the management of a firm breaks the law repeatedly, sooner or later it is bound to be found out. Where the abuse is not actually illegal, aroused public opinion generally brings about a change in the law, or compels management to desist from a practice which is morally wrong. On the positive side, large corporations have shown themselves to be increasingly anxious to cultivate

---

[17]e.g., Eugene Grace, President of the Bethlehem Steel Co. received, between 1918 and 1930, bonuses which averaged $814,993 per year. Over one three-year period when the Company paid no dividends to common shareholders, its directors voted themselves $6,800,524 in bonuses.

[18]Occasionally such efforts are made. John D. Rockefeller Jr. spent huge sums in 1928-29 to obtain enough proxy votes in the Standard Oil Company of Indiana to defeat the incumbent board of directors in the 1929 shareholders' meeting. Robert Young successfully waged a powerful campaign several years ago to oust the board of the New York Central Railway and install his own nominees as directors.

public goodwill. In order to be regarded as "good citizens" they are, with few exceptions, prepared to conform to the general view of what is fair and proper.

COOPERATIVES

British Origins

The modern cooperative movement, founded over a century ago, has as its objectives both long range social reform and immediate individual advantage. Its first great prophet was Robert Owen, a wealthy English manufacturer, who preached the new gospel in the first decades of the nineteenth century, in the dawn of the Industrial Revolution. Up and down the country he advocated the establishment of a society in which all would work cooperatively for the common good, instead of each for his private advantage. Drawing on his personal wealth, he founded four model communities organized on a cooperative basis, one each in England, Ireland, Scotland and the United States.

These utopian experiments all failed. But in 1844 twenty-nine followers of Owen, in the little Lancashire town of Rochdale, founded an organization whose effects have been enduring. With each contributing one pound to its capital, they formed the Rochdale Pioneers Equitable Society, to operate a retail store on cooperative lines. For the operation of its little store, the Society laid down these principles, which have guided the cooperative movement ever since:

> The store would be controlled by the Society.
> Membership in the Society would be open to all.
> Each member would be entitled to only one vote, regardless of how much capital he had contributed.
> Members would receive a fixed rate of interest on their contributions toward the store's capital.
> Only first quality goods would be sold.
> Sales would be for cash only.
> Surpluses earned would be returned to members in proportion to their purchases.
> Some portion of the surplus would be spent on educational work to propagate the doctrine of cooperation.

Widespread Adoption

From its humble beginning in Rochdale, the practice of consumer cooperation went forward steadily. In Great Britain today thousands of cooperative societies operate retail stores; the stores jointly own and operate wholesale and manufacturing plants, even tea plantations and wheat farms. The British example has been widely followed; a particularly strong cooperative movement has come into being in the Scandinavian countries. The first cooperative store in Canada was set up in Nova Scotia in 1861; today cooperative stores exist in every province. In each province the retail stores have cooperated to establish a wholesale supply house; the various provincial whole-sale firms have in turn established a national organization which supplies them with a limited number of products.

Producers' cooperatives have become quite common, particularly in the market-ing of agricultural products. The typical society is organized to market a single pro-duct grown by the farmers of a particular locality. The principles according to which producer cooperatives operate are much like those of consumer cooperatives. Mem-bers supply the capital (though capital may be borrowed as well from outside sources); each member has one vote only; surpluses are divided up among the members in proportion to their patronage.

Credit unions, first developed in Germany in the 1840s, have by now been organized in a good many countries, Canada included. The typical union is set up by persons who already have some degree of association, e.g. are employed in the same industry, or are members of the same parish. Members deposit savings with the union; the funds so deposited are available to be loaned out to other members who wish to borrow.

Advantages and Difficulties

To many people the objectives of the cooperative movement carry a strong appeal. They are attracted by the idea of cooperation rather than competition as a way of life. And they may be impressed by the idea of eliminating the middleman's profits, leaving more for both the producer and the consumer. However, cooperative organizations have their problems and difficulties too. They are unlikely to be able to raise as much capital as corporations can, since they appeal to a much smaller class of investor. In the retail field, competition is not easy against powerful and efficient department and chain stores which operate on the basis of very low profit margins. The fact that there are so many co-owners may give rise to managerial problems. There may be difficul-ties in recruiting staff; able and aggressive men who would make excellent managers may feel that they could get further ahead in private enterprise. Fortunately for them-selves, cooperatives have frequently been able to recruit first class people who, be-cause of their devotion to the idea of cooperation, were prepared to work there for less than they could have earned elsewhere.

PUBLIC ENTERPRISE

Various Forms

In Canada, as in the United States, the major proportion of goods and services is produced by privately owned business firms such as those described in the foregoing pages. But the minority produced by governments is nowadays a substantial one. Our three levels of government together provide, free to all, defence, education, police and fire protection, and a host of other services. In addition they sell, on a commercial basis, water, electricity, public transit, telephone and postal services. Most of these public services are provided by departments which are under the direct control of elected representatives of the people; a considerable number, however, are produced by organizations which governments own, but upon which they have deliberately conferred semi-independence. The government which owns the property of such an organization appoints a person or group of persons as its controlling authority, with very wide powers and a lengthy tenure of office. Examples of such semi-independent bodies are the provincial liquor control boards, and the federal government's crown corporations.

Merits and Demerits

Even in a private enterprise economy, government must play an important role. It alone will provide those services which are needed by the country but cannot be produced with profit. It must perform a great variety of regulatory functions, to ensure that the private enterprise system operates effectively and equitably. Quite properly, it undertakes to provide certain essential goods and services which must inevitably be produced on a monopolistic basis, such as water and telephone service. A privately owned monopoly producing essential services might take advantage of the public to maximize its profits; a publicly owned monopoly presumably will aim primarily to serve the public well. Public enterprise furthermore provides for the lodgement of economic power in the hands of people who are responsible to the general public and removable from their office by public will, expressed at the next election.

While it has its place, public enterprise suffers from grave, inherent weaknesses. It is liable to inefficiency and inequity. All too often political expediency takes precedence over administrative efficiency and the equitable distribution of burdens and benefits. The inevitably bureaucratic character of government operations reduces efficiency by prohibiting flexibility and stifling initiative. Everything must be done according to rigid rules, and in a good many cases these rules fit badly. Goods and services may be produced which the public does not really want; defective methods of production may be employed. When private enterprise commits such errors, the market ruthlessly exposes them: unwanted, inefficiently produced goods have to be sold at prices which do not cover their costs and their production must be discontinued. But public enterprise, drawing on the long purse of the government, need not cover its costs; it can persistently produce what the public does not want, or steadfastly employ inferior methods of production.

Federal crown corporations, together with provincial boards and commissions, represent attempts by government to overcome the disadvantages of government enterprise. By setting up semi-independent organizations in the image of private enterprise corporations, governments hope to achieve the latter's flexibility, vigorous initiative and freedom from political interference. Some of these bodies have been highly successful. Others have been much less so, reflecting the difficulties which may arise with organizations which draw their funds from the public purse, but are virtually immune from control by the public's representatives.

THE ORGANIZATION OF BUSINESS IN CANADA

There were in Canada in 1961 a total of 480,903 farms and approximately 300 thousand separate business establishments. The great majority of the farms—nearly 73 per cent—were operated by the owners with another 21 per cent operated partly by owners and partly by tenants; a little less than 6 per cent were operated entirely by tenants and less than half of one per cent were operated by hired managers.

While proprietorships constituted the majority of the 300 thousand or so business establishments, their aggregate contribution was small, in terms both of employment provided and business transacted. Incorporated companies, while very much fewer in number, employed the great majority of the Canadian labour force and transacted the great bulk of business done. Only in the fields of retail trade and service did proprietorships (together with partnerships) do an appreciable proportion of the total volume of business. In the fields of finance, transportation, mining, wholesale trade and manufacturing, incorporated companies were heavily dominant; the proportion of business handled in these fields by other types of firms ranged from small to nil.

Table 1 below indicates the relative importance, for the year 1961, of the various types of firms in the four industries for which statistics are available. In the manufacturing industry, incorporated companies constituted 54 per cent of the total number of firms, but produced 96 per cent of the total output; in wholesaling, incorporated companies constituted 52.3 per cent of the firms, but had 77.7 per cent of the sales volume. In both retail trade and retail service, however, incorporated companies constituted a much smaller proportion of the total number of firms, and accounted for only slightly more than half of the total business volume.

In retail trade, corporations formed 18.1 per cent of the total number of firms, and did 58.5 per cent of the total business. In retail service they formed 13.8 per cent of the total number of firms, and did 50.3 per cent of the total business.

While the corporation is the dominant form of business organization in Canada, a few specific industries furnish important exceptions. In the marketing of agricultural products, producers' cooperatives play an important role, handling about one-third of each year's produce. Establishments owned by provincial and municipal governments play a major role in the public utilities field. The federal government operates a heterogeneous array of enterprises, including a transcontinental railway and airline, a nation-wide radio and television broadcasting network, and a factory which produces synthetic rubber substitutes.

Table 1

BUSINESS ORGANIZATION IN CANADA IN FOUR MAJOR INDUSTRIES, 1961*

	Individual Proprietorship	Partnership	Incorporated Company	Cooperative	Misc.
Wholesale					
Total Number of					
Firms Reporting	11,642	1,942	16,136	1,105	30
% of total number	37.7	6.3	52.3	3.6	.1
Sales ($ millions)	2,079	652	15,117	791	814
% of total sales	10.7	3.3	77.7	4.1	4.2
Retail Trade					
Total Number of					
Firms Reporting	110,642	12,209	27,262	849	1,294
% of total number	72.4	8.0	18.1	.6	.9
Sales ($ millions)	4,964	995	9,391	168	556
% of total sales	30.9	6.1	58.5	1.0	3.5
Services					
Total Number of					
Firms Reporting	63,543	8,779	11,715	199	529
% of total number	74.8	10.4	13.8	.3	.7
Sales ($ million)	1,066	365	1,500	15	33
% of total sales	35.8	12.3	50.3	.5	1.1
Manufacturing					
Total Number of					
Firms Reporting	11,160	3,058	17,439	758	—
% of total number	34.4	9.4	54.0	22	—
Sales ($ million)	425	231	23,221	366	—
% of total sales	1.7	1.0	96.0	1.3	—

*Based on 1961 Census figures for wholesale trade, retail trade and services, and figures obtained from the *General Review of the Manufacturing Industries of Canada, 1961*.

United States Domination in Some Sectors

One highly significant feature of the Canadian economy, to which many citizens are acutely sensitive, is the degree to which it is externally controlled. A number of key sectors are dominated by firms which are the branches or subsidiaries of American corporations, and are owned wholly or partly by the parent organization. Thus in 1963, 97 per cent of the capital employed in the Canadian automobile (and parts) industry was under foreign control, as was 97 per cent of the rubber industry, 78 per cent of the chemical industry and 77 per cent of the electrical apparatus industry. In each case the whole, or virtually the whole of foreign control was American. The British investment in Canada is also significant in size, though only a fraction of that contributed by the United States. No major industry is dominated by British capital in the same way that several are dominated by American capital. While the large American investment has contributed indispensably to Canada's rapid economic development, a number of people feel misgivings about having major sectors of the nation's economy owned and controlled by foreign interests.

In part the problem has arisen because it has been difficult to raise in Canada the large aggregations of risk capital required in substantial business ventures. To remedy this deficiency the federal government in 1971 established the Canada Development Corporation, to have a capital of some $2 billion, of which $250 million would be provided by the government of Canada and the remainder by private Canadian investors. Possessed of this immense capital the Corporation would be capable of financing large undertakings which could not obtain their capital from any other Canadian source.

SUMMARY

Business organizations, generally established by private initiative and privately controlled, produce the bulk of Canada's annual output of goods and services. The capital required by these business organizations may be raised by different methods, each method involving a particular mode of exercising control; a firm may be a proprietorship, partnership, corporation, or cooperative.

In a proprietorship the capital is raised and control is exercised by a single individual.

In a partnership two or more persons contribute to the firm's capital, and together exercise control.

In a corporation a great many individuals subscribe capital; control is exercised by a board of directors elected by the shareholders, each shareholder having one vote per share.

In a cooperative capital is subscribed by the members; additional capital may be borrowed from outsiders. The members exercise control, each having one vote only.

The government also performs a number of economic activities. These may be administered either by departments which are directly controlled by elected representatives, or by semi-independent bodies whose executives have been appointed by the elected representatives.

In Canada, as in the United States, the proprietorship form of business organization is the most numerous. However, corporations, while fewer in number, are generally much larger in size, so that the majority of Canada's workers are employed by corporations, and these produce the major portion of our annual output.

A notable feature of business organization in Canada is the extent of foreign, particularly American, control. A great many corporations operating in Canada are controlled by parent firms in the United States.

FOR REVIEW AND DISCUSSION

1. If you owned common stocks in a company, would you favour retaining some of the profit in the firm each year as Undistributed Profit. Why or why not?
2. Government enterprise is bound to be less efficient than private enterprise. Do you agree? Justify your answer.
3. A well known book refers to the separation of ownership and control in the modern corporation. What do the authors have in mind?
4. You are planning to set up a small factory to produce men's shirts. Which form of business organization would you choose to adopt? Justify your choice.
5. "Within a generation there will be no more small firms; the big firms will have taken over everything." Do you agree? Why or why not?
6. Comment on the following. "A stock exchange is nothing more than a special kind of gambling den."
7. "It really is ridiculous to have so many different types of corporation security." Do you agree?
8. "Human nature being what it is, cooperatives are unlikely to be very successful." Comment.
9. "Canada should take steps to restrain the growth of American control over business enterprise in this country." Do you agree? Justify your answer.

APPENDIX ON ACCOUNTING

Every incorporated company is required to issue, yearly or oftener, three fundamental reports: a *balance sheet*, an *income statement*, and a *statement of earned surplus*. The balance sheet describes the firm's position at a point in time, usually the last day of the fiscal year; on the left-hand side will be shown what resources are employed in the business, and on the right will be shown the obligations which exist to whoever contributed these resources. The income statement indicates what revenue and expenses the firm had during the period covered and what profit was earned. The statement of earned surplus indicates how the net profit was disposed of: how much was declared in dividends and how much was retained in the firm to be added to the retained profits of previous years.

To illustrate the main features of these reports, the following pages contain, for hypothetical Company X Limited:

Its balance sheet as of December 31, 1971

Its income statement for the year January 1 to December 31, 1972

Its statement of earned surplus for the year ending December 31, 1972

Its balance sheet as of December 31, 1972 (which shows how the firm's position has changed as a result of the year's operations).

Table 2

BALANCE SHEET OF COMPANY X LIMITED, AS OF DECEMBER 31, 1971

ASSETS			LIABILITIES AND CAPITAL		

CURRENT ASSETS

Cash		$20,000			
Govt. of Canada bonds,					
at cost		40,000			
Accounts receivable					
(net)		30,000			
Inventory, at lower of cost					
and market		60,000			
Total current assets		$150,000			

CURRENT ASSETS

- Cash — $20,000
- Govt. of Canada bonds, at cost — 40,000
- Accounts receivable (net) — 30,000
- Inventory, at lower of cost and market — 60,000
- Total current assets — $150,000

FIXED ASSETS, at cost
- Buildings $1,000,000
- Less accumulated depreciation $550,000 450,000
- Equipment $500,000
- Less accumulated depreciation $200,000 300,000
- Total fixed assets 750,000

INTANGIBLE ASSETS
- Patents 50,000

TOTAL ASSETS $950,000

CURRENT LIABILITIES
- Accounts payable $55,000
- Note payable—bank 90,000
- Total current liabilities $145,000

LONG TERM LIABILITIES
- Industrial Development Bank note at 8%, due 31/12/1975 100,000
- 8% Bonds, payable 31/8/1990 400,000
- Total long term liabilities 500,000

CAPITAL STOCK
- Authorized*:
  - 1500 10% preferred shares at $100 each
  - 40,000 common shares of no par value
- Issued and fully paid:
  - 1000 preferred shares 100,000
  - 20,000 common shares 200,000
  - Retained earnings 5,000
- Total Capital and surplus 305,000

TOTAL LIABILITIES AND CAPITAL $950,000

*The terms of its charter authorize each incorporated company to issue specified numbers of common shares; in some companies, where the promoters wish it, the issue of certain numbers of preferred shares may also be authorized. A company which, for the time being needs only a certain amount of capital, may choose to offer for sale only portions of these authorized amounts.

The Current Assets

The asset column lists, in summary fashion, the firm's possessions. It has $20,000 in cash, $40,000 of bonds, and inventory of $60,000 (composed of materials, goods in process, and finished goods). Customers to whom it has sold its products owe the company $30,000. These items are all classed as current assets because they consist of actual cash or because cash will be obtained for them, in the ordinary course of business, in less than one year: the customers who owe the $30,000 will, within a matter of weeks, make their payments; finished goods on hand will soon be sold;

raw materials on hand will be processed into finished goods; the bonds can be converted into cash at any time when cash is needed.

Fixed Assets: Depreciation

The firm's buildings and equipment are fixed assets; they are not going to be turned into cash within twelve months. In listing them, the balance sheet shows an historical record of their cost minus the proportion of that cost which has been treated as expenses of operations to date; the difference is sometimes referred to as "book value", but "unamortized portion of cost" would be a more accurate description. In each year's accounting report a portion of the firm's outlay on fixed assets is reckoned as being part of that year's costs. The sum of these annual allowances for "depreciation" would equal the cost of the assets, so that the total cost of fixed assets is charged against the revenue not of a single year but of a large number of years.

How does the accountant decide how much to allow each year for depreciation? The candid answer is that his figure is an estimate, based upon an engineering estimate of physical life minus an allowance for possible obsolescence. Once an estimate of the length of useful life has been obtained, several methods may be used to calculate depreciation, of which the following three are perhaps the most common: the *straight-line* method; the *constant-percentage* method; the *unit of service* method.

A business management using the straight-line method will assume that a building or piece of equipment will last a specific number of years, and will allocate the same fraction of that cost to each year. Thus the buildings of Company X might have been bought in 1960 for $1,000,000, with the expectation that they could last 20 years. Using the straight-line method of depreciation and assuming no salvage value, the enterprise would show the buildings as depreciating each year by 1/20 of their original cost. Hence, by 1971, depreciation would amount to 11/20 of $1,000,000 or $550,000.

Management might assume that expenses relating to initial cost of buildings or equipment could be fairly charged against yearly revenues at a figure determined by a constant percentage of the residual cost each year. In that case the absolute amount of depreciation expense would become smaller each year. If, for instance, the constant rate was fixed at 10 per cent a year, then in the first year the depreciation on a $1,000,000 building would be reckoned as being $100,000, in the second year as $90,000, in the third as $81,000, and so on.

The unit of service method is likely to be used only in calculating depreciation of equipment. Management will estimate how many units of work can be performed by a particular piece of equipment in its whole lifetime and, each year, will reckon depreciation according to how much work the equipment did that year. Thus if a truck which cost $5,000 was expected to run for 100,000 miles, then depreciation of 5 cents would be charged for each mile it was operated. In a year when it was driven 10,000 miles, the depreciation would be considered to be $500, and so on.

Intangible Assets

The figure attributed to "Patents" would represent a price paid by the firm for the right to use a particular method or process. Cost is a fact relating to an actual transaction, and must be recorded either as an expense of one year's revenues or of the revenues of a series of years. A patent is good only for a specified number of years and its cost must be allocated as an expense of earning the revenues of those years. Each year an appropriate proportion of its original cost must be charged as an expense of that year and that figure must be "written off," i.e. the patent must be deemed to have lost that much of its original value during the year.

The Current Liabilities

The accounts payable figure would represent money owing to suppliers on account of goods delivered to Company X, but for which it had not yet paid. The "note payable—bank" item would probably refer to money owed to a chartered bank. These two items are classified as current liabilities because they are a charge against current assets, representing promises to make payment within a year or less.

The Long Term Liabilities

The Industrial Development Bank note item refers to a loan received from this source. The Bank's capital is provided by the federal government and it is operated by the Bank of Canada with the object of making long term loans to small companies that could not obtain long term capital otherwise.

The bonds payable item refers to bonds which the company sold in the past in order to obtain funds; the figure shown would represent the total indebtedness to bondholders, a sum that would have to be paid to them when their bonds fell due. Because both the I.D.B. note and the bonds are due to be paid off some years hence, they are classed as long term liabilities.

Shareholders' Equity

Company X is owned by the shareholders; the stated amount attributed to their rights of ownership is the difference between the amount of everything the firm possesses and the amount of its indebtedness to outsiders. Thus Company X has resources of a stated amount of $950,000, but owes a total of $645,000 to suppliers, banks and bondholders. So far as the shareholders are concerned, therefore, the stated amount of the ownership rights in the company is $305,000. This figure would be referred to as the shareholders' equity in the company. It has no relation to the actual market value of their holdings: this would depend upon expectations of the company's future earnings.

The Income Statement[19]

During the calendar year 1972 Company X Limited manufactures and sells its products. At the end of the year it will prepare an Income Statement showing what its total revenues and expenses were during the year, and what profit it earned. In a separate Statement of Earned Surplus it will indicate how much of this profit was paid out to shareholders and how much was retained in the company.

Table 3

COMPANY X, LIMITED, INCOME STATEMENT
FOR THE YEAR ENDED DECEMBER 31, 1972

Sales Revenues		$800,000
Less: Manufacturing cost of goods sold:		
Materials	$240,000	
Labour cost	165,000	
Depreciation and amortization	105,000	
Local taxes (property and business)	45,000	
Miscellaneous	40,000	
Manufacturing cost of goods sold		$595,000
Gross margin		205,000
Less: Selling costs		50,000
Administrative costs		41,000
Net operating margin		114,000
Less: Fixed interest charges		49,000
Net profit before income taxes		65,000
Less: Corporation income tax		25,000
Net profit after taxes		$ 40,000

Most of the items in these statements need very little comment. Company X took in $800,000 from sales during the year, spent $240,000 on materials and paid out $165,000 to factory labour. Its buildings, equipment and patents were considered to have depreciated by $105,000 between January 1 and December 31. It had to pay local taxes amounting to $45,000. Miscellaneous costs, comprised of such items as light, power, repairs, amounted to $40,000.

With receipts of $800,000 and manufacturing costs of $595,000, the gross margin was $205,000. Selling costs, consisting of advertising expenditures, salesmen's commissions and the like, amounted to $50,000; administrative costs, comprised of office salaries and other office expenses, amounted to $41,000. After paying these costs the firm is left with a net margin of $114,000. Interest on the notes payable, on the Industrial Development Bank note and on the bonds outstanding, amounts to $49,000. The remaining $65,000 represents the company's profit for the purpose of the corporation income tax. On profit of this amount the tax payable is $25,000, leaving $40,000 for the shareholders.

[19]Also referred to as the Profit and Loss Statement.

The Company's Statement of Earned Surplus shows how this profit of $40,000 was used. Preferred shareholders were paid the $10,000 that was due to them, leaving $30,000 for the common shareholders. However, instead of paying out this full amount in dividends to common shareholders, the directors paid out only $5,000 in dividends on common shares, retaining the other $25,000 as *earned surplus*.[20]

Table 4

COMPANY X LIMITED, STATEMENT OF EARNED SURPLUS
FOR THE YEAR ENDED DECEMBER 31, 1972

Balance—December 31, 1971		$ 5,000
Add. Net profit for the year		40,000
		$45,000
Less dividends paid:		
10% preferred	$10,000	
Common	5,000	15,000
Balance—December 31, 1972		$30,000

The nature of this earned surplus must not be misunderstood. Very likely it will not consist of a sum of cash, but rather will take the form of an increase in the firm's assets and a reduction in its indebtedness to outsiders, both of which serve to increase the shareholders' equity in the Company. The point will be made clearer when we examine the firm's balance sheet as of December 31, 1972, at the end of the twelve months covered by the statement of profit and loss.

Some asset items are up while others are down, but the total of $960,000 is greater than that of last year by $10,000. As a result of the year's depreciation, the book value of buildings and equipment is down by $100,000 and of intangible assets by $5,000; but cash is up by $20,000, accounts receivable are up by $55,000, and bonds are up by $40,000.

Long term liabilities are unchanged from last year, but current liabilities are reduced by $15,000: while there is now a tax liability of $25,000 (owing to the government on account of the profit earned), accounts payable are down by $10,000 and notes payable by $30,000.

Now we can tell what happened to the $25,000 of earnings that was retained in the company. It was used to increase assets by $10,000 and reduce indebtedness by $15,000, thereby increasing shareholders' equity by $25,000, from $305,000 to $330,000. Shareholders benefited from this $25,000 of the Company's profit not through receiving it in actual dividends, but through the increase in the value of their ownership rights.

This brief appendix provides a very elementary introduction to business accounting; we shall make use of this knowledge later on in the book.

[20]Also referred to as "retained earnings".

Table 5

BALANCE SHEET OF COMPANY X, AS OF DECEMBER 31, 1972

ASSETS				LIABILITIES AND CAPITAL			
CURRENT ASSETS				CURRENT LIABILITIES			
Cash	$40,000			Accounts payable	$45,000		
Govt. of Canada bonds,				Note payable—bank	60,000		
at cost	80,000			Taxes payable	25,000		
Accts. receivable (net)	85,000			Total current liabilities		$130,000	
Inventory, at lower							
of cost and market	60,000			LONG TERM LIABILITIES			
Total current assets		$265,000		Industrial Development			
				Bank note, at 8%, due			
FIXED ASSETS, at cost				31/12/1975	$100,000		
Buildings $1,000,000				8% Bonds, payable			
Less accumu-				31/8/1990	400,000		
lated depre-				Total long term liabilities		$500,000	
ciation $600,000 $400,000							
Equip-				CAPITAL STOCK			
ment $500,000				Authorized:			
Less accumu-				1500 10% preferred			
lated depre-				shares at $100 each			
ciation $250,000 $250,000				40,000 common shares			
Total fixed assets		$650,000		of no par value			
				Issued and fully paid:			
INTANGIBLE ASSETS				1000 preferred			
Patents, at cost				shares	$100,000		
less amount				20,000 common			
written off $45,000		$45,000		shares	200,000		
				Retained earnings	30,000		
				Total capital and surplus		$330,000	
TOTAL ASSETS		$960,000		TOTAL LIABILITIES AND CAPITAL		$960,000	

PART TWO

THE THEORY OF PRICE

3   Demand, Supply, and Price

WHAT DETERMINES PRICE AND OUTPUT?

An enormous variety of goods is produced and sold in Canada each year. Each type of commodity is produced in a specific quantity and is sold at its particular price. What decides how much is produced of each type of commodity, and the price at which it is sold? Last year, for instance, there were produced and sold in Canada approximately 200 million dozen eggs, and the price averaged about 60 cents per dozen. Why was this so? Why wasn't the output of eggs 500 million dozen, or just ten million dozen? Why wasn't the price one dollar per dozen, or only 10 cents? Was it merely chance that caused the output of eggs during the year to be 200 million dozen, and the price to be 60 cents, or were there definite forces at work which caused the output and price of eggs to be exactly what they were?

To this last question the economist answers yes. The quantity of eggs produced, and the price at which they were sold, were determined by the forces which he calls *demand* and *supply*. To find out how these forces work, let us observe them in a typical situation. Of the 200 million dozen eggs sold in Canada last year, about five million dozen were sold in Winnipeg. Let us see how demand and supply determined that the price in Winnipeg would be 60 cents per dozen, and sales five million dozen per year, or roughly 100,000 dozen per week.

Demand

The demand for eggs in Winnipeg at any given time would reflect the attitudes of all potential buyers, determined by both their liking for eggs and the amount of money they had to spend. Probably as a matter of course each housewife would have considered all possible uses that she might have for eggs and classified them in order of importance. Thus Mrs. Allen might know that she could use a dozen eggs per week for each of the following purposes, listed in order of importance:

1. her children's lunches,
2. her husband's breakfasts,
3. her own breakfasts,
4. baking,
   etc.

41

Very likely Mrs. Allen would attach to each of these uses for eggs a money value that reflected both family income and the importance that she attributed to that use. Thus she might feel that it was worth a dollar to her to be able to provide her children with egg sandwiches, and she would therefore be prepared to pay a dollar for the dozen eggs to be used for that purpose. However, she woud be prepared to spend only 90 cents to provide her husband with eggs for breakfast and only 80 cents to provide eggs for herself.

If this is how she feels then clearly if the price of eggs were a dollar a dozen she would buy only one dozen — to serve her children; if the price were 90 cents she would buy two dozen, the second to be served to her husband; at 80 cents she would buy a third dozen; and so on.

Other housewives would react in the same general way, with variations reflecting differences in family income and their families' liking for eggs. Thus Mrs. Bell may be the same as Mrs. Allen in every respect except that her children do not care for eggs; in that case she would buy no eggs if the price were a dollar, one dozen if the price were 90 cents, 2 dozen if the price were 80 cents, and so on. Mrs. Clark's family may have exactly the same taste for eggs as does Mrs. Allen's, but they have less money. Accordingly, Mrs. Clark is prepared to buy eggs for her children's lunches only if the price is 80 cents a dozen, and to buy eggs for her husband's breakfasts only if the price is 70 cents, and so on.

The attitude of each of the three ladies reflects what the economist calls "diminishing marginal utility": whenever one of them increases her purchase of eggs she uses the additional quantity to satisfy a less important purpose than those being served thus far. This is why she will buy more than she has been buying only if the price is lowered.

Table 1. represents the quantities of eggs that would be bought at various possible prices by our three housewives and, in the final column, the total that would be bought collectively by all Winnipegers at these prices.

Table 1

DOZENS OF EGGS BOUGHT PER WEEK IN WINNIPEG

(1) Price per Dozen	(2) Bought by Mrs. Allen	(3) Bought by Mrs. Bell	(4) Bought by Mrs. Clark	(5) Bought by all Winnipegers
$1.00	1	0	0	20,000
.90	2	1	0	40,000
.80	3	2	1	60,000
.70	4	3	2	80,000
.60	5	4	3	100,000
.50	6	5	4	120,000
.40	7	5	4	140,000
.30	7	5	4	160,000

Columns (1) and (5) together would represent the *market demand* for eggs in Winnipeg. This demand, it should be noted, does not consist of the desire to buy just one specific quantity of eggs; it consists instead of the *willingness to buy any one of a number of different quantities, depending on the price charged.*

Supply

Let us assume that all the eggs sold in Winnipeg are produced on farms located near the city, each operated by a different person. Although the farmers would all be paying the same price for feed, equipment and so on, each would have his own attitude regarding the price he expected to get for eggs. Some might be prepared to keep chickens even if the price of eggs were quite low: they might have buildings and equipment that could be used for no other purpose; members of the family might have much spare time in which they could look after chickens; some people would prefer keeping chickens to other types of farming even though it was less profitable.

If the price of eggs rose it would become more profitable to keep chickens, and any farmer who was already keeping some would no doubt decide to keep more. In addition, some entirely new people might enter the field—perhaps farmers who previously raised cattle only, or other people who had not even been farmers but were now convinced that they could become rich by raising chickens.

Table 2 represents the quantities that would be produced, at various possible prices, by three typical farm operators; column (5) indicates how many dozen would be produced by all farm operators together at these prices.

Table 2

DOZENS OF EGGS PRODUCED PER WEEK BY FARMERS NEAR WINNIPEG

(1) Price per Dozen	(2) Produced by Mr. Black	(3) Produced by Mr. Gray	(4) Produced by Mr. White	(5) Produced by All Farmers
$ .30	0	0	5	10,000
.40	0	5	10	40,000
.50	5	10	15	70,000
.60	10	15	20	100,000
.70	15	20	25	130,000
.80	20	25	30	160,000
.90	25	30	35	190,000
1.00	30	35	40	220,000

Three significant points are illustrated in this table, analogous to those which were illustrated in Table 1.

1. When the price rises, the farmer who is already producing some eggs, decides to produce more.

2. When the price rises, some persons who were previously not producing any eggs at all, become willing to produce some.
3. Each rise in price brings about an increase in total ou:put, because of the combined effect of (1) and (2) above.

Columns (1) and (5) form a schedule which indicates how many dozen eggs would be produced, by all the farmers together, at different possible prices. This schedule would represent the *market supply* of eggs in Winnipeg. The supply, like the demand, does not consist of one specific quantity. Rather, it consists of *the willingness to produce any one of a number of different quantities, depending upon the price offered.*

Equilibrium Price

Table 3 shows both the market demand schedule and the market supply schedule, as they were derived from the attitudes of housewives and farmers. Let us examine the two sets of figures to see how demand and supply together determine the price of eggs in Winnipeg, and the amount produced.

(For convenience in exposition, the market supply schedule is presented here in a different order from that used in Table 2. Here the top price and corresponding quantity are listed first.)

Table 3

DEMAND AND SUPPLY OF EGGS IN WINNIPEG

Demand		*Supply*	
Price	No. of dozen that would be bought each week	Price	No. of dozen that would be produced each week
$1.00	20,000	$1.00	220,000
.90	40,000	.90	190,000
.80	60,000	.80	160,000
.70	80,000	.70	130,000
.60	100,000	.60	100,000
.50	120,000	.50	70,000
.40	140,000	.40	40,000
.30	160,000	.30	10,000

Common sense tells us that in the situation represented by Table 3, the price will have to be 60 cents per dozen, and the quantity produced will have to be 100,000 dozen per week. At this price the quantity which housewives are willing to buy is exactly equal to the quantity which farmers are prepared to produce. At no other price would such an equality exist.

If the price were higher, if say it were 70 cents, then producers would produce

130,000 dozen. Housewives would be willing to buy only 80,000 dozen at this price, and there would be a surplus of 50,000 dozen on the market. To dispose of this surplus the producers would have to lower the price below 70 cents. Obviously, therefore, a market price of 70 cents is too high to last; it gives rise to a surplus on the market which makes necessary reduction of the price to below 70 cents. Had the price been set above 70 cents, an even greater surplus would have developed, and the downward pressure on price would have been even greater.

On the other hand, if the market price happened to be set below 60 cents, say at 50 cents, then producers would produce only 70,000 dozen per week, while housewives would want to buy 120,000 dozen. There would now be a shortage of eggs: housewives would want to buy, *at the going price*, 50,000 dozen more eggs than were actually available on the market. What would be the result? Housewives who were unable to get eggs at the going price would indicate their willingness to pay more, rather than do without. Once it became evident that more could be sold than were currently available, and at higher prices, the price would tend to rise; middlemen, believing that they could profitably resell to consumers, would offer higher prices to producers. As the price rose, the shortage would diminish; farmers would produce more eggs, while housewives would decide to buy fewer of them.

Thus, a market price which is higher or lower than 60 cents per dozen cannot last. If the market price ever happened to be set above 60 cents, it would be pushed down; if it were set below 60 cents, it would be pushed up. Only if the market price were actually at 60 cents, would there be no tendency for it to change. In this example, we would refer to 60 cents as the *equilibrium price*, meaning thereby the price at which the market stays if it is already there, and towards which it will move if it is not there. At the equilibrium price there is neither a surplus nor a shortage on the market. Every seller is able to sell as much as he cares to produce at this price; every buyer is able to buy as much as she cares to buy at this price.

The Consumer's Expenditure Pattern

Once the market price is established each consumer is able to decide what actual quantity to buy. Suppose the market price for eggs were 60 cents per dozen, the equilibrium price according to Table 3. Now according to Table 1 a first dozen of eggs is worth $1.00 to Mrs. Allen, a second dozen is worth 90 cents, and so on. Evidently, when the price is 60 cents she should buy five dozen. If she bought six dozen, the sixth—which cost her 60 cents like all the rest—would bring her only 50 cents worth of satisfaction. On the other hand she should buy more than just two or three dozen. If she bought only two, for instance, she would be passing up the opportunity to buy, at 60 cents, a third dozen that was worth 80 cents to her and a fourth that was worth 70 cents. A fifth dozen would be just worth buying; it would provide satisfaction exactly equivalent to its price.

As a matter of fact, Mrs. Allen should apply the same logic to all her purchases, buying that quantity of each good such that the satisfaction she derived from the marginal unit bought corresponded to the price at which the good was being sold. If her family's preference for steak is such that a fourth pound is worth 80 cents to her, then, when the price is 80 cents she should buy four pounds; if a sixth pair of shoes would be worth $15 to her, then when shoes sell at $15 she should buy six pairs; and so on.

GRAPHICAL DESCRIPTION OF DEMAND AND SUPPLY

The foregoing analysis of how the equilibrium price for eggs in Winnipeg is determined may be illustrated graphically, with demand and supply being represented by curves on a graph. (Economists often find it helpful to use graphical analysis: it enables important theoretical points to be demonstrated clearly and simply.) Let us see how the ideas contained in the last few pages can be expressed graphically.

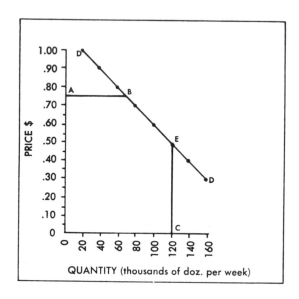

Figure 1.
The demand curve

The Demand Curve

We set up a graph whose vertical axis represents price, and whose horizontal axis represents quantity. (Figure 1.) We plot the points in the market demand schedule (taken from Table 3) and join them to form the continuous curve DD[1]. This curve

---

[1]The demand and supply data in our simple illustration are represented by straight lines; had the figures been different, the lines might have been curved.

represents the demand for eggs by the housewives of Winnipeg, indicating to us what quantity of eggs the housewives will want to buy at any particular price. If, for instance, we would like to know how many dozen they would buy if the price were 75 cents, we would simply draw a horizontal line out from the price axis, at 75 cents, to touch the demand curve, as shown in Figure 1. The length of this line AB would represent the quantity which housewives are willing to buy at this price.

We can derive from the demand curve an additional and highly useful piece of information. We can find out from it what price could be charged when any particular quantity is offered for sale. Suppose, for instance, that we wanted to know what price could be charged when 120,000 dozen weekly were being put on the market. We would draw a vertical line from the quantity axis, at 120,000 dozen, up to the demand curve. The length of this line CE would represent the maximum price per dozen at which the entire quantity could be sold.

The Supply Curve

We set up a graph with the same axis as in Figure 1. On it we plot the points represented by the market supply schedule in Table 3. Joining these points, we obtain the continuous curve SS, shown in Figure 2. As from the demand curve, we can derive from it two types of valuable information. We can tell how many dozen eggs will be produced at any particular price. Simply draw a horizontal line from the price axis, at that price, to the supply curve. The length of this line would represent the quantity that would be produced when farm operators were receiving this price: the line FG represents the quantity of eggs that farmers would produce, if paid 45 cents per dozen.

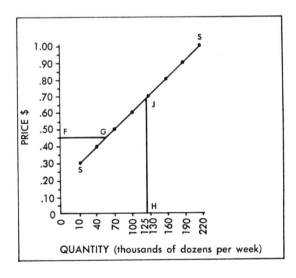

Figure 2.
The supply curve

We can tell also what price must be offered to suppliers to induce them to produce any particular quantity. Draw a vertical line from the quantity axis, at that quantity, up to the supply curve. The length of this line would represent the price which must be paid to bring forth that output. Thus the line HJ represents the price which must be paid per dozen to suppliers, to induce them to put 125,000 dozen on the market.

Equilibrium Price

If we draw the demand curve and the supply curve on the same graph, as in Figure 3, we can demonstrate graphically why the equilibrium price will be 60 cents, with 100,000 dozen being produced and sold. It is at the point which has these coordinates that the two curves intersect. If the market price happened to be higher, say at 75 cents, the quantity produced would be AC, while consumers would wish to buy only the quantity AB. The quantity BC would constitute a surplus on the market which would compel a reduction in price. Only when the price was pushed down to 60 cents would there cease to be a surplus.

If the price were set lower than 60 cents, say at 45 cents, there would be a shortage. At this price consumers would wish to buy the quantity FH, but producers would only be producing the quantity FG. The distance GH would represent the additional quantity of eggs which housewives would like to buy at this price, but could

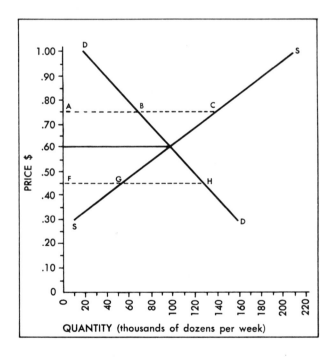

**Figure 3.
The equilibrium
Price**

not buy, because not enough eggs were available on the market. As we have already seen, disappointed housewives would indicate their willingness to pay a higher price, rather than do without, and the price would rise. It would keep rising until it reached 60 cents, at which price every housewife would be able to buy as many eggs as she desired and was willing to pay for at the rate of 60 cents per dozen.

The point of intersection of the demand and supply curve therefore represents the equilibrium price and quantity. At this price, the amount which housewives wish to buy is precisely equal to the amount which farmers will offer to sell. There is no surplus to push the price down, no shortage to push the price up.

Changes in Demand and Supply

We have demonstrated, by two different methods, how demand and supply determine that the equilibrium price for eggs in Winnipeg shall be 60 cents per dozen, and that the quantity sold shall be 100,000 dozen per week. But note this: 60 cents is the equilibrium price, and 100,000 dozen per week the equilibrium quantity, only so long as there is no change in demand or supply. If either or both change, we will have a new equilibrium price and quantity.

Change in Demand

Next year the demand for eggs in Winnipeg might be quite different.
It might turn out that many housewives would now be willing to buy more eggs than last year, even at the same prices. Possibly many of them had more money to spend

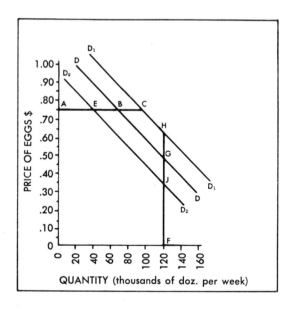

Figure 4.
Changes in demand

because their husbands were now earning more money. Perhaps the price of meat and fish had gone up, and so they had decided to use more of substitute foods such as eggs. Or possibly a recent article in a popular magazine had quoted authorities to the effect that an egg diet would make a woman plump or slender, whichever she wanted to be. The population might have increased; there might be more housewives wanting eggs.

If any such developments had occurred we would find the housewives of Winnipeg more anxious to buy eggs than they had been last year. Whereas last year at a price of $1.00 per dozen they would have bought only 20,000 dozen per week, this year at that same price they would buy 30,000 dozen per week; last year at a price of 90 cents they would have bought 40,000 dozen; this year they would buy 50,000 dozen; and so on. Graphically, this new demand schedule would be represented by a new demand curve D_1D_1 which would lie above and to the right of the original demand curve DD, as in Figure 4.

We might, of course, find that housewives were less anxious to buy eggs than they had been the year before. They might have less money to spend because many hubsands were out of work. Meat and fish might have fallen in price; housewives might be buying more of these foods and would need fewer eggs. A magazine article might have quoted impressive authority to the effect that eating eggs gives a woman the sort of figure she does not want to have. The population may have decreased. If such developments had occurred, we would find that, at the same prices, housewives would buy fewer eggs than they had done last year. Whereas last year they would have bought 20,000 dozen when the price was one dollar per dozen, now they will buy only 10,000 dozen; at 90 cents they would have bought 40,000 dozen last year; this year at 90 cents they will buy only 30,000 dozen. This new demand schedule would be represented graphically by a demand curve D_2D_2 lying below and to the left of the original DD curve, as in Figure 4.

A simple example will illustrate the significance of the relative position of the three curves. At price OA, housewives originally were prepared to buy the quantity AB; if D_1D_1 represents their new demand, then at this same price they would now be prepared to buy AC; if D_2D_2 represents their new demand, then at this same price of OA they would now be prepared to buy only the quantity AE.

Similarly, when they had the original demand DD, housewives would have bought the quantity OF at a price of FG per dozen; if their demand shifted to D_1D_1, then they would be prepared to buy the quantity OF at a price of FH per dozen; if, however, their demand shifted to D_2D_2, then they would buy the quantity OF only if it were offered to them at a price of FJ per dozen.

"Change in Demand" Defined

From our analysis thus far it is evident that housewives may buy more eggs for two different types of reason. First, they may buy more eggs because the price has fallen;

secondly, they may buy more eggs, even though the price is unchanged, because they have more money to spend or want eggs more eagerly than they did before or because there are more housewives than before. To avoid ambiguity in discussion we must distinguish clearly between an increase in purchases attributable solely to a reduction in the price, and an increase in purchases which is attributable to causes other than change in price. Economists call the two by different names. If the community wished to buy more eggs even though the price was unchanged, the economist would say that "demand had increased". If the community wished to buy more eggs purely because the price had been reduced, he would say that there was now an "increase in quantity demanded."

As indicated earlier in the chapter the noun "demand" refers to an attitude on the part of people, i.e. their willingness to buy any one of different possible quantities, depending on the price charged. If price is reduced and people buy more it would not mean that their attitude had changed: they were always prepared to buy more at lower prices. It would be correct to say that their "demand," i.e. their attitude, had changed only if they bought a larger quantity when the *same* price was being charged.

A similar distinction must be drawn between a reduction in the desire to purchase a good which is attributable strictly to an increase in its price and a reduction in desire to purchase attributable to reduced need or interest. The first we call a reduction in quantity demanded, the second a reduction in demand.

Change in Supply

If we surveyed the farm operators next year, we might get a different set of data regarding them too. The cost of feed and the wages of hired help may have gone up. Other types of farming may have become more attractive. The farmers might now report that whereas last year at a price of 30 cents per dozen they would have produced 10,000 dozen, this year at that price they would not produce any eggs at all; that while last year at 40 cents they would have produced 40,000 dozen, this year they would produce only 20,000 dozen; and so on. Graphically this new supply schedule would be represented by a new supply curve, S_1S_1, lying above and to the left of the original curve, SS, as in Figure 5.

On the other hand, we might find that farmers are more anxious to produce eggs than they had been the year before. The cost of labour and feed may have fallen; other types of farming may have become less profitable and a number of farmers may have decided to shift into egg production. Now at a price of 30 cents per dozen the local farm community would produce 25,000 dozen whereas last year they would have produced only 10,000 dozen; and so on. Graphically this would be represented by a new supply curve S_2S_2, located below and to the right of the original curve SS.

An example will demonstrate the significance of the relative positions of the three curves. At a price of OA, suppliers were originally prepared to produce the quantity AB. When their supply curve shifts to S_1S_1, then, at this price they would produce only the quantity AC; if their supply curve had shifted to S_2S_2, then they would be prepared to produce, at this same price, the quantity AE.

Last year, in order to induce them to produce the quantity OF they had to be offered a price of FG per dozen. If this year their supply curve had shifted to S_1S_1 then they would now require a price of FH per dozen to produce the same quantity. On the other hand, if their supply curve had shifted to S_2S_2, then they would now be prepared to produce the quantity OF even if they were only offered the price FJ.

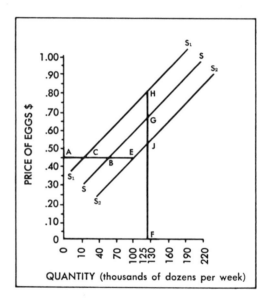

Figure 5.
Changes in supply

The Equilibrium Price Shifts

Just what the equilibrium price will be at any given time will depend on what the demand is and what the supply is *at the time*. In Figure 6, two different sets of curves are shown. If on a particular date D_1D_1 represents the existing demand, and S_1S_1 represents the existing supply, then the equilibrium price at that time will be P_1. If at another time D_2D_2 represents the prevailing demand and S_2S_2 represents the prevailing supply, then P_2 will be the current equilibrium price.

General Validity of Demand and Supply Analysis

Using our common sense, we have been able to analyse the working of the forces which determine the price and output of eggs in Winnipeg. Experience suggests to us that the price and output of every good and service everywhere is likely to be determined in the same general way. Every commodity and service has, at any time, its own particular demand and its own particular supply, and these determine the current equilibrium price and output. As demand and supply change, the equilibrium price will change correspondingly.

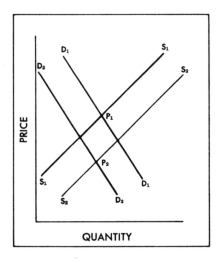

Figure 6.
Changes in the equilibrium price

INTERRELATED GOODS

Interrelated in Demand

The demand for one commodity may be affected by a change in the price of another commodity. Suppose that two goods are substitutes, as are beef and veal for instance. If the supply of beef increases and the price therefore falls, people will likely buy more —and consequently need less veal. The price of veal is likely to fall, therefore, because of the reduced demand. On the other hand, if the supply of beef declines and the price rises, people will presumably buy less—and turn to veal instead; because of the increase in demand its price will rise too. Evidently the prices of substitute goods will tend to move up and down together.

If two goods are complementary in use, if, that is, in using one we require the other, then their relationship will be precisely the reverse. If the supply of one good increases so that its price falls, more of it will be bought and demand will therefore increase for the complementary good, causing its price to rise. Similarly, we would find that when the supply of a good declined causing its price to rise and less to be bought, demand would fall for the complementary good and its price would fall. A striking illustration of this relationship occurred following the Suez crisis of 1956 when, following closure of the Suez Canal, oil and gasoline products were in desperately short supply throughout Europe and their prices soared; the price of automobiles declined heavily.

Interrelated in Supply

Two goods may be joint products, in that they are always produced together, as are beef and hides. In such a case when the demand for one rises (and therefore the price), more will be produced and more of the joint product will also be produced. The price of the joint product is accordingly likely to fall. Thus, if the demand for beef increases, its price will rise and more cattle will be slaughtered. More hides will be produced too, and the increase in their output will probably bring a reduction in their price; i.e., an increase in the price of beef is followed by a decline in the price of hides, the joint product. Correspondingly, a fall in the price of beef is likely to cause a rise in the price of hides.

Two goods may be competitive products from the point of view of the supplier: they both require the same resources for their production. For instance, wheat and barley can be grown on the same land, so that a farmer has the choice of growing one or the other. A rise in the price of wheat will likely induce farmers to sow more wheat and less barley. As a result barley will become less plentiful and its price will tend to rise. A reduction in the price of wheat will probably cause farmers to produce less wheat and more barley. Barley will therefore become more plentiful, and its price will fall. Evidently where two goods are competitive from the supply side, requiring the same resources for their production, their prices will tend to move up and down together.

EXCEPTIONAL TYPES OF DEMAND AND SUPPLY

In general, when the price of a commodity falls, people will buy more of it; when its price rises they will buy less. But this rule is not universally valid. Some people tend to buy more of something when its price rises and less when its price falls, exhibiting this perverse kind of behaviour for two possible reasons:

They may feel that something can be good only if it is expensive, so that if the price is lowered they buy less and if the price is raised they buy more.

They may believe that a recent change in the price of some good will soon be followed by an additional change in the same direction. For example, the price of a certain share may fall on the stock market. Speculators may conclude that it is likely to fall even further. Instead of buying more of these shares because their price has fallen, they actually buy less or none at all; they are waiting for the price to fall further before they buy. A rise in the price of a stock, on the other hand, may induce them to buy more of it, because it leads them to believe that the price will soon rise even higher.[2]

A corresponding perversity may exist in regard to the *supply* of some goods or services, i.e., at higher prices less may be produced. This perversity of supply is most likely to be found in the supply of the services of human beings. A person who earns

---

[2]A person's demand for certain types of *inferior goods* may also be perverse in that when he becomes richer he buys more of better quality goods and less of inferior goods. For example, a person might, when he was poor, buy second-hand furniture; when his fortunes improved, however, he would likely buy only new furniture.

his income by working may set himself the objective of earning a specific amount of money, and may not be particularly interested in earning more. If he is paid at a low rate for his labour, he will have to do a good deal of work in order to earn his target income. If he is paid at a high rate, he will be able to earn that income with very little work. Every time the price of his labour is increased, he provides less of it. Graphically, this kind of supply would be represented by a curve which looks like a demand curve; it would slope downward and to the right, indicating that at a high price only a small quantity would be offered, and that with each decline in price more would be offered.

ELASTICITY OF DEMAND AND SUPPLY

Save for the exceptional cases just noted, it is generally true that consumers buy more of a good when its price falls, and suppliers produce more of a good when its price rises. However, if we are to use this knowledge in practical situations, we should know something further. We should know *by how much* consumers' purchases will increase as a result of any particular price reduction, and *by how much* suppliers' output will rise as a result of any particular price increase. We should know, for instance, whether a 10% reduction in the price of eggs will cause the amount bought to increase by 2%, by 10%, or by 50%; we should know whether a 10% increase in price will induce suppliers to increase their output by 10%, by more, or by less. What we should know is what the economist calls the *elasticity* of demand and supply.

Elasticity of Demand

By elasticity of demand the economist means the degree to which the amount sold of any good varies as a result of change in its price.[3] It is expressed numerically as follows:

$$\text{elasticity of demand} = \frac{\% \text{ change in quantity sold}^4}{\% \text{ change in price}}$$

[3]To avoid being cumbersome, all illustrations given here refer to the consequences of price reductions only. The student should appreciate, however, that elasticity of demand refers also to the ratio between a percentage *increase* in price and the consequent percentage *reduction* in amount sold. Similarly, elasticity of supply refers to the effect on output of a reduction, as well as an increase, in the price offered.

[4]A minor complication arises in the calculation of elasticity, as a result of the fact that the percentage change in price and quantity can be calculated in different ways, each yielding a different result. Thus suppose that the price of a certain good falls from $10 to $9, and that sales therefore increase from 1000 units to 1100 units. We might say that price had fallen by $\frac{\$1}{\$10} = 10\%$, or that it had fallen by $\frac{\$1}{\$9} = 11.1\%$; similarly, we might say that sales had increased by $\frac{100}{1000} = 10\%$, or that they had increased by $\frac{100}{1100} = 9.1\%$. In calculating the elasticity of demand in this case our result will depend upon which figures we use. For the sake of consistency, and as a reasonable compromise, a good many economists recommend that we consider, as the percentage change in each case, the figure yielded by relating the amount of the change to the *average* of the new and old figures. Thus in the above example the percentage change in price would be taken as being $\frac{\$1}{\$9\frac{1}{2}} = 10.52\%$; the percentage change in quantity would be considered to be $\frac{100}{1050}$ units $= 9.52\%$. The elasticity of demand would accordingly be $\frac{9.52\%}{10.52\%} = .905$.

Thus if the price of eggs were reduced by 10%, and the quantity bought consequently increased by 20%, we would say that the elasticity of demand for eggs was

$$\frac{10\%}{20\%} = 2.$$

If the amount sold had increased by only 5%, then the elasticity of demand would have been

$$\frac{5\%}{10\%} = \frac{1}{2}.$$

For convenience in analysis, the economist classifies, according to their elasticity, the following types of demand:

1. **Demand of unitary elasticity,** i.e. elasticity of exactly one. In this case any reduction in price causes the amount sold to increase by an exactly offsetting percentage so that the total value of sales therefore remains constant, regardless of what price is charged.[5]

2. **Inelastic demand,** i.e. demand of which the elasticity is less than one. Here a reduction in price leads to a decline in total sales receipts, since the increase in amount sold is insufficient to offset the effect of the reduction in price per unit.

3. **Elastic demand,** i.e. demand of which the elasticity is greater than one. Here a reduction in price results in an increase in total sales receipts, since the increase in amount sold more than offsets the effect of the reduction in price per unit.

4. **Perfectly inelastic demand,** i.e. demand such that people buy exactly the same quantity, regardless of what price is charged.

5. **Perfectly elastic demand,** i.e. demand such that consumers are prepared to buy an unlimited quantity at some particular price, but would buy none whatsoever if they had to pay anything more than that price.

The five different types of demand are graphically illustrated in Figure 7, in which as usual the vertical axes represent price, and the horizontal axes represent quantity.

Referring to Figure 7:[6]

(a) D_1D_1 is *inelastic*; a large price reduction produces only a slight increase in the quantity consumers wish to buy.

(b) D_2D_2 is *elastic*; a small price reduction produces a large increase in the quantity consumers wish to buy.

---

[5]To be strictly accurate, this is true only when the change in price is infinitesimally small. If the change is of significant size, then, even if the quantity sold varies by exactly the same percentage, there will be some change in the total value of sales. The point is a pretty fine one, however, and of little practical significance.

[6]In more advanced discussion, it would be pointed out that the slope of a demand curve does not conclusively indicate its elasticity. Slope is only one component of elasticity. The scales used in the graph will affect the steepness of the slope of the demand curve; an elastic demand could conceivably be represented by a steep demand curve. Furthermore, the elasticity of even a straight line varies as between different positions on the line. However, in our elementary analysis it is helpful to represent elastic and inelastic demands as in Figure 7, and we are not likely to fall into serious error.

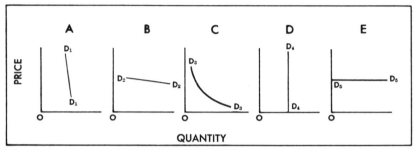

Figure 7.   Types of elasticity of demand

(c) D_3D_3 has *unitary elasticity*; any price reduction leads to an increase of the same percentage in the quantity which people wish to buy.

(d) D_4D_4 is *perfectly inelastic*; the same quantity OD_4 is bought regardless of what price is charged.

(e) D_5D_5 is *perfectly elastic*; an unlimited quantity will be bought at the constant price OD_5, but none will be bought if the price is in the slightest degree above OD_5.

Why is the demand for some goods elastic, while the demand for other goods is inelastic? The answer lies in the differing characteristics of the goods demanded. In general we will find that the demand tends to be inelastic for goods which have one or more of the following attributes:

1. A certain quantity is considered to be necessary, but anything above this quantity is considered to be of little additional use, e.g. salt.
2. Our total expenditure on the good is insignificant, so that even after a large percentage increase in price, the total cost is still a very small amount, e.g. mucilage.
3. It has no close substitute which could serve the same purpose, e.g. milk.
4. It is required in conjunction with some other good which is of very much greater value, e.g. shoelaces.

For goods which lack these characteristics, demand will tend to be elastic.

The elasticity of demand for a good is likely to be greater the longer the time period considered. It may not be easy for individuals to change their consumption habits abruptly; for a lengthy period after a price change has occurred they will buy the same goods and in the same amounts. Business firms are also likely to display a more elastic demand over a long period than over a short period. For example, for some time after a sharp fall in the price of aluminum, industrial firms may buy very little more, and continue to use steel for purposes where aluminum is equally satisfactory and now more economical. They may do this because it takes them a good deal of time to adjust their operations to the use of aluminum. Once they make the adjustment, however, they greatly increase their purchases of aluminum.

Elasticity of Supply

Elasticity of supply is analogous to elasticity of demand; it measures the degree to which producers increase their output as a result of a rise in price. If, when the price rose by 5%, producers increased their output of eggs by 15%, we would say that the elasticity of supply was $\dfrac{15\%}{5\%} = 3$. As with demand there are five categories of elasticity of supply. These are illustrated in Figure 8.[7]

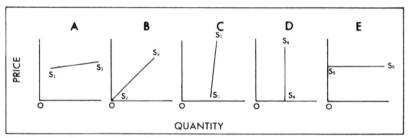

Figure 8.   Types of elasticity of supply

(a) S_1S_1 *elastic* (elasticity greater than one); a small increase in price induces a large increase in output.

(b) S_2S_2, *unitary elasticity*; an increase in price of a certain percentage induces an increase in amount produced of the same percentage.

(c) S_3S_3, *inelastic* (elasticity less than one); a large increase in price induces only a small increase in quantity produced.

(d) S_4S_4, *perfectly inelastic*; a constant amount OS_4 is produced, regardless of the price offered.

(e) S_5S_5, *perfectly elastic*; suppliers will supply any amount desired, at the price OS_5.

Whether the supply of a commodity is elastic or inelastic will depend largely upon the ease with which output can be increased or decreased. In general we will find that the supply of a commodity will tend to be elastic:

1. If, when producers change the scale of their operations, there is no marked change in their operating efficiency, and therefore no marked change in cost of production per unit;

2. If, when it is desired to increase output, the necessary additional factors of production can be readily obtained at prices little if any higher than the prices now being paid to the factors already employed;

3. If, when it is desired to reduce output, the factors of production which are no

---

[7]The qualifying comments in Footnotes 3 and 4 apply to supply curves as well.

longer required can be transferred to other employment, and there earn practically the same rewards.

Elasticity of supply, like elasticity of demand, *will depend upon the time period considered.* When the price of a particular commodity increases sharply, there may at first be very little increase in the amount produced. Supply appears to be inelastic. But this limited response may be only temporary, and attributable simply to the fact that it takes a good deal of time to arrange for a large increase in output. Because of a sharp increase in the price of their product, producers may wish to increase their output greatly but all they may be able to do at first to increase output is take on a few more untrained workers whose contribution to output would likely be small. To achieve a really large increase in output it may be necessary to build more plant, to acquire more equipment, to train more key personnel; all of these measures are likely to require a good deal of time. Hence, while producers may, in fact, decide right away to expand their output in response to a rise in price, the main part of the increase may materialize only after a considerable lapse of time. In such a case, if one considered only the time period immediately after the price increase, supply would appear to be inelastic; however, if one considered a longer time period, a period sufficiently long for plant capacity to be enlarged and additional personnel to be trained, then supply would appear to be elastic.

The Significance of Elasticity When Demand or Supply Changes

Earlier in this chapter we learned that, for any commodity, a change in the demand or the supply will cause a shift both in the equilibrium price and in the equilibrium output. An increase in the demand will cause the equilibrium price to rise and the equilibrium output to become greater. An increase in the supply will also cause the

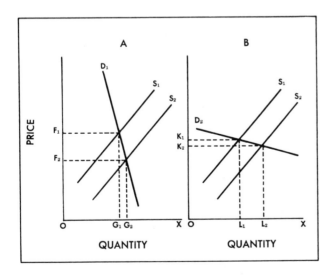

Figure 9.
Significance of elasticity of demand when supply shifts

equilibrium output to become greater, but will cause the equilibrium price to fall. While any change in demand or supply will thus alter both the equilibrium price and the equilibrium output, the effects will vary with different situations. In some cases, a change in demand or supply will primarily affect the equilibrium price. The equilibrium output may change very little; in extreme situations it may not change at all. Conversely, we may find in other cases that when demand or supply shift, it is the equilibrium output which is primarily affected; the price changes very little, and possibly not at all.

These differing responses to shifts in demand or supply will be attributable to *differences in the elasticities involved.* Thus, if demand is inelastic, then a shift in supply will cause a large change in the price, but only a small change in the quantity bought. If demand were elastic, the same shift in supply would cause only a slight change in the price, but a very large change in the quantity bought. Fig. 9 graphically illustrates these propositions.

In Fig. 9A, the demand curve D_1 is inelastic. When the supply shifts from S_1 to S_2, the equilibrium price declines heavily, from OF_1 to OF_2; the equilibrium output increases only slightly, however, from OG_1 to OG_2. In Fig. 9B, the demand curve D_2 is elastic. In this case, with the same change in supply, from S_1 to S_2, the results are very different. Here price declines only slightly, from OK_1 to OK_2; output increases greatly, from OL_1 to OL_2.

The real world offers many instances of elastic and inelastic demand such as is illustrated in Fig. 9. As was illustrated in Figure 7, however, there exists the theoretical possibility of three additional types of demand: demand which is perfectly elastic, demand which is perfectly inelastic, and demand which everywhere has an elasticity of exactly one. We are not likely to find examples of these theoretically conceivable types in the real world, but in some instances the actual demand may approach one or other of these extremes. Fig. 10 graphically illustrates what would happen when supply shifted, if the demand were one or other of these extreme types.

In Fig. 10A, the demand curve D_1 is perfectly elastic; when the supply shifts from S_1 to S_2, the price remains OM, exactly the same as before; the quantity produced increases, however, from ON_1 to ON_2. In Fig. 10B, the demand curve D_2 is perfectly inelastic; here the same shift in supply, from S_1 to S_2, causes the price to fall from OP_1 to OP_2; the quantity remains unchanged at OQ. In Fig. 10C, the demand curve D_3 is of unit elasticity; when the supply shifts from S_1 to S_2, the price falls from OR_1 to OR_2; the quantity produced increases by the same proportion, from OT_1 to OT_2.

In the same general way, the effects of a shift in demand will depend upon the elasticity of the supply involved. Where supply is inelastic, a shift in demand will cause a large change in the equilibrium price but only a small change in the equilibrium output. Where supply is elastic, a shift in demand will have a small effect on the price and a large effect on the output. The student may work out his own graphical illustration of these propositions.

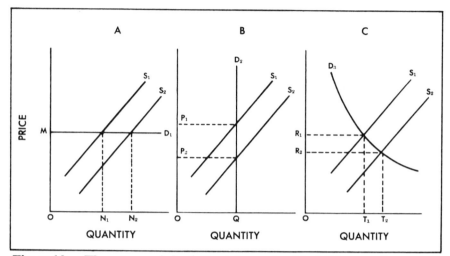

Figure 10.   Three types of elasticity of demand, with shifting supply

Arbitrage

When the same good is sold in different markets, then, all other things being equal, the prices in the different markets should differ by no more than the cost of transportation. For instance, if it costs 25 cents to ship a bushel of wheat from Montreal to Liverpool the price of wheat in Liverpool should not exceed the Montreal price by more than 25 cents. If ever a larger price differential developed, *arbitrage* transactions would quickly follow. If it ever happened, for example, that wheat was selling for $1.25 in Montreal and for $1.75 in Liverpool, dealers would rush to buy wheat in Montreal for shipment to Liverpool. Their actions would reduce the price differential: purchases in Montreal would push up the price there; sales in Liverpool would push down the price here. Such arbitrage transactions would continue until the price differential was reduced to its appropriate figure of 25 cents.

Speculation

Markets may be separated by time as well as by space; there is the same need for an appropriate relationship of prices. In Canada, for instance, wheat harvested in September is needed every day of the year. Because of the great quantity put on the market in September, the price would at that time tend to be very low; because no wheat was harvested in December the price would then tend to be very high. The *speculator* looks ahead to future market situations; he buys wheat at the low September price in order to sell it at the higher price expected in December. His actions serve to smooth out wheat prices over the year, raising them in September and reducing them in December. Prices will not be absolutely equalized, of course; because of storage charges, wheat should normally cost somewhat more in December than in September.

Hedging

Some business firms, because of the nature of their operations, are exposed to the danger of windfall loss due to unexpected price changes. A flour miller, for instance, may buy wheat in September which he proposes to grind into flour next March. Say that he pays $2.00 per bushel and that storage until March costs a further 10 cents per bushel. Suppose, however, that because of an adverse market situation the price of wheat drops to $1.90 in March; the miller will have lost 20 cents per bushel.

He could safeguard himself against this danger by *hedging*. He could sell wheat to a speculator at a price of $2.10 per bushel, to be delivered in March. In that case, if wheat drops to $1.90 the miller comes out even; he loses 20 cents on the wheat he bought in September but makes a profit of 20 cents on the deal with the speculator, since he can buy at $1.90 wheat which the speculator has under-taken to buy from him at $2.10.[8] If March wheat had risen above $2.10 the miller would achieve a profit on the wheat he had bought in September but would suffer an equal loss on his contract with the speculator. The effect of his hedge has been to eliminate the possibility of both windfall loss and windfall gain.

THE PRICE SYSTEM

We saw in Chapter I that the productive capacity of even the richest country has its limits, and that accordingly every country must take care to direct its economic activities efficiently. Watchful attention must be paid to ensure that the largest possible aggregate of goods is produced, with the amount of each type produced being in proper proportion. Furthermore, abundant though a country's output may be, it is still a finite quantity. There can never be enough to give an unlimited amount to everybody; there can never in fact be enough to give each person the full amount of goods which he would like to have. Some procedure must therefore be employed whereby the country's output of goods, which is limited in quantity, is divided up among people who would like to have far more.

The price system automatically performs the dual function of arranging what goods a country produces, and how these goods are divided up among the country's people. Demand and supply conditions determine what quantity of each commodity shall be produced, and how that quantity changes through time. As we have seen, an increase in the demand for a good, reflecting an increase in the public's desire for it,

[8]The speculator will make the deal because he expects that wheat will sell for more than $2.10 in March.

will bring a rise in its price and, therefore, will induce an increase in its output. A fall in demand, reflecting a decrease in public preference, will result in a fall in price, which in turn brings about a reduction in output. The public's expenditures represent a kind of balloting; each dollar spent on a particular commodity constitutes a "vote" in favour of its production, so to speak. Each commodity is produced in a quantity which reflects the number of "votes" cast in its favour by buyers. The "voting" goes on continuously, and the production of each commodity is adjusted continuously, in conformity with shifts in the degree to which it is favoured by the public. Changes in supply, reflecting changes in cost of production, will also have their effects on price and output.

The price system arranges as well for the distribution of a nation's product among its citizens. Each person receives an income, which itself is usually a price, being the price paid for his productive services, and determined, as are prices generally, by demand and supply.[9] The size of his income determines what share of the nation's product each person can obtain. For each commodity which is produced has its price, as we have seen, and the would-be purchaser must pay it. The available quantity of each commodity is "rationed out," so to speak, to the people who are willing and able to pay its price. Those people whose incomes are large will be able to buy more goods; those whose incomes are small will be able to buy less. So, through the price system, the real rewards of all people—the actual goods which they are able to obtain—are determined by the valuation placed by society upon the services they perform.

SUMMARY

The equilibrium price and output of any good is determined by the demand for it and the supply offered. The demand will reflect the desire of consumers; the supply will reflect the costs of producers. Changes in demand or supply will cause shifts in the equilibrium price and quantity.

The prices of some goods are interrelated. When goods are substitutes their prices will tend to move together in the same direction; the prices of complementary goods tend to move in opposite directions.

Elasticity of demand represents the degree to which the quantity which consumers wish to buy of some commodity is affected by a change in its price. Elasticity of supply represents the degree to which the quantity offered for sale by suppliers is affected by a change in price.

The demand and supply of all goods and services collectively give rise to a price system which automatically determines how a country's productive capacity is allocated and how its annual output is distributed.

[9]There are exceptions, however, as we shall see in later chapters.

FOR REVIEW AND DISCUSSION

1. The successful speculator is an asset to society; the unsuccessful speculator, besides losing his own money, is a social nuisance. Why?
2. It is not always necessary for a nation to reduce its current consumption in order to accelerate its progress. Do you agree?
3. The elasticity of a straight line demand curve would not be the same over the whole length of the line. Why not?
4. Which is likely to have the more elastic demand: milk or oranges? Explain.
5. A price system would be necessary even under Socialism. Do you agree? Justify your answer.
6. A French cabinet minister recently urged French housewives to cut down their food costs by buying each day only those foods which were cheap at the time. Was this economically sound?
7. It is a fact that as a nation grows wealthier, an increasing proportion of its work force becomes employed in service industries. Why should this be so?
8. Make up hypothetical demand and supply schedules for some commodity. Plot your data. Indicate the equilibrium price and explain why equilibrium could not occur at any other price.
9. Illustrating graphically and specifying the assumptions upon which your reasoning is based, describe the following:
   (a) The effects on the price and output of oranges of an insect blight which sharply reduces, over a period of years, all grapefruit crops.
   (b) The effect on the price of shoe leather of widespread decisions to become vegetarian.
   (c) The effect on the price of mutton of the development of synthetic fabrics which are effective substitutes for wool.

4

Applications of Price Theory

In the preceding chapter we worked out a theory which explained how the forces of supply and demand determine the price of any good and the quantity produced. Here, we shall make use of this theory in a discussion of practical issues. Governments nowadays impose sales taxes upon most goods, pay subsidies toward the production of some, and attempt, by means of "floors" and "ceilings," to control the prices of others. In this chapter we shall examine the theoretical implications of such measures and describe actual programmes of price support currently maintained in the United States and Canada.

THEORETICAL PRINCIPLES

Taxes on Goods Sold

Primarily in order to raise revenue, governments impose taxes upon goods sold.[1] For each unit sold the seller is required to pay a tax or duty to the government. This levy might be a fixed sum of money per unit or a percentage of the selling price.

To illustrate the effects of a tax on a commodity, let us refer back to the market for eggs in Winnipeg which we described in the preceding chapter. Suppose that the federal government, suddenly indifferent to the views and votes of chicken ranchers and housewives, were to impose a tax of ten cents per dozen on eggs. After the tax had been imposed, the producers, in order actually to receive for themselves any particular sum per dozen, would have to charge the consumer ten cents more than that sum. We saw, referring to the original supply schedule, that if producers are to produce 40,000 dozen, they must receive forty cents per dozen. Obviously once the tax has been imposed they must now receive from the consumer a price of fifty cents per dozen if they are to produce this same quantity. Similarly, whereas previously with consumers paying sixty cents per dozen, producers would have supplied 100,000

---

[1]The exceptions are important. Protective tariffs are in effect sales taxes imposed upon foreign goods primarily in order to discourage their importation rather than to raise revenue. Also governments may impose *sumptuary* taxes upon certain goods in order to make them dearer, and thereby discourage their consumption.

dozen, now they will supply that amount only if consumers pay seventy cents per dozen; and so on.

As indicated in Table 1, the producers' supply schedule has shifted. Column (2) indicates the prices which consumers had to pay, before the tax was imposed, to induce the production of the quantities shown in Column (1). Column (3) indicates the price which they must pay, after the tax has been imposed, to induce the production of the same quantities. Each price in Column (3) is ten cents higher than the corresponding price in Column (2).

Table 1

DOZENS OF EGGS PRODUCED PER WEEK BY FARMERS NEAR WINNIPEG

(1)	(2)	(3)
Quantity Produced per Week	Price Paid by Consumers (before tax)	Price Paid by Consumers (after tax)
10,000 doz.	$ .30 per doz.	$ .40 per doz.
40,000 "	.40 " "	.50 " "
70,000 "	.50 " "	.60 " "
100,000 "	.60 " "	.70 " "
130,000 "	.70 " "	.80 " "
160,000 "	.80 " "	.90 " "
190,000 "	.90 " "	1.00 " "
220,000 "	1.00 " "	1.10 " "

The full implications of this shift in the supply schedule are best illustrated through a graphical portrayal. In Figure 1 D_1D_1 represents the demand for eggs in Winnipeg, on the basis of the demand schedule given in chapter 3. The curve S_1S_1 represents the original supply schedule, which existed before the tax was imposed. The curve S_2S_2 represents the new supply schedule which comes into being after the tax has been imposed. Measuring vertically, S_2S_2 is ten cents higher than S_1S_1, at all points; i.e. each point on S_2S_2 is ten cents above the point on S_1S_1 which represents the same output.

Before the tax was imposed, output and price were determined by D_1D_1 and S_1S_1. Output was therefore OQ and price QP; since there was no tax, this sum represented both what the consumer paid and what the producer received. Following the imposition of the tax, price and output are determined by D_1D_1 and S_2S_2. The price paid by the consumer therefore becomes AT. But the producer cannot keep this full amount for himself; he must pay to the government the amount of the tax, equal to BT, and is therefore left with only AB per dozen as payment for his efforts. Output drops since if he receives only AB per dozen the producer will produce only the quantity OA.

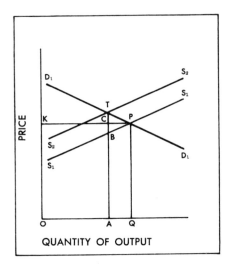

Figure 1.
Effects of a sales tax

As a result of the tax, the price paid by the consumer is higher than before, but the net amount obtained per dozen by the producer is lower than before. We can measure the degree to which the price to the consumer has risen and the return to the producer has fallen. Draw the horizontal reference line KP through to P. Because the point C is on this horizontal line, the length AC is equal to QP, which represents the price before the tax was imposed. If, after the tax, the consumer pays a price of AT, then obviously he is paying CT per dozen more than before. Similarly, if after paying the tax, the producer is left with AB per dozen, he is obtaining BC less than before. Thus the total burden of the tax (which is equal to BT) is distributed between consumer and producer: because of the tax the consumer pays CT more per dozen, while the producer receives BC less.

If the government were to impose a sales tax in the form of a percentage of the selling price, our graphical portrayal would differ in one significant respect. S_2S_2 would not be vertically higher than S_1S_1 by a constant amount; instead, at higher prices the difference between the two curves would be greater. The student is invited to analyze graphically for himself the effects of such a tax.

The Significance of Elasticity

What determines how the burden of a tax is shared, i.e. how much is borne by the producer and how much by the consumer? In our illustration the shares appeared to be approximately equal: the price increase to consumers (CT) was roughly equal to the reduction in return per dozen suffered by producers (BC). Such an equal distribution of the tax burden does not inevitably occur, however. As we shall now prove, the distribution of the burden will depend upon the elasticities of the demand

and supply involved. Figures (2) and (3) illustrate this proposition graphically.[2]

In Figure 2 the demand curve D_1D_1 is the same as D_1D_1 in Figure 1. The supply curve S_1S_1, however, represents a pre-tax supply schedule which is much more inelastic than that represented by S_1S_1 in Figure 1. If now, as before, we assume that a tax of ten cents per dozen is imposed, we obtain a new supply schedule represented by S_2S_2, which is vertically above S_1S_1 by ten cents at all points.

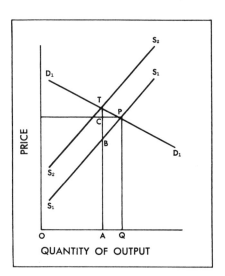

Figure 2.
Effects of a sales tax, with
supply inelastic

From Figure 2 it is quite clear that in this case the burden of the tax (BT) is borne mainly by producers. The price paid by consumers rises slightly, by CT; the return received per dozen by producers falls greatly, by BC. Evidently when supply is inelastic, the burden of a sales tax is borne chiefly by the producers, and only a small portion falls on the consumers.

In Figure 3 the supply curve S_1S_1 is the same as S_1S_1 in Figure 1, which represented the pre-tax supply schedule. However, the demand curve D_1D_1 is much more inelastic than is D_1D_1 in Figure 1. Assuming that a tax of ten cents per dozen is now imposed, the supply curve shifts to S_2S_2, vertically above S_1S_1 by 10 cents at all points.

It is evident that in this case consumers bear the main burden of the tax. Of the total tax LN, the large portion MN is borne by consumers in the form of an increase in the price which they pay. Producers bear a small portion of the burden; their return per dozen falls only by LM.

[2]We continue here with the convention, referred to in Chapter 3, that slope and elasticity are synonymous. Actually, the distribution of the burden of a sales tax will depend purely upon the *slopes* of the demand and supply curves. Elasticity of demand and supply determine by how much, *percentagewise*, price rises to the consumer and falls to the producer, following the imposition of a tax.

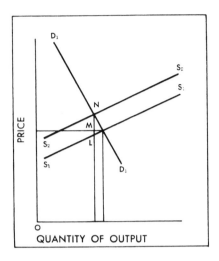

Figure 3.
Effects of a sales tax, with
demand inelastic

Students may devise additional examples to show how the burden of a sales tax will be distributed when demand or supply are highly elastic. They will find that this general rule holds in all cases: the more elastic the demand, the smaller will be the share of the tax borne by the consumer; the more elastic the supply, the smaller will be the share of the tax borne by the producer.

The Effects of a Subsidy

A subsidy is the exact opposite of a tax, and its effects are exactly opposite as well. Referring once more to the egg market in Winnipeg, if the government were to grant a subsidy on eggs of ten cents per dozen a new supply schedule would come into being. Whereas previously producers required forty cents per dozen from consumers if they were to supply 40,000 dozen, now they would supply this amount if consumers paid only thirty cents per dozen; the other ten cents which they require they will be getting from the government in subsidy. The same holds true for each possible output: to induce them to produce any particular quantity of eggs they will now require ten cents less per dozen from the consumers than before.

Table 2 indicates how the supply schedule would change as a result of a subsidy of ten cents per dozen. Column (2) shows the prices that consumers would have to pay, before the subsidy was granted, to induce producers to supply particular quantities. Column (3) shows the prices that consumers would have to pay, after the subsidy is granted, to induce producers to supply the same quantities.

Again let us resort to graphical demonstration. In Figure 4 D_1D_1 represents the demand schedule for eggs in Winnipeg; S_1S_1 represents the original supply schedule

Table 2

DOZENS OF EGGS PRODUCED PER WEEK BY FARMERS NEAR WINNIPEG

(1) Quantity Produced per Week	(2) Price Paid by Consumers (before subsidy)	(3) Price Paid by Consumers (after subsidy)
10,000 doz.	$ .30 per doz.	$ .20 per doz.
40,000 "	.40 " "	.30 " "
70,000 "	.50 " "	.40 " "
100,000 "	.60 " "	.50 " "
130,000 "	.70 " "	.60 " "
160,000 "	.80 " "	.70 " "
190,000 "	.90 " "	.80 " "
220,000 "	1.00 " "	.90 " "

which was effective before the subsidy; S_2S_2 represents the supply schedule which comes into being as a result of the subsidy and is vertically lower than S_1S_1 by ten cents at all points; i.e. each point on S_2S_2 is lower by ten cents than the point on S_1S_1 which represents the same output.

As is evident in Figure 4, the price paid by the consumer, originally QP, declines to FG following the granting of the subsidy. The total return per dozen to the producer becomes FK, comprised of the price FG paid by the consumer plus the subsidy GK given by the government. Output increases from OQ to OF. The benefit of the subsidy is shared between producers and consumers; producers benefit because they receive a return which is greater by HK than what they received before; consumers benefit because they pay a price which is lower by GH than what they paid before.

Like the burden of a tax, the benefit of a subsidy is distributed between pro-

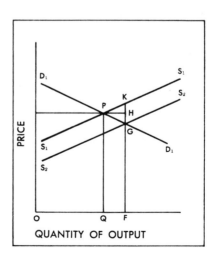

Figure 4.
Effects of a subsidy

ducers and consumers according to the elasticities of supply and demand. The more inelastic the supply, the greater will be the portion of the benefit realized by the producers; the more inelastic the demand, the larger will be the portion of the benefit realized by the consumers. Students may prove this for themselves by means of graphical demonstrations.

Price Ceilings

Governments sometimes impose ceilings on prices; i.e., they may order the suppliers of a particular product, usually a basic necessity, not to charge more than a stipulated maximum price for it. Almost invariably the occasion for such an order is a sharp rise in its price, or the threat of such a rise, which would drive the market price substantially above the level which has prevailed for a long time and which people have come to regard as normal and proper. Sharp increases in the prices of basic commodities usually occur, of course, only under conditions of emergency, such as during wartime. Supplies may then fall off because of shortages of shipping space, or because necessary raw materials and labour are used in the war effort instead. At the same time, demand may rise because a great many people enjoy increases in income; or perhaps because many provident people anticipate that later on goods will be in short supply and accordingly rush to lay in an ample stock "before the hoarders get it all." With supply reduced and demand increased, price is bound to rise substantially. In the case of a basic commodity which everyone needs, such as sugar, everybody feels the effect. For people with low incomes some degree of hardship may result. Suppliers are accused of profiteering, and the government is called upon to protect consumers by fixing ceiling prices.

Figure 5 illustrates the situation which develops and indicates the consequences of price control by the government. SS and DD represent the supply and demand which had prevailed for a long time previously and OP represents the price at which the commodity had customarily been sold. S_1S_1 and D_1D_1 represent respectively the new supply and demand which come to prevail during the emergency situation. OX therefore represents the current equilibrium price, the price at which the commodity would be sold if the current market supply and demand were its sole determinants.

To protect consumers, the government now declares OP (the customary price) to be the *ceiling price*, the maximum price which sellers may charge. But with their costs being what they are now, if suppliers can get a price of only OP, they will offer to sell only the quantity PQ (that we know from our discussion of price theory in Chapter 3). Consumers, on the other hand, wish to buy the quantity PR. What happens now?

It all depends upon what further action the government takes. Three alternative courses are available; each will produce a different result.

Firstly, the government may do nothing further. In that case suppliers will distribute, as they themselves see fit, the limited quantity PQ among the people who

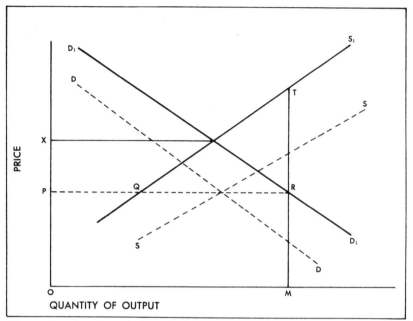

Figure 5.   A price ceiling

wish to buy the larger quantity PR. They may sell only to friends, to old or pretty customers, or to those who come to them first. All other would-be buyers will be disappointed; although willing to pay the market price, they will be unable to buy the goods they want.

Secondly, the government may introduce a formal system of rationing. In that case coupons would be printed, their number being equal to the number of units available of the commodity, that is, the amount PQ. The coupons would be distributed among the public, either on the basis of absolute equality or with some specially deserving persons being given more than others. To obtain a unit of the commodity henceforth, each consumer would be obliged not only to pay the price, but also to hand over a ration coupon. Thus each member of the public would be authorized to buy only his or her appropriate share of the quantity which was available.

Thirdly, the government may offer producers a subsidy. If the government would like all consumers to be able to buy as much as they wished, and at the ceiling price, then it should offer a subsidy of RT per unit. If that were done, producers would be prepared to produce the quantity PR. With the price MR ($=$ OP) being paid to them by the public and the subsidy RT given to them by the government, their total return per unit would be MT. Their supply curve being S_1S_1, a return per unit of MT would induce them to produce the quantity OM (which is equal to PR). The ceiling price would be observed, and the public would be able to buy all that it cared to at that price.

Floor Prices

Governments, as we have just seen, may intervene in the market to protect consumers against excessively high prices; they may also intervene to protect producers against excessively low prices. Because the price which a producer receives for his product is a prime determinant of his income, an extremely low price is likely to mean a disastrously low income. Therefore, when the price of a commodity falls, or threatens to fall, to a level which would be ruinous to its producers, the government may protect them by setting a *floor price;* i.e. it guarantees to producers that they will receive no less than this price. To be of any significance, of course, the floor price would have to be above the equilibrium market price which would prevail if market supply and demand were its sole determinants. If it were not above the equilibrium level, a floor price would merely be guaranteeing to producers something which they would receive anyhow.

In Figure 6, OJ represents the equilibrium price, or the market price which would prevail on the basis of the existing supply and demand situation. Because the government decides that this price will yield insufficient income to producers, it announces a floor price of OF. However, at a price of OF, consumers will buy only the

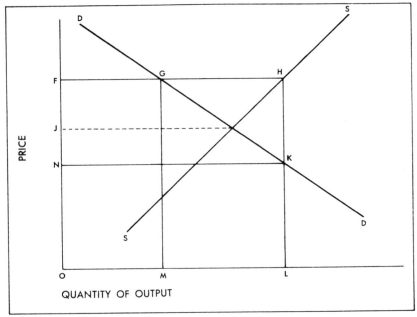

Figure 6.   A price floor

quantity FG, while suppliers will produce the quantity FH. If the government takes no further action a market surplus will develop, forcing the market price below the floor. What must the government do to ensure that its guarantee is effective, and that producers do in fact receive a price of OF on all their output?

It can do any one of three things. It can induce suppliers to produce only the quantity FG, presumably by offering them some kind of bonus for restricting their output. If output is held down to FG, no surplus will develop on the market. Consumers will buy this quantity, paying the floor price for it; producers will take in the amount OMGF in sales to the public, and will receive in addition whatever payments the government makes to induce them *not* to produce the additional output GH.

If the government does not induce producers to curtail their output, and if the market price is held at the floor price of OF, a surplus will emerge which the government must buy. With the public buying only FG and suppliers producing FH, the size of this surplus will be GH. The government pays the floor price, so that producers' total income would be represented by the area OLHF, of which OMGF represents receipts from sales to the public and MLHG represents receipts from sales to the government.

The government may offer to pay producers a "deficiency payment" amounting to the difference between the floor price and the price which they can get from the public when they put their entire output on the market. Since producers are thereby guaranteed OF per unit they will produce OL units; when they put this amount on the market, the price charged to consumers can be only LK. The government's deficiency payment, therefore, must be KH per unit, so that producers receive in total the promised OF per unit ($=LK+KH$). As in the previous case, the total receipts of producers will be OLHF, but here being made up of OLKN received through sales to the public and NKHF received in payments from the government.

The Significance of Elasticity

The elasticity of both supply and demand will affect the cost to the government of its price support operations. The more elastic supply is the more will a price support programme cost, whether it takes the form of the payment of bonuses for restricting output, the purchase of surpluses, or the payment of subsidies.

Figure 7 illustrates. DD represents the demand for a farm commodity while SiSi and SeSe are two possible supply curves, the latter being the more elastic.

I. If when the government introduces a floor price of OF and it turns out that SiSi is the supply curve, then the government must
   > *i* induce farmers to produce only the amount FB and not the amount FC; i.e. the government, presumably through some compensatory payment, must persuade farmers to produce BC less than they otherwise would have done at a market price of OF.

OR

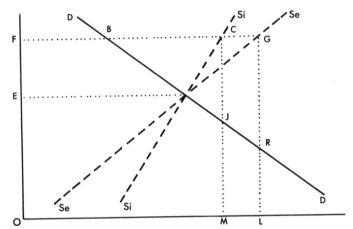

Figure 7.   Elasticity of supply and the cost of price supports*

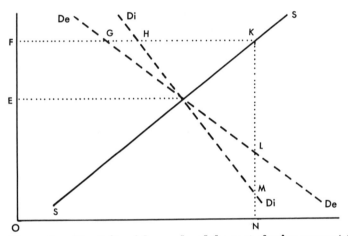

Figure 8.   Elasticity of demand and the cost of price supports*

ii purchase the surplus BC, at the floor price OF.

OR

*SiSi and SeSe must be drawn to intersect the demand curve at the same point in order to demonstrate conclusively the significance of elasticity of supply when a price support is introduced. If there were no price support then obviously it would not matter which curve represented supply: the market price would be OE whichever of the two supply curves was the applicable one. When, however, the price is raised to OF by government action it matters very greatly which is the applicable curve.

By analogous reasoning DiDi and DeDe in Figure 8 must be drawn so as to intersect the supply curve at the same point.

iii make a deficiency payment to farmers of CJ per unit, on the FC units they will be producing.

II. If however SeSe turns out to be the supply curve then to maintain a floor price of OF the government must

    i persuade farmers to produce BG less than they otherwise would have done at a price of OF. Since BG is greater than BC presumably larger compensatory payments would have to be made than in Ii above.

OR

    ii purchase the surplus BG, greater than the surplus BC in Iii above.

OR

    iii make deficiency payments of GR per unit on FG units, whereas in Iiii above it would have only paid CJ per unit on FC units.

The significance of elasticity of demand, in respect to the total cost of a price support programme, will depend upon which method of support is employed. Figure 8 illustrates. SS represents the supply of a farm commodity while DiDi and DeDe are two possible demand curves, the latter being more elastic.

I. If when the government introduces a floor price of OF and it turns out that DiDi represents the demand, then the government must

    i induce farmers to produce only FH and not FK; i.e. it must deter the output of HK.

OR

    ii buy the surplus HK

OR

    iii make a deficiency payment of KM on each of the FK units being produced.

II. If, however, DeDe turns out to be the demand curve, then the government must

    i deter the output GK, presumably therefore making greater compensatory payments than in Ii above.

OR

    ii purchase the surplus GK, greater than the surplus HK in Iii above

OR

    iii make a deficiency payment of KL per unit, less than the payment of KM per unit that would be required in Iiii above.

Evidently, if the object is to minimize government outlay on its support programme then payments to reduce output or the purchase of surpluses should be emphasized where demand is inelastic; deficiency payments should be favoured when demand is elastic.

The Problem of Surplus Disposal

A government which acquires surplus commodities through a price support programme must either sell them abroad at bargain prices or hold them indefinitely. The commodities cannot be sold abroad at the support price: if foreigners were willing to

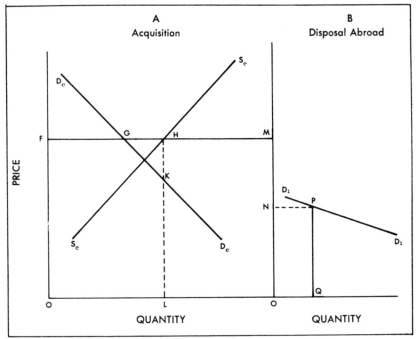

Figure 9.   Acquisition and disposal of surpluses

pay that much there would have been no need for the government to buy anything in the first place; domestic and foreign buyers would between them have bought the entire output at the support price, leaving no surplus for the government to buy. A surplus cannot be offered on the domestic market; if it were, then the domestic price would be forced down below the support level. Figure 9 illustrates the probem.

Figure 9A represents the situation in the country which supports prices through the purchase of surpluses. To maintain the price of OF, the government purchases the surplus GH. It dare not sell this on the domestic market. If it did so the total quantity on the market would become FH (=OL) and the price would be forced down to the level of LK. If there is to be no interference with the domestic price the surplus can be disposed of only by selling it abroad.

Figure 9B represents the demand for the commodity in the foreign country. To sell the surplus GS (=OQ) in this country a price of only QP would have to be charged. Accordingly if the price supporting country does in fact dispose of its surplus by selling it in the foreign country, it must accept a loss of MN per unit. It will be selling commodities at a price equal to ON, after it had bought them at a price equal to OM.

If, of course, at some future date market conditions improve, either at home or abroad, then the government may be able to sell accumulated surpluses at prices equal to, or greater than, the price it paid. Thus the Canadian government, which had acquired considerable stocks of wheat between 1930 and 1935 through price support operations, was able to sell all its holdings in 1936 at prices which fully covered the cost of buying and holding the wheat. As it happened, a series of world-wide droughts in the early 1930s caused crops to be generally poor for several years in succession, transforming glut into shortage; with the "bottom of the barrel being scraped" in 1936, the price rose sharply in that year. (Larger world crops in the next few years drove the price down again.)

PRICE SUPPORTS IN CANADA AND THE U.S.A.

The Case for Agricultural Support Prices

Support prices in Canada and the U.S.A. apply primarily to agricultural products. Cases are on record of such support extended to non-agricultural products, but their relative importance is slight. The major price support programmes maintained by the governments of these two countries apply to agricultural commodities, and are intended to protect the incomes of the farmers who produce them.

Upon what basis is this special assistance to agriculture justified? The government does not support the prices of automobiles, of shirts, of dresses; why should it support the prices of wheat, butter, hogs and potatoes?

The advocates of farm price supports base their claims upon the following:

1. Agriculture in recent years has not fared as well as have other sections of the national economy and requires special assistance if it is to share equally in the general prosperity. Our rising standards of living have not resulted in demand for more food; people may in fact be spending more on food, but their additional outlays are for packing, processing, freezing, and so on. Meanwhile, thanks to improved methods and equipment, the same amount of food can be produced by fewer farmers. Many farm-born people are reluctant to leave the land, however: some lack the educational qualifications for good jobs in cities; others wish to remain on the land, operating a "family farm."

2. The government already provides assistance to other industries by measures suited to their needs. Tariffs protect the nation's manufacturing industries (and incidentally burden farmers by forcing them to pay higher prices for manufactured goods). Price supports for agricultural commodities constitute assistance to agriculture which is no more than equivalent to the support which other industries receive from the government.

3. The bargaining power of the agricultural section of the economy is inherently weaker than the bargaining power of the rest of the economy, and this inferiority

becomes particularly significant whenever general downward pressure on prices develops. Non-agricultural goods are mostly produced under monopoly or semi-monopoly conditions, with the consequence that producers have the power to control output and price. Farm products, on the other hand, are produced by many thousands of individual farmers, so that there is no possibility of their exercising monopolistic control over output and price. Producers of non-agricultural commodities, therefore, are able to resist downward pressure on prices whereas farmers are not. The burden placed on farmers by the lower prices they receive for their products is increased by the fact that the prices of non-agricultural goods and services which they must buy, remain steady or actually rise. Price support for agricultural products are needed to compensate for the farmer's inferior bargaining power and to protect his real purchasing power.

4. Maintenance of the purchasing power of farmers supports other sections of the economy. Because farmers are enabled to maintain their spending at the normal level, the industries which sell to farmers are able to maintain their production and employment.

5. The farming community consists of a very large number of people and comprises an important segment of the total population. It is only reasonable and proper that the government should take whatever action it can to safeguard the interests of so large a number of its citizens. By the same token, the political strength which farmers enjoy by virtue of their numbers, obliges governments to heed their demands. Whether or not they are impressed by the other arguments in favour of price supports, governments must respond to the political pressure exerted by the agricultural community.

THE AMERICAN PRICE SUPPORT PROGRAMME

Although the American government undertook some measures in 1928 to support the prices of agricultural products, the modern programme really dates from 1933 when President Roosevelt launched his New Deal. Farm prices, which had been weakening during the closing years of the 1920s, collapsed utterly with the onset of the Great Depression of the 1930s and large scale aid to farmers was a major feature of the New Deal programme. The U.S. government has continued to support farm prices ever since, with the form and extent of support being periodically altered in accordance with changing circumstances and attitudes.

Surplus Disposal

The legislation of 1933 which inaugurated the modern price support programme created the Commodity Credit Corporation (the CCC) as the instrument for carrying it out. The Corporation was endowed with the authority to buy, store and sell agricultural products and to extend loans on the security of such commodities. The technique it chiefly employed to support prices was the following: a farmer was authorized to borrow from a bank an amount equal to the value of his crop, reckoning its value on the basis of the support price. If the market price was above this figure, he could sell his crop and repay the loan. If, however, the market price was below the support price he could repay the loan simply by turning over his crop to the CCC; the latter then reimbursed the bank which had extended the loan.

Since in most years the market price was below the support price (it was above during World War II and its aftermath and during the Korean and Vietnam war periods) the CCC acquired enormous quantities of agricultural products. To dispose of them a variety of measures were adopted.

1. Stockpiled commodities were sold to American exporters at prices which enabled them to re-sell to foreign buyers at prevailing world prices. The price realized was usually much less than the price which had been paid, (see Figure 9) the loss being absorbed by the government.

2. Commodities held by the CCC were bartered for the raw materials of other countries, these being placed in domestic stockpiles.

3. Farm products were sold to foreign countries, with the latter making payment in their own currency.

4. Commodities were given away to relieve distress in foreign countries and were donated to deserving causes and institutions in the Unted States itself. Surplus food has been used to provide free school lunches and has been distributed gratis to needy families. (In 1968 over 6 million persons were receiving food out of surpluses owned by the federal government.)

Acreage Diversion

The Soil Bank plan was introduced in 1956 under which payments were made to farmers who diverted part of their acreage quotas to the cultivation of other commodities not in surplus, or retired it from cultivation altogether. The scheme was discontinued in 1960 but another version appeared three years later: farmers who diverted or retired part of their acreage quotas were offered higher price supports for the crops they grew on land still cultivated. Legislation passed in 1965 authorized the Secretary of Agriculture to enter into 5 - 10 year contracts with farmers under which they would be paid to divert cropland to uses that would conserve water, soil, wildlife, and afford recreational opportunities; the payments would take the form of an annual rental based upon the value of the crops which could have been grown. In 1968, it was estimated, a total of 63 million acres were kept out of production by the government's diversion payments.

Problems of the U.S. Support Programme

While achieving its main purpose of maintaining agricultural prices at high levels, the U.S. price support programme has been characterized by anomalies, weaknesses and unfortunate side-effects. The degree of benefit which any individual farmer received from the price support applied to a commodity depended on how much he produced. Consequently, the main beneficiaries were the large, efficient operators who would probably have done very well for themselves even without any artificial boosts to the price of their products. Poor farmers who needed the most help got very little; producing only small crops they derived correspondingly small benefit from the support to prices.

The government was obliged to hold enormous stocks of farm products. As of June 30th, 1962, the Commodity Credit Corporation held in storage 1,097 million bushels of wheat, 659 million bushels of corn, nearly one and a half million bales of cotton and massive quantities of other farm products. The total value of stocks held was 4.5 billion dollars; storage and handling charges alone averaged over a million dollars *a day*.

Attempts to restrict the build-up of surpluses encountered fierce opposition or effective counter measures. Farm groups insisted that farmers be aided through high support prices rather than by any form of subsidies, even though under the latter method of support no surpluses would come into being.[3] The Soil Bank plan proved to be of little help in reducing output. Farmers generally withdrew their poorest land from cultivation and worked the remainder more intensively; output failed to decline in proporton to the reduction in acreage.

Attempts to dispose of stocks by sales abroad at very low prices antagonized other nations which produced the same commodities for export. Canada repeatedly protested to the United States that its virtual "givaways" of wheat to foreign countries caused those countries to buy less wheat from Canada than they otherwise would have done.[4] Donations to needy persons and worthy organizations in the U.S. and abroad did not raise objections, but if care were exercised not to displace commercial sales only a limited amount could be disposed of in this fashon.

The picture has been changing in the past several years. World prices for farm products have risen significantly, reflecting a shift in demand and supply relationships, and U.S. agricultural support policy has markedly changed its emphasis. Agricultural aid legislation passed in 1964 and 1965 provided for assistance primarily in the form of subsidies and payments for cropland diversion rather than high price supports. The Food and Agriculture Act of 1965 provided for price supports at or

---

[3]Price supports were considered to be less vulnerable politically than subsidies; under the former arrangement the government received something for the money it laid out, albeit at an artificially increased price; subsidies would be pure handouts.

[4]Actually, the mere existence of vast U.S. stocks, well publicized at that, was considered to exercise a depressing effect on farm prices throughout the world, and thereby harm the producers of other countries.

near world levels for the country's major crops, thereby removing the prospect that the government might have to purchase large surpluses; with support prices down to world price levels American farmers would presumably produce no more than could be sold at market prices. It may be that the era of huge surpluses, enormous government stockpiles and massive give-away programmes, is drawing to a close.

THE CANADIAN PRICE SUPPORT PROGRAMME

Canada's efforts in the direction of supporting farm prices have been much simpler and more modest than those of her great neighbour. Our main price support programme has been embodied in two pieces of legislation, the Canadian Wheat Board Act of 1935 and the Agricultural Prices Support Act of 1944. Neither exists today in its original form; since its introduction the Wheat Board Act has been considerably amended, while the Agricultural Prices Support Act was repealed in March, 1958, being replaced by the Agricultural Stabilization Act. At present, therefore, the Canadian support programme consists of the latter Act together with the current form of the Wheat Board Act.

The Wheat Board Act

This piece of legislation was introduced during the Great Depression of the 1930s, when the world price of wheat stood at a catastrophically low level, partly because of the prevailing economic conditions and partly because of an unprecedented world wheat surplus. The Act provided for the establishment of the Canadian Wheat Board, with authority to purchase wheat from the farmers of Western Canada, paying a price which would provide growers with a reasonable return. Western-grown oats and barley were subsequently included as well, to be treated in the same way as was wheat. The Board's procedure is as follows: each year it sets an initial price which is paid to farmers upon delivery of their grain. If, in selling the grain, the Board realizes a higher price, farmers are later given a supplementary payment amounting to the difference. If the Board realizes a lower price in its sales, the government absorbs the loss. Therefore, the initial payment made by the Board constitutes in effect a support price. The size of this initial payment is not determined according to any formula; the Board sets it each year in the light of the selling price which it anticipates and its judgment as to farmers' needs.

The operations of the Board have been complicated in recent years by the fact that there has been insufficient commercial storage capacity to hold all the grain which farmers had to sell. Several bumper crops occurred in succession, while sales opportunities abroad remained constant or actually declined, owing partly to the competition of the American "giveaway" programme. Thus while farmers were guaranteed an initial payment per bushel on delivery, they could not make delivery because the Board had nowhere to store additional grain. A system of quotas was introduced enabling each farmer to deliver a specified amount of grain in order to obtain some cash for his immediate requirements. As grain moved to export markets, releasing storage space in the country's elevators, the quotas were increased progressively. Since their inability to sell all their crop left many farmers badly short of cash, the government introduced a scheme under which farmers were enabled to borrow money from the banks, on the security of grain stored on their farms. In 1957, a new federal administration introduced a plan under which farmers could receive cash advances on grain which they held on their farms.

The Agricultural Stabilization Act

Price supports for agricultural products other than wheat commenced in Canada with the Agricultural Prices Support Act of 1944. Introduced during the later stages of World War II this Act reflected the views and anticipations which prevailed at that time. The possibility was envisaged that when peace came the prices of agricultural products would drop sharply from their wartime heights, with disastrous effect on farmers' incomes. Government support would be required in all likelihood if the transition from wartime to peacetime price levels was to be achieved without serious distress. Secondly, the government acknowledged itself to be under obligation to the farm community. During the war, when food supplies were short and demand very great it had imposed ceiling prices on farm products in order to repress inflation. Having denied farmers the full benefit of the highly favourable market which prevailed in wartime, the government agreed that it was morally obligated to protect them against the hazard of an extremely unfavourable market situation in peacetime.

A new federal administration repealed this first legislation, replacing it in 1958 with the present Agricultural Stabilization Act. Under this Act the prices of nine key commodities must be supported at not less than 80 per cent of the "base price," defined as the average of market prices over the preceding ten years. Additional commodities might also be supported if it was thought desirable, at levels approved by the government.

The nine commodities are: butter, cheese, eggs, cattle, hogs, sheep; and wheat, oats and barley grown outside of the Prairie areas designated under the Wheat Board Act.

The Agricultural Stabilization Board administers the Act, though since 1967 support operations for dairy products have been handled by the Canadian Dairy Commission, established in that year. Three methods are employed to boost farmers' receipts:

> An agricultural commodity may be purchased at the support price, stocks being subsequently disposed of by a variety of means, including gifts to international relief agencies, and sales abroad and in Canada at prices well below the support price.

Supplementary payments, subsidies in effect, are made to producers. These are not determined according to any formula, but are of such size as the authorities deem to be reasonable.

Deficiency payments are made, amounting to the difference between the market price and the selected support price.

(This has been the method chiefly employed in support operations).

During the early years of its operation the Agricultural Stabilization Board expended very large sums in supporting the prices of a lengthy list of agricultural products. In the later 1960s, reflecting the inflationary pressures of the time, the market prices of most agricultural products were above the designated support levels and there was little occasion for intervention to boost the prices received by producers. Only dairy products continued to receive support in substantial amount; the Canadian Dairy Commission spent over $130 millions on its support operations in the fiscal year 1969-70; sugar beets and wool were the only other agricultural products whose price was supported in that year, at a total cost of just over $2 million.

At the time of writing (midsummer 1971) there was the prospect of two new pieces of legislation intended to deal with significant problems of the agricultural economy. Parliament had before it Bill C.244, which was designed to reduce year-to-year fluctuations in the aggregate income of the prairie grain economy: levies would be imposed in good years on all grain producers and supplementary payments would be made in years when the aggregate value of all prairie grains was below the previous norm. Bill C.176 provided for the establishment of a number of government agencies to handle the marketing of agricultural products both within Canada and abroad (excluding dairy products and grains already being handled under the Wheat Board Act). Neither bill had been passed at the time of writing; Bill C.176 in fact had been temporarily withdrawn because of the heavy criticism levelled at it by members of the House of Commons.

INTERFERING WITH THE PRICE SYSTEM: GENERAL CONSIDERATIONS

We saw in Chapter 3 how, through the price system, the productive capacity of a country is automatically allocated in accordance with public demand as expressed in the market-place. We noted, too, that through the price system the rewards which people receive for their productive services are automatically arranged. Government interference with the working of the price system, of the sort described in this chapter, brings about a different allocation of the country's productive capacity, and a different distribution of its income.

Good intentions are not enough. As we have seen in this chapter, the effects of intervention in the price system are likely to be complex and characterized by unintended consequences that are quite unwanted. A sales tax imposed in order to raise revenue will discourage both production and consumption of the article which is taxed. A subsidy intended to lower the price paid for a commodity by consumers or to increase the price realized by producers, will induce increases in both production and consumption.

Price ceilings, laudably intended to protect consumers against exploitation, will cause reduction in output, possibly even a complete cessation of production. Protection of the consumer in such a case takes the form, dubiously helpful, of making it impossible for him to obtain the product altogether. Price floors, generously intended to help small-scale, poor producers, may benefit primarily large-scale well-to-do producers who need no aid; price floors may furthermore enable and encourage people to continue producing goods which the public does not want, when otherwise they would be compelled to shift to the production of goods which the public does want.

The fact that government interference with the price system has effects beyond those intended, does not of course mean that the government should never interfere. The verdict of the market-place in respect to resource allocation and income distribution is not necessarily the judgment which best reflects a country's basic, long-term needs. A government may in some cases be amply justified when it intervenes to set aside the verdict of the market-place; any adverse results may be more than offset by benefits gained. However, in some cases the balance may lie the other way. Unintended repercussions of government intervention may turn out to be more harmful than the difficulties which the intervention was intended to solve.

This does not mean, of course, that the government should refrain from assisting particular consumers or producers; it means that other methods of assistance should be employed instead: thus, where producers of a particular commodity are unable to earn a decent living the government might assist them, not by artificially raising the price of their product, but by helping them to establish themselves in some other industry whose products are in good demand and can be sold at remunerative prices.[5] Such alternative forms of assistance may serve the same purpose as would be achieved by intervention in the price system, without giving rise to the same undesired consequences.

SUMMARY

Sales taxes tend to raise prices and reduce output; subsidies tend to reduce prices and increase output. The burden of a sales tax is divided among producers and consumers, the apportionment depending upon both elasticity of demand and elasticity

---

[5]It might of course be very difficult for some producers to transfer out of a particular industry, —and perhaps socially undesirable that they do so. Such considerations would also have to be taken into account.

of supply. The benefit of a subsidy is also apportioned according to elasticity of demand and supply.

Price ceilings tend to cause reductions in output, so that rationing, or alternatively subsidization, becomes necessary.

Price floors tend to induce production in excess of the amount that can be sold commercially; the government becomes obliged to buy up surpluses, to pay subsidies, or to take measures to reduce output.

The American price support programme has tended to maintain the prices of certain farm products at levels above those which would have otherwise prevailed. The Canadian price support programme has tended to support the prices of farm products only during transitional periods and emergencies.

Interference by a government with the working of the price system, though well-intended, may give rise to unfortunate repercussions.

FOR REVIEW AND DISCUSSION

1. Suppose the equilibrium price of a certain good is $1.00. The government is considering whether to impose a tax of 10 cents per unit, or 10 per cent of the selling price. Would it make any difference which tax was chosen?
2. Indicate the circumstances in which a sales tax would be borne entirely by producers.
3. Contrast the Canadian and American agricultural price support programmes in the post-war era.
4. Who would bear the main burden if the Canadian government imposed a sales tax on (a) milk, (b) Volkswagen cars?
5. What relationship might exist, in your opinion, between acreage quotas and the demand for fertilizer?
6. A recent article in a popular Canadian magazine declared that Canadian farmers have too much voting power. If this is in fact the case, what are likely to be the economic consequences?
7. It is ridiculous to spend millions on research to improve agricultural productivity, and then spend more millions to induce farmers to restrict their output. Comment.
8. Because of its very advances, agriculture is a declining industry. Explain.
9. "Cattle raisers will not be happy if the government makes deficiency payments to hog producers." Why should they care?
10. A distinguished economist referred to the wartime American economy, when price controls were in effect, as a "disequilibrium system". What did he mean?
11. "If left alone, the Canadian agricultural problem will solve itself." Do you agree? Justify your answer.

PART THREE:

FIRM AND INDUSTRY

5

Firm and Industry Under Perfect Competition

The man in charge of a business firm is constantly obliged to make decisions, on all sorts of matters. He must decide exactly what features his product should have, how to make it, how to market it, what price to charge for it, how much to produce. Repeatedly, in the light of changing conditions, he must revise his decisions. In this chapter and the following we shall work out the principles which a business man ought to keep in mind when making his decisions on the last two issues: what price to charge, and how much to produce. As we shall see, the range of choice available to him will depend upon the degree of competition prevailing in his industry, whether he is a monopolist, whether his firm is one of only a few, or whether his firm is only one of a great many in the industry. Our analysis will deal with issues that were referred to in Chapter 3 in a very general way. There we saw that supply and demand determine price, and we noted that supply consists of the total offerings of many individual firms. Here we shall be examining the logic employed by the individual firm in deciding what to offer on the market.

In this chapter we shall describe the theoretical principles according to which a firm in a *perfectly competitive* industry decides what price to charge, and what quantity to produce. We shall see also how firm and industry are affected by changes in market demand, and by changes in the cost of production.

"PERFECT COMPETITION"

Let's make clear, first of all, what the economist means by a perfectly competitive industry. To qualify fully for this description an industry should have the following features:

Each firm's product is exactly the same as that of every other firm.

The number of firms in the industry is very large, and no single firm produces more than a small fraction of the industry's output.

There is no discrimination: each seller is prepared to sell on the same terms to all buyers; each buyer is prepared to pay the same price to all sellers.

There is complete knowledge on the part of every seller and buyer: each knows what prices are being asked by other sellers and what prices are being offered by other buyers.

It is possible for additional firms to enter the industry if they so desire.

We must admit that no actual industry fully satisfies all of the above conditions, though there are some, such as agriculture, which come fairly close. In any case, the conclusions which we derive from our analysis of the perfectly competitive industry are generally applicable even to industries which do not fit the description exactly.

If an industry were perfectly competitive, i.e. had the characteristics listed above, then at any given time there could be only one price for the product of all its member firms. The product being perfectly homogeneous, and every buyer and seller being fully informed, no buyer would pay more than any other was paying and no seller would take any less than any other seller was getting. The market price would be determined by market supply in relation to market demand, in the manner described in Chapter 3. No individual seller or buyer could significantly affect that market price. With each seller providing only a tiny fraction of the market supply, any variation in his output would have a negligible effect on the total quantity offered on the market and would therefore insignificantly affect the market price.

The same would be true of buyers. Since each furnishes only a small fraction of the total market demand, any variation in his demand would have an insignificant effect on that total and would therefore have virtually no effect on the price. Like the individual seller, the individual buyer would be powerless to affect the market price.

The Individual Firm in a Competitive Industry

A firm in a perfectly competitive industry does not decide, therefore, what price to charge for its product. The decision is in effect made for it by the market forces of supply and demand, to which it contributes a tiny element, but which it is quite powerless to control. This market-determined price is the price the firm will charge. It cannot charge more: no one would buy from it when he could obtain the identical commodity from other firms at a cheaper price. The firm would be foolish to charge less: it can sell all it cares to at the market price; there is no need to cut its price below that figure in order to make a sale or to increase sales.

Figure 1 shows the relationship between the sales possibilities of the individual firm and the market situation for the perfectly competitive industry as a whole. Figure 1A represents the market supply and demand situation for the industry as a whole. The curve SS represents the aggregate supply of all the member firms; the curve DD represents the aggregate demand of all the buyers. The market price must be OP. This market price of OP is in turn the price which will be received by each firm for its product; each can sell as much as it cares to at this price. The demand curve for the products of the individual firm, shown in Figure 1B, consists therefore

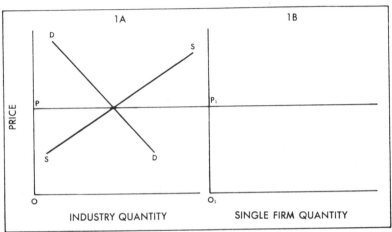

PRICE

1A

1B

D

S

P

P₁

S

D

O

O₁

INDUSTRY QUANTITY

SINGLE FIRM QUANTITY

Figure 1.   Demand for the product of the individual firm, under perfect competition

of a horizontal line at the height O_1P_1 ($=OP$). The demand, at this price, is perfectly elastic for the products of the individual firm: so long as it charges the price O_1P_1, it can sell any amount it likes.

With the decision on price in effect made for him by market forces, the businessman in a perfectly competitive industry has only to decide what quantity to produce. He can sell all he chooses at the market price; but what quantity should he choose? In very general terms the answer is obvious. Assuming that he wishes to achieve a maximum of gain for himself, he will produce and sell the amount at which the excess of receipts over costs is greater than it would be if he produced any other amount. To determine which output would yield this optimum result he would, of course, have to know just what his costs and receipts would actually be at each possible level of production.

Fixed Cost and Variable Cost

In examining the relevant figures he would become aware that his costs divided naturally into two distinct categories. There would be one group of costs which did not vary with changes in output, and in fact remained the same even if output were zero. In this group would be such items as interest on borrowed money, property taxes, rent, and the like. This category of costs would be referred to by economists as the firm's *fixed costs*. (Businessmen would refer to it as the *overhead*.) The other category would be composed of those costs which did vary with the volume of production, and were zero when output was zero. These are what the economist would call the firm's *variable costs*; they include wages, outlays on materials, expenditures on power, and the like.

The Short Run and the Long Run

A businessman does not have to pay his fixed costs forever; he is committed to pay them only for some specified period of time. If, for instance, his fixed cost consists of the monthly rental specified in a lease, then he is obliged to pay this cost only for the duration of the lease. Whatever form his fixed cost takes, at some date in the future he will be free of the obligation to pay it. However, if he wishes to stay in business he will have to commit himself to a new set of fixed cost obligations, once his present ones come to an end. For example, if he wishes to stay in business after his present lease expires, he will have to sign a new lease, thereby committing himself to a new series of fixed cost obligations in the form of monthly rental payments.

The economist refers to the time period during which a business man is committed to pay his particular fixed costs as the _short run._ A longer time period, i.e. a period long enough for his fixed cost obligations to come to an end, is referred to as the _long run._ Just how long a run actually is will vary from firm to firm depending on the time it will take for each firm's particular fixed cost obligations to come to an end.

The terms "long run" and "short run" are also used in reference to the time required for expansion. Short run in this context means a time period insufficiently long to enable a new firm to be established or an old firm to be enlarged. During such a period the industry's output can be increased only by increasing the output of existing plant. In this context, the long run accordingly means a time period sufficiently long to enable more firms to be built or existing ones to be enlarged.

Entrepreneurial Reward a Part of Cost

The economist defines the "cost" of a firm to include a fair return to the owner for his contribution to the firm, this return being referred to as _normal profit._ If a firm's receipts were insufficient to cover all its outlays on wages, materials, etc., and a to provide a normal profit to the owner, it would be considered to be operating at loss. If its receipts were greater than this figure the firm would be considered to be earning _super normal profit,_ i.e. the owner of the firm would be receiving a return for his effort and investment that was considered to be in excess of what was generally deemed to be adequate and fair. (There is of course no one figure which would represent a proper return in all industries. Each industry has its own difficulties and risks, and these would determine the general opinion as to what was a reasonable return to the owner of a firm in the industry.)

Variation of Costs with Output

The economist suggests that in the typical firm efficiency and cost of production vary with output in the following fashion. At a very low level of output cost of production per unit will be high. The firm will be operating inefficiently: its equipment will be under-utilized; workers will not be concentrating on their specialties; materials will be bought in small lots and therefore at high prices; by-products will be too few to be effectively utilized. As the firm's output is increased, cost of production per unit tends to fall. The disadvantages of a low level of output disappear. Manpower, materials and equipment are used to better advantage; supplies are bought in volume and therefore at lower prices; more effective methods of handling and distribution can be employed.

For every firm, however, there is some level of production at which it attains its maximum efficiency, and at which its cost of production per unit is the lowest possible. If output is increased beyond this figure, the firm's operations become less efficient and cost of production per unit rises. Overtime rates may have to be paid; less able workers may have to be taken on; distribution costs may rise as output is marketed over a wider area; management's control over operations may become less effective as the scale of operations becomes larger. For reasons such as these the cost of production per unit will begin to rise once a certain output has been passed, and will continue to rise with each further increase in output.

The Cost Structure of a Firm: An Example

Table 1 presents the cost data of a hypothetical firm; the figures have been designed to illustrate the general principles suggested in the preceding two paragraphs. Cost of production per unit is high when output is very low; each increase in output causes cost per unit to fall, but only up to a certain point; beyond this point each increase in output causes cost per unit to rise.

In Table 1:

Column (2) shows the *fixed cost,* which remains absolutely constant at $50 no matter how much is produced and even if output is zero. The firm is of course obliged to pay this fixed cost only during a short run period.

Column (3) shows what the *total variable cost* will be at each level of output. From the figures it is clear that variable costs rise less than proportionately when the firm increases its output from a very low level. When the firm increases its output from one to two units, or by 100%, variable costs rise from $50 to $90, or by only 80%. On the other hand when the firm, already producing at or beyond its optimum level, further increases its output, variable costs rise more than proportionately. When the firm increases output from five to six units, or by 20%, variable costs rise from $210 to $270, or by 29%.

Column (4) shows the *total cost* at each output, being the sum of the fixed and variable costs at that output. (The student is reminded that the total cost figure is assumed to include a reasonable return to the owner.)

Column (5) shows how the *average fixed cost* (AFC) steadily decreases as output increases, as a result of the fact that the constant fixed cost is being divided up among an ever larger number of units. (Businessmen would refer to this as "spreading the overhead".)

Column (6) shows how the *average variable cost* (AVC) per unit falls at first but then rises, as the firm gains in efficiency by increasing its output from a very low beginning level, but then loses efficiency when it increases its output beyond a certain

Table 1

PRODUCTION COSTS OF FIRM X FOR OUTPUTS 0-10 UNITS

(1)	(2)	(3)	(4)	(5)	(6)	(7)	(8)
Output Units	Fixed Cost	Total Variable Cost	Total Cost	Average Fixed Cost	Average Variable Cost	Average Total Cost	Marginal Cost
0	$50	$ 0	$ 50	$—	$—	$ —	$ —
1	50	50	100	50	50	100	50
1	50	90	140	25	45	70	40
3	50	120	170	16.6	40	56.6	30
4	50	160	210	12.5	40	52.5	40
5	50	210	260	10.0	42	52.0	50
6	50	270	320	8.3	45	53.3	60
7	50	340	390	7.1	48.6	55.7	70
8	50	420	470	6.3	52.5	58.8	80
9	50	510	560	5.5	56.6	62.1	90
10	50	610	660	5.0	61.0	66.0	100

point. Average variable cost per unit declines to a minimum at outputs of three and four units, but rises when output is increased to five units, and becomes progressively larger with each further increase in output.

Column (7) shows the *average total cost* (ATC), this being simply the sum of the AFC and AVC; the figures here indicate how the average total cost declines to a minimum, and then rises. One seeming anomaly should be noted. While the minimum AVC occurs at the outputs three to four units, the minimum ATC is achieved at an output of five units. The reason is of course that the higher AVC at five units is more than offset by the lower AFC. At an output of four units the average total cost is $52.5 ($40+$12.5); at an output of five units the average total cost is $52 ($42+$10).

Column (8) *Marginal Cost* (MC) represents the amount by which the total cost of production increases as a result of the production of one more unit. As is evident from the figures, each unit produced is responsible for its particular marginal cost. The marginal cost of the third unit is $30: total costs rise from $140 to $170 when output is increased from two to three units. The marginal cost of the eighth unit is $80, because costs rise from $390 to $470 when output is increased by the eighth unit.

DECISIONS ON OUTPUT BY THE INDIVIDUAL FIRM

Table 1 gives us all the information we need to have about the firm's costs; from these figures we can determine exactly how much the firm ought to produce, given any particular market price.

(a) **When the Price Equals the Minimum ATC** one point is obvious at once. The market price must be at least $52, the minimum ATC, if the firm is to cover its full cost. A price of exactly $52 will just enable the firm to cover its costs, provided it produces five units; at any other output cost per unit would be greater than $52 Our first conclusion then is that if the firm is to cover all its costs, the market price must at least equal the minimum average total cost, here $52. And, given a market price exactly equal to the minimum average total cost, the firm must produce the specific output at which this cost per unit is achieved.

(b) **When the Price Is Below the Minimum ATC** of $52 the firm will not necessarily close down. If it stops production altogether, it will lose the fixed cost of $50 which must be paid, during the "short run", whether goods are produced or not. If the firm can cut its loss below $50 by continuing to produce, then of course production should be carried on. And in fact, provided the price is not too low, a smaller loss can be achieved. If, for instance, when the market price was $45 the firm produced four units, its loss would be only $30 (costs being $210 and receipts being $180).

If the price falls very low indeed it will be better to shut down. Thus if the market price were $35 and the firm produced four units, its loss would be $70, receipts being $140 and costs $210.

Just how low can the price go before the firm finds it more advantageous to shut down rather than continue production? In our example the "cut-off" price is $40. With the price above $40 the firm is better off if it continues to produce; below $40 it should shut down. At a price of exactly $40, it doesn't matter which course the firm adopts; its loss will be the same in either case. (Where production of any units will neither improve nor harm a firm's position we assume that the firm will produce those units. This assumption is made purely in order to achieve consistent results. In our example therefore we would say that the firm would produce four units if the price were exactly $40, but would shut down if the price were anything less.)

What is the significance of the $40 figure in our example? It is the *minimum average variable cost* that the firm can achieve: by laying out as little as $40 per unit for labour, materials, etc., the firm will be able to produce four units which it can sell. If the selling price is anything above $40, it will take in more than the $160 it paid out on variable costs. The $50 loss on account of fixed cost will be reduced by whatever is taken in over and above the $160 spent on variable cost items. Expressed in another way: if the firm shuts down, it pays out $50 and takes in nothing. If it produces 4 units, it pays out a total of $210, but if the selling price per unit is over $40 it will take in more than $160 and its loss will obviously be less than $50. If the selling price per unit were under $40 and the firm produced four units, its loss would be greater than $50; the firm would be paying out $210 and getting back less than $160.

In the long run, of course, the firm will cease altogether to operate if the price is below $52. Because of its obligation to pay the fixed cost, the firm finds it advantageous to operate in the short run when the price is below $52 (but above $40). In the long run, as we have defined it, these fixed cost obligations come to an end. If the firm is to stay in the industry once its present fixed cost obligations expire it must assume a new set. However, if the market price has been less than $52, the firm will have been losing money. It operated in the short run only because it lost less that way, but it will not remain in the industry once its existing fixed cost obligations expire, if the price remains below $52, the firm will finally close down.

(c) **When the Price Is Above the Minimum ATC.** Enough of this gloomy talk of losses. What if the market price proves to be favourable, rising well above $52? Suppose for instance, that the market price were to rise to $65. How many units should our firm produce then?

We could laboriously establish the most profitable output by checking to see what the costs would be at each level of output, and calculating what the receipts would be at each level of output on the basis of a selling price of $65. The optimum output would be the one at which receipts exceeded costs by the largest amount. There is, however, another method whereby we can find optimum output, a method which involves the application of an important and fundamental principle.

We know that the businessman will produce five units if the price is $52. When the price rises to $65, should he increase his output? We know that for each additional unit that he produces he will take in an additional $65. What will be happening to his costs? This we can tell from the marginal cost schedule: the marginal cost of the sixth unit is $60, of the seventh $70, and so on. If the firm produces six units the sixth will add $60 to costs and $65 to receipts, obviously increasing profit by $5; production of the seventh unit would add $70 to costs but of course only $65 to receipts; he would be worse off by $5 for producing it.

Evidently when the price is $65 an output of 6 units will result in the largest possible profit. The calculation by which we arrived at this figure is based on this fundamental principle: the firm should keep on increasing production so long as the additional output adds more to receipts than to costs. Bearing in mind our rule about consistency, we will assume that the firm will produce additional output even if the added receipts are just equal to the marginal cost.

What if the market price rises even higher, to $75, to $85? Our guiding principle tells us that at a price of $75 the firm should produce seven units; the marginal cost of a seventh unit would be under the selling price; the marginal cost of an eighth unit would be over the selling price. By analogous reasoning, if the price rises to $85 the firm should produce eight units, and so on.

Supply Schedule of the Individual Firm

We are now in a position to tell exactly how many units the firm will produce at any possible price; i.e. we are able to describe the firm's *supply schedule*. Below a price of $40, its minimum average variable cost, it will produce nothing; at a price of $40 to $49 it will produce four units; at a price of $50 to $59 it will produce five units; at a price of $60 to $69 it will produce six units; and so on. Evidently, the firm's supply schedule begins at its lowest average variable cost, and from then on corresponds to its marginal cost schedule. Table 2 indicates just what quantity the firm will produce, at any possible price.

Table 2 represents only the firm's *short run* supply schedule. As we have seen, if the market price remains below $52, the firm will, in the long run, leave the industry. What is more, if all member firms in the industry have the same cost pattern,

Table 2

SUPPLY SCHEDULE OF FIRM X

SELLING PRICE	QUANTITY PRODUCED
Under $40 (= minimum AVC)	0
$40—49 (derived from MC schedule)	4
$50—59 (” ” ” ”)	5
$60—69 (” ” ” ”)	6
$70—79 (” ” ” ”)	7
$80—89 (” ” ” ”)	8
$90—99 (” ” ” ”)	9
$100—109 (” ” ” ”)	10

and if new firms can produce at exactly the same costs, then in the long run the price cannot remain above $52 either. We shall investigate this point more fully later in the chapter.

Graphical Representation

Figure 2 graphically presents some of the data contained in Table 1; the AFC, AVC, ATC and MC curves represent the corresponding schedules in that table. The AFC curve falls steadily as output is increased. The AVC curve is saucer-shaped, reflecting the fact that at low outputs cost per unit is high, and that as output is increased the cost per unit declines until it reaches a minimum level and thereafter increases as output is further increased. The ATC is saucer-shaped too, with its minimum point occurring to the right of the minimum AVC. The ATC ordinate at any output is the sum of the AFC and AVC ordinates for that same output, e.g. CR=CK+CL. The MC curve falls at first, then rises steadily and, because of the relationship of marginal cost to average cost, it cuts both the AVC and ATC curves at their minimum points.[1]

The curves indicate graphically the average cost and marginal cost figures for each level of output. A vertical line drawn from any point on the X axis up to the AFC curve represents the average fixed cost at that output. A vertical line from the

---

[1]A simple non-mathematical explanation of this relationship is this. Where the marginal cost touches an average cost curve, marginal cost equals average cost. But if the marginal cost of some unit exactly equals the average cost then the production of that unit has neither raised nor lowered the average cost, i.e. the marginal cost is equal to the average where the average is neither rising nor falling. There is only one point on an average cost curve where *it is neither rising nor falling*, and that is the minimum point. Hence, marginal cost can equal average cost only at the latter's minimum.

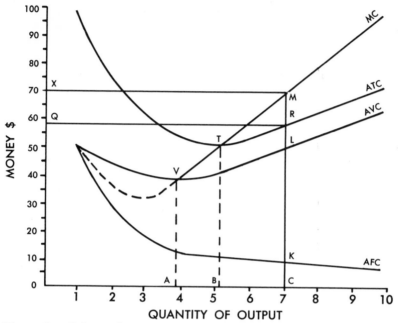

Figure 2.   Price and output of the individual firm, under perfect competition

X axis to the AVC curve represents the average variable cost per unit at that output; an ordinate drawn to the ATC curve represents the average total cost at that output. A vertical line to the MC curve represents the sum by which total cost is increased as a result of the production of that particular unit, e.g. the distance CM represents the sum by which costs increase as a result of production of the OCth unit;[2] CR

---

[2]Strictly speaking, marginal cost should be represented by a rectangle rather than a line, for it represents an absolute amount of money rather than just a rate. In Figure A, for instance, rectangle (1) represents the additional cost of producing the first unit; rectangle (2) represents the additional cost of producing the second; and so on. The smooth MC curve of Figure 2 has been derived by assuming that we can ascertain the marginal cost of a very small fraction of a unit of output, as in Figure B. Joining the tops of these rectangles we obtain the continuous curve MC.

represents the average total cost per unit when output is OC; CL represents the average variable cost at this output; CK is the average fixed cost.

The firm's supply schedule consists of the MC curve, beginning from the point V, the minimum average variable cost position, where the MC curve cuts the AVC curve. Thus with the price below AV the firm produces nothing; at a price of AV it produces OA units; at a price of BT it produces OB units; at a price of CM it produces OC units; and so on.

At a price of BT, the minimum average total cost, the firm can just break even, if it produces OB units. With output at OB, the average total cost per unit will just equal the selling price. With the price above BT, the firm will earn super normal profit. For example, if the price were CM, the firm would produce the output OC at which average total cost per unit is CR. The firm's total costs are therefore OCRQ (the average cost CR multiplied by the OC units produced). With the selling price CM, total sales receipts are OCMX; hence the firm achieves a super normal profit of QRMX. Since our cost figure included a reasonable return to the owner, the sum QRMX represents earnings received by the owner over and above an adequate and normal return.

Given a price of CM, the quantity OC represents the optimum output. If the firm were to produce any additional units their marginal cost would be greater than the selling price CM, and the firm's profit would be reduced. If the firm produced less, sales receipts would fall by more than cost; again profit would be less. The amount OC represents the most profitable output, and the sum of money QRMX therefore represents the maximum profit which can be earned, when the price is CM.

FIRM AND INDUSTRY UNDER PERFECT COMPETITION

As we saw earlier in this chapter, a perfectly competitive industry consists of a very large number of firms, each of which produces only a small fraction of the industry's total output. In this section we shall examine inter-relationships between the industry as a whole and the individual firms of which it is composed. Specifically, we shall see how firm and industry react, in the short run and in the long run, to changes in market demand and to changes in the cost of production. For simplicity's sake we shall use as our illustrative example an industry which consists of one thousand firms, each of which has a cost structure identical with that given in Table 1.

Reduction in Market Demand: Short Run and Long Run Effects

At a market price of $52, equal to the minimum average total cost, each firm would produce five units and manage to cover exactly all its costs (including of course a reasonable return to the owner). With each firm producing five units the output of the industry as a whole would be 5000 units. Now suppose that the market demand for the product declines, so that the market price falls to $45. From our previous analysis we know that each firm will continue to produce, despite the fact that it is now losing money. In the short run it is committed to pay its fixed costs whether it produces or not; during the period that it is bound by this commitment it is more advantageous to produce than to close down, provided of course that the market price is above $40, the minimum average variable cost.

However, fixed cost obligations do not last forever. Eventually one firm's fixed cost obligations come to an end, and it will cease to operate. Other firms will subsequently do likewise when their fixed cost obligations terminate. The number of operating firms in the industry consequently drops to 999, to 998, to 997, and so on. As the number of firms decreases the industry supply declines. Instead of the industry's output being the output of one firm multiplied by 1000, it becomes the output of one firm multiplied by 999, by 998, and so on. In a graphic representation, as in Figure 3, the industry supply curve would shift to the left.

As the market supply declines, the market price rises. Eventually, when a sufficient number of firms have ceased to operate, the market supply will have declined to such a degree that the market price will rise to $52. Once a market price of $52 is restored, the firms which are still carrying on are again able to cover fully their costs of production. Accordingly, no more firms will close down. Now any firm whose fixed cost obligations terminate will not leave the industry; it will elect to remain, even though it could leave without loss if it wished. The number of firms will therefore remain stable at the figure which makes possible a market price of $52, despite the reduction in market demand from its original level. The industry will once again be in *long run equilibrium*, i.e. tending neither to expand nor contract.

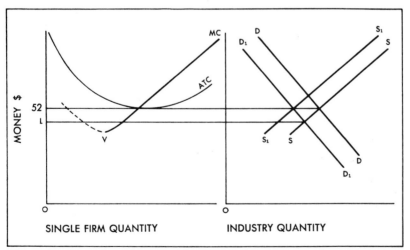

Figure 3.   Reaction of competitive firm and industry to change in price

Figure 3 graphically represents the analysis described above. Figure 3A shows the ATC and MC of an individual firm, with minimum ATC at $52. The firm's minimum AVC occurs at the point V, and the firm's short run supply curve consists therefore of the MC curve above and to the right of V.

The original market demand is represented by DD; the original supply, produced by 1000 firms, is represented by SS. The original market price is therefore $52, equal to the minimum ATC of each firm.

Market demand now declines to D_1D_1. In the short run, before any firm can advantageously leave the industry, the market supply remains at SS. During this period the market price becomes OL, being determined by the intersection of D_1D_1 and SS. At this price every firm will be losing money. But this is only a short run situation; in due course the fixed cost obligations of some firms come to an end and they leave the industry. As they leave, the supply curve shifts to the left, since the industry's output is being produced by an ever diminishing number of firms. Eventually, when enough firms have left, the supply curve becomes S_1S_1 which intersects D_1D_1 at a price of $52. At this price the remaining firms are once again able to cover their costs, and will therefore remain in the industry; i.e., when so many firms have left the industry that the supply curve has shifted to S_1S_1, the situation becomes stabilized; the industry will once again be in equilibrium.

A Permanent Increase in Market Demand

If an increase in market demand causes the market price to rise above $52, then the member firms of the industry will all be earning super normal profit; the owners will be obtaining returns over and above what would be fair and adequate for the investment and effort involved. Since there is no obstacle to entry, other businessmen, attracted by the high returns, will enter the industry. They will not be able to do so immediately, of course, for it will take time to build and equip new plants. New firms will be established only in the *long run*, after sufficient time has elapsed for new plants to be built and equipped.

Once the additional plants begin production, however, the market supply will increase. Eventually, when a sufficient number of new firms have established themselves, the market supply will have increased to such an extent that the market price is driven down to $52. Once this point is reached, the industry will no longer be unusually profitable. No additional firms will enter; the number in the industry will become stabilized at the figure which, under existing demand conditions, causes the market price to be $52. (The student is invited to work out the graphical analysis for himself.)

A Change in Production Costs

A permanent change in the cost of production will have effects analogous to those brought about by a change in market demand. Suppose the cost declines, of the materials, labour, or equipment required to make the product; the ATC of every firm will accordingly be reduced.[3] In this event, even with market demand unchanged and the market price $52, every firm will be abnormally profitable. New firms will wish to establish themselves in the industry and, in the long run will do so. Ultimately, so many additional firms will enter that the market price will be forced down to the level of the reduced minimum ATC of each firm. Once this stage is reached, every firm yields only normal returns and no more newcomers will be attracted to the industry.

A decline in costs of production, as we have just seen, may lead to expansion of the industry. It is also the case that expansion of the industry may be responsible for a decline in costs. Thus, suppose demand were to increase, enabling more firms to be in the industry; with the industry enlarged it may become feasible to establish specialized facilities to produce materials and components required by all firms; it may prove feasible as well to set up new facilities for the training of workers. Each firm thereupon is able to obtain materials, components and labour more cheaply; its costs fall, not because it has changed its operations in any way, but because there are more firms in the industry. Such developments are referred to as "external economies," for they arise outside the individual firm. The long run supply curve of such an industry would be downward-sloping, reflecting the fact that with more produced—because there were more firms in the industry—a lower price would be acceptable to each firm.

On the other hand, the growth of an industry may in itself cause the costs of individual firms to rise. With more firms in the industry, competition is likely to be keener for labour, materials and other requirements. Their prices may rise, while no offsetting reductions occur in other costs. Each firm, therefore, finds that its costs of production have risen, not because of any change in its own operations, but purely because the number of firms in the industry has increased. In this case the long run supply curve of the industry would be upward-sloping: with more firms in the industry and more being produced, each firm would require a higher market price for the same output.

External Economies: Graphical Representation

Figure 4 graphically illustrates how, purely because of external economies, the long run supply curve of an industry may be downward sloping. For simplicity the assumption is made that all firms have exactly the same cost structure, and that the most efficient output of each firm is 10 units, i.e. the minimum ATC is always achieved at this output.

Figure 4A shows how the ATC curve of each firm drops as the industry expands. When the industry has only 1,000 firms, each firm's costs are represented by ATC_1; the minimum ATC, achieved at an output of 10 units, is $60. When the number of

---

[3]If the reduction is made in some fixed cost item, then MC and AVC will remain unchanged. If the reduction is in some variable cost item such as labour, materials or power, new and lower MC and AVC schedules will come into being.

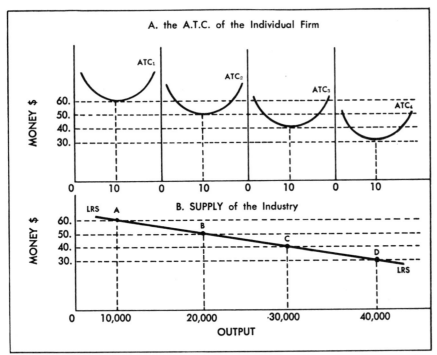

Figure 4.   A.T.C. of the firm, and industry supply, with external economies

firms increases to 2,000, then, because of external economies, each firm's costs drop to ATC_2; now the minimum ATC is $50. With 3,000 firms in the industry each firm's costs become ATC_3, with the minimum at $40; and so on.

Accordingly, in the long run, allowing sufficient time for any number of new firms to be built, the industry would be able to produce as follows:

  10,000 units, produced by 1,000 firms, @ $60.
  20,000 "   "   " 2,000 " @ $50.
  30,000 "   "   " 3,000 " @ $40.
  40,000 "   "   " 4,000 " @ $30.

This schedule is plotted in Figure 4B. Points A, B, C, and D represent the industry's equilibrium price and output when there are, respectively, 1,000, 2,000, 3,000, and 4,000 firms. By joining these points we obtain the continuous curve LRS, which represents the long run supply of the industry.

Industry Supply When Member Firms Unequally Suited

In our analysis of the competitive industry so far, we have made the assumption that all firms in the industry have exactly the same cost structure. On the basis of that

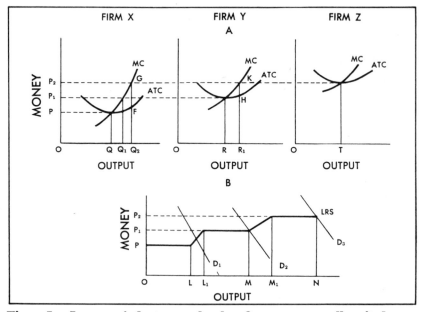

Figure 5.   Long run industry supply when firms are unequally suited

assumption, we analyzed the consequences of: a decrease in demand for the industry's product; a change in production costs; the existence of external economies.

Now let us make the assumption—probably more representative of many actual situations—that some firms are better suited to the industry than others, so that costs vary as between different firms. In agriculture, for example, farmers operating on fertile land close to markets will have lower costs per unit of output than farmers who are less favourably located. In mining, rich ore bodies can be worked at lower cost than poor ore bodies. In manufacturing, the superior management of some firms will enable them to achieve lower production costs. The industry supply curve will reflect the cost differences which exist among its member firms, as illustrated in Figure 5.

Figure 5A represents the ATC and MC schedules of three different firms. Firm X, the most efficient, can produce for as little as OP per unit; firm Y achieves its minimum ATC at OP_1; firm Z's minimum is higher still, at OP_2.

Figure 5B shows the industry's supply curve, representing the quantities that it would put on the market at various possible prices. If market price were OP only firm X could operate, producing the quantity OL (= OQ in Fig. 5A). At a price of OP_1, firm Y could enter production with an output of L_1M (= OR in Fig. 5A); firm X would meanwhile have increased its output to OL_1, (= OQ_1 in Fig. 5A). At a price of OP_2, firm Z could afford to produce the amount M_1N (= OT in

Fig. 5A); firms X and Y would increase their output by a total of MM_1 (= to Q_1Q_2 plus RR_1 in Fig. 5A).

The LRS line in Figure 5B is the industry's long run supply curve; the position of the demand curve will decide the market price and therefore the number of firms that will actually be able to operate in the industry. If demand were only D_1, then obviously only firm X could afford to operate; if demand were D_3, resulting in a market price of OP_2, all three firms could operate. If demand were actually D_3, then firms X and Y would be getting a price in excess of their average cost of production per unit; in the case of firm X the excess would be FG per unit; in the case of firm Y the excess would be HK per unit. These margins would be attributable to whatever factors were responsible for the superiority of firms X and Y; in principle these factors might demand and might be paid the full amount of the difference between each firm's total costs and total receipts. If the owners of firms X and Y had to make such payments, then, so far as they were concerned, their total cost of production would be exactly equal to the selling price (and to the cost of production of firm Z).

SUMMARY

A perfectly competitive industry is one which contains a large number of firms producing a completely standardized product, with no one firm producing a significant fraction of the total industry output. In such an industry, market demand and supply would determine the price; an individual firm would have to decide only how much to produce.

Presumably the firm will wish to produce that output at which its profit, i.e. the excess of receipts over costs, is maximized.

In the short run a firm will continue production even though it is suffering losses, so long as the price received exceeds average variable cost. In the long run the market price will tend to be equal to the minimum average total cost at which the firm can produce.

A permanent increase in market demand will cause, in the long run, an increase in the number of firms; a permanent decrease in demand will cause, in the long run, a decrease in the number of firms.

The production costs of an individual firm may rise or fall as a result of the entry of new firms into the industry. The competition of new firms for labour and materials, etc., will tend to raise costs; on the other hand, because the industry has expanded, some necessary goods and services may become available at lower prices to all its member firms.

FOR REVIEW AND DISCUSSION

1. Under perfectly competitive conditions price can never remain for long above the minimum cost of production per unit. Accordingly, no member of such an

industry ever has any inducement to introduce new methods or new products. Comment.

2. Cite an example of a "decreasing cost" industry, i.e. one in which cost of production per unit fell *because* the number of firms had increased and output had therefore been expanded.

3. Under perfectly competitive conditions the individual firm can have no "price policy." Why?

4. Fixed costs are "water over the dam." Explain.

5. For the perfectly competitive firm, Price = Marginal Cost. Which would be the independent and which the dependent variable in this statement?

6. A certain perfectly competitive industry is characterized by external economies. Show how an individual firm in this industry would become adjusted, in the long run, to a permanent increase in market demand.

7. For a firm considering the construction of a new building, the "short run" is quite short; for a firm which has already built a building, the "long run" may be quite long. Explain.

8. Why does the economist believe that the ATC and AVC curves are both "U" shaped?

9. The minimum average variable cost of a firm is a critical figure. Why?

10. From the cost schedules of the individual firm we derive its supply schedule; from the supply schedule of all the firms in an industry we derive the market supply schedule. Explain.

11. Illustrating graphically, demonstrate what will happen to the individual firm in a perfectly competitive industry, and to the industry, when a reduction occurs in the cost of an important raw material. Distinguish between the short run and long run effects.

Derive the long run supply curve of an industry in which the member firms are not equally well suited to the industry.

6

Firm and Industry in Imperfect Competition

In the preceding chapter we analyzed the behaviour of the individual firm in a perfectly competitive industry. We saw that the selling price of the individual firm would be determined by the forces of market supply and demand, and that it would decide only how much to produce at that price. In this chapter we shall examine the behaviour of the individual firm in industries where perfect competition does not prevail, whether because of the fewness of the firms, or because their products are not exactly the same. At the end of the chapter we shall assess the degree to which our theory of businessmen's behaviour applies to the real world.

MONOPOLY

A One Firm Industry

The diametric opposite of perfect competition is absolute monopoly. A monopoly situation is said to exist when one firm is the sole producer of a particular product and this product has no close substitutes. Anyone who wishes to buy this type of good or service must buy from this firm; there is no other source, and no satisfactory alternative.

Monopoly may exist in a great variety of situations, and for a great variety of reasons. A firm may control all the supplies of a particular natural resource, e.g. the International Nickel Company of Canada controls most of the free world's nickel deposits. A firm may be the sole producer of some item because it holds a patent which forbids others to copy, or because other firms simply could not duplicate its procedures: its organization may be unique in the scale of its operations, or in the skill and teamwork of its staff. It may be that for technical reasons the market is best supplied by a single firm: a local telephone system really ought to be operated by one company only. The market may be too small to support more than one firm of efficient size; for example, in a small country town there might be room for only one movie theatre. Through massive advertising, or through the careful cultivation of customers' goodwill, a firm may gain a unique position in the minds of the general public; other firms which produced goods that were identical or virtually identical might attract very few customers. A firm which holds a monopoly position may preserve it by dealing ruthlessly with attempts at competition. It might sharply reduce its selling price, incurring losses itself in the process, but forcing upon any competitor the hopeless alternative of either matching an unprofitably low price, or not selling at all; a small rival with limited resources would soon be driven to the wall. Illegal methods, including violence or the threat of violence, might be employed to frighten away would-be competitors.

The Monopolist's Market Power

We saw in Chapter 3 that, given any particular market demand for a product, the price would depend upon how much of it was offered by suppliers. If only a small quantity were placed on the market, a high price could be charged; if a large quantity were offered, only a low price could be charged. We saw in Chapter 5, that where there are a great many firms in an industry, no single firm can significantly affect the total quantity put on the market. That total is determined by the collective action of all the firms. An individual firm is powerless to prevent the total quantity offered to the market from being so great as to force the price down to a point where it barely covers costs. Restriction of its own output would have only an insignificant effect, and it cannot induce the other firms to reduce their output. Each seller, acting independently, finds it to his advantage to increase output so long as selling price exceeds marginal cost. With every firm acting in this way the market price will be kept down to a figure which equals the average cost of production of each firm, operating at its most efficient level.

The monopolistic firm possesses the market power which a competitive firm lacks. Being the sole producer of its type of product, a monopolistic firm can decide what quantity shall be offered to the market. It can restrict production to the quantity which, given the prevailing demand, will enable a profitable price to be charged. The same effect can be achieved in an industry which is composed of a number of firms if, by collusion, they charge higher prices than are necessary to cover costs, and appropriately restrict their output.

An Example

Let us see, on the basis of a simple example, how, in theory at any rate, a monopolist would decide what output to produce, and at what price to sell. Suppose that Company X, a monopolistic firm, has a cost schedule as shown in Table 1A, and that demand for its product is as shown in Table 1B.

Company X can elect to produce and sell whatever quantity it cares to. Each quantity that it may choose involves a certain level of costs and a particular selling price. For example, if the monopolist were to produce two units his total costs would be $280, and his selling price would be $150; his total receipts would therefore be $300, yielding a profit of $20. If he were to produce five units, total costs would be

Table 1

COST AND DEMAND SCHEDULES OF COMPANY X

A: Cost			B: Demand	
Output	Total Cost*		Quantity	Selling Price
1	$ 200		1	$ 160
2	280		2	150
3	340		3	140
4	420		4	130
5	520		5	120
6	640		6	110
7	780		7	100
8	940		8	90
9	1,120		9	80
10	1,320		10	70

*Includes Fixed Cost of $100.

$520 and the selling price would have to be $120, yielding total receipts of $600, and a profit of $80.

How can the company determine which level of output will be the most profitable? To answer this question properly, we must draw up a somewhat more elaborate schedule of costs and receipts, as is done in Table 2.

Columns (1) to (4) are all familiar, being similar to figures we presented in Chapter 5 for a hypothetical competitive firm. Column (5), taken from Table 1, indicates how the price which could be charged per unit will depend upon the quantity put on the market. Column (6) shows what total receipts will be realized at each

Table 2

COST AND DEMAND SCHEDULES OF COMPANY X
(Showing Average and Marginal Figures)

(1)	(2)	(3)	(4)	(5)	(6)	(7)
Output	Total Cost	Average Total Cost	Marginal Cost	Price Per Unit	Total Receipts	Marginal Revenue
1	$ 200	$200	$100	$160	$160	$160
2	280	140	80	150	300	140
3	340	113.3	60	140	420	120
4	420	105.0	80	130	520	100
5	520	104.0	100	120	600	80
6	640	106.6	120	110	660	60
7	780	111.4	140	100	700	40
8	940	117.5	160	90	720	20
9	1,120	124.4	180	80	720	0
10	1,320	132.0	200	70	700	−20

level of output, taking into account the price at which each unit must be sold. Column (7), the marginal revenue (MR) column, indicates how total receipts will vary with each additional unit sold. For example, the sale of two units instead of just one causes sales receipts to increase from $160 to $300; the marginal revenue of the second unit is therefore $140. The sale of eight units instead of seven causes total receipts to become $720 instead of $700; the marginal revenue of the eighth unit is accordingly $20, and so on.

Marginal Revenue Less Than Price

Except where only one unit is sold, the marginal revenue (MR) attributable to any particular unit is always less than the price at which that unit is sold. For example, the selling price of the third unit is $140 but its MR is only $120, the selling price of the ninth unit is $80, but its MR is zero. The tenth unit sells for $70 but its MR is actually negative.

The reason is that whenever the monopolist produces an additional unit, he must, in order to sell it, charge a lower price than before. But he must charge this lower price not only for the additional unit, but also for all the other units which he could otherwise be selling at a higher price. For example, if the monopolist produces only two units he can charge $150 each; if he wishes to sell three units he must lower his price to $140. But he must charge $140 not only for the third unit, but also for the other two, which he could have sold for $150 each, *provided he sold only them*. Hence his receipts, when he increases his sales from two to three units, rise by only $120. He sells the third unit for $140, but because he is selling it, he is obliged to accept $10 less for each of the other two units. His net receipts therefore rise by $20 less than the price at which he actually sells the third unit. The same kind of result occurs, at any level of output, when he increases output by one unit.

Non-Discriminatory Pricing Assumed

The foregoing discussion of marginal revenue assumes that the monopolist must charge the same price to all customers. The assumption is not universally valid; a monopolist may be able to discriminate between customers. If he is able to conceal from each customer the price which all the others are paying, he can sell the same product to different people at different prices. From the buyer who is willing to pay $150, he may ask $150; from the buyer who is willing to pay only $140, he may ask only $140, and so on.

How general this practice is, no one can tell. It is the accepted procedure in oriental bazaars, where the price charged to each customer is the outcome of lengthy haggling, and may differ considerably from the price charged someone else for the identical article. In Western countries business firms generally announce their prices publicly. They may grant secret reductions to large and favoured customers who wield considerable market power;[1] they are unlikely to sell for less to some small buyer whose purchases are insignificant just because that person is unprepared to pay more—almost inevitably this would become known and the firm would be forced to sell at the same price to all buyers. In our analysis of monopoly, accordingly, we make the assumption that the firm does not discriminate among its customers, but always charges the same price to all.

The Most Profitable Output and Price

On the basis of the figures in Table 2, the most profitable output is four units. We can establish this by comparing total receipts with total costs for each level of output. With output at four units total receipts exceed total costs by a greater margin than at any other output. We can arrive at the same result by using the "marginal" method introduced in Chapter 5; i.e. commencing with the minimum level of output we note how receipts and costs are affected when output is increased. So long as additional output adds more to receipts than to costs, it is worthwhile; additional output which adds more to costs than to receipts is not worthwhile.

Applying the "marginal" method to our example, we proceed as follows. If the monopolist produces one unit, his total costs will be $200 and total receipts $160. If he produces and sells two units, however, costs will rise by $80 (the MC of the second unit), while receipts rise by $140 (the MR of the second unit). Production of two units is obviously better than production of only one unit; it adds $60 more to receipts than to costs, and converts a loss of $40 into a profit of $20. Production of three units is even better; the MC of the third unit is $60, while its MR is $120; hence production of the third unit will add a further $60 to profit. Production of four units is better still. The MC of the fourth unit is $80 while its MR is $100; with a fourth unit produced, total profit goes up by another $20. But production of five units would be foolish; the MC of the fifth unit is $100 while its MR is only $80. Whatever the total profit was when four units were being produced, it would be reduced by $20 if five units were produced. Any further increase in output would reduce the firm's profit even more.

Maximum profit will be realized with output at four units. Having established what his output will be, we can tell what price the monopolist will charge. Column (5) in Table 2 indicates that with four units being put on the market, the selling price will be $130 per unit. Here then is the answer to the question with which we started. The monopolist, to achieve maximum profit, should produce four units, and sell them at a price of $130 each; his average total cost being $105 at that level of output, the profit would amount to $100.

It may seem a little odd that the monopolist, getting a price of $130, should

---

[1]In some countries, of which Canada is one, the charging of different prices to different customers is actually illegal in some circumstances.

refrain from selling a fifth unit: after all, its marginal cost is only $100. But if he were to sell a fifth unit, his receipts would not go up by $130; they would go up by only $80. To sell that fifth unit he would have to cut his price to $120, *and would have to charge this lower price on the four units which he could have been selling for $130 each*. The fifth unit would therefore only bring a net increase in receipts of $80, the $120 at which he sells it *minus* the $40 reduction in receipts gained from the sale of the other four units. This is why the production of a fifth unit, though it would sell for $120, would fail to cover its marginal cost of $100.

Graphical Representation

In Figure 1 the average and marginal figures of Table 2 are graphically portrayed. The ATC and MC curves represent the data in columns (3) and (4) respectively; the D and MR curves represent, respectively, the data in columns (5) and (7). We can obtain from the graph the same information as from the schedule. To find the average cost and receipts and marginal cost and receipts for any level of output, we simply draw a perpendicular from the X axis, at that quantity, up to intercept the various curves. For example, at output OV, the MR of the OVth unit would be VW; the ATC per unit would be VX; the marginal cost of the OVth unit would be VY; the selling price per unit would be VZ.

According to the graph the most profitable output will be OQ, the output where the MC curve intersects the MR curve, and where therefore MC=MR. A higher or lower output would be less profitable. Beyond OQ the MC curve is consistently above the MR curve; hence any output beyond OQ would add more to costs than to receipts. To the left of OQ, the MR curve is consistently above the MC curve; hence if output were reduced below OQ, receipts would fall by more than would costs.

Having established the most profitable output, we can go on to determine the average cost of production, the selling price, and therefore the total profit. With output at OQ, the ATC will be QL; selling price will be QP; profit per unit will be LP. The total profit will be the shaded area TLPN, being the number of units produced (TL) multiplied by the profit per unit of LP. This is the maximum profit which can be earned under the given cost and demand conditions. If the firm changes its price and output *in any way*, its total profit will become smaller.

THE EFFECTS OF MONOPOLIZATION

Figure 1 in the previous chapter presented the cost figures of a hypothetical firm, the firm's minimum average total cost being $52, achieved at an output of 5 units. It was demonstrated later in the chapter that in a competitive industry composed of 1000 such firms (and with additional firms free to enter if they so desired) the market price would tend to be exactly $52. Each firm would produce 5 units and earn exactly the normal rate of return on its effort and investment.

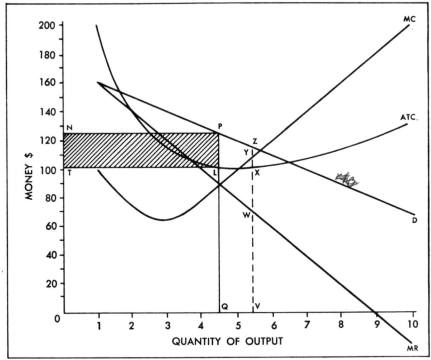

Figure 1.   Price and output of a monopolist

Suppose now that this industry were to become a monopoly as a result of one firm acquiring control over all the others, and that new firms were no longer able to enter. Suppose further that the market demand for the product is as follows:

Price	Quantity
$84	1000
76	2000
68	3000
60	4000
52	5000
44	6000
36	7000
28	8000
20	9000
12	10000

Under perfectly competitive conditions the industry would have produced 5000 units selling at a price of $52; once it becomes monopolized, output is held down to

4000 and the selling price is $60. Total costs are then $210,000 and total receipts $240,000, giving a monopoly profit of $30,000. This superior result derives from the fact that the additional 1000 units cost an extra $50,000 to produce (the marginal cost of the fifth unit being $50 in each producing firm) but the sale of another 1000 units increases total receipts by only $20,000; whereas 4000 units can be sold at a price of $60 for a total of $240,000, it becomes necessary to lower the price to $52 to sell 5000 units, for a total of $260,000.

So long as perfect competition prevails, with each firm considering only its own interests and having no regard to the effects of its actions on the market situation, the industry will inevitably produce 5000 units. If ever it happened that each firm was producing 4 units, so that the market price were $60, each firm would see an opportunity to increase its profit by producing another unit—the marginal cost would be only $50 while the addition to receipts would apparently be $60. But with every firm doing this, the industry's output becomes 5000 units and the market price must be lowered to $52. The opportunity for additional profit which everyone sees is a mirage that disappears as soon as everyone tries to grasp it. A monopolist, however, knowing that an increase in the industry's output to 5000 units would cause profits to disappear, uses his power of control to ensure that output is held to 4000 units, enabling a price of $60 to be charged and a monopoly profit to be earned.

The figures in the foregoing example are of course carefully contrived. But the basic principle which they illustrate is absolutely valid: replacement of a competitive situation by a monopoly creates the possibility of monopolistic profit through reduction in output and increase in price.

Monopolies Not Always Profitable

Company X in Table I is lucky; not all monopolists do so well. The possession of monopoly power does not guarantee the earning of monopolistic profits. Some monopolists earn only normal returns; others actually lose money. A person who had a monopoly of the sale of air conditioning equipment in the Antarctic, for instance, would find the pickings poor. Just how profitable a monopoly will be, depends upon the relationship between its cost and demand curves, as shown in Figure 2. Three different firms are represented here, each with its own particular cost-demand relationship, and therefore its own opportunity—or lack of opportunity—for earning profit.

If a firm is to earn monopoly profit, selling price must—at some level of output —exceed the cost of production, as in Figure 2A where the firm is able to earn a monopoly profit of ABRP. The firm represented in Figure 2B is able to cover its cost and no more; at its optimum output of OL the average cost of production and the selling price are exactly equal at LM. The firm shown in 2C will, at its optimum output, lose the amount HKFG; the cost of production per unit will be EG while a price of only EF can be charged.

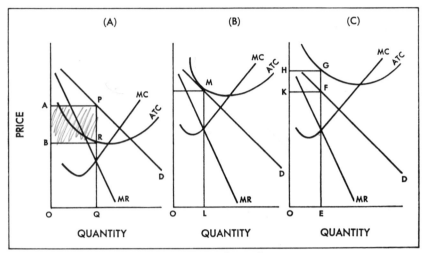

Figure 2.   Costs, demand and monopoly profit

Few firms are likely to remain profitable monopolies forever. There will always be rivals eager to share in the super normal profits and, whatever the basis of the monopoly power, if it can be imitated they will do so. They may not be able to duplicate the monopoly's product but manage to come pretty close. Where a firm's monopoly power derives from the special characteristics of its product, a rival may develop a product which is similar, as the Pepsi-Cola Company did in creating a product which resembled hitherto unique Coca-Cola. Where a profitable monopoly derives from the occupying of a special location, a rival may set up in the vicinity; a store which does a roaring trade because it is the only one in a particular district, is likely to find itself joined by other stores which locate themselves nearby. Where monopoly power is derived from effective advertising and public relations, rival firms are likely to adopt similar advertising and similar measures designed to build up customer goodwill. Only monopoly power based on technical grounds, as in the case of a telephone system or a town water supply, is secure against infringement.

Rivalry may come even from firms producing products which are altogether different in character. For, though completely different, they may be capable of serving the same general purpose. For example, a firm may have a monopoly in the production of glass bottles. If its profits are large, firms which produce plastics may devise plastic bottles to replace glass bottles; steel firms may develop light-weight steel containers which could be used in place of bottles altogether. While its monopoly in glass bottle production may remain intact, the firm would find itself under heavy pressure from competitors.

MONOPOLISTIC COMPETITION

Long Run Equilibrium Under Monopolistic Competition

An industry may be composed of a large number of firms whose products, while generally similar, are not identical. Every firm is likely to have some customers who prefer its particular product and will pay more for it if necessary; each firm could raise its price, therefore, without losing all its customers. It will, of course, lose some business when it raises its price: there will be some customers whose preference is not very strong and who will buy substitutes rather than pay the higher price. Such customers in fact might stop buying even if the firm did not raise its price: they could be lured away by another firm which offered a cheaper or more attractive product.

Where the foregoing conditions prevail, the economist says that the industry is one of *monopolistic competition.* Monopoly is present, since each firm is the sole producer of its particular product. There is competition, too, since all the firms are trying to sell substantially similar products to the same customers.

In such an industry, the member firms cannot earn monopoly profits for very long. If ever firms are especially profitable, new firms will enter the industry and attract away some of the customers of original firms. With demand for their products reduced, these firms will earn smaller profits; eventually, they are likely to earn no more than a fair and reasonable return.

Figure 3 indicates what is likely to happen to the sales and profits of Company Z, a typical member of an industry characterized by monopolistic competition. Figure 3A shows the position of Company Z before additional firms have entered the industry. It produces the quantity OQ_1 (this being the output at which MC = MR), charges the corresponding price of Q_1P_1, and earns profit represented by the shaded rectangle $FBCP_1$. Figure 3B shows its position after other firms, attracted by the profits being earned by Z and all the others, have begun to put their similar products on the market. Some of Company Z's customers buy the competitor's products, so its demand curve falls to D_2. Average total cost and marginal cost remain the same. With the demand curve down to D_2, and the marginal revenue curve correspondingly down to MR_2,[2] the new optimum output is OQ_2; at this output MC equals the reduced MR. Selling price accordingly must be reduced to Q_2P_2; profit is now only the shaded rectangle of Figure 3B, $LGHP_2$.

Although demand has fallen off, Company Z is still able to charge a price which exceeds the cost of production. Accordingly, it still is earning a return over and above what would be adequate for the effort and investment involved. More firms will be tempted to enter the industry, introducing similar products or products which could be used for the same purpose. Company Z may hold its market despite all the new challenges, and continue to earn profit as shown in Figure 3B. But it may lose more

---

[2]Every demand schedule has its own corresponding marginal revenue schedule. When the demand curve shifts from D_1 to D_2, the MR curve must shift therefore from MR_1 to MR_2.

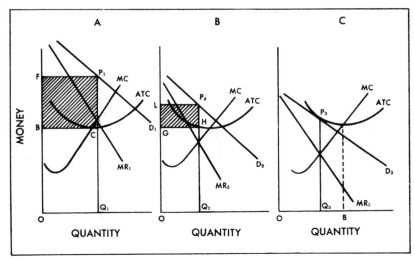

Figure 3. Monopolistic competition

customers to fresh rivals, so that the demand for its goods declines to D_3 in Figure 3C. In this case, Company Z will earn no monopolistic profit whatever; now, at its optimum output, its selling price will exactly equal its cost of production per unit.[3] If Company Z is forced into the position illustrated in Figure 3C, the situation is likely to become stabilized. Since the company—the typical firm—is now only just covering its costs, it is unlikely that any firms will develop new products to compete for its market. That market is no longer particularly attractive. The economist would say that an equilibrium situation has been achieved, there being now no tendency for additional firms to enter the industry, nor for existing firms to leave.[4]

The "Wastefulness" of Monopolistic Competition

If Company Z does end up in the position illustrated in Figure 3C then it appears to be operating inefficiently. Its level of production, OQ_3, is well below the output OB where its average cost per unit is a minimum. Other firms in its industry will be in the same position; each will be producing less than the output at which it is most efficient. From society's point of view, resources appear to be wasted. The same total output could be achieved if there were fewer firms in the industry but each produced more.

Such a situation is frequently encountered in the real world. We should, however, temper any urge to rush out and rationalize an industry, by shutting down some

---

[3]It could well happen that rival firms draw off so many of its customers that company Z winds up losing money. Demand for its products may decline to such a degree that, at its optimum output, selling price is less than cost, as illustrated in Figure 2C.

[4]Since cost is defined as including an adequate return on effort and investment, a firm will remain in the industry so long as its selling price equals its cost.

firms and concentrating production in the remainder. The fact is that each firm's product has its own particular features, and these may be attractive to some people. Sometimes, admittedly, the differences between the product of different firms in an industry are only trivial, and customers would be just as pleased to have one as to have the other. But other times the differences are significant: members of the public would be annoyed if they could not obtain the special product which they liked, even though they could obtain a corresponding standard product at a lower price.

It may be, too, that we are too hasty in our judgment of what constitutes excess capacity. In some industries demand is concentrated in certain peak periods. To serve properly the peak load demand, facilities must be installed and staff maintained which are used only partially during off-peak periods. Frequently there is no help for this apparent waste. If capacity were just sufficient for off-peak periods, peak load demands would be very badly handled.

In some industries, notably retail trade and retail service, the convenience with which the customer is served, is hardly less important than the product itself. People like to make their purchases whenever they please, and without waiting. A store or service establishment must have staff and facilities on hand which are not actually "producing" anything, but simply stand ready to give customers immediate attention. The much maligned filling station industry offers excellent illustration. No doubt the retail distribution of gasoline could be rationalized. In any North American city, probably a fraction of the existing filling stations could serve the local market. With fewer stations, and each operating more intensively, distribution costs might be reduced somewhat. But then the motorist who wanted a tankful of gas would likely have to make an appointment to buy it, or queue behind a long line of other cars. To most motorists the convenience of being able to buy gas whenever they happen to think of it, and without waiting, is worth the extra money which it costs. It may well be the case that to distribute gas with the present degree of convenience to motorists, something like the present number of filling stations is required.

OLIGOPOLY

An oligopolistic industry is one which contains only a small number of firms—say fewer than a dozen. The economist distinguishes two types of oligopoly: the *homogeneous oligopoly,* in which the products of all firms are identical or virtually identical; the *differentiated oligopoly,* in which there are significant differences between the products of the different firms, and buyers have preferences for one over another. Examples of homogeneous oligopoly are furnished by such industries as the following: petroleum products, rubber tires, chemicals, aluminum; the automobile industry would be an example of differentiated oligopoly. Each of these industries is composed, in Canada and the U.S., of fewer than a dozen firms.

Price Under Homogeneous Oligopoly

Since the products of all the firms in the industry are identical, or virtually so, they must sell at the same price. No customer will pay to one firm a higher price than is being asked by another firm for exactly the same product. How is this price determined?

To this question there is no categorical answer. The oligopoly price will likely lie somewhere between an upper and lower limit. It could be as low as the price which would prevail under perfectly competitive conditions, i.e. be exactly equal to the minimum average total cost of production of the individual firm. Or it could be as high as the price which would prevail under monopoly conditions, i.e. be equal to the price which would be charged if all the firms were under a single ownership, with the owner setting the price which would maximize total profit.

The oligopoly price will be between these upper and lower limits, but precisely where no one can tell beforehand. Its exact position will depend upon the degree of collusion, or cooperation—to be more polite—which exists among the firms. If there is none whatsoever, the price will be at the competitive level. Any firm which tried to charge more would immediately lose its customers to rivals who offered them the same thing for less. If the firms of the industry cooperate completely, the profit earned by the industry as a whole will be the maximum possible. Less than complete collusion will cause the industry's profits to be correspondingly smaller than the maximum attainable.

Output Restriction

Earlier in this chapter we saw that a monopoly firm is able to charge a profitable price because it is able to hold output below the level which would be produced under competitive conditions. In the same way, an oligopolistic industry, if it is to achieve a profitable price, must arrange for a restriction of output by its member firms.

Figure 4A shows the market demand and supply of an oligopolistic (homogeneous) industry which is comprised of three identical firms; Figure 4B shows the ATC and MC curves of one of the firms. If perfectly competitive conditions prevail, then each firm will produce the quantity OR (in B) and the total output of the industry will be OQ (in A). The market price will be OP, and each firm will just cover its costs. If, however, each firm restricts its output to OF, industry output will be only OI; with the smaller quantity OI being offered on the market, the price OM can be charged. Each firm is now able to earn profit. Its cost of production per unit is FG (its output being OF); selling price per unit being equal to FH, it earns a profit of GH on each of the OF units which it sells, for a total profit amounting to the shaded area LKGH.

In order for all firms to achieve this profit, each must keep output down to OF, so that the output of the industry as a whole is only OI, enabling firms to charge a market price of OM. The agreement may be in the form of a binding contract, a

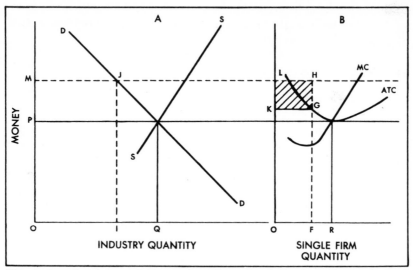

Figure 4.   Output restriction under oligopoly   A: In the industry   B: In the firm

verbal undertaking, or perhaps an unspoken "understanding." It may require each firm simply to charge the price OM, with the total potential sales of MJ to be divided up among the firms on some agreed basis—or perhaps with the division reflecting the outcome of a competitive struggle. As is evident from Figure 4 each firm will be tempted to cheat by offering—perhaps secretly—to sell for a little less than OL; additional sales which it thereby gains will be highly profitable since the marginal cost of additional output is far less than OL. In collusively setting their price the members of an oligopoly may in fact take care to keep this sort of temptation to a minimum: in the United Kingdom eight major tire companies were accused in 1966 of setting a price which was "the highest which the manufacturers dared charge without one of the members suffering an irresistible urge to undercut."[5] A more detailed description is given in the next chapter of the various methods whereby oligopolists may achieve such collusion.

Differentiated Oligopoly

Where the products of the firms in an oligopolistic industry are significantly differentiated, a firm may raise its price without losing all its customers. It will lose some sales, the extent of the loss presumably depending upon the degree of substitutability between its product and those of the other firms. If one firm cuts its price the effects will depend upon the reaction of other firms. If they continue to sell their products for the same prices as before, the price-cutting firm may achieve a substantial increase

[5]*The Guardian*, May 10, 1966, p. 5.

in sales. If they cut their prices, the original price-cutter may find his sales unchanged. Quite possibly the other firms might retaliate with such sharp price reductions that the original price-cutter actually experiences a reduction in sales.

Cooperation Facilitated if the Firms are Few

The fact that an oligopolistic industry contains only a few firms renders it relatively easy to achieve unanimous agreement and absolute conformity to a common policy. With a large number of firms in the industry, it might well prove impossible to persuade each and every owner to observe a prescribed price and output policy. It could happen that each one of even a large number of persons conforms absolutely, but the likelihood of absolute conformity is very much greater when only a small number of persons is involved. Furthermore, any individual firm contemplating a breach of the agreement is subject to particularly powerful deterrence when the number of firms in its industry is very small. Let us see why.

If one firm sells for less than the agreed price and therefore increases its sales, the extra business is done at the expense of the rest of the industry. Since the number of firms in an oligopolistic industry is small, if one firm increases its business substantially, each of the remaining firms will lose heavily. For example, if business is equally distributed in a three firm industry, then if one firm increases its sales by 100 per cent, each of the other firms must be losing 50 per cent of its sales. A firm which was threatened with so large a loss of sales would be forced to take defensive action; it would have to match the lower price offered by an aggressive rival; it might even retaliate by offering to sell at a still lower price. Once the firms which were attacked responded in this fashion, the aggressive firm which first cut the price would find that its sales were back to about their usual level, or perhaps were even lower. It would be worse off than it was originally, however, because it would now be selling at a much lower price. All the other firms would be worse off too.

In an industry which contains a large number of firms, on the other hand, a single firm may not provoke a reaction when it cuts its price. Although it gains customers from the other firms, the loss suffered by each other firm may be too small to justify counter-measures on its part. For example, suppose an industry consists of 100 firms. If one firm, by cutting its price, manages to increase its sales by 100%, then each of the other firms will, on the average, lose only $1/99$ of its custom.[6] So small a loss would not justify counter-action on the part of any one firm. Accordingly, in such an industry, each individual firm may understandably assume that it can safely

---

[6]It may happen of course that all the increase in sales gained by a price cutting firm is at the expense of just one or two other firms nearby. In that case they may find it necessary to match price cuts. Another group of firms may be affected in turn by *their* price cuts. For example, one filling station located on a particular street may reduce the price of its gasoline. Nearby stations are obliged to match the reduction. But when they cut their price, other stations near them, but far from the original price cutter, are obliged to match the reduction. A further group becomes affected, until by such a series of chain reactions all filling stations in the area wind up selling at the low price.

cut prices in order to increase sales, without having to worry about retaliation by its competitors. But with *each* firm pursuing such a policy, the price will ultimately be cut to the bone.

Significance of the Price-Marginal Cost Ratio

Where fixed costs constitute a very large proportion of total costs, selling price is bound to be very much greater than marginal cost. In such a case each additional unit sold means a handsome increase in profits, giving rise to a strong temptation on the part of an oligopolist to shade his price below the agreed level in order to increase sales. Where fixed costs are not so large a proportion of total costs the temptation is correspondingly weaker. Table 3 illustrates by comparing the consequences, for two different member firms of an oligopoly, of shading the price below the agreed figure. Firm A has high fixed costs and low variable costs; Firm B has relatively low fixed costs but high variable costs. The price, set through collusion, is $1500 and each firm is expected to sell 100 units.

Evidently the firm with heavy fixed costs would gain far more through price shading, under identical demand conditions. Firm A, by cutting its price $50 below the agreed level and thereby increasing sales by 10 units, would increase its profit by $7500; Firm B, doing the same thing, would increase its profit by only $500. Presumably Firm B would be much less tempted to "chisel"; the prospective gain would be small and probably would not warrant the risk of retaliation by other members of the oligopoly. Firm A, on the other hand, might easily be tempted to take the risk.

Table 3

IMPLICATIONS OF THE FIXED COST / VARIABLE COST
RATIO IN AN OLIGOPOLY SITUATION

	Firm A	Firm B
Fixed Cost	$100,000	$ 30,000
AVC = MC	200	900
Total Variable Cost (100 units)	20,000	90,000
Total Cost (100 units)	120,000	120,000
No. of units sold at price of $1500	100	100
Total receipts at price of $1500	150,000	150,000
Profit selling at price of $1500	30,000	30,000
No. of units sold at price of $1450	110	110
Total costs at price of $1450	122,000	129,000
Total receipts at price of $1450	159,500	159,500
Profit at price of $1450	37,500	30,500

Our examples reflect actual experience. In the real world "price wars" have tended to occur particularly in those oligopolistic industries which are characterized by heavy fixed costs, e.g. railways and ocean shipping companies. These "wars" generally arose out of price cutting by a single firm, and in such industries, as we have just seen, the temptation for an individual firm to cut its price is particularly strong.

Restriction of Entry Into the Industry

Oligopolistic profits are likely to be earned on a continuing basis only in industries which new firms cannot enter, or can enter only with great difficulty. With the member firms earning handsome profits, new firms would naturally like to enter the industry. But if they do enter, the profits of firms presently in will inevitably decline. If the new firms offer to sell at a lower price, member firms will suffer whether, to keep their customers they match this price, or whether, accepting the loss of some customers, they continue to charge the usual price. Even if the new firms sell at the generally agreed price the original firms will suffer, since the market will now have to be shared among more firms, leaving fewer customers for each one.

Oligopolistic profits are likely to be earned on a sustained basis only in industries which are closed, or virtually closed, to new firms. A good many industries are in this category. Some industries are virtually closed to newcomers because of the enormous amounts of capital required to establish a new plant; others are, in effect, closed because a particular site, resource or skill is required, and the available supply is completely controlled by the existing firms. In some industries, the existing firms may keep out newcomers by threatening them with ruinous price wars. The use or threat of physical violence is not unknown as a means of restricting entry into an industry.

International Oligopoly Agreements

The world's output of a number of natural commodities, such as tin, tea, natural rubber and sugar, is concentrated in a relatively small number of countries. For example, Malaya, Nigeria, Bolivia, Siam and Indonesia are responsible for something like 90 per cent of the world's annual output of tin. India, Ceylon and Indonesia produce about 80 per cent of the world's tea. While wheat is grown in practically every country in the world, the world's major wheat exporting countries are only a few—Canada, the United States, Argentina, Australia, France. In the case of each of these commodities the governments of the main exporting countries have at one time or another entered into agreements whereby each undertook to restrict exports thereby enabling all to charge a more profitable price on the world market. Within each country production was typically carried on by a large number of private producers; each signatory government was accordingly obliged either to buy up and hold off the export market a portion of the crop grown by its nationals, or to induce, perhaps compel, individual producers to restrict their output.

In the case of some manufactured goods, virtually the entire world supply has been produced by a handful of giant firms of different nationality. For example, during the 1920s a small group of American, British, German, Dutch, Japanese,

Hungarian and French firms produced practically the entire world's output of electric light bulbs. In such cases the firms involved might enter into an agreement to divide up the world market among themselves. Each firm would be allocated a particular sector of the world market, and thereby be assured of freedom from competition. The leading producers of electric light bulbs entered into such an agreement in 1924. During the 1930s, the world's giants in the chemical industry, America's Du Pont, Britain's Imperial Chemical Industries and Germany's I.G. Farben, entered into various market-sharing agreements.

MONOPSONY

A "Monopoly" Buyer

Monopsony is said to exist when there is only a single buyer for a particular good or service. The reason may be that the buyer is a large firm, and the market area can support only one. For example, a cannery may be the sole buyer of vegetables grown in a particular locality, since the local farmers can produce enough to supply only one firm of efficient size. Or only one firm may possess the technical skill or the capital equipment required to make use of some good or service. Those people who have such goods or services to sell can therefore sell to this firm only; no one else can use them. For example, the Canadian Broadcasting Corporation is virtually a monopsonist in regard to the services of many types of professional entertainers in Canada.

Market Power of the Monopsonist

Being the sole buyer, the monopsonist can set the price which he will pay. He need not fear that competitors will outbid him. But he cannot *force* people to accept a low price. Some people will accept whatever he offers because they have no better alternative, but others will refuse to sell if the price he sets is very low. The monopsonist accordingly must take note of the fact that if he sets a low price he will be able to buy only a little; if he wishes to buy more he will have to pay a higher price. He does, however, have the *freedom to select the price, and the corresponding purchase quantity, which suits him best.* The perfectly competitive buyer has no such option; he can buy only at the competitively determined price, although at that price he can buy all he likes. Under monopsony conditions, the selling price of a good will be lower, and less will be sold, than under competitive conditions. For an illustration of the effects of monopsony, see Chapter 9.

Oligopsony

Oligopsony refers to the situation where the number of buyers for a particular product or service is very small. The reasons will be similar to those given for the existence of monopsony; i.e. the market area may be able to support only a few firms of efficient size; or only a few firms possess the facilities required to make effective use of the good or service in question. The significance of oligopsony will, as with oligopoly, depend upon the degree of collusion practised by the member firms. If, by an agreement or through an understanding, each firm agrees to pay no more than a certain price and to buy no more than a specified quantity, the firms can all pay the same low price as would be paid by an absolute monopsony. If, on the other hand, each firm acts independently, the price will be bid up to the higher level which would prevail under conditions of perfect buyers' competition.

QUALIFICATIONS TO THE THEORY OF THE FIRM

Assumptions Not Universally Valid

Our theory of the firm presented in this and the preceding chapter has been based upon two key assumptions: firstly that the firm possesses all relevant information, i.e. it knows exactly both the cost schedule and the demand schedule for its product; secondly, that the firm adopts the course of action which will maximize its profit. In practice neither of these assumptions is strictly true. Some firms can not even predict with assurance how their costs will vary with changes in output. Furthermore, while a firm in a perfectly competitive industry may know exactly what the demand is for its products, a monopolistic or oligopolistic firm can only guess. The competitive firm *knows* that it can sell as much as it cares to at the market price; the monopolistic firm must *estimate* how much the public will buy at the price it sets. Furthermore a businessman in any industry, competitive or monopolistic, may have other objectives than maximization of his profits; he may therefore quite deliberately refrain from following the course of action which will yield him the highest net income.

Monopoly Pricing: A "Realistic" View

The typical businessman will deny that his firm "restricts" output, as our theory of monopoly has suggested; he will, on the contrary, insist that his firm tries to sell as much as possible. This is quite true; even a monopolistic firm will, in practice, vigorously attempt to expand its sales—once it has set the price.

But how does the monopolist choose his selling price? If he wishes to achieve the maximum profit possible he will probably proceed in something like the following fashion. Firstly, he will estimate the demand schedule for his product, i.e. the quantity that could be sold at each possible price. Then, multiplying each price by the corresponding quantity he will calculate the total sales receipts that might be expected on the basis of each possibility. He would then estimate the cost of producing each quantity, and would select the price/quantity combination that promised the biggest margin of receipts over costs.

If his judgment of demand was absolutely correct he will turn out to be producing exactly the quantity, and selling at exactly the price, which our theoretical analysis indicated as being the most profitable. A monopolist, in effect, applies the logical reasoning we have analyzed not to the actual demand schedule—he does not know what it is—but to his *estimate* of the demand schedule. Only if his estimate of the demand schedule is incorrect will his price and sales volume diverge from their theoretically derived optimum values.

Figure 5 illustrates how the results achieved by a monopoly firm which announces a specific selling price, will depend upon the demand which materializes for its product.

Suppose that a monopolist has marginal and average total costs as shown in the graph. Suppose that he anticipates that demand for his product will be D_4. Now MR_4, the corresponding marginal revenue curve, cuts the MC curve at an output of OD. Accordingly, OD appears to be the optimum output and OX—the price at which it can be sold when demand is D_4—appears to be the optimum price. The monopolist accordingly announces OX as his selling price. If D_4 turns out in fact to be the demand then he will indeed achieve the maximum profit possible under the circumstances. Suppose, however, that demand proves to be only D_1. He will sell OA units at the announced price of OX, but at this output his cost of production per unit is AL; he loses LF per unit. If the demand were D_2, he would just cover his

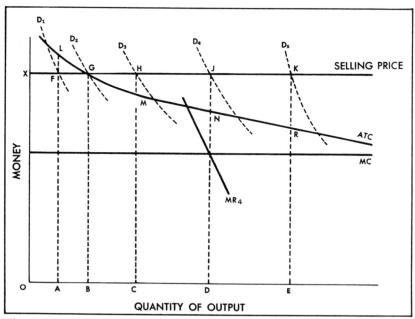

Figure 5.   Price setting by a monopolist, with demand estimated

costs; his cost of production per unit and selling price would be exactly equal at BG. If demand were D_3 he would earn profit, but less than anticipated: i.e., he would be earning a profit of only HM per unit on only OC units, whereas he had expected to earn a profit of JN per unit on OD units. If demand were D_5 however, he would earn KR per unit on OE units, a better result than he had counted on.

If the demand turns out to be less than D_4, the monopolist will be more than disappointed; he will be exasperated with his poor judgment. For he would have done better had he charged a price lower than OX. Similarly his gratification when demand turns out to be D_5 is tinged with regret: he would have made even more profit yet had he set his price above OX.

Whether or not his profit turns out to be the largest attainable under the circumstances can be demonstrated graphically, as in Figure 6.

D_4 represents the demand curve which the monopolist estimates to exist; MR_4 is its corresponding marginal revenue curve so that the optimum output is OD. At this output a price of DJ could be charged, and the monopolist announces this as his price. Suppose, however, that the demand curve turns out actually to be D_5. In that case, at his announced price of DJ ($=OX$), he will sell XK units. But the marginal revenue curve to D_5 (MR_5) cuts the MC line at an output coordinate of

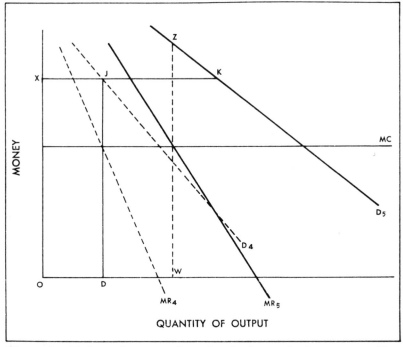

Figure 6.   Estimated vs. actual results of price setting by a monopolist

OW; i.e., demand being D_5, his optimum output would have been OW, with selling price WZ. It can similarly be shown that if the demand curve were to the left of D_4, his optimum price would have been lower than OX.

Price Rigidity

One phenomenon commonly encountered in monopolistic or oligopolistic industries is price rigidity. Some firms have maintained the same selling price over extended periods of time during which demand and supply conditions altered substantially; in response to shifts of demand they varied their output but not their price. Thus the International Nickel Company of Canada, from 1925 to 1940, held the price of nickel at 35 cents per pound; however, during the period 1929 to 1932 it reduced output by more than 80 per cent.

Price rigidity would seem to indicate entrepreneurial irrationality. If a certain price was right under a given set of demand and supply conditions, then it cannot still be right when those conditions change—unless miraculously the changes all offset one another. Why then do firms neglect to change their prices when market conditions change? Several reasons may be suggested. Firstly the price was likely set in the first place on a fairly arbitrary basis—at a certain proportion of the labour cost, for instance, or on the basis of a vague estimate of demand. No one could claim with assurance that this was the optimum price; quite conceivably this price is better suited to the new conditions of demand and supply than it was to the old. In any case since it was never very closely related to known market conditions, it need not be changed because these conditions have changed.

Secondly, to introduce a change in price may be a costly and difficult procedure. A good deal of administrative work may be required; in the case of an oligopoly a price change might have to be preceded by prolonged negotiation among the member firms. Accordingly there might understandably be a tendency for firms to maintain a particular price even after they knew it was inappropriate, and only to change it once its inappropriateness was really extreme.

Thirdly, once a price has been in effect for some time it acquires a status of its own. Buyer and seller alike come to feel that this is a just price, or *the* price. Not being schooled in the niceties of economic theory, they see no inexorable relationship between the price of a product and conditions prevailing in the market in which it is sold. A change in a long established price represents to them irreverent tampering with a familiar institution. Maintenance by a firm of *the* price through thick and thin furthermore tends to confer prestige. It demonstrates integrity and power: integrity in its disdain to snatch chance opportunities for earning extra profits; power in its capacity to withstand, unshaken, the turbulences of the market.

Non-Economic Motivation

Many businessmen have other goals in mind besides the earning of profit, and quite knowingly sacrifice additional profit in order to achieve these objectives. Some men prefer to spend in pleasurable pursuits time and energy which, devoted to their business, would have brought an increase in its profits. Some businessmen deliberately operate on a smaller basis than the most profitable in order to reduce the burden of their responsibility. Other men expand their operations even when it is disadvantageous to do so, in order to gratify their craving for additional power. Some firms deliberately earn lower profits than would be possible, in order to avoid attracting competition or intervention by government. Some firms deliberately pass up short term gains because, by doing so, they achieve long run advantages. Some businessmen, out of a sense of justice and fair play, charge no more than what they think is right. The fact is that while the profit motive is no doubt the most important single determinant of businessmen's behaviour, it is by no means the sole determinant. Human nature is after all infinitely complex, and each personality is unique. It would be fatuous to assume that in business, as in any sphere of human activity, the motivation of different persons is rigorously simple and absolutely uniform.

J. K. Galbraith has forcefully argued that the executive hierarchy—"the technostructure" he calls it—which controls the typical giant corporation directs the operations of the firm so as to further its own interests, not those of the stockholders. The latter, it is true, would like to have the firm earn maximum profits so that it could pay them the largest possible dividends, but they are not in control. The technostructure is likely to have several objectives, ranged in order of priority. Characteristically, its primary goal will be to retain full control over the corporation. To do so it must earn enough profit to maintain a decent earnings record so as both to keep stockholders quiescent and capital markets satisfied that the firm is being competently managed: steady profit is therefore more important than maximum profit. What is more, the personal interests of members of the technostructure are likely to be better served by alternatives to mere profit maximization. Expansion of sales and output, the development of new products and new production techniques, will likely generate possibilities of promotion and of increased authority to pay, as well as conferring prestige and providing keen personal satisfaction to members of the organization. While growth and technological progress may indeed bring larger profits they are not undertaken primarily with this object in view but rather because they are desired by the firm's controlling hierarchy.

SUMMARY

A monopolist has the power to determine the total quantity marketed of his product and therefore the price at which it can be sold. Presumably he will choose the output which, having regard to the price at which it can be sold, will yield a higher profit than he could have achieved by producing any other output and charging any other price.

Where monopoly prevails the market price will likely be higher, and output smaller, than would have been the case if perfectly competitive conditions had prevailed.

If its product can be imitated, a profitable monopoly is likely to become subject to competition. Other businessmen will produce similar goods, or goods which will serve the same purpose, and encroach upon the monopolist's market. The demand for his product will accordingly decline; his extraordinary profits may shrink to zero.

An oligopoly is said to exist when a small number of firms produce an identical or virtually identical product. In such a situation the market price may be anywhere between that which would prevail under perfect competition, and that which would prevail under monopoly.

Where oligopoly prevails some kind of collusion is almost bound to exist. Each firm, in considering what price and output policy to adopt, must take into consideration the probable reactions of the other firms in the industry. Since other firms are likely to retaliate fiercely, each firm will probably be inhibited from adopting aggressive price-cutting policies. In oligopolistic industries characterized by heavy fixed costs and low marginal costs a firm which can increase its sales will greatly increase its profits; in such cases the temptation will be very strong to shade prices in order to gain sales.

Monopsony and oligopsony refer respectively to situations in which there is just a single buyer in the market or only a very small number of buyers.

The theory of the firm developed in this chapter and the preceding one represents actual practice only approximately, for two chief reasons. Firstly, businessmen are unlikely to have all the information which would be needed for a rigorous application of the theoretical principles. Secondly, they may knowingly refrain from adopting the most profitable procedure because they have other objectives beside the earning of profit.

FOR REVIEW AND DISCUSSION

1. In which industry is the customer likely to be given the most solicitous treatment from a firm with which he deals: in a monopoly; in an oligopoly; in a perfectly competitive industry? In which type of industry are we likely to find heavy expenditures on advertising? Explain.
2. "The greedy monopolist who wishes to maximize his profit will of course charge the highest price possible." Is this necessarily so?
3. In the city of X there is only one firm which provides electricity to householders. Does it necessarily follow that this firm has no competition? Explain.
4. Money received by the CBC from programme sponsors represents a clear gain for the people of Canada. Do you agree? Justify your answer.
5. What basis is there for the argument that advertising actually results in lower prices for purchasers?

6. Why do some retail stores prefer to locate in downtown districts, near their chief competitors?
7. The perfectly competitive buyer always pays the same price, no matter how much he buys. The monopolist pays a higher price, the more he buys. Why, therefore, should it be of any benefit to have monopsony power?
8. In a small community in Canada, the local housewives once entered into a "gentleman's agreement" not to pay cleaning women more than 50 cents per hour. What economic principles were involved in this agreement?
9. Mr. Jones owns one of several dozen firms that manufacture ladies' house dresses in Canada. This year he experiments with a new material and finds that the public likes the new garments very well indeed. Illustrating graphically, describe the likely short and long run consequences for Mr. Jones' firm, in terms of price charged, quantity produced, and profits earned.
10. The member firms of a certain oligopolistic industry containing only four firms agree to sell at a designated price. One firm "chisels" by offering to sell for a little less to all buyers, including its own regular customers. The owner explains to his wife that he just couldn't resist the temptation. Illustrating graphically, explain the nature of his temptation.

7

Public Control Over Monopoly

FAIR PRICE–DIFFERING DEFINITIONS

A platitude which few people have ever disputed is that prices should be "fair". But what is "fair"? Various criteria of fairness have been offered at different times. Medieval philosophers propounded the doctrine that the "just price" for any good or service was that which would yield the seller an income appropriate to his station in life. In modern times the belief is general that a "fair" price is that one which emerges from the free and unhindered operation of a fully competitive market, i.e. a market which is composed of a large number of buyers and sellers, each of whom is incapable, through any act of his own, of significantly affecting the market price. It is considered that in such a market, price is determined by "natural" forces, and is not manoeuvred this way or that by selfish parties, to their advantage and the detriment of others.[1]

The Size of the Market

Perfect competition, as defined in Chapter 5, has been a rather rare phenomenon in human history. At few times, in few places, in few commodities, have there been markets where very large numbers of buyers dealt with very large numbers of sellers. Until the nineteenth century the small size of the typical community necessarily meant that within each individual market there was only one enterprise, or at the most a few, in any particular branch of industry or commerce. Local firms enjoyed virtually complete control of the local market, for the difficulty and cost of transportation practically prohibited customers from buying their needs outside their own community. Prices characteristically were set, not by the interplay of impersonal

---

[1]This view of what is a fair price is not of course universally accepted, and its adherents are not always loyal. We saw in Chapter 4 that even a competitively determined price may be condemned by many people if it diverges, to their detriment, from an earlier price which had prevailed for a considerable time. The fact that the price shift is attributable to the movement of market forces does not reconcile them to it. Hence we find consumers demanding price ceilings when market shifts drive prices sharply upward, and producers demanding price floors when market shifts drive prices sharply downward.

market forces, but rather through the conscious exercise of their power by individuals who possessed monopoly power or achieved such power through collusion. The tradition of guild solidarity, handed down from medieval times, probably reinforced in many cases the selfish tendencies of businessmen in a particular trade to join together for their collective advantage. Adam Smith, writing in the 1770s, remarked on the tendency of businessmen to get together to set prices.

It is only in relatively recent times that large numbers of buyers and large numbers of sellers have been able to have effective contact with one another. The great cities, thronged by buyers and sellers of every conceivable commodity or service, are mostly of fairly recent origin. So are the means of transportation and communication which link together into a single market individuals living in widely separated communities. With the advent of the railway, the steamship and the tele-graph in the mid-nineteenth century, whole nations, and in some respects the whole world, became a single market. The truck, automobile, airplane, telephone and radio, developed later, knitted separate communities even more closely together into single, gigantic markets.

Increase in Industrial Concentration

The emergence of national, as opposed to local markets, did not necessarily bring into being nation-wide competition in place of local monopoly and oligopoly. In a great many industries the scale of the typical enterprise increased enormously; the superior efficiency of large machines and heavy equipment and of large and highly specialized staffs, enabled a giant firm to produce far more cheaply than could small firms. The railroads quickly and economically transported over a wide area the goods that were efficiently produced in a single large plant. The corporate form of organiza-tion enabled the assembly of the immense amounts of capital required to finance immense industrial projects. Corporate organization in turn enhanced the advantages of size: firms already large were generally able to obtain additional capital more easily and on better terms than could their smaller rivals. The large firm could carry out "vertical integration"; i.e. it could acquire control over the sources of its neces-sary materials; it could establish its own outlets for the sale of its own products, or acquire control over those firms which constituted its market. By reducing its de-pendence upon outsiders for supplies and markets, the large firm correspondingly reduced its risks and uncertainties.

Developments of the twentieth century added further to the advantages enjoyed by the large firm. In many fields competition took the form, primarily, of rivalry in the production of new and improved products; only the giant firm could afford to maintain the elaborate and costly research organizations required to develop and test new products. Finally, the enormous importance of advertising in the twentieth century powerfully confirmed the market superiority of the large firm. Experts agree that successful advertising is generally that which is carried out on a large scale, in the form of sustained and widespread newspaper, magazine and billboard campaigns, nation-wide radio and television broadcasts; only the giant firm could afford advertising expenditures on the largest and most effective scale.

AMERICAN EXPERIENCE

The phenomenon of the giant firm serving national and even international markets, was not unique to any one land; to a greater or lesser degree, it occurred in every country in the world. But it was in the United States that it attained its most spectacular form, and caused the most powerful and the most widespread repercussions. The development of "Big Business" in the United States, a phenomenon of world-wide interest, deserves special study by Canadians. American influence and example have been of paramount importance to Canada, and a substantial portion of the Canadian economy is American controlled. Accordingly, the next few pages are concerned with the American scene.

Emergence of National Markets

American "Big Business" emerged in the latter half of the nineteenth century. A conjuncture of developments contributed to the rise of enterprise on a gigantic scale: the great increase in the nation's population, the settlement of the West, the development of large-scale machinery and equipment of superior efficiency, the construction of railways, the introduction of corporate organization. Able and aggressive men grasped the opportunities inherent in laying down the railways and in building the giant firms made possible by the existence of the national market which the railways brought into being. Their methods were sometimes unethical and ruthless, outrageous to the public conscience. Not without cause they were collectively referred to as the "robber barons".[2] From small beginnings they built up large firms which they expanded to mammoth proportions, often by absorbing firms established by others.[3]

The Powerful Monopolies

Not uncommonly a single firm, organized and dominated by one man, controlled virtually the entire national supply of a particular good or service. The Standard Oil Company, built up and dominated by John D. Rockefeller, at one time controlled over 90 per cent of the nation's oil refining capacity and nearly as large a proportion of the nation's oil marketing facilities. The American Tobacco Company, whose

[2]The original robber barons were medieval lords who robbed or exacted tolls from merchants and wayfarers who crossed their estates.

[3]Their personal rewards were correspondingly large; Andrew Carnegie received in one year a personal income of $22 million (in an age when no income tax was levied and the value of a dollar was probably several times greater than it is today).

chief architect and master was James B. Duke, produced about 80 per cent of the nation's tobacco products. The United States Steel Corporation, built around the firm established by Andrew Carnegie, produced at one time about 70 per cent of the nation's steel products. Great railway empires, each exercising domination over a large part of the country, were built up by Edward H. Harriman, Jay Gould and James J. Hill. At one time, Harriman's influence extended over railway companies whose trackage totalled 60,000 miles.

In some industries monopoly was inevitable on technical grounds. For example, in the provision of gas, water, electricity, telephone and railway service, competition would involve wasteful duplication. In other industries, however, monopolies were deliberately contrived. A large firm could earn a fair profit through the scale and efficiency of its operations; if it possessed monopoly power, it could reap monopolistic profit as well. At one time, the Standard Oil Company was able to charge for its marketing services over three times the amount that independent experts considered to be fair and adequate; on an invested capital of $70 millions, the company in eight years earned some $500 millions in profits. But additional profit was not the sole gain derived from the possession of monopoly power. The firm which achieved a monopoly thereby gained security against the possibility of suffering harm through the action of rivals. Plans could be laid more confidently when there existed no competitors who might upset them.

The methods for contriving a monopoly were various. One firm might eliminate competitors by buying them out or, using ruthless and predatory tactics, by forcing them out. A number of hitherto competing firms might agree to amalgamate into a single concern which would have monopoly power. Ingenious arrangements were devised whereby individual firms, without losing their own identity, became subject to the control of a single authority. The first arrangements were the *trusts*; when these were outlawed, *holding companies* were devised.

The Trust, a Device for Concentrating Control

The "trust," the first of which was built up by John D. Rockefeller in 1879, was an arrangement whereby control over a number of companies was transferred to a small executive group. Voting control over each firm in the trust was handed over to a "Board of Trustees" nominated by the member firms. Holding the major voting rights in each firm, the Board of Trustees was able to ensure that each charged the price and sold the quantity which would produce maximum profits for the industry as a whole. The arrangement was widely copied, trusts being organized in numerous industries, notably those producing sugar, rope, cotton, rubber, oil, beer and whiskey.

The Holding Company

The Sherman Act of 1890 rendered the trust illegal, but legislation introduced in New Jersey in the previous year paved the way for its successors. A new state law authorized the incorporation of a company for the sole purpose of acquiring shares in other companies. A "holding company" could now be organized, its assets consisting solely or partly of a controlling block of shares in each of a number of other companies. Whoever held the dominating interest in the holding company accordingly controlled all the other companies whose shares it held.

The holding company device made it possible for a gigantic aggregate of property to be controlled by a small but strategic investment. Suppose that industry X consisted of six firms, each of which had assets worth $110 million, the capital having been raised in each case through the issue of $100 million of bonds, and $10 million of common shares. Each firm accordingly could be controlled by an investment of $5 million in its common shares. A holding company might be organized, raising say $24 million through the issue of bonds and $6 million through the issue of shares; its total capital of $30 million would be used to acquire $5 million of shares, a controlling interest, in each of the six firms of industry X. Then, the holding company itself would be controlled by whoever held a majority interest in *its* common shares. Hence, whoever invested $3 million in the shares of the holding company thereby acquired control of the six firms of industry X, whose assets were worth a total of $660 million.

Control of the six firms might, in fact, be achieved with an even smaller investment. We saw in a previous chapter that a minority shareholding in a company might be sufficient to confer control. The holding company in our example might therefore be able to acquire control over the firms of industry X by purchasing a good deal less than half of the common shares of each one; it, too, might be controlled by the holder of a minority interest. Furthermore, a "second degree" holding company might be organized to purchase a controlling interest in the first one. This second holding company might have a capital of $3 million, raised by selling $2 million of bonds and $1 million of common shares. Whoever held half a million dollars worth of common shares of this second holding company controlled it, and therefore controlled the first, which in turn controlled the six firms of industry X. Additional layers of holding companies could be added, each reducing further the investment required to exercise ultimate control over industry X. This procedure, technically known as "pyramiding", was in some cases carried to inordinate lengths. One financial wizard, Samuel Insull, built up a pyramid composed of eight layers of holding companies. Two brothers named Van Sweringen, with an investment of $1 million, gained control over a dozen railways whose total assets were valued at $1 billion.

The "Leverage" Effect

Shareholders of the holding company not only possessed control over the operating companies involved, but thanks to "leverage" were able to realize a far higher rate of return than was paid to shareholders of these companies. "Leverage" arose from the fact that of the dividends which the holding company received on the shares it held in other companies, only a fixed sum had to be paid to its bondholders, and the remainder went to its shareholders. Suppose that in the industry X of our example, each operating company earned a profit of $7 million in one year and that all bonds (including those of the first holding company) were issued at 6 per cent interest. In that case, each company's bondholders would get $6 million (6% × $100 million) leaving $1 million for the common shareholders. On their investment of $10 millions this would represent a rate of return of 10 per cent. But the (first) holding company owns half the shares of each company; it therefore receives $½ million in dividends from each, for a total of $3 million. It must pay its bondholders 6 per cent on the $24 million they have contributed, or $1.44 million. There is left $1.56 million for the common shareholders of the holding company; on their investment of $6 millions this amounts to a return of 26 per cent, over two and half times the rate received by shareholders in the operating companies.[4]

Collusion Among Oligopolists

Where a few large firms dominated an industry, they could, through collusion, achieve the same profitable results as a complete monopoly. A variety of means were employed at one time or another to effect such collusion. During the 1870s "pools" were organized in a number of industries, each "pool" constituting an arrangement whereby the available business was divided up among members of the industry. Its market secure, each firm could charge a profitable price. The era of pools did not last more than a decade or two, however. The public was intensely hostile to them and pool members tended to violate their undertakings to one another (which were not enforceable in the courts).

The general use of corporate organization in the latter half of the nineteenth century provided a basis for effective inter-firm cooperation. One firm might purchase stock in others, thereby acquiring a degree of control over their operations. The same individuals might serve as directors of several firms in the same industry; such "interlocking of directorates" ensured that firms would pursue mutually helpful policies. In

---

[4]A reduction in profit earned by the operating companies would of course also be compounded. Thus, in this example if earnings of the operating companies dropped from $7 million to $6.48 million or less, shareholders of the holding company would get no dividend whatever. With each operating company earning $6.48 million, its shareholders would get $.48 million after bond interest had been paid, for a return of 4.8 per cent. The holding company would receive $.24 million from each company (since it held half the common shares of each). Its total receipts from all six companies would be $1.44 million—just sufficient to pay its bondholders.

The "leverage"principle operates in any enterprise where money borrowed at a specified rate of interest is used together with the owner's own investment. Thus suppose a business man puts $2 million of his own money into his firm and borrows an additional $6 million at 7 per cent interest. Suppose the profit realized in a particular year is $1 million, constituting a 12¼ per cent return on the $8 million of capital invested. With $420,000 (7 per cent of $6 million) going to the outside suppliers of capital, $580,000 is left for the owner; on his investment of $2 million this constitutes a return of 29 per cent.

If, however, the firm achieved a total profit of only $420,000—5.25 per cent of the total capital of $8 million—the owner would receive zero returns on his own investment. All of the profit would have to be paid to the outside suppliers of capital to give them the promised 7 per cent on the $6 million they had provided.

some industries a single investment banking house might have arranged the financing of all or most of the member firms. It would have representation on the boards of all the firms, and use its influence to ensure that all worked harmoniously together, avoiding competition which would generally reduce prices and profits.

Informal understandings would sometimes suffice to maintain cooperation among a few giant firms. The largest might set a pattern which the others would obediently follow, with or without urging on its part. For example, in 1907 and 1908 when prevailing depression raised the possibility that some steel firms would sharply cut their prices, Judge Elbert H. Gary, Chairman of the Board of the U.S. Steel Corporation, gave elaborate dinners to which the heads of the country's major steel firms were invited. He announced on these occasions that U.S. Steel would hold the line on prices, and urged the others to do likewise. They did. In some industries an all-embracing trade association might "suggest" prices which its member firms ought to follow. In a good many industries, with no agreement or understanding of any kind, firms nevertheless "played ball" with one another; each knew that it would gain only a temporary advantage, and would suffer in the end if it did not.

PUBLIC ANTAGONISM TO PRIVATE MONOPOLIES

The ruthless tactics of giant firms, their market power, the "public be damned" attitude evinced by some, roused widespread concern and hostility. Farmers were particularly vehement in their denunciation of industrial and railway monopolies. In their roles of consumer and shipper, they were obliged to bear the burdens of high prices for manufactured goods and high railway rates; unlike urban workers, they did not derive at least the benefit of employment in the profitable factories and railways.

Largely reflecting the farmer's point of view, public opinion insistently demanded that governments take action against the monopolies which were reaping immense profits by extorting high prices from consumers. Governments—federal, state and municipal—responded with three broad categories of protective measures. These were: government ownership, public utility regulation, and legislation to enforce competition.

Government Ownership

Governments, especially those of states and municipalities, bought out many of the private companies which supplied public utility services, such as gas, water, electricity, and public transit. In some cases, a government provided a public utility service from the very beginning and private enterprise was never involved. With such natural monopolies state-owned, there could be no abuse of their monopoly power. The rates charged would usually be sufficient only to cover costs; if profit was earned, it would become part of the general public revenue to be used for the public good.

But while public ownership eliminated private monopoly profit, it had drawbacks of its own. The administration of publicly owned enterprises tended to be distinctly less efficient than that of privately owned firms, and the possibility existed—and was all too often realized—that some groups in the community would, by dint of political influence, manage to obtain preferential treatment from a public enterprise.

Public Utility Regulation

A second protective measure introduced by governments was the establishment of boards and commissions upon which was conferred jurisdiction over the rates and prices charged by specified industries. The first such body was the Interstate Commerce Commission, established by the federal government in 1887 to control railway freight rates. Since then, a host of similar regulatory bodies have been set up, mostly by state governments. In general these bodies have been given jurisdiction over public utilities such as water, telephone and electricity companies, which provide vital services and which, for technical reasons, are bound to be monopolies. In the course of time, public regulation over prices was extended to serve industries which were not monopolistic in character, for example, the distribution of milk. In general, public authorities appear to have taken the view that public regulation is justified in any industry which provides a commodity or service which is of great concern to the public, and in which market forces alone cannot be relied upon to produce fair and reasonable prices.

In setting the prices to be charged by the industries they supervise, regulatory boards seek to ensure that firms receive only a "fair" return on their investment. This objective seems straightforward enough, but in actual cases can be interpreted in dozens of extremely divergent ways. First of all, what is a "fair" rate of return? The appropriate figure will vary from industry to industry in accordance with the degree of risk considered to be involved. In practice regulatory bodies have usually settled on some figure between five and eight per cent, their exact choice being, to a considerable degree, arbitrary. In the second place, what valuation is to be placed on a firm's investment? Shall it be valued on the basis of its actual, *original cost*, or shall it be valued at its present-day *replacement cost*? Whichever method is adopted, what rate of depreciation is to be assumed? Furthermore, if some of the firm's investments were unnecessary and foolish, is the firm entitled to receive a return on them too?

Here obviously are happy hunting grounds for lawyers, economists and accountants. Almost invariably when a public regulatory body has been called upon to set a rate or approve a change in a rate, there have paraded before it two opposing armies of experts, each attacking as utterly unfounded the claims of the other. This public board, usually consisting of laymen, has to decide which of the opposing sets of experts is right. Small wonder that some of their decisions have been a good deal less than perfect.

Legislation to Enforce Competition

The third type of governmental measure introduced to protect consumers was legislation which outlawed monopoly and oligopolistic collusion. State after state passed legislation during the 1880s which prohibited trusts from operating within its borders, and in 1890 a virtually unanimous Congress passed the Sherman Act which has ever since been the cornerstone of American anti-monopoly legislation.

The Sherman Act's first section declared to be illegal "every contract, combination in the form of trust or otherwise, or conspiracy, in restraint of commerce." Later sections detailed the action to be taken against violators. Where the government's law officers believed that a company had violated the Act they would launch a prosecution in the courts. If they found the defendants guilty, the judges were authorized to impose fines and even prison terms. The government might furthermore, under the Act, request the court to order the dissolution of an already existing monopoly, and to forbid any one from undertaking a contemplated action which would result in the establishment of a monopoly. Finally the Act provided for redress to private individuals or firms which had suffered damage through the actions of a monopoly: they could sue in the courts for *treble* the damages they had suffered.

Two decades of experience revealed major shortcomings in the Sherman Act. Its provisions were sufficiently general to allow considerable latitude in interpretation; the courts, in actual cases, adopted interpretations which a good many people felt were at variance with the motivation and spirit of the Act. Although it was intended to be used against industrial monopolies, the Act was, during its early years, applied largely against trade unions. Furthermore, the discovery and effective prosecution of violators of the Sherman Act were hampered by the lack of an appropriate enforcement authority. The intricacy and uniqueness of the issues rendered ordinary police officers and government attorneys inadequate for the task of enforcement.

Congress accordingly in 1914 passed two new laws designed to supplement and strengthen the operation of the Sherman Act. The Clayton Act specifically named and outlawed a number of practices by which monopolistic combines were established and by which they maintained their power. In addition it specifically exempted trade unions from the provisions of the anti-monopoly legislation. The Federal Trade Commission Act provided for the establishment of a permanent authority, staffed by experts, whose responsibility it would be to detect unfair business practices, investigate complaints regarding such practices and, where offence was proven, order the offending party to desist.

Anti-Monopoly Legislation Qualified

New problems and situations, arising in the course of time, gave rise to legislation which partly compromised the original anti-monopoly laws. Just after World War I, American firms complained that in their dealings abroad they had to compete with powerful foreign cartels which in many cases were supported by their respective governments. Congress accordingly passed, in 1918, the Webb-Pomerene Act which authorized American firms to organize themselves into export associations for the more effective promotion of their foreign operations. During the 1930s small retailers became hard pressed by the competition of mail order, department and chain stores which, because of the volume they handled, were able to extract preferred prices from suppliers. To assist the small retailers, Congress passed in 1936, the Robinson-Patman Act which forbade producers to sell at discriminatory prices to the different classes of distributors. During the 1930s, as another means of aiding small retail stores, state after state passed "fair trade" laws which forbade retailers to sell branded merchandise at cut prices. In 1937 Congress passed the Miller-Tydings Act which exempted such laws from federal anti-monopoly legislation.

The Enforcement of Anti-Monopoly Legislation

Congressional laws failed to guarantee the maintenance of vigorous competition. The means of enforcement were always inadequate, for a long time grossly inadequate. The Anti-Trust Division of the Department of Justice was established in 1903 with a tiny staff and a correspondingly small appropriation. For years it lacked the resources to launch a significant number of investigations and prosecutions under the Sherman Act. With each case requiring years of investigation and preparation[5] only a few could be undertaken. Successive federal administrations varied in their zeal for the enforcement of the anti-monopoly laws. In the early 1900s, under the vigorous leadership of President Theodore Roosevelt, the "Trustbuster," some notable successes were achieved. A gigantic railway amalgamation was prevented; action was launched which culminated, in 1911, in the dissolution of the Standard Oil Company and the American Tobacco Company. During the period of Republican[6] rule from 1920 to 1932, however, the federal government showed little enthusiasm for the anti-monopoly laws, and the business world enjoyed a virtual moratorium from their enforcement. A brief backward step was taken in 1933. As part of the New Deal of Franklin D. Roosevelt, the attempt was made to establish "codes" for the regulation of industries; most of the codes contained price-fixing provisions; many provided for the restriction of output and the allocation of markets. The United States Supreme Court declared these codes to be unconstitutional in a decision handed down in 1935.

Commencing in 1938 a new era of anti-trust law enforcement began. The staff and appropriation of the Anti-Trust Division were sharply increased; more prosecutions were undertaken in the next decade than during the preceding half century. Action was stayed during the war but following the end of hostilities was vigorously renewed.

---

[5]A case completed in less than four years was considered to have been handled with great despatch. One case, against the U.S. Steel Corporation, went on for a decade.
[6]Theodore Roosevelt had been a Republican, but a most unorthodox one.

The Court's Interpretation of the Law

In the administration of the Sherman Act and its associated legislation, the attitude of the courts has been crucial. It was the courts which judged whether or not a firm or individual was actually guilty of an offence, and prescribed the punishment to be imposed upon those found guilty. To dissolve a monopoly, or to prevent one from coming into being, a court order was required. The Supreme Court, the nation's final tribunal, for many years adhered to the so-called "rule of reason" in its judgment of cases under the Sherman Act. The Court generally interpreted the Act as outlawing only those monopolies which were obviously detrimental to the public, i.e. those which raised prices to unreasonable levels, or curtailed output, or lowered the quality of the product. Where a firm attained great size, even a monopoly position, through legitimate means and without harm to the public, the Court held that the Sherman Act was not being violated.[7]

Since 1945, however, the Court has taken a more rigorous stand against monopolistic organizations and anti-competitive practices. In 1948 the cement industry was ordered to discontinue a price-fixing arrangement[8] which had been in effect for decades; three years later the steel industry, which had maintained a similar practice, agreed to abandon it. A number of giant corporations were ordered to divest themselves of a substantial portion of their properties; reduced in size and performing fewer functions they would no longer be able to dominate their respective industries. Large firms, already enjoying great market power, have been forbidden to acquire companies which supplied their materials (backward integration) or companies which bought their products(forward integration), on the grounds that competitors would suffer reduction in access to materials and markets. Firms already possessing a significant share of the market have been barred from merging with a competitor (horizontal integration), on the grounds that the result would be an undesirable increase in the share of the market controlled by one firm.

Broadly speaking, the view of the U.S. courts has been that great size and even monopoly are not to be condemned if they are the result of successful innovation or superior operational efficiency; the objection is to actions and practices which are intended to reduce the degree of competition prevailing in any industry. The prospect of superior economic performance has not been accepted as justification for the impairment of competition, and the prospect that economic performance will suffer has not deterred the courts from ordering the break-up of large consolidations. (In gen-

---

[7]This view was most succinctly expressed in the U.S. Steel case of 1920 when the Supreme Court refused to order a dissolution of the company, holding that "the law does not make mere size an offense, or the existence of unexerted power an offense."

[8]The "basing point system", under which a price was set for each section of the country, and every firm charged that price, no matter where it was itself located. The price in a specified centre where the commodity was produced, (Pittsburgh in the case of the steel industry), was designated as the "base" price. The price in any other locality was arrived at by adding to the "base" price the cost of transportation from Pittsburgh to that locality. All firms charged this same price, even those located at the purchaser's doorstep.

eral, the courts have assumed that increased competition is bound to produce improved efficiency).

No scores can be kept of actions that were contemplated but never committed. Observers generally agree, however, that U.S. anti-trust legislation has exercised widely deterrent effects. They are convinced that because of these laws, many American firms have refrained from buying or selling their products at discriminatory prices, from buying materials or selling output on long-term contracts, from buying the patents of rival firms, from backward, forward and horizontal integrations.

THE CONTROL OF MONOPOLY IN CANADA

Public Ownership and Public Utility Regulation

In general, governmental action to protect consumers in Canada has followed the American pattern. Provincial and municipal governments have acquired or established public utilities such as water, gas, electricity and telephone services, operating them as publicly owned enterprises. The federal and the provincial governments maintain regulatory boards which are endowed with authority to set the prices charged by specified industries. The federal Board of Transport Commissioners has jurisdiction over railway and air freight and passenger rates; the federal Board of Grain Commissioners has authority to fix maximum charges for services rendered in connection with the handling of grain. The federal Energy Board, established in 1959, has been given control over the rates charged by gas and oil pipeline companies. Provincial regulatory boards have jurisdiction chiefly over the rates charged by local public utilities.

Canadian legislation to safeguard competition actually antedates that of the U.S. An amendment to the Criminal Code of 1889—one year before the passage of the Sherman Act—forbade suppliers to "prevent, limit or lessen unduly" the production, distribution or sale of any commodity, or to "enhance unreasonably" its price. A good many additonal enactments were subsequently passed, with all the relevant legislation consolidated in 1960 in the Combines Investigation Act. Essentially, this Act outlawed oligopolistic collusion and monopolies that harmed the public interest; it forbade as well specific business practices that were deemed to be inequitable or harmful; thus it banned "price discrimination,"[9] "predatory price cutting,"[10] "resale price maintenance,"[11] and misleading advertising.

A new approach was adopted in 1971 to the issue of safeguarding competition in

[9]i.e. the practice followed by some suppliers of selling to favoured distributors at especially low prices.

[10]i.e. the offer of goods at drastically cut prices as "loss leaders" to attract customers away from competitors.

[11]i.e. the requirement, laid down by some manufacturers, that retailers sell their product at a specified price. An amendment of 1960 authorized "resale price maintenance" in some designated circumstances.

Canada. The Competition Act introduced in that year and superseding the Combines Investigation Act, provided for the establishment of a Competitive Practices Tribunal which would have wide authority over the conduct of business. The Tribunal, to be composed of up to seven men appointed normally for ten-year terms, would have jurisdiction over matters which hitherto had been adjudicated in the courts. Its members would presumably possess more business experience and a deeper knowledge of economic principles than would most judges in a court of law, and would therefore be better qualified to render judgments on matters that were essentially economic in character.

The Competition Act extended the already long list of forbidden business practices and empowered the Tribunal to issue orders prohibiting activities by business firms which it considered to be against the public interest. As well the Act decreed that where any merger was proposed of firms whose assets or gross annual revenues totalled more than $5 million, the approval of the Tribunal was required. If it felt that such a merger was not contrary to the public interest the Tribunal would give its consent; if, however, it felt that the public interest would be adversely affected the Tribunal would prohibit the proposed merger. It could, as well, order the dissolution of mergers previously consummated, if it considered them to be against the public interest.

From time to time the Tribunal might issue draft guidance rules for the benefit of the business community, in which it indicated what practices it would allow and what it would forbid. Such rules might be formulated on the basis of research conducted by the Tribunal and perhaps following public hearings in which it heard representations from business interests likely to be affected.

THE OPPOSITION TO ANTI-MONOPOLY LEGISLATION

The legislative attempts to enforce competition do not command universal approval. Businessmen generally condemn the legislation as being vague, ill-defined, and arbitrary in its application. They complain that they have no means of knowing whether or not they are in fact committing an offence. Only when they are tried in court and convicted, is it made clear what their offence was. Furthermore, businessmen contend that the objective of the legislation is unrealistic, arguing that under modern business conditions, many of the business practices upon which the law frowns, are perfectly fair and reasonable.

A strong body of academic opinion now sides with the businessmen.[12] Economists recognize that in many fields the very large firm can produce more efficiently than can firms of smaller size. It is in society's interest therefore that production in

---

[12]Probably the foremost exponent of this view was the late J. A. Schumpeter of Harvard University, who set forth his opinions in the book *Capitalism, Socialism, and Democracy* (New York, 1942).

such fields be carried out in very large firms. But in any industry, if the member firms are to be of giant size, their number must be small. In some cases the number can be no more than one.

The Benefits of Monopoly

Monopoly, furthermore, has positive virtues, say the critics. The firm which enjoys monopoly power enjoys a degree of security which enables it to make long term arrangements and to undertake ventures which will bear fruit in the distant future. That these arrangements are made and these ventures undertaken is to the advantage of society generally. The small firm in a highly competitive industry cannot afford to take the long view. Its very existence is in daily peril; constantly faced with the threat of extinction, it may be driven to adopt desperate measures simply to survive.[13]

Even monopoly profit serves a useful social purpose, it is argued. The prospect of earning super normal profit furnishes the incentive to undertake costly and risky research and experimentation. Without some degree of monopoly power, large profits could not be earned through risky ventures. Where perfect competition prevails the market price tends to move to the level of bare equality with costs. The originator of a useful new development would, in a perfectly competitive situation, enjoy no permanent advantage over his inevitable imitators; because the gain would be only short-lived, few people might be prepared to apply the time, effort and investment needed to bring a bright idea to fruition. Finally, monopoly profits earned in the past may furnish a large part of the capital required to finance new development.

"Creative Destruction"

Admittedly monopoly does result, at any given time, in less output and higher prices than would be the case if perfect competition prevailed. But this monopoly which is responsible for restricting output, is also responsible for bringing about major improvements in the quality of output, sweeping reductions in costs of production, and the production of totally new goods. Monopoly in fact produces a superior form of competition. The competition does not consist of the offering of the same good at a slightly lower price. Its nature is far more devastating, and of far greater ultimate benefit to the consumer; it consists of the offering of new and superior products, or the offering of radically lower prices made possible by a major improvement in the method of production. Existing firms do not merely lose some of their business; they are utterly destroyed. But the destruction is "creative", for it involves the introduction of new and superior goods, new and superior methods of production.

---

[13]e.g. In the Canadian pulpwood industry, large firms have tended to be conservation-minded; small operators have not. The large firm, endowed with strong market power and certain that it will continue in business for a long time to come, plans for its long term future needs, and is prepared to make present sacrifices to ensure that those needs will be met when they arise. The small firm, its existence precarious, is understandably unwilling to sacrifice present opportunities for the sake of a future which may never materialize.

The "Reasonableness" of Oligopolistic Collusion

Collusion among oligopolists should not be condemned out of hand. By entering into a price-fixing agreement with the other firms in its industry, each firm achieves primarily *security*. Such an agreement provides assurance that no firm will cut the price, thereby forcing the others to match or retaliate, with possibly disastrous consequences for all. The plain fact is that where the number of firms in an industry is small, they simply cannot be expected to act as they would if the number were large. As we saw in the previous chapter, a price reduction adopted by one firm in an oligopoly will materially affect the other firms in the industry and, therefore, compel them to react. If he is to act sensibly, the oligopolist who contemplates a price reduction must take into consideration the likely reaction of the other firms in his industry. The member of a perfectly competitive industry is under no such compulsion. The other firms in his industry are not likely to react to any action of his; in arriving at business decisions he need not take into account the probable reaction of other firms.

Non-Price Competition

The opponents of government interference argue further that, despite price-fixing agreements, oligopolists do in fact compete. Each firm does try to increase its business, not admittedly by price-cutting, but by advertising, or by providing superior quality and service, or by offering better terms of delivery and payment. The consumer benefits from such rivalry, perhaps as much as he would from price cutting. Such competition, however, is not "destructive"; it does not have the damaging effects upon the industry as a whole which price competition produces. The fact that firms agree not to employ tactics which involve mutual slaughter, does not mean that their competition is not genuine. One might as well argue that when nations at war agree not to use poison gas against one another they are fighting a "phony war." Price competition is in effect the "ultimate weapon"; once invoked in an oligopoly situation all firms are bound to lose. Non-price competition, on the other hand, enables at least some to win. Rational businessmen will inevitably make arrangements under which there exists the possibility of gain for some, rather than tolerate procedures which involve the certainty of loss for all. Anyone who expects them to do otherwise is being hopelessly doctrinaire, unrealistic, and probably hypocritical.[14]

Latent Competition

Every firm faces not only actual competition from other firms already in existence, but also the possibility of competition from firms which may be built in the future. If the profits of existing firms are inordinately large, new firms are likely to arise and invade the market. Monopoly power does not afford complete protection; satisfac-

---

[14]cf. the following acid comment "Restraints on competition and the free movement of prices, the principal source of uncertainty to business firms, have been principally deplored by university professors on lifetime appointments." J. K. Galbraith, *The Affluent Society,* (Boston, 1958), p. 99.

tory substitutes may be developed. The high profits of a monopolist (or oligopolistic combine) will stimulate the search for substitutes and render their discovery more likely. The greedy monopolist in effect ensures the emergence of competition, and this ever present threat warns against the exploitive use of monopoly power.

"Countervailing Power"

J. K. Galbraith has recently suggested another source of competition for monopolists and oligopolists: their customers. His thesis, briefly, is that almost inevitably strong sellers beget strong buyers. The customers of a powerful monopolist have a strong incentive to create a single, powerful buying organization which will be able to bring great pressure to bear on the seller. The customers of an oligopoly will similarly tend to organize a strong buying organization which can effectively play off one seller against another. When bargaining for lower prices the strong buyer is able to pose the highly effective threat of producing the commodity himself. In 1937 the A. & P. grocery chain, after carrying out a survey, ascertained that it could profitably produce its own corn flakes. It would cost $175,000 to build a plant; valuing the product at the price currently charged by suppliers, a return of 68 per cent would be realized on the investment. The A. & P. Company accordingly forced its suppliers to lower their price by ten per cent, threatening to produce its own corn flakes if they refused to do so.

This "countervailing power" of consumers, Galbraith argues, acts as an effective restraint upon the possessors of monopoly power. That it should come into being is assured. The greater the power of a monopolist the greater is the incentive to his customers to organize a countervailing power. America's massive retailing organizations represent, according to Galbraith, the countervailing power brought into being by monopoly and oligopoly in manufacturing. The great department, mail order and chain stores protect the public against exploitation by monopolistic manufacturers. Applying their market power, they compel the latter to sell to them at low prices and pass the benefit on to the consumer, depending for profit upon sales in great volume at relatively low mark-ups.

The Need for Discrimination

No one of course will argue that *all* monopolistic practices have desirable consequences of the sort outlined earlier in this chapter. Some monopolists have no redeeming features. They restrict output and charge high prices, and do not use their profits to achieve technical progress. They may in fact use their profits to stifle progress: they may buy up new inventions and keep them off the market, thereby eliminating a threat to their own security.

The critics therefore do not unreservedly condemn anti-monopoly legislation. What they demand is that the law should be selective and prohibit those business practices which harm, but tolerate those practices which serve the long run interests of society, even though they are "monopolistic" in character. Accordingly the critics argue that each case should be judged on its merits; the judges should consider not simply whether a particular practice is being carried on, but what are likely to be its consequences. J. K. Galbraith, already referred to, singles out for special derision those judicial decrees which order a monopoly to be broken up into several independent firms. He suggests that these firms will likely collude; the courts have merely dissolved a monopoly into an oligopoly which will act like a monopoly anyway.

Attack on the Critics

The critics have their critics. A good many economists stoutly defend American and Canadian anti-monopoly legislation, and urge not that it be relaxed but that it be more vigorously enforced. They are skeptical of the argument that a single giant firm will be more efficient and more progressive than firms which are not so large. They point out that in a good many industries in the United States, a single firm may hold a dominating position thanks to its ownership of a number of different plants. Each plant may be sufficiently large to achieve all possible economies and to engage in all worthwhile research. The fact that several plants are under a single ownership does not produce benefit of any kind; it merely brings into being monopoly power with its consequences of reduced output and higher prices.

The opponents of monopoly bring to bear a powerful non-economic argument. They urge that on political grounds great concentrations of private economic power ought not to be tolerated. The persons who wield this power are able to control, to a significant degree, the very destiny of the country, without being responsible to the public or subject to any kind of public control. They may use their power to exercise a malignant influence in the nation's political life. Democracy would be more secure and better served if economic power were more widely dispersed. Although the possibility of some economic gains is thereby sacrificed, great concentrations of private economic power ought not to be tolerated in a democratic society.

INDUSTRIAL CONCENTRATION IN CANADA

The Canadian economy is characterized by a high degree of industrial concentration. In a number of industries the great bulk of the industry's output is produced by a handful of large firms, and these firms employ the great majority of the industry's workers. The degree of industrial concentration is actually greater in this country than in the United States. Firms are, on the average, almost as large as in the United States, but the Canadian market is very much smaller. A higher degree of concentration is therefore inevitable: where a market is small and the member firms are large, they are bound to be few.

Figure 1 graphically represents the degree of concentration in ten Canadian industries in 1948.

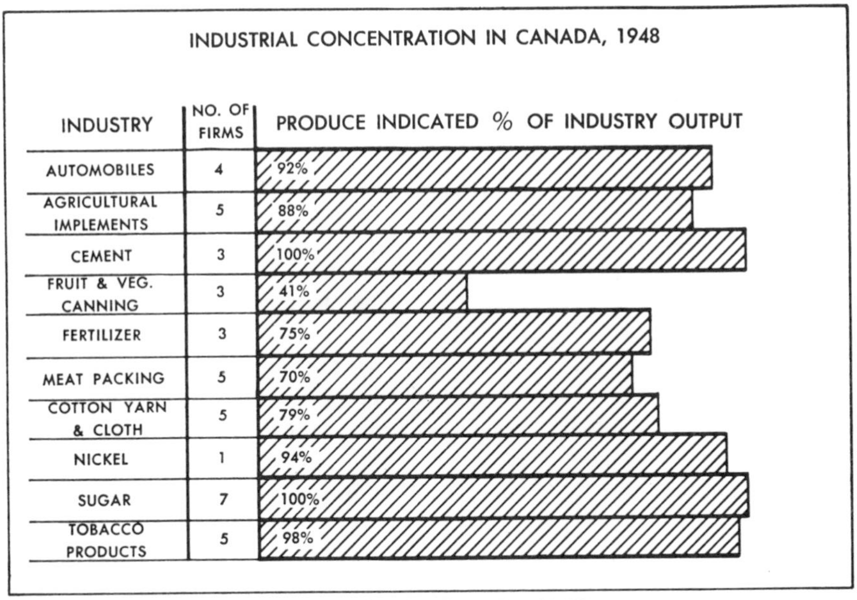

INDUSTRIAL CONCENTRATION IN CANADA, 1948

INDUSTRY	NO. OF FIRMS	PRODUCE INDICATED % OF INDUSTRY OUTPUT
AUTOMOBILES	4	92%
AGRICULTURAL IMPLEMENTS	5	88%
CEMENT	3	100%
FRUIT & VEG. CANNING	3	41%
FERTILIZER	3	75%
MEAT PACKING	5	70%
COTTON YARN & CLOTH	5	79%
NICKEL	1	94%
SUGAR	7	100%
TOBACCO PRODUCTS	5	98%

Figure 1.   Industrial concentration in Canada, 1948

(Based on Table 5 in *Industrial Concentration* prepared for the Royal Commission on Canada's Economic Prospects, June, 1956.)

While a high degree of concentration, such as that indicated in Figure 1, is fairly common in Canada, there are nevertheless a substantial number of industries in which concentration is very much less. In a good many industries the typical firm is small, and even the very largest firms produce only a small fraction of the industry's total output. Among such industries are those which manufacture wearing apparel, processed foods, wood, metal and cement products. Furthermore, available evidence suggests that during the past few decades, as the Canadian market has become larger, the degree of industrial concentration has tended to decline. The size of firms has increased as markets have enlarged, but their number has increased to an even greater degree.

SUMMARY

The giant firm operating on a nation-wide basis became common during the nineteenth century, particularly in the United States. Whole industries came to be dominated by a single firm or a handful of firms.

To protect the public against exploitation by powerful private monopolies, the government operated certain natural monopolies as public enterprises, set up regulatory bodies with authority over the prices and rates charged by certain industries, and introduced measures to ensure that competitive conditions prevailed wherever possible.

In the United States the Sherman Act, passed in 1890, has been the cornerstone of legislative attempts to enforce competition. However, the significance of anti-monopoly legislation varied according to the vigour of enforcement and the attitude of the courts.

In Canada the Competition Act of 1971 specifies offending business practices and provides for a tribunal which will have extensive jurisdiction over the conduct of business.

A number of prominent economists oppose existing anti-monopoly legislation on the grounds that monopolies in some industries are inevitable and in fact desirable. They suggest that powerful natural safeguards exist against the abuse of power by monopolists, and that government intervention is not necessarily desirable.

Other prominent economists urge the retention and strengthening of present anti-monopoly legislation. They argue that great concentrations of private power are undesirable in themselves, and that anyhow most of the real benefits which society gains from the existence of giant firms would still be available if these firms did not have monopoly powers.

FOR REVIEW AND DISCUSSION

1. So long as entry into a particular industry is not barred to newcomers, it cannot be said that consumers of the industry's products are being exploited. Do you agree?
2. Would you predict that in the future more and more industries will come under the domination of one or a few firms? Why or why not?
3. "The giant American monopolies and oligopolies have done more to raise the North American standard of living than have the competitive industries". Do you agree? Justify your answer.
4. It is claimed that where one or a few firms dominate an industry, they will deliberately cultivate a few small competitors. Does this appear to be likely?
5. Would you favour a government programme which gave special assistance to small firms? Why or why not?
6. Would any advantage be gained, in your opinion, if a cartel were transformed into a single monopoly firm? Explain.
7. "The absence of unreasonable profit in an industry is sufficient proof that the public interest is not being harmed." Comment.
8. What in your view would be "reasonable" restraints of trade? What restraints would be unreasonable?

9. Suppose that your local telephone company were to apply for an increase in its rates. Upon what basis would you decide what would be a reasonable increase?
10. Contrast American and Canadian legislation and procedure in respect to the restraint of business practices deemed to be contrary to the public interest.
11. Giant firms are undesirable even if they do not have monopoly power, or have it but don't abuse it. Do you agree? Justify your answer.

PART FOUR:

DISTRIBUTION OF INCOME

8 Principles of Income Distribution

The Size of Individual Incomes

The income earned by any individual will depend upon two basic considerations: the amount of productive service he performs, and the rate at which his type of productive service is paid. Thus the income of a factory worker will depend upon the number of hours he works and the hourly rate at which he is paid. The income of an investor will depend upon the amount of his investment and the rate of return he receives. The amount of productive service any individual is able to perform is a matter of individual ability and good fortune. The number of hours a man works, for instance, will depend upon his health and strength and the job opportunities available to him. The amount of capital an investor possesses will reflect his own savings and accumulation, and, quite often, the amount of his inheritance. Any individual may, furthermore, perform several different kinds of productive service and therefore earn income from several sources.

The Factors of Production

The productive services which people perform can be classified into four broad categories. Each category of service is performed by what economists call a *factor of production*, and each receives its own type of payment.

Labour performs work and is paid by wage or salary.

Capital consists of all man-made things required for production, including not only plant and equipment but also the man-made materials which are used up in the production process, such as cloth, leather, lumber. The owners of capital receive interest and dividends.[1]

Land consists of natural resources for the use of which rent is paid.

Entrepreneurship establishes and directs business enterprises, and receives profit.

What determines the rate at which each factor of production is paid? In other words, what determines the levels of wages, rent, interest and profit? The answer

[1]The term "capital" is commonly used to refer to the money used to buy capital goods; strictly speaking, interest and dividends are paid to the people who supply this purchasing power.

runs along familiar lines: since each of these is a price, it must be determined by demand and supply. If the rate of payment to some factor of production appears high or low at any given time, the reason will be found in the demand and supply situation. If the rate of payment changes from one time to another, it will be because demand, or supply, or both, have changed.

In the real world each of the four factors of production is comprised of an immense number of sub-groups. "Labour" in Canada consists of carpenters, clerks, airplane pilots, professors, farm workers, and the members of literally thousands of trades and professions employed across the length and breadth of the country. "Land" consists of land in Saskatchewan on which farmers grow wheat, and the land along Dorchester Avenue in Montreal and University Avenue in Toronto, on which stand some of Canada's largest office buildings.

The Demand for Factors of Production

In Chapter 3 we analyzed the demand of housewives for eggs. We noted that, because of diminishing marginal utility, the typical housewife would increase her purchase of eggs only if the price were lowered; additional eggs would be used for less important purposes and would be worth less to her.

The demand for a factor of production resembles and differs from the demand for a consumer good. It differs in that it is a *derived demand*: the purchaser wants the factor not for itself but because it will contribute to the production of something he expects to sell. A builder hires a carpenter not because he enjoys watching the man work but because he helps put up a building. A factor's productivity determines its worth. Like the utility of a consumer good, the productivity of a factor will tend to decline with each additional unit acquired. Corresponding to diminishing marginal utility, there is *diminishing marginal productivity*. The market demand for a factor of production will resemble the demand for a consumer good in that at a high price only a small amount will be bought and that more will be bought as the price is lowered. Like the demand curve for the typical consumer good, the demand curve for the typical factor will slope downward to the right.

The Supply of Factors of Production

The supply of a factor represents the different quantities that will be offered at various possible prices. At any time, in any particular locality, the quantity offered at each price will depend upon how attractive that price is compared to prices being paid elsewhere. Thus if in some part of the country low wages are paid in a particular trade compared to wages paid in the same trade elsewhere, few people will be prepared to work here. If high wages are paid here compared to elsewhere, many people will offer to work here. Every increase in the rate of wages paid will tend to attract additional people, with the new arrivals coming from different parts of the country, from other occupations, and perhaps from different countries.

Factors of production may show great versatility and, with the exception of land, great mobility. Whenever a new industry arises in some area which promises superior rewards to those engaged in it, a great inrush of factors is likely to occur. The Alberta oil boom of the late 1940s and early 1950s provided striking illustration of this fact. Once it became evident that major oil pools existed under the surface of the province, huge quantities of capital flowed in—capital which otherwise would have been invested in other countries and in other industries. Workmen who had been employed in other occupations and in other countries came to Alberta to operate drilling rigs, to lay pipelines, to build and staff refineries. Businessmen who previously had been engaged in merchandising or manufacturing organized oil exploration and drilling companies. For all these factors of production the Alberta oil industry promised rewards superior to those which could be achieved in their present employments or in other opportunities available.

Land, while not mobile, is versatile. Agricultural land can be used to grow any of a variety of crops; a farmer's decision to grow a particular crop reflects his view that such a crop will be more rewarding than the possible alternatives. Hence farm land may be shifted from one use to another, in accordance with the changing comparative attractiveness of its various possible uses.

Changes in Factor Prices

As we have seen, the price of a factor depends at any given time upon demand which reflects productivity, and supply which reflects alternative opportunities. Both may shift in the course of time. The productivity of a factor may change in the course of time for three distinct reasons: a change in the efficiency of the factor; a change in the quantity of other factors employed; a change in the price of the good that is being produced. Thus the productivity of carpenters may increase because: carpenters become more skilful thanks to additional training; the use of more and better equipment enables carpenters to accomplish more in the same period of time; the market price of houses rises. If any of these developments occurred, the productivity of carpenters would be higher so far as building contractors were concerned and they would be prepared to pay them higher wages.

New developments may change the balance of advantage compared with other employments, and therefore change the supply of factors in any occupation or locality. When the Distant Early Warning line was built in northern Canada, for instance, large numbers of electricians and other building tradesmen were needed for the project. The attractive wages offered drew men from a number of Canadian cities; in these cities, at the same rate of pay as heretofore, fewer men offered their services.

Factor Employment by the Individual Firm

Market demand and supply determine the price of each factor of production. Having regard to the price which has been established by market forces, the owner of a firm must decide how much of each factor to employ. Each additional unit adds progressively less to output; he should ideally employ that number of each factor such that the last unit taken on adds exactly as much to the value of output as it adds to cost. Suppose, for example, that the productivity schedule of borrowing money to some business man were as follows:

First $100 borrowed adds annually to output*	$14
Second $100 ” ” ” ”	$12
Third $100 ” ” ” ”	$10
Fourth $100 ” ” ” ”	$ 8
Fifth $100 ” ” ” ”	$ 6
Sixth $100 ” ” ” ”	$ 4
Seventh $100 ” ” ” ”	$ 2

*Over and above what must be set aside toward repayment of the money borrowed.

If the market demand and supply situation caused the rate of interest to be 6 per cent, the businessman should borrow $500. Borrowing of the first $400 is obviously desirable; each of these dollars adds more to annual output than to costs. The fifth hundred dollars borrowed is marginal: it neither helps nor hurts. Borrowing in excess of $500 would be harmful; the additional borrowing would add more to costs than to value of output.

A change in the market rate of interest would cause the businessman to revise his decision; if the interest rate rose to 10 per cent he would borrow only $300; if it fell to 4 per cent he would borrow $600.

Graphical Illustration

The argument is depicted graphically in Figure 1. Figure 1A represents the operations of the market as a whole; the market demand and supply cause the rate of interest to be OM. Figure 1B represents the operations of the individual firm. Rectangle (1)

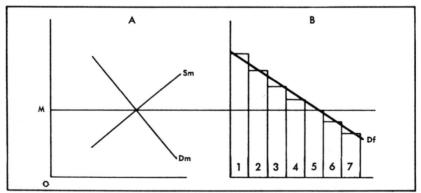

Figure 1.   Factor employment by the individual firm

represents the increase in receipts which results from the borrowing of $100; rectangle (2) represents the increase resulting from the borrowing of a second $100; and so on. Evidently, the firm should borrow exactly $500: when it does so the increase in receipts attributable to the final $100 borrowed exactly equals the increase in cost involved. The continuous line Df has been drawn to represent the firm's demand schedule, on the assumption that very small amounts of money can be borrowed and that it is possible to ascertain the addition to receipts produced by each amount.

Buyer's Monopoly

If the firm which requires a particular factor of production is merely one of a great many requiring the same factor, its own purchases will have no noticeable effect on the market price of that factor. Consequently it will pay the same price, no matter how much or how little it purchases. If the firm is the sole user of any particular factor, however, its purchases will very definitely affect the market price. In deciding how much to buy, the firm should take into account the fact that the more it buys the higher will be the price it has to pay. Because this type of situation is most likely to occur in relation to the employment of labour, we shall reserve detailed study of this phenomenon for our chapter on wages.

"Lumpiness" of Factors

Factors of production may come in fairly large units which must be bought entirely, or not at all. Where such is the case, a firm may not be able to employ the precise quantity which it would like of a particular factor. (If a large number of firms find themselves in this position in respect to the identical factor of production it will likely prove profitable for someone to acquire a few large units and rent them to firms that need them on a part-time basis only. Equipment and truck rental firms perform this kind of function, in effect breaking down large lumps to small pieces that users can digest.)

Elasticity of Demand for Factors

Two basic considerations determine the degree to which the quantity demanded of any particular factor of production will vary with its price; these are what economists refer to as the *output effect* and the *substitution effect*. The output effect refers to this fact: when the price of a factor of production changes, the total cost of producing the finished product in which it is used will change; the product's selling price and therefore the amount sold will likely change. Because a different amount of the finished product is now being sold, a correspondingly different amount of each factor of production involved will be needed. For example, if the price of road building machinery declines, road construction will become cheaper and more roads will therefore be built; because more roads are being built, more machinery will be required.

The substitution effect refers to the fact that as one factor of production falls in price it will be used to a greater degree in place of alternative factors; if its price rises, other factors will be substituted for it. When the price of road building machinery falls, more machinery will tend to be used and fewer workmen; machines will be substituted for human labour. The two effects would thus reinforce each other. The increased purchases of road building machinery which would follow a reduction in its price, would reflect the working of both the output effect and the substitution effect.

Evidently the elasticity of demand for any factor of production will depend on the size of these two effects: if the price of a factor is reduced, then the greater the increase in output of finished product that follows and the greater the degree to which it is used in place of other factors, the more elastic will its demand prove to be. In general terms it is possible to indicate the considerations which will determine the size of the two effects.

Size of the Output Effect

We will find that the output effect will be small (and demand for a factor of production will tend to be inelastic) in the following circumstances:

Where the demand for the finished product is inelastic. If the demand for men's shoes were inelastic, for instance, then a reduction in the price of shoemaking machinery, which enables shoes to be produced more cheaply, would not lead to any great increase in the quantity wanted of such machinery. With demand inelastic people would not buy very many more shoes, despite the lower price, and little additional machinery would be required.

Where expenditure on the factor whose price has changed is only a small fraction of the total cost of producing the finished product. Thus if interest charges payable by a firm constituted only $4,000 out of a total production cost of $100,000 a year, then if interest charges rose by as much as twenty-five per cent, total expenses would rise from $100,000 to only $101,000, or by just one per cent. Only a slight increase in price would be necessary to offset this extra cost, and sales would probably drop only negligibly as a result. Because sales were down hardly at all, practically the same amount of capital would be required. The demand for capital would therefore appear inelastic: despite a sharp percentage increase in its cost, the quantity demanded would be almost as much as before.

Where, for administrative reasons or prestige purposes, the selling price of the finished product is held constant, despite changes in the cost of production. Where this policy is followed, a change in the cost of a factor of production has no effect on the selling price, hence no effect on the quantity sold of the finished product. Because the same quantity is sold, the same number of factors of production will be required. Therefore a change in the price of any particular factor of production will have no effect on the quantity demanded.

Size of the Substitution Effect

The substitution effect will be small, and elasticity of demand for any particular factor of production will be small, when the following circumstances prevail:

When the factor of production has no good substitutes and no alternative uses. Despite an increase or decrease in its price, the same number will be required. Thus if plumbers' wages were to rise sharply, there would be little substitution of other factors for plumbers; on the other hand, if plumbers' wages were to fall sharply, plumbers would not be hired for a great many new purposes.

When the supply of suitable substitutes is inelastic. Suppose that land and fertilizer are substitutes, in the sense that a particular output could be achieved by using any one of various combinations of land and fertilizer. If the price of land rises, farmers will tend to use less land and more fertilizer. But if the supply of fertilizer is highly inelastic, so that an increase in demand sharply drives up the price, then very quickly there will be no advantage in substituting fertilizer for land. Despite the higher price for land, nearly the same proportion of land will continue to be used.

Elasticity of Supply of Factors

We have already noted that the supply of any particular factor of production in any particular area can be increased by the entry of additional such factors, or decreased by the exodus of some now present. There may be substantial obstacles, however, in the way of new factors seeking to enter. To induce additional factors actually to enter, the reward for their services might have to be increased sharply; i.e. their supply would be inelastic. If, on the other hand, it were easy for additional factors to enter, only a slight increase in the price offered might serve to attract them; supply would be elastic.

Similarly, the response of factors to a decline in the price paid them will depend upon the ease with which they can transfer to other employment. If they cannot easily turn to something better they may stay where they are, despite the lower reward. Their supply would be inelastic. In our discussion of the individual factors of production in the next few chapters, we shall note the sort of considerations which decide how easy it is for them to move in or to move out of particular employments. These will be the prime determinants of the elasticity of their supply.

Free Government Services: A Part of Income

At the beginning of this chapter we observed that people's incomes were determined by the prices they received for the products and services they supplied. A realistic qualification must be added here. The populations of modern countries have a large number of benefits provided freely by their respective governments. They have the free use of roads, streets and parks; extensive educational and other public services are available to them without charge. In some countries, and Canada is one, governments grant free pensions to older persons and allowances for children. The money which an individual earns is not, therefore, the sole determinant of his real income; to what he can buy with his earnings must be added what he gets free from the government. In the case of poor people, this free income may constitute a very large proportion of total income.

These "free" services and allowances are, of course, paid for by taxation. But while taxes nowadays are borne primarily by the middle and upper income groups of a country, government services, pensions, and allowances are available to all; the poor obtain more than their proportionate share. Hence the effect of increasing government taxation and spending has been to make our society more equalitarian than it would be if all people's incomes consisted exactly of the reward paid for the factor services which they provide. Real income has been reduced for those who receive large rewards for their productive services; real income has been increased for those who receive small rewards for their productive services.

Income Distribution and the National Product

The relative size of factor rewards, and of government taxation and spending policies, affect not merely the distribution but also the character of goods produced. Working people constitute in any country the great majority of the population and if wages are relatively high while profits and property incomes are relatively low, then the great bulk of the nation's output will consist of consumption goods and services designed to serve the majority. If, on the other hand, wages are relatively low while profits and property incomes are high, a large proportion of the national output will consist of luxury goods for a rich minority, together with the capital goods in which they invest their savings. One important effect of increased government taxation and spending on services and transfer payments has been to alter the proportions in which the various types of goods and services are produced. In comparison with bygone eras, rather less is produced today of investment goods and of extravagant luxuries for the very rich. More free public services are provided, however, and more goods and services designed for general consumption.

The Distribution of Income in Canada

Table 2 in Chapter 23 sets forth how much income the people of Canada earned in the years 1966-70, indicating how much was earned through each type of productive activity. Wages generally constituted about two-thirds of the total earned; property income, i.e. rent, interest and dividends, generally was in the vicinity of 20 per cent; farmers' income ranged from 2 to 5 per cent and the income earned by persons (other than farmers) who were in business for themselves, was generally about 7 per cent; military pay and allowances accounted for about 1½ per cent.

Table 1 of this chapter shows how income was distributed in 1961, as between the receivers of small, medium and large incomes. (A family living together is here considered to be receiving one income.)

Table 1

INCOMES OF FAMILIES AND UNATTACHED INDIVIDUALS, CANADA 1961*

Income Bracket	Number	Percent of Total Number	Total by Incomes	Percent of Aggregate Income
Under $1,000	475,000	9.9	$ 249,000,000	1.1
$1,000–1,999	501,000	10.4	741,000,000	3.2
$2,000–2,999	575,000	12.0	1,442,000,000	6.2
$3,000–3,999	662,000	13.8	2,340,000,000	10.2
$4,000–4,999	706,000	14.7	3,176,000,000	13.7
$5,000–5,999	596,000	12.5	3,237,000,000	14.0
$6,000–6,999	431,000	9.0	2,753,000,000	11.9
$7,000–7,999	280,000	5.8	2,055,000,000	8.9
$8,000–9,999	313,000	6.5	2,801,000,000	12.1
$10,000–14,999	188,000	3.9	2,313,000,000	10.0
$15,000 and over	73,000	1.5	2,006,000,000	8.7
Total	4,800,000	100.0	23,113,000,000	100.0

*Based on Tables 1 and 2 in *Distribution of Non-Farm Incomes in Canada by Size, 1961*. Published by the Dominion Bureau of Statistics.

SUMMARY

The productive capacity of a nation is classified into four broad categories, called the factors of production. Income is paid to individuals for providing one or more of these factors, the amount depending on the quantity supplied and the ruling price for that factor.

The demand for any productive service is derived from its productivity; the supply offered of any service in any particular situation will depend upon the total quantity in existence and the alternative opportunities available.

The elasticity of demand for any productive service will depend upon the output effect and the substitution effect. When the price of a particular productive service is altered, the quantity then wanted will depend firstly upon how the total sales of the product in which it is used have been affected. Secondly, it will depend on the extent to which, because of the change in its price, relatively more or less of it is used in conjunction with other productive services.

The elasticity of supply of factors of production will depend, in any particular enterprise, upon the ease with which additional productive factors can move in, and existing ones move out.

Because of the principle of diminishing marginal productivity, each additional unit of any factor employed tends to add progressively less to total output (other factors being held constant). The individual firm will increase its employment of any factor so long as the value of the extra output achieved exceeds the additional cost involved.

The prices paid for the various factors of production are socially significant, since they determine the incomes and welfare of individuals. However, modern governments provide a great many free public services and an individual's total income consists of what he purchases with his earnings plus what he receives free from the government. For people with low earnings, the latter portion of their income may bulk large.

FOR REVIEW AND DISCUSSION

1. When urged by his son to hire another man, Farmer Jones replied, "It wouldn't pay unless we get another section of land." What economic principles did he have in mind?
2. Just how much inequality of real income would be "reasonable", in your opinion?
3. There should be absolute equality of opportunity. Everybody should be rewarded according to his deserts. Are the two foregoing statements contradictory?
4. The degree of prosperity prevailing in Great Britain will have a bearing on the number of airplane mechanics available in Toronto. Why?
5. If American steel workers gain a substantial wage increase in the near future, what output and substitution effects are likely to follow?
6. "It's only in theory that factors of production are versatile; in actual practice they tend to be immobile." Do you agree?
7. A government can provide too many free services. Comment.

9　Wages

Our task in this chapter has been foreshadowed in the last. We saw there that the reward of any factor of production takes the form of a price, the price paid for its services. But any price, of any good or service, is determined by demand and supply, save where intervention is carried out to prevent prevailing forces of demand and supply from having their full effect. In this chapter we shall investigate the nature of the demand for labour, of the supply, and then go on to note the various reasons why the market price may not correspond to the equilibrium figure which would prevail on the basis of market forces alone.

THE THEORY OF WAGE DETERMINATION

The Demand for Labour

The demand for any kind of labour is derived from the productivity of that labour. An employer desires the services of workers, and is willing to pay for them, because those services help to produce saleable product. What determines the dimensions of his demand? What wages will he be prepared to pay? How many workmen will he wish to employ? According to the economist the employer will make his decisions on these matters in accordance with the principle of *diminishing marginal productivity*. Let us see, through an example, how the principle works.

Diminishing Marginal Productivity: An Example

Suppose that in a certain agricultural district in Canada 1,000 different people operate farms. Suppose further that the farms are exactly alike, all being of the same size and fertility, and having exactly the same equipment. All farms produce the same crop which sells for $2 per "unit."

Each farmer knows exactly how much work he can get out of hired men. Each farmer knows that only one hired man, working a normal day, could not possibly look after all the jobs which might usefully be done. The farmer would, of course, instruct him to leave undone the less important jobs, and spend his time only on those which were more important. Each farmer knows, accordingly, that if he were to take on a second hired man, the work he did would be less important than that being done by the first man. Perhaps even two men could not do all the jobs which might be done; the farmer would make sure that they did the most useful tasks only, and did not bother with less important ones. If he hired a third man, this man would inevitably be doing work which was less important than that done by the second man. Similarly, a fourth man would do less important work than the third; and so on.

Because of the fact that each successive worker did work of progressively less importance, each additional worker would add progressively less to the farm's total output. Total output would increase each time another worker was taken on, but the increase would become smaller with each additional man. All the workers might be equally capable and work equally hard; the fact that each additional worker added progressively less to output would be due simply to the fact that there would be less important work left for him to do.

Table 1 below represents the results which might be realized on each of the 1,000 farms with different numbers of workers employed. (The simplifying assumption is made here that labour is the only factor of production which need be applied to the land, and that wages are the farmer's only expense.)

Table 1

WORKER PRODUCTIVITY ON A SINGLE FARM

(1) Number of Workers	(2) Total Output	(3) Marginal Physical Product	(4) Marginal Revenue Product
1	1,000 units	1,000 units	$2,000
2	1,900 "	900 "	$1,800
3	2,700 "	800 "	$1,600
4	3,400 "	700 "	$1,400
5	4,000 "	600 "	$1,200

Column (3) in Table 1 shows the *marginal physical product,* the additional output for which each additional worker is responsible. Column (4) shows the *marginal revenue product,* the value of the additional output attributable to each man, this being in each case simply the physical product multiplied by the price at which each unit is sold.

From column (4) in Table 1 we can deduce the number of workers which each farmer will want to hire at any particular wage. Quite obviously if wages were above $2,000 a farmer would hire no one at all. If he did hire a man, that man would produce $2,000 worth of crop but would have to be paid more than that in wages. If wages were exactly $2,000 it would be barely worth a farmer's while to hire one man: one man would produce just enough to pay for his wages. The farmer would not hire two men at a wage of $2,000 per man; if he did take on a second man output would rise by only $1,800 worth, while the wage bill rose by $2,000; the farmer would be worse off by $200 for having hired two men instead of just one.

If wages were $1,800 it would just pay to hire a second man; at this wage he would be costing the farmer in wages exactly what he was adding to the value of the product. By the same reasoning if wages were $1,600 it would just pay to hire three men. At this wage a third man would be costing exactly what he added to the value of the product, but if wages were anything above $1,600, say $1,625, then it would not pay to hire a third man.[1]

The Market Demand Schedule

Column (4) in Table 1 indicates to us what a single farmer's demand schedule for labour will be. Since the community is composed of 1,000 farms, all exactly alike, the community or market demand for hired men will be the demand schedule of a single farmer multiplied by 1,000. If at wages of $2,000 each individual farmer is willing to hire one worker, the community would be willing to hire 1,000; and so on. Table 2 presents the market demand for labour in the local community, the market demand consisting simply of the sum of the demands of all the individual farm operators.

We should note here that our assumption that all 1,000 farms are exactly alike has been made purely for arithmetical convenience. It is not necessary to the argument. If the farms differed in size, fertility and equipment used, then presumably different farmers would have different demand schedules for hired men, based upon

Table 2

INDIVIDUAL AND MARKET DEMAND FOR FARM LABOUR

(1) Wage Level	(2) Number of Workers Wanted by Each Farmer	(3) Number of Workers Wanted by All Farmers
over $2,000	0	0
$2,000	1	1,000
$1,800	2	2,000
$1,600	3	3,000
$1,400	4	4,000
$1,200	5	5,000

[1]An important point to note is that with wages at $1,625 the farmer who hired three men would not be losing money on his overall operations. His total wage bill would be $4,875, while the total value of his crop would be $5,400 (2,700 units worth $2 each). Receipts would exceed the total wage bill therefore by $525. But if he hired only two workers his wage bill would be $3,250 and the value of his crop $3,800, making a difference of $550. Hiring of the third worker is unwise therefore not because it brings losses, but because it reduces profits from the higher figure which could have been achieved if only two workers had been employed. This result follows from the fact that the third man adds $1,625 to the wage bill, but only $1,600 to the value of the product.

worker productivity in each case. But there would still be a market demand schedule which would represent the total number of workers demanded at each wage level by all the farmers together. This schedule would have the same general characteristics as the one given in Table 2.

The Supply of Labour

Strictly speaking the total quantity of labour provided during any time period depends not only upon the number of workers, but also upon the amount of work put forward by each individual worker. Let us begin our analysis of supply with the simplifying assumption that every worker always works the same number of hours per week, and with the same intensity of effort. In that case the quantity of labour performed would depend strictly upon the number of workers employed.

What in fact will determine the number of workers in any particular employment in any particular locality? Two considerations chiefly: the number of people capable of handling this sort of job; and the comparative attractiveness of this kind of work compared with the alternative opportunities which are available to workers of the type involved.

Applying these principles to the farm community whose demand schedule for labour was worked out in Table 2, we can say this: The local supply of farm workers will depend upon the number of people who are already employed, or could be employed here as farm workers, and upon the attractiveness of jobs on the farms of this community compared with other jobs which these people could have if they chose. If wages here are low, few people will be prepared to work here, probably only those who have strong ties to the neighbourhood and are unwilling to move away. With wages higher, more people will be persuaded to stay here rather than move away. Very high wages might induce additional workers to come in, including perhaps farm workers hitherto employed elsewhere, workers till now employed in other industries, and possibly people who did not have to work and who normally would not be working.

The Market Equilibrium

The supply schedule of farm labour in this community would therefore be something like that presented in Table 3B.

From Table 3 it is evident that $1,600 will be the equilibrium wage, with 3,000 workers being employed. A higher or lower wage would not last very long. If wages were set at $1,800 for instance, then farmers would want to hire only 2,000 men, while 4,000 men would be offering their services. If every person were completely free to do as he chose, the extra 2,000 men who could not get jobs would offer to work for less, and the wage would be driven downward. Only when the wage had been pushed down to $1,600 would the number of workers offering to work cease to be in excess of the number farmers wanted to hire.

Table 3

MARKET DEMAND AND SUPPLY OF FARM WORKERS IN
COMMUNITY X

A: Demand		*B: Supply*	
Wage Rate	No. of Workers Wanted	Wage Rate	No. of Workers Offering to Work
$2,000	1,000	$1,200	1,000
$1,800	2,000	$1,400	2,000
$1,600	3,000	$1,600	3,000
$1,400	4,000	$1,800	4,000
$1,200	5,000	$2,000	5,000

If wages were set at $1,400 there would be a shortage of workers. Farmers would want to hire 4,000 men, but only 2,000 would offer their services. Those farmers who were unable to get men would likely offer to pay more, pushing the wage rate upward. It would continue to rise until it reached $1,600; only then would every farmer be able to obtain all the men he was prepared to hire at the going wage.

Equilibrium Position of the Individual Employer

Market demand, which depends upon productivity, and market supply, which depends upon alternative opportunities, together determine the equilibrium level of wages. Once the wage rate is established, each farmer is able to decide exactly how many men to hire.

Each will hire three, because the value which a third man adds to output is just equal to his wage. The demand expressed by every single farmer contributes to the determination of the market price; that price in turn determines how many men each farmer will actually employ.

Increasing Returns

Some students might object, and quite rightly, that our assumption of diminishing marginal productivity is far from being universally valid. They will be able to suggest all sorts of instances where a larger group of men constitute a more effective working team than does a smaller group. The reasons are several. Specialization may be carried further; some large jobs can be handled only by many men together; facilities which are needed, no matter the number of employees, will be used more intensively and therefore more economically when more men are being employed. Where such is the case each additional man taken on will cause output to increase more than proportionately. This is actually the sort of development which we have already discussed in Chapter 5; there we saw that as a firm increased its output from a very low level its efficiency would likely increase.

As we also noted in Chapter 5, the economist assumes that in every firm there is some output figure such that when production is pushed beyond it, efficiency declines. Similarly, the economist assumes that, while at first additional workers may add progressively more to output, eventually the stage will be reached when additional workers will add progressively less to output. An initial period of *increasing returns* is bound to be followed by a permanent condition of *decreasing returns*.

Table 4 illustrates this assumption. While one man produces 1,000 units, a second man adds to output by 1,200; a third adds by 1,400; a fourth by 1,600; however, a fifth adds by only 1,200; a sixth by 1,000; and so on. Increasing marginal productivity is experienced only up to the fourth worker; after him each additional worker causes output to increase less than proportionately.

On the basis of Table 4, what will be the farmer's demand schedule for hired men? What is the highest wage he will be prepared to pay, and how many men will he be prepared to hire at different wage levels?

Clearly the maximum wage the farmer can afford to pay is $2,600, equal to the highest output per worker that can be attained. If he hires four men, the working crew of most efficient size, he will have a total output worth $10,400 or $2,600 per man. He would therefore be able to pay each man this wage. If wages were any higher, then no matter what number of workers he hired his wage bill would exceed the value of his output. But note this: with wages at $2,600 *he must hire four workers* in order not to lose money. If, for instance, he hired only three at this wage, his total wage bill would be $7,800, while the value of his output would be only $7,200.

Table 4

WORKER PRODUCTIVITY ON A FARM
UNDER CONDITIONS OF INCREASING AND DECREASING RETURNS
(Each "unit" of output sells for $2)

(1)	(2)	(3)	(4)	(5)	(6)	(7)
No. of Workers	Total Output (Units)	Output of Marginal Worker (Units)	Average Output per Worker (Units)	Value of Total Output	Value of Output of Average Worker	Value of Output of Marginal Worker
1	1,000	1,000	1,000	$2,000	$2,000	$2,000
2	2,200	1,200	1,100	4,400	2,200	2,400
3	3,600	1,400	1,200	7,200	2,400	2,800
4	5,200	1,600	1,300	10,400	2,600	3,200
5	6,400	1,200	1,280	12,800	2,560	2,400
6	7,400	1,000	1,233	14,800	2,466	2,000
7	8,200	800	1,171	16,400	2,342	1,600
8	8,800	600	1,100	17,600	2,200	1,200

If wages were lower than $2,600 he would want to take on more than four workers. If men could be hired for $2,400 then he would hire five men; the fifth would add $2,400 to the wage bill, but would also add $2,400 to the value of the farm's output. If wages were $2,000 it would be feasible to hire six men, and so on. The farmer would add to his work force until the value added to output by the last man was just equal to the wage which he had to be paid.

On the basis of Table 4, the farmer's demand schedule for labour will be as shown in Table 5. This schedule does not differ greatly in its general character from the demand schedule in Table 2, which was based on the assumption that diminishing marginal productivity set in with the very first man hired. Here, too, there is a maximum, which the farmer is prepared to pay; here, too, at lower wage levels he will hire more workers. The sole difference between the two demand schedules is this: where increasing returns prevail for some time, the farmer will, at the highest wage he can afford to pay, employ more than one worker; at this wage rate he will employ the number which forms a working crew of the most efficient size. Where diminishing returns set in at once, on the other hand, he will employ only one worker at the highest wage he can afford to pay.

Table 5

DEMAND SCHEDULE FOR LABOUR ON A SINGLE FARM
UNDER CONDITIONS OF INCREASING AND DECREASING RETURNS

(1)	(2)
Wage Rate	Number of Workers Demanded
Above $2,600	0
$2,600	4
$2,400	5
$2,000	6
$1,600	7
$1,200	8

A Monopolist's Demand for Labour

We have dealt so far with the demand for labour of firms in competitive industries. In any such industry the individual firm gets the same price per unit no matter how many it sells. In a monopoly situation, on the other hand, the single firm which constituted the industry would find that when it increased its output it would have to reduce its selling price. This fact would significantly affect its demand for labour.

Suppose, for instance, that the physical productivity schedule of some monopoly firm is the same as that given in Table 1, and that the price at which the firm can sell its product varies with the quantity produced, in the following way:

Output	*Price that can be charged*
1000 units	$2.20 per unit
1900 units	$2.10 per unit
2700 units	$2.00 per unit
3400 units	$1.90 per unit
4000 units	$1.80 per unit

The increase in receipts achieved whenever an additional man was taken on would be represented by column 5 in Table 6.

Table 6

THE PRODUCTIVITY OF WORKERS EMPLOYED BY A MONOPOLIST

(1) Number of Workers	(2) Total Output	(3) Selling Price	(4) Total Value of Output	(5) Marginal Revenue Product
1	1000 units	$2.20	$2200	$2200
2	1900 units	2.10	3990	1790
3	2700 units	2.00	5400	1410
4	3400 units	1.90	6460	1060
5	4000 units	1.80	7200	740

The increase in sales receipts which results from the hiring of another man is less than the amount for which his output is actually sold. For example, while the third man adds 800 units to output and these are sold at $2 per unit, sales receipts increase by only $1410 as a result of his being taken on. The reason is that if only two men had been employed their output of 1900 units could have been sold at a price of $2.10 per unit, but when output is enlarged by the 800 units contributed by the third man it becomes necessary to lower the price to $2. The output of the third man sells for $1600 but, because of him, the amount realized from selling the output of the first two men declines by $190.

Evidently, a monopolist would hire fewer workers than would a competitive firm under the same conditions. With output selling for $2 per unit and wages set at $1600 the firm in a competitive industry would hire three workers whereas the monopolist would hire only two; the monopolist would hire three workers only if wages fell to $1410.

The Bases of Wage Differentials

Our analysis of wage determination suggests an explanation for the differences in wages paid to workers in different occupations—the differing conditions of demand and supply. If the demand for a particular type of labour is strong while the supply is weak, wages will tend to be very high. Reverse these conditions and wages will tend to be low.

A strong demand for certain workers will reflect the high value of the product, the superior productivity of this class of worker, attributable perhaps to their natural skill and energy, perhaps to their required training, or perhaps to the rich natural resources and abundant equipment with which each worker operates. A small supply will reflect the fact that there are few persons capable of doing this particular type of work, or that of those who are capable few wish to do it, because it is dangerous or disagreeable, or because of the long period of training required.

Hence we have the paradox that a hockey star, whose labour consists of play, is paid ten times as much as the man whose job it is to empty garbage cans. In the one case demand is very strong and supply very limited; in the other case demand is weak while the supply is very large.[2]

Our analysis also serves to explain why there are differences in the wages paid for the same work in different countries. Why for instance does a machinist in Canada get wages considerably higher than those received by an equally skilled machinist in Japan? The answer lies primarily in the differing conditions of supply and demand. The Canadian machinist is more productive because he has available more equipment and superior natural resources; what is more, his product, having unobstructed access to the Canadian market, brings a higher return. On the other hand, the supply of machinists is more limited in Canada because the number of people who could be machinists is very much smaller,while there are a great many alternative, attractive employments available to them. There are a great many other industries in Canada where, thanks to the abundant resources available and the extensive capital employed, the productivity of workers is high. Employers in these industries are therefore prepared to pay high wages. The pay offered to machinists must be high enough to attract them away from these other employments.

Causes of Wage Movements

Why do wages change over a period of time in the same occupation? At the risk of appearing parrot-like, a familiar answer must be given: primarily because of changed conditions of demand and supply. Demand could increase because additional or superior capital equipment was brought into use, causing the same workers to become more productive. Or perhaps the selling price of the product may increase: worker productivity would then become greater simply because of the higher value of the same physical output.

---

[2]It might be noted that in Canada the supply of menial labour has recently been declining. The persons who do such work have been recruited chiefly from the ranks of unskilled immigrants and poorly educated native born. Not being qualified for better jobs, such persons crowded into the unskilled employments; with the supply large, wages were low. But the two groups which furnish the bulk of the unskilled labour force have been declining in recent years. The day may not be far off when the wages of garbage collectors will have to be higher than the wages paid in more agreeable jobs. With everyone capable of filling a pleasanter job, it will become possible to recruit garbage collectors only by offering appropriately higher pay than can be earned in more agreeable occupations.

The supply situation in any occupation may change too. The number of suitable workers may fall off. Alternative opportunities may become more numerous and more attractive; workers will stay only if wages rise sufficiently to counter the growing attraction of jobs elsewhere. Thus the sharp rise in farm workers' wages in Canada in recent years has reflected changes in both demand and supply. The demand for such workers increased as a result of their greater productivity (largely due in turn to the increase in the price of farm products and the more extensive use of mechanical equipment); the supply declined as a result of the very great increase in the number and quality of alternative employments.

Variation in Work Performed by a Single Individual

Early in our analysis of wage determination we made the simplifying assumption that each worker always performed the same amount of work. This assumption must now be qualified. The fact is that a worker is generally able to vary, deliberately, the amount of time he works and the effort he puts into the job. Hence the quantity of labour provided in any given market situation may vary without any change in the number of persons employed, but simply because of variation in the amount of work performed by each individual worker.

An upper limit exists to the amount of time which any individual can work and the effort which he can apply. This limit varies from one employment to another according to the nature and conditions of the work. Thus in farming where a man does a variety of jobs, mostly out in the fresh air and in circumstances generally healthful, he could probably work eleven or twelve hours a day without becoming really tired. In industry, on the other hand, where a job may consist of performing a monotonously repetitive task in a noisy, evil-smelling factory, a man may well become exhausted after seven or eight hours.

When the need arises, most people can put extra effort into each day's work, but usually only over a limited period of time. If they work for very long beyond their normal daily limit, they become exhausted. Efficiency declines; they may produce less in long hours of work than they would in shorter hours. Great Britain has had experience of this. During the nineteenth century, output actually increased in some factories when the number of working hours per week of employees was reduced.

Within the maximum imposed by the limitations of the human constitution then, an individual worker can deliberately vary the amount of work that he performs. What will determine the supply schedule of the individual worker? How is he likely to vary the amount of work he offers in response to different wage rates?

Contrasting responses are possible. The worker may offer to work more if a higher wage is paid; many workers will be prepared to put in overtime if they receive more than the normal rate of pay. Some workers will apply themselves more conscientiously and with greater effort if they are paid higher wages. On the other hand some workers may actually work less if their rate of pay is increased. They may have only a fixed number of material wants and need only a specific sum of money to buy them. They have little or no use for the additional money which could be earned by working additional time and they would prefer to have the additional leisure. Accordingly, because an increase in their wage rate enables them to earn the money they need with less work, they work less.[3]

REALISTIC QUALIFICATIONS TO THE THEORY

The analysis of wage determination outlined in the foregoing pages is neat and plausible, but it describes only an approximation to reality. The facts of life are always a good deal more complicated than the theory assumes and in some cases they may be altogether different. In any particular case we will likely find that the actual wage differs from the theoretical figure, the figure which would exist if theoretical assumptions were perfectly valid. Just what are these assumptions, and how may they differ from the hard facts of particular cases?

Worker Productivity Never Precisely Known

Firstly, employers may lack the detailed and accurate knowledge of workers' productivity which we have assumed in our example. It is very easy for the writer of a text-book to make up an example showing that the productivity of one worker is 1,000 units, the productivity of a second is 900, and so on. In real life the facts are never so clear and precise. Generally in actual life an employer can only attempt a rough estimate of workers' productivity. His estimate is likely to consist of a range, rather than a specific figure. His demand schedule will accordingly lack the sharp and precise outline of those in our examples. Graphically presented, his demand schedule would consist of a broad band, rather than a single line. An actual demand schedule would consist not of a single, specific wage figure for each given number of workers, but of a broad range of possible figures for each number of employees.

Imperfect Competition Among Employers

Secondly, there may be less than perfect competition for workers on the part of employers. The example which we used to illustrate the theory assumed that there

---

[3]This kind of behaviour pattern is characteristic of primitive people. In North American society modern advertising effectively stimulates public desire for additional goods. Advertising may therefore be given credit for contributing to North American willingness to work hard. Had they not been made sharply conscious of the existence of a vast array of goods, and had their desire for them not been aroused, many North Americans would probably feel less anxious to earn large incomes, and would likely work less.

On the other hand even in North America few people have a burning desire to accumulate goods indefinitely. It would probably be true of most people that, once they were earning enough to support a reasonable standard of living, they would, like primitive people, prefer additional leisure to more material satisfaction. They may in fact *need* more leisure time in order to enjoy fully their already abundant material possessions.

was a large number of employers in the market, each of whom bid independently for workers, on the basis of their productivity in his particular establishment. But suppose that monopsony conditions prevailed instead, i.e. that there was only one employer in the market. The case would be very different. Let us see how the equilibrium wage would be changed in our example if we assumed that instead of the 1,000 farms being owned by different people, they were all owned by the same person. Table 7 shows how the equilibrium position would be shifted even though worker productivity and the workers' supply schedule remained the same as before. (To keep the arithmetic within manageable proportions we assume that the single owner of all the farms hires 1,000 workers at a time.)

From Table 7 the following points emerge. If the owner of all the farms hired just 1,000 workers, presumably he would take on the men who were willing to work for $1,200. If he decided to hire an additional 1,000 men he would take on the the men who were willing to work for $1,400. But once he takes them on, and pays them $1,400 each, he must also pay $1,400 to his previously hired workers, for in all likelihood, he must pay the same wages to all workers; once he pays $1,400 to some, he must pay $1,400 to all.

The consequence is that when he hires the second 1,000 men his wage bill rises by $1,600,000, i.e. by the wages these men must be paid *plus* the additional wages which it becomes necessary to pay to employees previously hired at a lower wage. Similarly, if he were to hire a third 1,000 men, his total labour costs would rise by $2,000,000, by the $1,600,000 which he must pay these men, plus the extra $400,000 he must now pay the 2,000 workers who previously were getting only $1,400 each.

On the basis of the figures in Table 7, the single owner of all the farms will hire only 2,000 workers. If he were to hire 3,000, the third 1,000 men would cause his wage bill to rise by $2,000,000 while they would add only $1,600,000 to the value of his output. Thus under monopsony conditions the equilibrium wage is

Table 7*

THE DEMAND FOR LABOUR UNDER MONOPSONY CONDITIONS

(1) No. of Workers	(2) Total Value of Output	(3) Value Added by Each Additional 1,000 Workers	(4) Wage Rate	(5) Total Labour Costs	(6) Labour Costs Added by Each Additional 1,000 Workers
1,000	$2,000,000	$2,000,000	$1,200	$1,200,000	$1,200,000
2,000	3,800,000	1,800,000	1,400	2,800,000	1,600,000
3,000	5,400,000	1,600,000	1,600	4,800,000	2,000,000
4,000	6,800,000	1,400,000	1,800	7,200,000	2,400,000
5,000	8,000,000	1,200,000	2,000	10,000,000	2,800,000

*Based on figures in Tables 1 and 3.

$1,400, with 2,000 workers hired, whereas under competitive conditions the equilibrium wage would be $1,600 with 3,000 men hired.

Something like the above results occur in the real world when employers of the same type of labour agree not to compete against one another for the same workers. Wages will tend to be lower and fewer workers will be hired, than would be the case if there were no such collusion on the part of the employers. The more effective such collusion is, the closer will the actual wage be to that which would be achieved under completely monopsonistic conditions.

Employer Irrationality, Non-economic Motivation

We must acknowledge the fact that employers sometimes act irrationally; they pay wages which are to high or too low, hire too many or too few workers. Such behaviour may be attributable to mistakes in judgment and also to the possibility that the desire to earn profit is not the employer's only motive. He may be anxious to provide employment for worthy people. He may be an empire-builder who takes on too many employees in order to maximize his own power and prestige. He may hire fewer workers than the economic optimum because he does not want to bear the strain and responsibility of supervising a large staff. He may refuse to hire the cheapest available labour because of personal prejudices and dislikes. Such considerations do very frequently influence the decisions of employers; a theory which ignores them is bound to provide a less than complete explanation of wage phenomena.

Realistic Considerations Regarding the Supply of Labour

The supply of labour is also likely, in real life, to exhibit characteristics not allowed for in our theory. We have assumed that workers are always perfectly familiar with all the opportunities available to them and make their choices on the basis of careful, logical calculations. Our theory, as developed early in the chapter, further assumed that each worker acts quite independently and competes unrestrainedly for the jobs offered by employers. Each of these assumptions represents only an approximation to reality.

Limited Knowledge, Immobility

The fact is that many workers are not aware of all the job opportunities available to them. Many a man works at his particular job because of chance rather than as a result of a considered selection among all the alternatives open to him. This may have been the first job he heard about, perhaps through a relative or friend. Once established in the job he may prefer to remain, even though he subsequently learns of superior opportunity elsewhere, The better job may be far away, so that it would require him to move away from the midst of friends. If the better job is in another country, immigration barriers may prevent him from settling in that country. There may not be absolute assurance that he can get the better job. To quit his present one would therefore be risky; a man with family responsibilities might understandably be deterred from taking the risk of ending up without employment altogether, or having to accept a job worse than the one he left.

J. M. Clark has dealt in delightful fashion with the postulate of economic theory that workers make their decisions regarding jobs according to the strictest logical principles.

> "He is a somewhat inhuman individual who, inconsistently enough, carries the critical weighing of hedonistic values to the point of mania. So completely absorbed is he in his irrationally rational passion for impassionate calculation that he often remains a day laborer at pitifully low wages from the sheer devotion to the fine art of making the most out of his scanty income and getting the highest returns from his employers for such mediocre skill as he chooses to devote to their service. Yet he cannot fail to be aware that the actuarial talent he lavishes outside of working hours would suffice to earn him a relatively princely salary in the office of any life insurance company."[4]

Restraints Upon Demand and Supply

Furthermore, there exist today powerful restraints upon competition among workers; it is uncommon nowadays for one worker to offer to work for a lower wage than is being paid to someone else, in order to get the latter's job. In many occupations, wage rates are established by negotiation between employers and union representatives. Union members work at the contract wage or not at all. We shall in Chapter 11 examine in some detail the nature and functions of trade unions. Suffice here to say that a union may cause the actual wage in an industry to be considerably different from what it would have been in the absence of the union.

Finally, governments may intervene in the wage setting process. In wartime, when extraordinary demand developed for labour, governments have introduced wage ceilings. In peacetime, governments have laid down minimum wages for specific occupations, usually after consultation with representatives of the employers and workers involved. Most provinces of Canada have such "fair wage" legislation on their statute books and in addition have a basic "minimum wage," less than which no worker may be paid, in any employment.

TECHNICAL PROGRESS AND THE DEMAND FOR LABOUR

Every day, every hour, some new machine is devised which enables the same production to be achieved with fewer workers than before. What happens to the workers

---

[4]J. M. Clark, "Economics and Modern Psychology", I, *Journal of Political Economy,* January 1918, p. 24.

whose work is taken over by machines? Let us see what may happen, by way of an illustrative example.

Suppose that a machine is developed which enables a laundry worker to iron a man's shirt in two minutes instead of the six minutes required to do the job by hand iron. First of all, it should be noted, new jobs will come into being in the manufacture, servicing and repair of these machines. Secondly, if the laundries, now that their labour cost is reduced, lower the price for ironing shirts, more will be sent to them. If demand is sufficiently elastic they may need as many people as before to iron shirts and even if demand is only moderately elastic they will need more personnel than before for other tasks: the increased volume of business will require additional delivery men, counter clerks, accounting and supervisory staff. In that case, though fewer ironers are employed, total employment in laundries may be as great as before or greater. It is true that if demand for laundry service is very inelastic then total employment in laundries will fall as a result of the introduction of the new machine. However, in this case the public, sending in virtually the same number to laundries but paying a lower price, will be spending less money to have its shirts ironed; it will therefore have money to buy other things. Demand will increase for other products and services and there will be more job opportunities in the industries which produce them.

Suppose though that laundries do not reduce their charges for ironing shirts. (If the industry were competitive this would be practically impossible; a price reduction would be virtually bound to occur.) Presumably the public will send no more shirts to laundries than before. Laundry operators will earn increased profits; very likely their remaining workers will demand and receive wage inceases.

What do laundry operators do with their additional profits, and laundry workers with their additional wages? Presumably they will spend the money; when they do they will provide increased employment opportunity in the industries whose products they buy with the additional money.

The foregoing example illustrates the key fact that while the introduction of a labour-saving machine may reduce the need for one type of labour it will also bring about an increase in the demand for other types of labour. The total demand for labour may well become greater than before; there is no necessary reason why it should be less. Furthermore, because the new machines enable more goods to be produced with the same labour, it becomes possible for the nation as a whole to produce a larger aggregate of goods than before.

Lags and Hindrances to Adjustment

Our argument must be qualified in one major respect. The individuals who have been displaced by machines may not be able themselves to obtain the other jobs which come into being as a result of the introduction of the machines. A long time interval may elapse before the new jobs actually come into being; or the new jobs may become available in localities distant from the homes of the displaced workers; or the new jobs may require strength and skill which these workers do not have and cannot acquire.

If such obstacles to transfer do indeed exist, then the workers displaced by machines may remain unemployed for a long time, perhaps for the rest of their lives. Such indeed was the fate, in the early nineteenth century, of thousands of English hand-loom weavers, following the introduction of mechanical looms. Adjustment to the new technology may be made only by the next generation. Young people who would normally have entered the traditional occupation, instead enter one of the new occupations where opportunity has increased. Being young, adaptable, without deep roots in a particular locality, unburdened by family responsibilities, they are quite prepared to move away from the industry where the new machines have cut down the number of jobs, and head for the industries which are expanding.

The Historical View

Historical record bears out the fundamental truth of the above propositions. Despite the immense number of labour-saving machines which are constantly being developed, the number of persons employed goes on increasing. Use of these machines has enabled us to increase our production of goods and services, and thereby to improve our material well being. But while the introduction of more effective machinery has been ultimately beneficial to society, it has admittedly caused distress to particular individuals. This need not be so. It should not be beyond human ingenuity to devise means to ensure that advances which promote the welfare of a nation as a whole do not cause irreparable harm to individual members of that nation. In fact various protective measures have been worked out, and are in effect today.[5]

The Value of Education

Higher educational levels would eliminate many of the difficulties now caused by the introduction of labour-saving machinery. While new machines give rise to new job opportunities, many people are unable to take advantage of them. Because of their limited education they cannot be retrained to qualify for the new jobs which become available. If they had obtained a better general education to start with, however, they would have had the capacity to acquire a new skill when their old one became obsolete. To poorly educated people who cannot learn, new machinery is indeed a fearful threat; to well-educated and adaptable people, new machinery means new and better opportunity. The current and prospective rate of technological change emphasizes the need for high adaptability on the part of labour; experts declare that the typical person must expect that the skill he has acquired will become obsolete within a dozen years or so and that he will have to learn two or three different skills

[5]e.g. Unemployment insurance, re-training facilities available free to displaced workers, grants toward the cost of transportation to new jobs.

in the course of his working career. It will be vital to have a firm educational base acquired in youth which will enable the effective acquisition of new skills in middle age.

SUMMARY

The equilibrium price for any kind of labour will be determined by demand and supply. The demand of an individual employer will depend upon the productivity of labour in his enterprise, and will reflect the principle of diminishing marginal productivity. The market demand will consist of the aggregate of the demands of all the individual employers. The market supply of each type of labour will depend upon the total number of such workers available and the alternative opportunities open to them.

Wage differentials among different categories of workers are attributable to differences in demand and supply. Changes through time in the wages paid to a particular category of worker result from changes in the demand-supply situation.

The quantity offered of any particular type of labour will depend upon the number of workers, and the amount of work each is prepared to perform. This latter quantity may vary perversely with wage changes if workers have only a fixed level of material aspiration.

Actual wages may diverge from the equilibrium figure because: worker productivity may not be perfectly ascertainable; because competition among employers may be imperfect; because of non-economic motivation on the part of both workers and employers; because governments and trade unions may intervene in the wage-setting process.

Technical progress, which enables the same output to be achieved with fewer workers, effects an improvement in living standards, and does not necessarily result in unemployment. New employment opportunities are bound to arise as a result of the new developments, and these may cause the total demand for labour to be as great as before or even greater.

FOR REVIEW AND DISCUSSION

1. What arguments would you advance in favour of, and opposed to, a minimum wage for all workers?
2. Workers should unite to fight automation because it threatens their jobs. Do you agree?
3. "Labour is after all just like any other commodity, and its price should be determined strictly by demand and supply." Do you agree?
4. According to David Ricardo, the well-being of the working class could never rise

in the long run. For, he said, if ever workers are granted a wage increase, they will breed larger families, so that their real welfare will be no greater than before. Does this doctrine seem reasonable to you?

5. The handsome salaries once offered to engineers by electronics firms with large defence contracts, had a noticeable influence on academic salaries. Why should this have been the case?

6. It is nonsense to say that wages have risen faster than productivity. The employer always pays workers whatever their productivity is; if wages have gone up it must be because worker productivity has risen in the same degree. Do you agree?

7. It is altogether likely that, in some occupations, if wages are raised workers will do less work rather than more. Comment.

8. Suggest why Hollywood actors are paid more than barbers; why steeplejacks are paid more than housepainters; why street cleaners are paid less than carpenters.

9. Mr. X who operates a small business, has advertised a job. One of the men who replies to the advertisement demands a higher salary than Mr. X is prepared to pay and he explains as follows why he cannot pay the man what he asks. "I could probably afford to pay you that salary if it was a matter of paying it only to you; but I would have to pay it to the four people who are working for me now and I simply could not afford to do that."

Make up a set of figures which would reflect the situation in which Mr. X finds himself.

10

Trade Unions: Historical Development

GREAT BRITAIN

Trade Union Origins: The Industrial Revolution

The trade union movement is a product of modern capitalist society, originating in Great Britain in the dawn of the Industrial Revolution, nearly 200 years ago. There had been, it is true, occasional associations of workers even before this time; bodies of workers had staged mass protests against their conditions of work and had attempted, by united action, to bring pressure upon their employers. Some associations of workers had come into being as mutual insurance societies, with members paying regular dues and the society furnishing assistance when needed because of sickness, unemployment, or death. But there was no trade union movement as we know it today, characterized by permanent associations of workers, joined into national organizations which in turn are linked together in huge federations.

Modern industrial society produced the conditions which gave rise to modern trade unionism. Before the Industrial Revolution the characteristic unit of industrial enterprise had been the small shop, in which a master employed a few apprentices and journeymen. In some branches of the clothing industry, families worked at home, on the raw material brought to them by a merchant employer or which they had themselves bought in the local market. With the means of production relatively simple and cheap, a good workman could reasonably aspire to becoming some day a master for himself. Comprehensive state legislation safeguarded workers, though not always fully, against predatory employers who sought to exploit them. The law laid down the wages to be paid in the various employments, and prescribed as well the maximum number of workers a master might employ.

The Industrial Revolution produced the modern factory system, characterized by the use of large and costly equipment, the employment of a great many workers under a single roof, the concentration of scores of factories and thousands of factory workers in large industrial cities. For most workers there was henceforth no prospect that they would some day become masters in their own right; they were destined to spend their lives as employees. In response to pressure exerted by the rising capitalist class and with the blessing of the early economists, the ancient legislation which regulated the conditions of work was repealed or ignored. Now the wages which the worker received, and the conditions under which he worked, depended upon the terms laid down by his employer. Deprived of the prospect of some day becoming a master, and deprived also of the protection of government, the worker's main hope for maintaining and improving his earnings and conditions of work lay in effective bargaining with his employer.

Collective Action by Workers

In dealing with an employer, the bargaining power of a single worker is generally slight. Bargaining power in the final analysis reflects capacity to harm; in any negotiations the side which possesses superior bargaining power is the side which can impose the greater harm on the other, and threatens to do so if its own terms are not met. The harm which an individual worker, acting within the law, can inflict upon his employer is normally very small. He can, legally, harm the employer in only two possible ways: by refusing to work for him, and by refusing to buy his products. Neither is likely to damage the employer seriously. If the worker refuses to work for him, the employer can easily replace him. If the worker stops buying the goods produced by the employer, the reduction in the latter's sales and profits is negligible. The employer, however, can harm the worker greatly. He can fire the worker, and it may be very difficult for the man to get another job. The employer in such a case has the power to deprive the worker of the means to support himself and his family. The distribution of bargaining power is grossly uneven.

But when all the workers employed by an employer act together their bargaining power is of altogether different dimensions. If all the workers refuse to work, i.e. *go on strike*, the employer may be obliged to shut down his plant. While he can without difficulty replace a single worker, he may find it impossible to replace his entire staff. Even if there are people who might be able to replace his regular staff, the latter might persuade them not to accept the jobs offered. They might *picket* the premises, accosting the replacements and urging them not to work. If they could not dissuade the replacements,[1] they could *boycott* the firm's products, and urge the general public to do the same. Sympathetic workers in other establishments which used the firm's products, might refuse to handle them, so that these establishments would be forced to discontinue their purchases from it.[2] Collective action might enable workmen furthermore to maintain themselves and their families while they were on strike and earning no money. The group might have accumulated funds in the past which could now be drawn upon; sympathetic outsiders might contribute additional assistance.

The power which workers would have if they stood together was clear and

---

[1]Who would unflatteringly be referred to as "scabs".

[2]Such supporting action by workers in another establishment is referred to as a "secondary boycott".

obvious. Use of that power would redress the balance between them and their employers. The logic was compelling. The natural leaders among the labouring classes accordingly set about, in the early years of the modern factory system, to organize workers into unions which would possess and exert the power conferred by collective action.

The Pattern of Union Organization

The first trade unions met with bitter hostility from the authorities. Parliament, with the horrors of the French Revolution still fresh in mind, feared that they might be conspiratorial societies aiming to overthrow the regime and banned them entirely in 1800. Despite the ban, unions continued to exist, clandestinely. Members were recruited furtively; meetings were held in fields at night; the identities of members and of leaders were guarded secrets. New legislation passed in 1824 authorized unions to exist, but subjected them to closely confining restraints.

Once their existence was legalized, British unions grew in size and number. During the 1850s there emerged the type of organization which became characteristic of trade union movements the world over. National unions were organized, each open only to the members of a particular skilled occupation. In each locality in which the union had enrolled members, there was a *local* which administered the affairs of the local members according to the union's constitution. Each local was self-governing in most respects, although in some matters, such as the decision to hold a strike, it was subject to the jurisdiction of the national officers. The affairs of the union were conducted, at the national level, by full-time, salaried officers, usually union members who had shown marked administrative capacity. The national unions in turn joined into a loose federation, called the Trades Union Congress, which included virtually all organized work-people in the country. The officers of the Congress accordingly came to be the official spokesmen of organized labour, leading the campaign for legislation favourable to the working classes, and for public sympathy and support for the trade union movement.

Status of Trade Unions

The advantages gained by workers through bargaining collectively constitute the main *raison d'être* of trade unions. However, if unions were to exploit effectively the possibilities of collective action, two requirements had first to be met. They had to have special privileges at law, and they had to have acceptance from employers, i.e. willingness of employers to deal with them. Each of these requirements was achieved only after many years of struggle.

The common law rules that when two or more persons act together to bring about a reduction in the trade or production of a third party, they may be charged with "conspiracy in restraint of trade," a criminal offence. Under the common law, furthermore, any one who causes financial loss or property damage to another person may be ordered by the courts to make restitution. Accordingly, the leaders and members of a union which staged a strike were liable to be charged with conspiracy in restraint of trade, because their action interfered with the employer's trade, and were liable to be sued by him for any losses he might have suffered because of the strike. It was only during the 1870s, after decades of pressure and struggle, that the British Parliament passed legislation which conferred on trade unions a special exemption from the common law's provisions regarding conspiracy in restraint of trade, and exemption also from liability for loss and damage inflicted upon an employer in the course of a strike.

The second principal requirement for effective trade union action, acceptance by employers and by the community at large, came gradually in the course of time. Effective public relations and level-headed dealing allayed the early fears that unions would make irresponsible and wholly unwarranted demands. Two great strikes, one in 1888 by girls employed in match factories, and the second in 1889 by London dock workers, brought to light terrible conditions of work and pay, and roused widespread sympathy for labour's cause. Most employers came to take for granted the obligation to bargain with union representatives. Collective bargaining frequently proved actually to be advantageous to employers, as unions took upon themselves responsibility for employee discipline, ensuring that individual workers abided by the terms laid down in agreements. By the early years of the twentieth century, trade unions had become accepted in Britain as part of the administrative machinery of the state.

The government in fact introduced legislation to increase the effectiveness of collective bargaining. Under the Conciliation Act of 1896 the government undertook to assist both parties in a labour dispute to reach an amicable agreement. The Industrial Courts Act, introduced in 1919, provided for the establishment of a permanent Industrial Court to which labour disputes could be referred for voluntary[3] arbitration. If the disputant parties preferred, the Minister of Labour was empowered, under this Act, to name a single arbitrator or to set up a special *ad hoc* Board of Arbitration.

THE UNITED STATES

Early Beginnings

The American trade union movement originated in the 1870s. Individual unions had of course existed before; a union of shoemakers is known to have been organized in Philadelphia in 1794, and in the same year a printers' union in New York. Numerous other workers' associations were formed subsequently in other trades and in other centres, but a nation-wide labour movement came into being only in the 1870s.

---

[3] i.e. the Court's award was not binding on the parties involved.

Massive industrialization had taken place during the 1860s, partly to supply the combatant armies of the Civil War, and the first transcontinental railroads had been completed during this decade. By 1870 there had come into being in the United States numerous large industrial centres, employing great masses of workers and linked by railroads into a single, integrated, powerful economy. By 1870 too, a number of national unions had been organized along British lines, each composed of locals which included only the members of a particular skilled trade.

The Knights of Labor

In 1869, nine Philadelphia tailors formed an association, on which they conferred the modest title of "The Noble and Holy Order of the Knights of Labor." Branches, called "Assemblies", were formed in other centres and these were joined in 1878 into a national organization. The Order emphasized the dignity of work, and sought to take into one fold all those who made their living through honourable toil. Admission was refused only to lawyers, bankers, liquor sellers, stock-brokers and professional gamblers.[4] Its objectives were idealistic and humanitarian; emphasis was placed on the achievement, through public discussion, of political and social reforms which would improve the lot of working men.

The local assemblies were of three broad types: some included only the members of a particular trade, such as carpenters; others included only the members of a particular industry, such as railway workers; others were "mixed," the membership including workers employed in various trades and industries. The Order expanded enormously in a short space of time. By 1886 it was composed of 5,892 local assemblies, with a total membership in excess of seven hundred thousand. This was its high water mark, however. Ineffective leadership, a series of disastrous strikes, problems arising out of extremely rapid growth, the opposition of skilled workers to the admission of large numbers of unskilled workers, all combined to bring about the decline and ultimate disintegration of the Order. Its decay proceeded with the speed of its growth; by the early 1900s it ceased to exist.

The American Federation of Labor

Reflecting more than coincidence, the American Federation of Labor (A.F. of L.) was formed in 1886, the year in which the fortunes of the Knights of Labor began to ebb. This new organization consisted of a loose association of national unions, each of which included, as did British trade unions, only the members of a single, skilled occupation. Its chief executives were elected from among the heads of the national unions. The A.F. of L. had no authority over member unions; in the administration of their internal affairs all were strictly autonomous. It did, however, have power to adjudicate jurisdictional disputes between unions, i.e. disputes in which two or more unions made conflicting claims for authority.

[4]A welcome was extended even to employers, those who had themselves been workmen once.

The main functions performed by the A.F. of L. fell into two broad categories. Firstly, it acted as spokesman for organized labour, lobbying in Congress and state legislatures for legislation favourable to the interests of organized labour, and presenting to the general public its problems and views. Secondly, it laid down the working principles of the trade union movement.

The working principles developed by the A.F. of L. reflected the philosophy of the first and long-time president, Samuel Gompers. (He was president for 37 years, from 1886 down to his death in 1924; in only one year, 1894, was he voted out of the office.) The trade union movement was to emphasize the organization of skilled workers into craft unions. Its emphasis was to be not on social or political reform, but on the practical goal of improving wages and working conditions. When asked once what labour wanted, Gompers replied simply, "More."

In its dealings with management, Gompers insisted, labour should not look to the government for assistance. It should rely upon its own economic power, the power it could wield through collective bargaining and collective action. What was required from government therefore was scrupulous non-interference in labour disputes, leaving labour free to exercise its powers without hindrance or restraint. Organized labour ought to be strictly non-partisan in politics, though it would support or oppose individual candidates according to their records in regard to labour legislation; labour's friends would be rewarded and its enemies punished.

Such were the guiding principles of the main body of organized labour in the United States for half a century. The number of trade unions, and enrolled membership, increased greatly during the early years of the twentieth century, especially during World War I. By the end of the War, more than five million workers were members of trade unions.

Employer Opposition

The work of organizing new unions, and of enrolling additional workers in existing unions, was carried out in the face of fierce opposition by employers. Many firms maintained among their staffs "labour spies" who immediately reported to management on any workers who attempted to organize a trade union. Such employees would be discharged; their names might be put on a "blacklist" so that nowhere could they get a job. Some employers compelled workers, as a condition of being hired, to sign a "yellow dog contract," an undertaking not to join a union while in the firm's employment. Some firms deliberately organized "company unions," unions which were entirely composed of, and led by, their own employees. Such "company unions," being under the thumb of management, did not fight aggressively on behalf of workers; the fact that the workers were already unionized served, however, to prevent their being enrolled by outside organizers into national unions.

When workers did strike, employers frequently imported professional strike-breakers, supplied by the notorious Pinkerton agency and similar organizations.

Clashes between strikers on the one hand and strikebreakers, police or soldiers on the other, were characterized by savage violence and bloodshed. In 1877 twelve people were killed in the course of a strike in Baltimore; twenty-five were killed in the same year during a strike in Pittsburgh. Ten were killed in a strike at the Homestead plant of the Carnegie Steel Company in 1892. During the 1870s the "Molly Maguires", a secret miners' association in the Pennsylvania coalfields, resorted to sabotage, destruction and assassination to terrorize employers. A bomb thrown into the midst of a group of policemen during a workers' rally in Chicago's Haymarket Square, led to a battle in which eleven people were killed and more than a hundred wounded.

The I.W.W.

In 1905 the International Workers of the World (I.W.W.)[5] came into being, its membership composed chiefly of Western miners, lumberjacks, migratory farm hands, and Eastern factory workers. Its leaders urged that the country's workers take over the means of production and establish a socialist state. When the United States entered World War I, the I.W.W. refused to support the war effort, and called upon its membership in the mines to go on strike. For this action it was outlawed. The American Communist Party, which was organized in 1919, in effect took over the philosophy and the role of the I.W.W.

Attitude of the Courts

In one major respect American trade unions gained the support of the courts even before their counterparts in Great Britain. In a famous decision handed down in 1842, a Massachusetts judge ruled that a strike staged by a union in order to advance the interests of its members did not necessarily constitute a conspiracy in restraint of trade. This ruling constituted a precedent; thereafter, a union which called a strike could not automatically be charged with conspiracy. Only thirty years later did British trade unions gain a corresponding exemption from the provisions of the common law.

During the early years of the twentieth century, however, American courts generally favoured management in labour-management disputes. Judges interpreted the Sherman Anti-Trust Act of 1890 as applying to trade unions, when actually it had been intended to prevent combines among industrial firms. In the famous case of the Danbury Hatters the courts awarded damages of $252,000 against a union which had called for a nation-wide boycott of the hat manufacturing firm whose workers were on strike.[6] On a good many occasions, when workers threatened to

---

[5]Referred to as the "Wobblies."
[6]Under the Sherman Act the party harmed by an illegal combine could sue for treble the damage he had suffered.

go on strike, judges, at the request of the employers involved, issued injunctions forbidding the strikes to be carried out.[7]

Attitude of Congress

Congress was generally more favourable to labour than were the courts. The Clayton Act, passed in 1914, declared that labour was not an "article of commerce," and expressly exempted trade unions from the provisions of the Sherman Anti-Trust Act. Under the Railway Labor Act of 1926, railway employees were assured the right to organize into unions without "interference, influence or coercion" by their employers. The Norris-LaGuardia Act, passed in 1932, outlawed the "yellow dog contract," severely restricted the use of injunctions in labour disputes, and declared it to be public policy that all workers have full freedom to associate into unions, without interference from their employers.

It was during President Franklin D. Roosevelt's New Deal era, however, that labour received its strongest legislative support. The Wagner Act of 1935 specifically forbade all anti-union practices, such as the firing of workers for attempting to organize, or for joining, trade unions. Workers were guaranteed the right to organize and to bargain collectively through representatives of their own choosing. A National Labour Relations Board was established to ensure that labour's right to organize was implemented in orderly fashion, without interference from employers. The Board would supervise elections in individual enterprises in which workers would vote for the union of their choice. The union which won such an election in any firm would be certified by the Board as the sole bargaining agency for all the workers concerned; the management would henceforth be legally obliged to bargain "in good faith" with the representatives of this union. The Board would also hear and adjudicate complaints of unfair practices which contravened the provisions of the Wagner Act.

The Wagner Act represented the high water mark of legislation favourable to organized labour. Massive strikes by workers in powerful unions during World War II and immediately after, notably the coal miners and the railway workers, threatened to paralyze the country; extreme wage demands pressed by union leaders contributed to inflationary pressure. Accordingly, 30 states introduced restrictive legislation in 1947, and in the same year, Congress passed the Taft-Hartley Act which imposed restraints on unions comparable to those imposed on employers by the Wagner Act.

---

[7]Under law, where an act intended by some person or group is likely to cause irreparable harm, the threatened party may ask the courts to prohibit the performance of that act. An employer, claiming that a strike would cause him irreparable harm, accordingly would seek a court injunction against the strikers. Once an injunction had been issued, a strike was illegal; the leaders and participants in such a strike would be charged with the criminal offence of contempt of court.

However, though bitterly denounced by labour leaders, the Taft-Hartley Act does not appear to have affected seriously the basic rights conferred on labour by the Wagner Act.

The C.I.O.

A development of key significance during the 1930s was the emergence of the Congress of Industrial Organizations, the C.I.O. Time-honoured doctrine had dictated that unions should be composed of skilled workmen, each particular craft being organized into its own union. During the early 1930s, a number of labour's foremost leaders became convinced that such unions were unsuited to the needs of a large proportion of American labour. By now the great mass production industries, which employed chiefly unskilled or semi-skilled labour, were accounting for a very large fraction of the nation's total output and employment. If the workers in these industries were to be organized, it could not be on the basis of their crafts, for they had none. They would have to be organized into industrial unions, each such union including all the members of a particular *industry*.

Furthermore, where a single firm or industry employed tradesmen of several different crafts, collective bargaining with the employer could be carried out more effectively if all were members of a single union. Where the various types of tradesmen were all organized into separate unions, the employer might play one off against the other. The necessary coordination of action required to deal with him effectively might not be achieved. Thus the United States Steel Corporation had been able to break a great strike in 1919, partly because the strike was led by an unwieldy and un-coordinated committee representing 24 different trades employed in the firm.

Led by John L. Lewis, the chief of the United Mine Workers, a group of union heads formed the Committee for Industrial Organization in 1935, for the purpose of organizing into industrial unions the workers of the great mass production industries. The unions which they headed were promptly expelled from the A.F. of L. Powerful organizing drives,[8] and the support of the Wagner Act, enabled the Committee to organize industrial unions in the country's greatest industries, the steel, automobile, rubber, oil industries, and a score of others.

The new unions affiliated with the Congress of Industrial Organizations,[9] which became comparable in size to the A.F. of L. At the end of World War II the total membership of A.F. of L. unions was 6,800,000 while the membership of C.I.O.

---

[8]Including, in the automobile industry and in several other industries, "sit-down strikes," in which strikers occupied the premises to keep out scabs and strikebreakers until their demands were met.

[9]The initials C.I.O. referred initially to the Committee which was set up to organize industrial unions, and later to the federation in which these unions were joined.

unions totalled 6,000,000. After years of bitter rivalry, jurisdictional disputes and mutual raiding, the two great federations amalgamated in 1956 to form the A.F.L.-C.I.O., so that once again the great majority of American organized labour was enrolled within a single federation.

CANADA

The Growth of Trade Union Membership

The course of the trade union movement in Canada has reflected the character and pace of the nation's economic development. Right down to the outbreak of World War I Canada was largely an agricultural country: the total membership of trade unions was only 166,163 in 1914.

During the course of World War I, Canadian manufacturing industry expanded greatly, producing munitions on a huge scale and a great many manufactured goods which had formerly been imported from abroad. With the very large increase which occurred in industrial employment, trade union membership more than doubled. As in the United States, membership declined sharply during the postwar recession, recovered slightly during the prosperous years of the later 1920s, and then declined heavily during the Great Depression of the 1930s. Increasing trade union enrollments accompanied the improving conditions of the later 1930s, and by the outbreak of war in 1939 trade union membership in Canada was 358,967, or approximately at the level attained twenty years earlier. As had been the case during World War I, Canadian industrial employment soared during the course of World War II; reflecting primarily the huge industrial expansion, trade union membership almost doubled during the course of the war, amounting to 711,117 in 1945. With Canada's industrial growth continuing at a rapid pace and unions recruiting aggressively, the number of locals and enrolled membership continued to grow rapidly following the end of the war, membership attaining the figure of 1,454,000 in 1958. Over the period 1958-60 a slight decline occurred, but the upward trend was resumed in 1963. Figure 1 graphically depicts the growth of trade union membership in Canada over the half century 1914-69.

The Trades and Labour Congress

It was only during the 1850s that trade union organization in Canada attained proportions which were of any significance. A few unions had been established much earlier: printers in Toronto and Montreal had organized locals as early as the 1820s. During the 1850s, however, established British and American trade unions gave their support to the organization of unions in Canada. Two great British unions of engineers and carpenters, organized locals in this country. Much more important, the Reciprocity Treaty, effective between Canada and the U.S. in the years 1854-66,

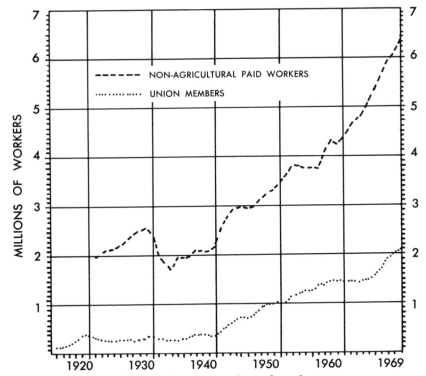

Figure 1.   Non-agricultural workers and number of union members, Canada, 1914-69

brought a very great increase in commercial relations between the two countries and contributed to a marked prosperity and expansion in Canada. As a consequence, with the Canadian economy thriving, growing, and more closely related to that of the United States, American organizers enrolled Canadian craftsmen into American unions, establishing locals in Canada. These American unions to which Canadian locals were affiliated, became known henceforth as "International."

In 1881, the Knights of Labor, then rapidly expanding in the United States, entered Canada. The Order was well received and acquired a large following, particularly in Quebec. In 1886 the first national labour federation was established, the Trades and Labour Congress (T.L.C.), centred on a solid core of Canadian locals of international unions. Assemblies of the Knights of Labor were at first recognized and accredited but in 1902 the T.L.C. expelled them, ruling firmly against dual unionism, i.e. the enrollment of the same type of worker into two different unions. No union was henceforth accredited which infringed upon the jurisdiction of an established international union.

The T.L.C. served as the voice of Canadian organized labour, lobbying for such measures as state support to technical education and restrictions on immigration. Because its member unions were predominantly the Canadian locals of American trade unions, however, the T.L.C. could not attempt to develop working principles to be followed by the Canadian labour movement. Canadian locals were bound in each case by the rules set down by their headquarters, located in the United States. These in turn reflected the philosophy of the American trade union movement, as developed by the leaders of the A.F. of L.

The Canadian Congress of Labour

We have already noted the deep division which existed within the American trade union movement from 1935 to 1955. The same division existed in Canada, based upon the same grounds—conflicting views as to the basis upon which unions should be organized. But in Canada further causes existed for disunity, notably differences in race, religion, and language, and conflicting views as to the desirability of having the Canadian trade union movement fully autonomous and independent of American labour organizations.

In 1926 a group of purely Canadian unions, barred from the T.L.C. because they competed for membership against international unions, formed a rival federation, the All Canada Congress of Labour. Fourteen years later, in 1940, this group was joined by the Canadian sections of C.I.O. unions, these having been expelled in the previous year from the T.L.C. (The American sections of these unions had been expelled from the A.F. of L. in 1935, four years earlier.) The new federation, thus comprised of a group of all-Canadian unions and Canadian branches of C.I.O. unions, was named the Canadian Congress of Labour, and became in effect the Canadian counterpart of the C.I.O. in the United States. In 1956, only a few months after the A.F. of L. and C.I.O. amalgamated in the U.S., the two Canadian federations joined together to form the Canadian Labour Congress.

The Catholic Unions

A distinctive feature of the Canadian trade union movement has been the existence of the Catholic trade unions. Early in the twentieth century the Catholic Church of Quebec began to participate actively in labour affairs, organizing trade unions along the lines recommended by Pope Leo XIII in his Encyclical Rerum Novarum, issued in 1891. The characteristic feature of these new unions, all located within the province of Quebec, was their close association with the Catholic Church. Each union had a chaplain named by the religious authorities, and he had the right to participate in the union's councils. Each union conformed in its proceedings to the rules laid down by church authorities. The various Catholic unions joined together in 1921 to form the Confédération des Travailleurs Catholiques du Canada; in 1960 the name was changed to Confederation of National Trade Unions.

The change of name in 1960 reflected profound changes that had occurred in membership and outlook. Until World War II the Catholic unions had been based to a very large extent upon the province's building trades and their members were almost exclusively Catholic; non-Catholics were permitted to join but only as associate members without voting rights. During the War mass production industries proliferated in the Montreal area, and came to employ large numbers of non-French, non-Catholic workers. To forestall expansion by the internationals in Quebec the Catholic unions recruited these workers, thereby significantly changing their own character. Since they now included large numbers of non-Catholics who insisted on equal membership rights, unions de-emphasized religious affiliation and devoted themselves to furthering the material interests of their members in every possible way; many dropped the word Catholic from their title. New leaders emerged, many of them trained at Laval University, who were aggressively radical in their political and economic views and the hitherto docile unions manifested an unprecedented militancy. The new spirit was dramatically revealed in the great strike staged in 1949 by asbestos workers against the Johns Manville Company. The long and bitter contest served to polarize opposing factions: the CCL, hitherto benignly regarded by the provincial government became quite alienated from it; the Church, on the other hand, sided with the strikers.

Table 1 shows, as of January 1969, the total number of locals in Canada and the total membership of each of the various labour federations.

Table 1

UNION MEMBERSHIP BY CONGRESS AFFILIATION, 1969*

Congress Affiliation	No. of Locals	Membership Number	Per cent
AFL-CIO/CLC	4,460	1,106,861	53.4
CLC only	2,924	481,790	23.2
Total Canadian Labour Congress	7,384	1,588,651	76.6
Confederation of National Trade Unions	984	207,983	10.0
AFL and CIO only	10	604	—
Unaffiliated international unions	345	111,111	5.4
Unaffiliated national unions	463	109,853	5.3
Independent local organizations	124	56,414	2.7
Total	9,310	2,074,616	100.0

*Labour Organizations in Canada, 1969, p. xiii.

Labour Legislation

Through a series of enactments between 1872 and 1892 Parliament conferred on Canadian trade unions substantially the same privileges as those accorded to British unions during the same period: notably, exemption from the conspiracy laws and from liability for damages suffered by an employer because of a strike. Later Canadian legislation introduced procedures under which the government would contribute to the settlement of trade disputes. The Conciliation Act of 1900 authorized the Minister of Labour to appoint a Conciliation Board of three men, when requested to do so by either labour or management. The Railway Labour Disputes Act introduced the principle of compulsory investigation: in a dispute involving railway employees a board of arbitration might be set up which would have all necessary powers to carry out a thorough investigation, including the right to compel witnesses to appear and testify. Following its investigation the board would report its findings and make its recommendations to the Minister of Labour; these recommendations were not binding, however, on either party.

The Industrial Disputes Investigation Act of 1907 constituted a landmark in the history of Canadian labour legislation. It extended to all mines and public utilities the principle of compulsory investigation that had been introduced in the Railway Labour Disputes Act of 1903.[10] Secondly, it prohibited any strike or lockout before a Board of Conciliation and Investigation had been set up and had reported its findings and recommendations to the Minister of Labour. As laid down in the earlier legislation, the board's report was not binding; it was hoped, however, that, out of deference to public opinion, the disputant parties would both abide by the board's recommendations.

The Industrial Disputes Investigation Act was extensively used. In the period 1907-25, 619 applications were made under the Act for the appointment of boards and 441 boards were established; strikes were avoided in all save 37 cases. However, in 1925 the courts ruled that the Act was ultra vires, being beyond the jurisdictional authority of Parliament. The British North America Act had allocated to the provincial legislatures jurisdiction over matters affecting property and civil rights, and the courts ruled that contracts of employment involved civil rights. Parliament thereupon amended the Act, limiting its coverage to those industries that were subject to its jurisdiction, such as railways, canals, telegraphs. Within a few years, however, each province except Prince Edward Island passed legislation extending the coverage of the Act to industries within its own jurisdiction.

Wartime Gains of Organized Labour

The passage of the Wagner Act in the U.S. in 1935 furnished powerful legislative support to the American trade union movement, as we have seen; corresponding legislation was introduced into Canada only nine years later. Provincial legislatures did enact some of the provisions of the Wagner Act during the 1930s, but without

---

[10]Actually, the Act authorized the Minister of Labour to set up a Board of Conciliation and Investigation to deal with a dispute in *any* industry. There was this proviso, however. In the case of a dispute in one of the specified industries (mining or public utilities) the Minister could set up a Board upon the request of only one of the parties involved. In the case of a dispute occurring in some other industry a Board could be set up only if *both* parties requested it.

effective arrangements for their enforcement. During World War II, the federal government, using its emergency powers, issued a number of Orders-in-Council designed to win the wholehearted cooperation of Canadian labour in the war effort. In 1944, following a comprehensive investigation of the labour scene, the federal government issued Privy Council Order 1003, a landmark in the history of the Canadian trade union movement. Privy Council Order 1003 instituted the main provisions of the Wagner Act (together with some restraints on labour not in the Act) and included the provisions for the settlement of labour disputes that had been incorporated in the Industrial Disputes Investigation Act of 1907.[11] The application of P.C. 1003 was extensive: in 1944 the major portion of Canada's industrial capacity was engaged in war production and was subject to the jurisdiction of the federal government.

Postwar Labour Legislation

With the end of the war, the federal government's emergency powers lapsed, and its control over the major portion of the industrial economy came to an end. Accordingly in 1948 Parliament passed a new Act, the Industrial Relations and Disputes Investigations Act, which was in effect a slightly amended version of the wartime P.C. 1003. This Act applied to only the limited number of industries which were subject to federal jurisdiction in peacetime. It was hoped, however, that provincial legislatures would introduce legislation modelled on the federal Act.

This hope has been fulfilled. Each provincial legislature has indeed passed legislation along the lines of the federal Act of 1948. The provincial statutes vary somewhat from one province to another, but only in matters of detail; the main outlines are fairly uniform. Hence there now exists on the statute books of every province of Canada, legislation along the following general lines:

Workers are guaranteed the right to organize themselves into unions of their own choosing.

Employers are forbidden to engage in anti-union activities, such as the firing of men for joining a union.

A provincial Labour Board "certifies" the bargaining agency (union) which has been chosen by the workers in any establishment. The Board may "certify" a union on the basis of an election which it has supervised, or on the basis of evidence submitted to it by a union organizer which conclusively indicates that the majority of the workers want this union as their bargaining agency.

---

[11]Actually, one important provision of the Wagner Act had already been introduced in Canada on a nation-wide basis and others on a regional basis. Parliament passed legislation in 1939 forbidding an employer to fire a worker—or to refuse to hire him—on account of union membership. In 1943, just months before P.C. 1003 was issued, British Columbia and Ontario had enacted legislation under which employers were required to bargain in good faith with the accredited representatives of their employees.

An employer is legally obliged to bargain in good faith with the representatives of the union which has been "certified" for his establishment.

Each provincial government has on its staff "Conciliation Officers" whose services are available without charge to the parties involved in a labour dispute. Upon request by either party to such a dispute a Conciliation Officer will contribute his assistance toward the reaching of an agreement.

If the Conciliation Officer fails to bring about an agreement, a Conciliation Board may be established, consisting of one nominee of labour, one of management, and a neutral chairman. After hearing both sides the Board draws up its recommendations as to how the dispute shall be settled, and these are publicly announced.[12]

The recommendations of a Conciliation Board are not binding on either party to a dispute; it is hoped merely that the two sides will abide by these recommendations, out of deference to public opinion.

No work stoppage may take place while the dispute is subject to conciliation procedure, i.e. while a Conciliation Officer is attempting to bring about agreement, or while a Board is studying the issue and preparing its recommendations.

Once a contract has been signed, then, for the duration of that contract, any disputes which arise between labour and management *must* be settled by arbitration.

Some categories of worker whose services are absolutely vital for public health and safety, are denied the right to strike or allowed this right only in very circumscribed form. Policemen and firemen are generally forbidden to go on strike; some provinces prohibit strikes by school teachers; in some provinces strikes by public utility employees are altogether forbidden; in other provinces such employees have the right to strike, but subject to close limitation and restraint.

Compulsory Arbitration in British Columbia

British Columbia has introduced arrangements for the compulsory arbitration of labour disputes which threaten serious harm to the public interest. A provincial Mediation Commission was set up in 1968 with wide powers to prohibit strikes or lockouts and to terminate any that were already in progress. Whenever the government felt that a labour dispute was likely to harm the public interest the Commission would be authorized to intervene and impose a settlement that would be binding on both sides.

The Public Interest in Labour-Management Relations

Two other provinces have recently introduced legislation prohibiting strikes in essential industries. The government of Ontario passed an act in 1965 forbidding strikes in

---

[12]It should be pointed out that the governments of several provinces have become reluctant to set up Conciliation Boards, preferring to see disputes settled by the parties themselves, without government intervention. Manitoba, New Brunswick, Nova Scotia and Quebec have tended particularly to adopt this attitude.

hospitals: henceforth contract disputes would have to be settled by arbitration, with the arbitrator's award binding on both parties. An act passed by the legislature of Saskatchewan in 1966 empowered the government to prohibit any strike by the employees of the provincially-owned power corporation, which distributes natural gas and electricity throughout the province. (In Quebec, on the other hand, a long-standing ban on strikes by hospital employees was removed in 1964; legislative changes made the following year authorized strikes by teachers and permitted provincial civil servants to bargain collectively. Subject to the proviso that essential services must be maintained, the latter too were given the right to strike.)

A number of attempts were made in the early 1960s to improve labour-management relations in Canada; permanent organizations devoted to that purpose were established in two provinces. In Nova Scotia where labour and management had displayed a deep mutual distrust for years, the Dalhousie Institute of Public Affairs convened a joint study committee in 1962, composed of representatives of both groups. The primary objectives were to develop mutual understanding and goodwill and, in particular, to bring to an end the annual series of demands made by each side on the provincial legislature for amendments to existing trade union legislation—with acrimonious objections and counter-demands by the other side. Both would be better served, it was felt, if there were less government participation in labour-management disputes and if the two sides were left alone to compose their differences through negotiation. A similar body has come into existence in Manitoba, where the provincial government set up a labour-management committee to consider legislation in respect to labour relations and labour standards.

Vexing specific problems gave rise to a series of large scale government investigations and new techniques of accommodation. Comprehensive inquiries have been carried out into major industries characterized by serious labour disputes, in order to ascertain root causes and achieve lasting solutions. A royal commission was set up to consider the impact upon railway workers of technological advance in the industry; the Commission recommended that workers be consulted whenever major changes were introduced. *Ad hoc* studies have since been carried out in other industries where new equipment drastically altered the volume and pattern of employment. Another Royal Commission studied the use of the court injunction[13] in labour disputes; in New Brunswick a commission was set up to study the public interest in labour-management conflicts. Reacting to the large-scale labour disputes that erupted in 1966—over 5 million man days of work were lost during the year through strikes—the federal government set up a "task force" of experts to study the entire field of labour relations in Canada and to recommend appropriate legislative changes.

---

[13]An injunction is a court order forbidding the performance of a particular act; they have frequently been issued by the courts in labour disputes, e.g. injunctions have limited the scale of picketing that strikers might carry on and have ordered groups of workers to return to work.

SUMMARY

A large and distinct class of industrial workers came into being in Great Britain with the Industrial Revolution. Production became concentrated in large establishments in which numerous workers served a single employer.

Trade unions were organized by workers to increase their bargaining power in dealings with employers. The first unions typically included only the members of a single skilled trade or craft.

A nation-wide trade union movement emerged in Britain around the middle of the 19th century. Trade unions were accorded important legal privileges and by 1900 had become generally accepted as part of the administrative apparatus of the state.

In the United States a nation-wide trade union movement came into being following the construction of transcontinental railways and the emergence of an integrated national economy. The American Federation of Labor was organized in 1886 to become the spokesman of organized labour in the United States.

The American trade union movement encountered bitter hostility from employers and obstructionism by the courts. During the 1930s, however, the movement was powerfully endorsed by Congress; obstructionism by employers was prohibited by law.

A schism developed within the American labour movement during the 1930s, with the formation of the C.I.O. to organize unskilled workers in the mass production industries. In 1956, after a generation of conflict, the two great federations amalgamated.

The trade union movement in Canada achieved significant proportions only in the twentieth century when the country's industrialization attained appreciable dimensions. It was from the beginning strongly influenced by its American counterpart, a great many Canadian workers being members of locals affiliated with American unions.

The Trades and Labour Congress, organized in 1902, constituted the Canadian counterpart of the A.F. of L. in the United States. Other labour federations emerged, notably the Canadian Congress of Labour, and an association of French Catholic workers in Quebec. The T.L.C. and C.C.L. amalgamated in 1956, shortly after their counterparts in the U.S. had taken this step.

The B.N.A. Act conferred jurisdiction over labour matters on provincial governments, and most of Canada's labour legislation is in the form of provincial statutes. Within its sphere of jurisdiction the federal government has passed important legislation dealing with labour matters. A federal labour statute introduced in 1948 has served as a model for all provinces. Present legislation in each province guarantees to workers the right to organize themselves into unions, and provides for government assistance toward the settlement of labour disputes.

FOR REVIEW AND DISCUSSION

1. "There is no earthly reason why taxpayers' money should be used to help settle disputes between workers and their employers." Comment.
2. If no employer ever hired more than three or four workers, there would never be any need for trade unions. Do you agree?
3. In both the United Kingdom and the United States, labour's present privileges were not gained easily. Explain.
4. Canadian labour should shake off American domination. Do you agree?
5. Industrial unions, as opposed to craft unions, were an inevitable development of the twentieth century. Why?
6. Canada should have a single labour code which would apply uniformly across the whole country. Do you agree?
7. Labour legislation in Canada has been simply British and American legislation, introduced here after a few years' time. Assess the validity of this statement.

11 Trade Unions: Activities, Achievements, Problems

UNION ACTIVITIES

A trade union, according to one famous definition, is "a continuous association of wage earners for the purpose of maintaining or improving the conditions of their working lives."[1] The definition suggests the two categories of activity which trade union leaders must always be carrying on. Firstly, they must take whatever action is required to ensure that the association is in fact a continuous one. They must at all times keep a watchful eye on the health and strength of the union, and adopt any measures which will contribute to that health and strength. Any development which weakens the union or endangers its existence, must be prevented by all means possible. Secondly, union leaders must employ the collective power of the union on behalf of its members. In whatever field this power can promote their interests, there the power must be applied.

Let us now examine the various policies and measures which trade union leaders adopt, in the serving of these broad and basic purposes.

TO KEEP THE UNION STRONG

Obtaining "Recognition"

The main *raison d'être* of a trade union is to provide an agency through which workers can deal collectively with their employer. Expressing their collective will and wielding their collective power, the union negotiates with the employer on behalf of its members. But negotiations with the employer can be carried on only if he is willing; it is of paramount importance, therefore, to obtain the employer's agreement to deal with the union. If this consent is not achieved, the very existence of the union loses a good deal of its point.

Union leaders accordingly strive to achieve "recognition" of their unions by employers. In Canada and the United States, the law today requires an employer to

[1]Sidney and Beatrice Webb, *The History of Trade Unionism* (London, 1911), p. 1.

recognize as sole bargaining agency a union which has been "certified" by the local Labour Board,[2] and to bargain in good faith with that union's representatives. Since "certification" is granted to a union only when it has enrolled the majority of a plant's employees, the first goal of a union leader nowadays is to recruit, and retain, enough members to qualify the union for "certification."

The "Check Off"

To survive, and to operate effectively, a union must have a regular income. It must pay salaries to its officers; it must purchase office equipment and materials; it must rent office space; it should accumulate financial reserves out of which to pay benefits to members who are unemployed, sick, or on strike. This income can only come from the dues contributed by members; union leaders must therefore see to it that members pay their dues. To ensure that dues are in fact paid fully and regularly, and with a minimum of collection expense, union leaders nowadays demand the "check off," that is, that the employer deduct union dues from workers' wages, and hand the money over directly to the union. The "check off" is now fairly general in North America, less common in Great Britain and Europe.

"Closed" or "Union" Shop

The benefits won from an employer through the union's efforts must be available only to its own members. If non-members benefit equally from the union's achievements, then membership loses its point. Members might, understandably, object to paying dues to a union which brings them nothing more than it brings to outsiders who do not pay the dues. Hence union leaders demand the "closed shop," or the "union shop." The "closed shop" provides that only union members may be hired in a particular plant;[3] the "union shop" permits non-union personnel to be hired, but requires that they join the union within a specified period.[4]

TO PROMOTE MEMBERS' INTERESTS

A union battles for its members on four major fronts. It fights to protect their jobs, to maintain or improve their pay, to maintain or improve the conditions under which

[2]Through the procedure described in Chapter 10.

[3]Provincial legislation in Canada generally requires that when a "closed shop" agreement is arrived at between a firm and union, workers *already employed* by the firm are to be free to remain outside the union if they choose. The obligation that employees be union members is to apply only to workers hired *after* the agreement has been signed.

[4]Both the "closed shop" and the "union shop" are legal in Canada today. In the United States, however, the Taft-Hartley Act of 1947 banned the "closed shop" throughout the entire nation, while a number of individual states have in recent years passed so-called "right to work" laws which in effect prohibit the "union shop" as well. These laws expressly prohibit agreements under which a person becomes compelled to join a trade union as a condition of obtaining employment.

they work, to bring about beneficial legislation by governments. Bringing to bear the collective power which it wields, the union in each field defends the interests of its members against threats, and seizes opportunities for achieving gains.

Job Protection

The defence of workers' jobs requires a variety of measures and tactics, according to the nature of the threat. Where there is a danger that present members of the union may lose their jobs because of the competition of a horde of new members, the union may limit the number of newcomers which it will accept. This it may do by levying very high initiation fees, by insisting upon extremely long periods of apprenticeship, or simply by refusing outright to accept additional members. Where there is a danger that newcomers to the country will compete for the jobs of unionists, union leaders will campaign for a reduction in immigration.

Where the introduction of a labour-saving machine threatens to displace members, the union may resist the introduction of the machine. Where such resistance is hopeless, the union may insist that its members be employed to operate the machine, even though their particular skill is not really required. The union may "featherbed," insisting that its members continue to be hired, even though there is no longer any useful work for them to do. The union of course can only effectively exercise pressure if, despite the new machine, some at least of its members continue to be necessary in the production process; its power would derive from the fact that it could interfere with production by calling these men out on strike.

Because of fears that only a limited amount of work was available for its members, a union might order them to work at a slow pace, in order to make jobs last longer.[5] One union may challenge another union, each claiming that a particular kind of work should be done by its members only.

Collective Bargaining

The main function of the typical trade union nowadays is, of course, to serve as the agency through which workers deal collectively with their employer. Bargaining on behalf of its members, the union will enter into a contract with the employer. The contract will be for a specified time period, usually from one to three years, and will set forth the terms and conditions under which employees will work during that period. The clauses regarding pay will prescribe such matters as the hourly rate for each classification of employee, the size of periodic increments, the number of paid holidays per year, the employer's contributions to health, pension and other programmes.[6] The clauses regarding the conditions of work will specify arrangements

---

[5]e.g. Some bricklayers' unions are reputed to have instructed members to lay only a limited number of bricks per day, some painters' unions to have limited the width of the brushes which members might use.

[6]The benefits which a worker receives over and above the cash paid to him for work done, are generally referred to as "fringe benefits."

for the safety and convenience of workers, and the seniority rules to be followed when it becomes necessary to lay off or rehire personnel. Anticipating the possibility that some clauses in the contract might be differently interpreted by the two sides, or that disputes might arise in regard to matters not specifically dealt with, the contract would stipulate the procedure to be followed in such situations.[7]

In the negotiations leading up to the signing of a new contract, each side naturally seeks to protect and promote its own interests. Characteristically the union will ask for more than it expects to receive; the employer will offer less than he expects ultimately to pay. Each side presents arguments supporting its own case. The union representative will point out how workers need more because the cost of living has risen, how they deserve more because their productivity has risen, how the company can afford to pay more because its profits are large. The employer will counter by pointing out that productivity and the cost of living have really risen only slightly, that the firm's profits are needed to build up financial reserves or to finance future expansion, that wage increases would make necessary higher prices for the product, and that this in turn would reduce sales and therefore employment.

In a good many cases neither party knows what its "real" position is: the union is not certain what minimum it will insist upon; the employer does not really know what maximum he is prepared to give. On each side views and attitudes are likely to be affected by the bargaining procedure itself, and therefore to alter in the course of the negotiations. In the great majority of cases agreement is finally reached, usually on the basis of some compromise between the initial positions of the two sides. In the negotiations for a new contract, a union may begin by asking for $5.00 per hour, while the employer counters with an offer of $4.50. Eventually, despite earlier protests that a wage rate in excess of $4.50 per hour would ruin the firm, the employer agrees to pay $4.75. The union, despite earlier protests that its members could not possibly be expected to work for less than $5.00, agrees to accept $4.75.

Unsuccessful Bargaining: A Strike

Suppose, however, that the employer in the above example absolutely refuses to go above $4.60 per hour. He may feel certain that, given the current selling price of his product, a wage rate in excess of this figure would render the business a losing one. He may refuse to pay more than $4.60 per hour because he feels that the workers will accept this figure rather than strike. He may be confident that if they should strike, he could replace them. He may feel sure that even if he could not replace them easily,

---

[7]Nowadays, a good many contracts provide that disputes which occur in the course of the contract be settled by arbitration. In some cases a single person or a specific group of persons might be specified in the contract as the permanent arbitration authority, to which all disputes would be referred. Usually, the contract further specifies that the award of the arbitrator shall be binding upon both parties. In Canada, as we noted in the previous chapter, provincial legislation generally decrees that disputes which arise during the period of a contract, *must* be settled by arbitration.

very soon the striking workers would be in desperate financial straits, and would be forced to come back to work on his terms. And so, either because he feels that he simply cannot afford to pay more, or because he is confident that he really does not have to pay more, he refuses absolutely to improve on his offer of $4.60.

The union members have their own views. They may feel that the employer could afford to pay $5.00, and would pay it if he were forced to. The union holds a strike vote; the men vote in favour and a-strike is called. Striking workers picket the plant, carrying placards which proclaim the fact of the strike to the general public. If the employer hires other workers, the pickets will attempt to dissuade them from going into the plant. The law permits them to employ peaceful persuasion to this end, but understandably tempers sometimes flare and violence erupts. If the employer does manage to maintain production, the pickets will seek to dissuade customers from patronizing the firm. The union may declare a boycott, inviting the general public to join.

The strike, if it goes on for any length of time, is damaging to both sides. If the plant has been forced to shut down, the employer loses the profit he would have earned on the goods which could have been produced. There may be permanent damage as well: some customers may shift to other suppliers, and may continue to deal with them even after the strike ends. The workers suffer loss of income. Some may have savings upon which they can draw; the union may provide some help out of its reserves; other unions may contribute donations; local storekeepers may furnish supplies on credit. But these are likely to be poor alternatives to a regular wage. The typical striker and his family will be obliged to reduce drastically their standard of living, and may suffer real privation. The grim possibility looms that, after the strike ends, there will be no job to go back to; a non-striker may have taken over, or the firm may simply not need anyone to do the job.

The losses and sacrifices which both sides suffer as a result of a strike serve to soften rigid attitudes. Each side realizes that in expecting the other to surrender tamely to its demands, it was nursing an illusion. To avoid further losses the employer may improve upon his last offer; to avoid further privation the union agrees to make further concessions. Agreement may eventually be reached, with the hourly rate being set at $4.80. The strike is over.

Was This Strike Really Necessary?

Almost inevitably, after a major strike, someone points out the obvious truth that both sides would have been better off had the strike not taken place. The extra few cents per hour which workers receive as a result of carrying out the strike, will probably never make up for the hundreds of dollars of wages which they have lost. The temporary losses and the permanent damage suffered by an employer as a result of the strike may heavily outweigh the cost of granting the workers a few cents more per hour, an act which would have prevented the strike. The fact that a strike took place apparently reflects economic irrationality on both sides.

But is it really so? What would happen for instance if a union, on the grounds of economic rationality, determined never to go on strike, even when an employer refused to meet its demands? In that case the employer would pay no attention to the demands of the union's bargaining representative. Why should he? No penalty or harm would come to him if he did not.

The fact is that to achieve its demands a union must bring pressure to bear upon the employer. The pressure takes the form of a threat to call a strike if he does not comply, and the threat must be a real one. If the employer defies the union, it must be invoked. Otherwise the threat to strike is a hollow bluff to which the employer will pay no attention.

By the same token the employer must be ready to put up with a strike rather than give in to a union's excessive demands. If, on the grounds of economic rationality, he is always prepared to give in in order to avoid a strike, then there is no limit to what the union might ask. Why should the union not ask for more and more? They would get it, and without a strike. If, in negotiating, the employer grimly claims that he is prepared to have a strike rather than accede to the union's demands, he must mean it. If he is only bluffing, and the union becomes aware that he is only bluffing, it will pay no attention to his threat.

It does seem then that some strikes are inevitable. Where the union and management take completely incompatible positions, how is their disagreement to be resolved? Government-sponsored conciliation procedures do manage to bring the two sides together in a good many cases, but not always. When, despite conciliation attempts, disagreement persists, each side must choose between surrender to the other or a fight in which it will itself suffer. If it chooses to surrender tamely then the other side may make exploitive demands. If it threatens to fight rather than surrender, the threat must be a real one. If it is merely a bluff, and the other side knows it, its effect is nil. Hence the logic of circumstance sometimes brings about strikes from which no participant benefits, just as it sometimes brings about, between nations, wars from which no participant benefits.

Plant vs. Industry-Wide Bargaining

Where an industry consists of a number of firms whose employees are all members of the same union, how shall collective bargaining be carried on? Should the union bargain individually with each firm, negotiating a separate contract with each one, or should it bargain at once with all the firms of the industry, negotiating a single contract which will apply uniformly to the entire industry?

From the point of view of both union and management, industry-wide bargaining has important advantages. The union may find it easier to obtain concessions. An individual firm might be unwilling to grant a wage increase if its competitors were not at the same time going to increase the wages of their workers. Negotiation of an industry-wide contract removes the fear of the single firm that, in granting a wage increase, it will incur a competitive disadvantage. Employers, too, may benefit from industry-wide bargaining, and may voluntarily associate for that purpose. A single small employer may be no match for a powerful union. If each firm dealt individually with the union it might be forced to grant very large concessions; if all firms held together they might more successfully oppose the union's demands. Both union and management may achieve important economies through industry-wide bargaining. The number of contracts to be negotiated is greatly reduced; each side can afford to employ highly skilled representatives in the contract negotiations.

Sometimes the contract negotiated by a union with one firm becomes the pattern for subsequent contracts with all other firms in the industry. This is particularly likely to become the case if the firm plays a dominant role in the industry. Some provisions of the contract negotiated with a major firm may in fact be copied in other industries. Thus, in the U.S., the 1950 agreement between General Motors and the United Automobile Workers became the model for subsequent agreements in a good many other industries. In Canada, a formula devised to help settle the strike staged in 1946 against the Ford Motor Company of Canada, has been widely applied in many other Canadian industries.[8]

Labour's Interest in Government Legislation

The policies followed by governments materially affect the welfare of working class people nowadays, as they do indeed of everybody. The federal government's fiscal, monetary, tariff, and defence policies influence the number and type of jobs available in the country, the cost of living, and the extent of tax reductions from wages. Immigration policy will affect the total number of jobs and the degree of competition for certain types of jobs. Welfare legislation, which provides benefits to older persons and disabled persons and grants toward the cost of rearing children, is of special significance to working people whose wages are low. Provincial legislation fixes minimum rates of pay for workers, and requires that provision be made for their safety and convenience. Other provincial labour legislation provides various forms of support to trade unions, enabling them the more effectively to promote the interests of their members.

Understandably, union leaders seek to induce governments to pass legislation which will be favourable to the interests of their members. The benefits derived from favourable legislation may be as significant as the gains achieved through bargaining with individual employers. In addition to demanding legislation of specific interest to

[8]The "Rand formula", proposed by Mr. Justice I. C. Rand of the Supreme Court of Canada, who was called upon to help settle the strike. Under the formula all employees were obliged to pay dues to the union via the "check off," but were not obliged to be or become members of the union. If the union violated the contract in any way, the Company was authorized to withhold dues which it had collected through the "check off." The Rand formula has been widely applied in Canada, except in the province of Quebec, where it was declared illegal by the provincial courts. (A Supreme Court ruling reversed this ruling. In a judgment handed down in 1959, the Supreme Court ruled, with four judges in favour and three dissenting, that the Rand Formula was not contrary to the laws of Quebec.)

labour, trade union leaders have in recent years tended to express their views in regard to broad issues of concern to the nation as a whole. For example, in their capacity of spokesmen for a very large body of Canadian citizens, Canadian trade union leaders repeatedly demanded that the federal government recognize Communist China.

Political Activities: Great Britain and the U.S.

The specific procedures adopted to influence legislation vary from one country to another. In Great Britain the trade union movement has produced its own political arm, the Labour Party, which is one of the country's two great national parties. Its membership is not confined to trade unionists; a great many non-working class persons have been attracted by its programme and some play prominent roles in the party organization.

The trade union movement of the United States has not attempted to form its own political party, nor is it officially committed to the support of either of the major political parties. (However, the majority of working class people are considered to lean toward the Democrats.) Instead, American labour leaders have tended to be politically opportunistic, supporting or opposing individual candidates on the basis of their records in regard to labour legislation, "punishing labour's enemies and rewarding labour's friends".

Political Activities in Canada

From the time that it was formed, in the 1930s, the C.C.F. party received a certain degree of support from organized labour. Among the organizers of the C.C.F. party were several trade unionists who shortly afterwards helped to organize the Canadian Congress of Labour. The Congress officially expressed support for the new political party; a number of the member unions of the Trades and Labour Congress also expressed support for the C.C.F. party, but the T.L.C. organization never did so.

Events took a new turn in 1958, two years after the C.C.L. and the T.L.C. united to form the Canadian Labour Congress. At its convention of that year the new Congress decided to launch discussions with the C.C.F. party with a view to establishing a new political party in Canada which would embrace members of the C.C.F., organized labour, farmers, and all "liberally-minded people." The president of the C.L.C. expressed the view, however, that the C.L.C. should not itself affiliate with the new party; he urged instead that member unions affiliate on an individual basis. The proposal to launch a new political party was realized; at a founding convention held in 1961 the New Democratic Party was brought into being.

City and Provincial Federations

In most countries the trade union movement attempts to influence the policies not only of the federal government, but also of local governments. In Canada, and practice is much the same in other countries, there exist city and provincial federations of labour which include all of the union locals within a particular city and province. Besides sending delegates to conventions of the nation-wide labour Congress, these local federations watch over labour's interests within their particular locality. For example, a city federation will demand that the city government award contracts only to unionized firms; a provincial federation will seek to procure favourable treatment of labour by the provincial legislature.

Graphical Representation

Wages, it has been emphasized, are a type of price, and are determined primarily by the forces of supply and demand. When a union seeks to maintain or improve the wages of its members it must use its power to achieve one or more of the following four objectives:

(1) Reduce the supply of the type of labour furnished by its members.

(2) Increase the demand for this type of labour.

(3) Achieve, through negotiation with the employer, a wage rate which is above the level which would prevail on the basis of the current supply and demand.

(4) Where the equilibrium wage rate is ill-defined, press for the maximum figure the employer is prepared to concede.

Figures 1, 2, 3 and 4 graphically represent the effects achieved by each of these courses of action.

Figure 1 shows the effects of a reduction in supply. In the absence of action by a trade union the supply of the labour performed by its members would be the curve SS. With demand DD the equilibrium price would be BC, and the quantity OB would be employed. The union however restricts the supply to S_1S_1. Accordingly the equilibrium price is B_1C_1 with only the quantity OB_1 being employed.

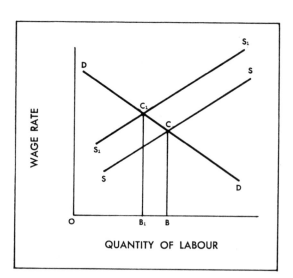

Figure 1.   Effects of a reduction in the supply of labour

Such a restriction of supply could be achieved by a variety of measures, notably the following:

Limiting entry into the union.[9] This might be achieved by setting high initiation fees, by requiring a long period of apprenticeship, or simply by refusing to accept new members.

Limiting the amount of work which a union member might perform. This might be achieved by restricting the hours which a man was authorized to work, or by reducing the effectiveness of his work: a painters' union might order members to use brushes of no more than some specified width.

Opposing immigration to the country of persons who might enter the trade.

Figure 2 shows the effects of an increase in demand. The union applies its power and influence to increase the demand for its members' services from DD to D_1D_1. The equilibrium price becomes therefore Q_1P_1 instead of QP, and the number employed is OQ_1 instead of OQ.

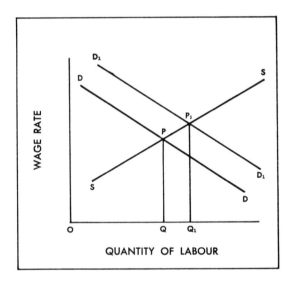

Figure 2.   Effects of an increase in the demand for labour

Such an increase in demand might be achieved by a variety of measures. The union could:

Increase the productivity of its members. This might be achieved by providing them with training courses to increase their proficiency. Alternatively, the union might help an employer to improve the efficiency of his plant; it might even lend

[9]Limiting entry into the union, or limiting the amount of work done by union members, might not effectively reduce the supply of a particular type of labour. If non-union workers could serve just as well, then the union's restrictions would be pointless. They would be really effective only where, to do the work, men had to be members of the union.

him money for the purchase of modern equipment. Worker productivity would rise if the plant were modernized and its efficiency increased; the employer would consequently be able to pay higher wages.[10]

Promote the sale of goods produced by its members. The union might urge an increase in the tariff protecting the industry which employed its members. Or it might urge the public to buy the goods produced by its members. Or it might demand that the government award contracts only to firms which employed its members.

Arrange that specific tasks be performed by its members only. A painters' union might insist that the job of applying preservative to fence posts be reserved for its members. Or the union might "featherbed," insisting that its members be employed at tasks which were quite unnecessary.

Figure 3 shows how a union may, through bargaining power, impose a wage rate which is above the equilibrium level. Here, with demand DD and supply SS, the equilibrium wage rate would be OE, and the number of workers employed would be EX. The union insists that employers pay a wage rate of OF, and the latter sign contracts to this effect. If they have to pay a wage rate of OF, however, employers will hire only FG workers. But there are FH workers who would like to work at this wage; GH of them will be disappointed. Many of these disappointed persons would be prepared to work for less than OF, but employers are forbidden to pay less than this figure. And since employers will hire only FG workers at this wage, the other GH workers will have to look for jobs elsewhere. So far as the union is concerned the ideal result would be achieved if the FG workers who were hired were

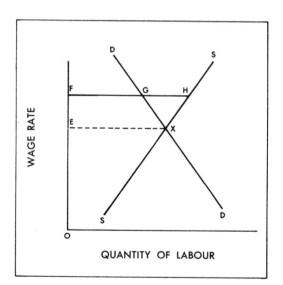

Figure 3.   The wage rate above the equilibrium level

QUANTITY OF LABOUR

WAGE RATE

[10]The International Ladies Garment Workers Union has on occasion extended such assistance to employers.

all its own members, while the GH workers who were disappointed were all non-members. In that case its members would all be employed, at the highest possible wage. It could happen of course that some union men were among those who were not being hired. Such a situation might still be acceptable to the union, provided the number of unemployed members was small. A reduction in the wage rate might induce employers to hire more men, so that all union members could have jobs; but those members who were employed at the high wage might be unwilling to accept anything less.

Where the equilibrium wage rate can only be vaguely estimated, a union may press for the highest figure that the employer is prepared to concede.

In Figure 4 both the demand for labour and the supply are represented by broad bands rather than lines, reflecting uncertainty on the part of an employer as to exactly what the marginal productivity of labour is in his plant, and vagueness on the part of workers as to just what wage rates they will absolutely insist upon. Given this uncertainty on both sides the equilibrium wage rate could be anywhere between XE and XF: OX workers would be prepared to work for as little as XE while the employer feels they might be worth as much as XF to him; the actual wage rate in such a situation would be determined by a bargaining process and could be anywhere between XE and XF.

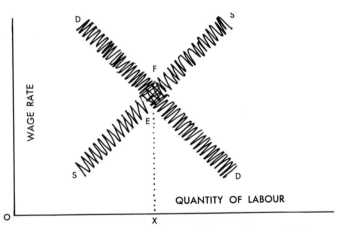

Figure 4.   Wage setting under conditions of uncertainty

UNION ACHIEVEMENTS

Have unions raised wages? Are working people better off than they would be if there were no unions? Superficially the answer seems obvious. During the past century, as the trade union movement firmly established itself and fought for the interests of working people, real wages increased tremendously. It is common knowledge, furthermore, that the members of trade unions generally receive higher wages than do workers who are not so organized.

The Expansion of Output

These facts are not absolutely conclusive, however. It is true that in Western countries working people are, in material things, much better off than were the workmen of times past. But the same is true of all other classes of society. The basic reason for this general increase in material well-being is the enormous increase in national productive capacity. Where a nation produces more, all its citizens can have more.

Have trade unions been responsible for these increases in productive capacity? Hardly if at all. The productive capacity of Western nations has expanded primarily because of the creation of more and superior capital equipment, the introduction of more efficient methods, the improved skill and training of workers, the discovery and exploitation of hitherto untapped natural resources. These developments came about primarily as a result of investment by business firms and by governments, and thanks to innovations carried out and risks run by businessmen and by government authorities. It is true that trade unions have sometimes spurred on business firms to greater efficiency, and that organized labour has campaigned for investment by governments in development projects; but it is also true that at times trade unions have resisted attempts to improve the efficiency of production. It could be argued, therefore, that the contribution of the trade union movement toward the expansion of productive capacity has been minor, or even negative.

On the other hand, it can be claimed that trade union activities have caused available productive capacity to be employed more fully, and to better advantage. Wage increases which unions achieved for their members have increased consumer purchasing power and therefore supported a higher level of output. (Because they also increased costs, wage increases in some instances may have had the opposite effect.) Furthermore, it can be argued that trade unions have desirably affected the *composition* of the national product, causing a larger proportion of productive capacity to be devoted to goods and services which are beneficial to working people. Accordingly, the charge that trade union pressures have caused the aggregate of output to be smaller than could have been achieved, is of limited significance even if true. The curtailment of output may have been primarily in respect to mansions and yachts; large gains in output may have been achieved in respect to public educational and welfare services, together with working men's housing, food, clothing and amenities.

Labour's Share of the National Product

Have unions increased the *share* of the national product which goes to labour? Here, contradictory views are held. According to some investigators, labour's share of the national product has increased significantly during the past generation (earlier figures are not available). According to other researchers, however, labour's share of the national product has remained virtually constant, at about 60 per cent in the United States, and presumably at about the same figure in Canada. Whether labour's share has increased or not during this era of powerful trade unions, we can only speculate as to what it would have been had there been no unions. Quite conceivably, labour's share of the national product would have fallen during the last several decades; in that case the fact that it has actually stayed the same would represent an achievement on the part of trade unions.

It may be plausibly argued that the pressure exerted by the trade union movement was an important factor in bringing about existing social legislation. While benefits conferred by the various pieces of welfare legislation now in effect are not actually part of anyone's wages, they nevertheless contribute importantly to well-being. Since the taxes from which they are financed come largely from higher income groups, and the benefits are realized mainly by lower income groups, such welfare programmes involve a redistribution of the national product in labour's favour. If the trade union movement did in fact help to bring such programmes into being, then it may fairly claim to have increased labour's share of the national product.

That union members generally receive higher pay than non-members in itself proves nothing. Union members are generally skilled tradesmen; unorganized workers are in many cases unskilled, so that with or without unions they would be earning lower pay. It may well be that in the absence of unions the pay of skilled workers would exceed that of unskilled by an even greater margin than exists today. On the other hand there are a good many instances where non-unionized workers receive higher pay *because* unions exist. Some employers, terribly anxious to keep out a union, pay very high wages, in order that their workers will not gain anything by joining a union. Some people who are employed in non-union occupations could easily get jobs in another occupation which is unionized. Since this alternative is available to them, their present employer must pay them wages equivalent to what they could earn in the unionized occupation. Housemaids, who have no union, must be paid very well nowadays, partly because they can readily get jobs at union rates in factories.

Reduction of Wage Differentials

Some writers claim that an important effect of trade union activity has been to reduce wage differentials among different classes of workers. This may well be so. It is entirely probable that regional and skill differentials have been diminished through the actions of trade unions. It is also likely that union organization has reduced or eliminated differentials which would otherwise have existed between the wages of different individuals, within the same trade and in the same locality. With all being paid at a single rate, the superior workman quite probably earns less than he might have done, while the inferior workman may earn more.

Psychological Benefits

There may be doubt as to whether union organization has been a significant factor in the improved material welfare enjoyed by working people. There is absolutely no doubt that unions have brought them major psychological benefits. A union member has the satisfaction of knowing that, through the union, he is able to exercise some control over the wage he is paid and the conditions under which he works. He enjoys security against discriminatory treatment and arbitrary dismissal. He is no longer subject to the caprice or malice of a boss or foreman. He must be treated according to rules which he himself has helped to establish and to which he has agreed. He has the comforting assurance that he is not alone; his fellow workmen stand together with him in a strong fraternal association. These are considerations of the greatest significance. Whether or not union efforts have increased the material welfare of their members in the long run, it is altogether probable that their existence would be justified by the psychological benefits which they confer.

PROBLEMS OF TRADE UNIONISM

Any kind of association is liable to have weaknesses and shortcomings. It may suffer from organizational defects; because of poor leadership it may serve its members poorly. In promoting the interest of its members it may create difficulties for society at large. From such shortcomings trade unions are by no means exempt.

Structural Weaknesses

As in a good many associations only a small minority takes an active interest in the administration of the typical union. Its affairs are likely to be administered in accordance with the views of this minority, and these may not reflect the feelings of the membership at large. In some unions the leader has the authority to make appointments to numerous executive positions. Once he attains leadership it may be practically impossible to unseat him because his supporters control all the strategic offices. In some unions challenges to the leaders' authority may be dangerous for the challenger, or futile.[11] The constitutions of some unions authorize the national leadership to suspend the elected officers of a local, and to appoint a "trustee" to administer the local's affairs. While intended as a purely temporary arrangement, there are instances where such "trusteeship" has been imposed for years.

Bad Leadership

Congressional investigations in the United States have brought to light grave abuses on the part of some union leaders. It has been revealed that some officials have used

---

[11]In some unions a member may be charged with such vague offences as "improper conduct," "disturbing the harmony of meetings," "insubordination" or "just and sufficient cause," and the executive which laid the charges also sits in judgment.

union funds for their own purposes. Others have negotiated "sweetheart" agreements with employers: in return for a bribe from the employer they have agreed to a low rate for union members. In a few unions Communists, practising gangsters, and ex-convicts have attained positions of authority.

Union Pressure on the Employer

Abuses by union leaders of the sort described above are fortunately few, but even responsibly led trade unions will likely create problems for management, and quite possibly for society at large. A strong union in a plant infringes upon the authority of management, and may prevent management from operating the plant in the manner regarded as most advantageous. Union wage demands, featherbedding, and deliberate slowdowns of work may raise production costs, thereby reducing profits and perhaps even endangering the very existence of the firm. Jurisdictional strikes render management the innocent victim of disputes between unions.

Repercussions on the Community

The community at large may be unfavourably affected by trade union activities. A strike which shuts a firm down obliges the public to do without the good or service which the firm normally produces. This deprivation will at best impose inconvenience; at worst, if the strike curtails production of an essential product like milk, or an essential service like railway transportation, the public's health and safety may be endangered.

Inflationary Wage Increases

The gains achieved by unions through collective bargaining may have adverse repercussions on the general public. Unions may act as agents of inflation. The higher wages won for its members by a union may force the employer to raise the price of his product.[12] If the product is an important one in wide use, such as steel, the production costs of the numerous products in which steel is used will rise also, and their prices must rise too.

Unions in other industries will also demand wage increases. As a result of the price increases, the cost of living will have risen and workers in other industries will need higher incomes to maintain their standard of living. They will need wage increases, too, in order to restore the customary relationship between their rates of pay and wage rates in the industry which has won an increase. Union leaders in other industries will be under pressure to win corresponding increases for their members; failure to do so will imply that they are less effective bargainers and, perhaps, ought to be replaced. Union bargaining agents are particularly likely to be successful in

---

[12]Employers may raise prices in fact by more than the increase in labour costs; they may allow for increases in other costs or elect to take advantage of a highly favourable market situation, the wage increase furnishing them with a useful pretext for raising prices.

winning wage increases for their members when inflation already exists or threatens. At such times business tends to be very good and employers, anxious to maintain without interruption their highly profitable operations, are likely to offer little resistance to union wage demands.

But the higher prices which come in the wake of sharp wage increases erode the effects of those increases. Workers whose wages have risen by less than prices have actually become worse off. What is more, rapidly rising prices produce disturbing effects on the national economy, giving rise to distortions in production, inequities in distribution, and a widespread mistrust in the economic system which seriously impairs its overall performance.

In chapter 27, Economic Stabilization by Government Action, we shall deal more fully with the problem of inflationary wage increases, examining other facets of the problem and suggesting ways of dealing with it.

Clouds on the Horizon

The North American trade union movement has made spectacular progress during the past generation; some observers now feel that its progress during the coming years will be a good deal less rapid. There appear to be some sharp rocks on the path ahead.

Public opinion has become very much concerned about the gangsterism and criminality which has been revealed in some American unions. There has been widespread hostility to large wage demands which have had the effect of raising prices, and considerable exasperation induced by strikes which cause severe inconvenience to great numbers of people.

Employers have become less vulnerable to strike threats. In some highly automated plants, a few supervisors can maintain operations for a long time, despite a strike by rank and file employees. Many firms have considerable excess capacity; where a firm is capable of producing a year's supply in nine months, a strike of three months or less will cause very few problems. The firm might slyly welcome such a strike, since it would have to close down for a period anyhow.

Enrolment of new members into unions is becoming more difficult. Automation has reduced the number of "blue collar" jobs in manufacturing and in transportation; the men employed in such jobs have traditionally been among the stalwarts of trade unionism. The same process of automation has produced new jobs—but chiefly for engineers, technicians, white collar workers; such personnel have proven difficult to attract into trade unions. Furthermore, a good many firms, anxious to recruit and retain capable people, voluntarily offer high wages and superior working conditions, without any pressure from unions. What is more, many of the benefits which unions fought for in the past have now been won and are quite generally established; they do not still have to be fought for. In many industries, therefore, there is relatively little that union organization can gain for the workers; a generation ago it could gain a great deal for them.

All this does not mean that unions no longer have a place. It does indicate, however, that serious problems are looming for them on the way ahead. We should not be surprised if they advance less rapidly in the future than they have done in the past, and perhaps in different directions.

SUMMARY

The trade union leader has two broad objectives: to maintain and strengthen the union, and to use the power of the union to promote the interests of its members.

To increase the power of the union, leaders seek legal privileges, assurance of "recognition" by employers, and economic security through the "check off." Unions assist their members by attempting to protect their jobs, to achieve improvements in their pay and working conditions, and to bring about legislation favourable to labour.

Workers bargain collectively with an employer, their union acting as their representative. Where agreement cannot be reached a strike is likely to follow, with harmful effects on both sides.

It is not clear to what extent, if any, labour's increased real income is attributable to union organization. It is indisputable, however, that unions have provided important psychological benefits to workers.

Like any associations, trade unions may be subject to organizational weaknesses. In particular they may become controlled by minority groups which do not really represent the will of the membership at large.

The activities of trade unions may create problems for management and, at times, difficulties for the general public.

FOR REVIEW AND DISCUSSION

1. Illustrating graphically, describe the various means whereby trade unions can use their power to raise the wages of their members.
2. You own a shoe factory in Ontario. The union to which your workers belong demands that you grant a twenty per cent wage increase. What arguments would you advance in opposing that demand?
3. "While superficially it may appear obvious that unions raise wages, the fact is that workers would probably be materially better off today if there were no unions." Comment.
4. "The government should set up a board to mediate all labour disputes, and its judgment should be binding." Do you agree?
5. "Within trade unions the national headquarters has tended to become more important, and the locals less important." What reasons can you suggest for such a tendency?

6. "Strikes by the employees of public utilities should be forbidden." Do you agree?
7. Under conditions of full employment, trade unions are unnecessary. Do you agree?
8. The obligation to join a trade union represents an unwarranted deprivation of a worker's rights and freedom. Do you agree?
9. Countries A, and B each have 8 workers and each has only two industries, X and Y, owned by local businessmen in each case. Labour is the only cost and worker productivity in the two countries is as follows:

In country A

	In Industry X	In Industry Y
The first worker employed produces output worth	$10,000 a year	$8,000 a year
The second worker adds output worth	9,000 "	7,000 "
The third " " " "	8,000 "	6,000 "
The fourth " " " "	7,000 "	5,000 "
The fifth " " " "	6,000 "	4,000 "
The sixth " " " "	5,000 "	3,000 "
The seventh " " " "	4,000 "	2,000 "
The eighth " " " "	3,000 "	1,000 "

In country B

	In Industry X	In Industry Y
The fiirst worker employed produces output worth	$ 6,000 a year	$8,000 a year
The second worker adds output worth	5,000 "	7,000 "
The third " " " "	4,000 "	6,000 "
The fourth " " " "	3,000 "	5,000 "
The fifth " " " "	2,000 "	4,000 "
The sixth " " " "	1,000 "	3,000 "
The seventh " " " "	700 "	2,000 "
The eighth " " " "	500 "	1,000 "

(a) Assuming that there are no restrictions on immigration from one country to another and no costs involved, and that everyone is determined to live where he can earn the highest possible income, what migration would occur between the two countries? What would be the prevailing wage rate in them?

(b) Assuming that migration is not possible between one country and another what will be the prevailing wage rates in the two countries? How would you answer employees of Industry Y in country B who demanded wage parity with their counterparts in country B on the grounds that their productivity was the same?

12   Rent

A Payment for the Use of Property

Rent, as everyone knows, is the price paid to the owners for the use of their property. Land and buildings are the main categories of property for which rent is paid, although machines, furniture, even clothing, are also sometimes rented. Every piece of property has, at any time, its own particular rental rate: wheat land in Saskatchewan may rent currently at $3 per acre a year; a store on Yonge Street in Toronto may rent for $2,000 a month; a suite in a Vancouver apartment block may rent for $275 a month. Why? What decides the rental rate in each case? Why is the tenant willing to pay, and why is the landlord willing to accept the amount paid?

Our answer is given in terms of demand and supply. Since rent is a price, its level must be determined essentially by demand and supply. To understand why rental rates are what they are, we must first of all investigate the nature of the demand and the supply. Sometimes there is intervention designed to prevent market forces from having their full effect. We must accordingly find out what sort of intervention may be carried out, and what consequences it is likely to have.

While in everyday usage the term rent is applied both to payments for the use of land and payments for the use of buildings, equipment and the like, economists have drawn a distinction between the two types. David Ricardo, writing in the early 1800s, defined rent as the price paid for "the use of the original and indestructible powers of the soil." Alfred Marshall, writing a century later, introduced the term "quasi-rent" to refer to the payment made for the use of man-made property.

The basis of the distinction between the payment made for the use of land and that made for the use of buildings or equipment is as follows. Land exists without need for any human effort or sacrifice; properly cared for, it will last forever. The available amount is fixed and cannot be enlarged in response to any increase in price. Buildings and equipment, on the other hand, are produced by human effort and involve a certain degree of sacrifice; to construct them requires resources which could have been used instead to produce consumption goods for immediate enjoyment. The number of man-made structures is not absolutely fixed. They wear out in time and their number may therefore decline; in response to an increase in their price more can be built. (Decreases or increases in their number may take a considerable period of time, of course. Buildings are generally durable, wearing out only after a long lapse of time; to build new ones may require a considerable length of time, particularly if they are large and complicated.)

The statement that the amount of land is "fixed," must be qualified. While the total of all the land in the world is fixed in quantity, the *usable* amount can be increased by human effort. Swamp lands can be drained, arid soils can be irrigated, tree-covered soils can be cleared, land under shallow seas can be diked and the covering water pumped off. When hitherto useless soil has been rendered productive through such human effort, the payment made for its subsequent use represents a return on the investment that has been made. Similarly, where land that is usable in its natural state is improved by drainage, fertilization or terracing, part of the payment made for the use of such land represents a reward for human investment rather than simply payment for "the original and indestructible powers of the soil."

The Rent of Agricultural Land

The farmer who pays rent for agricultural land does so because use of the land enables him to produce a crop which he can sell. The amount of rent he is willing to pay will depend upon the value of the crop and the amount of other expenses he must incur. For land which is better located or more fertile he will be prepared to pay a higher rent, because such land will enable him to produce a more valuable crop with the same expense, or the same crop with less expense. In all likelihood, too, the farmer will find it advantageous to work better land more intensively, that is, to apply more labour, material and equipment to it than he would to inferior land.

The following hypothetical example illustrates the point.

Suppose that there were just three grades of agricultural land. Suppose further that, to produce a crop, only labour need be applied so that wages are the only expense. Finally, to avoid an extraneous complication, suppose that the farmer who hires labourers does not perform any function himself and therefore does not expect any reward for his own services.

On each grade of land the application of labour is characterized by diminishing marginal productivity: each additional worker adds progressively less to output. Table 1 represents the output that might be achieved by working an equal area of each grade of land.

The marginal product of each worker, on each grade of land, would be as shown in Table 2.

Now suppose that the price of the product is $2 per unit and that the prevailing wage rate per worker is $2,000, both figures having been established by the demand and supply situation in their respective markets. Evidently, it would pay to hire two men to work on Grade A land: the first would produce output worth $2,200; the second would be responsible for output worth $2,000—an amount just equal to his wage. Any farmer who rented grade A land could afford to pay $200 a year for it: use of the land enables him, by spending $4,000 on wages, to obtain a crop

Table 1

TOTAL OUTPUT ON THREE GRADES OF LAND, WITH ONE TO FIVE WORKERS EMPLOYED ON EACH GRADE

	Total Output on Grade A Land	Total Output on Grade B Land	Total Output on Grade C Land
With one worker employed	1,100 units	1,000 units	800 units
" two workers "	2,100 "	1,900 "	1,500 "
" three " "	3,000 "	2,700 "	2,100 "
" four " "	3,800 "	3,400 "	2,600 "
" five " "	4,500 "	4,000 "	3,000 "

Table 2

OUTPUT ATTRIBUTABLE TO EACH ADDITIONAL WORKER, ON EACH GRADE OF LAND

	On Grade A Land	On Grade B Land	On Grade C Land
Output due to first worker	1,100 units	1,000 units	800 units
" " second "	1,000 "	900 "	700 "
" " third "	900 "	800 "	600 "
" " fourth "	800 "	700 "	500 "
" " fifth "	700 "	600 "	400 "

worth $4,200. The farmer on grade B land would hire only one man and would not be prepared to pay rent: the crop he realizes has a value just equal to the wages he must pay. Grade C land is sub-marginal; even if it were available free it would not be used, since the crop it grew would be worth less than the wages that would have to be paid.

If the price of the product increased, farmers would produce more, with the increase in output being achieved in two distinct ways. First, land already in use would be worked more intensively; second, hitherto sub-marginal land would be brought under cultivation. Thus suppose the price of the produce rose to $2.50 per unit. In that case it would pay to hire four farm workers on grade A land, and output on such land would increase from 2,100 units to 3,800 units. It would pay as well to hire three men on grade B land so that output there increased from 1,000 units to 2,700 units.[1] Finally, it would pay to cultivate grade C land, employing one man on it; such land would then yield an output of 800 units.

The rental value of grade A land would increase to $1,500: with the application

[1]The fourth man on grade A land and the third man on grade B land are each responsible for an addition to output of 800 units. With a unit selling for $2.50, each of these men adds to the value of output by an amount exactly equal to his wage of $2000.

of labour that cost $8,000, the land would yield a crop worth $9,500 (3,800 × $2.50). Grade B land could now pay rent of $750; grade C land would now be worth cultivating, but no one would pay rent for the use of it.

Canadian experience provides illustration for the foregoing analysis. As a result of the desperate Allied need for our foodstuffs during World War I, the price of wheat rose sharply in 1915. Canadian farmers thereupon worked their land more intensively and brought into cultivation a good deal of land which hitherto had been sub-marginal. The rental value and sale price of good land rose steeply.[2]

Location as a Factor in Rent

If all land is of equal quality, but some is closer to the market, then obviously the better located land will command a higher rent. The same output can be achieved on this land with less transportation cost; the use of such land will be worth more.

An improvement in transportation will tend to increase the value of land that is distant from the market. With transportation costs reduced, there will be a reduction in the expense involved in cultivating this land and marketing its product; use of the land becomes more valuable. Furthermore, an improvement in transportation is likely to render it worthwhile to cultivate land which was hitherto unusable because of prohibitive transportation costs.

When new land is brought into use because of an improvement in transportation, rent is likely to fall on land near the market that was already being cultivated. This effect comes about by repercussion rather than direct impact. The products of the new land, added to the market supply, cause the prices of such products to fall. Any land on which these products were already being grown, declines in market value. Of this proposition British experience furnishes illustration. During the last quarter of the nineteenth century, immense areas of land suitable for cereal cultivation were opened up throughout the world as railroads drove into the continental interiors of North and South America, Australia, Russia and India, while steamships linked their seaboards to the ports of Europe. From all these vast and fertile plains a flood of wheat, cheaply grown and cheaply transported by railway and steamship, poured into the markets of Europe. In Britain, where no tariff barriers stood in the way, wheat prices fell to record lows. The rental value of English wheat land declined heavily; a great deal of such land was shifted to other products and some was taken out of agricultural use altogether.

Changes in Technology or Wage Rates

An improvement in agricultural implements or methods is likely to cause an increase in the value of agricultural land. If because of technological advance the same crop

---

[2]As shown later in the chapter, the capital value of any property depends upon the return it promises to yield to its owner in the future. An increase in the annual rental value of a piece of agricultural land, as in the above illustrations, would raise the price at which it would be sold outright.

can be obtained with less expense than before, then obviously the land is worth more to the farmer. A change in wage rates will also affect the value of the agricultural land: an increase in wages would tend to lower rental value; a decrease would tend to raise rental value.

"Shifting" of Land to Other Uses

While the total of all land is fixed, the amount that can be used for any particular purpose is not. The area of land used to grow wheat, for instance, could be increased by sowing to wheat land which previously had been sown to coarse grains or left in pasture. Similarly, the amount of wheat land could be reduced by shifting some to other uses.

Such shifts from one use to another are caused by changes in the rent that could be paid by different users. Thus if a large city arose in the middle of a wheat growing area, the value of fresh vegetables which could be grown near the city might greatly exceed the value of wheat grown on the same land. Market gardeners would offer to pay higher rents than wheat farmers and land would be "shifted" from wheat farming to market gardening. Not all land might be so shifted, of course. There would likely be a limit to the amount of land that could economically be devoted to market gardening. If too much land were used for this purpose the price of fresh vegetables would fall to very low levels and market gardeners might find themselves unable to pay as much rent as wheat farmers.

Rent: A Cost to the Individual Farmer

While land is a free gift of nature, it is by no means free to the individual who would like to have the use of it. Any land which will be useful to him is likely to be useful to other people as well. They will be prepared to pay a rent for the land corresponding to the value to them. The individual who does get the land must pay the owner a rent at least equal to what the owner was offered by others. So far as that individual is concerned the rent he pays is one of his costs; if he does not pay it he does not get the land. While it is true that, for the country as a whole, land is a free gift of nature, any individual must pay for its use. The amount that he pays will reflect the value of the land in the alternative uses to which it could be put. The money is paid to the owner, not for any function that he performs, but simply because of his ownership rights.

The Rent of Urban Land

Urban land varies in quality, the differences being based solely on location. The best commercial land is that in the downtown area where crowds are largest and where stores, shops and offices therefore have the largest possible market. Commercial land located away from the downtown area tends to be less valuable; the small number of passers-by provide a meagre market. The best residential land is that located in some scenic spot or conveniently accessible to the downtown area. Some land is "choice" simply because fine homes have already been built in the vicinity.

We saw how better agricultural land will be used more intensively; so it is with better urban land. On the most valuable downtown sites the tallest commercial buildings tend to be built; on the choicest residential land are built the costliest homes and apartment blocks. The explanation corresponds to the reason for intensive use of agricultural land. Capital applied to a downtown site is extremely productive; only after a very great deal of it has been applied does the product of the marginal unit equal its cost. Accordingly, a large amount of capital should be applied; in other words, a large building should be built. Capital applied to a choice residential site is similarly productive and, in the form of a large and costly residence, should be abundantly applied.

Quasi-Rent

The rent of a building may be more or less than is required to pay its construction cost and furnish the owner with an appropriate return on his investment. If it is less, it will be because investment, once made, cannot be withdrawn. A building cannot be "un-built." The materials cannot be recovered and restored to their original condition; the labour that put them together cannot be taken back and used elsewhere. Once built, the rent of a building will be determined by its productivity, by the value it has to prospective tenants. The highest rent which the landlord can expect to charge will be the productivity of the building when employed in its most productive use. This market-determined rental rate may turn out to be a good deal lower than was anticipated, and the owner may, during the entire lifetime of the building, receive a rent insufficient to cover its construction cost and provide a reasonable return on the investment involved.

On the other hand, thanks to the prevailing market situation, the rent of a building may exceed the amount required to cover its construction cost and yield a fair return. Because the market supply cannot be quickly increased, landlords may enjoy these inappropriately large rents for some considerable time. However, their good fortune will not last forever. The high profitability of this type of building will induce other people to construct others like it; once these are erected, the larger quantity available will force rents down. But until the additional buildings are built— and the interval may sometimes be long—owners of existing buildings will enjoy abnormally large earnings on their investment.

Thus at any given time the rental rate of buildings would be determined by demand in relation to a quantity that was temporarily fixed. The returns received by owners would resemble the rent of land, which is determined by demand in relation to a permanently fixed quantity. For this reason such returns have been designated "quasi-rents." In the long run, of course, given the lapse of enough time for existing buildings to wear out or for new ones to be built, the quantity of buildings will become such that owners receive an appropriate return on investment—no more and no less.

Changes in Construction Costs

A rise or fall in construction costs will affect the rentals of existing buildings. If construction costs rise, rentals of existing buildings will tend to rise. New buildings, constructed at higher cost, will require higher rents than those which would provide an adequate return on older buildings built at lower cost. If the new buildings are needed to meet the demand which exists, the people who wish to occupy them will have to pay this higher rent. If the older properties serve tenants' needs just as well as do the newer properties, then people will be willing to pay just as much rent for them as they are required to pay for accommodation in new buildings.

A fall in construction costs, if it ever occurred, would lead to a decline in rents. The owners of new buildings would be prepared to accept lower rents than those required in older buildings. A tenant naturally would refuse to pay high rent for accommodation in an old building when he could obtain the same kind of accommodation at a lower rent in a new building. Since any number of new buildings could be built, every tenant would have the opportunity of renting space in a new building; owners of old buildings would only attract tenants if they offered their premises at the same low rentals as were being asked by the owners of new buildings.

Market Imperfections

Our analysis of rent has been based upon a number of key assumptions. It was taken for granted that there would always be a large number of tenants bidding for any property, that both tenants and landlords would always be fully informed, and that they would always be guided by purely economic considerations. These assumptions do not always fit the facts. There may be only a limited number of bidders for a particular property; in such a case a tenant may pay rent considerably lower than the value of the property to him. Suppose that Morrison and Smith are the only two people interested in renting a certain building. Use of the building may be worth $15,000 a year to Morrison, but only $10,000 a year to Smith. In that case Morrison may be able to rent the building for as little as $10,000, no more than the landlord could have got from the only other possible tenant.

Tenants may, through ignorance or inertia, pay more rent than is being charged for equally good accommodation elsewhere. Landlords may ask for less than they could get. They may not realize how much rent they could charge, or they may employ some rule of thumb to determine the rental rate; the resulting figure may fit poorly. Landlords may, on non-economic grounds, let a tenant have a bargain. The rents stipulated in long leases may, after a time, cease to correspond to the current rental value of the premises; market conditions may have changed drastically, and the rental value established when the lease was negotiated may have become unrealistic.

Rent Controls

For many families the payment of rent requires a large fraction of their income. Any substantial increase in rent would bring considerable hardship to them. Hence governments have in the past taken action to prevent sharp increases in rent. During emergencies such as in wartime, the demand for accommodation may increase greatly, while the quantity available remains the same or even decreases. Inevitably rents tend to rise sharply. At such times governments have intervened to limit rent increases or prevent them altogether.

Such action laudably prevents bloated landlords from squeezing more money from helpless tenants. We must temper our approval, however. In our society the price of a commodity, as we saw in Chapter 3, performs three distinct functions. First, it constitutes the income of the seller. Second, it determines who shall get the available supply: this goes to the people who are able and willing to pay the price. Third, price influences future output: a high price tends to induce an increase in production; a low price tends to bring about a decrease in production.

When the government limits rents, it does more than merely prevent rich landlords from exploiting poor tenants. It affects the way property is used; it makes it possible for property to be used to less than best advantage. Suppose, for instance, that the rent of a certain suite is fixed by the government at $75.00 per month, all that the present occupant is prepared to pay. Suppose that someone else needs the suite badly and would be willing to pay $100 per month for it. If there were no controls he would offer $100 and get the suite. But with controls in effect the suite remains occupied by the person to whom it is worth only $75. The would-be tenant may be obliged to live in adequate and unsatisfactory quarters because the rent controls prevent him from obtaining the suite he needs at a rent he is quite prepared to pay.

During wartime the lack of labour and materials may render it impossible to build new housing. Under such conditions the de-control of rent could not possibly bring about an increase in the quantity of housing available. However, once the war is over shortages of labour and materials come to an end. But new rental housing will be built only if it promises to be profitable, only if prospective rents are sufficiently high to cover construction costs and yield an appropriate return to the investor. If, by government order, rents are held below this level, additional housing will not be built. The controls turn out to be self-perpetuating; they cause the shortage of housing to continue and therefore the need for controls.

It may well be that at certain times, rent controls are absolutely necessary; the good they do exceeds greatly the harm. But we should be alert to changes in the situation which cause this balance to be reversed. Because of rent controls, available property may be mis-allocated and desirable new construction may be inhibited. These disadvantages may become so serious as to render undesirable the continuance of controls. Or, if the controls must be maintained, supplementary measures should be undertaken to allocate property appropriately, and to provide incentive for new construction. Otherwise, the remedy perpetuates the disease.

Economic Rent

Payment is made to any factor of production to induce it to provide its services. Because the supply may be very limited while the demand is very strong, the payment made to some factors may be greater than is necessary to induce them to provide their services. This excess is known as "economic rent." Thus a man may be willing to work at a certain job for $10,000 a year; because of keen demand for his services he may be paid $15,000; in that case it would be said that he was receiving economic rent of $5,000 per year.

Rent and Capital Value

Any rental property which yields a net income to its owner (the net income being the annual rent less expenses) has a capital value. Strictly speaking, this capital value will consist of the present worth of all the future net revenue, discounted according to the current rate of interest. Thus, if a piece of agricultural land yielded an annual net income to its owner of $1,000, and the rate of interest was five per cent, then the capital value of the land would be $20,000. Ownership of the land yields the same income as would $20,000 invested at the prevailing interest rate, and is therefore equivalent to the possession of $20,000. A rise in the annual net income yielded by the land would bring a proportionate increase in the capital value; e.g. if the net income rose to $1,500 a year, the value of the property would become $30,000.[3]

The capital value of a building which has only a limited lifetime can be calculated in the same general way. If the net income realized by the owner of a building amounted to $2,000 a year, and the building was expected to last 25 years, then the building's value would be the present worth of $2,000 received in each of the next 25 years, discounted according to the current rate of interest. If the interest rate were five per cent, this would amount to exactly $28,192. In reality, the calculation of the value of a piece of property would never be so precise. Its future net income would depend on the level of rentals in the future and the size of future expenses; these could only be roughly estimated. The better the estimate proves to be, the closer will the price paid for a property approach its true value.

SUMMARY

Rent is the price paid to owners for the use of their property. The amount paid will reflect the productivity of the property, which in turn will depend upon the value of the output achieved and the cost of other productive factors employed.

The amount of rent will vary from one property to another in accordance with differences in their productivity. While the rent of land may rise indefinitely, the rent

---

[3]A change in the rate of interest would also affect the capital value of the property. See Chapter 13.

of buildings will in the long run tend to be equal to a reasonable return on the capital investment involved in such buildings. In the short run, the rent of a building may be substantially more or less than this figure.

Rent controls designed to protect tenants against exploitation may have the undesirable consequence of preventing optimum use of property and deterring new construction.

Owing to market imperfections, the actual rent paid for a piece of property may not correspond closely with its productivity.

Any property which yields an income to its owner will have a capital value. This value will be determined by the size of the income derived, its distribution through time, and the prevailing rate of interest.

FOR REVIEW AND DISCUSSION

1. A tax on rent is preferable to a sales tax or profits tax because it will interfere less with production. Do you agree?
2. Rent is absolutely unearned, and should therefore be confiscated by taxation. Comment.
3. Under Socialism there would be no such thing as rent? Do you agree?
4. A suburban clothing store advertises that it can sell more cheaply than downtown stores because it is out of the "high rent district." Does this claim accord with economic principles?
5. "One reason farmers need higher prices for their products is because they have to pay such high rents." Would you agree with such an argument?
6. The rent of apartments may be too low for a long time, but is unlikely to be too high for very long. Why should this be so?
7. Make up:
   (a) a hypothetical demand schedule for apartment accommodation on a site close to the central business district of a large Canadian city.
   (b) a hypothetical demand schedule for apartment accommodation on a site in a distant suburb of the same city.
   Making appropriate assumptions regarding construction costs, prove by reference to your hypothetical demand schedules that it would be wise to build a bigger apartment block on the central site than on the suburban site.
8. (a) Argue the pros and cons of the following declaration:
   "One of the surest ways to bring down the price of single family housing in Toronto is to extend the subway system well beyond the present built-up area."
   (b) Subsidization of a public transit system out of local property taxation is likely to have different effects on different types of property: some will be favourably affected; other unfavourably. Explain.

(a) Rent controls are obviously helpful to the occupants of properties that are subject to control; they are harmful to others, however. Who is adversely affected by rent controls? Take into account both long run and short run considerations.

(b) The land speculator, whose motives are entirely selfish, may at times serve a useful social purpose. Do you agree? Justify your answer.

9. An increase in the wages of building tradesmen will have an influence on the value of all existing buildings but the effect will be far from uniform. Thus for instance the consequences for recently constructed buildings will not be the same as for old buildings in a poor state of repair. Explain, giving appropriate hypothetical examples.

10. A haberdasher and his partner consider whether or not to hire an additional salesman; they agree that it would not pay them to do so unless they moved first to larger premises. Make up your own example to demonstrate how the employment of another salesman in their present store would reduce profits while he would increase profits if he were employed in a larger store. Make sure to incorporate the principle of diminishing marginal productivity in your example.

13   Interest

THE PRICE OF LOANS

Interest is the price paid for the loan of money. A borrower typically undertakes to pay back more than the amount he has borrowed, the extra payment being interest. But why should a borrower be willing to repay more than he has borrowed? Why should a lender be able to insist on being repaid more than the amount of his loan?

Our explanation proceeds along lines now familiar. Since interest is a price, it must be determined by the forces of demand and supply; to understand what determines the rate of interest we must ascertain the nature of the demand and the supply. The broad outline of our explanation can be briefly set forth. The demand for loans is comprised of three main elements: the demand of consumers, the demand of businessmen, the demand of governments. The supply of loans comes from three main sources: money saved out of income by individuals, money retained by firms as depreciation allowance and undistributed profit, money created by the agencies legally endowed with the authority to create it.[1] Let us examine in turn each of these components of the demand and the supply of loans.

Consumer Borrowing—Time Preference

Smith would like to buy a car that sells for $2,400. He does not have that much money now, but could lay away $100 a month. Two years of saving would enable him to buy a car. But he does not want to wait two years; he would like to have that car right away. He feels what the economists refers to as "time preference." If someone would lend him $2,400 so that he could buy the car immediately, he would gladly undertake to hand over to the lender $100 a month for the next three years. He is willing to undertake to repay not just the $2,400 loan, but an extra $1,200 in addition. It is worth that extra money to him to have the use of the car immediately, instead of having to wait two years.

---

[1]A government which achieves a budget surplus may use its extra funds to purchase securities, thereby contributing to the supply of loans. Government surpluses occur irregularly and infrequently, however, and are usually small.

Different people have different degrees of time preference. Mulligan may be so impatient to have a car right away that he would agree to pay $150 a month for three years to anyone who would lend him the $2,400 he needs to buy it immediately. McDougall, however, does not believe in borrowing. He will buy a car only when he has saved up the price. He is quite prepared to wait.

Instalment buying constitutes a form of consumer borrowing. The purchaser of a good on the instalment plan in effect borrows the price from the seller, and undertakes to pay him back at a specified rate. A house mortgage represents a type of consumer borrowing. The buyer of a house borrows from the mortgage company the money he needs to pay for the house and undertakes to repay the loan, with interest, over a specified period of time.

The volume of consumer borrowing will vary in accordance with prevailing attitudes and customs, and with economic conditions. In European countries the tradition is strong that a person should buy only those goods for which he can pay in cash. In North America, on the other hand, there has long existed a widespread willingness to buy on the instalment plan. Prosperous conditions and the expectation of continuing prosperity, generally increase people's willingness to incur debt in order to buy goods. They expect to earn easily in the future the money they will need to meet their debt obligations. The expectation of inflation supports instalment buying because goods purchased right away are cheaper than they will be if bought later. Inflation, furthermore, will reduce the real value of money, and the money paid in future instalments will be worth less than money is worth today. The person who pays with future money, so to speak, pays with cheaper money.

The extent of the demand for large and costly (and usually durable) consumer goods will affect the scale of consumer borrowing. If people bought only such things as food, clothing and entertainment services, which can be bought in small quantities, they would be able to make all purchases out of current income. However, such major and costly items as houses, automobiles, furniture and appliances cannot generally be paid for out of current income. They have to be paid for out of the income of a considerable period; they must be saved up for over a long period, or, if bought on credit, the debt can only be repaid over a lengthy period. Where the purchase of such costly goods bulks large in consumer spending, as it does in North America, we are likely to find that consumer saving and consumer borrowing is correspondingly large.

Business Borrowing—The Productivity of Capital

Businessmen borrow money primarily because they expect to invest it productively. Characteristically, they propose to purchase with the borrowed money capital goods which will enable them to produce saleable output. They anticipate that the value of this output will exceed all the costs involved; the excess of the value produced over its cost will represent the productivity of the capital asset they propose to acquire. This return will be received by the owner of the asset. The businessman is prepared to pay interest for the money which enables him to acquire it, and thereby to gain the revenue it yields.

Thus suppose that a businessman calculated that the use of a certain machine will enable him to produce $40,000 worth of goods a year. Suppose that the machine costs $100,000, and will last exactly ten years. Suppose further that each year $15,000 worth of materials will be used up, and that $7,000 will have to be spent on labour to operate, service and maintain the machine. If the businessman borrowed the $100,000 needed to buy the machine, he could repay the loan and could pay interest as well. In each year of the machine's lifetime he would be taking in $40,000 in sales receipts, while spending only $22,000 in labour and materials. Out of the $18,000 left over he could set aside $10,000 toward repayment of the loan, leaving a surplus of $8,000 a year. This figure represents the net productivity of the machine, the value which it produces over and above what is required to meet all expenses, including its own cost.

It will be because of this return of $8,000 a year which the machine yields that the businessman will be able and willing to pay interest on the $100,000 loan. If someone agreed to lend him $100,000 at say 5% interest, the businessman would be happy to borrow. After meeting all his expenses, including principal and interest payments, he would have a handsome sum each year for himself. At the end of the first year, after paying over to the lender a $10,000 instalment on the principal plus $5,000 in interest, he would be left with $3,000. At the end of the second year he would be left with even more; the principal outstanding having been reduced to $90,000, he would now have to pay only $4,500 in interest. Each successive year the principal outstanding would decline by a further $10,000, reducing his interest by a further $500. At the end of 10 years, when the machine was quite worn out, he would have paid a total of $27,500 in interest, so that his return for the period would have amounted to $52,500 ($80,000-$27,500).

Through applying his own time and effort a person may be able to build a useful machine or a productive organization. If he is to do this he must have funds to support himself while he is applying his efforts to the task of creating the productive property. Money which he borrows for this purpose serves essentially the same purpose therefore as money borrowed to purchase plant and equipment, and interest will be paid out of the returns yielded by the productive property which is created by the borrower's efforts.

Government Borrowing

In our chapter on Public Finance we shall consider the subject of government borrowing in some detail. Suffice to say here that its government is the agency through which any community handles its affairs, and that borrowing by a government means simply borrowing by the community as a whole. A community is, after all, just like a giant family; we shall find that governments borrow for much the same reasons as do private individuals and families. Their revenues sometimes fall short of what they need to cover current requirements; they may suddenly need very large sums to cope with an emergency; they may wish to carry out large and durable projects which cannot be financed out of current income.[2]

The Market Demand for Loans

The aggregate demand for loans in any country will be the sum of the three categories referred to in the foregoing pages—the demands of the general public, of business firms, and of governments.[3] The total demand for loans will at any given time reflect the prevailing degree of consumers' time preference, the productivity of capital as anticipated by businessmen, the budget position of governments and their anxiety to equip their respective communities with large and durable public facilities. Presumably the demand will have some degree of elasticity: if the rate of interest rises, the amount people wish to borrow is likely to fall. Consumers with low time preferences will not pay high interest charges in order to have something sooner rather than later. Businessmen who anticipate only low productivity from new investment will not borrow the money needed for the investment if the rate of interest is high. Governments will hesitate to embark on large projects if the money for them must be borrowed at high rates which will heavily burden future taxpayers. At a low rate of interest, on the other hand, more money will be borrowed. Because finance charges are lower more people may buy on the instalment plan. If they can borrow money cheaply, businessmen will be prepared to undertake even ventures which promise relatively low returns. Governments will undertake public projects of fairly low priority.

Accordingly, the market demand schedule for loans at any given time is likely to have the characteristics of any normal demand schedule. As the price falls, the quantity demanded will tend to increase; as the price increases, the quantity demanded will tend to decline. As we shall see in Chapter 27, however, the degree of elasticity in the demand for loans is likely to be rather small. The desire to borrow, whether by consumers, businessmen, or governments, is affected by many considerations; the rate of interest is only one of them and generally a small one at that. Hence while a change in the rate of interest will have some effect on the desire to borrow, the effect is likely to be limited. The elasticity of demand for loans is likely to be low.

As any other demand schedule may do, the demand schedule for loans may shift about from one time to another. Changing desires and anticipations will bring about such shifts. Thus during a particular period of time consumers' time preference may be very strong, many businessmen may anticipate large returns from new

[2]At times governments may borrow for other reasons. As we shall see in Chapter 27, a government may deliberately spend more than its income, borrowing the difference, in order to counter a business depression. Furthermore, when inflationary pressure is very strong—such as in wartime —a government may borrow from its people not just because it needs the money, but because it wants them not to spend it.

[3]This aggregate may include the demand of foreigners—of foreign individuals, firms and governments.

investment, governments may be under strong pressure to spend more than they receive in revenue or to build costly projects which can be financed only by borrowing. At such a time the desire to borrow will be very strong, and sharp increases in the rate of interest will exercise relatively little deterrence. At other times all these attitudes and expectations may be reversed, so that even a very low rate of interest tempts few to borrow.

The Supply of Loans

The money that is loaned to borrowers is provided chiefly by private individuals and business firms. In the case of individuals, the money they lend out is money which they received as income but which, for various possible reasons, they have chosen not to spend. Some people save in order to spend at a later date; their time preference is negative. Some people save because they see nothing they are tempted to buy; they save by default, so to speak. Some people save because they have been brought up to believe that saving is prudent and virtuous; they save not to achieve any particular objective but to live righteously.

Business firms, too, acquire funds which they can lend out. Firms generally put some portion of their receipts into depreciation allowances, toward the cost of replacing present plant and equipment when they wear out. Until this money is actually spent on replacements it is available to be loaned out. Furthermore, corporations often do not pay out their full earnings in dividends to shareholders; they retain a portion to build up a reserve out of which to cover possible losses or to finance large expenditures anticipated in the future. This money, too, can be loaned out.

New Money from the Banking System

As we shall see in later chapters, the banking system of a country can create money. When it does, the new money brought into existence becomes part of the country's supply of loanable funds, augmenting the supply drawn from the savings of persons and firms.

Liquidity Preference

Individuals—and firms too—will not necessarily be prepared to lend out all the money they have saved. There are advantages to keeping one's savings in the form of cash; whoever lends out his savings sacrifices these advantages.

Economists point out two primary reasons why people should prefer to hold cash rather than lend it (or buy bonds with it). First, the *transactions motive*:[4] any-

---

[4] A supply of cash on hand may enable a person to meet unforeseen emergencies more effectively. Some economists consider this a distinct reason for holding cash, referring to it as the "precautionary motive." However, the transactions motive could be considered to relate to unforeseen as well as anticipated expenditures, and is so interpreted here.

one who expects to make purchases in the near future will want to have on hand the cash he will need to make the required payments. Second, the *speculative motive*: a person who uses his savings to buy bonds may suffer loss as a result of a decline in their value. It is true that he will receive interest, but the value of a bond may drop by more than the interest paid on it. A person who pays $100 for a 4 per cent bond which after one year declines to $95, would have been better off if he had just held his cash. Anyone who expects such a decline to occur will keep his savings in cash.

Because of the transactions motive and the speculative motive many people feel what the economist calls *liquidity preference*: they prefer to keep their savings in cash. If someone wishes to borrow their savings he must compensate them for giving up the advantages involved in having savings in the form of cash. The compensation is interest: interest can be regarded as the payment made to savers for their sacrifice of liquidity preference.

The Equilibrium Rate of Interest

As with any price, prevailing demand and supply will determine the equilibrium rate of interest at any given time: changes in either will cause the equilibrium to shift. The demand for loans will be large when consumers wish to buy a great deal on credit, when businessmen wish to invest heavily in plant and equipment, when governments borrow heavily to finance budget deficits or major public works programmes. The supply of money for loan will be large when incomes are high, when individuals have a strong desire to save, when business firms are accumulating large depreciation allowances and undistributed profits, when the banking system is creating new money, when savers have low liquidity preference and are quite willing to lend their money or to buy bonds. Change in any of these determining elements will affect the equilibrium rate of interest.

The Element of Risk

We have established that *even if a lender is fully repaid* he nevertheless sacrifices, during the period of the loan, the advantage of holding cash as opposed to holding someone's bond or I.O.U. For this sacrifice he must have compensation. There is yet another burden which he bears during the period of the loan; *he runs the risk that the borrower will not repay.* For enduring this risk he must receive additional compensation, over and above that which he requires as reward for exchanging liquid cash for an illiquid bond or I.O.U. The size of this compensation for risk-taking will vary according to the degree of risk involved in the loan.

All loans are not equally risky. A loan to the federal government is absolutely safe; no special compensation need be paid to persons who make such loans on the grounds that they are running the risk that they will not be repaid. A loan to a private firm or even to a provincial or municipal government, is not completely safe, however. There is a possibility, even in the case of provincial and municipal governments, that they will not be able to raise the money needed to pay off debt. The possibility of default is generally stronger in the case of private firms; it could easily happen that earnings fall short of the amount required to repay debt. Hence we find not just a single interest rate in a loan market at any time but a whole hierarchy of interest rates, with a different rate being paid for each different type of loan, according to the degree of risk involved in each case. Broadly speaking, one would say that in Canada the interest rate on federal government bonds represents the "pure" rate of interest; the rate on any other security is greater than this figure by a premium which reflects the degree of risk involved. Shifts in the demand and supply of loans cause this whole hierarchy of interest rates to move up or down together.

Long Term and Short Term Loans

Different loans are made for different periods of time. Banks may lend money to stock brokers for just a few hours; loans to governments sometimes provide for repayment only after half a century. Characteristically the rate of interest expected by lenders will be affected by the duration of the loan, higher rates being typically demanded for loans of longer term. For the longer the time period of a loan, the greater is the likelihood that the lender will suffer inconveniences through not having his cash. Furthermore, the greater becomes the possibility that something will happen which will render it impossible for the borrower to repay. Hence a higher rate of interest is normally called for on longer loans because the risk and the sacrifice of liquidity are both greater.[5]

Financial Intermediaries

In the last several pages we have described the supply of loans in terms of the amount of cash which individual savers are willing to lend to borrowers. This picture must now be qualified. The fact is that a great many people do not lend their savings directly to borrowers; instead they entrust their savings to financial institutions, and it

---

[5]On the other hand, the person who is anxious to keep his money invested may accept a lower rate of interest on long term loans than he would on short term. Lending for short periods only would require him to negotiate new loans repeatedly. By lending at long term he avoids the trouble and inconvenience involved in negotiating loans at frequent intervals; accordingly, he may be quite prepared to accept a lower rate of interest on long term loans than can be obtained on short term ones.

A lender may believe, furthermore, that the rate of interest on loans is currently higher than normal, and that it will therefore soon fall. In that case, too, he would be prepared to accept a lower rate of interest on a long term loan than he could get on a short term loan. *Example*: Suppose that the rate of interest, on a loan of one year's duration, is currently seven per cent. Suppose further that a lender anticipates that, within a year, the rate of interest on such loans will drop to three per cent, and will stay there. In that case he would be quite happy to make a 10 year loan to someone at an interest rate of five per cent. During the first year of such a loan he would admittedly be getting only five per cent on his money when he could have been getting seven per cent; but in the remaining nine years of the loan he will still be getting five per cent, when otherwise he would be getting only three per cent.

is the latter which actually lend the money to borrowers. In North America the institutions which chiefly perform this role of financial intermediary are the commercial banks, the life insurance companies, the trust and investment companies. The banks each year receive enormous amounts of savings lodged with them for convenience and safe-keeping. The life insurance companies each year also take in vast sums in the form of premium payments on policies. Only a portion of these payments represents the price of the actual insurance provided; the remainder constitutes a form of saving by the policy holders. Trust companies, which manage the estates of deceased persons, control huge amounts of capital. Investment syndicates nowadays take in large amounts of personal savings entrusted to them by private individuals, to be invested by their expert staffs.

The supply of funds to borrowers at any given time depends not merely upon the attitudes of the people who have saved the money, but also upon the attitudes of the firms to which they have entrusted their savings. Whether the administrators of these firms are currently cautious or liberal will affect the aggregate of funds offered to borrowers at any given time. Furthermore, the financial firms have very broad discretionary powers in regard to the disposition of the savings in their custody. Subject only to the provisions of their charters and relatively light government restrictions, they are able to decide for what purpose and to whom they will lend the money entrusted to them. Hence the supply of funds offered to any particular class of borrowers will depend heavily upon the attitudes of the financial intermediary institutions.

"Stickiness" of the Market Rate of Interest

In the preceding sections of this chapter we indicated what factors determine the demand and supply of loanable funds, and therefore the equilibrium rate of interest. However, the equilibrium rate is not necessarily the market rate, the rate actually paid by borrowers. As we learned in Chapter 4, the market price of a good may be deliberately held above or below the equilibrium figure. This may be done with the rate of interest too: despite changes in the demand and supply of loanable funds, the market rate of interest may remain the same, with results similar to those produced by any disequilibrium situation. Thus, suppose the demand for funds becomes very strong in relation to the supply. In a freely adjusting market, the interest rate would rise sharply, ultimately reaching such a height that many people would lose their desire to borrow. The limited funds available would be loaned out only to the people who were willing to pay the high rate. Because of the reduction in the number of would-be borrowers, the volume of loans demanded would not exceed the volume of loans offered; every borrower who was willing and able to pay the high market rate of interest would be able to obtain the loan he wanted.

With the rate of interest held rigid, however, the deterrent effect of a high rate is not brought into play. A situation develops comparable to that which emerges when the government imposes a price ceiling on some commodity. At the prevailing interest rate borrowers wish to borrow more than the banks have available to lend. The banks are accordingly obliged to refuse loans to people who are quite willing to pay the interest asked. Just which fortunate persons or firms do get loans from the banks will now depend upon other considerations than mere willingness to pay the bank's interest charges.

A fall in the demand for loans, relative to supply, may not induce an appreciable reduction in the bank rate of interest. We are likely to find, however, that banks adopt other measures designed to attract borrowers. Potential borrowers are canvassed more aggressively; special services and facilities are offered at no extra charge; less impressive security may be required. An increase in lending may thereby be achieved, without a reduction in the rate of interest charged.

THE INTEREST RATE AND PROPERTY VALUES

In Chapter 12, on Rent, we saw that any property which yields a net income will have a capital value. This capital value will consist of the sum of the present values of all future net income, discounted according to the current rate of interest. Thus a property which would yield an annual net income of $2,000 for 25 years would, when the rate of interest was five per cent, have a capital value of $28,192.

The capital value of the property will be affected markedly by changes in the rate of interest. The higher the rate of interest, the higher will be the discount on future receipts, and the lower therefore will their present value be. A low rate of interest will mean a low discount rate and correspondingly high present value of future income. Hence the capital value of any income-yielding property will vary inversely with the rate of interest. If the rate of interest were seven per cent, a property which yields a net income of $2,000 per year for 25 years would have a capital value of $23,307; with the rate of interest 3%, the same property will be worth $34,826.

SUMMARY

Interest is the price paid for the loan of money, taking the form of a percentage of the amount of the loan.

Being a price, interest is determined primarily by demand and supply considerations. The demand comes from consumers who wish to borrow on account of "time preference," from businessmen who wish to borrow for investment purposes on account of the productivity of capital, and from governments when it is inexpedient to raise needed funds by taxation.

The supply of loans comes mostly from individual and corporate saving. In return for interest, savers are prepared to lend their money to borrowers.

The interest rate will vary as between different classes of loans, according to the degree of risk and the length of time involved.

Savers regularly deposit their savings with financial intermediaries such as banks, so that the actual loans to borrowers are made by these institutions. Their attitudes and practices will affect the supply of funds actually available to borrowers and the rate of interest charged. Through its influence upon the nation's money supply, the banking system is also able to affect the rate of interest.

Changes in the rate of interest will change the capitalization of future income and therefore the value of properties which are expected to yield future income.

FOR REVIEW AND DISCUSSION

1. "Under socialism there would of course be no such thing as interest." Is this correct?
2. The rate of interest is governed ultimately by impatience to spend and opportunities to invest. Do you agree?
3. In an era of rapid technological change, the rate of interest is likely to be high. Why should this be so?
4. "If no individual item bought by customers ever cost more than one day's pay, there would be no need for consumer credit." Do you agree?
5. The elasticity of demand for loans both by consumers and businessmen is likely to be low. Why?
6. It is fundamentally unfair to add a risk premium on to interest charges. The result is that the honest person who meets his obligations is forced to pay more, on account of other people who do not meet their obligations. Discuss.
7. The virtually fixed rate of interest charged by banks constitutes a kind of price ceiling in boom times, and has all the effects of a price ceiling. Explain.

14   Profit

THE NATURE OF PROFIT

Profit is, in any business enterprise, the excess of receipts over costs, and is received by the owner as his income. The term "receipts" is clear enough, but we must define "costs" with some care in order to avoid ambiguity. By "costs" we mean the total value, reckoned at their market prices, of *all* the goods used up in the enterprise and all the services applied to it. We include in costs therefore the market value of any services performed by the owner. Profit is then purely the income which the owner of an enterprise receives *because he is the owner, and not on account of any services which he may perform.*

For example, suppose that the owner of a small corner grocery owns his building, has invested his own capital in the stock and fixtures, and works himself as a clerk in the store. Suppose that the building has a rental value of $2,000 a year. Suppose this his investment in stock and fixtures is $10,000, and that seven per cent would be a fair rate of return on money invested in this line of business. Suppose that the value of the job he does as a clerk is $4,000 a year—he would be paid that much if he did the same work for someone else.

Suppose now that, after paying all his expenses for the year, the grocer has $9,000 left for himself. Does all of this represent profit? The answer is no. Profit we have noted, is strictly the reward which the owner of an enterprise receives for being the owner, the "boss." In our example, of the $9,000 received by the grocer, $6,700 represents income due to him for other services he has provided; he would have received this much even if he had not been "the boss." He could have rented the building to someone else for $2,000. He could have invested his $10,000 in someone else's store and received a return of $700 per year on it. Had he worked for someone else the way he worked for himself, he would have been paid $4,000. Doing exactly what he did, but without being the owner of a business, he would have earned $6,700. If his actual income was $9,000, his additional reward for being the owner of a business is obviously $2,300. This figure is the true measure of his *profit*.

The Role of the Businessman

Just what are the functions which the owner of a business performs, and for which he receives profit as reward? How do his functions differ from the work of an employee? They differ in two key respects. Firstly, the owner is the person who makes the ultimate decisions. He decides what shall be produced, how, where, by whom; he decides how, where and at what price the product shall be sold. In a very large organization the owner probably would not make such decisions himself but would nominate and control the persons who did actually make them; through his control over the actual decision-makers, however, he would control the nature of the decisions. Secondly, the owner carries the ultimate responsibility for the decisions made. If wrong decisions are made, by him or by his subordinates, the losses will fall upon his shoulders. He will suffer financial penalties for making wrong decisions himself, or for having appointed subordinates who make wrong decisions.[1]

As a matter of course he tries to maintain the efficiency of his firm's operations, and to improve it in every way possible. Reduction in costs through increase in efficiency will widen the margin of receipts over costs. Slackness and inefficiency, on the other hand, will reduce that margin. The responsibility of the owner is to coordinate the various activities of his enterprise and to ensure that each is performed carefully and well. His income will depend in part upon how successfully he performs these purely administrative functions.

In Chapter 5 we drew a distinction between "normal profits," being a return generally considered adequate for the effort and investment involved, and "super-normal profits," being a return over and above this amount. The profit realized by an owner who administered his firm along traditional lines with reasonable efficiency would presumably be considered normal, save when he obviously had good or bad luck. But the owner of a business, we take it for granted, is always on the alert for opportunities to maximize his income and would like to earn more. In what directions does he look for opportunities to earn super-normal profits?

Reward for Innovation

The owner may introduce some trail-breaking innovation. He may develop a new product or service which catches the fancy of the public and which can be sold for a good deal more than it costs to produce. He need not have invented the new product himself; someone else may have done that. His contribution has been to appreciate the possibilities of the invention and to arrange for its commercial production and

---

[1]Actually, all of the people who are associated with a firm are likely to suffer as a result of wrong decisions made by those in charge. The owner loses the value of his investment, but workers lose their jobs. This loss may impose financial penalties on them too. They may have difficulty in obtaining other employment. They may find it impossible to use elsewhere the specialized skill, tools, housing, which they acquired in order to serve their firm; if the firm fails, they may lose all or part of such investments.

sale. Thus Marconi invented the radio, but David Sarnoff was responsible for the mass production of radios and the creation of the modern radio broadcasting industry. Marconi was the *inventor*, Sarnoff was what economists would call the *innovator*. The profits earned Mr. Sarnoff were, in large part, the reward for his successful innovation.

Every enterprising businessman is on the alert for a profitable innovation. It need not be so momentous as the radio; it may be something quite minor—a new wrapping, a delivery service, novel credit arrangements; it may take the form of a new method of production. Its main feature is that it is new and therefore different from what has been done before. If it meets with public approval or if it reduces costs, profit will be earned.

Reward for Uncertainty-Bearing

Uncertainties of all kinds beset every business enterprise. Labour and materials may prove to be unobtainable; it may prove impossible to sell the product. In a good many enterprises the consequences of entrepreneurial decisions are completely unpredictable. When an oil exploration company undertakes a search for underground oil pools, for instance, it is embarking upon a gigantic gamble, investing enormous sums without any assurance of a return. A key function of the owner is to bear the uncertainty which is inevitable in the conduct of any business enterprise. For despite the uncertainties involved, decisions must be made, action must be taken. The owner is the person who stands ready to shoulder the losses which will result if it turns out that the decisions were wrong. His reward for accepting responsibility for losses if the decisions prove to be wrong, is the profit realized if decisions turn out to be right.

Risks vs. Uncertainty: The Nature of Risk

In his book, *Risk, Uncertainty and Profit*, F. H. Knight drew a distinction which has become classic, between *risk* and *uncertainty*. His analysis proceeds along the following lines. The outcome of any act performed in the present will depend upon developments which will occur in the future. Because they will only occur in the future, these developments cannot be known. Some, however, can be confidently and precisely estimated. These are developments which will be of the same general type as others which have occurred on a great many occasions in the past. Because developments of this sort have occurred very frequently in the past, we have been able to formulate precise statistical laws to describe their behaviour. We assume, with considerable assurance, that they will behave in the future as in the past, and will therefore conform closely to the statistical laws which we have formulated to describe their past behaviour.

For instance, suppose that statistical records showed that out of every 2,000 homes in a certain city, one burned down each year. If this record extended back for a great many years, then this ratio could be regarded as a constant and reliable one. It could be assumed, with considerable confidence, that in the future too, one house would burn down each year for every two thousand in the city.

Each individual houseowner is subject to the danger that his will be the house which burns in any particular year. He can, however, secure himself against any possible loss by entering into a contract with an insurance company. By paying them a small sum per year, he obtains the company's assurance that if his happens to be the house which burns down, they will make good the loss to him. The houseowner thereby avoids all risk-taking. Even if his house does burn down he will lose nothing. *The insurance company takes no risk either.* It will have entered into similar contracts with a very great number of other houseowners. From each one it will be receiving an annual payment; to each one it will have promised full reimbursement in the event of his house burning down. However, the insurance company knows, as a virtual certainty, that for each two thousand householders with whom it has arranged such contracts, it will be called upon to indemnify *only one*. By joining together two thousand similar risks, all risk has been in effect eliminated, for both the houseowner and the insurance company. The company has merely to take care that the sum of the payments made annually by the two thousand insured parties is sufficient to enable *one* policy holder to be indemnified, and administrative expenses to be met.[2]

Uncertainty

The laws of probability, and common sense, affirm that a tendency which has manifested itself many times over in the past will, under similar conditions, continue to operate in the future. Because we have records covering many thousands of houses, we are able to calculate, with precision and reliability, what the probability is of any one house burning down. But what probability estimate can we attach to business decisions which are absolutely unique, or are of a kind seldom made before? Have we any basis for calculating the chances of success, for instance, when a business man sets up a new firm, or introduces a new product, or undertakes a search for underground gas, oil or metals? Obviously not. Either there is no precedent whatever upon which a judgment may be based, or precedents are so few that reliable conclusions cannot be drawn from them.

The businessman who undertakes a venture of this sort is in effect leaping into the unknown. He does not know, nor can anyone know, what are the chances of success. He cannot gain security by pooling his risk with the similar risks of a great

[2]Suppose every house was worth $20,000. Suppose further that an insurance company's annual administration costs amounted to $8 per house insured. In that case it should charge each houseowner an annual premium of $18. For every two thousand houses insured this would produce $36,000, enough to indemnify the one householder whose house burned down, and to cover the $16,000 of administrative expenses involved in dealing with the two thousand houses.

many other people, as does the homeowner who takes out insurance on his house.[3] As a matter of fact, even the businessman who follows a long established routine is not free of hazard. There is always the possibility that someone else will introduce a new development which will render long established practices outmoded and value- less. Whoever is in charge of a business operation, whatever its nature, must carry the burden of uncertainty. There exists always the possibility of loss as a result of unanticipated and unfavourable developments.

Not all people are prepared to have their livelihood depend upon such uncer- tainties. Many prefer to engage in activities whose results are more predictable. It is a distinguishing feature of the owner of a business that he is prepared to bear uncertainties. The businessman who wishes to increase his profits will deliberately enter into more venturesome undertakings; he will realize handsome profits if his decisions, all made in an atmosphere of uncertainty, prove to be mostly correct.

Windfall Gains

A businessman may do well through sheer good luck. As a result of circumstances which he had not foreseen, and which occurred through no effort of his own, he may reap a golden harvest.[4] Some business decisions that were really quite irrational, may turn out well because of purely chance developments which no one could have foreseen. Such "windfall gains" accrue to the owner of the business and form part of his profit. In a sense, they constitute reward for his bearing of uncertainty. When a businessman embarks upon an uncertain venture, among its unpredictable con- sequences are developments which will be highly favourable and yield the "windfall gains." Had he not undertaken the venture in the first place, with all its attendant uncertainties, he would not have been in a position to realize these "windfall gains." (Nor of course would he be in a position to suffer "windfall losses.")

The Element of Monopoly

Profit represents, as we have just seen, reward for the carrying out of innovation, and for the bearing of uncertainty; at times it may be the result simply of good luck. Whatever be the source of his profit, a businessman will actually receive it only if a key prerequisite condition prevails: he must enjoy some degree of monop- oly. It must be impossible for others to do exactly what he does. If other persons cannot be totally prevented from duplicating his activities, there must at least be a limit to the number who manage to do so, or it must be impossible for imitators to

---

[3] A qualification is in order here. Many large firms do in effect pool their risks nowadays by engaging in a large number and variety of enterprises. The firm which is able to achieve a pooling of risk through such diversification, does in fact appreciably diminish the uncertainty which surrounds its future.

[4] The government may decide to locate a military base near a small town; local merchants enjoy greatly increased business and profits as a result.

follow at once in his footsteps. If competition develops instantaneously and in unlimited degree, no one can earn profit. The innovator who develops a worthwhile product will find himself obliged to sell at a price which yields no profit, because of the quantities simultaneously put on the market by competitors who have duplicated his innovation. The uncertainty-bearer will earn no profit because a horde of competitors will immediately copy any decision of his which has proven to be correct. Even a windfall development will not be profitable if there is no limitation upon the number of people who can share in it.[5]

The rational businessman takes steps to ward off competition. If possible, he will patent his product so that close competition becomes prohibited by law. He may keep secret the nature of his operations so that outsiders, not knowing what he is doing, cannot copy him. He may acquire complete control over some indispensable ingredient, so that others cannot duplicate his product. He may, through advertising or the careful cultivation of consumer goodwill, establish himself so solidly in the market that competitors who come after, offering identical products, are less well received by the buying public. The businessman who fails to establish monopoly power on a permanent basis, by one or other of these means, will earn profit only during the limited period when other businessmen are making their preparations to enter into competition with him.

ECONOMIC ROLE OF THE PROFIT MOTIVE

The material progress of free enterprise societies has depended heavily upon the capacity and willingness of businessmen to carry out innovations and to undertake ventures whose outcome was uncertain. Each year, in such a society, businessmen introduce new manufactured products and search for new sources of natural materials. Society becomes richer for their efforts and uncertainty-bearing. Some of the new products and services which they develop are admittedly of little real value, but others contribute agreeably to our material welfare. With each passing year our material well-being rises, as a fresh group of products and services is added to the list of past innovations which have become permanently incorporated into our way of life. The new deposits of natural resources discovered each year make possible the maintenance and expansion of our output of finished products. The earning of profit is the characteristic motive for making the effort and bearing the uncertainties involved in such innovation and resource development. Hence the profit motive may be regarded as providing the vital stimulus of the forward drive which characterizes free enterprise economics.

[5]Referring to the example suggested in the previous footnote of the location of a military base near a small town: if there is nothing to stop new business firms from entering the town, established merchants may not specially gain from the base that has been established nearby.

Profit and Loss: Production Guides

The profits earned and losses incurred by firms in their operations serve as guides to production. The productive capacity of the nation is automatically directed into the right channels and away from the wrong channels. The fact that profit is earned in the production of any good or service reflects the fact that the public desires it warmly, and that more of it would be welcome. The profitability of present production will induce the increase in production which is socially desirable. Existing firms will expand and new firms will enter the field. Losses incurred by firms generally indicate, on the other hand, that the public does not want their products. Less of them, perhaps none at all, should be produced. The losses suffered will exercise the appropriate deterrence. Less of the nation's productive capacity will be channelled into these directions as firms close down or curtail their operations.

Personnel Selection and Rejection

Profit and loss perform yet another function in our society. They aid in the selection of the personnel who will exercise entrepreneurial authority. The businessman who has earned profit has thereby demonstrated his worth as a maker of decisions. He has directed well the productive capacity over which he had control and has earned the right to exercise authority over an even larger aggregation of factors of production. His profits make this possible. He can use them to acquire control over additional productive capacity, to hire more workers, to purchase more equipment and materials, to rent or build additional buildings. Lending institutions, impressed by his record, will be prepared to advance loans which confer additional economic power.

The businessman who incurs losses, on the other hand, has demonstrated his incapacity as a decision maker. It is in society's interest that his economic authority should be curtailed, or perhaps taken away altogether. His losses automatically bring about such a result; they diminish his capacity to hire workmen, to purchase equipment and materials. Banks become reluctant to lend. If his losses are large enough, he will lose completely his power to control any part of the nation's productive capacity; society will become desirably rid of an incompetent manager.

Abuses and Shortcomings

In the foregoing pages we have shown how profit induces the performance of necessary functions; how profit and loss guide the nation's productive capacity into the appropriate channels, and away from the inappropriate; how profit and loss ensure that control over the productive powers of the nation is conferred only upon those who are worthy. Our account is incomplete. There is a darker side; the arrangements are far from perfect; abuses and shortcomings are common.

Some people have earned profits through activities which are harmful to society. Their gains have been achieved through the ruthless exploitation of workers, through the deception of gullible consumers, through the innovation of useless frivolities, through success in gambles which served no useful purpose. The profit and loss system furthermore, may inappropriately direct the flow of productive capacity. The goods which are profitable to produce and whose production is therefore stimulated, may be undesirable in terms of the nation's long range interests. The goods and services on which losses are incurred and whose production is therefore deterred, may be genuinely desirable.

Under the profit and loss system, unworthy people can and do attain positions of economic authority. They may have acquired their wealth and therefore their power to control some part of the nation's productive capacity, without genuinely deserving it. It may have come to them through luck, through inheritance, or as a result of unlawful activities. The enormous profits which some people gain may be dissipated in lavish consumption; the use of productive capacity to indulge the grandiose tastes of tycoons represents a form of social waste.

The scale of such shortcomings has in the past been impressive but their dimensions appear to be a good deal smaller today. Collective action by organized labour, together with government legislation, renders it difficult nowadays to win profit through the exploitation of workers. A better informed and more alert public, and government watchfulness render it difficult to gain profit through deception of consumers. Steep succession duties limit the economic authority which is acquired through inheritance rather than personal deserts. Heavy income taxes curtail the capacity of the ultra rich to spend money wastefully. Governments support worthy projects which, because they operate at a loss, would not otherwise be carried on.

We are still a long way from the millennium. Our free enterprise economy, with its reliance upon the profit motive for its driving force, is far from perfect. Abuses and shortcomings still exist aplenty, as they likely will under any system. But the free enterprise system is working tolerably well nowadays, and in the workaday world this is probably the best that any system can do. Perfection is achieved only on paper and in dreams.

SUMMARY

Profit is the excess of receipts over costs achieved in a business firm, and is received by the owner as his income. It represents reward for performing the functions and carrying the responsibilities of ownership.

Profit will be earned when decisions, made in an atmosphere of uncertainty, prove to be correct or when superior new products or methods are introduced. Some degree of monopoly must exist if profit is to be earned on a sustained basis.

Profit and loss perform critical functions in a free enterprise society. They direct the flow of economic resources toward the production of what the public wants, and away from the production of what it does not want. Profit and loss serve as well to select or reject the personnel who will have authority over the nation's productive resources.

The profit and loss system has been characterized in the past by serious shortcomings and abuses; these have been very much fewer in recent times.

FOR REVIEW AND DISCUSSION

1. Strictly speaking, it is not necessary that businessmen actually earn profit; it is only necessary that they *expect* to earn profit. Does this seem reasonable?
2. Our present corporation profit taxes are far too high. Do you agree?
3. "Under socialism there would of course be no such thing as profit." Comment.
4. "The only way to earn profit is to keep ahead of your competitors." Comment.
5. Profits can not have any influence upon a country's economy if they add up to zero. Is this correct?
6. The Canadian economy is to be condemned because it produces not for people's use but for profit. Do you agree?
7. Describe an example of successful uncertainty-bearing which yielded profit.
8. You are considering the purchase of a small business which has been established by someone else. What information would you try to obtain before deciding how much you would be willing to pay for it?
9. A corporation manager is paid a bonus of $50,000 one year. Would you call this money profit or wage?
10. The inventor is a technician; the innovator is a businessman. Explain.
11. "The man who insures his house against fire, and then buys a lottery ticket, is really being inconsistent." Do you agree?
12. While admittedly they deal in risks, insurance companies cannot be said to engage in gambling. Explain.
13. When a drunken driver causes an accident it is not the fault of the automobile. In the same way undesirable results produced by the profit system are attributable to the shortcomings of people, not to the system. Do you agree? Justify your answer.

PART FIVE:

INTERNATIONAL
TRADE

15

The Physical Basis of International Trade

THE GAINS FROM SPECIALIZATION

Writing two centuries ago, Adam Smith cited an example of the advantages of specialization. He described a visit to a factory in which pins were manufactured, where the manager informed him that the firm was able to achieve a considerable output by having each employee perform a single task only. The raw material consisted of thin steel wire; to produce pins, it was necessary to cut the wire into short lengths, sharpen one end, attach a head to the other, and polish the whole. At one time each man performed all these operations himself, making the finished pin from the raw material. It was found, however, that by having each man perform one task only, a considerably greater output could be achieved.

Output was greater because every employee was being used to best advantage. Each man was assigned to the task for which he was best suited; by concentrating on that one task alone, he enhanced greatly his natural skill and adeptness; furthermore, he wasted no time proceeding from one task to another. With each man specializing in doing the one job for which he was best fitted, the total productive power of all was used to best advantage and the output of the plant was the greatest possible.

What was true for the pin factory described by Adam Smith is true everywhere. Any group of individuals will increase its collective output by having each individual member specialize in the performance of a single task. The same principle holds true for the nations of the world. Each nation is best suited, by reason of its natural endowment and acquired characteristics, for the production of particular goods and services. If each nation concentrated on the production of that which it produced best, the aggregate output of the world would be the greatest possible, and the amount of goods and services available for each nation would therefore also be the greatest possible.

The Bases of National Advantage

What are the characteristics which cause a nation to be particularly well suited to the production of particular goods and services? The following four are suggested as being the most important:

1. Climatic features, e.g. tropical countries are suited to the cultivation of spices and those fruits which can be grown only in permanently warm areas. The climate of western Canada, on the other hand, is favourable to the production of high quality wheat.
2. Possession of rare or unique natural resources: e.g. Canada has large deposits of nickel-bearing ores, such as are found in very few other countries of the world.
3. A unique labour supply; e.g. Switzerland has a very large number of craftsmen highly skilled in the manufacture of watches. The United States has very large numbers of engineers and skilled technicians who are capable of designing, installing and operating machinery and equipment of the most advanced types.
4. Superior capital equipment; e.g. the United States has highly efficient machinery and equipment which enable the production, at low cost, of many goods and services. Because these productive facilities are very large and complicated, few other nations are capable of duplicating them; furthermore the output of large and highly specialized machines is cheap only if they are operated at or near their capacity, which means in turn that there must be a correspondingly huge market available for their product. Thus the United States produces automobiles on gigantic assembly lines, at relatively low cost, primarily for a vast domestic market capable of absorbing automobiles on a mass basis.

(The last three characteristics, it is worth noting, are not eternal attributes. A country's natural resource endowment may become exhausted: agricultural lands may become worn out through poor husbandry; forests may be cut down; wild life populations may disappear as a result of heavy slaughter rates; mineral deposits are removed as a matter of course and ultimately the removal may be complete. Extensive training programmes may spread hitherto unique labour skills. Large scale investment programmes may enable other countries to become possessed of major capital facilities that were hitherto the unique possession of one particular country. Such developments have occurred in the past—and are going on now—significantly altering the relative suitability of the world's nations for the production of different goods.)

International trade consists essentially of the exchange among nations of their respective specialties, each nation exporting the goods and services for the production of which it is best fitted, thanks to its contemporary endowment, and importing goods and services for the production of which other nations are best fitted. Thus Canada exports wheat, newsprint, nickel, aluminum, and imports heavy machinery, Swiss watches, tropical fruits and spices. The results are beneficial all round.

It should be emphasized that international trade consists of the exchange of services as well as goods. Canadian banks, insurance companies and railways furnish their respective services to the nationals of foreign countries. Canadian hotels, motels and restaurants serve the tourists who come from other countries. Canadian hockey players perform their services for teams in United States cities. These sales to foreigners of the services of Canadian firms and individuals constitute Canadian exports in just the same way as do our sales to foreigners of wheat, aluminum and newsprint.

Comparative Advantage: An Example

Not all countries are equally well endowed. Some have limited natural resources, their workers possess no valuable skills, and they lack specialized capital equipment. In the production of no good do such nations excel; in the production of all goods they must admit inferiority to others. Is it possible for such countries to participate in international trade? Can they gain anything from exchange with better endowed countries? Can wealthier countries gain anything from exchange with them?

To these questions the answer is yes. It is entirely possible for mutually beneficial trade to take place between a country whose productivity is high and another whose productivity is low. The following example illustrates how this may come about.

Suppose that the world consists of just two countries, Canada and England, and each is capable of producing only two products, wheat and automobiles. Suppose that Canada is much better endowed than England, and is able to produce *both* wheat and automobiles more effectively than England. Suppose further that each country has three units of labour, and that labour productivity in each country is as follows:

> In Canada 1 unit can produce either 80 units of wheat or 10 autos.
> In England 1 unit can produce either 40 units of wheat or 8 autos.

Examination of the figures reveals this important point: while Canada is superior to England in the production of both wheat and autos, her margin of superiority is greater in the production of wheat than it is in the production of autos. Canadian labour is twice as productive as English labour in regard to wheat, but only 25% more productive in regard to autos. This difference furnishes the basis for mutually profitable trade between the two countries. (The economist would say that England has a *comparative advantage* over Canada in the production of autos, because here her inferiority to Canada is less; Canada, he would say, has a *comparative advantage* over England in regard to wheat production, because here her superiority is greater.)

Now suppose that each country attempted to be self-sufficient, devoting two units of labour to the production of wheat, and one unit to the production of autos. In that case their output would be as follows:

> Canada would produce 160 units of wheat plus 10 autos.
> England would produce 80 units of wheat plus 8 autos.
> Together they would produce 240 units of wheat plus 18 autos.

If, however, each country produced only that good in which it enjoyed a comparative advantage, Canada would devote all three of her labour units to the production of wheat, and England would devote all three of her labour units to the production of autos. In that case their output would be as follows:

Canada would produce 240 units of wheat plus   0 autos.
England would produce   0 units of wheat plus 24 autos.
Together they would produce 240 units of wheat plus 24 autos.

As a result of each country's specializing in the production of the good in regard to which it has a comparative advantage, their combined output is enlarged.[1]

The fact that with specialization their combined output would be greater by six autos, makes it possible for both countries to become better off. Thus, for example, if England produces only autos and gives Canada 12 autos for 80 units of wheat, she would be better off than she would have been without specialization, since she would end up with 80 units of wheat and 12 autos, as opposed to 80 units of wheat and only eight autos. Canada too would be better off, ending up with 160 units of wheat and 12 autos, as opposed to the 160 units of wheat and 10 autos which she would have if she produced both wheat and autos.

Specialization and trade does not make the two countries *equally* well off; Canada is richer before trade and remains richer after trade. If the exchange described in the preceding paragraph is carried out, the three units of Canadian labour obtain as reward 160 units of wheat plus 12 autos, while the three units of English labour receive as reward only 80 units of wheat plus 12 autos. The effect of trade is only to make each country better off than it would have been without trade.

The Terms of Trade

Specialization *enables* both countries to become better off, but if one country demands an excessive price for its exports, then the other country cannot gain from trade. Suppose Canada were to demand 17 autos in exchange for 80 units of wheat. In that event, England would be better off producing her own wheat rather than buying from Canada. If she produced her own wheat and autos, she would have 80 units of wheat plus eight autos; if she produced autos only and bought wheat on Canada's terms, she would end up with 80 units of wheat and only seven autos. Only if Canada is willing to accept 15 autos or fewer in exchange for 80 units of wheat, will England gain from specialization and trade. Similarly, Canada will gain from trade only if she obtains at least 11 autos from England in exchange for 80 units of wheat. If she gets only 10 autos, she is no better off; if she receives fewer than 10 autos, she would be worse off than she would have been without trade.

Obviously then, if both countries are to gain from trade, England must give Canada at least 11 autos, but no more than 15, in exchange for 80 units of wheat.

---

[1]An alternative method of illustrating the principle of comparative advantage is as follows: To produce one auto in Canada requires resources which could have produced 8 units of wheat instead. To produce 1 auto in England takes resources which could have produced 5 units of wheat. If Canada gives England 6 units of wheat for 1 auto, then that auto costs Canada 2 less units of wheat than a Canadian-made car. England, in obtaining 6 units of wheat for 1 auto is getting wheat cheaper than she can produce it herself. Had she grown wheat at home the production of 6 units of wheat have cost 1⅕ autos.

The terms of trade, the rate at which the two goods are exchanged for each other, must lie somewhere between these limits. While, to be mutually beneficial, the rate of exchange must be between these limits, the benefit derived by each nation will depend upon whether the actual rate of exchange is near the upper or lower unit. The fewer cars Britain has to give in exchange for the 80 units of wheat, the better off she will be; the more cars Britain gives for the 80 units of wheat, the better off will Canada be.

Granted that the rate of exchange must be somewhere between 11 and 15 autos in exchange for 80 units of wheat, what will determine the exact rate at which the two commodities are traded? This will be determined by the market forces which determine the relative prices of the two goods in the countries. If supply and demand cause the price of wheat to be relatively high in each country and the price of autos to be relatively low, then, when the two are exchanged, the terms of trade will prove to be favourable to Canada, the wheat-selling country.

REALISTIC QUALIFICATIONS

Our discussion so far, and the example we have worked out, have been over-simplified. We must now introduce a number of realistic qualifications which will modify our conclusions somewhat, but will not alter their basic character.

Increasing Costs

In our example of specialization and trade we tacitly assumed that costs of production, of both wheat and autos, do not change with the level of output, either in Canada or England. In real life we are likely to find that things are different. The production of wheat, for instance, is likely to be an *increasing cost* industry in both countries; the cost of production per bushel is likely to rise with each increase in the scale of output. For this reason, we will probably find that England does not obtain all her wheat from Canada, but produces a little for herself.

Canada will be the main producer because her cost of producing wheat begins at a lower level and rises more slowly than does England's. Nevertheless, as Canada's wheat output is increased, the cost of production per bushel would rise; once Canada's output was very large, a further increase would be achieved only at a very high cost per bushel (probably because this additional output would have to be grown on quite inferior land, the better land being all in use). There might be in England a small area of land fairly well suited to the growing of wheat. Accordingly, England might find it to her advantage to grow at home some of the wheat she needs, rather than obtain it all from Canada. If she relied on Canada for all her wheat then Canada, to produce the full amount required, might be obliged to grow some on her inferior land. The cost of wheat grown on inferior Canadian land

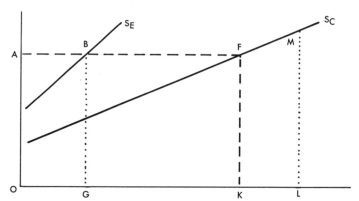

Figure 1. The implications of increasing costs in international trade

might exceed the cost of wheat grown on England's most suitable land. However, because the area of such land is very limited in England, that country's wheat output will be very small.

Figure 1 illustrates. SE represents the supply curve of wheat grown in England; SC represents the supply curve of wheat grown in Canada. Suppose that England wishes to have the quantity of wheat OL. If she were to obtain it all from Canada the price would have to be LM per bushel: that is the price which would elicit production of OL quantity in Canada. However, England could produce part of her needs at home for less than LM per unit: her optimum arrangement would be to produce the quantity OG at home (OG being equal to KL) and import the quantity OK from Canada; with this combination of domestic production and imports the cost would be OA per bushel, the lowest figure that could possibly induce supply of the quantity OL.

Decreasing Costs

Some industries, such as the manufacture of automobiles, are characterized by decreasing costs: the larger the scale of production, the lower will be the cost of production per unit. If, in the production of some good, this were true without limit, then the most economical production would be achieved by having a single firm produce the world's entire output. Such a development has not actually been realized (to the writer's knowledge), but has been approached; viz. the concentration of the world's jet airliner production among a very small number of firms in only a few countries.

Many Goods

Our example has assumed that Canada and England are capable of producing only two goods, and that each country specializes in the production of only one. In actual fact, Canada can produce thousands of different goods and so can England. Nevertheless, the fundamental principle of our example still holds true. Out of the thousands of goods which England can produce, she will concentrate upon those in which she enjoys a comparative advantage; Canada will do likewise. Thus Canada's production emphasizes wheat, newsprint, aluminum and nickel; Britain's production emphasizes airplanes, woollens, electrical machinery and small autos. Within each country, the emphasis placed upon the production of any particular commodity will reflect relative prices. If the price of electrical machinery is relatively high, England will produce relatively more of it, and relatively less of her other specialties such as woollens. If aluminum is in strong demand, Canada will produce relatively more of it and relatively less of her other specialties such as wheat.

Trade Among Many Nations

Our example has illustrated how two nations would trade with each other. Trade in the real world is of course more complicated; there are in the world several dozen different nations who all buy from one another in greater or less degree. This complication does not refute the principle embodied in our example, however. Each nation concentrates on the production of those goods in which it enjoys a comparative advantage, and tends to buy from other nations the products in which it is at a comparative disadvantage.

Trade Carried on by Individuals

Our example has referred to "Canada" selling wheat to "England," as though Canada and England each had a single corporate personality and this personality engaged in international trade. The truth is that thousands of individual businessmen and firms do the actual exporting and importing in each country. This complication does not affect our fundamental principle. Individuals and business firms carry on in each country those enterprises for which the country is best suited by reason of absolute or comparative advantage. Individual Englishmen find it advantageous to export autos to Canada; individual Canadians find it to their advantage to produce wheat for export to England. The effect is as if "England" exported autos, and "Canada" exported wheat.

The Use of Money

Our example has implied that the exchange between Canada and England has been conducted on a barter basis, with Canada swapping so much wheat for so many English autos. This of course is unrealistic; while such barter deals do occur they are not characteristic of the way goods are exchanged internationally. What normally happens in fact is that Englishmen sell autos in Canada for money, and Canadians sell wheat in England for money. The money realized by Englishmen from the sale of autos in Canada is the money they use to pay for our wheat. The money realized by

Canadians through the sale of wheat in England pays for the autos which we obtain from that country. Thus the exchange of Canadian wheat for English autos is characterized by the payment of money for goods bought, and the receipt of money for goods sold. However, the basic fact remains that Canada's wheat has been exchanged for England's autos; the money transactions reflect the movement of actual goods.

The use of money and the fact that many countries engage in international trade, make possible a further complication. One country may sell to, but not buy from, some other country; or its purchases from one country may not equal its sales to that country. Canada may sell wheat to England, but use the money proceeds to buy machinery in the United States. The United States may use this money to buy autos in England. In such event, no two countries actually exchange goods with each other, although each does pay with its exports for its imports. England pays for her wheat by sending autos to the United States; the United States pays for the autos by sending machinery to Canada; Canada pays for the machinery by sending wheat to England.

Such multilateral trade has three important advantages over strictly bilateral trade: each country is able to receive, in payment for its exports, the imports which it desires most. Each country is able to pay for its imports by exports to the country which most desires these goods. One country is able to import from another, despite the fact that it cannot export to that particular country.

Transport Costs

Finally, our example is unrealistic in that it ignores the cost of transporting goods from one country to another. For some items, those which are heavy and bulky in particular, transportation costs constitute a very large fraction of production costs. International trade in such commodities is feasible only if the differential in production costs exceeds the cost of transportation from one nation to the other. If it costs $1.00 to produce a bushel of wheat in Canada, and $1.50 to produce a bushel of wheat in England, then Canada will be able to sell wheat in England only if the cost of transportation between the two countries is less than 50 cents per bushel.

Every reduction in transportation costs reduces an obstacle which hinders the movement of goods from where they can be produced cheaply to where they are costly to produce. Every such reduction therefore induces an increase in the scale and diversity of international trade. The huge increase in the volume of international trade which occurred around the end of the nineteenth century was primarily attributable to the marked reductions which occurred in transportation costs. The newly developed steel steamship cheaply linked the continents of the world, while railways cheaply linked continental interiors to their respective seaboards. Wheat and cattle produced at low cost on the interior plains of North and South America could now be cheaply and efficiently carried to markets in Europe. Throughout the world, the rich resources of hitherto remote localities became feasible to develop and their products entered into international commerce.

TRADE IN LIEU OF FACTOR MOVEMENTS

A distinguished Swedish economist, Bertil Ohlin, has advanced the thesis that the movement of goods serves as a substitute for the movement of factors of production between nations. Labour may be abundant and therefore tend to be cheap in England; it may be scarce and therefore tend to be dear in Canada. Such a disparity would of course tend to foster emigration from England to Canada; this emigration in turn would tend to bring about equalization of wage levels in the two countries by reducing the abundance of labour in England and its scarcity in Canada.

There may be obstacles to migration from one country to another, however. The Canadian government may impose restrictions on immigration; the cost of moving workers and their families may be prohibitively high; many Englishmen may be unwilling to leave their native land. Even if such obstacles do restrict the movement of people from England to Canada, equalization of wage levels may still occur; the movement of goods from England to Canada will bring about the same equalizing tendencies as would be achieved by the emigration of labour from England to Canada. Because English goods are being sold in Canada as well as in England, the demand for the English labour which makes them will be strong, so that, despite its abundance, its price will not be unduly low. In Canada, because English-made goods are available, the need for labour will be less, so that despite its scarcity, the price will not be unduly high.

The same principle holds true for land. Because its products can be sold in England, Canadian land will have high value, despite its great abundance. Because the produce of Canada's land is available in England, land in that country will not be unduly high in price, despite its scarcity. The practical significance of this thesis was strikingly demonstrated in Great Britain in the latter part of the nineteenth century when the inflow of cheap grain and cattle from newly developed countries was followed by a drastic reduction in the rental rates for agricultural land.

FOREIGN GIFTS AND LENDING

It is not universally true that imports must be paid for by exports. A country may receive foreign goods and services as gifts, or may receive as a gift the money required to buy such goods and services. A conqueror may exact tribute from a defeated nation in the form of money or goods.

One country may obtain the foreign currency it requires to pay for imports, not by the sale of its exports, but by borrowing from abroad. To repay the loan, however, and to pay interest, it must earn foreign currency by the sale of its exports. In effect these subsequent exports pay ultimately for the imports which were bought with the borrowed money. An international loan, and its repayment, have therefore their physical counterparts. The loan involves the movement of goods from the lending to the borrowing country; repayment of the loan involves the movement of goods from the borrowing to the lending country.

The physical counterparts of an international loan and its repayment are not necessarily so direct, however; third parties might become involved. Venezuela may borrow $10 million in the United States, and use the money to buy wheat in Canada. Canada might then use this money to buy machinery in the United States. For the United States the physical counterpart of her lending is the export of $10 million worth of machinery to Canada; for Venezuela, the physical counterpart of her borrowing is the import of $10 million worth of wheat from Canada. The physical counterpart of the repayment might be similarly triangular.

CANADA'S TRADE PATTERN

Tables 1 and 2 list respectively Canada's ten leading exports and imports for the year 1970. Our large exports and imports of motor vehicles and parts reflect primarily the working of the Canada-United States Automotive Agreement of 1965 which provided for the removal of tariffs on motor vehicles and parts imported from one country into the other; manufacture of some types of vehicles and parts for the entire North American market became concentrated in Canada, while we henceforth obtained all our requirements of some automotive products from the U.S. The higher degree of international specialization resulted in increased exports and imports for both countries.

Aside from the large trade in motor vehicles and parts the figures generally correspond to theoretical expectations. Canada's other chief exports are commodities which we are well qualified to produce thanks to our rich natural resources: newsprint, wood pulp and lumber derived from our extensive forests, wheat from the prairies, petroleum from the large oil deposits of Alberta and Saskatchewan, minerals drawn from the great ore bodies of the Laurentian shield, aluminum, whose production requires vast amounts of electrical power and which Canada, with her abundant hydro-electric resources, has available cheaply.

Machinery of many types, motor vehicle parts, aircraft and parts, constitute Canada's main imports; these are goods which we are unable to produce as economically as other countries can (notably the U.S.), because we lack the skilled labour, do not have the technical equipment or because the domestic market is not large enough to support an efficient scale of production. The heavy imports of petroleum are a little odd: large oil pools and other petroleum sources, e.g. the McMurray tar sands, exist in Canada, and we export substantial quantities of petroleum, as evident from Table 1. The explanation lies in the fact that the great bulk of Canada's oil deposits are located in Western Canada and existing petroleum pipelines reach only as far east as Ontario. The large Quebec market is served chiefly by oil from Venezuela which is cheaply delivered by ocean tankers to Portland, Maine, and thence moved by pipeline to Quebec. To serve the Quebec market with Western Canadian oil would require the construction of another cross-country pipeline, to Montreal; a Royal Commission which considered the project in 1959 deemed it to be economically unjustified.

Table 1

CANADA'S TEN LEADING EXPORTS IN 1970*

	VALUE OF EXPORTS (Millions of dollars)
Motor vehicles	2,422
Newsprint	1,110
Wood pulp	785
Motor vehicle parts	782
Wheat	687
Lumber	668
Crude petroleum	649
Iron ore	509
Fabricated copper	475
Aluminum	458

*Based on figures in Table 3 of Section II, *Canadian Statistical Review*, April, 1971

Table 2

CANADA'S TEN LEADING IMPORTS IN 1970*

	VALUE OF IMPORTS (Millions of dollars)
Motor vehicle parts	1,653
Motor vehicles	1,212
Crude petroleum	415
Aircraft and parts	401
Communications and related equipment	378
Motor vehicle engines	373
Office machines	314
Primary iron and steel (other than plate and sheet)	312
Metal fabricated basic products	308
Measuring, control and scientific equipment	298

*Based on figures in Table 4, Section II, *Canadian Statistical Review*, April, 1971

Problems of transportation similarly cause Canada to import large quantities of coal, even though immense deposits exist within the country. The bulk of our requirements occur in the central provinces of Ontario and Quebec, while the main deposits are located many hundreds of miles away in Alberta and Nova Scotia. The cost of transporting Canadian coal to the chief Canadian markets is therefore extremely high; American coal, on the other hand, mined in fields just across the Great Lakes, can be cheaply transported to those markets, and primarily for that reason has supplied the major portion of their coal requirements.[2]

Other leading Canadian exports, though not among the first ten, are other metals—notably nickel and copper, natural gas, foodstuffs such as flour, meat, fish, and some manufactured products in the production of which Canada has become very proficient—aircraft together with engines and parts, farm machinery, communication apparatus and other types of equipment, several types of whiskey. Leading imports, aside from those in the first ten, include apparel of various types—high style items from the world's leading fashion centres and cheap clothing from low wage countries, industrial materials such as cotton, wool, plastics, chemicals, and foods that can be grown only in warmer climates such as tea, coffee, nuts, spices and various fruits and vegetables.

Canada's foreign trade pattern varies from year to year with the discovery of additional national resources, the changing demand of foreigners for our products and our changing demand for foreign goods. Thus during the 1950s Canada's exports of iron and uranium ore greatly increased, following the discovery and development of major deposits. Wheat exports have fluctuated considerably, in accordance with the needs of importing countries and the competition of other countries which have wheat to export. Because of poor crops in Russia and China we were unexpectedly able to sell hundreds of millions of bushels of wheat to those countries in the early 1960s. In recent years we have greatly increased our sales of petroleum and natural gas to the U.S., and have increased substantially our exports of minerals and wood products to Europe. Japan has become a large scale buyer of wheat, coal and other natural products. Our imports of machinery and other steel products in any year have reflected the current volume of construction undertakings in which such equipment and materials were required. Our imports of petroleum and some industrial products have fallen off in recent years as a result of the development or enlargement of domestic production.

---

[2]To enable Nova Scotia and Alberta Coal to compete at all in the main Canadian market, the federal government paid "subventions," i.e. subsidies, toward the cost of transporting coal from these provinces to Central Canada. By the late 1960s however, the price of American coal was rising steeply while marked advances were being achieved in the mining and transporting of Canadian coal. With the possibility that Canadian coal could, without government support, compete in Central Canada against imported coal, the policy of subventions was ended in 1970.

"Traditionally, the relatively high cost of Canadian coal at the mines, plus the high cost of transporting coal to central Canada, has prevented the establishment of a viable market for native coal in this highly industrialized market. Now, however, with modernization of the western Canadian mines and with the introduction of the modern technique of the unit-train transport, the price gap between the native and the imported coal is narrowing. Also, as indicated, the price of imported coal is sharply rising. The possibility therefore exists that, within the near future, the Ontario consumer particularly in the metallurgical industries can be supplied with quality western coals at competitive prices." *Annual Report of the Dominion Coal Board*, 1970, p. 10.

The Direction of Canada's Trade

For the first few years after Confederation, Canada's trade continued to be mainly with Great Britain. We sent most of our exports to that country and obtained from her the bulk of our imports. By 1883, however, our imports from the United States exceeded our imports from Britain. Following World War I, the U.S. became our most important market as well as the main source of our imports; Great Britain took second place in both respects.

Our massive trade with the United States reflects a number of considerations. Our exports to the U.S. consist primarily of raw materials—a few processed to some degree—that we are especially qualified to produce because of our resource endowment. American industry requires enormous amounts of raw materials, and Canadian supplies are conveniently close. We import a great deal from the U.S. for several distinct reasons. American capital equipment is oftentimes better suited to our requirements than that made in other countries; American firms operating in Canada tend to obtain equipment from home sources. We depend upon the U.S. for raw materials, notably cotton and coal, in the one case because we cannot produce it ourselves and in the other case because our own supplies are too far from the centres of demand. We import a variety of consumer goods and services from the U.S.: fruit and vegetables from southern states during winter months; movies, entertainers and

THE DIRECTION OF CANADA'S FOREIGN TRADE IN 1970
(millions of dollars)

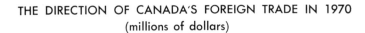

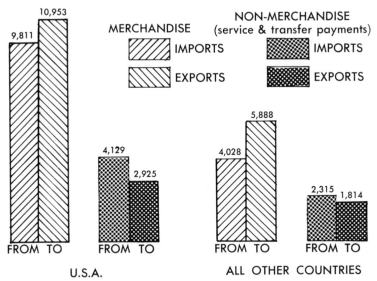

Figure 2. The direction of Canada's foreign trade in 1970

athletes; attractive luxuries and novelties developed in their larger and more advanced economy and which Canadians—exposed to the same advertising influence—are equally anxious to acquire.

In the two decades following World War II our trade ties with the U.S. became progressively closer as that country hugely expanded its industrial establishment and, having largely exhausted its own resource endowment, became more dependent on our natural resources. We at the same time adopted American technology and consumption styles to an ever increasing degree. Since the late 1960s, however, a distinct tendency has emerged toward more diversification in our trade relationships. Japan and Western Europe have been achieving very substantial industrial advance, thereby increasing their need for the kind of materials that we are able to supply, and enlarging their capacity to provide us with the kind of industrial products that we wish to have. Our trade with the U.S., while still of dominating magnitude, has become a slightly smaller proportion of our total international trade. Figure 1 represents the direction of our trade in 1970; a comparable graph for 1965 would have shown our trade with the U.S. as relatively larger and our trade with "all other countries" as relatively smaller.

SUMMARY

If each nation specialized in producing the goods which it was best fitted to produce, the output of the world as a whole would be the maximum possible.

Each country could benefit by concentrating on its specialties and purchasing its other requirements from those nations which specialized in producing them. Reflecting the principle of comparative advantage, even a nation which is generally superior can trade with a nation which is generally inferior, to their mutual advantage.

The degree of benefit achieved by each nation through specialization and exchange, will depend upon the *terms of trade* between its exports and imports.

While the basic theory of international trade is worked out on the basis of highly simplified assumptions, the theory remains obviously valid even when more realistic conditions are assumed.

The free international movement of goods serves as an effective substitute for the free international migration of people.

Canada's trade pattern reflects the principle of comparative advantage. Aside from the large trade in automotive vehicles and parts resulting from the 1965 agreement with the U.S. our exports consist chiefly of natural products. Our imports consist chiefly of manufactured goods.

The United States is our chief trading partner, purchasing the great bulk of our exports and furnishing the great bulk of our imports. Latterly, our trade with other countries has increased significantly in relative importance.

FOR REVIEW AND DISCUSSION

1. If international trade were absolutely free there would never be any point in migrating to another country. Do you agree?
2. "The United States can produce everything more efficiently than any other nation; therefore it has no need to trade with anyone else." If the first statement were true, would the second necessarily follow?
3. Make up an example to show how when three countries trade with one another, each may have total exports equal to total imports while its trade is not in balance with any individual nation.
4. Make up your own example to prove that specialization and trade may be mutually advantageous to two countries.
5. For both countries to benefit from an international exchange, the terms of trade must be between specific limits. Explain.
6. International specialization will be absolute only when the goods traded are produced under conditions of constant costs. Is this statement completely true?
7. The use of money does not affect the fundamental truth that international trade consists of an exchange of *real* goods and services. Explain.
8. When a country is very large in area, international trade may prove preferable to inter-regional trade within the country. Comment.

16

Monetary Aspects of International Trade

THE BALANCE OF INTERNATIONAL PAYMENTS

Each year, or oftener, a modern country carries out an accounting of its business transactions with foreign countries. All the individual transactions carried out during the period are aggregated in a statement known as the Balance of International Payments. The statement divides naturally into two parts, one dealing with current transactions and the other with capital transactions. The first part presents the total value of all goods and services imported and exported during the year, and is referred to as the Balance of Payments on Current Account. The second part indicates what loans, investments, loan repayments and the like have been made by its citizens in foreign countries, and what value of loans, investments and loan repayments foreigners have made within the country; it is referred to as the Balance of Payments on Capital Account. If the Balance of Payments on Current Account reveals that the country has exported a greater value of goods and services than it has imported, the country is commonly said to have a *favourable balance of trade*. If its imports have exceeded its exports in value, its balance of trade is called *unfavourable*.

In examining the balance of payments of any nation, we will find that if its exports and imports are not exactly equal in value, the difference will be matched by an equal difference in payments on capital account. Suppose that Canada exported $15 billion worth of goods and services last year, but imported only $14 billion worth. If foreigners bought $15 billion worth from us, they must have paid us that much. But they only earned $14 billion through their sales of goods and services to us. How could they have obtained the other billion which they paid to us? In 6 possible ways:

1. We might have given them $1 billion of Canadian dollars, under one of the programmes whereby we extend aid to less fortunate nations.
2. We might have loaned them $1 billion of our money, either in the form of short term credits to cover commercial transactions, or long term loans to corporations or governments.

3. We might have invested $1 billion in foreign countries; i.e. we might have established new enterprises in foreign countries or bought out already established ones, or we might have bought the securities of foreign companies and governments.
4. We might have handed over $1 billion to foreigners to pay off debt that we had previously incurred or to buy back Canadian stocks and bonds which they had previously acquired.
5. Foreigners might have possessed Canadian money which they had accumulated through previous earnings and investments in Canada.
6. We might have given them a billion dollars in Canadian funds in exchange for an equivalent amount of foreign currency, adding the money thus acquired to our reserves of foreign currency.

It would have been through any one of the above ways, or some combination of them, that foreigners would have acquired the billion dollars which, together with the $14 billion they earned in sales to us, enabled them to pay for the $15 billion worth of goods and services they bought from us. If we were to examine Canada's Balance of Payments on Capital Account for the year, we would find that, in such transactions, Canada had reduced her indebtedness to foreigners or increased her foreign assets, to a net total of $1 billion.

CANADA'S BALANCE OF INTERNATIONAL PAYMENTS IN 1970

Canada's Balance of Payments for 1970, as shown in Table 1, illustrates the points made above. The Current Account portion gives the value of our sales of goods and services to foreigners and the value of their sales to us. The column headed "Receipts" indicates how much we received from foreigners in each category; the column headed "Payments" shows how much we paid to foreigners in respect to the same categories. As is evident, we sold foreigners $3,002 millions more merchandise than we bought from them. In respect to services and transfer payments, however, we paid foreigners a good deal more than we received so that our surplus on current account was only $1,297 millions.

Two types of payment that we had to make to foreigners were primarily responsible for the fact that our balance on current account was only $1,297 millions when our balance on merchandise sales was more than twice that figure. We remitted to foreigners over one and a half billions as interest and dividends on their investments in Canada, a billion dollars more than we received as return on our investments in foreign countries. The $481 million deficit on "Other services" was largely attributable both to the immense foreign investment in Canada and also to our extensive utilization of various types of foreign expertise. Every branch of a corporation must make remittances to the head office as its share of the firm's total expenditure on general administration, engineering services, research and

Table 1

THE CANADIAN BALANCE OF PAYMENTS ON CURRENT AND CAPITAL ACCOUNT, 1970*
(millions of dollars)

ON CURRENT ACCOUNT	Receipts	Payments	Surplus + or Deficit −
Merchandise	16,841	13,839	+ 3,002
Gold	95	0	+ 95
Services			
Travel and tourism	1,219	1,454	− 235
Interest and dividends	513	1,524	− 1,011
Freight and shipping	1,048	1,012	+ 36
Other services	1,377	1,858	− 481
Transfer payments			
Inheritances and immigrants' funds	388	211	+ 177
Personal and institutional remittances	99	184	− 85
Official contributions	0	201	− 201
	21,580	20,283	+ 1,297

ON CAPITAL ACCOUNT, foreigners:			
Made direct investments in Canada	760		
Bought Canadian securities	1,346		
Repaid, retired debt to Canadians	45		
Paid re Columbia River Treaty	31		
Increased their deposits in Canadian banks	22		
Bought Canadian short term obligations	309		

ON CAPITAL ACCOUNT, Canadians:			
Made direct investments in other countries		215	
Bought securities from foreigners		220	
Retired old security issues		474	
Acquired bank balances and short term holdings abroad		376	
Bought back Canadian short term obligations		152	
Made short term loans abroad		373	

ON CAPITAL ACCOUNT, the Canadian government:			
Advanced to foreigners		142	
Gave export credits		136	
Made other long term loans		181	
Paid off short term liabilities to foreigners		11	
Totals	2,513	2,280	+ 233
Allocation of Special Drawing Rights	133		+ 133
Addition to international reserves		1,663	
Totals	2,646	3,943	− 1,297

*Based on preliminary estimates as given in Table 1 on pp. 24-8, in "Quarterly Estimates of the Canadian Balance of International Payments," Fourth Quarter 1970, published by the Dominion Bureau of Statistics, 1971.

advertising; these are services which are of benefit to all branches and toward whose cost all branches must contribute, including those located in foreign countries. In addition, business firms engage foreign consultants and technicians, use foreign-owned patents and copyrights; promoters engage foreign entertainers and hire foreign athletes. The category of "Other services" includes these types of payments; the size of the payments which we made under this heading reflects the great number of foreign firms operating in Canada and our heavy dependence on technical, entertainment and other services provided by foreigners; Canadians rendered such services to foreigners but the balance was heavily against us.

We applied the surplus of $1,297 millions achieved on current account to increase our reserves of foreign exchange. Actually, we enlarged our reserves during the year by more than this figure. As indicated in the Balance of Payments on Capital Account, foreigners invested a total of $2,513 millions in Canada during the year while Canadians invested a total of $2,280 millions in foreign countries. We added to reserves the $233 millions by which our capital receipts exceeded our capital payments, together with the $133 millions allotted to us as Special Drawing Rights. (A description of these is given later in the chapter.) Our reserves accordingly increased during the year by $1,663 millions, the sum of $1,297, $233 and $133 millions.

A Dramatic Turnabout in 1970?

Our balance of payments surplus of 1970 contrasted dramatically with the deficits we experienced in most of the previous two decades. From 1953 to 1969 we incurred an unbroken series of balance of payments deficits that totalled $14.5 billion for the 17-year period, averaging over $850 million per year with a high of $1,487 million in 1959. The main factors in each year's deficit were always the same: heavy remittances of interest and dividends and large payments for all manner of professional services; in only a few years did we import more merchandise than we exported.

Capital, chiefly American, poured into Canada during this period. Year after year Americans bought huge blocks of Canadian stocks and bonds; year after year they spent vast sums in plant to exploit our natural resources and in branch factories to produce manufactured goods for the Canadian market. We used these American investment funds to cover our annual deficits; a substantial portion of the money we borrowed was used to pay the interest due on past borrowing, further swelling our debt. We found ourselves in the perilous position of being absolutely *obliged* to borrow abroad: without such borrowing we would have been forced either to reduce our purchases from foreign countries or to default on our debt obligations to them.

On several occasions we encountered the possibility of being unable to borrow: for most of this period the U.S. was virtually the sole possible source of foreign capital and because of her own balance of payments problems became increasingly reluctant to provide funds to foreigners. In 1963 the U.S. government introduced an

"Interest Equalization Tax" designed to discourage foreign borrowing in the U.S. by adding fifteen per cent to the cost. Had Canadian borrowers in the U.S. been obliged to pay this tax the effect would have been to produce a general—and very undesirable —increase in the structure of interest rates in Canada. Fortunately, Canadian financial representatives were able to persuade the American authorities to exempt all new issues of Canadian securities from the tax. A more serious threat developed in 1965 when the U.S. Administration announced "voluntary guidelines" for American firms investing outside the country. In order to help eliminate the country's balance of payments deficit in 1966, non-bank financial institutions were asked to limit their purchases of foreign securities during the year and other corporations were asked to limit the amount of direct investment they carried out abroad. Again Canadian representatives successfully interceded, winning for Canada exemption from the first guideline, though not from the second. In 1968 mandatory restraints were introduced on U.S. direct lending abroad and financial institutions were asked to restrict further their lending abroad. Again Canada was accorded a degree of exemption from the restraints.

While Canada was able to continue borrowing on a large scale from the U.S. throughout the period 1953-69 despite that country's concern to reduce its foreign lending, our position was obviously hazardous. The Governor of the Bank of Canada expressed his concern in 1965:

> ". . . . But I believe that it would be unwise to take a detached view of the problems that arise from our dependence on continuing large imports of foreign capital. A situation in which Canada needs to import a great deal of capital from a country which is trying to restrict the export of capital is inherently unsatisfactory, and there is no easy or satisfactory way of dealing with it."[1]

One swallow does not make a summer. The balance of payments surplus we achieved in 1970 may turn out to be merely the good fortune of a single year rather than the herald of a new era; we may revert after 1970 to the pattern of 1953-69, incurring large deficits each year which we cover by borrowing. If, however, we continue to achieve big surpluses on each year's trade our position *vis-à-vis* the United States is likely to change significantly in the years ahead. We will no longer be obliged to borrow from that country to cover deficits; we will instead be in a position to pay off past borrowing.

As of the end of 1970 our gross indebtedness to foreigners, including the value of enterprises which they owned in Canada, totalled $49 billions. Canadians, however, owned foreign investments and assets valued at $21 billions, so that our net foreign indebtedness was $28 billions. Quite obviously if henceforth we regularly achieved balance of payments surpluses of the magnitude of that recorded in 1970, it would not take too many years to reduce our net foreign indebtedness to zero, using

---

[1]Bank of Canada, *Annual Report of the Governor to the Minister of Finance*, 1965, p. 10.

the surpluses either to increase the amount of our foreign investment or to pay off—
or buy out—foreigners who invested in Canada.

FOREIGN EXCHANGE RATES

Every independent country has its own currency: Canada has the Canadian dollar;
the United States has the American dollar; the British have the pound sterling; the
French have the franc; and so on. Within each country its own currency constitutes
the lawful money of the land, and is the money which people normally receive in
payment for goods sold or services rendered. Any person who wishes to make purchases in a foreign country must first acquire that country's currency, with which to
make payment. The cost to him of whatever he buys in the foreign country will depend on two factors: its price, expressed in its domestic currency; and secondly, the
price which must be paid by a foreigner to acquire that currency. If a Canadian buys
a bottle of wine in France the cost to him will depend upon the number of francs
charged, and also upon the number of cents he must pay to acquire those francs.

The rate at which a country's currency exchanges for the currency of another
country is known as its foreign exchange rate. While one country's currency may be
exchanged for any other in the world, exchange rates are usually expressed nowadays in terms of the U.S. dollar. The rate can be expressed as the number of U.S.
dollars obtained in exchange for one unit of the country's currency, or the amount of
its currency for which one dollar is exchanged. Thus if the Canadian dollar is worth
about 98 cents in U.S. funds this means that an American dollar is worth $1.02 in
Canadian funds.

What Determines the Rate of Exchange?

The answer runs along familiar lines. The foreign exchange rate is simply a price, the
price paid for the currency of another country; its equilibrium level is determined by
supply and demand and it changes as a result of shifts in supply and demand. As we
shall see, however, governments may intervene to establish some rate other than the
equilibrium figure.

In respect to the exchange rate of the Canadian dollar, the relevant demand is
the demand for our dollars expressed by foreigners who offer their own currency in
payment. The supply is the supply of Canadian dollars offered by Canadians who
wish to receive foreign currency in exchange.

The reasons why foreigners want our dollars is indicated in Table 1. They need
our dollars "on current account," that is to pay for goods and services they wish to
buy from us. Secondly, they want Canadian dollars "on capital account": to carry
out investment projects in Canada, to buy Canadian securities, to pay off debts owed
to Canadians, possibly just to hold their wealth in Canadian dollars because they

expect that the currency of their own country will soon decline in value or that our dollar will soon rise.[2]

These are the component elements in the demand for our dollars expressed on the foreign exchange market.[3] The corresponding supply consists of the very same elements, only with direction reversed; it is composed of the offerings by Canadians of dollars in exchange for foreign currency which they need to make purchases and investments abroad, to pay debts owed to foreigners, and so on.

The foreign exchange market is not unlike the market for a commodity with demand and supply curves of normal shape: if the price falls buyers will want more and sellers will offer less; if the price rises buyers will want less and sellers will offer more. The equilibrium rate of exchange will be at the point of intersection between the two curves. As with any commodity, shifts may occur in demand and supply between one period and another: foreigners might become more anxious to have our goods or to invest in Canada and therefore increase their demand for our dollars; Canadians might become less eager to have foreign goods and offer fewer dollars in exchange for foreign currency. When such shifts occur in demand and supply the equilibrium rate of exchange changes accordingly.

The supply and demand factors which together determine the demand for a nation's currency do in fact change continuously. Check a daily paper on two successive days, for instance, to see the rate at which the Canadian dollar is exchanged for U.S. funds. In all probability you will find that the rate changes, by just a fraction of a cent, between one day and the next. Over longer periods, after major shifts have occurred in the balance of market forces, the variation may be very large. Thus in 1933 the Canadian dollar exchanged for about 80 cents in U.S. money; at one time in 1959 it exchanged for more than $1.06 in U.S. funds. And, relatively, the Canadian dollar may be considered to have been fairly stable in value. The foreign exchange rates of other countries' currencies have varied over a far greater range.

Exchange Rate Instability, an Automatic Correction

Even without government controls, variations in the foreign exchange rate tend to be self-limiting. A shift in the rate, in either direction, brings into play a reaction which tends to restrict the movement away from the original position. Suppose that the Canadian dollar exchanges today for one American dollar exactly. Suppose that, tomorrow, Americans decide to increase greatly their investment in Canada and

[2]The Canadians who sell goods, services and securities to foreigners may accept foreign currency in payment. However, they will eventually want to convert this money into Canadian currency and will offer it on the foreign exchange market in return for Canadian funds. This foreign currency offered by Canadians therefore becomes part of the total supply offered on the foreign exchange market; the fact that it is supplied by the Canadians who acquired it, rather than the foreigners who first provided it, is of no significance.

[3]The "market" consists of the banks and financial institutions through which buyers and sellers carry out their transactions.

therefore increase greatly their demand for Canadian dollars. The Canadian dollar will of course rise in value; say it rises to $1.05 in American funds.

American importers are regularly buying Canadian goods and services; American newspapers, for instance, each year buy large quantities of Canadian newsprint. If the price of newsprint is $100 per ton in Canada, then American newspapers will find that because the Canadian dollar has risen to $1.05 in American funds, they now have to pay $105 for a ton of Canadian newsprint. Because Canadian newsprint now costs them more, American newspapers will likely buy less; they may turn to other countries or obtain more from sources within the United States. The fact that American newspapers now wish to buy less newsprint in Canada means that Americans will want fewer Canadian dollars.

An increase in the number of their dollars offered by Canadians is likely to occur as well. Canadians will now find themselves able to buy an American dollar for only 95 cents[4] in their own currency and very likely will increase their purchases in the United States. To obtain the additional American currency which they wish to spend, they will increase the amount of Canadian dollars which they offer in exchange.

Hence the rise in the Canadian dollar's foreign exchange rate will induce a reduction in the number wanted by some foreigners, and an increase in the number offered by some Canadians. These developments will tend to restrain the Canadian dollar's rise, and it will not move up by as much as it would have done had these restrictive reactions not come into play.

Similarly, if the foreign exchange rate of the Canadian dollar tends to fall, this will also induce reactions which will have stabilizing effects. If foreigners have to pay less of their money for our dollar, all Canadian goods will become cheaper as far as they are concerned and they are likely to increase their purchases in Canada. Canadians, on the other hand, will find that to obtain a foreign currency they now have to pay more. Presumably many will decide to reduce their purchases in foreign countries; because they need less foreign currency, they will offer fewer Canadian dollars in exchange for such currency. Hence, when the Canadian dollar tends to decline in value, foreigners will want to obtain more of them, while Canadians will offer fewer of them; the dollar's downward tendency will be restrained.

Disadvantages of Exchange Rate Instability

To businessmen engaged in international transactions, the variability of the foreign exchange rate constitutes a disagreeable hazard. It exposes them to windfall losses which are quite unrelated to the ordinary risks of their business. Suppose that an English importer buys one million bushels of wheat from a Canadian firm, at a price

---

[4]95.24 cents to be precise, or $\dfrac{100}{105} \times \$1.00$.

of $2 per bushel, and agrees to pay in Canadian funds. Suppose that the current exchange rate is £1 = $4. In that case the wheat costs the Englishman £500,000 in his own money, and he may contract to sell it to a British milling firm for £510,000.

But suppose that the pound suddenly drops in value from $4 to $3.80, as the result of shifts in supply and demand on the foreign exchange market which have nothing to do with Britain's wheat imports. The English wheat importer finds that the wheat will actually cost him £526,312; this is the amount which he will now have to pay in order to obtain $2 million in Canadian money. Instead of earning a profit on his contract with the miller, he suffers a substantial loss.[5]

Besides causing losses to individual businessmen, exchange rate fluctuations may have adverse effects on the national economy as a whole. Sharp changes in the foreign exchange rate will abruptly alter the prices of imports and exports, with undesirable effects on the general level of prices and perhaps on the distribution of the nation's productive capacity as between exports and goods for domestic use. Unstable foreign exchange rates will discourage international lending and borrowing.

Stabilization of the Foreign Exchange Rate

Despite constant variation in the supply and demand involved, the foreign exchange rate of a nation's currency need not be continuously shifting about. Governments have employed two effective techniques to maintain stability for the foreign exchange rate of their currency over long periods of time. These are described below.

The Gold Standard. During the half century which preceded the outbreak of World War I, practically all of the major countries of the world were on the *gold standard*. For a country to be on the gold standard meant four things:

Its currency was declared by the government to be worth a specified weight of gold.

A unit of its currency could always be exchanged for this weight of gold at the banks of the country.

The country's banks would buy gold, in any quantity, at this price fixed by the government.

The total money supply of the country was, at any given time, closely related to the country's current gold holdings. An increase in the nation's gold stocks would effect an increase in the total money supply; a decrease would require a decrease.[6]

With each country adhering rigidly to these rules, the stability of foreign exchange rates was assured. A simple example will illustrate. Suppose that the British

---

[5]Had the deal between the Canadian exporter and the British importer specified payment in British currency, it would have been the Canadian who bore the loss when the pound dropped in value. The £500,000 which he had agreed to accept for the wheat would have turned out to be worth only $1,900,000 in Canadian funds, instead of $2,000,000 as he had anticipated.

[6]The relationship would normally be in the form of a constant ratio; e.g., for every dollar's worth of gold there might be four dollars of paper currency. (The law would likely stipulate some such ratio as a maximum, and in practice the actual ratio would be near the authorized maximum.)

fixed the gold value of the pound sterling at 100 grains, while the Canadian government fixed the gold value of the dollar at 20 grains. In that case the rate of exchange
could not vary from the ratio £1 = $5.[7] If the market rate for the pound threatened
to fall below this level, an Englishman could simply go to his bank, buy gold, and
ship it to Canada. For each pound note he gave the bank he would get 100 grains of
gold. Shipped to Canada, these 100 grains of gold could be sold to any Canadian
bank for $5.

Actually the shipment of gold from one country to the other involved some
costs, of packaging, insurance, freight, and the loss of interest during the period when
it was in transit. These costs amounted to about 2 cents per 100 grains of gold.
Hence, because of these shipping costs, the Englishman who bought £1 of gold in
Britain and shipped it to Canada would realize only $4.98. He would, therefore, buy
and ship gold only if, in the foreign exchange market, he was offered less than $4.98
for a pound sterling. The figure $4.98 would be referred to as the *gold export point*,
being the exchange rate below which gold would be shipped out of Britain, but above
which it would not be shipped. Similarly, $5.02 would be referred to as the *gold
import point*; Canadians would send gold to Britain only if the exchange rate rose
above £1 = $5.02.

The Automatic Correction of Payments Imbalances. The fact that a country's
gold holdings determined the size of its total money supply assured that the value
of its imports and the value of its exports would be kept in appropriate relationship
to one another.[8] Excessive imports would initiate the shipment of gold out of the
country. Importers who needed large amounts of foreign currency to make payment
would be offering large amounts of domestic currency in exchange for the foreign
currency they required; these heavy offerings would drive the rate of exchange below
the gold export point, and gold would be shipped out of the country.

However, the shipment of gold would itself tend to correct the situation. With
its gold holdings reduced, the nation's total money supply would automatically be
contracted, by a multiple of the amount of gold sent out. The contraction of the
country's money supply would bring about a decline in prices and incomes. The lower
prices would tempt foreigners to buy more, and their need for the nation's currency
would increase. On the other hand, the country's own people, their incomes lowered,

[7]This particular rate of exchange never of course existed. It is used here in order to keep the
arithmetic simple and within the competence of the author. Actually, when Britain and Canada
were on the gold standard the gold content of the Canadian dollar was specified to be 23.22 grains
(the same as the American), and the exchange rate with the pound sterling was £1 = $4.866.

[8]The appropriate relationship is not necessarily one of equality. A country which is borrowing
abroad in order to finance a long range development programme will naturally have an excess of
imports over exports; the excess will represent the value of the foreign goods and services it requires to carry out its programme, and will amount to the sum borrowed. The country's imports
would accordingly be considered excessive only if their value exceeded the value of its exports
plus its long term foreign borrowing for developmental purposes. Similarly, a country which is
making long term loans abroad will naturally have a surplus of exports over imports which is
equal to the amount of its lending.

would be obliged to buy less from abroad. In any case, the lower prices prevailing at home would induce them to prefer domestic over foreign goods and importers' offerings of the country's currency in exchange for foreign currency would correspondingly decline.

Loss of gold would, in this way, correct the situation which was responsible for that loss of gold. Imports had been too large in relation to exports; the resultant loss of gold, as we have just seen, would bring about a reduction in imports and an increase in exports, and thereby would bring the two once more into appropriate relationship.

By the same token, if a country was receiving gold from other countries, it would be because its exports were inappropriately greater than its imports. The inflow of gold would bring about an expansion of the country's money supply and an increase in incomes and prices. With incomes higher, and domestically produced goods higher priced, imports would tend to increase. The higher domestic prices would discourage foreigners from buying as much as previously. Hence, because of the inflow of gold, imports would rise and exports fall until the two were once again in proper relationship.

Abandonment of the Gold Standard. The gold standard worked well until 1914, maintaining a degree of exchange rate stability which has never been matched since. The outbreak of World War I brought a general suspension of the standard, and postwar attempts to restore it came to grief. The prewar pattern of world trade had facilitated the smooth operation of the standard; the postwar pattern differed sharply, being characterized by sustained heavy exports from the United States to Europe and a markedly smaller flow of exports from Europe to the United States.[9]

Gold was shipped steadily from Europe to the United States, but this gold movement failed to bring imports and exports into proper relationship, either in Europe or America. European countries refused to allow their respective money supplies to contract, despite the outflow of gold; contraction of the money supply would have given rise to unemployment and a reduction of money incomes, and these the people simply would not tolerate. The United States refused to allow its money supply to expand in accordance with the gold flowing in: it did not want inflation. The movement of gold from Europe to America failed accordingly to bring about either an increase in European exports to America or a reduction in American exports to Europe. Gold continued to leave Europe until European countries had so little left that they were obliged to leave the gold standard. Great Britain abandoned the standard in 1931, and most of Europe promptly did likewise.

The United States, which by now possessed most of the world's gold stock, remained on the gold standard, although with qualifications. The U.S. government maintained its undertaking to buy all gold offered at the price it fixed—$20.67 per ounce before 1933 and $35.00 per ounce afterward. With its price thus firmly

---

[9]Other developments further hindered the successful operation of the gold standard during the inter-war era. These are described later in the chapter.

underwritten by the American government gold continued to serve as an international currency. While no longer observing the rules of the gold standard nations regarded their gold stocks as reserves of international currency and gladly accepted gold from other countries as payment of obligations.

Exchange Stabilization: "Pegging"

Abandonment of the gold standard exposed nations to the inconveniences and disadvantages of having the foreign exchange rate of their currency shift about in accordance with the vagaries of supply and demand. Most nations, to keep the rate stable, adopted the device of "pegging," i.e. guaranteed to maintain a specified rate regardless of the movements of demand and supply.

Figure 1 illustrates how the Canadian government might maintain the dollar at a fixed rate. The demand and supply conditions on the foreign exchange market are shown for four time periods; the conditions are different in each period and the equilibrium rate is different in each, being Q_1P_1 in Period 1, Q_2P_2 in Period 2, and so on. Suppose now that the government has fixed the exchange rate at OF, i.e. it has declared that a dollar will always exchange for OF in foreign currency.

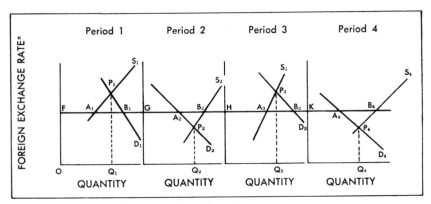

*Price paid by foreigners for Canadian Currency.

Figure 1.   A "pegged" foreign exchange rate

In the first period, foreigners, at the fixed exchange rate, wish to purchase the amount FB_1 of Canadian dollars; Canadians, however, wish to sell only the quantity FA_1. To enable foreigners to purchase all the Canadian dollars that they wish at the pegged rate, our government sells them the amount A_1B_1 taking their foreign currency in payment. In Period 3, when the same kind of situation prevails, the government sells A_3B_3 of Canadian dollars to foreigners.

In Period 2 foreigners wish to purchase only GA_2 of Canadian dollars at the pegged price, but Canadians wish to sell GB_2 (in order to obtain the corresponding amount of foreign currency). If the government has guaranteed that Canadians will be able to buy all the foreign currency they desire at the official rate, then it must offer for sale the quantity A_2B_2. In Period 4, the government would have to provide A_4B_4 of foreign currency, accepting Canadian dollars in payment at the official rate.

Where does the government get the foreign currency it sells to Canadians? As we have seen, the government will acquire foreign currency whenever the foreign exchange situation corresponds to that of Periods 1 or 3. The amounts acquired at such times may be adequate to meet the need that arises when situations develop like those in periods 2 and 4. So long as the amounts of foreign currency that must be paid out during periods like 2 and 4 are no greater than the acquisitions during periods like 1 and 3 the country's reserves will remain at a safe level. If, however, drains exceed acquisitions then reserves will be eaten into and may be consumed altogether. Faced with the problem of dwindling reserves a government may borrow foreign currency from another country or from an international agency such as the International Monetary Fund.

Persistent drains on a country's reserves of foreign exchange could be prevented by pegging the nation's currency at a lower rate.[10] If the peg was lowered acquisitions of foreign exchange during periods like 1 and 3 would be greater while drains during periods like 2 and 4 would be reduced. The student may verify this for himself by graphical demonstration.[11]

As we shall see in Chapter 28 a modern government, through its control over taxation and the banking system, is able to exercise a very considerable influence over the aggregate of incomes and spending in the country. Since a significant portion of income is typically spent on imports, policies which restrain the growth of incomes are likely to restrain, more or less correspondingly, the demand for imports and therefore the demand for foreign currency with which to pay for imports. Hence, in principle, by controlling the aggregate of national incomes a government might ensure that the quantity of foreign currency demanded by its people was no greater than the amount that could safely be provided to them, i.e., the amount that could be provided without impairing the government's capacity to maintain the pegged rate of its own national currency, in the manner described above. It was partly for this reason that the British government raised taxes and introduced its "wage freeze" in 1966; it hoped thereby to ensure that the quantity demanded of foreign currency

---

[10]If Period 1 and 3 situations occurred very often the government might accumulate reserves of foreign currency so great as to be considered unnecessarily large. In that case the government might peg the country's currency at a higher rate, as the government of West Germany did several years ago.

[11]Note that the vertical axis in Figure 1 represents the price paid in Canadian dollars for foreign currency. A lower exchange rate for the dollar would mean a higher price for foreign currency.

did not rise to proportions which would render it impossible to maintain the pound sterling at the pegged rate.

Foreign Exchange Control

Despite the fact that Period 2 situations were occurring all the time, the government might be unwilling, for one reason or another, to peg its currency at a lower rate. It might also be unwilling, or unable, to borrow foreign currency from any source. In that case it would institute foreign exchange controls which required all Canadians who acquired foreign currency to hand it over to the government, receiving in return Canadian dollars at the official rate. Canadians who wished to obtain foreign currency would have to obtain it from the government or from an agent designated by the government. If the government did not wish to draw on its foreign currency reserves it would permit Canadians to purchase (referring to period 2) only GA_2 of foreign currency, exactly the amount currently provided by foreigners. If the government wished to build up its reserves of foreign currency, it would not permit Canadians to buy even as much as GA_2 of foreign currency.

The government would no doubt attempt to ensure that the limited amount of foreign currency available was used to best advantage. Canadians who wished to obtain foreign funds would be asked how they proposed to spend the money. Those who indicated that they would use it to pay for a pleasure trip abroad or for the purchase of foreign-made luxuries would be refused. The GA_2 amount of foreign currency available would be allotted only to those Canadians who needed such funds to pay for foreign materials, machinery and the like, which would strengthen the national economy.

The International Monetary Fund

During the half century or so which preceded the outbreak of World War I, the gold standard, to which all the major nations adhered, had guaranteed a world-wide system of stable exchange rates. A universally acceptable money had existed in the form of gold and balances in London banks which could readily be exchanged for gold. The London money market served as pivotal centre for the world-wide system. International obligations were characteristically paid through the transfer of funds held in London; most international loans and transfers of funds were arranged by the City's powerful financial institutions.

However, the gold standard was able to serve its purpose well only in a favourable international atmosphere. In the pre-1914 era most nations generally had adequate supplies of foreign exchange. Countries of the New World obtained ample foreign exchange through the export of their foodstuffs and raw materials and through loans obtained in London or other European financial centres. Western European countries obtained ample foreign exchange through the export of their industrial goods together with their commercial and financial services and through the interest and dividends they received on overseas investments. The City of London functioned superbly as the key centre of the world-wide system, thanks to the skill, integrity and experience of its financial community and the immense wealth, the world-wide power and influence of Great Britain.

In the era which followed the end of World War I, the international situation was drastically different. European countries suffered chronic balance-of-payments deficits and London was no longer the financial centre of the world. Partially restored several years after the War, the gold standard worked haltingly during the later 1920s and was generally abandoned in the early 1930s. In the absence of a world-wide system to which all nations adhered, foreign exchange rates became wildly unstable. Difficulties with foreign exchange were partly responsible for the enormous decline which occurred in the volume of world trade. Governments faced with balance-of-payments deficits adopted exchange control or resorted to depreciation as a means of stimulating exports and discouraging imports. The instability of foreign exchange rates, resulting from frequent and widespread depreciation, served to reduce the flow of international trade practically as much as did the barriers and controls; businessmen, apprehensive of loss through unpredictable shifts in exchange rates, became reluctant to buy and sell in foreign countries.

Experts meeting at an economic conference held at Bretton Woods in the U.S. in 1944 foresaw how problems of foreign exchange might seriously restrict the volume of international trade in the postwar world. Accordingly they drew up plans not only for the World Bank, but also for an international agency which would arrange for exchange rate stability such as had existed in the era of the gold standard. The institution which they designed, the International Monetary Fund, actually began to operate in 1946.

The member countries initially contributed approximately $9 billion to its capital when the Fund was established; by 1970 this figure had been increased to $28.9 billion. Each country contributed 25 per cent of its quota in the form of gold or American dollars[12] and the remainder in its own currency. The money supply held by the Fund accordingly includes all the various currencies of its member countries.

The key function of the Fund is to assist any member country which is temporarily short of foreign exchange, so that the country is not obliged to depreciate its currency or to adopt restrictions on imports. Each member country may draw from the Fund the foreign currency which it requires to meet a balance-of-payments deficit. When subsequently the country achieves a surplus in its balance of payments, it is expected to repay to the Fund the foreign currency which it has drawn. Drawing rights are limited; no nation may, in any one year, draw foreign exchange in excess of a value equal to 25 per cent of its own quota. Nor may it continue drawing indefinitely; its total indebtedness to the Fund must at no time be greater than twice its quota.

---

[12]Or 10 per cent of its official holdings of gold and American dollars, if that amounted to less.

If a nation persistently draws on the Fund, its balance of payments is regarded as being in "fundamental disequilibrium"; i.e., that nation is regularly importing more goods than it has the means to pay for, and should take steps to correct the situation. Depreciation of its currency is likely to prove a remedy since it will tend to increase exports and to reduce imports, thereby closing the gap between the nation's earnings of foreign exchange and its requirements. A member country, when faced by persistent balance-of-payments difficulties, may depreciate its currency by as much as ten per cent without obtaining permission from the Fund's authorities. The approval of these authorities is required for any depreciation in excess of this figure.

Thus the Fund tries to maintain stable exchange rates, but where absolute stability is impossible it arranges for orderly adjustment to a new level at which stability can be achieved. The objective is to prevent foreign exchange difficulties from restricting the volume of international trade. A nation which is temporarily short of foreign exchange can borrow from the Fund, and is not obliged to reduce imports or to depreciate its currency. A nation which persistently tends to be short of foreign exchange will be advised to revalue its currency so as to correct this tendency.

A number of arrangements were developed during the 1960s to supplement the resources of the Fund and the assistance it was able to provide. The possibility existed that the currency of a particular country might be so strongly demanded by other countries as to deplete the Fund's holdings of that currency; to help safeguard against such an eventuality, ten of the world's leading industrial nations[13] undertook to lend their respective currencies to the Fund, up to specified amounts in each case, if ever the need arose. In addition, a group of central banks, including the Bank of Canada and the U.S. Federal Reserve System, formed a network for reciprocal short term credits. Completely *ad hoc* arrangements were made on several occasions to deal with balance of payments crises suddenly experienced by major powers: the central banks of several leading countries hastily formed a group to extend assistance to the Bank of England in 1967; another hurriedly organized group came to the aid of the Bank of France in the following year.

Special Drawing Rights

The international community evinced a new and pressing need during the 1960s—for an international currency that would be free of the disadvantages of those in use. For decades gold and U.S. dollars had been the universally acceptable media of international transactions, and nations had counted their holdings of gold and U.S. dollars as their solid reserve of foreign exchange. Gold, fascinating everyone with its glitter as in all ages past, was reckoned to be inherently valuable; U.S. dollars were the equivalent of gold since the U.S. government guaranteed to foreigners that they could

[13]The U.S., West Germany, the United Kingdom, France, Italy, Japan, Canada, the Netherlands, Belgium, Sweden.

at any time redeem dollars for gold at the rate of 35 dollars per ounce. Even without this guarantee the dollar would have been highly regarded throughout the world, for it was the means of purchasing the attractive American goods and services that foreigners ardently desired but could not produce as effectively for themselves. The British pound, universally acceptable during the heyday of the Empire, now served as an international currency only on a limited scale, chiefly within the confines of the Commonwealth.

During the 1960s both gold and U.S. dollars became increasingly unsatisfactory as international currency. The world's monetary gold supply was not growing proportionately to the expansion of international commerce, partly because only a relatively small amount of new gold was mined each year and partly because a considerable amount was being drawn off for industrial use. U.S. dollars lost a good deal of their mystique in the 1960s. The American economy was labouring under severe strains, experiencing a significant degree of inflation and incurring large balance of payment deficits. Inflation in the United States served to diminish the real value of dollars held by foreigners as international currency; as a result of a series of American balance of payments deficits foreigners came to hold greatly enlarged quantities of American securities and funds and their eagerness to acquire more distinctly cooled. A great many foreign holders of American dollars exercised their option of redeeming their dollars for gold, and the U.S. gold stock experienced heavy drains. The prospect emerged that the U.S. gold stock would be reduced to such a degree that the American government would be unable to maintain its guarantee that foreigners could redeem their dollars for gold any time they wished. With its prospects thus clouded, the dollar lost its quality of unquestioned and universal acceptability, and served less well as an international currency.

Remedial action was precipitated by events of 1967 and 1968. Great Britain, struggling with severe balance of payments deficits, devalued the pound in November, 1967. To many this act presaged even more damaging blows to the existing international monetary arrangements.[14]

A great many people became convinced that the price of gold, fixed since 1933 at $35 U.S. an ounce, would be sharply increased, and they bought large amounts in order to gain a speculative profit. Such purchases continued on a large scale for the next several months, the gold being drawn out of stocks held as reserves by monetary authorities. In March, 1968, the scale of gold buying by speculators reached crisis proportions; monetary authorities thereupon temporarily suspended gold sales to private parties. As a longer term measure they instituted a two-tier price for gold: the gold that served as monetary reserves would continue to be valued at $35 per ounce and would be exchanged at that price among national monetary authorities;

---

[14]The U.S. government, also beset by a balance of payments deficit, introduced a programme on January 1st, 1968, designed to curb the outflow of funds from the country; heavy opposition developed at once to some of its specific measures and it became evident that the programme was unlikely to realize its objective.

the gold that private parties wished to buy and sell, however, would henceforth be sold on private markets at whatever price prevailed in those markets.

The need remained to enlarge the supply of acceptable international currency. Monetary authorities were reluctant to achieve this by increasing the price of gold: an immense bonus would thereby be conferred on the nations which happened to hold large stocks at the time. It was agreed that the currency of a single country was an unsatisfactory form of international currency: the amount available to other nations would vary with the lending policies and the vagaries of the balance of payments of that country. What was needed was an international currency the supply of which could be deliberately regulated in conformity with the world's needs.

The solution adopted was creation of Special Drawing Rights, a form of international credit. On January 1, 1970, $3.5 billion of S.D.R.'s, were created, with each member country of the International Monetary Fund being allocated a share corresponding to its I.M.F. subscription quota. A further $3 billion were to be created in each of the next two years. These S.D.R.'s, "paper gold," constituted part of each nation's reserve of foreign exchange. Any nation in balance of payments deficit could acquire needed foreign exchange by transferring S.D.R.'s to the account of the country that supplied that foreign exchange; the recipient country would be paid interest, in S.D.R.'s, on the foreign exchange that it supplied.

The plan was instituted for a basic period of five years, with provision for review at the expiry of that period.

The role of the U.S. dollar as international currency, weakening throughout the 1960s, was gravely impaired by events of 1971. A full-blown crisis occurred in May of that year when holders of large quantities of U.S. dollars scrambled to exchange them for more highly regarded European currencies. In response to the strong demand Germany and other European countries took various courses of action which all had the effect of reducing the value of the dollar in relation to their own currencies. In August President Nixon suddenly announced a crisis programme designed to stop the drain of gold from the U.S. and to stem the outflow of dollars. Convertibility of dollars into gold was suspended and measures were introduced (described in Chapter 17) to reduce American imports; following the sudden announcement the American government urgently demanded of other free world countries that they revalue their currencies upward and, as well, that they increase their contributions to international defense arrangements and to programmes of economic assistance to underdeveloped countries. The foreign exchange rates of other national currencies did indeed quickly rise; governments pegged their respective currencies at higher levels in relation to the U.S. dollar or allowed them to "float" upward.

The overall object of these American measures was to reduce the country's outlays abroad and increase her foreign earnings, thereby shifting the U.S. balance of payments position from deficit to surplus. Inevitably this would diminish the role of the dollar as international currency: with the U.S. achieving surpluses in its balance of payments rather than incurring deficits foreigners would not be so readily able to acquire American dollars to use as an international medium of exchange or to hold as reserves. American authorities contemplated without regret the prospect that the dollar's international status would decline. The large and growing foreign holdings of dollars implied a large and growing international indebtedness on the part of the U.S.; this was undesirable in itself and involved the hazard of balance of payments crises—such as those which actually occurred—which could have seriously unsettling effects on the national economy.

STABILIZATION OF THE CANADIAN DOLLAR

Canada was on the gold standard until 1914, with the gold content of the dollar being set at the same weight as the American dollar, i.e. 23.22 grains. Gold payments were suspended when World War I broke out and not resumed until 1926, following Great Britain's resumption of the gold standard in the previous year. By 1929, however, Canada was obliged to restrict the export of gold from the country, thereby, in effect, going off the gold standard. Two years later, following Britain's departure from the standard, Canada formally abandoned it.

The foreign exchange rate of the dollar, now determined by demand and supply considerations alone, declined sharply; its value dipped at times to about 80 cents in U.S. funds. In 1933, however, the Canadian dollar rose briskly, attaining parity with the American dollar by the end of the year.[15] It hovered around this level until the outbreak of World War II in September, 1939.

Severe downward pressure quickly developed on the Canadian dollar as many people sought to exchange their Canadian funds for American dollars. Accordingly, on September 16, 1939, the federal government established the Foreign Exchange Control Board, to conserve the country's supplies of foreign currency and to stabilize the foreign exchange rate. The Board took over the Exchange Fund Account which had been established in 1935,[16] and henceforth strictly regulated all transactions by Canadians in which foreign currencies were involved. Canadians who sold goods or services to foreigners were obliged to turn over to the Board their earnings of foreign exchange; Canadians who wished to spend money in foreign countries could purchase

[15]The primary reason was the devaluation of the American dollar. Its gold value was reduced almost by half, when the U.S. government declared an ounce of gold to be worth $35.00, in place of the previous figure of $20.67.

[16]This Account had been established in 1935, to be used for stabilization of the Canadian dollar in foreign exchange. It was intended that the officials who administered the Account should carry out such purchases and sales of gold, U.S. dollars and British sterling, as were necessary to stabilize the external value of the Canadian dollar. But although the Account was set up in 1935, it was never actually used until it was taken over by the Foreign Exchange Control Board. The Act according to which the Account was to operate was formally proclaimed, and therefore became effective, only on that day. (Government intervention to stabilize the dollar had not really been necessary up to this time. As indicated above, market forces alone held the Canadian dollar quite steady, at about parity with the American, from 1933 till the outbreak of the War.)

the necessary currency only from agents of the Board, and only for purposes approved by the Board. For the next eleven years the Board "pegged" the Canadian dollar, the actual rate being varied, however, on two occasions. The initial rate, set on September 16, 1939, was $1.10 Canadian to $1.00 U.S., and this rate was maintained throughout the War. From 1946 to 1949 the Canadian dollar was held at parity with the American. In September 1949 the earlier rate of $1.10 Canadian for $1.00 U.S. was re-established and maintained until October of the following year. At that time the government abandoned its policy of maintaining the Canadian dollar at a fixed level, so that henceforth the rate was determined primarily by demand and supply. (Foreign exchange controls were retained for another year.)

While the Canadian dollar was no longer "pegged," the Exchange Fund Account was still maintained and periodically its management[17] purchased and sold foreign exchange, the objective being to prevent sharp and sudden changes in the external value of the Canadian dollar. No attempt was made to stop major shifts in the foreign exchange rate when these arose out of fundamental changes in the Canadian balance of payments. When such major changes became necessary, they were not prevented; instead the management of the Account attempted merely to slow them down, so that the movement to a new level took place gradually rather than suddenly. Businessmen were thereby protected against the danger of severe loss through sharp and sudden exchange rate fluctuations.

Significant departures from the established policy occurred in 1960-61. The Canadian dollar was above the U.S. dollar in value and there were widespread complaints that the high foreign exchange value of our dollar was unduly encouraging imports and discouraging exports, thereby contributing to unemployment. On at least two occasions the authorities intervened in the market not to smooth out fluctuations in the foreign exchange rate of the Canadian dollar but to reduce its average level.

Events took a new turn in 1961-62. For various reasons foreign demand for the Canadian dollar declined and its value tended to fall. To resist this downward pressure the Exchange Fund Account purchased Canadian dollars, using its previously accumulated reserves of U.S. currency; for a while the Canadian dollar was held at 95 cents in U.S. funds. The drain on our U.S. currency reserves became intolerably heavy, however. On May 2, 1962, the Minister of Finance announced that henceforth the Canadian dollar would be pegged at 92½ cents in U.S. Funds. Eight years later this action was reversed. Following a prolonged period of heavy demand for the Canadian dollar by foreigners, leading to the accumulation by Canada of large reserves of foreign currency, the Minister of Finance announced, on May 31, 1970, that until further notice the dollar would be allowed to "float," i.e. it would not be held at a pegged rate but would be allowed to move about in accordance with demand and supply.

---

[17]The account is managed by the Bank of Canada, on behalf of the Minister of Finance.

SUMMARY

Each nation regularly carries out an accounting of its transactions with other nations. The aggregates of imports and exports are ascertained, together with the aggregates of foreign lending and borrowing.

The foreign exchange rate of a nation's currency in effect constitutes the price which foreigners pay for that currency, in terms of their own money. Being a price, the rate is determined primarily by demand and supply. The demand comes chiefly from foreigners who wish to make purchases and investments within the country. The supply comes chiefly from nationals who wish to make purchases and investments in foreign countries.

Reflecting changes in demand or supply, the foreign exchange rate may vary from time to time. Such variations bring into play reactions which tend to restrict the degree of variation.

Since sharp variations in foreign exchange rates may deter international trade, governments have adopted special measures to keep them steady. The gold standard constituted a world-wide system under which general stability of exchange rates was assured. Furthermore, with nations adhering to the "rules" of the gold standard system, trade imbalances tended to be automatically corrected.

Following the general abandonment of the gold standard in the early 1930s individual nations attempted to stabilize their national currencies by "pegging" operations. A number of new international credit arrangements were introduced following World War II.

Following the first world war the American dollar served as the world's chief international currency; its status became significantly impaired, however, commencing in the 1960s.

Canada was on the gold standard until 1931, save for the period of the First World War. (Actually we went off the gold standard in 1929, the formal renunciation being made in 1931.) During World War II and for a few years after, the Canadian dollar was "pegged"; from 1950 to 1962 the dollar's value was permitted to vary with market conditions, the authorities seeking merely to prevent sudden and drastic fluctuations. In 1962, following an exchange crisis, the dollar was pegged at 92.5 cents in U.S. funds; in 1970 it was again allowed to "float".

FOR REVIEW AND DISCUSSION

1. A so-called favourable balance of trade would, by any rational person, be called unfavourable. Comment.
2. Would you advocate a return to the gold standard? Why or why not?
3. Under what circumstances would a country's price level tend to be more stable, when the country was on the gold standard, or when its exchange rate was permitted to fluctuate freely?

4. A nation's *total* balance of payments must always balance. Explain.
5. Explain why, when the Canadian dollar was pegged at 92.5 cents in U.S. funds, the actual rate of exchange could be slightly lower or higher.
6. When a country "pegs" its currency, it thereby inhibits the operation of forces which would automatically keep imports and exports in proper relationship. Explain.
7. In May, 1962, the Canadian dollar was "pegged" at 92.5 cents in U.S. funds. What was the purpose of this action? To what extent has this purpose been realized? Explain.
8. If the gold standard were restored there would be no need for an institution such as the International Monetary Fund. Do you agree?

17

Restrictions on International Trade

WHY RESTRICT TRADE?

We noted in Chapter 15 that each country has its own unique endowment of climate and natural resources; that through its past efforts, each has acquired a particular array of capital equipment; that the people of each country have their own special skills and aptitudes. Because of its particular attributes, the productive capacity of each nation is utilized to best advantage in the production of certain goods and services only. We saw, furthermore, how it would be to the general advantage of all countries if each specialized in the production of those goods and services which it was best fitted to produce. With each nation so specializing, the output of the world as a whole would be the maximum possible. Each individual nation could achieve the highest possible level of material well-being if it produced only its specialties, and, through trade, acquired from other nations the additional goods and services which it required, and which they were better qualified to produce.

In the real world we find, however, that most nations deliberately forgo the advantages to be reaped through specialization and apply a variety of measures which have the effect of limiting their international trade. Governments restrict the importation and foster the domestic production of goods which can be produced much more economically in other countries. Inevitably these measures involve reductions in the output and export of those goods for which the country's resources are best qualified. The severity of such restrictions varies from one country to another; within a single country the severity of restrictions varies as between different commodities. However, in greater or less degree practically every government in the world interferes in the nation's economic affairs, to lessen the specialization which the special character of the country's productive capacity would tend to promote. Why do they do it?

Broadly speaking, government intervention in international trade is designed to serve one or both of two main purposes: to improve the nation's balance of payments position; to assist particular industries within the country. Let us examine each of these objectives in turn.

The Desire for a Favourable Trade Balance

By restricting imports, a government will reduce the payments which the country must make abroad; by stimulating exports, it will bring about an increase in the payments due from foreigners. The objective is to achieve a favourable balance of trade, an excess of exports over imports; or, if an unfavourable balance is inevitable, to reduce the margin by which imports exceed exports. Why should nations pursue such objectives? On the face of it, they appear illogical. Imports after all consist of the goods and services we get from foreigners; exports consist of the goods and services we give them in exchange. Why this paradoxical striving to give foreigners more than we get from them?

The desire to achieve a favourable balance of trade has deep historic roots. When the modern nation states of Europe first emerged, during the fifteenth and sixteenth centuries, their leaders generally adopted economic policies designed to maximize both their economic and their military power.[1] Recognizing that economic power stems not so much from the possession of goods as from the capacity to produce goods, national leaders promoted home industry in every possible way. Bounties were given to domestic manufacturers and farmers; restrictions were imposed on the importation of foreign goods. The country gained through having a diversified, broad-based economy and, equally important, it acquired gold from abroad amounting to the excess of its exports over its imports; foreigners who bought its wares paid only partly with wares of their own, the remainder they remitted in gold. The gold which the nation thus acquired supported domestic prosperity, quickening the pace of activity by increasing the amount of money in circulation.

Economic power supported military power. The nation which possessed a strong and diversified economy possessed the means to recruit and maintain a powerful army and navy. If it were independent of foreign supplies, it could not be harmed if such supplies were cut off. On the other hand, if foreign nations were dependent on it for critical supplies, those nations were militarily subservient. The gold acquired as a result of a favourable balance of trade, besides stimulating domestic prosperity, contributed to national defence. The nation which had an ample stock of gold could readily hire mercenary troops, purchase military supplies and equipment, and give financial assistance to allies.

The Desire for a Favourable Trade Balance: Modern Times

In an era when war and the threat of war were commonplace, national leaders understandably emphasized those economic policies which enhanced their nation's military potential. The desire to maintain a favourable balance of trade persisted, however, even when wars had ceased to be commonplace and preparation for war was no longer the main preoccupation of national leaders. A favourable balance

---

[1]Historians have applied to these policies the label "Mercantilism."

of trade still reflected a comforting capacity on the part of the nation to pay its own way in the world; the gold or foreign exchange acquired through a favourable balance of trade constituted a desirable reserve which would enable the nation to withstand shocks and reverses. If its exports suddenly declined, reducing its foreign earnings, it could dip into these reserves to maintain its purchases abroad. If it had a sudden need for imports on a large scale, it could pay for them out of the reserves accumulated by favourable trade balances achieved in the past.

An unfavourable balance of trade was, on the other hand, disquieting. It reflected incapacity on the nation's part to pay its own way. While tolerable perhaps during the period when the nation was just beginning to develop its productive capacity, an unfavourable trade balance was not to be accepted indefinitely. Reserves of foreign exchange would be dissipated; indebtedness to other countries would attain ever increasing proportions.

We find, accordingly, that even in modern times governments restrict imports and artificially promote exports, in order to achieve more favourable trade balances. In some instances such intervention has been only temporary, designed to relieve a temporary difficulty. Shortly after World War II Great Britain, faced with the prospect of large balance-of-payment deficits, imposed drastic restrictions on imports, and by a variety of measures vigorously stimulated exports. Once she had regained a favourable balance of trade and accumulated substantial reserves of foreign exchange, she relaxed the restrictions on imports and suspended some of the measures which had been introduced to increase exports. Import curbs were imposed again in 1964, following another "balance of payments crisis." Similarly Canada, faced in 1947 with a serious drain on her foreign exchange reserves, adopted restrictions on imports. In 1950 when her reserves had been restored to an adequate level, the restrictions were removed. The U.S. introduced curbs on imports in 1968 as one means of alleviating her balance of payments difficulties; in 1971 President Nixon, confronted with a further deterioration of the country's balance of payments position, introduced the crisis measure of a 10 per cent tariff surcharge as a means of curtailing imports into the U.S.

It is obviously impossible for all nations simultaneously to achieve a favourable balance of trade and their attempts to do so are bound to be mutually inconsistent and mutually frustrating. The nation which manages to increase its exports is thereby increasing other nation's imports; the nation which reduces its imports thereby reduces some other nation's exports. It is simply impossible for *every* nation in the world to sell more than it buys. The total exported by all the nations is equal to— in fact, is the same thing as—the total imported by all the nations. If some nations have favourable trade balances, other nations must have unfavourable balances.

Government intervention to improve a nation's trade balance is a fruitful source of international friction. Each nation is concerned about having its own balance as favourable as possible. Each resents having its own balance, and its own exporters, adversely affected by the measures which another nation adopts in order to improve its balance. When Great Britain adopted restrictions on imports other countries protested strenuously; nor did foreign nations which exported to Canada joyfully hail the restrictions which we imposed from 1947 to 1950. The measures to curtail imports announced by President Nixon in August, 1971, provoked a world-wide storm of protest. For many countries the U.S. was their major foreign market; limitation on entry to that market would adversely affect a great many firms employing large numbers of employees. (In order to prevent the large scale unemployment which the U.S. action threatened, our federal government hastily st up an $80 million fund out of which grants would be paid to Canadian firms hard hit by the U.S. tariff surcharge, so as to enable them to maintain employment.)

Assistance to Domestic Industries

The second objective of government trade restrictions is, we noted, to develop particular domestic industries. When, because of import restrictions, a certain foreign good is no longer available or is available only at high prices, opportunity arises for domestic enterprises to fill the gap. If they were already producing similar goods they will be able to increase their output, taking over some of the market which previously was served by foreigners. Benefit accrues to the individuals who are associated with the new or expanding industries. The businessmen involved earn larger profits; the owners of the properties used obtain higher rents; some workers who were previously unemployed obtain jobs; some workers previously employed at inferior jobs now obtain better ones.

However, the import restrictions are harmful to other people in the country. Consumers become worse off through having to purchase the high-priced domestically produced goods instead of the cheap foreign equivalents. The people associated with the nation's export industries are likely also to become worse off. The foreign countries from which less is now being imported will reduce their own purchases abroad. Part, perhaps a very large part of this reduction, will be directed to the goods they buy from industries in the country which introduced the import restrictions. Accordingly, profit will decline in these exporting industries; the property which they use will decline in value; some workers will lose their jobs. The theory of comparative advantage, which was developed in Chapter 15, suggests that for the country as a whole, the losses caused by restrictions of imports will exceed the gains. The restrictions reduce the degree of international specialization; they stimulate expansion in industries for which the country is not well adapted and cause contractions in industries for which it is well adapted.

The effect is much the same when a government artificially supports a particular industry by granting it bounties or subsidies. In this case the cost of assisting the industry is borne by the nation as a whole, since the grants are paid out of the federal treasury to which the whole nation contributes. Assistance to a domestic producer in the form of a subsidy is, therefore, more fair to the consumers of the product; when assistance to a domestic industry takes the form of a restriction on imports, its consumers are made to bear a special burden from which other people are exempt. However, subsidies, like import restrictions, cause the nation's productive capacities to be diverted from their optimum channels. Furthermore, they present difficult and complex administrative problems and smack of favouritism. As a result, they are used infrequently; government assistance to particular domestic industries characteristically takes the form of a tariff on imports or some other restriction of foreign competition.

The Advocates of Protection

Who then advocates tariffs designed to aid particular industries when the harm appears to exceed the gain? Some people support tariffs and other import restrictions because, while they see the benefits, they are ignorant of the burdens or deliberately ignore them. The people who directly benefit from the tariff protection —the investors, managers, and workers in the protected industries—will understandably support measures which serve their own interests. Other people will be impressed by the employment which these protected industries provide, and by the markets which they furnish for the materials and services produced by other industries in the country. They take no account of the more than offsetting burdens to consumers and exporters.

FALLACIOUS ARGUMENTS FOR TRADE RESTRICTIONS

"Keep Money in the Country"

To justify tariffs some people bring to bear arguments which are inherently fallacious. It has been said, for instance, that when we buy goods in a foreign country, we get the goods and the foreigners get the money, while when we buy at home we have both the goods and the money.

But the fact is that when we spend money in a foreign country, that money *comes back* to us. Citizens of that country spend that money in our country to buy goods and services of ours which they want. General benefit results. When we spend our money in their country, we obtain their special products which we would like to have and which we cannot produce so well at home. When they spend, in our country, the money which we paid them, they are able to obtain our specialities which they cannot produce so well. If people always spend their money in their own countries, no one could derive these benefits; no one would be taking advantage of the specialized productive capacity available in other countries. In each country people would have for their use and enjoyment only the limited range of goods which their own country was capable of producing.

The Lower Wages in Foreign Countries

Other people argue that our producers must be protected against competitors in foreign countries where the wage level is only a fraction of our own. Superficially the argument seems plausible enough but it ignores the fundamental reasons *why* our workers are higher paid. The fact is that workers in our country are paid much more than are the workers of some other countries *because they are more productive*. They are more productive because they work with superior natural resources and capital equipment, or because they are more highly skilled, or because they are organized into more efficient productive teams. A Canadian employer is able to pay higher wages than can an employer in Hong Kong, because, thanks to such considerations, his employees produce far more for him.

Our workers do not possess the same degree of superiority in all fields of production. In industries where natural resources and capital equipment are relatively unimportant, a worker in Hong Kong may be able to produce nearly as much in a day as can a Canadian worker. It is quite true that in such industries Hong Kong manufacturers, paying only a fraction of Canadian wages, can undersell Canadian manufacturers.

This does not prove that we should protect these industries. What it proves rather is that we should not have them. Those industries of our which require protection against low-wage competitors are characterized by low worker productivity; we should not employ any of our people in them. Our workers should be concentrated in those industries for which the nation is best suited. Here their productivity is very great and their employers can readily afford to pay high wages. In some of these latter industries worker productivity is so great that their products can be exported to low wage countries. Thus Canada is able to export to Hong Kong products of her mineral and forest industries, whose workers are paid far more than are workers in Hong Kong. By protecting industries where worker productivity is low, we are actually reducing the size of the national product. We are causing part of our work force to be employed where they produce relatively little; without such interference, they would naturally be drawn into other industries where their productivity was high. If they were all in industries of the latter type, they would not need to be protected against the competition of low-paid workers in other countries.

Bargaining Power

Some people urge that their country should maintain a tariff wall in order to be able to bargain effectively on behalf of its exporters. They insist that in negotiating a trade agreement with another country, only the offer of a "concession," in the form of a tariff reduction, will induce the other country to offer a corresponding "concession"; a tariff is therefore needed, to serve as a bargaining counter. To extract concessions for its exporters in foreign markets, it can offer to lower the tariff; to deter a foreign country from harming its exporters in any way, it can threaten to raise the tariff against the products of that country.

This "realistic" argument contains a measure of truth. In actual practice countries do tend to lower their tariffs only in response to the tariff reductions introduced by other countries. However, the adherents of this doctrine overlook the fundamental fact that the tariff harms not only the countries against whose products it is imposed, but also the country which imposes it. By having the tariff, that country denies to itself the advantages of international specialization. It penalizes its own consumers and exporters, and the burden is likely to be considerable. Regardless of whether or not other countries reduce their tariffs, each country could improve its welfare by reducing its own; in so doing, it would cause a shift of productive capacity from industries for which the nation was ill adapted to other industries for which it was better adapted. The prosperity and power of Great Britain during the latter part of the nineteenth century, when it levied no protective tariffs whatsoever, suggest that Free Trade, too, can be a "realistic" policy.

VALID ARGUMENTS FOR TRADE RESTRICTIONS

There are advocates of tariffs who are neither hypocritical nor ignorant. They do not ignore the burdens which a tariff imposes. Their argument is that the existence of some industries within the country will serve broad national purposes. Because of the importance of these purposes, they urge, the burden of the tariff must be accepted.

Why might a particular industry be considered to be a national asset which serves in a crucial way the interests of the country, so that it is worthy to be maintained by government assistance when it cannot support itself? Why should the public be burdened in any way in order that a particular industry be able to exist within the country?

Because, the answer would be, the industry contributes to the nation's military security, or to its social and cultural development, or to its economic strength and stability. Let us examine this answer in detail.

Military Security

Any nation which anticipates that it might become involved in a war quite obviously should not permit itself to become dependent for vital supplies upon foreign sources which might be cut off in wartime. In an emergency the country might arrange to produce these goods, but if it had never been done before, their production might take a good deal of precious time to organize. Very likely the task would prove to be doubly difficult in wartime. A nation which did not regularly produce its own vital supplies might very easily lose a war for that reason alone. As a military precaution, therefore, a country ought to ensure that there existed, within its borders, those industries whose supplies would be vital in wartime. If such industries could exist only on the basis of government assistance such as subsidies or the restriction of cheap foreign imports, that support ought to be given.

On similar grounds, the export of strategic materials to a potential enemy might be justifiably prohibited, even though the sale was advantageous in all other respects. A good many people objected to American and Canadian shipments of scrap iron to Germany and Japan during the 1930s and their objections were justified by events.[2]

Claims for special assistance on account of contributions to national security are not always justified. Some industries, whose services would be of dubious value in wartime, claim that they would prove to be vital and demand special consideration from the government. American experience is suggestive. In 1954, President Eisenhower increased the tariff on Swiss watches as a means of giving aid to the American watch-making industry. The grounds were that watch-making personnel and equipment could, in wartime, readily switch over to the production of precision instruments for the armed forces and that it was vital to maintain the industry in a sound and flourishing condition. A good many observers were skeptical, however. In their view the military value of the industry was negligible; the increase in the tariff benefited not the nation as a whole but a small special interest which had advanced, successfully, a hollow plea on its own behalf.

Social Considerations

A particular industry may support a class of persons which was considered especially desirable for the country to have. Foreign imports which weakened the industry endangered the livelihood of the class. Its members would be obliged to enter new occupations; employed in these other occupations, their social value would be less. Thus France and Germany during the nineteenth century were both determined to maintain their peasant classes; they constituted a stable, conservative element in the national society, and furnished excellent recruits in wartime. When cheap wheat and cattle from America and elsewhere began to pour into Europe, threatening ruinous competition against small farmers in all lands, both these countries imposed steep tariffs against agricultural imports. A major objective in each case was to preserve the nation's peasantry. Without the tariff barriers, their domestic markets would have been deluged with cheap foreign food, offered at prices which a small European farmer could not possibly match.

---

[2]On the other hand of course, it can be argued that the refusal to maintain normal trade relations with other countries intensifies antagonisms and may be a contributory cause of war. Currently, a good many people urge that Western countries increase their commercial relationships with countries of the Communist bloc, as a means of easing world tensions.

Industrial Advance

During the twentieth century, particularly since the end of World War II, many countries with primitive, mainly agricultural economies, have promoted industrial expansion. A primary objective has been to create new opportunity for a backward peasantry. National leaders firmly believed that, following industrialization, unemployed and under-employed farm workers would be able to obtain factory jobs in which their productivity would be far higher than it had ever been on the land. As factory workers in industrial cities, they would enjoy a higher level of material well-being than they could achieve on the farm. General social progress would become possible, because industrial development would furnish the economic basis for large and modern cities in which cultural activities and artistic endeavours of all sorts could flourish.

Countries which export raw materials and import finished products have become increasingly restive in recent years. They view themselves in many cases as "hewers of wood and drawers of water" for others. They complain that they have only the primitive, ill-paid work of extracting resources from the earth, while the nations to which they export these resources have the superior, well-paid work of fabricating raw materials into finished goods. Some countries, to secure for themselves the superior work of fabrication, have restricted the export of their raw materials. Canada restricts the export of logs of the sort used in making paper;[3] foreign firms which wish to transform these logs into paper must set up their plants in this country.

The "Infant Industry" Argument. In a good many industries, an old established firm tends to enjoy a marked superiority over a newly established rival. The old firm has had time to build up a team of competent executives and skilled technicians. Through long experience, it has ascertained which are the best sources of supply, the best methods of production, the best markets and the best methods of marketing. It has built up a good reputation and can depend upon the patronage of a large body of loyal customers. These may be overwhelming advantages. For lack of them, the new firm's costs of production may be substantially higher than are those of the old firm. In such case, it could not compete. To cover its higher costs it would be obliged to charge higher prices; few people would be charitable enough to pay higher prices so that a new firm might get established.

The potentialities may all be there. People may be available who, with training and experience, could become executives and technicians as able and skilled as those of the old firm. In time, they could operate the new firm just as efficiently. In time, the new firm's production costs might be no more than those of its older rival and it might be able to sell at the same price, perhaps even at a lower price. How-

---

[3]The restriction takes the form of outright prohibition by provincial governments of the export of logs cut on Crown Lands, i.e. lands owned by the provincial governments. Logs cut on privately owned land may be exported. Since the major part of the nation's pulpwood reserves are on Crown lands, the prohibition of exports applies to the great bulk of the logs cut.

ever, time is a bottleneck. It may take years to acquire the skill, the experience, the contacts, which would enable the low production costs to be achieved. During that period, the infant firm might be smothered by its mature rival. It can be killed, not because of any inherent weakness, but simply because of the inevitable inferiority of an infant. If the new firm is to have the opportunity of reaching adulthood, it must be protected against adult rivals. Once it reaches that state, protection is no longer necessary; the firm will be able, without further assistance, to meet the challenge of older competitors.

This thesis offers a guide to national policy. A government might, by extending temporary assistance, bring about the development, within the country, of a whole new industry. The assistance might take the form of a tariff wall which restricted the entry of the products of old established foreign firms.[4]. Behind the shelter of this wall, the country's fledgling firms could safely grow to maturity. Once they did mature, the protective wall would become unnecessary. The country would then possess a valuable new industry which broadened and strengthened the national economy. It would no longer be necessary to burden the nation's consumers in order to protect member firms of the industry.

Historical experience suggests the validity of the "infant industry" argument for import restrictions. During the nineteenth century both Germany and the United States applied the doctrine effectively. In an era when British industrial firms were long established and pre-eminent in their fields, both countries erected steep tariff walls behind which new industries were able to develop. Eventually, some of their new firms were able to surpass in efficiency the older British firms against which they had at first required protection. Both countries gained new industries which immensely strengthened their respective economies; without the initial protection those industries might have never emerged at all, or would have come into being only at much later dates.

The application of the "infant industry" doctrine does not always produce the desired results. The "infant" may never grow up. Despite many protected years behind a steep tariff wall, the member firms may not manage to equal foreign firms in efficiency, and their costs of production may remain higher. Obviously their initial inferiority was due not merely to lack of experience which time would cure, but to basic inadequacies in the nation's resources or in the capacities of its people. If it is to survive in the face of foreign competition, the industry requires protection permanently. In such case, its existence in the country may be of no benefit. A nation may quite justifiably burden itself temporarily in order to develop an industry which will, in the long run, be able to stand on its own feet but if the burden must be borne forever the value of the industry becomes dubious.

There is a second danger. An industry which has been protected in its infancy

---

[4]In Canada assistance to a new industry has taken the form of subsidies as well as the restriction of competing imports. Thus for many years the Canadian government gave bounties to iron and steel firms, enabling them to sell at prices which were competitive with those of imports.

may, in time, achieve the efficiency which had been hoped for. It may become able to produce just as cheaply as do foreign rivals, and therefore may no longer need the protection of a tariff wall. However, the industry may plead, successfully, that the tariff be retained. The member firms may establish some sort of monopolistic arrangement which enables them to charge prices which are well in excess of their actual costs of production. The tariff protects the arrangement by shutting out the foreign competition which could force their prices down and thereby hold their profits to reasonable levels.

The Dangers of Specialization. A country's resources may be highly specialized in character. If the country were to produce only those goods for which it was best fitted, its economy would be a lop-sided one, with the employed population concentrated in a very few industries. In all probability the major proportion of the output of these industries would have to be exported, and the nation would have to import most of the varied consumer goods and industrial materials which it required.

The economy of such a nation would tend to be decidedly unstable. A reduced foreign demand for any one of its products would have severely damaging repercussions, affecting a large sector of its economy and a substantial proportion of its population. Periodic crises of this sort would be virtually inevitable. After all, the world demand for any single product shifts about constantly, varying with business conditions, with consumer tastes, with the availability and cost of substitutes. A nation which exports a wide range of goods is reasonably secure; a decline in the demand for one of its exports is likely to be offset wholly or partly by increases in the demand for its other exports, or, at least, by maintenance of the demand for them. A nation which exports only a few products cannot expect that a sharp decline in sales of one item will be offset by favourable developments elsewhere; when a decline occurs in foreign demand for a single one of its products, its economy will be severely shaken. If the nation exports its goods to only one foreign market, or to just a few, the risk of economic instability becomes even greater. Because of purely local conditions, the demand in any one foreign market is likely to fluctuate with special severity.

Foreigners may be undependable not only as buyers but also as suppliers; they may at times be unable or unwilling to supply their goods. Thus, some years ago because of a prolonged strike by their employees, American steel firms were unable to provide Canadian automobile manufacturing plants with their usual supplies of steel. The latter were accordingly obliged to suspend operations. (One group of workers in these plants thereupon demanded that Canada take steps to enlarge her steel industry, and so render herself independent of American supplies.)

Diversification to Achieve Stability

An economy which concentrates on the production of just a few exports which it sells in just a few foreign markets is virtually bound to be highly unstable. However, because of the specialized character of the country's resources, this may be the direction in which the economy tends naturally to develop. In such a situation it would not be unreasonable for the government to promote new industries, possibly by restricting imports, in order to achieve diversity and therefore a better prospect of stability. Its eggs would no longer be in just a very few baskets. With its population now employed in a larger number of industries, a setback suffered by any one industry would have less damaging consequences.

The stability afforded by artificially induced diversification has its cost of course. Resources devoted to artificially promoted industries will be less productive than they could have been if directed to the industries for which they are naturally favoured. So long as foreign demand continues to be strong for the product of these latter industries, the country could achieve its highest possible income by concentrating on them. A policy of deliberate diversification will only bear fruit when foreign demand for the country's natural specialties slumps, or when needed foreign supplies are unobtainable; at such times the fact that the country is less dependent on these exports or imports proves to be a blessing.

The foregoing discussion is particularly relevant to Canada. Our resources are highly specialized and we are particularly qualified to produce very large quantities of a limited number of staple products, chiefly newsprint, wheat, lumber, iron ore and several other metals. The United States purchases a major proportion of our entire output of many of these products. The Canadian economy is liable to serious instability because of its heavy dependence upon a narrow range of goods sold in a single foreign market. It could be argued that the Canadian government is justified in imposing import restriction, because they give rise to greater diversity in our economy and thereby contribute to stability.[5] Just how much diversity we should have, and how much income we ought to sacrifice to achieve it, is a matter of judgment, on which different people will hold different views.

TYPES OF IMPORT RESTRICTIONS

Tariffs

The tariff has always been, and remains, the chief instrument whereby nations restrict their imports. As we shall see in Chapter 19, the tariff was for centuries the main source of public revenue, because it could be imposed and administered even under primitive economic conditions. With goods brought in by ship to a few ports, it was a relatively simple matter to check cargoes as they were unloaded on the wharves, and to collect the appropriate duty. Since the duty made it necessary to sell foreign goods at higher prices, their sales were lower than they otherwise would

[5]As we saw in Chapter 15, Canada has been selling a larger proportion of her exports to countries other than the United States. This increased diversification, by making us less dependent on a single market, should help stabilize the volume of our exports and therefore contribute to general economic stability.

have been; the tariff, accordingly, brought about a restriction of imports. Other instruments for import restriction, such as quotas and exchange control, could only be employed effectively under modern conditions: they involve fairly elaborate record-keeping, require modern facilities for administration, and depend upon modern means of communication.

Consequences of a Tariff. The imposition of a tariff on a foreign good tends to increase domestic production but to curtail domestic consumption. Domestic output is increased because the country's producers, receiving a higher price, increase their output; domestic consumption falls because of the higher price. In the country which exports the good, on the other hand, the effects are exactly opposite. There the price falls, consumption is increased, and output is reduced. Figure 1 illustrates these various effects.

In Figure 1 D_eD_e and S_eS_e represent the demand and supply schedule prevailing for a certain commodity in the exporting country, which we call country E. D_iD_i and S_iS_i are the corresponding demand and supply schedules in the importing country, which we call country I. Before the importing country imposes a tariff the price is the same in the two countries, being O_eW in country E, and O_iH in country I.[6] At this price, output in the exporting country is WG and consumption is WF, leaving an export surplus of FG. In the importing country, output is HK while consumption is HL; the import surplus is KL, which is exactly equal to FG, export surplus of country E.

Suppose that the importing country imposes a tariff of the amount MX per unit. Henceforth, the price in the importing country will always exceed the price in the exporting country by this amount. In the importing country the price rises, causing domestic consumption to fall but domestic output to increase. In the exporting country, because of the reduced market abroad the price falls, causing domestic output to fall, but domestic consumption to increase. Equilibrium will be restored when the price settles at O_iX in the importing country and O_eQ in the exporting country. In the importing country output will now be XY, up from HK; consumption will be XZ, reduced from HL. In the exporting country output will have fallen to QT but consumption will have increased to QR. The price in the importing country exceeds that of the exporting country by the amount of the tariff MX; the export surplus of country E is down to RT, which is equal to the reduced import surplus YZ of country I. The government of the importing country will be receiving revenue amounting to MX per unit on each of the YZ units which still enter the country.

A "Prohibitive" Tariff. If country I had wished to shut out imports altogether, it would have imposed a "prohibitive" tariff amounting to HP or more. Making here the simplifying assumption that exporters in country E continue to demand the same price as before $(= O_iH)$, then, when a tariff in excess of HP is imposed the im-

[6]For simplicity, we assume that there are no transportation costs.

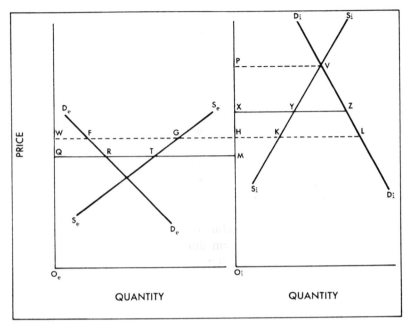

Figure 1.   Effects of a tariff

ported good must now sell for more than O_iP in the importing country. No one will be willing to pay such a price for the imported article; any one who is willing to pay O_iP can buy as much as he likes of the home produced article at that price. At the market price of O_iP the entire quantity that consumers wish to purchase is produced by local firms, and there are no imports whatever.

Rates of Duty. A country's tariff schedules will lay down different rates of duty on different goods and, most probably, different rates on the same goods, according to the country of origin. Lower rates will be applied to goods coming from those countries with which trade agreements have been signed,[7] or with which some special relationship exists. The Canadian tariff is a "three-decker," the lowest rates applying to goods originating in British Commonwealth countries, the intermediate (Most Favoured Nation) rates applying to countries with which Canada has entered into trade agreements, and the highest (General) rates applying to non-Commonwealth countries with which no agreement has been signed.[8]

The rate of duty varies furthermore from one class of goods to another,

[7]Usually the same tariff rate will be applied to the similar products of *all* the countries with which agreements have been signed. Most bilateral trade agreements contain a "Most Favoured Nation" clause, in which each signatory undertakes to extend to the other the benefit of any concessions which it grants in subsequent agreements with other nations.

[8]Imports are negligible from countries in the last category.

according to the degree of protection it is desired to provide. A substantial volume of goods enters Canada on the basis of a duty of 10 per cent of value, but on some goods the duty is 35 per cent. Generally, goods which are competitive with domestic products pay higher rates than those which are not.[9] An innovation of 1968, designed to encourage Canadian firms to instal superior equipment, provided that machinery which could not be made in Canada might be imported virtually duty-free. It would merely be necessary for the importer to prove that exemption from duty would be in the public interest and that no Canadian firm was capable of supplying the item in question.

Tariffs, furthermore, may be "specific" or "ad valorem." A "specific" tariff is one which consists of a specified sum of money per unit of the goods imported. Thus Canada imposes a specific duty of $4 per gallon on brandy with an alcohol content of 100 proof. An ad valorem tariff is one which takes the form of a percentage of the value of the good imported. The tariff on machinery cited in the footnote 9 is of this type. A combination of specific and ad valorem duties may also be levied on some goods; e.g., the Most Favoured Nation tariff rate levied by Canada on silk fabrics is 25 per cent of their value plus 5 cents per lineal yard.

Most countries levy special "dumping" duties against occasional shipments of merchandise which exporters sell for unusually low prices. It sometimes happens that a good has been over-produced in a particular country; producers, to avoid breaking the local market, export part of the output to a foreign country, and on such shipments are prepared to accept practically any price they can get. If such merchandise is sold at "clearance" prices, domestic manufacturers of similar products will be seriously harmed. A nation's tariff will likely contain some provision for an especially high rate of duty to be levied upon goods which are imported at prices below the level prevailing in their country of origin. The ultra high duty makes it necessary to sell such imported goods at something like the usual prices, thereby protecting domestic producers against sporadic competition of an unfair sort.[10]

The "Invisible" Tariff. The complexity of tariff schedules gives rise to problems of its own. The customs officials who actually inspect imports and assess the duties enjoy a considerable degree of administrative latitude. They decide in what classification a particular import belongs, and therefore what rate of duty it must pay. Furthermore, where they feel that the price paid by the importer is less than the fair market value of the good in its country of origin, they have the right to set their own

[9]e.g. The Canadian tariff on coin-operated soft drink vending machines is currently as follows:

Type of tariff	Rate
British preferential	10 %
Most Favoured Nation	22½%
General	35 %

[10]Until recently Canadian customs officials were authorized to decide whether an import was brought into Canada at a price below its fair market value in the country of origin and to impose a dumping duty amounting to the difference between import price and fair market value. Now they merely report instances of suspected undervaluation to a tribunal in Ottawa and the tribunal decides whether the public interest is being harmed and what dumping duty, if any, should be imposed.

valuation upon it and the duty is assessed upon this valuation. An importer can never be certain of the actual amount of duty he will have to pay upon any particular shipment of goods which he brings into the country. The total duty levied will depend, in the final analysis, upon how customs officials classify the merchandise and the valuation they attribute to it. There is likely to be provision for appeal to a judicial body against the decisions of these officials, but the cost, delay, and exasperation involved tend to inhibit such appeals. It has been suggested in fact that the delays, and the bureaucratic obstructions which are inherent in the actual administration of a tariff, constitute, in effect, an "invisible tariff" which may discourage imports even more effectively than do the actual duties themselves.[11]

Import Quotas

A tariff may not reduce imports to the degree hoped for by those who introduced it. The foreign exporters or the domestic importers may absorb most of the duty; because the foreign goods are offered to consumers at little more than the former price, the volume of sales may decline only slightly. Or, even if the full amount of the duty is added to the selling price, consumers may still buy practically as much as before. In either case domestic producers of similar goods do not derive much benefit from the tariff. Foreign goods will be selling in virtually the same quantity as before; the share of the market held by domestic producers will be little changed. Because of these possible consequences, a tariff imposed as a means of conserving foreign exchange, may similarly fail to produce the result desired. With the volume of imports down only slightly, if at all, the expenditure of foreign exchange will be the same as before, or down just a little.

To *ensure* that imports of a particular good are substantially reduced, a government may impose a "quota": it may permit only a specified quantity to be imported in a designated time period. The quota may be "global" or "allocated." The former merely indicates what aggregate quantity may be imported into the country, without specifying how much may come from any particular country. An "allocated" quota, on the other hand, authorizes a particular quantity of imports from each exporting country.

"Tariff quotas" are commonly imposed under which a specified volume of a good may be imported at a low rate of duty, while imports in excess of this figure are subject to a high rate. "Mixing quotas," imposed by some countries, require that a certain proportion of home produced goods must always be sold along with imported goods of a similar type. Great Britain, for example, requires its millers to use a certain proportion of domestically grown wheat in combination with imported wheat.[12]

---

[11]*Viz* the following offer. "Let me write the Administrative Act and I care not who writes the rates of duty." B. A. Levett *Through the Customs Maze* (New York, 1923) p. 11. (Quoted in G. A. Elliott, *Tariff Procedures and Trade Barriers* (Toronto, 1955).)

[12]The actual percentage required varies from year to year according to the size and quality of the British wheat crop.

A government may implement a quota on a particular good by limiting the amount which each of its importers may bring into the country. Each importer is issued a licence to import only a designated quantity; imports are not permitted beyond the amounts stipulated in the licences. By specifying the amount authorized on each licence the government is able to limit imports to whatever figure it considers to be appropriate.

Import quotas and licences give rise to problems and difficulties of their own. Global quotas tend to favour those exporting nations which are able to ship their merchandise very soon after the quota period begins; their shipments may completely fill the quota, so that other exporters are barred from the market altogether. Allocated quotas involve the possibility that the allocations will be made on an arbitrary basis or will be influenced by favouritism or bribery: a system of import licences ensures handsome profits to the fortunate people who get the licences, inviting corrupt practice in their issue.

Figure 2 indicates just what form this bonus takes. D_iD_i represents the domestic demand for a particular good that is imported; S_eS_e represents the supply schedule, so far as importers are concerned. It is perfectly horizontal, reflecting the assumption that the good is produced abroad under perfectly competitive conditions and that importers of any country can buy as much as they like at the competitive price. The government licenses importers to bring into the country the quantity OQ. Importers bring in the full amount allowed, paying the competitive price of OE per

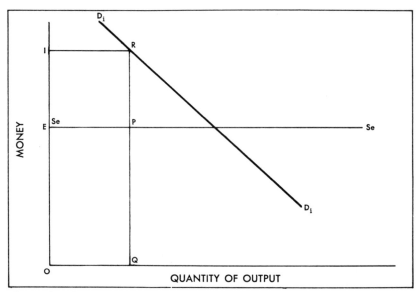

Figure 2.   Effects of an import quota

unit. If only this quantity is offered on the domestic market, a selling price of OI can be charged. Hence the government is, in effect, furnishing to importers a profit amounting to EI per unit. The total profit gained by all the importers will be represented by the area EPRI, this being the difference between the total amount they pay for the goods imported, and the total amount for which they can sell these goods.

Foreign Exchange Control

We saw in Chapter 16 how a country might "peg" the foreign exchange rate of its currency. We noted that, at the pegged rate, the quantity of foreign currency demanded by its citizens might chronically exceed the quantity supplied by foreigners. The government might institute a system of foreign exchange controls: exporters would be required to hand over to the government all their earnings of foreign currency; persons and firms who needed foreign currency would be obliged to buy it from the government or its designated agents, and the government would limit the total quantity it was prepared to sell. Private dealings in foreign exchange would normally be forbidden.[13]

Through its control of the nation's supply of foreign exchange, the government would be able to control imports. It could limit the import of any good or service simply by limiting the amount of foreign exchange it will sell to people who wish to import it. If it so desired, the government could, by this means, bar the importation of a particular good or service altogether. Normally the authorities would sell foreign exchange only to enable the importation of goods and services considered to be necessary and valuable to the country, and would refuse to sell foreign exchange for the purchase of non-essentials.[14]

Through its control over the nation's supply of foreign exchange a government may determine from what foreign countries the nation's imports will come. By refusing to sell to importers the currency of a particular foreign country, the government in effect prevents them from importing goods from that country. Such discrimination is likely to be practised where the government has only a very limited quantity of the currency of the foreign country in question. Immediately after the end of World War II, a great many countries were able to earn relatively few American dollars. Their respective governments accordingly made available to importers very limited quantities of American dollars, only enough to purchase just those goods which were absolutely essential and could not be obtained from any other source. When these countries acquired substantially larger holdings of American currency, they relaxed the restrictions, thereby modifying their discrimination against imports from the United States.

---

[13]There might however be a "free market" or a "black market" in which foreign currency acquired by unofficial or illegal means (e.g. from foreign tourists) would be sold at much higher rates than that charged by the government.

[14]Persons who were not permitted to purchase foreign exchange from the government might still of course obtain it, at inflated rates, on the local "black" or "free" markets.

Import Reduction by Persuasion

A country may bring about a reduction in its imports from another country by requesting the latter to restrict its exports. Presumably it would back up its request by the threat to impose import curbs of the usual type—high tariffs or quotas—if such "voluntary" restraints were not instituted by the authorities of the exporting country. The Canadian government has used such means to bring about reductions in Japanese exports of textiles, radios, and flatware to this country. (While complying with the Canadian request, the Japanese have hinted that their reduced earnings in Canada may force them to reduce their purchases of Canadian products.)

POSTWAR REDUCTION OF TRADE BARRIERS

Since the end of World War II a number of arrangements have been instituted to reduce or remove barriers to international trade. In each case they have been negotiated by a group of countries, each undertaking to reduce or remove obstacles which it imposed in the way of imports, in return for corresponding action by the other members of the group.

The International Trade Organization

In February, 1946, the United Nations Economic and Social Council established a Committee to produce a draft charter for an international authority on trade. The authority, to be called the International Trade Organization, was expected to serve as the agency through which nations would cooperate to reduce trade barriers. It would lay down the code of conduct which member nations were to follow in respect to trade practices, and would settle international disputes regarding trade. By August, 1947, the Committee produced a draft charter which was considered by the representatives of 57 nations at a conference held in Havana later that year. A somewhat modified version of the original draft emerged from the conference, and this version was approved by the representatives of 53 nations.

The Organization was to be established when the charter drawn up at Havana was ratified by a majority of the governments whose representatives had approved. The American Congress, unwilling that an international authority should have jurisdiction over American trade practices, refused to ratify the charter. Since American participation was indispensable to its success, the whole project thereupon lapsed.

G.A.T.T.[15]

The attempt to set up an international trade authority was not entirely fruitless, however. The Committee which prepared the draft charter sponsored a system

[15]General Agreements on Tariffs and Trade.

of voluntary agreements to reduce trade barriers. At the Committee's meeting in Geneva in 1947, 23 nations signed the General Agreements on Tariffs and Trade, in which each nation agreed to reduce its trade barriers on a broad list of goods imported from the other signatory nations.[16] The terms of the Agreements were to be binding for three years, but even after this time period had elapsed, could not be changed unilaterally by a single nation. Additional agreements have since been negotiated in which further reductions in trade barriers have been effected.[17] More nations have joined the Agreements. As of 1970 there were 78 full members and 12 associate members.

The OEEC

On the continent of Europe, major steps have been taken since the War toward the complete elimination of tariff barriers and the integration of separate nations into a single economic community. The Organization for European Economic Cooperation, established in response to the American offer of Marshall Plan assistance, has continued in existence. Largely through its efforts, the quota restrictions which the 17 member countries had imposed upon imports from one another were virtually abolished by 1956. The OEEC furthermore helped bring about a multilateral system of payments within Europe,[18] worked for the complete elimination of tariffs among groups of nations, and arranged for the movement of workers across national borders to relieve local shortages of labour and local problems of unemployment.

Benelux

Complete integration has been achieved of certain sections of the European economy. In 1948 Belgium, the Netherlands and Luxembourg formed the Benelux *customs union,* by eliminating all trade barriers among themselves and adopting a uniform tariff against the rest of the world.

The European Coal and Steel Community

Economic and political considerations brought about the formation of the European Coal and Steel Community in 1951. The coal and iron ore which supports the steel industries of several Western European countries comes from the same underground geological formations, artificially separated on the surface by national boundaries. Within each country, inefficient producers were kept going by subsidies; imports from more efficient foreign producers were prohibited or severely restricted. Needlessly

---

[16]The negotiations were conducted bilaterally; when they were concluded, however, every nation listed the concessions which it had granted in its negotiations with each other nation, and undertook to give all signatories the benefit of such concessions.

[17]At Annecy, France, in 1950; at Torquay, England, in 1951; at Geneva, in 1956; and at Geneva again in 1960-61. The so-called Kennedy Round began in May 1964, to consider the late President's proposal for an across-the-board tariff reduction of fifty per cent and was only concluded in 1968; the reductions agreed to were much less than fifty per cent.

[18]The European Payments Union.

high production costs meant that European users of steel were obliged to pay unduly high prices, while users on other continents looked elsewhere for their supplies. Furthermore, with each nation having full authority over its steel producing capacity, each, if it chose, could employ that capacity to build an arsenal which would support aggressive military policies.

M. Robert Schuman, France's Foreign Minister, advanced a plan whereby a single supra-national community would be formed to include the coal and steel industries of France, West Germany, Italy, Belgium, the Netherlands and Luxembourg. Within this supra-national community, all national restrictions and preferences were ultimately to be removed on coal and steel sales, so that production would become concentrated in the most efficient firms. The community would be administered by an international High Authority; no nation would henceforth possess sovereign jurisdiction over its own coal and steel resources; no one, therefore, would be able to embark unilaterally upon an armament programme. In the words of M. Schuman ". . . any war between France and Germany becomes not only unthinkable but actually impossible."[19]

The Common Market

The advocates of the European Coal and Steel Community hoped that it would be the forerunner of an even closer economic union among the six countries involved. This hope was realized. On March 25, 1957, the foreign ministers of these countries signed a treaty providing for the establishment of the European Economic Community (more generally referred to as the Common Market).[20] The treaty, which became effective on January 1, 1959, provided for the gradual elimination, within 12 to 15 years, of all trade barriers between the six countries. They would thereby come to constitute a single economic community of over 160 million people, comparable in size to the United States and the Soviet Union. A large single market would enable a high degree of specialization, the emergence of mass production industries, and the concentration of production in the most efficient establishments. The heightened productive efficiency of the area as a whole would make possible a corresponding increase in the material well-being of its population.

Tariffs would be retained against the rest of the world, with all member countries observing the same tariff rates. (Overseas colonies of member countries would be included in the Common Market.) The tariff rates charged on goods from outside countries would be roughly the average of the tariffs levied by member countries at the time the treaty took effect.

The architects of the Common Market had broader objectives in view than the mere establishment of a customs union. They hoped to bring about a high degree of

[19]Quoted in the *London Times*, May 10, 1950, p. 6.
[20]Provision was made in the same treaty for the establishment of the European Atomic Community (Euratom) to include the same six countries. Administered by the same authority as had been organized for the European Coal and Steel Community, Euratom would conduct a comprehensive programme of atomic research and development on behalf of the whole Community.

economic cooperation and integration, and as an eventual goal, looked forward to political integration, the establishment of some kind of federal state of which the six Common Market countries would be members. The treaty which they signed in Rome in March, 1957, accordingly provided that labour and capital were to be allowed to move freely from one country to another, unhampered by national boundaries; hours of work, social security and welfare payments, and pension regulations were to be harmonized. A European Investment Bank was to be established to lend money for the development of backward regions within the Market area. The Bank's capital, contributed by member countries, was set at one billion dollars. An Overseas Development Fund was to be established to make grants toward the development of the overseas territories of member countries. A total of $581 million was to be disbursed for this purpose over a five-year period. In addition, a Social Fund was established which would give aid to firms and workers adversely affected by the establishment of the Common Market, contributing to the cost of converting plants to new uses and to the cost of retraining and relocating workers.

Important milestones have already been achieved. By 1968, well ahead of schedule, the tariffs that the six countries had been levying on one another's industrial products were reduced to zero. Very serious consideration was given in 1970 to measures of further economic integration to be achieved during the next decade. Blueprints were drawn up of economic policies to ensure that exchange rates be absolutely fixed in relation to one another so that the currencies of the six member countries would in effect constitute a common currency. Plans were devised for the close alignment of national economic policies so that there would be no marked differences in the rates of price inflation experienced by member countries.

Britain refused to join the Common Market when it was first formed. If she became a member she would become obliged to impose the Common Market tariff on her imports from the British Commonwealth while allowing in, free, similar products from her European partners. Such discrimination against Commonwealth countries was simply out of the question on economic as well as political and sentimental grounds. Commonwealth countries supplied the bulk of Britain's food imports together with a great many of her raw materials and purchased a large proportion of her industrial exports.

Recognizing the advantages to be gained by membership in a group such as the Common Market, Britain spearheaded the formation of a rival organization of states, the European Free Trade Association. However, the Association proved to be an unacceptable alternative and Britain twice attempted to gain belated entry into the Common Market, in 1961 and again in 1966. On both occasions she was rebuffed, largely because of the virtual veto imposed by France. In 1971 Britain again sought membership in the ECM, as did Ireland, Denmark and Norway, the latter two being fellow members of the European Free Trade Association. At the time of writing all ECM countries had approved Britain's application for membership; there was uncertainty, however, as to whether the British Parliament would in fact agree to join.

Economic Integration in Latin America

In Latin America, too, groups of countries have negotiated agreements for closer economic integration. In 1960 four small Central American countries—Guatemala, El Salvador, Nicaragua, and Honduras—signed a treaty providing for the establishment of a customs union. Another small Central American country, Costa Rica, subsequently joined this regional association.

In 1961 representatives of seven larger Latin American countries—Argentina, Brazil, Chile, Mexico, Paraguay, Peru, Uruguay—ratified the Treaty of Montivideo which provided for the establishment of the Latin American Free Trade Area. The countries involved have a combined population of 200 million, about seventy per cent of the total population of Latin America. Under the treaty the signatory countries, within twelve years' time, were to remove all tariffs against one another. Each country, however, was free to set its own tariffs on goods entering from the rest of the world. More countries joined the Area once it was established; by 1966 Bolivia, Colombia, Ecuador and Venezuela were also members.

CANADA'S TARIFF RECORD

Canada's protective tariff originated in the "National Policy" advocated by Sir John A. Macdonald in the federal election of 1878. Until that time, duties had been levied on imports chiefly to raise revenue for the government; the protection which they afforded to Canadian producers was mostly incidental. The National Policy envisaged the creation of an integrated national economy. The transcontinental railway, already being built, would link together the separate regions of Eastern Canada, the Prairies and British Columbia. A protective tariff would promote the growth of industry in Eastern Canada, and its products would be carried by the railway to markets in the West. This east-west movement of goods would serve a double purpose; it would join the two regions by economic ties and assure traffic for the trans-continental railway. Without the tariff, the West might obtain its supplies of industrial goods from the United States to the south; in that case there would be little industrial expansion in Eastern Canada, and the trans-continental railway would be starved for traffic.

The tariff of 1879 implemented the National Policy. The customs duties were sharply increased on manufactured goods of the types which were being produced in Canada already or could be produced if some protection to Canadian producers were extended. During the next decade the rates were increased further, particularly on imports of textiles, iron and steel;[21] by 1887 Canada was a high tariff country.

A number of significant reductions were carried out during the next few decades. During the 1890s, in response to the complaints of farmers, the government

---

[21]The iron and steel industry was given further assistance in the form of bounties on output.

reduced the duties on agricultural implements. In 1897 imports from Great Britain were given preferential treatment, her exports to Canada being subjected to a lower rate of duty than were similar goods from other countries.[22] The preferences were increased in 1898 and again in 1900. Commencing in 1907, Canada negotiated bilateral trade agreements with a number of European countries, in which she granted tariff concessions on their exports to Canada in return for their concessions on Canada's exports to them. No such agreement was negotiated with the United States, however. An attempt was made in 1911 to bring about the removal of tariffs on all natural products[23] exported from one country to the other, but it produced a storm of controversy. The Laurier government which had made the attempt went down to defeat in the election of that year, its defeat being partly attributable to its attempt to achieve "Reciprocity" with the United States.

In 1930, following the onset of the Great Depression, the federal government sharply increased the tariff. Two years later, however, at a conference held in Ottawa, agreements were negotiated with other countries of the British Commonwealth in which each accorded, to all the others, preferential treatment over a wide range of goods. In 1935 a trade agreement was signed with the United States which reduced our barriers on imports from that country, the first such reduction since Confederation. Three years later, Canada signed another agreement with the United States in which each country granted additional concessions to the other. Following the end of World War II, Canada actively supported the world-wide movement to reduce existing barriers to international trade. We have been a party to each of the General Agreements on Tariffs and Trade which have been concluded since 1947, pledging ourselves to reduce our tariffs on a very wide range of goods imported from the other signatory countries. Since the United States, the source of most of our imports, is also one of the signatories, the great bulk of goods entering Canada is dutiable at the rates specified in the General Agreements. Goods imported from British Commonwealth countries are still granted some degree of preference. Our imports from other sources, i.e. non-Commonwealth countries with which we have not signed trade agreements, are negligible. As a result, practically all our imports enter under the rates accorded under the General Agreements, or under the slightly lower British Preferential rates.

As a result of the "Kennedy Round" of tariff negotiations carried out in the 1960s we undertook to reduce our tariffs on a great many items, making a specified reduction in each year of the five-year period commencing in 1968. As it turned out the reductions were made at a faster pace than had originally been considered. In June, 1969, the tariff rates involved were reduced to the levels that were supposed to have been reached only in the fifth and final year of the agreement period.

---

[22]The same preferential rates were extended to imports from Bermuda, the British West Indies, and British Guiana.
[23]i.e. Minerals, lumber, fish, farm produce.

SUMMARY

Nations impose restrictions on imports primarily to improve their trade balance or to assist particular domestic industries. Selfish interests frequently advance fallacious arguments on behalf of protection for particular industries; in some circumstances, however, valid arguments exist for such protection.

Import restrictions have generally taken the form of tariffs, although import quotas and exchange controls have been extensively applied in recent years.

Since 1945 a number of international arrangements have been instituted to reduce barriers to trade.

Canada became a high tariff country as a consequence of the introduction of the "National Policy" in 1879. A high tariff was conceived as a means of integrating Eastern and Western Canada and furnishing transcontinental railway traffic.

Preferences were extended to British Empire countries and trade agreements were negotiated with a number of European countries in the early 1900s.

With the onset of the Great Depression of the 1930s, the tariff was raised. Preferential trade agreements were negotiated in 1932 with other Empire countries. Trade agreements were negotiated with the United States in 1935 and 1938.

Canada has participated actively in the postwar attempts to reduce trade barriers.

FOR REVIEW AND DISCUSSION

1. The reduction or removal of tariffs ought to be attempted only in periods of high prosperity. Do you agree?
2. "International trade is really no different from trade within a single country. What does it matter if B.C. lumber is sold in California or Alberta?" Do you agree?
3. When we impose import restrictions in order to protect the Canadian standard of living, we actually reduce the Canadian standard of living. Comment.
4. A highly industrialized country and a primitive country may both impose import restrictions, but their motives are likely to be quite different. Explain.
5. During the inter-war era the United States demanded that European countries pay their war debts to her, and at the same time imposed high tariffs on imports. Was this behaviour logically consistent?
6. If we can buy something more cheaply abroad than at home, we should do so; no harm results to our own country. Do you agree?
7. Import quotas and exchange controls are actually more restrictive than tariffs. Explain.
8. If a particular industry demands tariff protection, what considerations ought the government to take into account before deciding whether or not to provide such protection?

PART SIX:

PUBLIC FINANCE

18 Public Finance

THE DOCTRINE AND PRACTICE OF LAISSEZ-FAIRE

There exists in the Anglo-Saxon world a long and cherished tradition of private enterprise and individual initiative. This tradition emerged, in its modern form, in Great Britain around the beginning of the nineteenth century, out of the Industrial Revolution and the writings of the early British economists. During preceding centuries the view had been generally accepted that if a nation was to achieve its full productive potential, the state must regulate all economic activity. Only close supervision by the state, it was believed, would ensure that each individual contributed his utmost to the nation's total production and that each received his due reward. Detailed, regulatory statutes gave effect to this belief.

The Industrial Revolution produced a host of new tools, new machines, new methods. Businessmen, anxious to adopt the profitable innovations, chafed at the state regulations which bound them to outmoded tools and practices. At the same time, Adam Smith and his followers advanced the view that the state would actually be promoting its own best interests if it allowed each individual to have complete economic freedom. They argued that an individual could advance his own interests only by activities which were beneficial to society as a whole. Hence each person who, with utter selfishness, sought only to maximize his own well-being, was thereby serving, as best he could, the interest of society.[1] Legislation which hindered the individual from pursuing his own selfish interests as he saw fit, prevented him from making his maximum contribution to the welfare of the nation. A government which desired to bring about a maximum of national output and welfare could do so only by strict adherence to the principle of *laissez-faire*—leaving people to do as they chose.

There was virtually no need, the early economists argued, for the state to perform any economic activities whatsoever. It should restrict itself merely to the provision of a few public services such as the administration of justice, arrangements for national defence, and the maintenance of national highways. Any other good or

---

[1]In a memorable phrase Adam Smith referred to the individual "being led, as by an invisible hand" to advance the interests of society.

service which was worth having would be provided by private enterprise. If society really needed and wanted any good or service, profit could be earned in its production. Inevitably and without delay, some private individual would become aware of this opportunity for profit-making and would arrange to supply the desired good or service.

Nor was there any need, the economists urged, for the state to protect any particular class of persons by special legislation. The free competitive market would adequately safeguard the interests of all. No employer could exploit his workers by paying them unduly low wages or by subjecting them to harsh conditions of work. Were he to attempt such exploitation, he would lose his workers to other employers who also needed them and who would entice them away with offers of better pay or superior conditions of work. Knowing what they were worth to other employers, workers would bargain effectively with their own employers, obliging them to pay the highest wages possible and to provide optimum working conditions. Nor could any businessman exploit his customers by charging exorbitant prices or by selling inferior goods; were he to do so, competitors would attract his customers away with offers of lower prices or better goods.

Such were the classic arguments in favour of laissez-faire, as expounded by the early British economists and elaborated by their successors. The doctrine spread far beyond the shores of Great Britain. Other nations, in Europe and America, followed in Britain's wake, adopting the industrial methods which she had pioneered, and, in varying degree, the economic philosophy which her economists had propounded.

In Britain, during the early years of the nineteenth century, the doctrine of laissez-faire prevailed triumphantly. The role of government was restricted to a minimum; the ancient, confining regulations on economic activity were discarded or ignored. Businessmen enjoyed virtually unrestricted freedom to order their affairs as they chose.

The Retreat from Laissez-Faire

The triumph of laissez-faire in Great Britain was relatively brief; it endured hardly more than a single generation. Beginning in the 1830s, successive governments intervened increasingly in the nation's economic affairs. In other countries, too, where some form of laissez-faire had been introduced, the original economic liberty accorded to individuals was progressively curtailed, and the economic role of governments became progressively more important.

Experience revealed that the key assumptions of laissez-faire were not fully warranted. The automatic safeguards against the exploitation of workers, impressive in theory, failed to be effective in real life, particularly if the workers were women and children. Governments accordingly introduced legislation designed to protect women and children against exploitation by employers and, in due course, legislation was introduced to protect adult males as well.

Modern nations developed wants during the course of the nineteenth century which private enterprise failed to satisfy. Low cost housing and free public school education could not be provided by private enterprise because no profit could be earned thereby. Railways, canals and other very large projects, could not be undertaken by private enterprise because the enormous sums required were, in most countries, beyond the capacity of private enterprise to raise. Furthermore, in the view of private enterprise, the risks involved in some such projects appeared excessive or the prospective benefits too remote. Hence many governments, including that of Canada, were called upon to play decisive roles in the construction of major national facilities such as railways and canals.

Industrialization gave rise to urbanization and it became necessary for local governments to safeguard the health, safety and convenience of populations congregated into towns and cities. Industrialization produced a class of persons completely dependent for their livelihood upon wages and therefore unable to provide for themselves in the event of unemployment, sickness, or old age. Governments accordingly introduced schemes designed to support workers whose earning power was interrupted or ended.

The proponents of laissez-faire had allotted to the state the role of referee in the economic arena, but in industrial societies even the functions of the referee became magnified and extended. The government was called upon to introduce elaborate regulations in respect to business practices and procedures and to maintain large staffs to enforce the regulations. To enable businessmen generally to carry on more knowingly and effectively, governments compiled and publicized vast masses of statistical information, operated large research institutions, maintained consular offices abroad which advised and aided private exporters and importers.

Evidence accumulated that competition among producers could not universally be relied upon to protect consumers. In some industries firms refused to compete and instead cooperated to exploit; governments were compelled to introduce special legislation designed to maintain competitive conditions. In some industries, competition was never feasible because of technical considerations; competition in the provision of water, electrical power and telephone service, for instance, would obviously involve wasteful duplication. Where monopoly was thus inevitable, governments operated such organizations as publicly owned enterprises, or set up authorities empowered to regulate the rates charged by privately owned firms.

Free enterprise economies proved to be liable to severe fluctuations, to alternations of dizzy boom and deep depression. Armed with newly acquired insight into the nature and causes of business fluctuations, governments undertook, beginning in the 1940s, the unprecedented responsibility of regulating the level of the nation's economic activity. The prosperity and relative stability which we have enjoyed since the end of World War II is attributable, in considerable degree, to government measures carried out in the fulfilment of this responsibility.

The Scale of Government Activities

Private enterprise still produces the bulk of the national product in North America and most countries of Western Europe, but the economic role of government is of major proportions. Through the evolutionary process just described, governments have extended and strengthened their regulation of the activities of the private business community. The extent of their ancient responsibilities has been vastly enlarged; the scale and character of modern warfare require the application of immense effort and resources to defence preparations, to actual warfare, to the rehabilitation of individuals and nations following a war. Within the past generation, governments have assumed greatly increased responsibility for the welfare of their less fortunate citizens. Aid has been extended to the victims of additional categories of misfortune; the scale of assistance to those already aided has been enlarged. What with new responsibilities and the increase in scale of old responsibilities, modern governments require in their service a goodly portion of the productive capacity of their respective nations. In Canada and the United States roughly one quarter of the national productive capacity is engaged in government service.

National and Local Governments

Practically every country in the world is composed of a number of distinct regions, these having emerged because of geographical factors or historical developments, or having been deliberately created for administrative convenience. Each region is in turn composed of a number of individual communities, villages, towns, cities and rural districts, each of which forms a single, distinguishable community. As a consequence, there exist in most countries three levels of government: national, regional (i.e. state or provincial), and local. The national government is characteristically responsible for those public services which are uniformly required by the nation as a whole and are best administered by a single authority. A regional government provides those services the need for which varies from one region to another, or which are best administered on a decentralized basis. A municipal government provides those services which are required only by the local community, and are most effectively administered by local people.

This division of responsibility is variable, and never precise. What is considered, in some countries, to be a local responsibility, may elsewhere be regarded as a regional or national responsibility. Within the one country, some functions may be performed by all three levels of government. Within the same country as well, a function may be transferred from one level of government to another, reflecting shifts of opinion as to whether the function is of local, regional or national significance. Canada's experience offers ample illustration, as we shall see in the next chapter.

THE FINANCES OF GOVERNMENT

To command the services of productive agents, even a government must have money. How do governments obtain the money they need to buy materials and equipment, to construct buildings, to hire personnel, to make welfare payments? The main source is taxation. A government has the authority to compel its citizens to contribute the money it requires, such forced contributions being known as taxes. Under certain circumstances, governments also raise money by borrowing. Some governments, unable to raise money either by taxation or borrowing, have simply created it by printing fresh supplies. (This last method is, however, extraordinary: usually it has been adopted by governments as a desperate expedient in a state of extreme emergency.)

The Nature of Taxation

Basically, there are only three different kinds of taxes: those which are levied on income; those which are levied on property; and those which are levied on goods sold. Governments levy taxes annually upon the incomes of private individuals and incorporated companies; they levy annual taxes on property owners, and special taxes on the occasion of property being inherited from a person deceased; they levy taxes on foreign goods imported into the country, and taxes on goods produced and sold within the country.

Equity in Taxation

There is universal agreement that taxes should be as fair as possible; views differ sharply, however, as to just what is most fair. Most people, it is pretty clear, feel that in all fairness, they should be paying less taxes and other people should be paying more. The taxes actually adopted generally consist of acceptable compromises; no individual tax, and indeed no tax system, has ever evoked the unqualified approval of those taxed.

Upon what grounds are we to judge whether a tax is fair or not? What shall be our standard? There are two possible criteria which may be used. Each sounds well, but unfortunately the two are frequently incompatible, so that if we employ one we must disregard the other. In actual cases, furthermore, there are likely to be conflicting views as to just what constitutes the appropriate application of a principle. The two principles are:

That people and firms should pay taxes in accordance with the *benefit which they receive* from government services.

That people and firms should pay taxes in accordance with their *ability to pay*.

The first principle seems reasonable enough, and is the basis of most transactions in the private sector of the national economy. People pay for the goods and services which private enterprise supplies to them. Unfortunately, it is simply not possible to charge citizens and firms in accordance with the benefits they receive from government services. In the first place, many beneficiaries are quite unable to pay. For example, it is out of the question that the recipients of public welfare pay for the assistance which they receive; the reason they need such help is that they have no money. In the second place, it is impossible to measure exactly how much benefit any particular person receives from government services. How could we decide, for instance, just how much benefit each individual citizen derives from the existence of the nation's defence forces, its courts of justice, its highways, its schools? Were any such estimate made it would be completely arbitrary.

Because of the limited applicability of the "benefits received" principle, governments levy most taxes on the basis of the alternative principle, that people should pay taxes according to their ability to pay. The concept of ability to pay requires careful definition, however. Strictly speaking, anyone who possesses or can raise the amount of a tax is able to pay it. Upon what grounds can we claim that some people are less able to pay a particular tax, when they could pay it if so required?

The grounds are these: we measure a person's capacity to pay a tax by the amount he would have left after paying it. The poor man who would have little left after paying a particular tax would be considered as being really unable to pay it; the rich man who would have a great deal left after paying the same tax would be considered as being amply able to pay it.

Progressive Taxation

Jones has an income of $3,000 a year, Pomeroy has an income of $100,000. If the government were to impose a tax of $500 on each man, Jones would obviously be much more heavily burdened than would Pomeroy. Suppose that the government, instead of taxing each man a fixed sum, were to tax each a fixed percentage of his income, say ten per cent. In that case Jones would pay $300, while Pomeroy would pay $10,000; each man's financial load would thus be related to his ability to carry such loads. According to a good many people, however, Jones would still be more heavily burdened even under this arrangement; the loss of ten per cent of his income hurts him more than the loss of ten per cent of his income hurts Pomeroy, even though the actual money sum paid by Jones is much smaller.

This argument cannot of course be proven, but it has wide acceptance, and is embodied in actual practice. Solicitous to ensure that the income tax makes all citizens equally unhappy, governments impose a higher *rate* of taxation on large incomes than they do on small. If Jones were taxed at the rate of ten per cent, Pomeroy would be taxed at the rate of fifty or sixty per cent; only so, it is felt, would he be made to suffer equally with Jones. A tax which is based upon this principle, that the rich should pay a higher rate, is known as a *progressive tax*; a tax which levies the same rate on rich and poor alike is referred to as *proportional*; a tax which takes a larger percentage of income from poor people than it does from rich people is called *regressive*.

TAXES ON INCOME

On Personal Income

Canada, like most modern countries, levies a tax upon the incomes of its citizens; the main features of the Canadian tax are fairly representative. Only income in excess of

$1,500 is subject to tax, and additional exemptions are allowed on account of marital responsibilities, charitable donations and extraordinarily large medical bills. The tax is progressive; in 1970 a taxable income of $1,000 was taxed at about 15% (varying slightly from one province to another), while a taxable income of $100,000 was subject to rates well in excess of 50%.

Although the progressive personal income tax is firmly established in a good many countries, it is by no means free of controversy and challenge. Opponents denounce it as inequitable because it takes away most from those persons who have worked hardest and deserved the most. They claim, furthermore, that a high rate of taxation on income discourages people from working as hard as they could; the nation as a whole produces less when some of its citizens, including the ablest, are deterred from putting forth all the effort of which they are capable. Finally they argue that the tax is liable to evasion and that the burden of the tax varies unfairly among individuals according to their capacity and will to evade it. Because the reward of successful evasion may be very great, the temptation at times is very strong: we have here a powerful source of pressure on the morals of honest, decent people.

Defenders of the progressive personal income tax deny that it significantly deters the receivers of high incomes from putting forward their best efforts. Such people, they claim, have status and prestige as their primary objectives; the money they earn is incidental, serving merely to measure the degree of their success. Since income earned *before tax* is the yardstick by which success and eminence are measured, it really does not matter how much the government takes away in tax; the money has already served its main purpose of attesting to the individual's achievement.

Defenders also claim that the tax is broadly justifiable on the basis of the "benefits received" principle. No individual, they argue, earns a high income through his own efforts alone; he requires the services of government and the efforts of others; he depends upon and utilizes the accumulated knowledge and capital of his society. By taxing the rich man heavily, the government merely ensures that society at large obtains its proper share of the national product.

The Corporation Income Tax

In most countries, every incorporated company must pay a tax on its net income. The net income upon which tax is payable is computed according to procedures carefully prescribed by the government, to ensure that no firm understates its net income by either understating its receipts or overstating its expenses.

Like the personal income tax, the corporation income tax is a fruitful source of controversy. Its advocates take it for granted that corporation profits represent income which has not been genuinely earned, and that no injustice is done when the state takes away a substantial portion. They claim that corporations derive great benefit from the services provided by government and should contribute appropriately to the cost of providing those services.

Opponents of the tax charge that it produces the inequity of double taxation of the same income. The profit earned by a company, which belongs to the shareholders, is taxed when it is earned by the company and is taxed a second time when, distributed as dividends, it becomes part of the income of shareholders.[2] They contend further that, in two ways at least, the tax is responsible for misdirection of the nation's efforts and resources. The tax deters corporations from undertaking new investments, since, even if these proved successful the net gain after tax might be too small to justify the risk and effort involved. Secondly, because additional expenditures reduce their taxable income and therefore their taxes, many firms quite deliberately engage in extravagance; of the money they waste, they would in any case have had to hand over a large proportion to the government in tax, so that the net cost of extravagant expenditures is small.

TAXES ON GOODS SOLD

Governments impose a wide variety of taxes upon the sale of goods within their respective countries. Such a tax must be paid over to the government by the seller, and is a stipulated amount of money for each sale made, being either a fixed sum per unit of goods sold, or a percentage of the selling price. The seller may of course recoup by raising his price to the consumer. The extent to which he is able to do so will depend, as we have seen in Chapter 4, upon the elasticity of demand in relation to the elasticity of supply.

Customs Duties

The duties or tariffs levied on imported goods are among the most venerable of taxes. Their relative ease of collection enabled them to be collected even in quite primitive times; goods imported from foreign countries would normally be brought by vessel to a limited number of ports, and it was a simple matter for revenue officers to check cargoes upon their being unloaded and assess the duties against them.

The customs duties have always served a dual purpose. They serve as a source of revenue to the government, and in addition protect domestic producers against the competition of foreigners. The two functions are necessarily performed alternatively, rather than in combination. If revenue is being collected, then obviously foreign goods must be entering the country and competing with those produced by domestic manufacturers; if the tariff really does keep foreign goods out, then no revenue can be collected.

Like most taxes the customs duties have features which are obviously inequitable. The burden tends to be imposed only on those citizens who require goods of the type subject to duty. If they buy these goods from abroad, they pay this form of

---

[2]Governments now recognize this. In Canada and the United States taxpayers are permitted to deduct from their taxable incomes a portion of the money which they have received in dividends.

taxation which no one else in the country is obliged to pay. If the duty effectively bars foreign goods, they are penalized through being obliged to purchase a more costly domestically produced good when, were it not for the duty, they could have bought the same thing more advantageously outside the country. Finally, as we saw in Chapter 17, customs duties which are protective restrict international specialization and reduce the volume of international trade; we noted in that chapter the losses such reductions involve.

Excise Taxes

Certain goods, whether produced in this country or imported, are singled out for special taxation by the federal government. These usually are in the luxury or semi-luxury class, such as radios, television sets, automobiles, cosmetics, china-ware, alcoholic beverages, tobacco products and smokers' accessories. In Canada, provincial governments levy taxes on admissions to theatres, to movies and to other places of amusement. The presumption is that people who are able to buy such goods and services are able to contribute extra tax revenue to the government. In most cases the tax is a percentage of the selling price (the percentage varying for different types of goods); in some cases the tax is a fixed sum of money per unit sold.

The tax on gasoline, levied by provincial governments in Canada, is a type of excise tax, although it possesses one important feature which sets it apart from the rest. Whereas excise taxes generally are simply means of raising revenue toward the general purposes of government, the gasoline tax is a so-called "user" tax. The public's use of automobiles and trucks obliges each provincial government to spend very large sums on roads, highways and bridges; in taxing the gasoline which fuels the vehicles, the government recovers the cost of these public facilities from the main beneficiaries. The gasoline tax represents an application of the "benefits received" principle of taxation.

General Sales Taxes

A general sales tax is levied as a percentage of the selling price of all goods sold, although usually some classes of goods may be exempted. In Canada the sales tax is not charged on most foodstuffs, farm products, farm equipment and a few other specified types of goods.

Two different types of sales tax are levied: the federal government imposes a sales tax at the producer's level, i.e. on sales made by a manufacturer or importer to a distributor; all provincial governments except Alberta levy a retail sales tax, i.e. on sales made to the general public by retail establishments.

The sales tax is widely criticized as being regressive in that it is paid equally by all, with no distinction made between rich and poor. This regressiveness, it should be noted, is in fact mitigated by the following considerations. Firstly, the necessities of life are customarily exempted. Poor people, whose total spending is small, and the bulk of whose spending is on necessities in any case, therefore pay a relatively small aggregate amount in sales tax. Wealthy people spend more, and a larger proportion of their expenditures is likely to be made on goods which are liable to sales taxes. Hence, although rich and poor do pay the same sales tax on any particular item, the aggregate amount paid by a rich person in sales tax is likely to be very much greater than the aggregate amount paid by a poor person.

TAXES ON PROPERTY

Succession Duties

These are levied, usually on a "progressive" basis, on the estates of persons deceased. Like all taxes, they have their pros and cons. In their favour it can be said that the heirs who bear the burden will, in all likelihood, have done nothing to deserve their inheritance; it cannot be argued, as with the income tax, that the succession duty takes away from a man money which he has earned through his diligent toil. What is more, the tax appreciably lessens social inequalities by diminishing the advantages enjoyed by rich men's sons over poor men's sons; each new generation starts out on a more equal footing than would otherwise have been the case.

On the other hand, the complexities involved render the cost of collection very high. Some persons evade the tax by moving to a jurisdiction in which a very low estate tax is imposed—or none at all. Finally, it is stoutly claimed that a good many men work hard to build up a going concern which they will pass on to children. Heavy succession duties may frustrate that intent: heirs to a family firm or farm may be forced to sell out in order to pay the estate tax that is due. Because his children will derive relatively small benefit from his achievement, a man may therefore refrain from putting forth all the effort of which he is capable.

Property Taxes

These are levied annually, primarily by municipal governments, on land and buildings located within the municipality. In some areas personal property such as furniture and clothing is also subject to taxation. The value of every piece of taxable property is assessed by municipal representatives, and the total assessment of all taxable property within the municipality is computed. The municipal authorities then determine the rate of taxation which, applied to this aggregate assessment, will yield the revenue which they will require in the coming year; each property owner is then taxed at this rate. Thus, suppose the total taxable assessment of a municipality were computed to be $100 million. If the local authorities decided in a particular year to raise $4 million from the taxation of property, they would set that year's tax rate at 40 mills. Each property owner would then be required to pay a tax amounting to $\frac{40}{1000}$ of the assessed value of his taxable property.

The property tax is widely criticized as being regressive, and the criticism is to a considerable degree deserved. A poor man with a large family may require a fairly large dwelling; a well-to-do person with a small family may live in a small one. If the latter's home, though small, is elegant and costly, it will be subject, of course, to a substantial property tax. However, a wealthy person may choose to live in a modest home, spending his money on other things; in that event, he might quite conceivably pay less in property tax than does a person with much smaller means.

Local Improvement Levies

The cost of street improvements such as sidewalks, pavements and sewers, is generally charged to the owners of properties located on the street where such works are installed. Characteristically, property owners are charged in proportion to the frontage of their properties, i.e. the width of their lots.

As with most taxes, the incidence of local improvement levies is frequently inequitable. The assumption that street improvements benefit only the owners of property on the street is often belied in practice. Other people may be the main users of the streets and sidewalks; the sewers may carry sewage which emanates mostly from elsewhere. In recognition of such considerations, many municipalities charge only a portion of the cost of street improvements against properties on the street, the remainder of the cost being borne by the municipality at large.

Business Taxes

Most municipalities levy a special tax on business firms, over and above the property tax which is payable on the land and buildings which they occupy. This business tax may take the form of a percentage of the rental value of the premises, or a levy based on the amount of space occupied, or a levy based on the value of the stock, fixtures and equipment employed.

Non-Tax Revenues

In addition to their receipts from taxation, governments may obtain income from the following sources:

1. Natural resources. In each province of Canada, all lands not owned by private persons or firms are legally the property of the provincial government. Should timber or mineral resources be discovered and exploited on such lands, the provincial government will obtain rents, royalties and similar payments.
2. Profits from government enterprises. A good many governments operate public utilities, supplying water, gas, electrical power and telephone service to their citizens. In some cases the government deliberately prices the good or service so as merely to cover costs; in other cases, however, the price is fixed at a level which will yield a substantial profit, and this money becomes part of the general revenue of the government. Most Canadian provinces, and some American states,

have reserved for themselves a monopoly of the sale of liquor within their respective jurisdictions, and earn substantial profits thereon.

3. Fees for licences and permits. When governments wish to exercise a measure of control over certain activities engaged in by private firms or individuals, they generally require those who wish to carry on the activity to obtain a licence or permit. Thus automobile drivers must obtain licences before they may drive; builders must obtain permits before they may build; distillers must obtain licences before they manufacture liquor. For such licences and permits fees are required. While the individual fees are generally nominal, even a nominal rate produces substantial revenue if a great many are collected, as is the case with automobile drivers' licences.

4. Court fines. The fines imposed on offenders against the law are a source of revenue for all levels of government.

5. Inter-governmental transfer payments. Grants paid by senior to junior governments constitute for the latter an important source of revenue. Thus in Canada municipalities receive annual grants from their respective provinces, while the provinces in turn receive grants from the federal government. Some are *conditional*; i.e. they are given toward the cost of specifically designated projects or services; others are *unconditional*; i.e. they may be spent in whatever way the recipient authority sees fit.

GOVERNMENT BORROWING

In addition to deriving income from tax and other sources governments frequently raise money by borrowing. The chief reasons and circumstances are the following:

1. Revenues may normally be received late in the year while expenditures must be made early. Under such conditions, governments are likely to borrow on a short term basis, repaying loans within a matter of months.

2. A government may be committed to a particular aggregate of expenditures but its revenues may fall short of the total required. Because it may be impossible or inexpedient to cut expenditures or to increase taxes, the government may borrow to cover the deficiency.

3. The government may wish to build a very large and costly project, such as a railway, canal or highway, which will be of enduring benefit to the country. To pay for such a project out of current revenues might be quite impossible and even if it were possible it might be undesirable. If the government pays for a permanent improvement out of current revenue, the cost of the project is imposed entirely on the current year's taxpayers; taxpayers of later years, who will derive equal or greater benefit, will obtain this benefit free. If the government finances the project by a loan which is repayable over an extended period, the cost burden is spread more equitably as between present and future taxpayers.

4. In periods of great emergency, such as during wartime, a government may be obliged to spend enormous sums of money both at home and abroad. To raise by taxation the full amount it must spend at home might be impractical; the government may raise by taxation as much as is considered feasible and obtain the remainder by borrowing from its own citizens. Large purchases which the government has to make in foreign countries may have to be financed by borrowing abroad. The country's exports may be too small to earn all the foreign exchange required, and its citizens may own few foreign assets which could be sold to obtain the currencies of those countries.

PUBLIC FINANCE AND THE NATIONAL ECONOMY

The financial operations of government bring about a considerable re-direction of the productive efforts of the nation. Suppose, for instance, that no government existed. Suppose, too, that the productive resources of the country were fully employed in the production of goods and services for private consumption and private investment. Suppose, now, that a government were to be organized, and that it imposed taxes to finance its expenditures. Because of the taxes which they were henceforth obliged to pay, firms and individuals would have less to spend on consumption and investment. Fewer goods and services for private consumption and private investment would be produced, but the government would now be providing public services, paid for by the money it took from the community through taxation. Hence in real terms the significance of the government's financial operations is that productive capacity which would have been used to turn out goods and services for consumption and investment by individuals, instead produces goods and services for the collective use of the community as a whole. Instead of having more shirts, dresses, automobiles and servants, we have roads, schools, jails, policemen and firemen.

We must be careful not to overstate the reduction in the output of consumer goods attributable to the government's financial operations. A considerable portion of the revenue raised by governments is distributed, in "welfare payments," to individuals considered to be in need of social aid. It may be presumed that the recipients spend this money on consumer goods. On the other hand, the people from whom the money was taken might not have spent it all on consumption, had they been allowed to keep it. Hence the reduction in the output of consumer goods for the benefit of taxable income receivers is offset, perhaps more than offset, by the increased production of consumer goods for the benefit of the receivers of welfare payments.

The illustration developed in the preceding paragraphs is unrealistic in that it assumes the possibility of having no government at all and therefore no public services whatsoever. The fact is that some public services are absolutely indispensable; even the private sector of a nation's economy could not function if these were not available. Our privately owned automobiles would be useless were there no public highways to drive them on; our privately owned business enterprises could not operate safely without publicly provided protection against fire, theft, and foreign attack; the education of our children is carried on primarily in publicly maintained schools.

While all agree that a minimum of government services is absolutely indispensable, views differ sharply on the question of how much service the government should provide beyond that minimum. The "liberals" favour expansion of public services; the "conservatives" urge that they be held down to a minimum, so that the nation's productive capacity can turn out the absolute maximum of goods and services for private consumption.

The foregoing discussion has indicated how the government's financial operations have the effect of altering the character and the distribution of the goods produced in the country. In Chapter 27 we shall see how the government's taxation and spending programmes may affect the *aggregate* of goods and services produced in the country as well. We shall see how governments may adopt taxation and spending policies which are designed not merely to finance desirable public services, but also to regulate the level of the nation's economic activity, preventing both depression and inflation.

SUMMARY

During the nineteenth and twentieth centuries governments were called upon to perform many new functions. Governments undertook to provide a variety of welfare services, to provide facilities and services which private enterprise could not provide, to maintain stable and prosperous economic conditions. Meanwhile, the traditional responsibilities of government, such as national defence, increased enormously in cost.

The large sums which governments require are obtained primarily through taxation levied on incomes, on property, and on goods sold. Taxes may be apportioned among people on the basis of ability to pay or on the basis of benefits received. Each type of tax has its drawbacks and inequities.

Governments may obtain revenue from non-tax sources, including profits of public enterprises, royalties on natural resources, fees and fines. Junior governments may receive grants from senior governments.

When it is inexpedient or impossible to raise needed funds in other ways, governments may borrow, either on a short or long term basis.

Modern governments deliberately manipulate their tax impositions, their expenditures, and their borrowing, so as not merely to finance desirable projects and services but also to maintain the national economy in a stable condition.

FOR REVIEW AND DISCUSSION

1. The corporation income tax is simply another means of taxing the rich. Do you agree?
2. An income tax structure which lightly burdened the rich and heavily burdened the poor would probably be conducive to rapid material progress. Do you agree? Justify your answer.
3. Governments generally spend their money wastefully; government expenditures should therefore be reduced. Comment.
4. What additional services do you think ought to be provided by the government? What services now provided by the government should be performed by private enterprise instead? Justify your answer.
5. If the government relied more on sales taxes and less on income taxes, we would all be better off. Do you agree?
6. Suppose that the government were able to levy only one tax; which one do you think it should be? Justify your answer.
7. Government expenditures simply represent expenditure for communal purposes. Comment.
8. Laissez-faire would be a perfectly acceptable economic system in a world of full employment. Do you agree?
9. Governments should never borrow except in emergencies. Do you agree?
10. The progressive income tax is really quite unfair. Do you agree? Justify your answer.
11. If it were possible for the government to raise all the revenue it needed by levying just one tax, would it be desirable to do so? Justify your answer.

19

Public Finance in Canada

THE ARRANGEMENTS OF CONFEDERATION

The British North American Act, which brought the Canadian nation into being, provided for the three levels of government which exist in Canada today. Each province was to retain its own legislature, with a federal parliament being established to administer the affairs of the country as a whole. A number of municipal governments already existed within each province, and additional ones were expected to be created. The B.N.A. Act enumerated the responsibilities of the new federal government and those to be retained by provincial governments. To the federal government was allocated responsibility for matters of broad national concern, such as relations with foreign powers, national defence, the administration of justice, and major public works which would develop the country as a whole; to the provincial governments was given the responsibility for matters considered to be of only regional or local concern, such as health and welfare services, education, roads, police and fire protection. A good many of the provincial responsibilities, it was anticipated, would be handed over to municipal authorities.

The Fathers of Confederation provided for the financial needs of the federal and provincial governments by allocating specific revenue sources to each. To the federal government was given the customs and excise; to each provincial government was given the right to charge fees for licences and permits, the public revenue yielded by the province's natural resources, and the right to impose direct taxation (i.e. taxes on incomes and property).[1] Municipalities would have as their main revenue the proceeds from taxation of property.

At the time of Confederation the customs and excise duties were overwhelmingly the nation's most important sources of public revenue. These the Fathers of Confederation allotted to the federal government because, in their view, the latter had been given the most onerous responsibilities. The revenue sources allotted to the provincial governments were small but then provincial needs were expected to be

---

[1]Defined by the courts as taxation imposed upon the person expected to bear the burden (as opposed to indirect taxation which the person paying is able to pass on to someone else).

332

small. The correspondence between revenues and financial needs was not exact, however. The customs and excise duties produced more revenue than the federal government required; the revenue sources allotted to the provincial governments produced less than they required. While admittedly the provincial governments could increase their revenues by levying direct taxes, these were unpopular and difficult to collect. It was arranged, accordingly, that the federal government pay an annual subsidy to each province, which would fill the gap between its revenues and its expenditures.

This solution brought new problems, for the revenue requirements of the different provincial governments were far from uniform. In Ontario and Quebec there existed by this time well-organized municipal governments, and these furnished a good many of the public services required by the local populations. The expenditures and therefore the revenue requirements of the provincial governments were correspondingly light. In the Maritime provinces, on the other hand, municipal organization barely existed. Here provincial governments had to supply practically all public services and their revenue requirements were correspondingly high. Thus, while the provincial government of Ontario estimated that it would require a federal subsidy of 38 cents per capita to cover its deficit, the government of New Brunswick estimated that it would need $1.33, and the government of Nova Scotia estimated that it would need $1.70. A compromise figure of 80 cents per capita was finally adopted, to be paid uniformly to all provinces. (In recognition of their special problems, additional subsidies were paid to the Maritime provinces, for a limited period after Confederation.)

In addition to the per capita subsidy, the federal government undertook to make "debt allowance" payments to the provinces which qualified. The genesis of these payments was as follows. Prior to Confederation, the various provincial governments had incurred heavy debts, chiefly in connection with railway and canal construction. By the terms of Confederation, the new federal government took over these provincial debts, so that they became consolidated into a single debt, which was the liability of the country as a whole. This involved unequal treatment of the different provinces. Some provinces, notably Ontario and Quebec,[2] had borrowed very heavily, and, with Confederation, became relieved of a very great burden of debt; other provinces had borrowed relatively much less and were relieved of only a much lighter burden. Furthermore, the people of these latter provinces now became obligated to help pay off the large debts incurred by the provinces which had borrowed heavily prior to Confederation. To eliminate this inequity, the federal government undertook to make "debt allowance" payments to those provinces whose debt at the time of Confederation was less than the national average. The average per capita debt for the Dominion as a whole was calculated to be about $25, and provinces whose debt was lower than this figure were to receive an annual grant of five

[2]From 1840 to 1867 these two had been united in the single "Province of Canada."

per cent of the difference; provinces whose debt was in excess of this figure were, on the other hand, to pay the federal government five per cent per annum on the excess.[3]

THE HISTORIC EXPANSION
OF GOVERNMENT RESPONSIBILITIES

In the century which has elapsed since Confederation, the Canadian economy and way of life have been transformed beyond recognition. The economy has massively expanded, in terms both of size and diversity. Primarily agricultural in 1867, it is now characterized by a high degree of industrialization and heavy emphasis on the exploitation of mineral and forest resources. Population has increased six-fold and has become primarily urban. The nation has participated in two world wars and has for years now felt obliged to maintain a large and costly military establishment. Carried along by world-wide currents, it has moved toward a new social philosophy which emphasizes state assistance to the unfortunate and the needy. These historic developments have brought about a huge increase in the range and scale of government activity at all three levels.

The increase in the number and size of urban municipalities and the complex needs of modern communities have multiplied the problems of local government. The authorities of towns and cities have been obliged to build and operate costly school systems; to install, on an extensive scale, sewers, water mains, streets and sidewalks; to maintain elaborate arrangements for safeguarding the health of their citizens and for protecting them and their property against fire and crime. Social assistance became necessary on a major scale as an urban and industrial society produced severe problems of destitution and family breakdown.

Provincial governments were obliged to share in the greatly increased education and welfare burdens of their respective municipalities. Following the large scale advent of the automobile, they had to build extensive highway systems and since the end of World War II all provinces have greatly expanded their health programs.

The federal government massively supported the construction of canals and transcontinental railways, and following their completion became responsible for their operating deficits. Two world wars required federal outlays on an unprecedented scale; veterans' pensions and benefits, together with interest on debt incurred

---

[3]Actually such payments *to* the federal government were never made. They were due only from Ontario and Quebec, resulting from the heavy debt incurred by them in the period 1840-67 when they had been joined together in a single province. Now that they were separated, the two provinces could not agree on what proportion each was responsible for, of the debt which they had incurred when joined together. It proved impossible, therefore, for the federal government to collect the interest for which the two provinces were liable and in 1873 the federal government itself assumed responsibility for these interest payments. To be fair to all the other provinces, it thereupon raised appropriately the annual "debt allowance" payments which it made to them. See J. H. Perry, *Taxes, Tariffs and Subsidies* (Toronto, 1955) Volume I, pp. 41-42.

to finance the war efforts, involved heavy federal expenditures even after the conclusion of the actual fighting. The potentially explosive international situation which
developed shortly after the end of World War II obliged the government to maintain
the nation's defence establishment at a level unprecedented in peacetime. As a
wealthy and responsible member of the community of nations Canada has contributed substantially, in money, services and goods, toward the needs of less fortunate countries, the federal government being, naturally, the main agency through
which the Canadian nation furnished this aid. Under the Tax Rental Agreements
the federal government obligated itself to pay large sums annually to the provincial
governments. Finally, the federal government undertook major welfare programmes,
notably in the fields of old age pensions, family allowances, and universal insurance
against hospital and medical costs.

THE EXPENDITURES OF CANADIAN GOVERNMENTS, 1939-67.

Figure 1 graphically indicates how government expenditure has increased since pre-
war. In 1939 all three levels of government in Canada together spent a grand total of
$1,321 million; in 1943, when wartime expenditures reached their peak, the total of
governmental expenditures in Canada was $5,509 millions, with the federal govern-
ment responsible for practically the whole of the increase. By 1967, twenty-two years

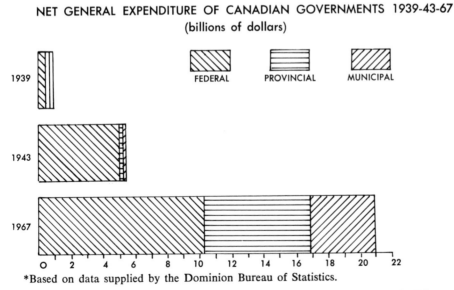

*Based on data supplied by the Dominion Bureau of Statistics.

Figure 1.   Net general expenditure of Canadian Governments 1939-43-67*

after the War ended, the total of government expenditures was nearly four times the peak wartime figure and sixteen times the 1939 figure.

The comparison of government expenditures in 1967 with those of 1939 is striking, but before leaping to conclusions we must take these four considerations into account:

1. The 1967 price level was approximately three times that of 1939. Fair comparison of 1939 with 1967 expenditures would require that we reduce the latter by two-thirds.

2. The population of Canada was 11.3 million in 1939 and 20.4 million in 1967. A substantial portion of the increase in expenditure was required simply by the near doubling of the nation's population.

3. A considerable fraction of the federal government's expenditures in 1967 was on defence and on obligations incurred as a result of our participation in two world wars, notably veterans' pensions and other benefits, and interest on the money borrowed to finance war effort.

4. The National Income increased very greatly, in real terms, between 1939 and 1967. We could afford a higher level of government outlay and we now required more and better government services; e.g. because many more privately owned automobiles were in use, governments had to spend far more on roads, bridges, traffic control and the like.

There are a good many people in Canada who deplore the great increase which has occurred since 1939 in the expenditures of our governments. They contend that this very great enlargement of public spending represents a rush towards socialism, or, at best, the construction of an immense and costly edifice of government which heavily burdens the people of Canada. The four considerations outlined above suggest that such contentions greatly exaggerate the case. The fact is that the very same government services cost a great deal more in 1967 than they did in 1939, because of price increases and population growth. In addition, the heavy expenditures by government on military pensions and defence represented inescapable commitments arising out of past wars and our moral obligation to contribute equitably to present international peace-keeping. And, if the standards of some publicly provided services have been raised it is because our national income and our living standards generally have risen. Some government services are complementary to private goods and services and must be improved and enlarged when the latter are improved and become more widely available. Furthermore, as we become wealthier we can afford to provide more adequately for the unfortunates in our midst—and must do so to avoid an intolerable contrast between a general well-being and grinding poverty suffered by those dependent on public assistance. Finally, it can be said that we are taking advantage of our enlarged productive capacity to provide ourselves with more and better publicly provided services as well as more and better products of private enterprise. Some people forcefully contend that governments should be spending even more money than they currently are, in order to provide us with still more and better public services, notably more and better educational services.

The Expansion of Government Revenue

The increase in their responsibilities obliged governments, at all three levels, to develop additional sources of revenue. Municipalities, while still mainly dependent for revenue upon property taxes, obtained steadily increasing grants from their respective provincial governments and imposed new taxes such as those upon gas, electricity and water sales. A number of municipalities in Quebec now impose a general sales tax.

Provincial governments were obliged, very soon after Confederation, to develop major new sources of revenue. By 1900, every province was taking advantage of its right under the B.N.A. Act to levy direct taxation; each was levying a personal income tax, a corporation profits tax, and succession duties. With the advent of the automobile, provincial governments obtained new revenue through taxes imposed on gasoline and through fees charged for vehicle and driver licences. During the 1920s most provinces set up government agencies to sell liquor on a monopoly basis, and the profits from liquor sales have since contributed substantially to provincial treasuries. All provinces except Alberta now levy a sales tax (at the retail level).

The federal government introduced, during World War I, a personal income tax and a tax on corporation profits, both additional to similar taxes already being levied by provincial governments. Shortly after the end of the war, the federal government introduced a general sales tax at the producer's level. Originally set at one per cent, it was increased in successive steps to its present level of twelve per cent. During World War II, the federal government sharply increased its personal and corporation income taxes and introduced special excise taxes upon a wide variety of goods, ranging from soft drinks to automobiles. A federal succession duty was introduced, additional to the similar duties already being levied by provincial governments.

The rate of federal taxation has declined since the end of World War II; some taxes have been lowered, and others suspended altogether. Nevertheless, the current rate of federal taxation is far higher than ever before in peacetime, reflecting particularly the government's heavy and continuing responsibilities in the fields of defence, health, and welfare, and the huge interest payments that must be made on debts incurred in wartime.

Government Revenue and Expenditure in Canada, 1967

Figures 2 and 3 indicate how the total revenue and expenditure of all three levels of government in Canada were composed in 1967. Inter-governmental transfers have been eliminated; the two graphs accordingly show how much money the people, the business firms, and natural resources of Canada contributed to the support of

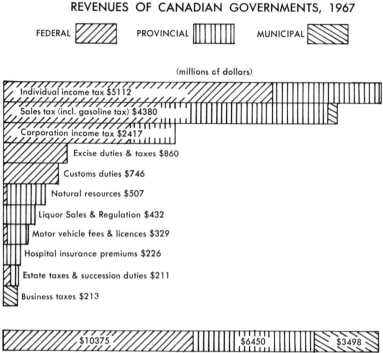

Figure 2.   Revenues of Canadian Governments, 1967

government, and how much was spent, by each level of government, upon the public services provided to the people.

(Note: Because of changes in classification it was not possible to obtain exactly comparable figures for all years upon which to base Figure 4. Thus the federal figures prior to 1950 represent "net debt" while the figures from that year on represent "debenture debt"; the provincial and municipal figures similarly are not completely consistent. Nevertheless Figure 4 does represent reasonably well the major movements in governmental debt over the period.)

Government Debt in Canada

Figure 4 graphically indicates how the debt of each of the three levels of government has increased during the last half century. The net debt of the federal government amounted in 1913 to just over $300 million, practically all incurred in connection with the construction of railways and canals. During the course of the next half dozen years the government borrowed heavily to finance the national war effort in World War I, and assumed the debt obligations of the two great railway

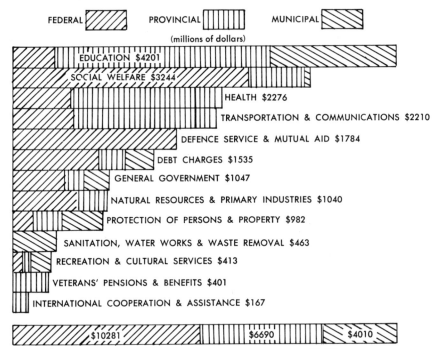

FEDERAL ▨ PROVINCIAL ▨ MUNICIPAL ▨

(millions of dollars)

EDUCATION $4201

SOCIAL WELFARE $3244

HEALTH $2276

TRANSPORTATION & COMMUNICATIONS $2210

DEFENCE SERVICE & MUTUAL AID $1784

DEBT CHARGES $1535

GENERAL GOVERNMENT $1047

NATURAL RESOURCES & PRIMARY INDUSTRIES $1040

PROTECTION OF PERSONS & PROPERTY $982

SANITATION, WATER WORKS & WASTE REMOVAL $463

RECREATION & CULTURAL SERVICES $413

VETERANS' PENSIONS & BENEFITS $401

INTERNATIONAL COOPERATION & ASSISTANCE $167

$10281 $6690 $4010

Figure 3.   Expenditures of Canadian Governments, 1967

systems which had in effect gone bankrupt in the course of the war. By 1920 the federal debt amounted to $2,249 million, over seven times the 1913 figure.

Budget surpluses during the 1920s made possible some reduction in the outstanding debt but heavy borrowing became necessary during the depressed 1930s and the federal debt rose to more than $3 billion in 1939. Immense borrowings to finance the war effort of 1939-45 swelled the debt to more than $13 billion in 1946. Budget surpluses during the next decade enabled the federal government to reduce its debt substantially, but a series of budget deficits after 1957 involved heavy further borrowing which raised the debt to over $18 billion by 1967.

Provincial and municipal debt, incurred chiefly to finance the construction of roads, bridges, streets, sewer and water systems and public buildings, rose steadily with population growth, urbanization, and increase in automobile ownership. Borrowing to finance new public works practically ceased during the Great Depression of the 1930s; provincial governments, however, borrowed substantial sums to finance their share of relief costs. During the 1939-45 war period, prosperous conditions prevailed and construction of public works might have been resumed but labour and materials were not available. Following the end of the war, with labour and materials again available, prosperous conditions continuing, and population—

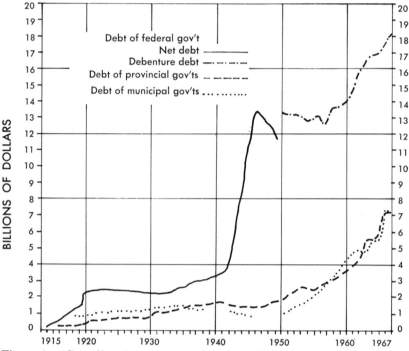

Figure 4.   Canadian Governmental Debt, 1913-67

both human and automobile—rapidly rising, the provincial and municipal governments embarked upon large scale public works programmes; these were financed, to a considerable degree by borrowing. As is evident, provincial and municipal debt rose much more rapidly in the postwar period than did that of the federal government; whereas in 1950 the aggregate debt of the two junior levels of government amounted to less than a quarter of the federal debt, by 1967 their aggregate debt amounted to over three-quarters of the federal figure.

CANADIAN PUBLIC FINANCE

Structural Weaknesses

In the three-quarters of a century after Confederation the structure of Canadian public finance had enlarged haphazardly, by uncoordinated additions. As it existed in 1930, the nation's tax system contained wasteful duplication; both the federal and provincial governments were levying personal income and corporation income taxes. There was serious regional inequality; the bulk of the nation's wealth and income was concentrated in the provinces of Ontario and Quebec, and the tax revenue which this wealth and income contributed went chiefly into the coffers of these two provinces.[4] The nation's public finances lacked coherence and centralized control; jurisdiction over its main elements was scattered among the federal government and nine provincial governments; there was little possibility of implementing integrated, national fiscal policies to counter tendencies to depression or inflation on the part of the nation's economy.

The great depression of the 1930s starkly revealed the weaknesses of Canada's system of public finance. Municipal and provincial governments, constitutionally responsible for the relief of destitution, were obliged to provide relief on an unprecedented scale to people who had become unemployed on account of the economic depression. Meanwhile the same depression caused their tax revenues to decline heavily. With revenues sharply reduced and expenditures on relief sharply increased, provincial and municipal governments were obliged to curtail drastically their normal services. Many municipalities defaulted on debt obligations; one provincial government partially defaulted. The problems of provincial and municipal governments were particularly severe in the Prairie and Maritime provinces, where the incidence of the depression was most severe. The federal government shared in relief costs, but the burden on junior governments was of crushing weight.

The Royal Commission on Dominion-Provincial Relations

Insistent demands developed during the depression for a major reorganization of the entire system of public finance in Canada. As a result, the federal government appointed a Royal Commission in 1937 to investigate Dominion-Provincial relations and make such recommendations as appeared appropriate. The Commission's report, presented in 1940, urged the following:

> That the federal government assume the debts of all the provincial governments.
>
> That the federal government assume responsibility for the total cost of unemployment relief.
>
> That the provincial governments henceforth refrain from levying personal income taxes, corporation income taxes and succession duties, these taxes to be levied by the federal government only.

---

[4]Other provinces claimed that some of this money rightfully belonged to them. They argued that because the head offices of most nation-wide corporations were located in Ontario or Quebec, the earnings of these concerns, gained from country-wide operations, all flowed into these two provinces and the tax revenue contributed on the basis of these earnings was received by these two provinces only. Firms paid provincial corporation income tax only to the province in which the head office was located; the major shareholders and high salaried executives, all living in Ontario or Quebec, paid provincial income taxes, and in due course their estates contributed succession duties, to the coffers of these two provinces. Other provinces, in which much of the money had been earned, received none of this tax revenue derived from it.

That the federal government pay to poorer provinces annual grants of such size as to enable them to provide normal services to their people, and without an oppressive rate of taxation.

These recommendations were designed to end the main weaknesses and inequities in Canada's system of public finance. There would be no further dual taxation of firms and individuals by the federal government and provincial governments. The less wealthy provinces would be assured of the means to provide an adequate level of service to their people. With the country's main taxes under federal control, it would become possible to employ variation in the rate of taxation as an effective weapon against the dangers of inflation or depression. With the federal government responsible for the full cost of unemployment relief, provincial and municipal governments would be relieved of the nightmarish possibility that they might be called upon, during a business depression, to spend huge sums on the care of the unemployed.

The Federal Provincial Tax Agreements

The Report of the Royal Commission, one of the most distinguished public documents ever produced in Canada, did not receive the careful consideration which was its due. Unfortunately, it was presented after World War II had begun, and at a time when relationships between leading political figures in the country were particularly acrimonious. A conference called in 1941 to consider the Report adjourned with no action having been taken. Nevertheless, since the Report was issued, the federal government has introduced important measures along the lines recommended by the Royal Commission.

In 1942, the federal government entered into the *Wartime Tax Agreements* with all the provinces, under which each province agreed to refrain, for the duration of the war plus one year after, from levying personal income and corporation income taxes. As compensation, the federal government undertook to pay to each province an annual cash grant equal to the total sum which that province had collected from these two taxes in the year prior to the Agreements.[5]

As stipulated, the Wartime Tax Agreements expired in 1946. In the following year the federal and provincial authorities entered into new agreements, to cover the next five years, in which again provincial governments would vacate tax fields, leaving them solely for the federal government and receiving cash compensation from the latter. When these agreements expired, in 1952, they were replaced by another set and new agreements have been drawn up to cover each five-year period since.

Each new set of agreements has contained its own distinctive provisions. Under the arrangements currently in effect, negotiated in 1967, the federal government maintains lower tax rates than it had previously been imposing on personal and

[5]An optional method of payment was also offered which was slightly more favourable to some provinces.

corporate income and on the estates of persons deceased, leaving room for provincial governments to impose their own taxes in these fields. To aid the poorer provinces where collections are small the federal government makes "equalization" payments according to a formula which takes account of fiscal capacity and provides for appropriately larger payments to be made to provinces with meagre revenue sources. Another significant feature of this agreement is the undertaking by the federal government to contribute substantially to the cost of post-secondary education in each province. The size of this contribution is determined by a rather complicated formula but the broad effect is to ensure that it amounts to approximately fifty per cent of operating expenditures on post-secondary education within each province.

FEDERAL CONDITIONAL GRANTS

The federal money paid to provincial governments under the tax agreements forms part of their general revenue and may be used by them however they will. In addition, the federal government makes contributions toward designated provincial projects and programmes, usually on the basis of formulas which make the federal contribution about fifty per cent of the cost. The federal payments are typically made on a matching basis; i.e. the province receives the federal money only if it carries out the designated project or programme, which means that it must provide the balance of the money required in order to qualify for the federal grant. Thus under the Hospital Insurance Plan introduced in 1958 the federal government shares the cost of provincial schemes which provide free hospital services for all their residents. Under the Canada Assistance Plan which came into effect in 1966 Ottawa pays one-half a province's outlays on virtually all forms of welfare assistance. Under the Medicare Act which became effective in 1968 the federal government contributes to the cost of provincial plans for universal medical insurance. In addition the federal authorities make grants to provinces for a variety of other purposes, including hospital construction, public health research, venereal disease control, vocational and technical education, the construction of highways that will lead to northern resources. When the Trans-Canada Highway was built, in the 1950s, the federal government contributed substantially to the cost incurred by each province in building its portion.

Both federal and provincial governments had cause to be unhappy with shared-cost programmes. The federal government has frequently found itself obliged automatically to increase its outlays, whenever provincial administrations enlarged the scale of shared-cost programmes and thereby qualified for larger federal grants. Federal authorities found this commitment particularly galling during the late 1960s when, to combat inflation, they were striving to limit federal outlays.

Provincial governments have their own reasons for being disgruntled. Ottawa in effect determines the nature of some programmes by insisting that designated features be included; provincial administrators exasperatedly claim that many of these federal requirements are irksome and pointless. They have another cause for dissatisfaction. On occasion, usually for budgetary reasons, the federal government has decided to terminate its contributions to a shared-cost programme, leaving provincial authorities the unpleasant alternative of dropping the programme or paying for it entirely by themselves.

However, despite their grievances, provincial governments are opposed to termination of the practice of federal-provincial cost-sharing. In 1968, when the federal government proposed to withdraw from cost-sharing programmes, compensating provinces by giving them enlarged revenue sources, provincial premiers expressed vehement opposition.

Regional Inequality

The payments made to provinces under the Tax Rental Agreements, together with the federal government's conditional grants, equalize to some extent the revenues of the richer and poorer provinces. Money collected by the federal government primarily from individuals and firms in the wealthier provinces is distributed on an equal basis to all provinces. Great disparities in provincial revenue nevertheless still exist. Every province depends for the major part of its revenue upon taxes which it continues to levy and upon the yield of its natural resources; these vary substantially in quality from province to province. The gasoline tax, drivers' licences, fees, amusement taxes and liquor sales, all yield much more public revenue in wealthier provinces than they do in poorer provinces. The provinces, furthermore, are unequally endowed with forests, mineral deposits and oil pools; thus, whereas in 1967 the government of Alberta received a total of $230 million as revenue from its natural resources, the government of Nova Scotia obtained only $1.5 million in revenue from its natural resources; Prince Edward Island obtained $34,000.

Great disparities exist as well within each province among its various municipalities. With municipal receipts derived primarily from the taxation of local property, public revenue depends upon private wealth. Municipalities, in which are located costly business buildings, expensive homes, or valuable farm land, enjoy an ample taxable assessment; their property taxes will be richly productive, Municipalities characterized by limited business development, cheap houses or poor land have a correspondingly meagre tax base from which to derive public revenue.

The disparities in public revenue sources among provinces and municipalities imply corresponding disparities in the quality and range of public services, unless the authorities of poorer jurisdictions impose steeper *rates* of taxation. Whichever course is adopted, whether the authorities of poorer provinces and municipalities provide inferior public services to their people, or whether they tax their people more severely to provide equivalent services, some provinces and municipalities will be better off than others. As a nation, we can accept this state of affairs; we are not committed to the belief that public services and tax loads ought to be exactly the same everywhere in the country. It is generally agreed, however, that even the poorest provincial or municipal government should be assured of the means to provide a decent minimum of public services, with taxation at a reasonable level. Just what is a decent minimum of services, and what is a reasonable level of taxation, are matters of social judgment and public debate in which decisions are made by our political representatives.

Metropolitan Areas

Since 1945 a new and pressing problem of local administration and finance has emerged in Canada, as in other countries. Much of the urban growth which has occurred during this period has taken place in suburban municipalities, located just outside the larger cities. Land in the central city was, typically, fully occupied by this time; furthermore, because they could commute by automobile to their work downtown, many people were enabled to enjoy the pleasures of a home in the suburbs. The emergence of large suburbs has given rise to many new problems. A city and its suburbs together form a single economic and social community, but the government of this single community may be divided up among a dozen or more municipal governments. If the politically divided community has problems in common, and requires public facilities and services in common, the structure of local government must be altered. It becomes necessary to create a new government to administer the area as a whole, to handle its common problems, to build the facilities which are jointly required, to administer the services which are best provided by one authority for the area as a whole, and to distribute equitably, over the whole metropolitan community, the costs involved.

Such an organization was brought into being in Greater Toronto in 1953, when the City and suburbs formed the federation known as the Municipality of Metropolitan Toronto. The new municipality is administered by a Council upon which all the municipalities have representation, the Council being responsible for the construction and financing of all metropolitan-type facilities and the administration and financing of all metropolitan-type services. Each municipality remains responsible for the administration of its own purely local affairs. Winnipeg established a metropolitan council in 1961;[6] other large Canadian urban centres where central cities have become surrounded by heavily populated suburban municipalities, are studying the advisability of reorganizing arrangements for local government within the metropolitan area.

---

[6]In its 1971 session the Manitoba legislature passed a bill providing for the amalgamation of Winnipeg and its suburbs into one city to be administered by a single council; the first such council was elected in October of that year.

SUMMARY

The B.N.A. Act allocated to each level of government responsibility for a specified group of services, together with revenue sources out of which to finance its expenditures. The federal government was given the larger responsibilities and therefore the more lucrative revenue sources; provision was made for an annual federal subsidy to each provincial government.

Following Confederation, the expenditures of all three levels of government increased enormously, as a result of population growth, wars, inflation, and public demand for additional services. All three levels of government became obliged to raise their tax levels and to seek additional sources of revenue.

By the 1930s the structure of public finance had become unwieldly, inequitable and inefficient. Provincial and municipal governments became obliged during the Great Depression to bear extremely heavy burdens while their tax base was shrinking. The dispersion of taxing power rendered it virtually impossible to carry out desirable fiscal policies which might have alleviated the depression.

The Royal Commission on Dominion-Provincial Relations recommended sweeping changes in Canada's system of public finance, but the war had already broken out when its report was presented and no action was taken.

The Wartime Tax Agreements between the federal and provincial governments brought a streamlining of the tax structure during the war period. The Tax Rental Agreements negotiated after the war proved to be particularly beneficial to the less wealthy provinces.

Despite the equal treatment meted out to all provinces under the Tax Rental Agreements, considerable inequality persists in the revenues of different provincial governments.

Where large suburban municipalities have come into being around central cities an imperative need has arisen for reorganization of local government.

FOR REVIEW AND DISCUSSION

1. In your opinion which federal taxes ought to be reduced in Canada and which, if any, increased? Justify your answer.
2. What additional public services do you think the federal government should perform? Should provincial and municipal governments administer some of the services now provided by the federal government?
3. Is it fair, in your opinion, that tax revenues collected by the federal government in one province should be distributed among other provinces?
4. A very large fraction of the federal government's expenditure is, and has always been, attributable to war. Comment.

5. The federal government's conditional grants represent an unwarranted intrusion on provincial independence. Do you agree?
6. During the next generation, there are likely to emerge in Canada several more metropolitan governments like the one established in Greater Toronto in 1953. Comment.
7. A government should always be obliged to raise the money it spends because, inevitably, it will spend in irresponsible fashion money which it has not been obliged to collect for itself. Do you agree?

PART SEVEN:

MONEY AND BANKING

20

The Money Supply and Price Levels

THE NEED FOR A MEDIUM OF EXCHANGE

We use money to make payment for goods and services which we purchase from other people. The need for money exists, accordingly, only in an exchange society, a society in which individuals do not provide all their needs for themselves, but rely upon obtaining some from other people. If every person were completely self-sufficient, there would be no need for exchange, and therefore no need for money as a medium of exchange.

Exchanges could of course be effected on the basis of barter. Each party to the exchange could give to the other real goods or services of equal value. But satisfactory barter deals may be difficult to arrange. To be consummated, a barter deal requires the double coincidence that each party offers what the other wants, and wants what the other offers. A farmer may have an extra pig and need a new suit; to effect a barter deal he must find a tailor who has a suit to dispose of and wants a pig in exchange.[1]

The use of money obviates the need for barter. It becomes unnecessary for each of the parties to a transaction to want for his own use exactly what the other has to offer. There is now a seller and a buyer. The buyer pays with money for the good or service offered by the seller who can subsequently use the money to buy whatever he pleases from other sellers. In a money economy, the farmer who has an extra pig and needs a suit, simply sells the pig to a dealer in pigs and obtains money which any tailor will accept in payment for a suit.

The Nature of "Money"

The "money" which is used as a medium of exchange can be just about anything. In modern countries money consists of small metal coins, of pieces of specially engraved

[1]Under barter condition each party may ultimately manage to get what he wants, but the process is likely to be complicated. Viz. the following account, by an American officer, of his difficulties in buying a boat in Africa. "Syde's agent wished to be paid in ivory, of which I had none; but I found that Mohammed Ibn Salib had ivory and wanted cloth. Still, as I had no cloth, this did not assist me greatly until I heard that Mohammed Ibn Gharib had cloth and wanted wire. This I fortunately possessed. So I gave Ibn Gharib the requisite amount of wire; whereupon he handed over cloth to Ibn Salib, who in his turn gave Syde's agent the wished for ivory. Then he allowed me to have the boat." Quoted in W. F. Foster and W. Catchings, *Money* (Boston, 1923) p. 35.

paper, and of figures in bankers' ledger books. However, these are not, by any means, the only things which can serve as money. In different places, at different times, all sorts of different commodities have been used: cattle in classical Greece,[2] rock salt in Asia and Africa two thousand years ago, wampum by North American Indians three centuries ago, cigarettes in prisoner-of-war camps during World War II, stones with hollow centres on the island of Yap today.

ESSENTIAL CHARACTERISTICS OF MONEY

To serve as money in any society, a thing must have one characteristic, first and foremost. It must be universally acceptable as money to all members of that society. Every one must be willing to accept it in payment for whatever it is that he has to sell. An individual will accept in payment for his goods or services an object which itself is of no use to him, only if he is fully confident that other people, who sell what he does want, will accept this object in payment. Any object which has this characteristic of *universal acceptability* will serve as money.

However, to serve efficiently, whatever is used as money should have additional characteristics as well. In a highly developed economy an enormous number of transactions are carried out daily. Millions of individuals purchase the varied goods and services which they need for their daily living; innumerable firms purchase the goods and services which they need to carry on their operations. In Canada the number of transactions in which money is paid out amounts to many millions daily, ranging in scale from the purchase of a penny lollipop by an anxious four-year-old to the purchase of a multi-million dollar business concern by calculating financiers. To serve as an efficient medium of exchange in the immense number of transactions which are carried out day after day, and whose scale ranges from the tiny to the gigantic, the things used as money should have, along with universal acceptability, the following attributes as well:

> Units of money should be absolutely uniform in appearance, so that any one can be instantly recognized; the precise size of each unit should also be evident at a glance, without any need for measurement.

> Very small units of money should exist, to serve as the medium of exchange in small scale transactions.

[2]The word *pecuniary*, meaning having to do with money, stems from the Latin "pecus" meaning cattle. The word *money* has an interesting "non-monetary" origin. In the year 390 B.C., a band of invading Gauls attempted one night to climb the walls of the citadel of Rome. The sacred geese, kept in the temple of Juno, cackled loudly, rousing the sleeping guards. The alarm having been given, forces were quickly mustered and the attack was repulsed. The temple became known henceforth as the temple of Juno Moneta, i.e. Juno who gives warning. Many years later equipment was set up in the basement of the temple to produce coins. The coin-making establishment became referred to as the "Moneta", after the name of the temple in which it was installed, and the same word was applied to the coins which it produced. Thus originated the words *money, mint,* and *monetary.*

Units of money should, for convenience, be light and easily carried about. The value of money should remain stable through time, so that a person who holds money, wishing to use it later, does not suffer a penalty or gain a reward for doing so. To meet this requirement, money should be made of some durable stuff, so that it does not deteriorate physically with the passage of time and the quantity in existence must not change rapidly.

Gold and Silver as Money

No class of object has proven to be a perfectly satisfactory money, possessing all of the features listed above. One kind of money, however, did serve civilized nations very well for many centuries: money made out of gold and silver. The present monetary systems of most countries grew out of systems which used these precious metals, and gold and silver still play a role in the monetary systems of many countries. Because they were used for ornamental purposes, gold and silver were considered to have intrinsic value whether or not they were used as money. Furthermore, they possessed in satisfactory degree the qualities which money ought to have: easy recognizability, uniformity, divisibility, portability, durability, and stability of value through time.

Coinage

When the precious metals first came into use as money, prices were measured in terms of specified weights of metal. Payment for a purchase was made by handing over the required weight of precious metal. The seller of a good or service who had been paid in gold or silver would, when subsequently making purchases himself, weigh out and hand over some of this metal. The practice of coinage emerged to dispense with the need for weighing and re-weighing the very same pieces of metal each time they passed from one hand to another. A quantity of metal would be melted down and cast in the form of a coin; an insignia would be impressed on it indicating the weight of precious metal the coin contained, and by whose authority it was issued. Henceforth, there was no need for weighing the metal in a coin; its weight was indicated on the coin's face.[3] Coins of base metal—copper usually— were minted as well, to serve in transactions of small value.

---

[3]Coins were often referred to in terms of the weight of the metal which they contained. Thus the words *pound, livre, lire, shekel,* which designate amounts of money, represent also, in their respective languages, units of weight.

Dishonest practices reduced the efficiency of coins as a medium of exchange. Some authorities, anxious to augment their money supply, issued coins which contained base as well as precious metal; the inscriptions impressed upon them claimed that they were of precious metal only. The wary individual would test coins offered to him; a frequently used test consisted of dropping a coin on a stone surface and listening to the ring. People who possessed coins might scrape the surfaces and edges; if they could then pass the lightened coins on at their face value, they would net a profit consisting of the grains of gold they had scraped off. Accordingly, when offered small, thin coins, many people insisted on weighing them, disregarding the inscription on their faces which declared what weight of precious metal was contained.

Paper Money: Goldsmiths' Receipts

A new kind of money emerged in seventeenth century England—paper notes.[4] Its derivation was the practice adopted by Londoners of entrusting their gold and silver to goldsmiths for safekeeping; valuables kept in the home might easily be stolen. A goldsmith, having large amounts of precious metals and other valuables always in his shop, necessarily arranged more effective protection of his possessions than could an ordinary householder. His vaults would be very strong and difficult to break into; his shop would be located near the centre of town where police surveillance was most thorough.

The goldsmith who agreed to hold someone's coins for safekeeping, would give the depositor a receipt. When the depositor wanted his coins back he would present the receipt and they would be returned to him.[5] The goldsmith's receipt, a slip of paper, itself came to serve as money. An individual who had entrusted coins to a goldsmith for safekeeping might, to pay off a debt or to pay for a purchase, simply hand over the receipt which the goldsmith had given him. The debtor or seller would be quite happy to take it in payment. The receipt was as good as the gold itself, since the holder could at any time obtain gold for it by presenting it at the goldsmith's shop. By using a goldsmith's receipt, payment could in fact be made more conveniently than with actual coin. The person making the payment would not be put to the trouble and risk of withdrawing his coins from a goldsmith's shop to hand them over to some other person who very likely would promptly deposit them for safekeeping with the same or another goldsmith. By handing over his receipt to someone else an individual transferred to the other person his *ownership* of the coins. For many sellers and creditors this was perfectly satisfactory; they did not want physical possession of the coins, with its attendant inconvenience and risk. It was preferable simply to have the ownership of coins which were safely lodged in a goldsmith's vaults, with the right to take possession at any time.

The total value of the notes issued by many a goldsmith exceeded the value of the gold coin actually in his vaults. The reason was two-fold: discovering that much of the gold brought in to them for safekeeping was not demanded back, save perhaps long afterward, many goldsmiths adopted the practice of lending out much of the gold entrusted to them. On such loans they collected a handsome interest which they kept. Furthermore, some goldsmiths extended loans simply by giving borrowers some of their paper notes, these being generally acceptable as money. Goldsmiths' notes served effectively as money until 1672, when King Charles II, who had borrowed heavily, refused to repay his loans. The goldsmiths involved became unable in turn to pay the holders of their notes, and public confidence in goldsmiths' notes was gravely impaired.

[4]While it made its first appearance in Europe in the seventeenth century, paper money had been used for centuries in China.

[5]They did ot have to be the very same coins which he had brought in, but merely coins of equal value.

Paper Money: Bank Notes

In 1694 the Bank of England was organized, and given the right to issue paper notes up to a maximum prescribed by the government. These bank notes soon replaced goldsmiths' notes in general circulation. Substantial increases were subsequently authorized in the Bank's note issue and Bank of England notes, for over two centuries now, have constituted virtually the entire paper currency of Great Britain. Banks in other countries, following the example of the Bank of England, also issued paper notes and these bank notes came to constitute the main form of paper currency in circulation.

Bank Deposits

During the course of the nineteenth century, an additional type of money came into general use—the *bank deposit*. Individuals who deposited money in a bank were credited with a *deposit* in the books of the bank. A deposit is in effect a claim on a bank, representing the obligation on the bank's part to return his money to the depositor whenever he asks for it, just as the goldsmith's receipt represented an obligation on the part of the goldsmith to return his coins to a depositor whenever he asked for them. This claim on a bank is just as good as money itself since the owner can demand money from the bank up to the amount of his claim. Deposits can be transferred by means of *cheques*, a cheque being a brief and stereotyped letter in which a depositor requests the bank to hand over to someone else all or part of his claim on the bank.

Payment by cheque has proven to be even safer and more convenient than did payment by the transfer of paper notes. Creditors and sellers are prepared to accept a cheque in payment, knowing that it can be "cashed", i.e. exchanged for money at the depositor's bank. It is just as good as the money itself and in several ways is even better. No one but the person designated can "cash" it and consequently no harm is suffered if a cheque is lost or stolen. A cheque, furthermore, is a superbly convenient means of transferring money, since by one small slip of paper an amount of any size can be transferred exactly to the penny. Thanks to the safety and convenience of payment by cheque, bank deposits have come to constitute by far the largest portion of the national money supply, and an overwhelming proportion of payments are now made by cheque.

MONEY IN CANADA

Our Monetary Unit

During the French regime the monetary units of Canada were those of France; the most commonly employed were the *livre,* worth approximately one franc, the *sou,* worth one-twentieth of a livre, and the *denier*, worth about one twenty-fifth of a sou. Following the British conquest in 1760, new kinds of money entered into circulation in the country. British merchants and soldiers brought in Britain's sovereigns, pounds, shillings and pence; Canadian fishermen and merchants trading with Spain's American colonies brought back Spanish silver dollars; merchants trading with the United States brought in silver dollars which that country's traders had obtained chiefly in the Spanish possessions.[6]

The simultaneous circulation of different currencies created awkward problems. Exchange rates among different currencies varied from one part of the country to another. Thus in Halifax a dollar was reckoned as being worth five shillings, whereas in Montreal (as in New York) a dollar was valued at eight shillings. Buyers could pay for their purchases in any of the various currencies then circulating in the country, each being valued at its particular rate.

Reflecting the country's close commercial connections with the United States, the bulk of commercial transactions was in dollars and in 1857 the government of (the province) Canada, decreed that the dollar, exactly similar to the American, was to be the country's monetary unit. The public accounts were henceforth to be kept in dollars and cents, assuring their legal status.[7] In 1870, shortly after Confederation, a federal statute decreed that the dollar was to be the monetary unit throughout the entire Dominion.

Coins and Notes

The first money consisted of coins. During the French regime silver and copper coins were imported from France, to be used as the medium of exchange in Canada. Following the British conquest, British coins of various denominations and Spanish silver dollars constituted the bulk of the money supply.

However, coins were always scarce. It was no easy matter to acquire them, and they were very quickly drawn out of the country to pay for imports. With the means of payments generally in scarce supply, business tended to be hampered; various forms of paper money were consequently introduced to serve in lieu of coins. Signed playing cards were used as money for a time during the French regime; these

---

[6]These coins were actually Spanish *pesos*, which English-speaking people generally called "dollars". First issued by Ferdinand and Isabella around the year 1500, the peso was worth eight *reales*, and was the famed "piece of eight" of pirate legend and story. The colloquialism "two-bits", meaning a quarter of a dollar, traces back to the era when the dollar was a "piece of eight".

The word "dollar" itself is of German origin. Early in the sixteenth century, coins were minted out of silver taken from a rich mine at St. Joachimsthal in Bohemia. These and similar silver coins circulated widely in Europe for centuries, being referred to as "thaler", and various versions of "thaler" such as, "daalder", "tallero", "daler".

[7]The British government tried to persuade the Canadian authorities to adopt pounds, shillings and pence as their monetary units, in order to conform to the British system. The Canadian government refused on the grounds that dollars and cents were simpler and that conformity to the American system would be advantageous for Canada.

were followed by government notes (ordonnances). During the later years of the eighteenth century the main circulating medium of the country consisted of bills issued by merchants which were redeemable at their stores.

The Bank of Montreal, established in 1817, issued the country's first bank notes; other banks, established soon afterward, issued their notes, and the new paper currency quickly came to serve as the country's main circulating medium. An additional kind of paper money appeared in 1866 when the provincial government of Canada authorized the issue of $8 million of government notes, backed in part by gold.[8] In 1870, just after Confederation, Parliament passed legislation which prohibited the banks from issuing notes of value other than five dollars and multiples of five dollars; the issue of one-dollar and two-dollar bills was reserved to the federal government. Subsequent legislation authorized greatly enlarged issues of these government notes.

For the next six decades the form of Canada's paper currency remained as decreed in the statute passed in 1870. A major change occurred only following the establishment of the Bank of Canada in 1934[9]; the Bank took over responsibility for the issue of all denominations of paper currency. The other banks were given a number of years in which to withdraw their notes from circulation and these continued to circulate, in decreasing quantity, until 1950.

Bank Deposits

For many years after the banks were established in Canada, their notes constituted the chief means of payment in the country. Gradually, however, people and firms became accustomed to keeping their liquid cash in the form of a bank deposit rather than in actual currency, and widely adopted the practice of making payments by writing cheques on those deposits. During the past century, the total of bank deposits held by the public in Canada has increased far more than has the total of currency in circulation and the great bulk of payments is now made by cheque.

Canada's Money Supply Today

Canada's money supply now consists of three basic elements—coins, bank notes, and bank deposits. The coins are of small denominations, ranging in value from one cent to one dollar, and serve as the medium of exchange in small transactions. These coins are all of the "token" type: the face value of each coin is greater than the value of the actual metal in it. Coins are "legal tender" only up to specified limits; a

---

[8]Strictly speaking, these were not the first government notes issued in Canada. The government of Nova Scotia had issued such notes as early as 1812, and in Canada special government notes had been issued during the War of 1812.

[9]Canada's central bank. How it came to be established, and what its functions are, are described in Chapter 22.

creditor is not obligated to accept an immense number of coins in payment of a debt.[10]

The bank notes are all issued by the Bank of Canada, as has already been indicated. The notes range in denomination from one dollar to one thousand dollars, the largest denominations being used chiefly in inter-bank transactions. Reflecting its lineal descent from the old goldsmith's receipt, each of our bank notes carries on its face the promise that the Bank of Canada will pay to the bearer on demand the number of dollars indicated. This inscription is now anachronism; the Bank of Canada is not legally obligated to pay out gold or anything else to anyone who presents a paper bill. According to our present legislation, a Bank of Canada note is itself lawful money. It must be accepted by creditors in payment of debt, and no one who has such a note can demand "real" money in its place.

Bank deposits, which form the largest part of our money supply, are of two types, personal savings, and current or checking account. The former constitute the savings of individuals deposited in banks primarily for safekeeping; the latter represent chiefly the funds held in banks by individuals, firms and organizations for convenience, in order to be able to pay out funds speedily and efficiently.

MONEY'S UNSTABLE VALUE

Our money supply, composed of coins, bank notes and bank deposits serves us admirably in most respects. Each of its component classes is absolutely uniform, enabling easy recognition. Our money is easily carried about and readily transferred from one person to another when this is desired. It includes small units to handle small transactions. Unfortunately, it falls down badly in one important regard: its value is liable to marked instability through time. Sharp changes in the general level of prices may occur, as we know from ample experience, and these will correspondingly affect the purchasing power of money.

The Equation of Exchange

What determines the general level of prices at any given time, causing it to be perhaps higher or lower than heretofore? In very general terms the following truism serves as reply: the general level of prices in any period will depend upon the aggregate of expenditures made during the period in relation to the aggregate of goods and services which were purchased by those expenditures; as this ratio changes, so will the general level of prices change.

---

[10]An offer to pay money in coins is a "legal tender", which a creditor must accept, only up to the following limits: twenty-five cents in the case of bronze one-cent pieces; five dollars in the case of nickels; ten dollars in the case of dimes and coins of higher value.

Thus suppose that Canada produces one single product, which we call X. Suppose further, that last year 1,000,000 of X were produced. If the total of expenditures in Canada was one million dollars last year, then obviously each unit of X must have cost, on the average, one dollar. If, this year, our output of X increases to 1,250,000 units, while the aggregate of expenditures rises to $1,500,000, then obviously each unit of X will, on the average, cost $1.20 this year ($1,500,000 ÷ 1,250,000).

One point should be noted immediately. For Canadians to spend one million dollars in Canada last year, it was not necessary for that much money to exist in the country last year; nor must $1½ million exist now if they are to spend that much this year. As we all know, a particular unit of money may be spent over and over again. I may pay a garage mechanic a ten dollar bill for an engine tune-up; he may hand over the same bill as payment for a tailoring job; the tailor may spend that same bill on groceries; and so on. That ten dollar bill might possibly in the course of a year, be received by a hundred different people. That one bill would accordingly serve to make a total of a thousand dollars worth of payments during the course of the year. The economist would say, if this were the case, that the bill had a *velocity of circulation* of 100.

Suppose now that the velocity of circulation of all money in Canada was actually 100, so that each unit of money, on the average, was paid out 100 times during the course of a year. In that case, we could have, with an actual money supply of only $10,000, expenditures totalling $1,000,000 for the year. Obviously, too, the aggregate of expenditure in the country might change from one year to another either because the money supply had changed, or because the velocity of circulation had changed, or both. The aggregate of expenditure might increase from $1 million in one year to $1½ million in the next year, because the money supply had increased from $10,000 to $12,000 and the velocity of circulation had increased from 100 to 125.

Developed by the American economist, Irving Fisher, the equation of exchange $MV = PT$ expressed precisely the relationships, for any time period, between total spending and the things bought with that spending. In the equation,

M = the money supply
V = the velocity of circulation
P = the average price of all things bought
T = the total quantity of things bought

To establish P, the average price of all things bought, we simply express the equation in the form of $P = \dfrac{MV}{T}$.

The price level could be established for any period by inserting in the above equation the values of **M**, **V** and **T** which prevailed during that period. Thus, if one year, **M** was $12,000, **V** was 125, and **T** was 1,250,000, then **P** would be equal to

$$\frac{\$12,000 \times 125}{1,250,000} = \$1.20.$$

This equation, unfortunately, does not permit us to predict accurately the movement of prices; the reason is of course that we can never forecast the size of the component elements with any degree of precision. Nevertheless, the equation is not without value in the formulation of policy. Having reagrd to the relationships it reveals, the economist will caution that expansion of the money supply or substantial increase in the velocity of circulation, originating in whatever causes, is likely to produce a sharp increase in the price level—unless accompanied by a corresponding expansion in the output of goods and services.

MEASUREMENT OF CHANGES IN THE PRICE LEVEL

We learned in Chapter 3 that the equilibrium price of any particular good or service is determined by the prevailing demand for it in relation to the prevailing supply. Our discussion in this chapter does not contradict this basic rule. Changes in M, in V, in T, affect the prices of individual goods because they cause a change in their demand or supply, or both. An increase in the money supply will cause the demand for individual goods, hence their prices, to rise; a reduction in the money supply will cause the demand for individual goods, hence their prices, to fall.

The effects of a change in the total of all expenditures will vary from one good to another. The prices of some goods are fixed by law or by contract; for example, the price of beer sold at retail is, in most Canadian provinces, fixed by law; the rents of many buildings are fixed by long term contracts; the interest payable on some loans is set for a lengthy period of time. Some prices, of goods produced under monopoly or oligopoly conditions, are held rigid for long periods despite large changes in market conditions. Where situations such as the foregoing exist, the prices of the goods involved remain unchanged, despite increases or decreases in the aggregate of expenditure. Furthermore, the demand for some goods tends to respond sharply to changes in the price level and money incomes; the demand for other goods responds sluggishly. Thus in periods of rising money incomes, the demand for luxury goods, and their prices, tend to rise sharply; the demand for necessities and their prices tend to rise more slowly. Finally, for reasons which are unique to themselves, the prices of some goods may vary in a fashion contrary to the general trend. During the past two decades, while the prices of most goods have increased very substantially, the prices of major electrical appliances in Canada have remained virtually stationary or have actually fallen, chiefly as a result of very great improvements in the methods of production.

Since the price of each good and service responds in its own way to the forces which cause shifts in the price level, we must use an *average* figure to represent the movement of goods and services generally. What we do is calculate the percentage change in the price of each good, over the time period with which we are concerned, and then calculate the average of all the percentage changes. We may wish to consider separately the price movements of different classes of goods; in that case we would, for each particular class of goods, work out the average percentage change in the prices of all the individual members of the group. Our Dominion Bureau of Statistics calculates separately price movements of all sorts of different classes of goods, ranging from food products to farm machinery and building materials. Separate calculations are made, in many cases, for price movements in different parts of the country.

Price Indexes

In order to present data on price movements in a standard, easily understood fashion, statisticians generally employ *price indexes*. They specify some particular past time as the *base period*, and show how prices, in each time period since then, have compared, percentagewise, with the prices which prevailed during the base period. The base chosen would be some year or succession of years during which prices were generally considered to be "normal." A very simple index might be made up to show the prices of bread, meat and milk in 1970 and 1971 compared with their prices in 1939. The index maker would ascertain the prices charged for each of these foods in these three years, and calculate the percentage relationship of 1970 and 1971 prices to the 1939 prices. The following table indicates the way he would proceed.

	1939 Price	1970 Price	1971 Price	1970 price as % of 1939 price	1971 price as % of 1939 price
Bread	10¢	25¢	26¢	250	260
Meat	25¢	80¢	85¢	320	340
Milk	12¢	30¢	32¢	250	267

On the average, 1970 prices therefore constituted the following percentage of 1939 prices:

$$\frac{250 + 320 + 250}{3} = 273$$

On the average, 1971 prices constituted the following percentage of 1939 prices:

$$\frac{260 + 340 + 267}{3} = 289$$

The index maker would then list these percentage figures for 1970 and 1971 in a series, as follows:

Food Price Index
(1939 = 100)

1970	273
1971	289

The index would represent the fact that food prices in 1970 were, on the average, 173 per cent higher than they had been in 1939, and in 1971, were on the average 189 per cent higher than they had been in 1939. One great advantage gained in building up an index in this fashion is that it enables ready comparisons to be made of year-to-year changes, as well as comparisons between a particular year and the base year. In our little index we can readily see that *from* 1970 to 1971 prices rose by 16 points, the difference between 273 and 289. Price *trends* over a lengthy period could be clearly represented by an index which showed the average level of prices in each of a succession of years, compared with the level of prices in the base year.

PRICES IN CANADA: 1913-1970

Figure 1 graphically portrays, for the half century 1913-70, the General Wholesale Price Index maintained by the Dominion Bureau of Statistics. As the graph

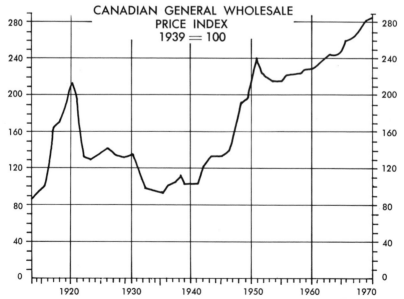

Figure 1.   The Canadian General Wholesale Price Index (1913-1970)

indicates, prices rose sharply during the course of World War I, reaching a lofty peak in 1920, two years after the war ended. They crashed precipitously in that year, and declined gently throughout the 1920s. The onset of the Great Depression drove them sharply downward during the early 1930s. They rose slowly and fitfully after 1933, despite the persistence of depression conditions, until the outbreak of World War II in 1939. The pace of increase accelerated significantly during the war, despite the price controls which were introduced. With the removal of controls, two or three years after war's end, prices rose more sharply than they had done during the wartime period itself, and reached a peak during the Korean War. With the ending of the war they declined abruptly and continued to sag during the brief post-Korean recession. They rose again during the 1956-57 "boom period" and remained nearly constant during the years of stagnation from 1957 to 1961; thereafter, as the pace of economic activity quickened, the price level rose appreciably.

SIGNIFICANCE OF CHANGES IN THE PRICE LEVEL

Major price level movements, such as Canada has experienced, generally have profoundly disturbing repercussions.[11] They may significantly affect the level at which the economy operates, and are likely to bring about pronounced shifts in the real wealth and income of different members of the community.

Deflation

The marked deflations of 1920 and the early 1930s were accompanied by sharp reductions in the levels of profits, employment, and production. Businessmen who had acquired large inventories at high prices, lost heavily when prices fell. Falling prices generated pessimism in regard to the future and a general hesitation to produce goods for future sale or to undertake investments which would yield their benefit in the future. A great many workers lost their jobs and production declined heavily. Debtors became heavily oppressed as falling prices increased the real value of their debts and of their interest obligations. In many cases the falling prices at the same time sharply reduced debtors' incomes. Thus farmers of Western Canada who had borrowed large sums to purchase more land and equipment, were reduced to desperate straits when the prices of farm products fell heavily. With incomes sharply reduced, the obligation to pay a fixed amount of interest each year proved to be a crushing burden. They suffered in this way in the early 1920s and again in the 1930s.

[11]Compared however to the inflations experienced by some other countries, ours has been relatively mild. In the great German inflation of 1923, for instance, prices increased a trillion-fold.

Not all people were adversely affected by deflation, however. People who had savings in the form of cash or fixed value securities such as bonds, found that the real value of their savings had increased. With prices lower each dollar of their savings could buy more than before. People whose incomes were fixed in terms of money similarly benefited from the deflation. Pensioners receiving fixed pensions, bondholders who received fixed amounts of money as interest, employees who continued to receive their usual salaries—all found that the deflation had increased their real incomes. Not all bondholders and salaried employees were so lucky, however. Many bondholders were unable during deflationary periods to collect money due them and many salaried employees lost their jobs. The seemingly "fixed" incomes turned out not to be "fixed" after all.

Inflation

The consequences of inflation are pretty well the reverse of those produced by deflation. When prices rise, businessmen enjoy windfall profit through appreciation of the market value of their assets. The business outlook tends to appear hopeful so that businessmen generally are anxious to enlarge their plant capacity. Employment and production tend to rise. (Unless of course they are already as high as can possibly be.) Debtors gain relief because of the fall in the real value of their debts and their interest obligations. Their gain is the creditor's loss.

The decline in the purchasing power of money imposes losses on people who hold their wealth in the form of cash or fixed value securities. Persons on fixed incomes, such as pensioners and the recipients of insurance benefits, suffer a decline in real income. If it becomes perpetual or severe, inflation may produce a general disruption of the economic system. If the purchasing power of money falls steadily, lenders are likely to insist on inordinately high rates of interest, to compensate for the prospective decline in the real value of the sums which they will receive each year as interest and the prospective decline in the real value of the principal when it is repaid. If the purchasing power of money falls very rapidly, people may refuse altogether to accept it in payment for goods or services. They know that when they come to spend the money offered to them, it will be worth less than it is currently worth. In such cases money can no longer perform its role as medium of exchange; transactions must be carried out in the clumsy and wasteful basis of barter.[12]

SUMMARY

The use of money as a medium of exchange eliminates the need for clumsy barter arrangements. Any commodity will serve as money so long as it is universally accept-

[12]The inflation which occurred in Germany after the end of World War II produced such a breakdown. Many people lost faith in the currency, and insisted on being paid in real goods. Confidence was restored only when the government introduced a new kind of money, and firmly undertook to issue it in limited quantity and so maintain its value.

able. To serve efficiently it should have the additional qualities of easy portability, easy recognizability, divisibility, durability, and stability in value.

For many centuries money consisted exclusively of metal coins. Paper money in the form of goldsmiths' receipts came into use in seventeenth century England. These were supplanted by bank notes; during the nineteenth century bank deposits came to serve as money also, and are now the most important form of money in modern countries.

The quantity of money in existence, together with the velocity of its circulation, will determine the aggregate of expenditures in any period and therefore strongly affect the price level.

Changes in the price level can be represented by means of price indexes, which show the average change in the prices of many goods over a period of time.

The Canadian price level has risen considerably, though unevenly, during the present century. Its sharpest increases have occurred during wars and in the immediate aftermath of wars.

Major price level shifts have important economic effects. The level of economic activity is liable to be adversely affected, and a redistribution of real wealth and income is liable to occur as between different groups of persons in the country.

FOR REVIEW AND DISCUSSION

1. Discuss the pros and cons of the proposition that old age pensions should be tied to the cost of living.
2. If the money supply were to be increased by ten per cent, would the price level necessarily also rise by ten per cent? Why or why not?
3. Construct a price index of at least four commodities.
4. How is the price level likely to be affected by each of the following methods of financing government expenditures: taxation; borrowing; the printing of new money?
5. Suggest why cigarettes came to serve as money in German prisoner-of-war camps during World War II.
6. If wages are tied to the cost of living, then price level changes will tend to be cumulative. Explain.
7. What consequences would likely follow if everyone came to feel that the value of money was going to decline regularly by five per cent per year?
8. "Money is what money does." Do you agree? Justify your answer.
9. Had it not been for wars, we would have had perfectly stable prices in Canada in the last half century. Do you agree? Justify your answer.

21

The Banking System: Commercial Bank Operations

FRACTIONAL RESERVES

We noted in the last chapter that a seventeenth century goldsmith might lend out a large fraction of the gold which had been deposited with him. On such loans he collected interest, which he kept. One significant result of this procedure was that he had in his shop only a small fraction of the gold which had been brought in by his customers, and for which he had issued receipts. But the goldsmith had absolutely guaranteed to pay gold to anyone who presented a receipt and asked for gold. How could he fulfil this guarantee when he had in his possession gold equal in value to only a small fraction of the receipts outstanding? He did in fact manage to do it. When we realize just why this was possible we will have learned the fundamental principle involved in modern banking.

An illustration

Suppose that 100 people each deposited $1,000 worth of gold coins with Mr. Gould, a London goldsmith. He would issue to each customer a receipt for $1,000 in which he undertook to return the money to the depositor whenever he presented this receipt. (He would not undertake however to give the depositor the very same coins which he had brought in; instead he would only promise—and this of course would be perfectly acceptable—to give back coins of exactly the same value.) Now suppose that Mr. Gould puts the $100,000 away in two boxes of different size. Into the larger one he puts $90,000, and into the smaller one the other $10,000. The large box he stores in his vault; the small box he keeps readily accessible at the front of his shop, so that when depositors come in, presenting their receipts and asking for their gold back, he has a ready-to-hand supply out of which to pay them. The goldsmith plans that when the front box is emptied he will replenish it from the large box in the vault.

His experience confounds his expectations. On the first day after he has received the deposits three individuals come in, present their receipts, and ask for $3,000 of gold. The goldsmith gives them the money, leaving $7,000 in the box. But the same day three new depositors come along and deposit another $3,000 in gold, so that at the end of the day the box is again full. The next day and every day thereafter the same sort of thing happens; he pays out some money to a few people who present receipts but takes in other money from new depositors. Withdrawals and new deposits are not exactly equal each day, of course, On some days withdrawals exceed fresh deposits and at the end of such days the level of gold in the box is down. On other days deposits exceed withdrawals and at the end of such days the level of gold in the box is up.

At the end of a year the goldsmith finds, to his astonishment, that *at no time has that small box ever been completely empty.* The amount of gold in it has fluctuated, decreasing with withdrawals and increasing with deposits, but at no time was there no gold in it at all. At no time, therefore, was it necessary for the goldsmith to go to the large box in his vault to replenish the supply of coins in the small box he kept in the front of his shop. The gold in that large box has just lain undisturbed all year; it was never actually needed to make payments to depositors.

A shrewd goldsmith would realize that he had here a wonderful opportunity for gaining extra income for himself. He could lend out the $90,000 of gold in the big box, and collect interest on the loan. No one would be harmed. If matters proceeded in the future as they had in the past, he would still be able to pay gold to everyone who presented a receipt and asked for gold. The gold kept in the small box would be sufficient to meet all actual demands, provided that, as before only the occasional receipt holder came in on any one day to ask for his money, and provided too that new depositors from day to day brought in fresh gold. There would be trouble only if a large number of receipt holders simultaneously came to the shop and demanded their money; in such a case he could not possibly fulfil his undertaking to give each depositor his gold on request. But such a development was most unlikely. Depositors actually needed their gold only when they wished to spend it; provided they were confident they could get it whenever they wanted it, the great majority would be content to leave their gold with the goldsmith, making only the occasional withdrawal. Out of the little supply he kept in the small box, replenished as it was by fresh deposits, the goldsmith would easily be able to pay gold on all occasions when receipt holders so requested.

BANKS ALSO LEND OUT DEPOSITORS' MONEY

A commercial bank operates on the very same principles as did the old-time goldsmith. The banker knows that of the money deposited with him for safekeeping only a small fraction will be asked for by the depositors at any particular time. Just like the goldsmith, he is prepared to lend out the greater part of the money lodged with him. He will keep on hand a relatively small *cash reserve;* out of this cash, replenished as it will be by fresh deposits, he expects to be able to meet all requests by depositors to have their money back (and also the requests for cash by people who have received cheques from depositors). Knowing that he can safely and profitably lend out their money, the banker will in fact attract people to deposit their money with him. His attractions will take the form of an offer to pay the depositor interest on his deposit and to perform, free of charge, a number of useful clerical and accounting services on the depositor's behalf.

These are the main functions of modern banks: to receive deposits and to make loans out of the money deposited; their income consists mainly of the interest they receive on these loans. Most banks perform, on a commission basis, a number of services relating to the handling of money and valuables: they buy and sell the currencies of foreign countries, arrange for the transfer of money from one locality to another, and maintain safety deposit boxes in which customers may store their valuables. These are generally only minor elements in their total operations; the primary business of commercial banks is to receive deposits and make loans.

Lending by Canadian Banks

Present legislation requires Canada's chartered banks to keep a cash reserve ratio of 12 per cent against their demand (current and checking) deposits and 4 per cent against their notice (i.e. savings) deposits. As their cash reserve the chartered banks may consider the actual currency—Bank of Canada notes—which they hold plus deposits which they have in the Bank of Canada.

In accordance with British practice, Canadian banks have concentrated on short term loans, of less than one year's duration. They favour the loan which finances a business operation which, within a matter of weeks or months, will yield to the borrower the money he requires to repay the loan. In this category are loans to merchants to purchase goods which they will soon sell; loans to manufacturers to purchase raw materials which they will shortly transform into finished products which they will market; loans to farmers in the spring for the purchase of seed, fuel, and the like, to enable them to produce a crop which they will harvest and sell in the fall. Our banks also lend money, for short periods, to governments, organizations and private individuals. They also lend substantial sums to investment dealers and stock brokers to enable them to purchase stocks and bonds for clients or for themselves. Only in limited degree to they make loans to finance the purchase of machinery, equipment, land and buildings, since such loans can normally be repaid only after a period of years. Federal legislation has contributed to this reluctance by expressly prohibiting banks from making loans upon the security of real estate.[1]

This legislative restriction, together with the banks' reluctance to make loans of long duration, gave rise to a great many difficulties and complaints. Farmers, fishermen and small businessmen who required implements, equipment and machinery, could not readily borrow the necessary funds from the banks, since they

---

[1]A bank may however accept such security in respect to a debt which has already been incurred.

would only be able to repay the loans out of several years' earnings.[2] Homeowners who wished to carry out major repairs to their homes could not borrow the necessary money from banks, since they could only undertake to repay the loans over a period of years.

Parliament in due course introduced measures designed to remedy these specific deficiencies. By offering to share part of the losses which a bank might incur in making such loans, the government has encouraged the banks to lend money to farmers and fishermen for the purchase of implements and equipment, and to homeowners for the repair of their homes. The banks have been authorized, furthermore, to extend loans to farmers and fishermen on the security of property. An Act of 1961 authorized the chartered banks to make loans to small business firms for the purpose of improvement and modernization of equipment and premises.[3]

Legislation introduced in 1954 authorized Canada's banks to extend loans toward the construction of houses and apartment buildings. The reason for this new departure was the government's fear that the main sources of funds for such purposes, the life insurance companies, would be unable to supply all the money required. The possibility existed, therefore, that home construction might be curtailed because builders would not be able to borrow enough money. With the banks authorized to lend for home construction, a major new source of funds would be available to builders. So far as the banks were concerned the loans would be virtually risk-free, being guaranteed to the extend of approximately 98 per cent by the federal government's Central Mortgage and Housing Corporation.

BANK INVESTMENT IN SECURITIES

One important qualification must be made here. The typical commercial bank does not simply set aside an appropriate cash reserve out of the money brought in by depositors, and then lend out *all* of the remainder to borrowers. Most commercial banks will use some of the money at their disposal to purchase federal government bonds. Such securities have two attractive features. They yield interest to the holder, and they can be readily bought or sold in the market at any time. It often happens that banks have surplus cash which no one wants to borrow; there is after all no guarantee that reliable people will always stand ready to borrow the

[2]Large business firms could raise long term capital by the sale of stocks or bonds, and were therefore not particularly troubled by the fact that they could not borrow from the banks for long term purposes.

[3]In effect this legislation supplemented something which already existed. The Industrial Development Bank had been established in 1944 as an agency which would lend money to small business firms on longer terms than could be obtained from the regular commercial banks. The Industrial Development Bank was a government enterprise, however, being a subsidiary of the government-owned Bank of Canada, our Central Bank (whose responsibilities and operations are described in the next chapter).

exact amount which a banker has available to lend. The banker, when he has funds which he does not need for reserve purposes and for which there are no borrowers, will use these funds to purchase government bonds. By doing so he earns interest on money which otherwise would have been idle.

Secondary Reserves

These securities may later stand a banker in good stead. He may suddenly need large amounts of cash, possibly because depositors are making heavy withdrawals which threaten to reduce his cash reserve below the minimum permissible figure. The loans which he has made may all be perfectly sound, but the borrowers are not obligated to repay until specified future dates.[4] He may need cash right away to meet depositors' demands and maintain a sufficient reserve. At such times he can sell some of his securities and thereby obtain immediately the cash he needs. Hence in effect his security holdings constitute a secondary reserve, thanks to the ease and speed with which they can be converted into cash.

Banker Preference for Early Maturing Securities

But there is the danger that when the banker decides to sell his securities the prevailing market price will be unfavourable, and that he will be obliged to accept a price lower than the one he himself paid for them. The fact is that the market price of bonds shifts about constantly, in accordance with shifts of supply and demand. The face value of a bond, the amount which the bondholder is to receive on its maturity, never changes, but the holder is assured of receiving that sum only at the time specified as the redemption date. If he wishes to sell the bond before then, he must sell it in the market for whatever price investors are prepared to pay. That price will reflect the prevailing demand and supply situation, and may be substantially above or below the bond's face value.

In the case of bonds which are due to be redeemed in the near future, the divergence between market price and face value is unlikely to be large. Very soon the bondholder will receive the face value, and he would be unwilling to sell now for very much less. In the case of bonds which are due for redemption only in the distant future, however, the divergence between the market price and face value may be very great. There is no assurance that the holder will soon receive a specified amount of money for the bond; for a long time to come its market price will be determined by the vagaries of demand and supply.

To avoid the possibility of having to sell securities at a heavy loss, banks prefer to hold those which will mature within a year or two. Because of the proximity of their redemption dates, the prices of such bonds cannot diverge too greatly from their respective face values. The banks, therefore, generally prefer to purchase short

[4]A banker may demand immediate repayment of "day-to-day" loans, described later in this chapter.

term bonds or long term bonds which were issued a long time before and are therefore due to mature in the near future. Canadian banks also purchase large quantities of federal government treasury bills, most of which have a maturity period of only 91 days.[5]

"Day-to-Day" Loans

Since 1954, Canada's banks have been employing in a new way those funds which they are prepared to invest for only very short periods. In addition to purchasing treasury bills on their own behalf, they have been lending spare cash to investment dealers which the latter in turn use to buy treasury bills (The dealers are continuously purchasing these bills on behalf of clients or for their own portfolios, and therefore very frequently need bank loans to pay for these purchases.) These bank loans to dealers are made on a "day-to-day" basis: the bank has the right to demand repayment of the loan at any time. Once the bank demands repayment, the dealer must repay the loan within a matter of hours. To the banker these "day-to-day" loans are even more liquid than treasury bills; they can be converted into cash more speedily, and they involve no risk whatsoever of capital loss.

A banker who has made a loan to a "day-to-day" borrower can count on getting back exactly the amount he loaned out; a banker who has bought treasury bills, on the other hand, may ruefully discover that because of an adverse market development they have lower value than he had anticipated. The rate of interest received on "day-to-day" loans is of course always lower than the rate currently earned on treasury bills, but the banks are willing to accept the lower interest in order to avoid the element of risk.

These "day-to-day" loans are distinct from the "call" loans which banks normally extend to stock brokers to finance the purchases of ordinary securities. Each bank makes "call" loans only to its own clientele; while it has the legal right to demand repayment of such loans at any time, in practice it will give up to 30-days notice in order not to embarrass and alienate regular customers. "Day-to-day" loans

---

[5]These bills are in effect short term bonds. The federal government, which needs cash at all times to meet its current expenses, offers treasury bills for sale each week (currently about $200 million worth). These are offered for sale on a tender basis as in an auction sale. The bidders are the chartered banks and a select list of the country's largest investment dealers; each bidder indicates how much he is prepared to pay for treasury bills and the quantity he wishes to buy at that price. The price paid determines the interest he will receive; this will consist of the difference between that price and the face value of the bill, which the government will pay to the holder on the maturity date.

The short maturity date of treasury bills makes them an excellent investment for a bank which has cash to spare but does not wish to commit that cash for a lengthy period. Furthermore, if a bank buys bills regularly, it will regularly receive cash for bills which mature. If a bank buys $1 million worth of 91 day (13 week) treasury bills every week, then each week it will receive $1 million from the federal government in redemption of the bills which it had bought 13 weeks before. If ever the bank wished to increase its cash in any week, it could simply refrain from buying any new bills that week; its cash would automatically rise by $1 million through the redemption by the government of bills which currently became due for repayment.

are made, however, on a completely impersonal basis; dealers borrow the money from whatever bank is prepared to lend and the banks are prepared to lend to any dealer who wishes to borrow. A bank has no hesitation in demanding the immediate repayment of such a loan; the borrower knows that this may happen and is in no way offended when immediate repayment is demanded. He simply arranges to borrow from another bank the money he needs to meet the call. As we shall see in the next chapter, if he cannot borrow from another commercial bank he can always obtain cash by selling bills to the Bank of Canada.

SUBSCRIBED CAPITAL— A PROTECTION TO BANK DEPOSITORS

If a banker shows poor judgment and makes bad loans which are not repaid, then depositors may lose their money; when they come to ask for it, it is simply not there. The possibility of a Canadian depositor losing his money is very remote nowadays, however. Our banks are all giant institutions, well managed, closely supervised, and subject to rigorous federal controls.[6] Furthermore, if a bank does suffer losses through bad loans, the depositors are protected by a substantial buffer in the form of the capital subscribed by the bank's stock holders. Losses must be met firstly out of this capital; depositors will suffer only if losses exceed the bank's subscribed capital[7] Thus suppose that a bank has $100,000 of capital subscribed by its shareholders. Say that depositors bring in a total of $500,000, of which the bank lends out $450,000. If $75,000 of these loans were not repaid, the loss would be borne entirely by the shareholders. Depositors would lose only if the bank's losses were in excess of the $100,000 capital provided by the shareholders.

DEPOSIT CREATION BY A BANKING SYSTEM

A modern banking system creates money. The money is in the form of bank deposits and the amount created will depend upon two basic determinants: the amount of cash deposited by the public in the country's banks and the cash reserve ratio maintained by banks against their deposits. Let us see, by way of a simple example, just how a banking system brings into being money which never existed before.

---

[6]In the U.S. practically all deposits are now insured by the Federal Deposit Insurance Corporation. In April 1967 Parliament approved the establishment of a new crown corporation, the Canada Deposit Insurance Corporation, to protect depositors in the chartered banks and in federally incorporated trust companies that take deposits from the general public.

[7]In Canada, bank shares for many years carried *double liability*. In the event of a bank's failure, its shareholders could be called upon to contribute, toward redeeming the notes which the bank had issued, an amount equal to the value of their shares. This feature of bank shares was eliminated after the banks ceased to issue their own bank notes.

An Example

Suppose that we have a large number of banks in our country, each one of which has had $100,000 deposited in it by its customers. Suppose further that the banks generally maintain a cash reserve ratio of 10 per cent, and therefore lend out 90 per cent of the money deposited with them. In that case each bank will be in this position:

ASSETS		LIABILITIES[8]	
Cash	$10,000	Deposits	$100,000
Loans	90,000		

Suppose now that a Mr. Adams deposits $1,000 in cash in one of the banks, which we shall refer to as Bank A. Let us examine the effects on Bank A, and trace the repercussions on all the other banks in the country.

Cash Deposited in One Bank. As a result of Mr. Adams' deposit, Bank A's position will become as follows:

Cash	$11,000	Deposits	$101,000
Loans	90,000		

As matters now stand, Bank A has $900 in excess reserves. It has $11,000 in cash, whereas 10 per cent of its total deposits of $101,000 amounts to only $10,100. Since a cash reserve of 10 per cent of deposits is perfectly adequate, it is quite unnecessary to hold more. Accordingly, if some businessman whose credit is good comes to Bank A and asks to borrow $900, the manager will gladly lend it to him. If kept in the bank that $900 will serve no useful purpose; if loaned out to the businessman it will earn interest for the bank.

Two Methods of Lending. The banker may lend the money by simply handing over $900 in actual cash to the borrower or he may write, in the bank's books, a deposit of $900 in the borrower's favour. Where the loan takes the latter form of a deposit, it will be because the borrower wishes to make payments by cheque. Once he is credited with the deposit he will issue cheques totalling $900. These will be presented for payment at Bank A; the bank will thereupon pay out $900 in cash and reduce the borrower's deposit accordingly. It makes no real difference therefore, whether Bank A extends a loan by giving a borrower cash, or by writing a deposit in its books in his favour. In either case it will pay out cash to the amount of the loan. In the one case it pays out the cash at once; in the other case it pays out the cash in a little while, when the cheques which a borrower has issued against his deposit are presented for payment.

Having loaned out $900, Bank A's position will become as follows:

Cash	$10,100	Deposits	$101,000
Loans	90,900		

---

[8]These deposits are assets to the depositors, but *liabilities* to the bank; i.e. deposits represent money which a bank *owes* to the people who have made the deposits. The loans which the bank makes are bank assets; the borrowers owe that money to the bank.

Its cash amounts once again to exactly 10 per cent of its deposit liabilities.

Repercussions on Other Banks. Now suppose that the person who borrowed the $900 from Bank A uses it to pay off Mr. Bell, who deals with Bank B. Mr. Bell does not care to hold this cash about him and therefore deposits it in his account in Bank B. This bank's position becomes therefore as follows:

Cash	$10,900	Deposits	$100,900
Loans	90,000		

Now Bank B has $810 of excess cash reserve. It holds $10,900 in cash when, to maintain a 10 per cent reserve against its deposits of $100,900, it needs only $10,090. If some reliable person asks to borrow $810, the manager of Bank B will be pleased to make the loan. Once the loan is made Bank B's position will be as follows:

Cash	$10,090	Deposits	$100,900
Loans	90,810		

Bank B's cash amounts once more to exactly 10 per cent of its deposit liabilities.

Now suppose that this last borrower uses the $810 to pay off Mr. Cameron who is a customer of Bank C. Not wishing to hold the cash on his person or in his till, Mr. Cameron deposits the money in his bank. Bank C's position becomes therefore as follows:

Cash	$10,810	Deposits	$ 100,810
Loans	90,000		

Bank C now has $729 of excess reserves. Whereas it needs to hold in cash only $10,081 (10 per cent of its deposits of $100,810) it actually has $10,810. Accordingly the manager of Bank C will be prepared to lend out $729. Once he makes the loan his books will appear as follows:

Cash	$10,081	Deposits	$100,810
Loans	90,729		

Bank C's cash amounts once again to 10 per cent of its deposit liabilities.

Deposits Have Come Into Existence. At this point let us stop to consider the significance of what has been taking place. In each bank deposits are now above their original figure of $100,000. Bank A has Mr. Adams' deposit of $1,000, which began the whole sequence. Bank B has Mr. Bell's deposit of $900; Bank C has Mr. Cameron's deposit of $810. What has happened is that because of the original deposit of $1,000 in Bank A, $\frac{9}{10}$ of $1,000 was subsequently deposited in Bank B, and $\frac{9}{10}$ of *that* was subsequently deposited in Bank C. If we were to keep on tracing the repercussions, we would find that $\frac{9}{10}$ of the money deposited in C was later deposited in another bank, $\frac{9}{10}$ of that in another bank; and so on. Ultimately the following series of deposits would be created, distributed among the various banks of the country:

$$\$1,000 + \tfrac{9}{10}\,\$1,000 + (\tfrac{9}{10})^2\,\$1,000 + (\tfrac{9}{10})^3\,\$1,000 + \ldots + (\tfrac{9}{10})^n\,\$1,000$$

The sum of all the elements in this series is $10,000 (the original deposit of $1,000 multiplied by the reciprocal of the reserve ratio).

This $10,000 of bank deposits belongs to members of the public, to Messrs. Adams, Bell and Cameron, who have the deposits in Banks A, B and C respectively, and to all the other persons and firms who subsequently will have acquired deposits in the other banks of the system. But these deposits are money: the owner of a bank deposit can pay for things by issuing cheques against that deposit. Hence the banking system has increased the public's money supply from $1,000 to $10,000. The nature of this money supply has been changed in the process, however, from cash to bank deposits. The public no longer possesses any of the $1,000 cash; that is now all held by the banks as reserve against deposits. Bank A holds $100; Bank B holds $90; Bank C holds $81; and so on.

Bank Loans Have Also Increased. While deposits have increased, the total of loans made by the banks has also increased. Bank A's loans have increased by $900; Bank B's by $810; Bank C's by $729; and so on. Ultimately the following series of loans will have been made by all the banks of the country:

$$\$900 + \tfrac{9}{10}\,\$900 + (\tfrac{9}{10})^2\,\$900 + (\tfrac{9}{10})^3\,\$900 + \ldots + (\tfrac{9}{10})^n\,\$900$$

The sum of all the elements in this series is $9,000.

Let us recapitulate briefly. As a result of Mr. Adams' initial deposit of $1,000 cash in Bank A, there has occurred a $10,000 increase in the public's ownership of bank deposits, and a $9,000 increase in loans made by the banks to the public. These increases in the country's money supply and bank borrowings have occurred because bankers followed their customary rule of lending out $\tfrac{9}{10}$ of the money deposited with them, and because all money borrowed from one bank was subsequently deposited in another bank.

DEPOSIT DESTRUCTION BY A BANKING SYSTEM

Withdrawal of Cash from One Bank. Suppose now that Mr. Adams, instead of depositing $1,000 in Bank A, had *withdrawn* $1,000 from his account. How would Bank A have been affected, and what repercussions would have been experienced by the other banks of the country? (We assume that Mr. Adams simply holds the cash, or pays it out to someone else who holds it, so that *it is not re-deposited* in any of the country's banks.)

As a result of paying out $1,000 in cash to Mr. Adams, Bank A's position will become as follows:[9]

Cash	$ 9,000	Deposits	$99,000
Loans	90,000		

[9]It is assumed, as before, that each bank in the country has previously received $100,000 in deposits, and has loaned out $90,000, keeping $10,000 in cash as reserve.

Bank A is now short of cash reserve by $900. If it is to maintain a 10 per cent cash reserve against its $99,000 of deposits it should have $9,900 in cash; it has only $9,000. But Bank A has $90,000 out on loan, with the loans varying in size, duration and maturity dates. Every day some loans fall due for repayment; every day, therefore, borrowers bring money in to the bank to pay off their loans. Normally when loans are repaid the bank would hasten to lend the money out again, in order to keep earning interest on it. Now, with its cash reserve too low, the bank will not re-lend all the money brought in by borrowers repaying loans. It will retain $900 to build up its cash reserve to the $9,900 figure it needs.[10] The total of its outstanding loans declines therefore by $900, to $89,100. Its position becomes as follows:

Cash	$ 9,900	Deposits	$99,000
Loans	89,100		

Repercussions on Other Banks. The matter does not end here. The $900 of cash that was paid over to Bank A came from somewhere; someone now has $900 less cash than before. That person will likely want to restore his cash balance to its customary level. Assuming that he is a customer of Bank B, he will draw $900 in cash from his account in that bank. Bank B's position will then become as follows:

Cash	$ 9,100	Deposits	$99,100
Loans	90,000		

Bank B is now short of cash reserve, by $810. It should have 10 per cent of $99,100 or $9,910; it has only $9,100. Out of loans repaid by borrowers, Bank B will retain $810 of cash to build up its reserves to the required level. When it does so its position becomes:

Cash	$ 9,910	Deposits	$99,100
Loans	89,190		

This $810 also came from somewhere. Someone's cash balance is now down by $810; to restore his cash holding to its usual level that person will draw $810 from his bank account. If he is a customer of Bank C, then its position will become as follows:

Cash	$ 9,190	Deposits	$99,190
Loans	90,000		

Bank C is now short of cash by $729. It should have 10 per cent of $99,190 or $9,919; it has only $9,190. Out of money it receives through the repayment of loans it will retain $729 to build up its cash reserve. Its position will then become:

[10]The Canadian banker need not wait for loans to mature. As we saw earlier, some of his loans will have been made to investment dealers for the purchase of treasury bills and he has the right to demand, at any time, the immediate repayment of such loans. Accordingly, the banker who needed cash would be likely, first of all, to call for the repayment of these loans.

| Cash | $ 9,919 | Deposits | $99,190 |
| Loans | 89,271 | | |

Reductions in Deposits and Loans. Let us stop now to consider what has happened. Deposits in Bank A have declined by $1,000, in Bank B by $900, in Bank C by $810; i.e. as a consequence of the original withdrawal of $1,000 from Bank A, deposits in Bank B fell by $\frac{9}{10}$ of $1,000, and in Bank C by $\frac{9}{10}$ of that. If we were to trace the repercussions further we would find that deposits in some other bank would subsequently fall by $\frac{9}{10}$ of that; and so on. The total reduction in deposits throughout the banking system would be represented by the series:

$1,000 + \frac{9}{10} \$1,000 + (\frac{9}{10})^2 \$1,000 + (\frac{9}{10})^3 \$1,000 + \ldots + (\frac{9}{10})^n \$1,000$

As we already know, such a series has a total value of $10,000.

Loans too will be down everywhere, by $900 in Bank A, by $810 in Bank B, by $729 in Bank C, and so on. The total reduction in loans throughout the banking system will be composed of the series:

$$\$900 + \frac{9}{10} \$900 + (\frac{9}{10})^2 \$900 + \ldots + (\frac{9}{10})^n \$900.$$

And this series, as we know, has a total value of $9,000.

Thus the withdrawal of $1,000 in cash from the banking system produces effects precisely opposite to those produced by a deposit of $1,000 in cash. In our example, as a result of Mr. Adams' withdrawing $1,000 in cash from Bank A, without that money being re-deposited in any other bank, the deposits held by the public in the various banks of the country declined by $10,000, and the total of bank loans outstanding declined by $9,000.

EFFECTS OF BANK PURCHASE AND SALE OF SECURITIES

We have assumed in the above illustration that banks always use excess cash to increase their loans, and make up deficiencies in cash reserves by reducing loans. In fact, as we saw earlier, banks may also invest excess cash in government bonds and may build up their cash by selling bonds. The same multiple creation of deposits takes place when banks use excess cash to buy bonds and the same multiple destruction of deposits takes place when banks sell bonds to build up cash reserves. Suppose in our example that after Mr. Adams deposited $1,000 cash in Bank A, the bank, instead of increasing its loans by $900, purchased $900 worth of bonds. In that case the person who sold them might deposit the money he received for them in Bank B. Bank B might now purchase $810 of bonds. The $810 cash which it paid would find its way into another bank. If this sequence proceeded indefinitely, a total of $10,000 of deposits would be created, as in our original example. However, instead of $9,000 being loaned out, $9,000 of bonds would be purchased by the banking system. Similarly, if the banks always sold bonds to bolster their cash reserves, then if Mr. Adams withdrew $1,000 from Bank A, the ultimate consequences would be a reduction in bank deposits of $10,000, and a reduction of $9,000 in bank holdings of bonds.

REALISTIC QUALIFICATIONS

Our example illustrating the operations of a banking system has been overly simple and its conclusions are exaggerated. Cash deposits and cash withdrawals do not, in real life, have as great an effect on aggregate loans and deposits as our example indicates. In actual practice two developments are likely to occur which will considerably diminish the repercussions of increases and decreases in the cash of any one bank.

Cash Retained by the Public

Firstly, not all of the money which has been borrowed from one bank, becomes deposited in another bank. A goodly portion of this cash may be kept by the public, being held by firms and individuals in pockets, vaults and tills, or being passed about in circulation without being deposited in a bank. Thus, when Bank A lends out $900, it may be that only $700 of this cash is subsequently deposited in Bank B. In that case Bank B can lend out only $\frac{9}{10}$ of $700, or $630, and not $\frac{9}{10}$ of $900, or $810, as in our original example. Similarly, the whole of the $630 loaned out by Bank B might not be deposited in Bank C and Bank C will be able to lend out only $\frac{9}{10}$ of $430, or $387.

If this sort of thing happens, then the total of deposits which are brought into being in just the first three banks as a result of Mr. Adams' deposit in Bank A will be: $1,000 in A + $700 in B + $430 in C; in our original example, deposits were: $1,000 + $900 + $810 + $729. Furthermore the total of loans created will also be much less if the public retains some of the cash brought in by Mr. Adams. New loans will consist only of: $900 loaned out by A; $630 by B; $387 by C; in our original example, loans amounted to: $900 loaned out by A; $810 by B; $729 by C.

Variations in Cash Reserves Ratios

Our second realistic consideration is this: banks may not try to keep exactly the same reserve ratio at all times. Where the government requires that they keep a certain minimum ratio they cannot keep less but they may choose at times to keep more. The fact that banks may be willing to hold a cash reserve ratio over and above the required minimum means that a deposit of cash does not necessarily lead to a multiple creation of loans and deposits throughout the banking system. In our example, when Mr. Adams deposited $1,000 in Bank A, thereby increasing its cash reserve ratio above ten per cent, the Bank might have decided to keep its reserve ratio at this higher level. In that case it would not lend another $900, and there would not take place the sequence of deposits in, and loans made by, Banks B, C, and all the other banks of the country. Similarly, if Bank A had excess reserves of $1,000 or more, then when Mr. Adams withdrew $1,000, its remaining cash would still amount to more than ten per cent of its deposit liabilities. The bank would not be obliged to reduce loans or sell securities in order to rebuild its cash reserve, and there need be no reduction of the deposits in and loans made by Banks B, C, and all the rest.

Because of the two practical considerations just described, an increase in a country's cash supply is likely to bring about a smaller increase in bank loans and deposits than was indicated in our original example. Similarly, a withdrawal of cash from a bank will likely lead to a smaller reduction of loans and deposits than our example indicated. Both the public's desire to hold cash and banks' desire to hold excess reserves vary from time to time. The way in which total bank loans and deposits respond to increases and decreases in bank cash will also vary from time to time, therefore, depending upon whether the public wants to hold more or less cash, and whether the banks want to hold more or less excess reserves.

A Single Bank vs. a Banking System

We have established that a *banking system* can create deposits amounting to several times the cash deposited in it; but what a banking system can do a *single* bank cannot do. A bank which attempted to expand its deposits by a multiple of the cash which it received would quickly fall into difficulty. Let us see why.

Suppose that when Mr. Adams deposited $1,000 in Bank A, the bank immediately loaned out $9,000 in the form of deposits. The bank credits borrowers in its books with $9,000 of deposits, so that they can issue cheques to that amount. Its position would become as follows:

Cash	$11,000	Deposits	$110,000[11]
Loans	99,000		

So far so good. The cash reserve is exactly ten per cent, even after $9,000 of deposits have been created in favour of borrowers. But the borrowers are going to issue cheques on those deposits, and a good many of those cheques are going to be deposited in other banks in the system. Those other banks, after crediting depositors' accounts with the value of these cheques, will present them to Bank A for payment. Suppose for instance that the $9,000 worth of cheques issued by the borrowers are all deposited in other banks. The other banks will in due course present them to Bank A in order to have them cashed. After cashing them Bank A's position would be:

Cash	$ 2,000	Deposits	$101,000
Loans	99,000		

Bank A's total deposits would be down to $101,000, the borrowers' deposits of $9,000 having been reduced to zero when the cheques they issued were cashed; but having cashed those cheques, Bank A's cash would be down to only $2,000, far less than ten per cent of its deposits.[12]

---

[11]Comprised of the original $100,000, plus Mr. Adams' deposit of $1,000, plus the $9,000 of deposits credited to borrowers.

[12]If Bank A were the only bank in the country, then it might be able to lend out, with safety, $9,000 in deposits for each $1,000 of cash brought in. All of the cheques issued by borrowers against these deposits would be received by customers of Bank A, there being no other bank. In that case (provided that no one asked for actual cash) Bank A would not experience any withdrawal of cash. It would simply reduce the deposits of those persons who issue the cheques and correspondingly increase the deposits of those who received the cheques. Its total deposits would remain at $110,000, and its cash would remain at $11,000, ten per cent of its deposit liabilities.

CANADA'S COMMERCIAL BANKS

Canada's first bank, the Bank of Montreal, was organized in 1817, and a good many more were subsequently established in the nineteenth century in other localities. At one time, there were some forty chartered banks operating in the country; but, chiefly through amalgamations and mergers, the total number was reduced to seven by 1971. Save for one which was only recently established by foreign interests, each one of Canada's banks is a very large institution, operating hundreds of branches throughout the country.[13] In a compilation carried out in 1954, three of Canada's banks were ranked among the twenty-four largest in the world.

In Canada, only the federal Parliament can grant the charter which a bank requires in order to operate. Originally, each bank's charter was separately drafted so that each operated under its own particular set of legal privileges and responsibilities. All of the charters had a good deal in common, however, each having been modelled on the charter of the first Bank of the United States. (This institution had been established in 1792, with a charter drawn up on the basis of British precedent and experience.) In 1871, Parliament passed the Bank Act which henceforth, with its subsequent amendments, governed the operations of all banks in Canada.[14] Provision was made for a revision every ten years to remedy revealed weaknesses and to bring the Act abreast of current conditions. We have already noted, earlier in the chapter, some of the main revisions made in the Bank Act in recent years.

CANADA'S CHARTERED BANKS:
BALANCE SHEET AS OF DECEMBER 31, 1970

Table 1 presents the aggregate assets and liabilities of all of Canada's chartered banks, as of December 31, 1970; the first asset listed, $1,703 million of Bank of Canada notes and deposits, constitutes their total cash reserves; their deposit liabilities totalled approximately $30 billions.

COMMERCIAL BANKING IN THE U.S.

In the United States there exist two distinct categories of commercial banks. *National* banks are those which are organized according to specifications laid down in the National Bank Act, a federal statute introduced in 1864. All national banks hold

---

[13]The operations of two Banks, the Banque Canadienne Nationale and the Banque Provinciale du Canada, are confined mainly to the Province of Quebec.

[14]This Act icorporated many features of the existing bank charters, so that Canadian banking law continued in the British tradition.

Table 1

THE CHARTERED BANKS OF CANADA
AGGREGATE ASSETS AND LIABILITIES, DECEMBER 31, 1970*
(Millions of dollars)

ASSETS		LIABILITIES	
Bank of Canada notes and deposits	$ 1,703	Deposits	
Canadian day-to-day loans	310	Government of Canada	$ 1,257
Treasury bills	2,689	Provincial governments	214
Government of Canada bonds	3,910	Personal saving	16,615
Net foreign assets	158	Other notice	4,450
Call and short loans	593	Other banks	270
Municipal, provincial loans	883	Public demand	7,083
Loans to grain dealers	705	Acceptances, guarantees and	
Loans for purchase of Canada		letters of credit	1,484
Savings Bonds	246	All other liabilities	161
General loans	16,123	Debentures issued and outstanding	40
Insured residential mortgages	1,100	Accumulated appropriations	
Other residential mortgages	357	for losses	604
Municipal, provincial securities	806	Shareholders equity	1,596
Corporate securities	843		$33,774
Canadian dollar items in transit	1,044		
All other assets	2,306		
Total of Canadian and Net			
Foreign Assets	$33,774		

*Compiled from *The Canadian Statistical Review,* April, 1971.

their charters from the Comptroller of the Currency, an officer of the federal Treasury Department. *State* banks, on the other hand, are organized under the laws of their respective states and obtain their charters from the appropriate state authorities. The requirements specified for national banks are a good deal more stringent than those laid down for most state banks. They must have larger amounts of subscribed capital; they are more closely restricted in respect to the types of loan they may make; they are subject to more rigorous supervision. A good many state banks are very large institutions, however, and comparable in all respects to national banks.[15]

In contrast to Canada's banks with their numerous branches throughout the country, American banks are generally of the "unit" type. (A *unit* bank is one which is an independent concern having no branches whatever.) Several states prohibit branch banking altogether; some permit a bank to operate branches within one city or county; a few, notably California, allow state-wide branch banking; but under current legislation, no bank may operate branches in more than one state. Thus,

[15]Approximately one-fifth of the country's state banks are members of the Federal Reserve System (whose organization and functions are described in the next chapter). To be members, they must meet the requirements specified for national banks by the National Bank Act.

while as of December 31, 1968, there were in Canada nine different commercial banks operating 5,956 branches, there were in the United States, on the same date, 14,199 different commercial banks, with a total of 20,131 branches.[16] (Despite the strict limitations in respect to the operation of branches, large numbers of banks— some in different states—are linked together and subject to centralized control through holding companies. As of December 31, 1969, there were 83 such companies[17] in the U.S., collectively controlling 715 different banks with a total of 3,353 offices. The largest, the Western Bancorporation of Los Angeles, controlled 23 banks in 11 different states; its member institutions operated a total of 611 offices and held over $81 billions in customers' deposits.)

Branch vs. Unit Banks

Both the branch and unit banking systems have their vociferous advocates. On behalf of the branch banking system it is argued that:

1. A bank to be successful, must hold the confidence of the public, and a large institution is more likely to inspire confidence than a small one.
2. A branch can place at the disposal of its customers all the varied and specialized services provided by the entire organization.
3. A bank which operates many branches throughout the country is less likely to fail. Its operations are diversified; its loans are made to many different industries and in many different localities. A small bank, on the other hand, operating in one locality only, may be ruined as a result of a single calamity which renders a very large proportion of its borrowers unable to repay their loans.
4. A branch is able to lend safely the very large sums which may be needed by a large local enterprise. A small local bank would not be able to lend so much, or would not dare to commit so large a proportion of its funds to a single borrower.
5. A bank with many branches automatically shifts capital about the country, from where it is accumulated to where it is required. During the early 1900s, for instance, Canadian banks customarily received large savings in their branches in old established Eastern districts, and transferred the funds to their Western branches to be loaned out to people who were just setting themselves up in the country.

On behalf of unit banks it is argued that:

1. With banks numerous and small there can be no dangerous concentration of economic power in a few hands.
2. A locally controlled bank can adapt its operations to the particular needs of the community, whereas a branch bank necessarily operates according to rigid rules

---

[16]Head office locations were not included in the figure for branches; hence the total number of bank offices was 34,330.

[17]As defined in the Bank Holding Company Act of 1956.

laid down by its head office. Furthermore, in a locally controlled bank, decisions are made on the spot and do not have to be referred to a distant authority.

3. The local owner of a bank is likely to feel more closely identified with a community and more anxious to promote its progress than will the manager of a branch. The latter typically has no roots in the community and does not expect to stay very long in any case.

4. A bank branch may simply be a medium for sucking the savings out of a community and sending them elsewhere, with the result that they are not available to support local development.

All of the above arguments, on both sides, have validity and can be supported by reference to actual experience. It would be presumptuous, in the author's view, to claim that one system is absolutely and everywhere superior to the other. The fact is that the institutional environment in which a banking system operates, and the people who operate and staff the banks, all vary from one place and time to another. Quite possibly under one set of conditions one system might prove more desirable, while under different conditions, it would prove less desirable. Furthermore, it may be that neither system is ever unequivocally superior to the other. Each always carries its own dangers and offers its own opportunities; different people will always differently assess the perils and possibilities involved.

SUMMARY

A modern bank receives deposits of money for safekeeping, from the general public and business firms, and invests or lends out the greater part of such deposits, keeping only a small fraction as cash reserve. A bank is able to do this safely because very few depositors ever demand their money back at any one time, while fresh deposits are constantly being made by other customers.

Banks generally use some of their funds to purchase bonds, and these constitute a secondary reserve since they can be sold for cash at any time.

Canadian banks purchase short term treasury bills which are regularly sold by the federal government, and make loans to dealers to enable them to purchase such bills.

The operations of a country's banking system increase greatly the national money supply, the additional money being in the form of bank deposits. The amount of bank deposits created will depend upon the amount of cash deposited in the banking system and the cash reserve ratio maintained by the banks. Withdrawal of cash from the banking system will likely lead to a multiple reduction in the volume of bank deposits.

The Canadian banking system consists of a very small number of very large banks, most of which operate hundreds of branches throughout the country. The

American banking system consists, on the other hand, of thousands of independent banks; several are giant institutions, but the great majority are, by Canadian standards, very small. Each system has its merits and its advocates.

FOR REVIEW AND DISCUSSION

1. A single bank dare not do what a banking system can safely do. Explain.
2. Assuming that all banks in the country keep a 20 per cent cash reserve ratio, what consequences would follow from a deposit of $5,000 in cash in one of the banks? What would happen if $5,000 were withdrawn from one of the banks (and not redeposited in any other)?
3. "Banks should be obliged to keep a 100 per cent cash reserve ratio; this would provide absolute security to depositors, and would not interfere in the slightest with their capacity to make loans." Do you agree?
4. To operate successfully a bank must have, first and foremost, the confidence of the public. Explain.
5. "The banks should all be owned and operated by the government." Do you agree? Why or why not?
6. "Canada would have made more rapid economic progress if we had had the American system of unit banks." Do you agree? Justify your answer.
7. The regular issue of treasury bills is beneficial both to the banks and to the government. Explain.

22

The Banking System: Central Bank Operations

THE NEED FOR A CENTRAL BANK

We saw in the preceding chapter how the commercial banks of a country create money in the form of bank deposits, by lending out cash deposited with them or by using such cash for the purchase of securities. These bank activities contribute indispensably to the smooth working of a modern economic system. In any modern country the money which the banks create constitutes by far the largest portion of the total money supply; the loans which the banks make, together with their investments in securities, finance a major portion of the nation's economic activities.

To Regulate the Money Supply

These operations of commercial banks inherently contain two grave dangers. Firstly, the total amount of money created by the banking system at any time and the total volume of loans which it extends, may be inappropriate to the current needs of the country. At times the money supply and the volume of loans may be too large, giving rise to inflation and very likely to a decline in the foreign exchange rate of the nation's currency. At other times the volume of money created and loans extended may be too small, giving rise to deflation and unemployment. Such occasional excesses and deficiencies can easily occur where the banks are privately owned institutions whose primary concern is to earn profit. It could happen that at a time when the money supply and the volume of loans were already excessive, individual banks might find it profitable to increase their loans, and so contribute to a further enlargement of the nation's money supply. It could happen, as well, that at a time when the money supply and the volume of loans were both too low, each individual bank might deem it inadvisable to increase its loans, so that the volume of loans and deposits remained deficient. These are not merely hypothetical possibilities; on a good many occasions, in Canada and in other countries, banking systems have created too much or too little money and have extended too many or too few loans, in relation to the needs of the country at the time.

An Ultimate Source of Cash

The second danger arises from the fact that each commercial bank, and therefore the

385

banking system as a whole, maintains only fractional reserves against deposit liabilities. The amount of cash which each bank possesses at any time is only a small fraction of the total claims for cash (i.e. bank deposits) which the public holds against it. If ever a substantial number of a bank's depositors simultaneously demanded their cash, the bank's reserves would be exhausted. If other banks were experiencing similar withdrawals, or feared similar withdrawals, a bank whose cash reserves were being drained would be unable to replenish them. The bank might have loaned out its money to perfectly reliable people or invested it in perfectly sound securities, but no one would be willing to advance to it the cash which it needed to meet its depositors demands. Being unable to honour its undertaking to pay depositors their money, the bank would be obliged to close its doors. The failure of one bank might precipitate a general panic. Depositors in other banks might become fearful that their money too was in danger and rush to withdraw it before it was too late. Mass withdrawals from the other banks would in turn drain their cash reserves and force them to close too. This too is not merely a hypothetical possibility: a good many countries have experienced such financial crises and panics, each involving the failure of numerous financial institutions and severe disruption of the economic life of the country.

The First Central Bank

The *central bank* has evolved as the institution which has the responsibility and the power to counter the dangers inherent in the operations of commercial banks. The need for such an authority was not evident at once with the introduction of modern commercial banking; it became manifest only in the course of time. The world's first real central bank, the Bank of England, came to perform the key functions of a central bank gradually and reluctantly, often protesting that it was not really obligated to perform them. It was a private firm,[1] and the responsibilities of a central bank which it was called upon to discharge frequently involved considerable risks, the foregoing of possible profit, and the incurring of actual loss. However, the Bank's immense prestige and authority and the unique role which it played in the British banking system, compelled it to assume responsibility for the financial system of the country and not merely the dividends of its shareholders. The techniques developed by the Bank to regulate the British money market came to serve as models for central banks established subsequently in other countries, including Canada.

CENTRAL BANK RESPONSIBILITIES AND POWERS

The key responsibilities of a central bank are twofold. It must regulate the size of the nation's money supply, using the various means in its power to check tendencies to excess or deficiency. Secondly, it must act as a "lender of last resort": it must stand

---

[1]From 1694, when it was established, till 1946, when it was nationalized by the British government of the day.

ready at all times to lend cash to commercial banks and other financial institutions whose loans and investments are sound, but which need immediate cash to meet depositors' demands and can obtain it from no other source. In discharging the first responsibility the central bank will contribute to the nation's economic stability, including the stability of the foreign exchange rate of its currency. In discharging the second responsibility the bank guarantees against the possibility that sudden panics by depositors will wreck basically sound financial institutions and bring on painful economic crises.

The typical central bank possesses a variety of powers and performs a variety of functions. It will likely be the authority which issues the country's paper currency. This currency, together with deposits in the central bank, would constitute the lawful money of the country; the cash reserve of the country's commercial banks consists of the notes of the central bank which they hold together with the deposits they have in the central bank. The central bank simply creates this money. It can have notes printed and issue them; it can create deposits, claims against itself, by writing figures in its books. Unlike commercial banks the central bank can in fact create money by "the stroke of a pen." It will create and pay out such money either as a loan, or as payment for securities which it purchases. The country's parliamentary authority may set some upper limit on the amount of money which the central bank may create, but the restrictive effect of such ceilings is usually slight. Generally the limit is set well above the maximum figure which is likely to be realized; if the limit does in fact prove restrictive it is likely to be raised or withdrawn altogether.[2]

The central bank is a "banker's bank." It holds deposits of the commercial banks and stands ready to lend them money. Its relations with the commercial banks parallel their relations with the general public. Because the central bank holds deposits of all the commercial banks it is able to act as a clearing house through which banks settle their mutual obligations. When one commercial bank wishes to pay another, the central bank transfers the money simply by deducting the appropriate amount from the deposit of the paying bank and adding that amount to the deposit of the receiving bank.

While a central bank usually has a good deal of independent authority, its relations with the country's government are likely to be close. It will probably be the fiscal agent of the government, handling its borrowings and repayments of loans, and ensuring that the government at all times has the funds it needs. The senior officials of the central bank may act as advisers to the government in economic matters; they are, after all, men of considerable experience and acumen who are in close and constant touch with the nation's financial affairs.

[2]e.g. Canada's central bank, the Bank of Canada, was originally required to create money, in the form of its notes and deposits, not in excess of four times its holdings in gold. Following the outbreak of World War II, however, it became necessary to increase the money supply well beyond this limit. Accordingly, in May, 1940, the limit was suspended and has never been restored.

While the operations of a central bank are likely to be profitable, the earning of profit is not of primary concern. It is taken for granted that the bank will always adopt those measures which are in the best interests of the country, even if in doing so it incurs substantial loss. Where the central bank is owned by the government, its profits become simply part of the general public revenue. Where the bank is privately owned there is likely to be a limit on the amount of profit which may be paid out to shareholders, profit over and above the specified limit being appropriated by the government.

To regulate the nation's money supply, a central bank may employ four basic measures, singly or in combination. These are: *open-market operations, variation of commercial banks' minimum cash reserve ratio, variation of Bank Rate, moral suasion.*

Open-Market Operations

We saw in the preceding chapter how an increase in the cash lodged in a country's banking system will bring about a multiple reduction in the volume of bank loans and deposits. The central bank may deliberately arrange such increases or decreases in bank cash, by the procedure referred to as *open-market operations*. If it feels that the the volume of bank loans and deposits is too small, it will buy federal government bonds or treasury bills. It will pay for these securities by *new cash which it creates*. This cash will in due course be deposited in one of the country's commercial banks, and will give rise to a sequence of loans and deposits such as was described in Chapter 21.

To illustrate: assume that the commercial banks always try to maintain a 10 per cent reserve ratio, and that the public always brings into the bank any extra cash which comes into its possession. Suppose now that the central bank decides that it would be a good thing if the total of deposits in commercial banks increased by $10 million and bank loans to businessmen and the public increased by $9 million. It will go into the market and *buy* $1 million of securities, giving the seller a cheque on itself for $1 million. He will deposit this cheque in his bank, and this bank will present it to the central bank for payment. The central bank will "cash" the cheque simply by crediting the commercial bank with another $1 million in its deposit. But the deposit of the commercial bank in the central bank is cash reserve; the commercial bank's reserves have therefore increased by $1 million. Its liabilities have also increased by $1 million of course, since it credited, in its own books, $1 million to the deposit of the person who brought in the cheque drawn on the central bank.

The commercial bank wants to maintain a cash reserve amounting to exactly 10 per cent of its deposit liabilities. So far what has happened is that its deposit liabilities and its cash reserves have both increased by $1 million. The bank will accordingly lend out $.9 million to borrowers, or purchase that value of securities. This $.9 million will become deposited in another bank; a sequence of loans and deposits will ensue, as described in Chapter 21, which will cause total deposits throughout the banking system to become $10 million greater than they were originally, and loans (plus security holdings) of the banks $9 million greater. This, of course, is the result which the central bank wished to achieve.

If, on the other hand, the central bank feels that the country's money supply is excessive, it will *sell* bonds. (Having purchased bonds in the past it will have an ample supply of them.) Suppose that it sells $1 million worth. It will be paid by the purchaser with a cheque on some commercial bank, which it will "cash" simply by deducting that amount of money from the commercial bank's deposit with it. Since this deposit of the commercial bank is cash reserve, its reserve becomes reduced by $1 million; its reserve ratio will now be less than 10 per cent of its deposit liabilities to its own customers. The commercial bank accordingly becomes obligated to reduce its outstanding loans in order to restore its cash reserve to the proper proportion. There will follow a sequence of deposit and loan reductions which will cause, throughout the banking system, the former to fall by $10 million and the latter by $9 million.

The foregoing examples exaggerate the effects of central bank open-market operations. The calculations were made on the assumption that banks always try to keep a 10 per cent reserve exactly and that the public never changes its holdings of actual cash. These assumptions are unrealistic, as we have already noted in Chapter 21, and the central bank's security purchases and sales are likely in practice to have rather smaller repercussions than our examples suggest. It may be that when the central bank buys $1 million of bonds the consequent increase in commercial bank deposits is just $5 million. This would not weaken the central bank's powers: it would mean simply that to achieve a $10 million increase in deposits the central bank would have to buy $2 million of bonds; similarly, to achieve a $10 million reduction in deposits it would have to sell $2 million worth.

A central bank may sell bonds, not to cause a reduction of bank loans and deposits, but *to prevent a possible increase.* If the commercial banks have reserves in excess of the legal minimum, then they have the capacity to enlarge their loans and deposits. But the central bank may be anxious that no such increase occur. In that case it will sell enough bonds to "mop up" the commercial banks' excess reserves. Purchasers of these bonds will pay with cheques on their banks; the central bank will reduce, by the amount of these cheques, the cash reserves of these banks[3] and they will no longer be in a position to expand their loans and deposits.

Effects on the Interest Rate

The purchase and sale of securities by the central bank directly affect the market rate of interest. When the bank buys bonds in order to increase the cash available to the commercial banks, the price of bonds tends to rise and the rate of interest earned

[3]Which are in the form of deposits in the central bank.

on them automatically declines.[4] Because the rate of interest charged on all types of borrowing tends to move up and down with the rate earned on government bonds, interest rates generally are likely to be pulled down and borrowing becomes more attractive. Thus bond purchases by the central bank have a double-edged effect: they increase the capacity of the commercial banks to lend and, by lowering the rate of interest, increase the desire of the public to borrow.

Security sales by the central bank have a double-edged effect in the opposite direction. They reduce commercial bank cash and, by depressing the price of securities, cause the real rate of interest earned on them to rise; interest rates generally will therefore rise. Hence the central bank's bond sales will reduce the commercial banks' capacity to lend and, at the same time, reduce the public's desire to borrow.

Variation of Commercial Bank Reserve Ratios

A central bank may have the authority to vary the minimum cash reserve ratio which commercial banks are obliged to keep. By reducing this figure the central bank enables the commercial banking system to maintain, with the same amount of cash, a larger volume of loans and deposits. By increasing this figure the central bank compels the commercial banking system to maintain, with the same cash reserve, a smaller volume of loans and deposits.

Suppose for example that the required reserve ratio is 10 per cent, and that the collective position of all the country's commercial banks is as follows:

Cash	$10 million	Deposits	$100 million
Loans	$90 million[5]		

If now the central bank authorizes commercial banks to maintain just a five per cent reserve ratio, then it becomes possible for the banking system to achieve the following position:

Cash	$10 million	Deposits	$200 million
Loans	$190 million		

i.e., deposits can be doubled and loans more than doubled.

---

[4]Suppose a certain $100 bond had been issued in the past to yield 3 per cent interest; until the redemption date the owner would each year get $3 in interest. Suppose now that the central bank bought large quantities of bonds, driving their price up to $150. In that case the real rate of interest being earned on this bond would become only 2 per cent, since the owner would be getting the same $3 per year on an investment which would now be worth $150. Similarly, if the central bank were to sell bonds to such an extent that the price dropped to $75, then the rate of interest earned on this bond would become 4 per cent. The owner would be getting $3 per year on an investment worth only $75. (The figures in this example are not entirely accurate; for simplicity no account was taken of the change in the present value of the $100 to be paid at the redemption date.)

[5]The banks will likely have used some of their depositors' funds to purchase bonds as well as to make loans. For the sake of simplicity it is assumed here that depositors' funds are used only to make loans.

On the other hand, if the central bank requires commercial banks to maintain a 20 per cent cash reserve, then they must reduce loans and deposits until their collective position is:

Cash	$10 million	Deposits	$50 million
Loans	$40 million		

i.e., deposits must be reduced by half, loans by more than half.

We noted in our discussion of open-market operations that a central bank may sell bonds, not to reduce the supply of bank credit but to prevent possible increases. The central bank, we said, may "mop up" excess reserves of the commercial banks which might be used to support an increase in bank loans and deposits. As an alternative, the central bank may achieve the same effect by raising the minimum legal cash reserve ratio, thereby "immobilizing" the excess cash. Suppose that when the minimum cash reserve ratio is 10 per cent, the commercial banking system is in the following position:

Cash	$12 million	Deposits	$100 million
Loans	$88 million		

As matters stand the banks have $2 million of excess reserves; the banking system could legally expand its deposits to $120 million and its loans to $108 million. If the central bank wishes to prevent such an increase, it may simply announce that henceforth all banks are required to maintain a cash reserve ratio of at least 12 per cent. In that case, with their $12 million of cash the banks could legally have no more than their present $100 million of deposits and $88 million of loans.

Variation of Bank Rate

The central bank, as we have already seen, is the "lender of last resort" to whom commercial banks can always turn for additional cash needed to fulfil their obligations. The bank implements its guarantee by standing ready to buy all treasury bills offered to it, paying in legal cash—i.e. deposits on itself—a price equal to their face value minus a publicly announced discount. The rate of discount, known as "Bank Rate," is raised or lowered from time to time depending on whether the bank wishes to discourage or to promote an increase in the country's cash supplies. A high Bank Rate which would presumably deter the holders from selling bills to the bank, would be announced when the bank feared inflation and was unwilling to increase the amount of cash in existence; a low Rate would represent the bank's willingness to assist in monetary expansion.

Bank Rate, as periodically announced, serves important functions even when the financial community has no need of cash from the central bank. The level of Bank Rate reflects the central bank's views of the current financial situation, and implies the general policy which it intends to follow. While the banks may currently have no need of additional cash, the situation may abruptly change. Depositors may make sudden, large withdrawals, sharply reducing the commercial banks' cash holdings and forcing them to seek more cash to restore their reserves. A low Bank Rate will encourage banks to lend their money freely; if ever they do need to replenish their cash they will be able to do so cheaply. A high Bank Rate will induce commercial banks to keep a tight rein on their lending; if ever they find it necessary to obtain additional cash they will get it only at a "penalty rate."

"Moral Suasion"

The central bank may simply request the commercial banks to adopt the lending policies which it feels are required at the time. At a time when inflation threatens, the bank may request that the commercial banks refrain from increasing their loans to businessmen and the public. The banks might have cash which they could lend out, or they could readily obtain such cash by selling some of their securities. It might be safe and profitable for them to lend out more money and ordinarily they would do so. As we have already noted, the central bank could prevent them from increasing their loans, either by selling bonds or by raising the minimum cash reserve which they must maintain. In some situations, however, it may prove more expedient simply to *request* commercial banks not to lend out more money. The central bank may, furthermore, request that certain categories of loans be particularly restricted. It may, too, request other financial institutions besides the banks to keep a close rein on their lending.

THE BANK OF CANADA — ITS ORIGINS

While the Bank of Canada, our central bank, was only established in 1934, one important central banking function had been performed in Canada since 1914. Arrangements existed since that year whereby the commercial banks could obtain additional cash whenever they so desired. These arrangements had been inaugurated during World War I to forestall financial crisis and panic. When the war broke out, Canada was on the gold standard, and the nation's supply of lawful money consisted of the gold which the commercial banks and the federal treasury held, together with the dominion notes issued by the federal treasury; these in turn were backed by the government's gold holdings and were exchangeable for gold upon request. Following the outbreak of war, Canada's bankers feared that panicky depositors might seek to convert their deposits into gold and drain the banks of their reserves. Parliament accordingly passed the Finance Act in August, 1914, which authorized the federal treasury to advance dominion notes to the banks when the latter pledged approved securities as collateral.[6] No ceiling was placed on the amount of such advances.

---

[6]This authorization was actually first granted by an Order-in-Council of August 3, 1914. The Finance Act itself was passed by Parliament on August 22, 1914, embodying the principles of the Order-in-Council.

Since these notes were legal tender the banks would be able to meet depositors' demands for cash on any scale; they could always pay off depositors in these notes, and replenish their supply by pledging further securities with the federal treasury.

The 1914 Finance Act was intended strictly as a war measure; one of its terms provided that it lapse within two years of the end of the war. But its operation had proven useful, providing a welcome degree of elasticity to the nation's supply of cash. In 1923 Parliament passed a new Finance Act, closely modelled on the original. Provision was made for the Act to be administered by a Treasury Board, which would consist of a committee of the federal cabinet.

The Finance Act suffered from a grave deficiency. The treasury board which administered it had no responsibility to ensure that the advances made to the banks were of a size appropriate to the current needs of the country. The banks alone decided what cash they would obtain under the Act. Once they handed over the necessary collateral securities the Treasury Board automatically handed over the cash which they requested. The possibility existed—and materialized—that the scale of advances made under the Act would not be of the size best suited to the country's monetary needs.

Following the onset of the Great Depression of the 1930s, widespread demands developed in the country for a reorganization of the nation's monetary system. The federal government appointed a "Royal Commission on Banking and Currency in Canada" to conduct an enquiry and to recommend appropriate changes.[7] The Commission's report, presented in September, 1933, strongly advocated the establishment of a central bank, and the following year Parliament passed the Bank of Canada Act which implemented that recommendation. The Bank actually began to do business in 1935.

Following the example of the Bank of England, the Bank of Canada, as originally established, was a private institution whose stock was owned by the general public. In 1936, however, following a federal election which brought a new party into power, the government acquired a majority interest in the bank. Two years later the government acquired the stock which had been privately purchased, so that the Bank became, and has since remained, wholly owned by the federal government.

---

[7]Like the recommendations of a good many Canadian royal commissions, this one advocated a measure upon which the government had already resolved. Viz. the following declaration by Mr. R. B. Bennett, Prime Minister and Minister of Finance from 1930 to 1935, referring to Canada's foreign exchange problems in September, 1931, following Great Britain's abandonment of the gold standard. "I learned to my surprise that there were no direct means of settling international balances between Canada and London, that the only medium was New York, and the value of the Canadian dollar would have to be determined in Wall Street. I made up my mind then and there that this country was going to have a central bank because there must be some financial institution that can with authority do business for the whole of the Dominion with the other nations of the World. If Canada was to be financially independent there had to be a means of determining balances, of settling international accounts, and a central bank would furnish this." Canadian Press Despatch, December 7, 1933. Quoted in M. L. Stokes, *The Bank of Canada* (Toronto, 1939), p. 65.

The Bank's Responsibilities

The preamble to the Bank of Canada Act declared the main responsibilities of the Bank to be "to regulate credit and currency in the best interests of the economic life of the nation, to control and protect the external value of the national monetary unit and to mitigate by its influence fluctuations in the general level of production, trade, prices and employment so far as may be possible within the scope of monetary action, and generally to promote the economic welfare of the Dominion." In addition, the Bank, as do central banks generally, acts as economic adviser to the government, issues the country's paper currency, holds the reserves of the commercial banks, and acts as clearing agent for the commercial banks, arranging inter-bank payments simply by making appropriate credit and debit entries in the accounts which it keeps of all of the banks. Since April 1, 1938, the Bank has managed the public debt; it has been the federal government's agent in respect to the flotation of new bond issues, the payment of interest on federal government bonds, and their redemption upon maturity. During World War II the Bank acted as adviser and agent to the Foreign Exchange Control Board.[8] Currently the Bank manages two major government accounts: the Exchange Fund Account, which is used to stabilize the foreign exchange rate of the Canadian dollar; the Securities Investment Account, which invests funds accumulated by a number of federal government agencies. The Bank does not do business with the general public; it deals only with governments, the commercial banks, and a limited number of investment firms.

Control Over the Bank of Canada

The Bank of Canada is managed by a governor and deputy governor, both appointed for seven-year terms, and twelve directors, each appointed for a three-year term. The board of directors meets at relatively infrequent intervals, and the effective directing body is the Executive Committee, which consists of the Governor, Deputy Governor, and one director. The Deputy Minister of Finance is a member of both the board and the Executive Committee, but without voting rights; his task is essentially that of maintaining liaison between the Bank and the federal government.

When opinions of Bank officials are divided, the will of the majority does not necessarily prevail. The Governor has the power to veto any decision of both the Executive Committee and the board of directors. If ever he does impose his veto, however, he must report the fact within seven days to the Minister of Finance. The latter will inform the federal cabinet, and the cabinet may confirm or disallow the Governor's veto.

The relationship between the Bank and the federal government is characterized by a certain degree of ambiguity. On the one hand the Bank of Canada Act requires the Governor to regulate the Canadian money supply in what he conceives to be the best interests of the country. On the other hand, the Bank is wholly owned by the federal government and the Governor should therefore carry out the will of the

[8]The Governor of the Bank acted as Chairman of this Board

government. What if the Governor feels that the government is demanding a course of action which is against the best interests of the country? By fairly general concensus the second obligation is regarded as being the crucial one: the Bank must heed the will of the government. The Governor of the Bank, as early as 1938, declared in a public address that "the policies of central banks must conform to the policies of their respective governments."[9] The following statement by Mr. Louis Rasminsky, made in 1961 when he became Governor of the Bank of Canada, clearly sets forth the current view.

"I believe that it is essential that the responsibilities in relation to monetary policy should be clarified in the public mind and in the legislation. I do not suggest a precise formula but I have in mind two main principles to be established: (1) in the ordinary course of events, the Bank has the responsibility for monetary policy, and (2) if the Government disapproves of the monetary policy being carried out by the Bank, it has the right and responsibility to direct the Bank as to the policy which the Bank is to carry out.

"The first principle is designed to ensure that the Bank has the degree of independence and responsibility necessary if it is, in the language of the Bank of Canada Act, to regulate credit and currency in the best interests of the economic life of the nation. To discharge this duty the Bank must be sufficiently independent and responsible in its operations to be able to withstand day-to-day pressures from any source. But in the longer run, if there should develop a serious and persistent conflict between the views of the Government and the views of the central bank with regard to monetary policy, which after prolonged and conscientious effort on both sides, cannot be resolved, the Government should be able formally to instruct the Bank what monetary policy it wishes carried out and the Bank should have the duty to comply with these instructions. The exercise of this authority by Government would place on Government direct responsibility for the monetary policy to be followed. If this policy, as communicated to the Bank, was one which the Governor felt he could not in good conscience carry out, his duty would be to resign and to make way for someone who took a different view."[10]

[9]Quoted in E. P. Neufeld *Bank of Canada Operations and Policy* (Toronto, 1958), p. 11.
[10]Statement by the Governor of the Bank of Canada issued August 1, 1961, in *Submission by the Bank of Canada to the Royal Commission on Banking and Finance, May 31, 1962*, p. 23.
Conflict between the federal government and the governor of the Bank of Canada may be resolved in dramatic fashion, as shown by the events which occurred in the summer of 1961. On May 30, the Minister of Finance demanded of the current governor, Mr. James E. Coyne, that he resign. In making this demand, the Minister charged, among other things, that Mr. Coyne had followed restrictionist policies and had refused to cooperate with the government. Mr. Coyne denied these charges and refused to resign. In a series of public statements he castigated the government and justified his administration of the Bank. The government introduced a bill in Parliament to dismiss him. (Having been appointed by Parliament he could be dismissed only by Parliament.) The Commons passed the bill, but on July 13 the Senate, having heard Mr. Coyne present his side of the case, refused to give its approval. His honour vindicated by the Senate's rejection of the bill of dismissal, Mr. Coyne immediately resigned.

Open-Market Operations of the Bank of Canada

As we saw in the last chapter, the commercial banks of Canada regularly submit bids for the ninety-one day treasury bills which the government offers for sale each week. The Bank of Canada submits bids along with all the rest. When it purchases bills at these weekly offerings, it pays by crediting the government's account with the appropriate sum. At the same time the government will be paying the Bank money to redeem treasury bills bought by the Bank in the past and which have currently become due. The government's deposit in the Bank of Canada will only increase, therefore, if the Bank's current purchase of treasury bills is greater than the value of the bills which the Bank owns and which the government must now pay off. The government's deposit in the Bank will decrease, on the other hand, if the Bank's new purchases of treasury bills amount to less than the total of the old bills which it holds and which mature that week. Thus the Bank of Canada can readily vary the size of the government's account with it by varying the amount of treasury bills which it purchases.[11]

The government's deposit in the Bank of Canada is legally cash; if the government spends that money, it will in due course become deposited in one of the commercial banks and give rise to the usual multiple creation of loans and deposits by the commercial banking system. Since matured treasury bills are redeemed each week and new treasury bills are issued each week, the Bank is able, through its transaction in treasury bills, to vary the nation's cash supply from week to week.[12] In fact transactions in treasury bills may occur every day; the Bank always stands ready to purchase them from commercial banks and dealers who need cash and are not willing to wait until their bills are due for redemption. When the Bank does purchase bills from commercial banks and dealers it pays with deposits on itself, thereby further increasing the nation's supply of legal cash.

The Bank deals in long term bonds as well as in treasury bills. Generally its

---

[11]A rider must be attached to this statement. As the government's fiscal agent, the Bank must ensure that the government always has sufficient funds. Now it could happen that the commercial banks, in a particular week, tendered for only a small part of the government's current issue of treasury bills. If nothing further were done the government might in that week be short of necessary cash. Accordingly, the Bank of Canada always submits a reserve bid in addition to its regular bid, to ensure that the government sells all its bills each week and obtains all the cash it needs.

[12]For example, if the Bank of Canada had regularly been buying treasury bills at the rate of $10 million worth per week then each week $10 million would be deducted from the government's deposit in the Bank. Through this deduction the Bank would obtain redemption for the bills it owned and which had now become due for repayment. Accordingly, if the Bank wished to reduce the country's cash supply by $10 million in a particular week, it could simply refrain from buying bills that week. In that case, while the usual $10 million would be deducted from the government's deposit as redemption of old bills there would be no offsetting payment of $10 million into the deposit, representing the Bank's payment for new bills. On the other hand, if the Bank wished to increase by $10 million the government's deposit (and therefore the country's supply of cash), it would buy $20 million of treasury bills. If it wished to keep the cash supply unchanged, it would buy just $10 million worth.

treasury bill dealings are designed to vary the country's cash supply in accordance with changing short term or seasonal requirements while its bond dealings are designed to bring about long term changes in the cash supply. In the usual manner of central banks, as described earlier in the chapter, the Bank buys bonds in order to increase the cash supply and sells bonds in order to reduce the cash supply. It appears too that the Bank manages the securities investment account in accordance with its open-market operations policy.

Control Over Commercial Bank Reserve Ratios

The 1954 amendment to the Bank Act authorized the Bank of Canada to vary the cash reserve ratio which commercial banks are required to keep, between eight and twelve per cent. (Hitherto the law had merely required the banks to keep no less than five per cent, although they had actually kept a ratio of about ten per cent.) The Bank in fact never called on the banks to maintain more than an 8 per cent reserve ratio, the minimum stipulated by the amendment of 1954. The reserve requirement was revised again by the amendment made to the Bank Act in 1967; henceforth banks were required to keep a cash reserve of 4 per cent against notice (savings) deposits and 12 per cent against demand deposits.

As we saw in the preceding chapter the commercial banks hold, as part of their assets, treasury bills and day-to-day loans to investment dealers. For each bank, these assets constitute a highly liquid reserve which can be turned into cash in a few hours' time. The Bank of Canada has since 1955 required the commercial banks to maintain at least a minimum amount of such assets. According to the regulations issued in 1969 the banks must keep a secondary reserve ratio of at least eight per cent against their deposit liabilities.[13]

"Bank Rate" in Canada

On only a very few occasions has Canada's financial community been obliged to turn for cash to the Bank of Canada. Accordingly the Bank Rate[14] periodically announced by the Bank on such advances has not been of prime significance. Prior to 1956 it was left unchanged for years at a time; changes were made primarily to signal the kind of monetary policy which the Bank intended to follow. When the Bank commenced operations in 1935, Bank Rate was set at two per cent. There it remained until 1944, when it was lowered to 1½ per cent as indication of the Bank's intention of maintaining a pattern of low interest rates into the postwar era. It was only changed in

---

[13]A bank's secondary reserves are defined as being the sum of its treasury bills, day-to-day loans to investment dealers and that portion of its cash holding which is in excess of the cash reserve requirement.

[14]Defined by the Bank of Canada as ". . . the minimum rate at which the central bank will lend for short periods to the chartered banks and the money market on the security of Treasury Bills and short-term Government bonds." Bank of Canada, *Annual Report* for the year 1955, p. 7.

October 1950, being then raised to two per cent. Inflationary pressures had developed as a result of the outbreak of the Korean War, and the increase in Bank Rate signalled the Bank's view that measures of monetary restraint were in order.

Table 1

BANK OF CANADA: ASSETS AND LIABILITIES 1966-70, AS OF DEC. 31
(Millions of dollars)

ASSETS	1966	1967	1968	1969	1970
Government of Canada Treasury Bills	409.1	538.3	453.4	477.7	621.2
Bonds	3,010.2	3,209.8	3,431.3	3,580.1	3,620.1
Foreign currency assets	226.9	101.6	106.7	160.6	194.5
Investments in Industrial Development Bank	281.8	315.2	354.0	403.3	469.6
All other assets	278.8	246.7	290.2	266.6	499.6
Total Assets	4,206.8	4,411.6	4,635.6	4,888.3	5,405.0
LIABILITIES					
Notes held by chartered banks	438.1	484.6	568.9	543.5	526.1
Notes held by public	2,295.5	2,494.4	2,660.3	2,902.7	3,106.2
Deposits of Government of Canada	34.1	42.2	47.4	80.9	228.0
Deposits of chartered banks	1,111.3	1,062.0	1,114.3	1,108.8	1,176.4
Other Canadian dollar deposits	29.7	37.9	38.4	42.0	37.9
Foreign currency liabilities	36.9	34.8	28.3	23.6	32.6
All other liabilities	261.2	255.7	178.0	186.7	297.8
Total Liabilities	4,206.8	4,411.6	4,635.6	4,888.2	5,405.0

In 1955 the Bank announced that henceforth Bank Rate would be made more flexible and would bear a closer relationship to shortterm interest rates prevailing in the market. Periodic changes were made in the Rate, in general accordance with the movement of these short term interest rates. Commencing November 1, 1956, Bank Rate was rigidly tied to short term interest rates, being set at ¼ of one per cent above the average rate on treasury bills.[15] In June 1962, however, as one of the measures designed to deal with the critical foreign exchange situation which had developed, Bank Rate was temporarily fixed at the high figure of 6 per cent. Since then the Bank has from time to time announced changes in Bank Rate, in accordance with its assessment of the prevailing situation.

Informal Agreements

The fact that there are a very small number of commerical banks in Canada renders it relatively easy for the governor of the Bank of Canada to meet informally with their

[15]Specifically, the average rate established at the most recent auction of such Bills.

chief executives, and indicate to them the policies he would like them to follow. A number of such meetings have been held since the end of World War II, at which the banks agreed to follow the policies suggested. In meetings held in February, 1951, the banks agreed not to expand their loans or investments any further; the Bank of Canada sought such a "ceiling" on bank credit as a means of repressing the inflationary pressure which had developed following the outbreak of the Korean War. In the fall of 1955, urgent anti-inflationary action again became necessary; to supplement its open-market operations and recent increases in Bank Rate, the Bank called upon the commercial banks to keep a tight rein on new lending. In addition, the Bank requested the instalment finance companies to restrict their lending, and the department and chain stores to restrict their credit sales. The response by these firms was not completely satisfactory. The chartered banks, however, which supplied a large proportion of the funds employed by finance companies and retail stores, limited their advances to them, and thereby brought about a restriction of their credit dealings.

The Bank of Canada's Operations: 1966-70

Table 1 indicates the main features of the Bank of Canada's open-market operations in the period 1966-70. Before referring to the table, let us recapitulate briefly some of the key points made earlier in this chapter and in Chapter 21.

The Bank of Canada creates the legal cash of the country;[16] this cash takes the form of currency which the Bank issues, and the deposits with which it credits the chartered banks and the federal government. The Bank creates this cash to pay for its purchases of treasury bills and federal government bonds. Whenever it buys these securities it increases correspondingly the country's supply of legal cash; when it sells such securities this supply decreases correspondingly.

When the Bank, through its purchase or sale of securities, varies the country's supply of legal cash, it brings about a much larger variation in the country's *total money supply*. The bulk of the nation's money supply consists of deposits credited to the public in the chartered banks. Against these deposits the chartered banks must hold a specified cash reserve ratio. Between 1966 and 1970 the volume of deposits in Canada's banks increased very substantially, for two quite different reasons. Firstly, because the Bank of Canada during the period bought additional treasury bills and bonds, the chartered banks acquired larger cash reserves, in the form of notes and deposits in the Bank of Canada. Their total cash reserve rose from $1,583 millions as of December, 1966, to $1,747 millions as of December, 1970. Secondly, and much more important, the banks were able in 1970 to maintain a smaller cash reserve *ratio*. Until 1967 they had been required to maintain a cash reserve of eight per cent against all their deposits. The amendment of that year to the Bank Act required them henceforth to maintain a cash reserve of twelve per cent against demand deposits and

---

[16]Except for the coins, these being issued by the Mint.

four per cent against savings deposits. Since savings deposits substantially exceeded demand deposits the overall effect was to bring about a reduction of the required ratio of cash reserve to total deposits; throughout 1970 the total amount of cash held by all the chartered banks amounted usually to something over six per cent of their total deposits. Consequently, while in 1966 they had aggregate deposits of $19,496 millions, or 12.3 times their cash reserve, in 1970 they had aggregate deposits of $28,589 millions or 16.4 times their cash reserve.

THE FEDERAL RESERVE SYSTEM

The Federal Reserve System performs for the U.S. the main functions of a central bank. It was organized in 1913, primarily because of a financial panic in 1907 which starkly revealed the inadequacies of the banking system as it existed at that time. Frantic depositors had drained lending institutions of their cash, and there had existed no "lender of last resort" from whom additional cash could be borrowed. Unable to meet depositors' demands for cash, many banks had closed their doors, bringing on a severe financial and economic crisis. Following a lengthy investigation of the nation's monetary system, Congress passed the Federal Reserve Act in 1913.

Under this Act the United States was divided up into twelve Federal Reserve Districts. Each District has a Federal Reserve Bank which serves in effect as the central bank for the District. It holds the reserves of member banks, issues paper currency, advances loans to member banks, and arranges for the efficient payment of inter-bank obligations. The capital of each Federal Reserve Bank is subscribed by banks within the District which are "members"[17] of the system, and they select six of its nine directors.[18] Member banks are required to maintain reserves as specified by the Federal Reserve System, and are rigorously supervised by their respective Reserve Banks.

The operations of the twelve Federal Reserve Banks are supervised and coordinated by a seven-man Board of Governors which maintains its office in Washington. Members of the Board of Governors are appointed by the President of the United States for fourteen-year terms, the terms being so arranged that every two years one man's appointment terminates. Both Reserve Banks and member banks are subject to the authority of the Board, in respect to important aspects of their operations. The Board's chief power derives, however, from the fact that its mem-

---

[17]All national banks are required to be members, while state banks may become members if they meet the requirements stipulated for national banks. A good many state banks have deliberately refrained from joining the System. In actual practice non-member banks may obtain practically all the benefits available to member banks without being subject to the costs, the restrictions, and the rigorous inspection.

[18]The other three are selected by the Board of Governors of the Federal Reserve System.

bers form a majority on the Federal Open-Market Committee, which determines what open-market operations are to be carried out by the System.[19]

SUMMARY

In a modern banking system some authority is required to perform two key functions: firstly, to ensure that the nation's money supply is of the proper size; secondly to serve as "lender of last resort" to banks which need cash in order to meet extraordinary demands from depositors.

The central bank performs these strategic functions, and generally some others as well. Because of the importance of its responsibilities a central bank is either an agency of the federal government, or is subject to the control of the government.

To regulate the size of the money supply, the central bank can employ a variety of measures. It can: engage in "open-market operations"; vary the cash reserve ratio which commercial banks are required to keep; vary the rate at which it discounts treasury bills; apply "moral suasion" to commercial banks.

Under the Finance Act of 1923 there existed in Canada a "lender of last resort," but without the responsibility or means to regulate the size of the money supply. The Bank of Canada, our central bank, was established in 1934.

FOR REVIEW AND DISCUSSION

1. Commercial bank profits are likely to be high during a period of "tight money." Why?
2. Had the Bank of Canada existed during the 1920s, it might not have been necessary for Canada to leave the gold standard in 1929, as in effect she did. Why?
3. If the federal government wished to sell more bonds to the commercial banks it might prove necessary to sell, first of all, some bonds to the Central Bank. Explain.
4. Suppose that the Bank of Canada, which hitherto has been buying $10 million worth of treasury bills per week, decides one week to buy only $5 million worth. How would the nation's money supply be affected?
5. There can be no financial panic in Canada so long as the Bank of Canada exists. Why?
6. Suggest reasons why the various control techniques which the central bank can employ to regulate the national money supply, may fail to be effective.
7. The banks of Canada generally opposed the establishment of a central bank in

[19]The other five members of this twelve-man Committee represent five different Reserve Banks.

1934, on the grounds that no need for it existed. Were they right or wrong, in your opinion?
8. Do you approve of the method by which "Bank Rate" is now set in Canada? Why or why not?
9. Suppose that the public's deposits in a certain banking system total $1,000 million, and that the banks maintain, as required, a 10 per cent cash reserve. Indicate the measures which the central bank might employ to bring about (a) an increase of $100 million in the total of the public's deposits; (b) a reduction of $100 million in these deposits. Indicate how the volume of bank loans and investments would be affected in each case.

PART EIGHT: NATIONAL INCOME

23 National Product and National Income

THE NATIONAL PRODUCT

Canada is a land richly endowed. In our Western plains we have millions of acres of fertile land; underneath them, randomly scattered, lie dozens of valuable desposits of oil and natural gas. Throughout the Pre-Cambrian Shield occur numerous pockets of ore rich in valuable minerals. The thin soil cover of the Shield supports trees which can be transformed by modern technology into paper. Forests of trees suitable for lumber and paper-making cover vast areas of British Columbia; underneath this province's soil lie major deposits of minerals and natural gas. Throughout the Maritime Provinces, in Central Canada and in British Columbia, occur pockets and extensive areas of good farm land. Off both our Atlantic and Pacific coasts, a dozen varieties of edible fish swarm seasonally. To the freely given bounty of nature, man has added his laboriously built fabrications. Generations of Canadians, aided by tools, materials and skills supplied by foreigners, have laid railway lines and highways across the land, constructed factories, stores and warehouses, schools and hospitals, churches and homes.

The people of Canada apply their brains and energy to the rich natural resources of the country, availing themselves of the tools, machinery and buildings accumulated in the country. They apply themselves in a thousand different ways, each helpful; they work as farmers, lumbermen, factory hands, executives, doctors, engineers. Each year their efforts produce an immense quantity and variety of goods—hundreds of millions of loaves of bread, hundreds of millions of pounds of meat, millions of shirts, hundreds of thousands of automobiles, thousands of houses. And in addition to these tangible goods, they produce intangible services, activities which are valuable in themselves; doctors heal the sick, teachers educate the young, members of the armed forces stand guard, performing artists entertain.

The sum total of tangible goods and intangible services which the people of Canada produce in any year we call Canada's National Product for that year. Its size will reflect the richness and variety of our natural resources, the size, skill and energy of our working population, the abundance of helpful equipment and tools, the intelligence and organizational ability with which we direct our energies and employ our capacities.

The Composition of the National Product

For purposes of analysis the National Product is classified into four broad categories as follows:

1. Consumption goods and services: those goods and services which are required by the general public for everyday living, such as food, clothing, shelter, recreational and personal services.
2. Investment goods: buildings, machinery, equipment and materials, which are required by business firms for purposes of production, replacement, modernization and expansion; the houses and apartment blocks required to house our growing populations and to replace dwellings torn down or destroyed by fire.
3. Government goods and services: the public works which governments build, and the services of education, protection, and administration which federal, provincial and local governments provide.
4. Exports: the goods and services which we sell during the year to foreigners. [However, as we shall see shortly, the value of imports must be deducted.]

Just How Big Is the National Product?

Economists would like to know—we shall see later why—what the size of the National Product is each year. How can we measure something which consists of thousands of heterogeneous items? How can we add bushels of wheat to men's shirts and surgical operations and come up with an answer which means anything?

In fact, it is not impossible. All we need do is find out the money value of each of the goods and services produced, and then add up these individual money values. This aggregate will be the total money value of all the goods and services produced during the year, and this figure will represent the size of the National Product for the year. Suppose our National Product for the year consisted of only three items: 500 million bushels of wheat valued at $2 per bushel, 100,000 houses which sold for $15,000 each, and concerts attended by 20 million people, with each person paying an admission charge of $3.50. In this case the value of our National Product would be $2,570 million, being comprised of $1,000 million worth of wheat, $1,500 million worth of houses, and $70 million worth of entertainment.

The Danger of Exaggeration

The money value of Canada's National Product for any year is supposed to represent the value of all the goods and services produced by the people of Canada during the year. In measuring this total we must be very careful, however. It is all too easy to give ourselves more credit than we deserve. If we merely added up the values of all the goods and services produced and sold in Canada during any year, and claimed the resulting total as our National Product for that year we would be over-stating, for *three* reasons.

Double Counting. If we simply added up the market values of all things that were produced in Canada during the year, we would be counting the value of some things more than once. Thus suppose that during the year we produced $10 million worth of wheat, all of which was milled into flour, the flour having a value of $15 million. Say that this flour was then baked into bread, which sold for $27 million. Now the wheat, the flour, and the bread might have all been produced in Canada in the same year. But if we included in our National Product the value of the wheat *and* the value of the flour *and* the value of the bread, we would be double and triple counting. For the value of the flour *includes* the value of the wheat which went into it, and the value of the bread *includes* the value of the flour which went into it. Accordingly, if in computing the National Product we counted in all three, we would be seriously exaggerating. We would be counting the flour twice, once as flour and the second time as part of the bread and we would be counting the wheat three times, once as wheat, once as part of the flour, and a third time as part of the bread.

To avoid such double and triple counting, we must make sure to exclude from our calculation of the National Product any good or service which is used up during the year to produce something else. Its value is embodied in the thing which it helps to produce, and is consequently being allowed for when we count the value of that product. Accordingly, we should count as part of the National Product only the goods or services which are ultimately produced; we should not include the *intermediate products* which are used up in the production process, since their value is incorporated in the value of the *final products*. Hence in the example given above we should include the $27 million of bread in our National Product, but not the $10 million worth of wheat, nor the $15 million worth of flour.[1]

Imported Goods and Services. We must make allowance for the fact that foreigners have contributed in various ways to the production of the goods and services sold in Canada. Some of the goods sold in Canada were grown or manufactured in foreign countries; many of the goods and services produced in Canada were produced with the aid of materials, skilled labour and capital supplied by foreign countries. Our National Product in any year is supposed to represent the output achieved through the efforts of the Canadian people in that year; from the total value of goods and services sold in Canada during the year we must therefore subtract the value of foreign goods, materials and assistance. Only the balance represents the value of *our own* production.

---

[1]Theoretically we might use an alternative method of calculating the National Product which would also ensure against multiple-counting. We might include in our National Product only the *value added* at each stage of production. Thus we could say that farmers produced a value of $10 million of wheat; millers contributed a value of $5 million by transforming $10 million of wheat into $15 million of flour; bakers added a value of $12 million by transforming $15 million of flour into $27 million of bread. This procedure yields the same result—$27 million—as is derived from the method of counting final products only. The *value-added* method is not used in actual practice, however, since it would require far more statistical effort than does the final products methods.

Depreciation of Capital. We must allow for the following consideration. The buildings and equipment which exist in Canada and which are used to produce a year's National Product, suffered loss of value during the year, through wear and tear in use and through obsolescence with the passage of time. Prudence requires that we set aside a sufficient portion of the year's output to restore and replenish our heritage of physical capital. Otherwise in future years we would find that our productive capacity had diminished, owing to the un-compensated deterioration of our buildings and equipment. Prudent reckoning dictates that we consider as the National Product for any year only what is left after we have subtracted from our total output an amount sufficient to offset the depreciation incurred by our physical capital during that year.

Gross and Net National Product

In our National Accounting, we distinguish between two versions of the National Product, as follows:

Gross National Product, being the total value of goods and services produced by our nation in one year. (Avoiding double-counting, of course, and excluding the value of imported goods and services.)

Net National Product, being Gross National Product *minus* the depreciation which occurred during the year in the value of the physical capital which we possessed at the start of the year.

Gross and Net Capital Formation

In computing the value of the capital goods (buildings, machinery, equipment, inventory) which we produced during the year, we likewise distinguish between two versions, as follows:

Gross Capital Formation, being the total value of capital produced during the year.

Net Capital Formation, being the value of capital goods produced during the year *minus* the depreciation incurred by the stock of capital goods which we possessed at the start of the year.

The NNP Figure not Practical to Use

While prudence dictates that we consider the Net National Product as being the appropriate measure of our production for any year, economists in fact generally use the Gross National Product to represent the amount of a nation's annual product. The reason is simple: We can compute the GNP with reasonable precision; it consists of the goods and services actually produced and sold during the year and can therefore be measured quite closely. The NNP, however, can only be estimated. It consists of the GNP minus the depreciation incurred during the year on our capital equipment. Just what the value of this capital was, and what amount of depreciation it suffered during the year, can never be precisely ascertained. Different persons would make different estimates, and we could have a wide range of figures put forward. Our Net National Product figure would depend accordingly upon which of the various estimates of depreciation we decided to subtract from the Gross National Product.

To avoid this confusion economists use the GNP figure to represent a nation's output for the year. It has the merit of being derived strictly from ascertainable facts, with no element of conjecture involved. As a measure of a nation's annual production the Net National Product figure is logically superior, but it is inferior from the practical point of view. Since we wish to use the concept of National Product for highly practical purposes, practical superiority wins out over logical excellence.

Two Methods of Measuring the GNP

How do statisticians ascertain the total value of all the goods and services which compose the GNP? There are in fact two methods that may be used; both should yield the same result.

The Expenditures Method. The statistician finds out how much was actually paid for all the goods and services produced in the country during the year (avoiding double counting, of course, and excluding payments for imports). This figure would be the market value of everything produced during the year by the people of the country and would therefore represent the GNP.

The Income Method. All of the money paid for the goods and services that were produced was received by the people who produced them. This money constituted their earned income for the year. Accordingly, if we found out how much income was earned by the people of the country during the year, that figure should correspond to the value of what they had produced. (We shall note two relatively minor qualifications.)

The following highly simplified example illustrates why the expenditures method and income method must yield the same result. Suppose that Farmer Brown produces a crop in 1970 which he sells for $10,000. The $10,000 paid to him by the purchaser would naturally be taken as representing the value of Brown's production for the year. But this $10,000 becomes his income for the year; his income therefore also represents the value of his production.

Canada's GNP and National Income, 1966-70

Tables 1 and 2 set forth the size and composition of Canada's GNP in each of the years 1966-70. Table 1 shows how the GNP is derived using the expenditures method: it corresponds to the aggregate of expenditures made to purchase the goods and services produced by the people of Canada. Table 2 shows how the GNP is derived using the income method: it corresponds to the money paid out to the persons who produced the goods and services which comprised the GNP. However, the amount earned by people is not fully equal to the value of the country's output, for two reasons: a part of the market value of the country's total output is allocated to depreciation, and another part is paid to governments in various types of sales tax. What remains after these two deductions is the income earned by the people who produced that output.

Table 1

Canadian Gross National Expenditure, 1966-70*
(millions of dollars)

	1966	1967	1968	1969	1970
Personal expenditure on consumer goods and services	34,480	37,714	40,916	46,531	48,995
Government expenditure on goods and services	11,169	12,377	13,329	16,732	19,054
Private residential construction	2,178	2,337	2,831	3,843	3,537
Private non-residential construction	4,811	4,716	4,683	4,773	5,253
Private outlays on machinery and equipment	5,225	5,556	5,239	5,574	5,919
Value of physical change in inventories	995	225	660	1,043	122
Exports of goods and services	13,073	14,748	16,735	18,468	20,969
DEDUCT:					
Imports of goods and services	−14,280	−15,415	−17,067	−19,435	−19,833
Residual error of estimate	−273	−149	42	1,031	452
GROSS NATIONAL EXPENDITURE AT MARKET PRICES	57,738	62,109	67,368	78,560	84,468

*Compiled from *Canadian Statistical Review,* 1967-70.

Personal Income

The National Income is the total income earned by the people of the country, earned as a reward for the productive services which they have contributed during the year and which collectively have produced the Gross National Product. The income which people *earn* is not, however, identical with the income which they actually *receive.* Four reasons are cited below, why *earned income* does not correspond to *received income.*

1. Many workers nowadays receive part of their earnings not in cash but in benefits; employers, for instance, may pay medical insurance premiums on behalf of their staffs; the cost of these premiums represents money which the employees have earned and which employers pay out for their benefit, but not in actual cash which workers receive.

2. The government imposes a tax upon profits earned by firms. The profit of a firm represents the reward for the productive services performed by shareholders;

Table 2

CANADA'S NATIONAL INCOME AND GROSS NATIONAL PRODUCT, 1966-70*
(Millions of dollars)

	1966	1967	1968	1969	1970
Wages, salaries and supplementary labour income	29,324	32,389	35,225	43,203	47,043
Military pay and allowances	621	704	696	898	906
Corporation profits before taxes	5,187	5,020	5,877	7,852	7,364
Deduct: Dividends paid to non-residents	−797	−798	−841	−818	−906
Rent, interest and miscellaneous investment income	3,903	4,339	4,758	3,187	3,614
Accrued net income of farm operators from farm production	2,204	1,698	1,796	1,695	1,369
Net income of non-farm unincorporated business (inc. rent)	2,949	3,194	3,422	4,410	4,551
Inventory valuation adjustment	−318	−291	−305	−549	−171
NET NATIONAL INCOME AT FACTOR COST	43,073	46,255	50,628	59,878	63,770
Indirect taxes less subsidies**	7,800	8,705	9,521	10,647	11,251
Capital consumption allowances and miscellaneous valuation adjustments	6,591	7,000	7,260	9,066	9,898
Residual error of estimate				−1,031	−451
GROSS NATIONAL PRODUCT AT MARKET PRICES	57,738	62,109	67,368	78,560	84,468

*Compiled from *Canadian Statistical Review*, 1967-70.

**As noted above, part of the money taken in by business firms through the sale of their products must be paid to the government in sales (indirect) taxes, and is therefore not paid out by firms as income. But the government also pays subsidies to some producers. The net amount by which governments reduce the amount available to be paid out as income is therefore the total of indirect taxes which they impose on business minus the aggregate amount which they pay to firms in subsidies.

through its tax on corporate profits, the govenment takes away a portion of the money which investors have earned, before it can be paid to them as income.

3. Not all the profits left to firms after government taxation are paid out to investors; directors frequently retain some portion, in the form of undistributed profits, for re-investment in their respective companies.

4. Some people receive cash income which they have not actually earned. Many individuals receive so-called *transfer payments*, usually from the government, and consisting of such items as old age pensions, family allowances and welfare assistance. They receive these payments, not in return for any productive services which they have rendered, but on essentially humanitarian grounds.

If we are to find out what money income the people of Canada *actually received* in any year, we must subtract from the National Income items one to three above, which represent money earned but not received, and add item four, which represents money received but not earned. The resulting total would be the income *actually received* by people during the year, and this figure we would call the nation's *Personal Income.*

Disposable Income

One point more: the money income which people receive is not wholly theirs to do with as they please. The government levies a personal income tax which compulsorily exacts from a great many people some portion of their incomes. It is only the remainder which they can spend as they like, or save if they choose. The aggregate of money income which people have left after paying their personal income taxes, is known as the nation's *Disposable Income.*

Table 3

SOURCES AND DISPOSITION OF CANADIAN PERSONAL INCOME, 1969-70*
(millions of dollars)

Sources	*1969*	*1970*
Wages, salaries and supplementary labour income	43,203	47,043
Military pay and allowances	898	906
Net income of farm operators from farm production	1,644	1,162
Net income of non-farm unincorporated business, including rent	4,410	4,551
Interest, dividends and miscellaneous investment income	4,961	5,400
Transfer payments from government	6,060	6,804
Other transfer payments	222	234
Equals PERSONAL INCOME	61,398	66,100
Disposition		
Expenditures		
On goods	28,843	30,123
On services	17,688	18,872
Income taxes	7,469	8,779
Contributions to social insurance and government pension funds	2,341	2,420
Other transfer payments	1,623	1,931
Personal savings	3,434	3,975
Equals PERSONAL INCOME	61,398	66,100

*Compiled from *Canadian Statistical Review,* March, 1971, Tables 1.4 and 1.5

National Income Concepts: Summary

The following schematic table presents in summary fashion the relationship between the concepts of Gross National Product, National Income, Personal Income, and Disposable Income.

| GNP | Consumption Goods and Services + | Investment Goods + | Government Goods and Services + | Exports minus Imports |

less: Indirect taxes,
       Depreciation allowances,

equals

| National Income | Earned labour income | Total + Earned Profit | + Rent | + Interest |

less: Non-cash labour income,
       Corporation profit taxes,
       Undistributed profits
plus: Transfer payments

equals

| Personal Income | Cash labour income + | Distributed Profits + Rent + Interest + | Transfer payments received |

less: Personal Income Tax,

equals

| Disposable Income | Spending on personal Consumption + | Personal Saving |

When Making Comparisons, Beware

We must not draw hasty conclusions from simple comparisons of Canadian GNP figures for different years. For five different reasons, changes in these figures might not properly reflect the actual change in the output of the country and the material well-being of its people.

1. Change in the Price Level. The price level might have risen or fallen. The Canadian GNP was $57,738 million in 1966 and $84,468 million in 1970, or 46 per cent greater. However, the Consumer Price Index was 17 per cent higher in 1970 than in 1966 so that a dollar could buy only $\frac{100}{117}$ as much in 1970 as a dollar bought in 1966. The goods and services produced in 1970, which sold in that year for $84,468 million, would have sold for only $72,287 million if prices in that year had been at the same level as in 1966. Part of the 46 per cent increase in GNP was due to the rise in prices; in real terms the increase in output between 1966 and 1970 was only 25 per cent.

2. Change in size of Population. The Canadian population increased from 20,015,000 in 1966 to 21,377,000 in 1970. The GNP *per capita* amounted to

$2,885 in 1966 and to $3,951 in 1970, an increase of 37 per cent. If we allow as well for the fact that a 1970 dollar was worth only $\frac{100}{117}$ of a 1966 dollar, then the increase in real output per capita was only 17 per cent. Table 4 compactly summarizes these figures.

Table 4

CANADA'S GNP, POPULATION AND GNP PER CAPITA, 1966-70

	1966	1970	Change 1966-70
GNP at current prices	$57,738 million	$84,468 million	+46%
Consumer Price Index, 1961 = 100	111	129.7	+17%
GNP valued at 1966 prices*	$57,738 million	$72,287 million	+25%
Population of Canada	20,015,000	21,377,000	+6.8%
GNP per capita, at current prices	$2,885	$3,951	+37%
GNP per capita, at 1966 prices	$2,885	$3,382	+17%

*The Consumer Price Index is used as deflator.

3. Some Welfare Gains not Reflected in GNP Figures. The number of hours worked per week by the average Canadian declined slightly between 1961 and 1970; the gain in leisure constituted an improvement in our well-being but was not reflected in National Income statistics. Another factor which affects our well-being is the amount we possess of durable goods such as automobiles and furniture; the more we possess of them, the more satisfaction we have. This element in our welfare is not included in our GNP figures, since these figures refer only to goods and services produced and sold during the year. In 1970 we had more automobiles, furniture, and the like than in 1966 and therefore derived more satisfaction from their use; the increase in this element in our well-being was not reflected in the official statistics.

4. Value of Goods and Services Produced at Home. A change may have occurred in the volume of goods and services which people produce for themselves at home and whose value is not recorded in the statistics of National Income and GNP. Years ago, for instance, housewives made jam at home while today most housewives buy their jam in grocery stores. When they made their own jam the value was not included in the GNP figures and the value of work done was not included in the National Income. Today when jam is produced in a factory its value is included in the GNP and the value of the work done is included in the National Income. Our national income figures overstate the gain in real welfare which has occurred in the past generation or so by the extent to which people now buy commercially produced goods and services which formerly were provided at home.[2] On the other hand, our

[2]This sort of consideration has given rise to the sardonic observation that if a man marries his housekeeper then the GNP and National Income would go down—as probably would also the quality of his housekeeping.

current figures do not include the value—and it is substantial—of the goods and services produced at home on a do-it-yourself basis.

5. Varying Composition of the GNP. As we noted earlier in this chapter, the composition of the GNP may vary from one year to another. The variation may be substantial, and highly significant in respect to people's material well-being. In wartime, for instance, a nation's GNP may be large, but the production of consumer goods and services may be very limited. Even in peacetime a nation's GNP may contain a relatively small proportion of consumer goods and services; munitions and military services may bulk large, while a high proportion of civilian output may consist of capital goods.

Why Bother with All This?

Economists have painstakingly worked out precise definitions of Gross National Product, National Income, and related concepts. Each year statisticians laboriously collect mountains of statistical data in order to ascertain the value of the year's GNP, National Income, and their component categories. The work is agreeable and the pay is good but is there any useful purpose served by all this careful labour?

The answer is yes. The assembly of all this statistical data serves more than merely to satisfy our curiosity and provide appropriate employment for statisticians. After being properly classified, the figures on production and income reveal to us the rate at which our economy has been growing, and indicate whether or not we are currently utilizing to the full our productive capacity. Analysis of the composition of the GNP indicates in what proportion we are currently producing the various categories of goods and services which collectively constitute each year's output. Examination of the composition of the National Income reveals how the National Product is being distributed among different categories of persons.

It may well happen that the GNP and the National Income turn out to be greatly different, in size and composition, from what we consider to be appropriate. In recent years a variety of measures have been devised whereby both the aggregate and the composition of our nation's production and income can be affected. Intelligent application of these measures requires accurate knowledge of the problem to be dealt with—accurate figures on the actual size and composition of the Gross National Product and the National Income. It is in order to furnish us with this information that statisticians laboriously collect the multitudinous details of each year's production and income, and classify them into precisely defined categories.

SUMMARY

The National Product of a country is simply the total of the goods and services which its people produce during a year. It is composed of four broad categories of product: consumption goods and services, capital goods, government goods and services, and exports.

The size of the National Product is ascertained by totalling the money values of its component elements. Care must be taken to avoid double counting; the value of goods and services supplied by foreigners must be excluded.

The National Product is the nation's real income, for the goods and services which the country produces during the year belong to its people as their income. The money value of the National Product is distributed to the people of the country as money income, each person receiving his appropriate reward for his contribution toward the National Product. Not quite the whole value of the National Product is earned as income by people; a portion of that value is appropriated by the government in duties, sales, and excise taxes; another portion is set aside by businessmen in depreciation allowances.

Personal Income, the cash income which people actually receive, differs from National Income because: many people do not receive in cash all of the income which they have earned; many people receive cash income which they have not actually earned.

Disposable Income, the money which people have available to spend or save, is less than Personal Income by the amount of personal income taxes which individuals have to pay.

Comparison of a country's GNP for different years provides unreliable testimony as to how the real welfare of the people has changed in the interim.

Governments nowadays collect detailed statistics regarding the GNP and National Income each year, in order to have a factual basis for major policy decisions.

FOR REVIEW AND DISCUSSION

1. Which figure in your opinion, would serve as a better measure of real welfare, Personal Income or Disposable Income? Justify your answer.
2. The interests of all economic groups in the country are fundamentally in conflict. One group can gain only at the expense of others. Do you agree? Why, or why not?
3. Why should we include the value of exports, but exclude the value of imports, in computing the GNP?
4. Which would constitute a better measure of a nation's product for a year, the GNP or the NNP? Justify your answer.
5. The GNP and National Income are essentially the same thing. Comment.
6. A simple comparison of the GNP or National Income figures of two different years is liable to be very misleading, Explain.

24

Expenditure, Production and Income

DETERMINANTS OF THE NATIONAL PRODUCT

The national product, as we saw in the last chapter, is the aggregate of goods and services which a nation produces in a year and constitutes the nation's real income for the year. This total varies greatly from one country to another and, within the same country, may vary considerably from one year to another. Why? What factors determine the size of any country's total output in any particular year?

We begin our explanation with a truism. The actual production of any organization will depend upon two basic determinants: firstly, upon its physical capacity to produce, secondly, upon the degree to which it employs that capacity. This is as true for the performance of an individual and the output of a factory as it is for the production of an entire nation. Differences in actual achievement may be attributable either to differences in capacity, or to differences in the degree to which capacity is used, or to both. Having regard to this fundamental truism, if we are to understand why the national product of a country was of a certain size in any year, we must find out what its productive capacity was, and if its actual output was less than this maximum amount, we must search out the reasons why.

National Productive Capacity

Self-evidently, a nation's productive capacity depends upon the following four general considerations:

1. *The size and quality of its work force.* This in turn will reflect the size of the total population, the proportion of the population which is in the labour force, the skill and training of workers, the time and energy they devote to their tasks.
2. *The country's natural resources.* Quite obviously a nation which is blessed with much fertile land, rich mineral deposits, extensive forests and agreeable climate, will be able to produce much more than it could if it were less well endowed by nature.
3. *The amount of capital equipment available.* A nation which possesses an extensive, well-equipped railway network, ample and well-constructed highways and

airfields, modern power generating plants, well-equipped factories, will be able to produce more because it has this abundance of equipment and facilities.

4. *The mode of industrial organization.* Nowadays, in a great many industries, efficiency increases with the size of the individual plant. Workers and equipment will produce a great deal if organized into large plants which emphasize specialization of tasks and assembly line methods of production. Organized into small shops the same workers and equipment are likely to produce much less.

The Utilization of Capacity

The better endowed a nation is, in terms of the attributes described above, the greater will be its productive capacity; the less well endowed, the smaller will be its capacity. However, its potential, whether great or small, may not be its actual production. The nation may fail, sometimes by a wide margin, to produce all that it is physically capable of producing. During most of the 1930s Canada's annual production probably amounted to only about two-thirds or three-quarters of the total which could have been produced with the means available. A great many workers and machines were idle or only partially employed; the goods and services which they could have produced in that idle time were simply not produced.

How Is Productive Capacity Activated?

Just what determines the extent to which a country's productive capacity is actually utilized? The nature of its society is a prime factor. In a slave state, for instance, it will be the vigilance and competence of the overseers which determines how completely the available productive capacity is utilized. Slaves do only what they are commanded to do; it is the responsibility of the overseers to watch over their charges continuously, giving an incessant stream of orders. Failure on the part of overseers to issue the right commands at the right times would result in slaves being temporarily idle, for lack of orders as to what to do next. Their output would be less than it might have been; it could have been greater had the overseers been more vigilant and more prompt to issue orders for new tasks the instant old tasks had been completed.

In a modern, free society, productive effort is performed not in response to the commands of overseers, but in response to the payment of money. It is the payment of money which induces workers to work, businessmen to manage their concerns, landlords to make available their property, capitalists to subscribe their capital. Money talks, orders and persuades. Whereas in a slave society the utilization of avaliable productive capacity will depend upon the commands issued by the overseers, in a free society the utilization of capacity will depend upon the total amount of money spent.

THE AGGREGATE OF EXPENDITURES: ITS COMPONENTS

What determines the total amount of money spent? What causes this figure to vary from year to year within the one country, producing variation in the degree to which productive capacity is actually used?[1] To answer these questions we must find out on what things people spend their money, and why they vary their expenditures on these things from time to time.

We saw in the last chapter that a nation's product consists of four broad categories of goods and services: consumption goods and services, capital goods, government goods and services, and exports. The total amount of money spent in a country in any year will be the aggregate of the expenditures on these four categories of goods and services. To appreciate why the total amount spent in a country is at any particular level and why the figure varies from one year to another, we must know the considerations which determine the amount expended on each of the four categories listed above.

1. Consumption Goods and Services

Income the Main Determinant. The total amount of money spent by a nation upon consumption goods and services is simply the sum of all the expenditures made by the individual families which form the nation. On the basis of our own experience and such research studies as have been carried out, we know that for any individual family the consideration which will chiefly determine its spending will be its income. A family with a low income will spend little; a family with a high income will spend a great deal. The family of a low paid labourer eats poor food and in limited quantity, buys new clothes only occasionally and then at low prices, lives in poor housing, and enjoys few luxuries. The family of the millionaire eats the choicest of foods, in some cases wasting a great deal, frequently purchases expensive clothes, occupies a large and handsome dwelling and enjoys elaborate recreational activities.

There are some wealthy eccentrics who live very meanly, but they are exceptions. We shall be right, by and large, if we take it for granted that their income is the single most important determinant of the amount that people spend, and that the larger their incomes the more do people spend.

Income Is Not Everything. "Money isn't everything", ran a once popular song, "so long as you have dough." In any examination of the determinants of spending on consumption, it becomes evident that income is not everything, particularly where incomes are large and a substantial proportion of consumer spending is on luxuries. Since the need for them is not strong, the spending on them is not steady. At any given

---

[1]As we have already noted in Chapter 23, not all of the money spent in a country on the purchase of goods and services is received by factors of production. Some of this money is spent on imports; some is taken by the government in indirect taxes; some is set aside in depreciation allowances. It is the remainder—that is actually paid out to factors of production—which activates productive capacity.

time people's spending decisions will be affected by a broad variety of considerations, quite apart from the amount of income they have available to spend. Let us look at the reasons why people may vary their spending between one time and another, although their income may not have changed at all.

People's need and desire for goods may be different at different times. If they already possess an ample supply of the sort of goods they need to maintain their standard of living, they unlikely to be anxious to buy more. On the other hand, if people are short of the sort of goods they want, they are likely to be eager buyers, prepared to spend their full incomes. Quite possibly, by borrowing or drawing on savings, they might spend even more than their incomes. Immediately after the end of World War II, for instance, people everywhere were anxious to buy goods of all kinds. On this continent there was a wild scramble for automobiles, appliances, clothes, houses, furniture, all things which had not been produced during the preceding five years. Within a few years this backlog of demand had been largely filled, and people's eagerness to spend declined substantially. This change in their desire to spend reflected not so much changes in their incomes as changes in the stocks of goods which they already possessed.

The attractiveness of consumer goods, which may vary from one year to another, will also determine how much of their income people will spend. When the automobile firms turn out attractive new models, sales tend to be higher; when the new models lack appeal, the year's sales tend to be lower. Variation in the appeal of advertising may also be responsible for variation in the level of consumer spending.

The expectations which people hold, in regard to future prices and their own future incomes, will determine in part their present spending. When people expect prices to rise they will buy as much as possible now, while prices are still low. When people expect their incomes to rise in the future, they will feel free to spend their current incomes. When they have such expectations they may in fact spend more than their current incomes; they may borrow or buy on the instalment plan, expecting to repay their obligations easily in the future when their incomes will be larger. On the other hand, when people expect that prices will be lower in the future, or that their incomes may be lower in the future, they will tend to reduce their present spending.

The length of time a person has had his present income may be a factor in his spending decisions. If a person suffers a decline in income, he may not immediately adjust his standard of living to his new, lower income; he may borrow or draw on savings rather than give up the manner of living to which he has become accustomed. By the same token, a person whose income has increased may continue for some time to live on his former scale, being unwilling to leave his old friends and his old neighbourhood, even though he could afford to do so.

People's expectations in regard to their future need for money will also affect their present spending decisions. Those people who anticipate needing a good deal of money in the future—to put children through college, for a rainy day, for their old age—will for that reason refrain from spending all of their income, preferring to save a fair proportion. Here it may be noted that the general drift in recent years toward the "welfare state" has profoundly affected the desire and need of people to save on such account. With governments providing free a good many of the things which people formerly had to provide for themselves out of savings, the motivation for saving is now smaller than it used to be; many people feel free to save less and spend more than they did formerly. Government (and privately subscribed) grants now provide free, or nearly free, college education to very large numbers of young persons; parents need not save so much for this purpose. Governments provide old age pensions, free hospital treatment, unemployment insurance benefits. Governments have also committed themselves to maintaining full employment in their respective countries. For every worker there is less danger that he might some day lose his job and be unable to find another. With governments guaranteeing shelter on "rainy days", and promising to eliminate some of the rainy days altogether, the need for the individual to provide his own umbrella through saving is correspondingly less.

Furthermore, the pressure on the individual to save money for anticipated future needs will depend upon *how large his savings are already*. The person who has managed to accumulate a substantial bank balance or a goodly number of bonds, has already secured himself against the future. On the other hand, the person who possesses no savings at all is for that very reason under pressure to save. The size of a person's past savings is likely to influence his present spending: the larger his savings, the larger is likely to be his spending; the smaller his savings, the smaller is his spending likely to be. For example, when World War II ended, a great many people possessed far larger savings than they had ever managed to accumulate before; the reason was, in many cases, that they had been unable to spend as much money during the war as they would have liked, because the goods they wanted were simply not available. When goods became available after the war, these people rushed to buy. Unquestionably the fact that they possessed large savings was a powerful support to their demand. Many people spent their savings to buy what they needed, so that their expenditures actually exceeded their incomes. Others, while not drawing on savings, were quite prepared to spend their full incomes; they considered their savings to be adequate and felt no need to save any more.

Finally, *the availability of credit* may be a limiting factor on consumer expenditures. A great many people who have no cash would like to buy goods on "terms," paying in instalments over an extended period. At times merchants may be quite happy to sell on "terms." Their own suppliers may be prepared to wait for payment; or the merchants may have ample cash out of which they could pay suppliers; or they could readily borrow from the banks the money they need to pay suppliers. At other times, however, merchants may be unable or unwilling to sell on credit. Suppliers may demand immediate payment for goods; the merchants may have no cash of their own; the banks may be unwilling to lend. At such times, merchants would only sell to those people who were able to pay cash for their purchases. Variation in the degree to which credit is available would be responsible for variation in the scale of consumer spending. What is more, the extent to which people have bought on credit in the past will affect their capacity to spend in the present. If they must make large monthly payments on account of goods bought in the past, less of their income is available for current purchases.

In the light of the various considerations outlined above, we must not assume that there exists in fact a rigid, unvarying relationship between income and expenditure. At various times the strength of these other determinants may cause the actual expenditures of individuals, and of an entire nation, to diverge markedly from what one might expect on the basis of individual incomes and the National Income.

2. Capital Goods

With probably very few exceptions, businessmen spend money on plant, machinery and equipment for one reason: to earn profit. The total amount spent on such capital goods by the businessmen of a country during any one year will depend, therefore, upon the number and size of the profitable opportunities which they see during that year. What are these profitable opportunities? What sort of development will induce businessmen to invest in the construction of additional plant and equipment? (An important cautionary warning must be issued here. In the context of national income analysis the term "investment" is applied only to the spending of money on the construction of *new* buildings, *new* machinery, *new* equipment and the like. The purchase of already existing capital goods by a businessman is not reckoned to be part of the country's investment for the year since it merely brings about a transfer of ownership from one person to another of something which the country already possesses. From the national standpoint investment is carried out only when the country as a whole acquires additional capital goods.)

The Expansion of Sales Opportunities. If businessmen expect that they will be able to sell more of their product than they can turn out with their existing plant, they will presumably wish to enlarge their plant or to build an additional one. They may have such an expectation for any of several reasons. The country's *population may be growing* and, therefore, the number of customers for the firm's products may be growing. *Incomes and living standards may be rising*, and people may be buying more of most types of goods and services than they did formerly. The rise in incomes and living standards may appear likely to continue, giving rise to an ever increasing demand for goods.

Additional markets may develop in new geographical areas. Possibly as a result of trade agreements or improvements in transportation, markets may emerge in foreign countries. New markets may come into being within the same country, as land hitherto vacant becomes settled and the settlers become customers. The settlement of Western Canada during the three decades 1885-1914 furnished a major new market for the factories, wholesale firms and financial institutions of Eastern Canada, and they greatly expanded their plant and facilities during that era.

Innovation of Attractive Consumer Goods. The development of new customer goods which have strong public appeal will give rise to investment. Businessmen, anticipating that profit can be earned in the production of these goods, will build the plant and equipment required to produce them. The more attractive and costly the new goods which are developed, the greater will likely be the investment made to produce them. The introduction of the automobile was the basis of a huge aggregate of investment, in factories to produce parts, in plants to assemble the parts, in filling stations, garages and show rooms. The invention of the electric stove and refrigerator gave rise to heavy investment in the plants required to produce them. The introduction of television involved heavy investment in plants to produce T.V. sets, and investment, on a very large scale, in transmitting stations, coaxial cables and relay stations.

The Discovery of Valuable Natural Resources. With each passing year the world's industrial plants consume an ever larger volume of raw materials—iron, coal, copper, zinc, lead, aluminum, oil. Each year the world's increasing automobile population requires more gasoline and lubricants. At all times the search goes on for new mineral deposits, for new sources of gas and oil, to replace sources which have been exhausted and to furnish the additional amounts required each year. When new ore bodies or oil pools are discovered, large scale investment follows in the physical plant required to recover the resources from the earth, to transform them into usable form, and transport them to where they can be used. The discovery of oil at Leduc, Alberta, in 1947, for instance, has been responsible for billions of dollars' worth of investment in Western Canada, in exploration activities, in the drilling of oil wells, in the construction of pipelines and refineries. The discovery of vast iron ore deposits in Quebec and Labrador has been responsible for massive investment in mining plant, in railway lines to carry ore to an ocean port, and in loading facilities at that port.

The Development of Superior Capital Goods. If new machines are invented which enable goods to be produced more cheaply than before, businessmen will presumably wish to acquire and use them. Businessmen who are reluctant to invest in the new equipment may find themselves forced to do so: competitors who have introduced the new machines will be underselling them.

The goods or services produced by some types of capital goods may be of strategic significance to the entire economy, being required in the production of all sorts of other products. All industries require transportation services, power supplies, communications equipment; a very great number of industries require steel in some form or other. If as a result of technical advances these strategic goods and services can be produced more cheaply, reverberations will be felt throughout the entire economy.

Thus the introduction of the railroad during the nineteenth century gave rise to massive investment in a host of industries whose growth previously had been limited by high transportation costs. The development of modern hydro-electric power involved not merely heavy investment in generating plants, but made possible the expansion of a host of industries producing goods which involved the use of electricity. The discovery of the Bessemer, Siemens and Thomas processes of making steel during the latter part of the last century enabled steel to be produced cheaply; cheap steel in turn furnished the basis for expansion in a multitude of steel-using industries.

The Stock and State of Existing Capital Goods. The size of expenditures made on capital goods at any given time will depend in part upon how much has previously been spent on such goods. If recent investment has been very large, so that most firms are possessed of ample plant and equipment, there will be, for that very reason, less need for additional investment. One reason given for the decline in investment expenditure in the United States and Canada during 1957-58 was the very large expansion programmes of the immediately preceding years. The capacity of a great many industries had been substantially enlarged, rendering unnecessary any further construction for some time to come.

The physical condition of existing capital equipment may also affect the scale of current investment. Damage inflicted upon European factories by bombing and shelling during both World Wars made necessary large scale reconstruction programmes when peace came. Plant and equipment which had not actually suffered war damage was nevertheless in poor condition when war ended, for lack of proper maintenance during the war. Plant and equipment in North America, too, far from the actual theatres of war, experienced deterioration on this latter account. When war ended, huge sums had to be expended in North America and Europe, and in fact throughout the whole world, to restore plant and equipment that had been allowed to deteriorate during the war years when the materials and manpower required for maintenance were not available.

The Psychological Atmosphere. The investment decisions which a businessman makes are never based exclusively upon objective, concrete facts. The plant and equipment whose acquisition or construction he is presently considering will serve him only in the future. His decision on whether or not to invest in new facilities will therefore depend upon his anticipation of how the future will turn out, specifically on how useful it will prove in the future to have additional plant and equipment over and above what he has already.

How does he arrive at his anticipation of what the future will bring? Through his interpretation of relevant, available information. But this same information may be differently interpreted by different persons, and in fact may be differently interpreted by the same person, according to the psychological mood he happens to be in. Ironically, our hard-headed, hard-boiled businessmen have turned out on many an occasion to be as temperamental as prima ballerinas. At some times they have viewed the prevailing situation optimistically and have been prepared to carry out substantial investments; at other times they have viewed practically the same situation pessimistically, and have shrunk back from undertaking investment. Their different behaviour at different times was primarily to be accounted for, not by differences in the objective situation, but by changes in their mood.

The Availability of Funds. Decisions of businessmen to invest, arrived at for any of the reasons suggested above, are subject for their implementation to one overriding proviso. The necessary money must be available. Firms which wish to invest in new plant and equipment must either have their own funds, in the form of subscribed capital and accumulated profits, or must be able to borrow from the public or from financial institutions. However attractive investment opportunities may appear to a businessman, if he has no funds of his own, and cannot borrow on reasonable terms, he will not be able to invest.

Variation in the amount of money available for investment may therefore be responsible for variation in the aggregate of expenditure on investment between one time and another. The amount of the funds available will constitute a limiting factor only if businessmen wish to invest more than this figure. The size of the available fund will not restrict them if they propose to invest less than this sum.

Variation in the terms upon which money can be borrowed may also affect the volume of investment actually carried out. A very high rate of interest demanded by lenders may deter businessmen from borrowing because the return which they anticipate from investment would be eaten up by interest charges; a lower rate of might make the same investment worthwhile. A reduction in the rate of interest will not necessarily bring about an increase in borrowing for investment purposes; if the investment outlook is poor, the fact that they can borrow money more cheaply is not in itself likely to induce businessmen to invest.

We shall see in Chapter 27 how the authorities may deliberately arrange for variation in the volume of loanable funds and the rate of interest, as a means of affecting the aggregate of borrowing done for investment purposes.

3. Government Goods and Services

As described in Chapter 19, the long run trend of government expenditures has everywhere been upward. Population growth and economic expansion have obliged governments to provide administrative and protective services on an increasing scale. The pressure of public demand has obliged governments to enlarge the range of their responsibilities. Because there are more people, to be provided with an ever growing range of services, the expenditures of government have been increasing, substantially and continuously. The international situation has required heavy annual expenditures on national defence.

Viewed realistically, it is clear that a large proportion of government expenditures are beyond the power of government to control, or to vary significantly from year to year. Programmes and services which governments have become committed to provide cannot suddenly be dropped; once a particular service has been initiated, it tends almost inevitably to become a permanent responsibility. With each new service introduced, expenditures tend to shift permanently to a higher level. The heavy defence expenditures are inescapable charges, forced on us by international concerns and commitments and reflecting the extremely heavy cost of modern weapons of attack and defence. A decision to adopt the most stringent economies would probably result in only a slight reduction in the expenditures on the majority of the services a government provides.

There is one major category of government expenditures which does lend itself to considerable variation between one time and another. Expenditures on public works—on the construction of streets, bridges, schools, public buildings of all types —can be deliberately increased or reduced. While such facilities may be necessary, their construction can be advanced or postponed; the scale and quality of the construction can be adjusted. Even here there are limits: if there are more children to be educated, then more schools have to be constructed; if there are more vehicles in service, more and better roads have to be built. Nevertheless, there generally exists a fair degree of latitude in regard to public works expenditures. How a government may take advantage of this latitude to vary deliberately its expenditures on public works, we shall see in Chapter 27.

4. Exports

How much we export, that is, how much foreigners spend on the purchase of Canadian goods and services, will depend upon four broad considerations, which need only to be stated. These are:
(a) Their need for our products.
(b) Their ability to pay.
(c) The prices we ask for our exports compared to the prices asked by other countries which have the same goods to sell.
(d) The degree to which we are prevented, by tariffs and other obstacles, from selling our products to foreign countries.

Canada's postwar experience reflects the working of all these factors. Immediately after the end of World War II, Canadian exports to Europe were at a very high level. A devastated Europe desperately needed everything we were prepared to sell; huge American loans and gifts furnished European countries with the funds they needed to make payment. When their own productive capacity was restored, the urgency of European demands for Canadian goods abated. In the 1950s, the fact that the United States was giving away agricultural products, or virtually giving them away, reduced the volume of such products which Canada could sell abroad. The American business recession of 1957-58, involving a diminished need for raw materials by that country, brought a sharp decline in Canadian exports of those raw materials. During the 1960s we made very large grain sales to Russia and China when those countries harvested poor crops that were inadequate to fulfil their requirements. Through trade negotiations we achieved substantial reductions in the tariffs imposed on our products by other countries; much of the increase in our exports was attributable to reduction in the tariff barriers they had to hurdle.

The Expenditure Is Not All Income

We have just described the determinants of the four broad categories of expenditure made in Canada, on consumption goods and services, on capital goods, on government goods and services and on our exports. The sum of these four types of expenditure constitutes the aggregate of expenditures in the country. However, this entire amount is not paid out as income to Canadian factors of production. Some of the goods and services sold in Canada are produced by foreigners; the money spent on them is not received as income by Canadian factors of production. (In the same way, money spent by foreigners on imports from Canada is received by Canadians, rather than by nationals of their own countries.) Furthermore, as we have seen, some portion of the total amount paid by the public for goods and services is taken by the government in customs duties, sales and excise taxes; in addition businessmen set aside another portion in depreciation allowances. With these three reservations, it is correct to say that the aggregate of expenditures made in Canada will become the total payment made to Canadian factors of production, and that it will determine the amount of the services performed by those factors and, therefore, the degree to which the country's productive capacity is utilized.

Factors not Fully Shiftable

The fact that every productive agent, whether it be labour, land, capital or entrepreneurship, is employed in some specific enterprise and may not be able to shift, produces a further complication. Conceivably a reduction in expenditures on one type of good may be exactly offset by an increase in expenditures upon some other type, so that the aggregate of expenditures remains unchanged. However, the aggregate of effort performed and goods produced may fall; factors of production may not be able to shift from the industries where they are no longer demanded, to the industries which have experienced an increase in demand. Production declines in one industry, but does not rise in another. The increase in expenditures on the products of an industry may not lead to an increase in the amount produced but simply to an increase in their prices.

It might happen that people want to purchase more of something than is currently being produced but cannot, because there are not enough available of the particular factors of production required. If the price of the product is held constant, or nearly so, they may find themselves in the position of being unable to spend as much as they would like. In such a case, the fact that people *want* to buy more of one thing, would fail to offset the fact that they *actually buy less* of something else. The national aggregate of expenditure falls and so does the volume of productive effort which this expenditure calls forth.

For example, suppose that at a time when foreign demand for newsprint and base metals decreased, the desire of Canadians to build homes increased. Conceivably, Canadians might want to buy all the houses that could be built in Canada by all available personnel, including the men who had lost their jobs in newsprint mills and base metal mines. However, it may not be easy for the latter to get into the construction industry: they may lack the required skills, and they may live on the remote sites of newsprint mills and base metal mines while new housing is wanted primarily in large cities. Because they cannot readily transform themselves into building tradesmen at the right location they may remain unemployed, while at the same time fewer houses are being built than the Canadian people are prepared to purchase. The nation may produce less than the full amount of which it is capable, not because over-all demand is deficient, but because, given the distribution of that demand, our productive capacity is wrongly distributed and cannot readily shift.

Like all good things, mobility can be overdone too. If the decline in demand for our newsprint is only temporary, it might prove advisable to have the unemployed men remain at home during the short period that demand is slack. It would probably cost a good deal, financially and otherwise, to move from their homes to the cities where construction jobs could be had, and it might not be worthwhile to incur the various costs of moving away and back, for the sake of only a short period of employment.

SUMMARY

A country's output of goods and services in any year will depend basically upon its productive capacity and the degree to which it utilizes that capacity.

National productive capacity will depend upon the size and quality of the nation's work force, the abundance of its natural resources, the amount of its capital equipment and the manner in which its productive establishments are organized.

The degree to which capacity is actually utilized will depend primarily upon the aggregate amount of money spent in the country: by consumers, by businessmen, by the government, by foreigners in purchase of the country's exports.

Each of these categories of expenditure is highly variable, being determined by factors which fluctuate constantly. The aggregate of expenditure in the country, being composed of elements which vary in size from one time to another, also varies from one time to another.

FOR REVIEW AND DISCUSSION

1. In a free enterprise society waste appears in the form of unemployment; in a totalitarian society it is likely to take the form of misdirection of effort. Comment.
2. There may be unemployment even when the aggregate of expenditure in a country is at a very high level. Explain.
3. It would be unwise to assume that there existed a rigid relationship between the

size of people's incomes and the amount of their spending. Do you agree? Justify your answer.

4. Broadly speaking, the scale of business investment varies from year to year for only two reasons: the profit outlook changes; funds for investment are available in greater or less degree. Explain.

5. Government expenditures never go down. Comment.

6. Because its components are variable, the aggregate of expenditures made within a country is variable. Explain.

7. The aggregate of spending is likely to be less stable in a rich than in a poor country. Comment.

25

The Equilibrium Level of National Income

Economists have in recent years developed a theory to explain how the level of the national income is actually determined. In its most simplified form the theory is worked out for a hypothetical nation which neither imports nor exports, which has no government, whose citizens' spending decisions are determined absolutely by the size of their incomes, and whose businessmen's investment decisions are either absolutely fixed or determined according to an unvarying formula. Given these assumptions, it can be demonstrated that the actual size of the national income will be determined by the relationship between the schedules according to which the public make their spending decisions and businessmen make their investment decisions.

THE CIRCULAR FLOW

Suppose that we have a very simple economy which consists only of business firms and the general public; there is no government, and the country has no trade relationships with other countries. Suppose further that no one ever saves any money, that whatever income people earn they spend entirely. Finally, suppose that businessmen use no capital equipment whatever and, therefore, do not accumulate money for the replacement of such equipment.

Figure 1 illustrates the circular flow of payments that would go on in such an economy, when the total value of each year's production was $25 billion. Business firms would take in $25 billion through sales to the public, and would then pay out this full amount to the public in the form of wages, rent, interest and profit. Having received income of $25 billion the public would once again spend this amount in buying the output of the business firms.

The Circular Flow, with Saving and Investment

In Figure 2 two realistic qualifications are introduced. Allowance is made for the fact that the public does not spend all of its income, but saves a substantial portion. This saving takes the form of the holding of actual cash out of income received, or the depositing in a bank of a portion of income received.

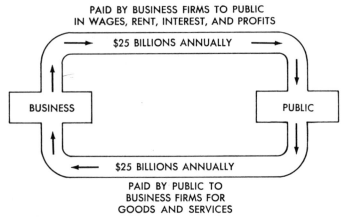

Figure 1. **The circular flow**

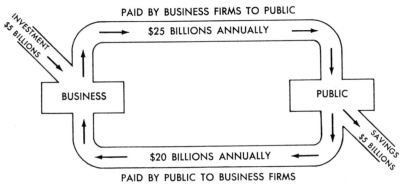

Figure 2. **The circular flow (with saving and investment)**

Let us investigate the consequences of a decision by the public to save. Suppose that in one year, having earned an income of $25 billion, people decided to spend only $20 billion and save the remainder. If nothing further happened, then businessmen, having taken in only $20 billion in sales, would have only that much money to pay out to the public in wages, interest, rent and profit; the public's income would therefore drop to $20 billion. Quite probably the public's income would ultimately fall even more; as we shall soon see, in our analysis of the "multiplier," once a decline occurs in the national income it is likely to bring about a further decline.

But now let us allow for the second realistic qualification. The fact is that business firms produce not only consumer goods for sale to the general public but also investment goods—buildings, machinery, equipment—for sale to other business firms. If, when the public decides to save $5 billion, business firms simultaneously decided to spend $5 billion on such investment goods, then the total outlay on goods would still be $25 billion. Business firms would be selling $20 billion worth of consumer goods plus $5 billion worth of capital goods. And, having produced and sold $25 billion of goods in total, businessmen would again be able to pay out that much to the public for services rendered. The public's decision to save would not have led to a change in its income, because simultaneously businessmen had decided to invest an exactly equal amount.

The public's income would continue at the $25 billion level *only if its decisions to save were precisely matched by business men's decisions to invest.* So long as these decisions were of matching size, business firms would take in from sales exactly as much as they paid out to the public. In our example, if saving and investment decisions were both $5 billions, or if they were both $4 billion, or any other figure, national income would continue to be $25 billion. Each year businessmen would pay out $25 billion as income; no matter how much the public decided to save, so long as businessmen decided to invest an equal amount, the country's firms would produce and sell a total of $25 billion worth of goods and services, and would pay out that much as income.

If saving and investment decisions were unequal, the national income would change from one period to another. Suppose the public decided to save $5 billion, but businessmen decided to invest only $4 billion. In that case the production and receipts of business firms would total only $24 billion. Having produced and sold only this much they would pay out only this much; national income would fall to $24 billion; ultimately, it would fall even lower, as we shall see. On the other hand if, while saving decisions totalled $5 billion, investment amounted to $6 billion, then business firms' production and sales receipts would be $26 billion and national income would become $26 billion; eventually it would rise even higher. Evidently, if saving decisions exceed investment decisions, national income will fall between one time period and the next; if investment decisions exceed saving decisions national income will rise. If they are equal it will stay constant.

EQUILIBRIUM AT ONE INCOME LEVEL ONLY

We have just demonstrated that the national income will remain in equilibrium, unchanged from one time period to another, so long as saving and investment decisions are equal. This will be true no matter what the level of the national income happens to be, and no matter how large or small these saving and investment decisions happen to be. We can now go on to prove something further: if the public's spending (and therefore its saving) depends absolutely on the size of its income, and if businessmen decide their investment according to a single rigid formula, then national income will be in equilibrium *only at one particular figure.* Only when the national income is at that level will saving and investment decisions be equal; only when the national income is at that particular level, will it tend to remain unchanged between one time period and the next.

Let us investigate the basis and the implications of this theory.

Does Spending Vary Proportionately with Income?

One knotty problem must be cleared away first of all. Shall we assume that the public always spends the same proportion of its disposable income, or shall we assume that the proportion varies with the size of that income? The statistical evidence is far from clear on the point and differing views are held as to which assumption best represents the public's actual behaviour.

It would be reasonable to expect that when the public's income was low, practically all would be spent. Most families would be poor and there would be scant opportunity for saving: poor families must spend all or nearly all of their income just to buy necessities. It is even conceivable that at a very depressed level of income people's spending would exceed their incomes; they might draw on savings, borrow, or receive some kind of charitable assistance. Suppose, however, that the public's income is not unduly low and most people are living comfortably. By how much would they increase their spending if they received an increase in income? Would they spend very little of the additional money, or would they spend most of it, and perhaps even all? On the one hand, it might be expected that since they were already living comfortably they would buy very little more and would save most of the additional money. On the other hand, if the increase in income was widespread, the country's standard of living might rise. What had previously been considered adequate might now be regarded as not good enough. People might use their additional income to achieve the new, higher standard of living that was becoming general, to keep up with the many Joneses. What is more, if a great many attractive new products were being introduced, people who were already living well might want to acquire them; if their incomes rose they would take advantage to buy these products.

The distribution of any increase in income would also be significant. If the additional income went primarily to people who were already well off, a relatively small proportion would likely be spent on consumption; if most of the additional income went to poorer persons, however, a larger proportion would probably be spent. (Some people claim that in fact an increasing proportion of the nation's disposable income has been going to poorer people, thereby ensuring that the level of spending by the general public is higher than it otherwise would have been.)

The Consumption Schedule: An Illustration

It is of no special significance here which assumption we make: that the public always spends the same proportion of its income, or that the proportion varies with the size of income. The fundamental theory of income determination can be demonstrated on the basis of either assumption. We will assume here that if the public's income were at a certain minimum figure it would spend it all, but that whenever income increases only a proportion of the increase is spent. For simplicity we will assume that this proportion remains the same for any addition to income and that when income is reduced, spending falls by this same proportion. The following hypothetical example illustrates:

In Country A everybody receives as income exactly what he earns. There is no government which imposes taxes or pays out pensions, allowances and the like. All earned profits are paid out to shareholders; workers receive all their earnings in cash —there are no wage supplements such as employer contributions to pension plans, medical schemes, and so on. Everyone gets as actual spendable income exactly what he has earned; Disposable Income equals National Income. With the national income at $50 billion, people spend exactly $50 billion. For each $10 billion increase in national income people would increase their spending by $8 billion; for each $10 billion reduction in national income they would reduce their spending by $8 billion.

The following simple table indicates how much spending and saving would occur, at various possible levels of national income.

Columns (1) and (2) together constitute the *consumption schedule* of Country A; columns (1) and (3) together constitute its *savings schedule*. The economist would say that in Country A the *Marginal Propensity to Consume (MPC)* is .8; this is the proportion of each addition to income that is spent on consumption. The *Marginal Propensity to Save (MPS)* is .2; this is the proportion saved of any addition to income.

Table 1

CONSUMPTION AND SAVING SCHEDULE OF COUNTRY A

(1) National Income	(2) Spending	(3) Saving
$ 30 billion	$34 billion	$ - 4 billion
40 "	42 "	- 2 "
50 "	50 "	0 "
60 "	58 "	2 "
70 "	66 "	4 "
80 "	74 "	6 "
90 "	82 "	8 "
100 "	90 "	10 "

The Equilibrium Level of National Income

Suppose now that the businessmen of Country A each year invest exactly $4 billion in new plant and equipment. In that case the total of spending in the country would vary with the size of the national income, as shown in Table 2 (still assuming, of course, that expenditures are made only for consumption and investment).

Table 2

SAVING AND SPENDING SCHEDULE OF COUNTRY A

National Income (billions of dollars)	Consumption Expenditure (billions of dollars)	Saving (billions of dollars)	Investment (billions of dollars)	Total Spending (billions of dollars)
30	34	- 4	4	38
40	42	- 2	4	46
50	50	0	4	54
60	58	2	4	62
70	66	4	4	70
80	74	6	4	78
90	82	8	4	86
100	90	10	4	94

From Table 2 it is evident that equilibrium will be achieved only when the national income is $70 billion. Only at this level of income would the public plan to save an amount exactly equal to that being invested by businessmen. Only here would the rate of total spending, on consumption and investment, equal the rate at which people were receiving income. If the national income ever happened to be higher than $70 billion it would tend to fall. If, for instance, national income were ever $80 billion, the total of spending would be only $78 billion; with only $78 billion being spent, only $78 billion could be earned. As we shall see, a $78 billion national income would still be higher than the equilibrium figure; further declines would occur. Similarly, if the national income were ever below $70 billion it would tend to rise. If, for instance, it were just $50 billion then total spending would be $54 billion; with $54 billion being spent, $54 billion would be earned. The rise would continue until the figure of $70 billion was reached.

From the standpoint of the business community, only when the national income was $70 billion would they be taking in from sales exactly as much as they were paying out in costs—in wages, rent, interest and profit. If national income were above this figure they would find that their sales receipts were running below their outlays; they would be forced to reduce outlays—thereby reducing incomes for the people to whom they paid out the money. If national income were below $70 billion, businessmen would find themselves taking in more in sales receipts than they had themselves been paying out. They would have more money than before to pay out; in doing so they would increase the national income.

Graphical Representation: Consumption Plus Investment

The conclusion arrived at in the preceding paragraphs may be represented graphically, as in Figure 3.

In Figure 3 the line CC represents the national consumption schedule as given in Table 1 and repeated in Table 2. An ordinate drawn from any point on the

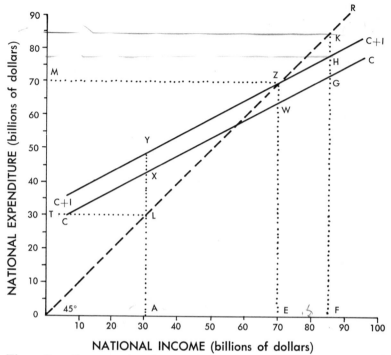

Figure 3. Consumption, investment, and the equilibrium national income

horizontal axis up to the CC line represents the amount of consumption spending which would occur if national income were at that level. If national income were OA, consumption spending would be AX; if national income were OE, consumption spending would be EW; and so on.

Businessmen each year invest $4 billion, which is equal to XY, to WZ, and to GH. Hence the C + I line, which is vertically above the CC line by $4 billion, represents the total spending which would occur in the country, at each possible level of national income. For example, if national income were OA, then total spending, on consumption plus investment, would equal AY; if national income were OE, then total spending would be EZ; and so on.

The reference line OR is drawn out from the origin at an angle of 45 degrees. The line having been drawn at this angle, each point on it is equidistant from the horizontal and vertical axes: the line LA is exactly equal in length to the line LT; ZE is exactly equal to ZM and so on. Since distance measured upward from the horizontal axis denotes spending, while distance measured sideways from the vertical axis denotes income, each point on the OR line denotes a position where income and spending are equal.

The C + I line, which indicates how much would be spent at all possible levels of national income, touches the OR line at only one point, at Z. Only here would the nation's total spending exactly equal its income. Only here would businessmen's sales receipts exactly equal the amount they were paying out to the public as income in the previous year. Therefore, only if the national income were OE, the income which gives rise to total spending of EZ, would there be an exact equality between income and spending, and only if income were OE would it remain unchanged from one year to the next.

An income greater than OE would inevitably be pulled down. If income were OF, total spending would amount to only FH, comprised of FG spent on consumption plus GH spent on investment. However, OF is equal to FK, K being on the 45° reference line. The nation's total spending, if it had an income of OF, would amount to less than OF; businessmen's sales receipts would be short of the amount they had just paid out as income to factors of production and they would now pay out less than before as income. As is evident from the graph this result would occur whenever income was in excess of OE, since, for all incomes in excess of OE, the C + I line is below the OR reference line. At any national income in excess of OE, therefore, total spending would be insufficient to maintain income at the same level.

The opposite result would occur if national income were lower than OE. If national income were only OA, then total spending would be AY, comprised of AX spent on consumption plus XY spent on investment. Since the point L is on the OR reference line, spending amounting to only AL would equal the national income of OA. Actual spending would therefore be in excess of the income earned. Businessmen would achieve sales receipts greater than the sum they had paid out to the public as income; they would accordingly, in the next time period, pay out a larger sum as income. This result would occur whenever national income was smaller than OE, since to the left of OE the C + I line is always above the OR reference line; whenever income was below OE, total spending would always exceed that income, giving rise to a larger income in the following time period.

Graphical Representation: Saving and Investment

The equilibrium level of national income can be determined in an alternative way, by reference to the saving and investment schedules. This method is demonstrated graphically in Figure 4.

In Figure 4 the SS line graphically represents the nation's saving schedule given first in Table 1 and repeated in Table 2. An ordinate drawn from any point on the horizontal axis, to the SS line, represents the amount of saving which would be decided upon if income were at that level. If national income were OX, people would decide to save *minus* XY; if national income were OA, they would decide to save AB; and so on. Businessmen are assumed to invest $4 billion a year, or OI, regardless of the level of the national income.

Only if income were OE would saving decisions equal investment; here saving decisions would amount to EG, which is exactly equal to the amount OI which

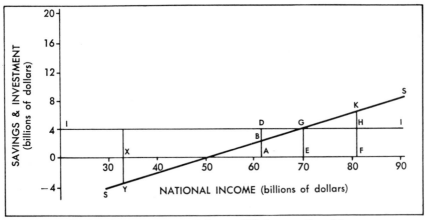

Figure 4.   Saving, investment, and the equilibrium national income

businessmen are investing. At no other income level would this equality occur. At an income OF, in excess of OE, people would decide to save FK, while investment would be only FH. At an income of OA, lower than OE, people would decide to save only AB, while investment would be AD. But we know that income will be in equilibrium only when saving and investment decisions are equal. If saving decisions exceed investment, income will move downward: if investment exceeds saving decisions, income will move upward. Only where saving and investment decisions are exactly equal will income remain unchanged between one time period and the next. In numerical terms the equilibrium income in Figure 4 is $70 billion, exactly the same amount as we derived from the arithmetic and graphical demonstrations that the equilibrium level of income is determined by the investment and consumption schedules.

THE MULTIPLIER

In spending his own income, a person creates income for someone else. The man who spends a hundred dollars a year on the services of a landscape gardener is providing the gardener with income of a hundred dollars a year. *Indirectly he is creating income for other people as well*: the gardener spends all or most of the hundred dollars, thereby providing income to other people. The people who earn the money spent by the gardener in turn spend all or most of that, thereby providing still other people with income, and so on.

Just how much income is created throughout the country as a result of this spending of one hundred dollars per year on landscaping? The answer will depend upon the prevailing marginal propensity to consume, the MPC. Suppose that all people had the same MPC of .75. In that case anyone who receives an addition to his income will spend three-quarters of the increment and save the remainder. The homeowner who spends one hundred dollars a year on landscaping services is therefore creating income as follows:

For the gardener	$100
The gardener spends $75, creating income for others of	$ 75
The people who get the $75, spend ¾ of it, creating income for others of the amount ¾ × $75	$ 56.25
The people who receive the $56.25 spend ¾ of it . . . etc. etc.	

Thus the person who spends $100 a year on his garden is responsible for a total income creation in the country of the amount

$$100 + \tfrac{3}{4}\ \$100 + (\tfrac{3}{4})^2\ \$100 + \ldots + (\tfrac{3}{4})^n\ \$100$$

The sum of the elements in this series is $400. i.e., the $100 spending by the individual on landscaping services is responsible for the ultimate creation of $400 of income throughout the country.

The ratio between the total income ultimately created and the initial expenditure to which it is attributable, is called the *multiplier*. In the above example the multiplier would be $\$400/100 = 4$. i.e., the expenditure of the individual on his garden would bring about additional income throughout the country amounting to *four times what he spends*.

The size of the multiplier will depend upon the magnitude of the MPC. Had the MPC been ⅔, then his expenditure of $100 on landscaping services would be responsible for creating income throughout society of the amount:

$$100 + \tfrac{2}{3}\ \$100 + (\tfrac{2}{3})^2\ \$100 + \ldots + (\tfrac{2}{3})^n\ \$100$$

The sum of the elements in this series is $300; hence with an MPC of ⅔, the multiplier would be $\$300/100 = 3$.

An easy way of arriving at the value of the multiplier is this: the multiplier is always the reciprocal of the MPS. For example, if the MPC were ⅗ the MPS would be ⅖; the reciprocal of the MPS, 5/2, would be the multiplier. If the MPC were ⅔, the MPS would be ⅓; its reciprocal, 3, would be the multiplier.

Up and Down with the Multiplier

Earlier in this chapter we noted that where investment exceeds saving decisions the national income will rise; we stated, without explanation, that income will rise by more than just the excess. Similarly, we stated that where investment is less than saving decisions, income will fall by more than the difference between them. We can now see why this should be so. Because of the multiplier any person's decision to spend more (and therefore save less) will produce a magnified increase in the national income; similarly a decision to spend less (and therefore save more) will produce a magnified reduction in the national income.

If, for instance, our homeowner decided one year to increase his spending on landscaping from \$100 to \$200, then, with the MPC being ¾, national income would become \$400 greater than if he had just spent the usual \$100 on landscaping. On the other hand if he decides one year to spend only \$50 on landscaping services instead of the usual \$100, then income will ultimately fall throughout the country by \$200, four times the amount of his reduction in expenditure. The gardener will earn \$50 less, and having \$50 less income, will spend ¾ × \$50 less; other people's incomes will thereupon fall by this amount, so that they will spend less; and so on. The series \$50 + ¾ \$50 + (¾)^2 \$50 + ... + (¾)^n \$50 represents the amounts by which people's incomes will decline; the total value of this series is \$200.

The homeowner's change of expenditure on landscaping services will only have the effects described in the above paragraph if it is not *offset* by a change in his expenditure on something else. If, for instance, he spends \$100 more per year on landscaping, but spends \$100 less per year on having his car washed, then the national income will remain unchanged. The increase in income of the landscaper, with its multiplier effects, will be exactly offset by the reduction in income of the car washer, with its multiplier effects. The homeowner's decision to spend more, or less, on some particular good or service will cause national income to rise or fall only if it represents a *net change* in his spending, and is not offset by a reduction or increase in his spending elsewhere.

The Multiplier: General Applicability

The multiplier applies to all types of expenditure. Our example has indicated the effects of an increase in spending on consumer services, but the same general consequences would be produced by an increase in business spending on investment goods, by an increase in government spending on public facilities and services, by an increase in foreigners' spending on our exports. In each case the increase in spending would produce an ultimate expansion of income amounting to the initial increase multiplied by the multiplier.

The nature of the increase in spending would still be of significance, since it would determine in what sector of the nation's economy the main expansion of income would occur. If businessmen increased their investment by purchasing more airplanes, the main benefits would accrue to the owners and employees of the airplane factories which got the orders and to the owners and employees of firms which supplied materials, goods and services to these firms and to their personnel. If the government increased its expenditures on highway construction, the main expansion of income would occur among road building contractors and their staffs and the firms which supplied road building machinery, materials, and the like. If foreigners increased their spending on our wheat, the main beneficiaries would be western wheat farmers, together with the retail establishments which serve them and the producers of the machinery, hardware, and clothing which they buy.

Some firms produce goods and services which are wanted by everybody, and these firms will benefit from an increase in expenditure in the country, no matter in which sector it originates. Anyone, anywhere, who achieves an increase in income is likely to purchase more of their products. Thus, factories producing clothing are likely to experience an increase in demand for their products whether it is the demand for airplanes which has increased, or government spending on road construction, or foreigners' spending on the purchase of our wheat. Hence the owners and employees of such factories are likely to be among those whose incomes are enlarged by an increase in spending, wherever this increase is initiated.

The Multiplier: Graphical Representation

Figure 5 graphically illustrates how the multiplier magnifies the effects on income of a decision to change the level of spending. Here it is assumed that the initial variation in spending arises out of a decision by businessmen to increase the amount of their annual investment. Originally, businessmen invested the sum of OI_1 per year; now they decide to invest the amount OI_2 per year. The line SS represents the savings schedule, which remains unchanged throughout.

With investment at its original figure of OI_1 the equilibrium level of national income is at OE_1, the income at which the I_1I_1 line cuts the SS line and where therefore saving decisions equal investment. When investment increases to OI_2, the equilibrium national income becomes OE_2, the level at which saving decisions equal the new and larger investment. The increase in the equilibrium income, amounting to the distance E_1E_2, is much greater than the increase in investment which amounted to I_1I_2. The increase in equilibrium income is in fact I_1I_2 multiplied by the multiplier.

This must be so. If income was originally at its equilibrium level, saving decisions must have been equal to investment. If investment is increased, equilibrium will again be attained only when saving decisions have increased by the same amount as has investment, so that the two are again equal. But if savings have increased,

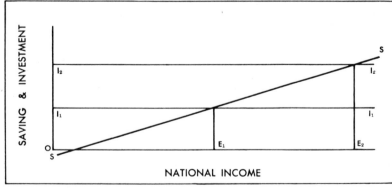

Figure 5.   The multiplier

incomes must have increased much more: people save only part of their incomes. Suppose, for example, that the economy of Country X is in equilibrium and that the marginal propensity to save is ¼. Suppose now that businessmen decide to increase their annual investment by $5 billion. In that case equilibrium will be restored only when the national income has increased by $20 million—by the figure such that the ¼ of it which is saved equals the additional investment of $5 billion. In other words, the increase in income amounts to the additional investment multiplied by the multiplier.

The Deflationary Gap

The equilibrium level of national income is the one toward which the nation gravitates as a result of its people's decisions in regard to consumption, saving and investment. *This is not necessarily the most desirable level of national income.* The most desirable is the one which the nation could achieve with full employment, when it would be producing the maximum amount of goods and services of which it was physically capable. The equilibrium national income may, in fact, be a good deal less than this. Referring to Figure 6, OF might be the full employment income, representing the volume of output that could be produced and the income that could be earned, if all the productive capacity of the country were fully utilized. The equi-

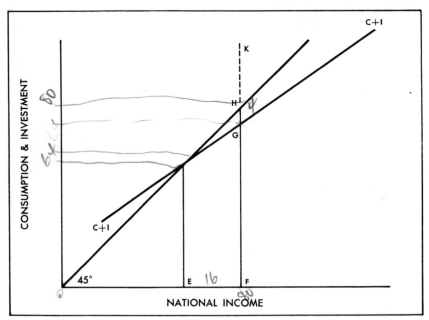

Figure 6.   The deflationary gap

librium income, however, is only OE, which is very much less. Because of the shape and position of the total spending schedule, the nation's income will tend toward OE, although it is physically capable of achieving the income OF.

The distance GH is referred to as the *deflationary gap*. If the nation decided to increase its total spending by that amount, the equilibrium national income would rise from OE to OF, and the national income would be in equilibrium at the full employment level. The difference between OE, the under-employment equilibrium, and OF, the full employment equilibrium, amounts to GH multiplied by the multiplier. Thus, if the nation were earning only the income OE, it need not decide to increase its expenditures by EF in order to achieve full employment. It need only arrange an increase in expenditures of GH; the action of the multiplier will bring about an ultimate increase in income of EF.

A numerical example of the foregoing would be this: suppose that the full employment level of national income in Canada were $80 billion, but that, because of prevailing attitudes to consumption and investment, our equilibrium level of income was only $64 billions. If the MPC were ¾, and the multiplier was therefore 4, we need only to arrange that expenditures increase by $4 billion. Due to the working of the multiplier, a $4 billion increase in expenditure, whether on consumption or investment, would bring about a $16 billion increase in income. So long as we maintain the new spending schedule we will remain in equilibrium at the $80 billion income level.

The Inflationary Spiral

A nation may spend too much. Referring to Figure 6, the nation's total spending ought ideally to be HF. The spending of this amount would induce the production of the full amount of goods and services which the country was physically capable of producing. This sum HF (equal to OF) would be received by the people as their income; provided they again spent HF, full employment and its associated income would continue. Suppose, however, that the nation, having earned an income of OF, decided to spend the amount FK. Since the expenditure of FH would purchase all the goods and services which the country could produce, the expenditure of a larger sum could not bring about the production of more goods: it could only give rise to inflation, to higher prices being paid for the same goods.

The inflation would likely prove cumulative or spiralling. If FK were spent, then this much would be received by people as income. Having larger incomes, people would spend more; but since physical output, being at its limit, could not increase, prices would rise even further as still more money was spent on the same amount of goods. The still higher prices would bring still higher incomes to people and, therefore, even greater expenditures on their part. Prices would rise again, and would continue to spiral upward until a general collapse occurred in the value of money and the economic system broke down altogether, or until the government took firm action to prevent any further upward movement of prices. We shall see, in Chapter 27, just what measures a government can adopt to choke off an inflationary spiral.

The Paradox of Thrift

So far in this chapter we have assumed that businessmen always invest a constant amount each year, regardless of the level of the national income. Let us now make the more realistic assumption that businessmen vary the scale of their investment according to the size of the national income, investing more when income is high, and less when it is low. If this assumption be made, it follows that, paradoxically, *a decision by the public to save more will actually result in the public saving less.* How this would come about is illustrated in Figure 7.

In Figure 7 the II line represents the investment schedule of the business community; its upward slope reflects the fact that with higher levels of national income, investment will be greater. The line S_1S_1 represents the original savings schedule; the line S_2S_2 represents the new savings schedule which develops when people become more anxious to save, so that out of the very same income they will now save more than before. Previously, when national income was OB, people would want to save BH; now at the same income OB they would want to save BY; previously, at an income of OC they would want to save CK; now they would save CZ; and so on.

The shift in the saving schedule brings about a shift in the equilibrium level of income. Originally, when the savings schedule was that depicted by the S_1S_1 line, the equilibrium level of income was OC. Now, with S_2S_2 representing the savings schedule, the equilibrium level of income is only OA. The decision to increase savings has caused the equilibrium income to fall by the amount AC.

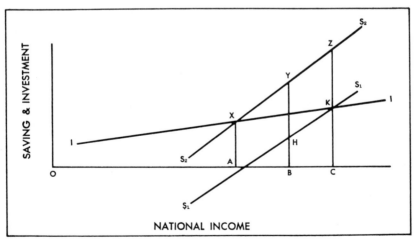

Figure 7.   The paradox of thrift

Paradoxically and ironically, savings as well as income will now be lower than they had been before. Originally, with the S_1S_1 line in effect and the equilibrium income at OC, savings had amounted to CK. Now, with the S_2S_2 line in effect and equilibrium income at OA, savings amount only to AX. Because people have decided to save a larger proportion of their income than before, income, *as a result,* has fallen so greatly that their aggregate savings are now less than before.

Government Taxation and Spending

In analyzing the forces which determine the size of the national income in our hypothetical economy, we made the unrealistic assumption that there was no government. Let us now be more realistic.

When we allow for the existence of a government we must change our analysis in two distinct ways. First, there will be taxes imposed upon individuals and business firms, the effect of these taxes being to reduce spending. Because of the taxes they must pay, private individuals will have less money to spend; business firms will have less money to invest (and because of the deterrent effect of taxes, may choose to invest less). Second, there will be a new component in our total of spending in the country: the spending of the government. The aggregate of expenditure in the country will now be composed of consumption spending and investment (both reduced, because of taxation, from the originally assumed levels) plus the spending of government.

Figure 8 illustrates. The CC line represents the consumption that would take place at any level of national income, when people must hand over part of their income to the government in taxes. The vertical distance between the C line and the C + I line represents the amount of investment carried out when business firms are subject to taxation. The vertical distance between the C + I line and the C + I + G line represents the amount of government spending.[1] The C + I + G line indicates what total of spending will take place at each possible level of national income; obviously the equilibrium level of income will be OE. It is evident that the government could shift this equilibrium by varying its own spending or by varying the taxes which it imposes. An increase in government spending, for instance, would raise the C + I + G line and therefore increase the equilibrium level of income. A reduction in taxation would have the same effect; it would tend to increase C and I, and therefore would also tend to raise C + I + G.

Handle with Care

The theory of income determination presented in this chapter constitutes a valuable addition to our knowledge, but it must be used with the greatest of care and circumspection. We must bear in mind that its limitations are severe. As we noted at the

---

[1]For simplicity it is assumed here that investment and government spending do not vary with the level of the national income.

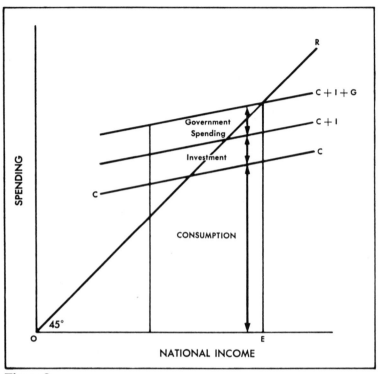

Figure 8.

beginning of the chapter, it has been developed for a hypothetical country characterized by the following features:

The public's spending on consumption is determined solely by the size of the
national income.
Investment is made each year according to a definite formula.
No economic relationships exist with other countries.

It must be admitted that these features correspond poorly to those which we
are likely to find in any real country. As we saw in the previous chapter, the public's
spending on consumption is not in fact determined solely by the size of the national
income. While income is the most important single factor, actual spending at any
one time will be affected by a host of other considerations as well. Also, investment
is not decided according to an invariant formula. We saw in the previous chapter
that the volume of investment will fluctuate, depending upon half a dozen or more
factors, each of which is highly variable and fundamentally unpredictable.

The assumption that the hypothetical country for which the theory is derived, has no economic relationships with other countries especially weakens the theory's relevance to Canada. The state of our export industries and the volume of foreign capital entering the country are major determinants of the level of national income in this country. Explaining what determines that level without reference to these factors would be like staging a performance of "Hamlet" without bothering to fill the title role.

The principles of the theory of income determination are logically valid and unquestionably are operative in reality, but the theory has been developed on the basis of highly restrictive assumptions. Considerations which are totally absent from the hypothetical model from which the theory is derived, bulk large in the real world. In attempting to apply the theory in a practical way we must, therefore, keep a weather eye out for these important characteristics of the real world which are not represented in the model.

SUMMARY

In a highly simplified economy which had no government and carried on no external trade, the level of national income would be determined by the relationship between decisions by the community to spend and save, and decisions by businessmen to invest.

The national income will remain the same from one period to another, only when people decide to save an amount equal to that which businessmen decide to invest. If people's saving decisions are governed strictly by the size of their incomes and businessmen determine their investment according to a rigid schedule, then the equilibrium national income can be one figure only.

Due to the working of the "multiplier", a person who spends money thereby gives rise to additional income throughout the country, amounting to several times the amount he spends. A reduction in expenditures will give rise to a multiple reduction in income.

If, when national income is at its full employment figure, total spending decisions amount to less than this figure, the deficiency is referred to as the deflationary gap. The equilibrium national income will be lower than the full employment figure by an amount equal to the deflationary gap × the multiplier.

If, at full employment, spending decisions are in excess of the full employment national income, an inflationary spiral will tend to develop.

The "paradox of thrift" reflects the fact that a decision by the public to increase its rate of saving may result in so great a decline in national income that the absolute amount of savings actually declines.

A word of warning is necessary. The theory of income determination has been developed on the basis of highly simplified models; its applicability to problems of the real world may be very limited.

FOR REVIEW AND DISCUSSION

1. It is ridiculous to claim that a nation can ever save too much. Comment.
2. Would the multiplier analysis be relevant to exports and imports? Explain.
3. Do you think that in the future Canadians will save a greater or smaller percentage of their incomes than they do now? Justify your answer.
4. There can be only one equilibrium level of national income at any one time. Explain.
5. We can never predict with assurance how consumption spending will be affected by an increase in the national income. Why not?
6. Even wasteful spending helps to increase the national income? Do you agree?
7. Once an inflationary gap develops it is likely to give rise to an inflationary spiral. Why?
8. The equilibrium level of national income is not the same as the full employment level. What is the measure of their difference?
9. There would be no "paradox of thrift" if the level of investment by businessmen was unaffected by the size of the national income. Explain, illustrating graphically.

26 Business Cycles

A HISTORICALLY RECENT PHENOMENON

In the two centuries which have elapsed since the Industrial Revolution began, production in Western countries has increased enormously. Rapidly growing populations have brought corresponding increases in the number of workers; their efforts have been immensely aided by the introduction of ever improving tools, machines and techniques, by the application of ever increasing amounts of power, by the use of ever growing quantities of natural materials. We have moved far from the days when most people lived on the land, producing by primitive means the narrow range of goods which furnished their meagre subsistence.

However, the advance has been an irregular one. In practically every branch of industry, production has been carried on chiefly by privately owned business firms whose objective it was to sell goods in markets at a profit. Markets have been capricious. At times they would readily absorb at profitable prices the full output of which firms were capable; at other times they would take much less. In many industries there were periods of intense activity when demand for the product was strong, followed by periods of slackened activity when demand was weak. Whole groups of industries, embracing a large proportion of a nation's entire productive capacity, moved upward and downward together. The term *business cycle* came to be applied to the fluctuations in which a very broad section of the total economy became involved. The following is a widely used definition:

"Business cycles are a type of fluctuation found in the aggregate economic activity of nations that organize their work mainly in business enterprises; a cycle consists of expansions occurring at about the same time in many economic activities, followed by similarly general recessions, contractions and revivals which merge into the expansion phase of the next cycle; this sequence of changes is recurrent but not periodic; in duration business cycles vary from one year to ten or twelve years; they are not divisible into shorter cycles with amplitudes approximating their own."[1]

[1]A. F. Burns and W. C. Mitchell, *Measuring Business Cycles* (New York, 1946), p. 3.

Problems Created by Business Cycles

Each different phase of the business cycle produced its own difficulties. In periods of depression when the tempo of activity was slack, the output of goods was below the volume which the economy was capable of producing. Great numbers of people suffered privation; because less was being produced their services were not needed, and they were unable to earn their customary livelihood. Periods of prosperity frequently produced problems too. Often they would generate sharp increases in the price level, bringing hardship to people on fixed incomes and reducing the value of monetary savings accumulated in the past. Serious distortions sometimes developed in the distribution of economic effort and resources, with the production of some goods being heavily over-emphasized. Worst of all, a period of high prosperity and rapid expansion appeared to bring on, as an inevitable aftermath, a following depression.

A Subject of Economic Analysis

Until about three-quarters of a century ago, economists made no real attempt to study the nature and causes of business cycles. The view was generally held that depressions were only temporary phenomena which would very quickly generate their own remedies. It was felt that if unemployment developed, then wages would fall; with wages reduced, employers would take on more workers. The problem of unemployment would thus solve itself. However, some depressions proved to be more severe, more lasting, than anyone had thought possible and views changed. As an ever increasing proportion of the population became drawn into the market nexus, dependent for their livelihood upon jobs and wages, downturns in business activity affected more people; the problem became too serious to be dismissed as unimportant. In recent decades, therefore, economists have studied intensively the phenomenon of the business cycle, gathering together a great many relevant facts and developing explanatory hypotheses.

Cycles in Individual Industries

In some industries a disturbance of their normal operations tends to produce a series of cyclical fluctuations. Such industries, to use a famous analogy, are like a rocking chair which responds to a shove with a series of swings. Industries which produce durable goods are likely to manifest a cyclical rhythm if ever they produce an unusually large output in a relatively short period. For, if a very large proportion of the total number of units required are produced in a single burst of construction, very few more will have to be built in following years. However, the units built during the period of concentrated construction will wear out in due course, *all at about the same time*, and, years later, there will occur another burst of construction to replace them. The residential building industry shows fairly clear evidence of such a cycle, as does the ship-building industry. Immediately after World War I, for instance, shipyards in Great Britain produced a tremendous number of ships to make up for losses suffered during the war from the German submarine campaign. The consequence was that in 1920 a very large proportion of the world's ships were new, and not due for replacement till 20-25 years later. Production and employment in British shipyards were at very low levels all through the 1920s and 1930s, partly for this reason.

In some industries an initial market disturbance may give rise to a series of cyclical fluctuations. Observers have noted that when the price of hogs is high in the U.S., farmers naturally tend to raise a great many. When the large number they have raised is marketed the price is driven down; then, because they received a low price, farmers raise fewer hogs. When these are ready for market they fetch a high price because the quantity supplied is so small. The high price induces farmers to produce a large output once again; and so on.

CYCLES IN GENERAL BUSINESS ACTIVITY

The "Cumulative Process"

A modern economy has a number of features which tend to produce "snowballing" effects. Movement in any direction tends to gather force; an original impulse which shifts the economy either upward or downward gives rise to repercussions which magnify the initial shift. The economy may be likened to an atomic pile in which an initial charge sets off a chain reaction. What are these attributes of a modern economy which are responsible for this "cumulative process?"

The Multiplier

We are already familiar with most of them. In Chapter 25 we learned of the multiplier, which magnifies the effect of an initial change in expenditures. We saw that when an individual spends money, he thereby brings about an ultimate increase of income and expenditure throughout the economy amounting to a multiple of the sum he actually spent. Similarly, when a person reduces his spending, he brings about a multiple decrease in income and expenditure throughout the country. Any initial shift in expenditure, because it brings the multiplier into action, gives rise to a magnified shift in the same direction.

The Banking System

In Chapters 21 and 22 we saw how the central bank and the commercial banks of a country can expand or reduce their nation's money supply. During a period of prosperity, the liberal creation of bank credit may strongly support and stimulate expansion. During a period of depression, restrictive lending policies adopted by the banks may speed the decline in general business activity.

Psychological Factors

In Chapter 24 we noted that the level of spending, by consumers and by businessmen, is influenced by the prevailing climate of opinion. An optimistic atmosphere is conducive to a high level of spending; pessimism serves to deter spending. Any developments which affect the prevailing mood bring these psychological factors into play. A new expenditure which induces optimism, for instance, thereby promotes a greater increase in spending; a decline in spending which gives rise to pessimism thereby produces an even greater decline.

The "Acceleration Principle"

There is yet another reason why upward and downward shifts in general business activity tend to be cumulative. Efficient production of most goods and services requires a great deal of real capital goods of a durable character—bulidings, equipment, machinery. If the existing plant which produces a particular commodity or service is already working to capacity, then, if output is to be increased, additional plant will have to be built.

An increase in public demand for a commodity or service may therefore give rise to investment in extensive and costly additional plant which is required to produce the additional output. The cost of this investment may substantially exceed the amount by which the public's annual expenditures on the product has increased. These expenditures on additional plant will be over and above expenditures made to replace worn-out or obsolete equipment. Investment carried out to satisfy an increase in public demand for a product is referred to as *induced investment*; the ratio between the amount of money so invested and the additional purchases of the product which induced it is referred to as the "acceleration factor."

The following example illustrates the working of the acceleration principle. Suppose that a certain airline operates 100 planes, each of which costs $5 million and has a service lifetime of 10 years. Suppose further that the company's planes have been acquired at regular intervals in the past, so that in 1975 ten become 10 years old and must be replaced; another ten are nine years old and will have to be replaced in 1976; another ten are eight years old and will have to be replaced in 1977; and so on. Finally, suppose that one million people use the airline each year, paying a total of $100 million in fares, for an average of $1 million per plane operated.

If the annual passenger load remains steady from year to year at one million persons, each year the airline will be spending $50 million on new planes to replace the ten old ones which annually fall due for replacement. Suppose, however, that the airline anticipates that commencing in 1976, another 100,000 persons per year will want to fly in its planes, so that its passenger load and revenue will rise by 10 per cent. To fly 1,100,000 people the airline will require 110 planes; in 1976 twenty planes will therefore be ordered, ten to replace the old ones which are due for replacement, and another ten to build its fleet up to 110. Assuming that the airline's forecast is correct, the acceleration factor is five. The public's expenditure on air travel will increase by $10 million in 1976 and because of this increase, the airline will increase its investment in airplanes that year by $50 million. In 1976, instead of purchasing the usual $50 million worth of new planes, it will purchase $100 million worth.

Like most numerical illustrations the foregoing one is a gross oversimplification of reality. In the real world, increases in consumer demand do not immediately induce precisely related amounts of investment. In most firms an increase in demand can be met by using existing capacity more intensively, or perhaps by stretching out deliveries. Some firms simply decline to fill the extra orders. Where capacity is actually enlarged, the expansion may be undertaken only after the need has existed for some time. On the other hand, expansion may be carried out before the need arises: some businessmen build ahead of demand in order to "get in on the ground floor," or to be ready to meet the demand the moment it develops. However, these realistic qualifications should not be allowed to obscure the important measure of truth represented by our illustration. Albeit not with the mechanical precision of our example, the acceleration principle does operate in the real world and its operation is an important feature of business cycles.

ALTERNATIVE INTERPRETATIONS OF PAST FLUCTUATIONS

It has been said, with a good deal of justice, that if all the economists in the world were laid end to end, they would not reach a conclusion. Nowhere probably is their occupational proclivity for controversy better illustrated than in business cycle analysis. Economists disagree as to when business expansions and contractions actually began and ended. They disagree as to whether there is just one type of cycle or several. They offer different explanations for its causes, and suggest different measures for its cure.

These disagreements are understandable. The historical record of business activity is by no means clear and exact. Our impressions of the state of business throughout the nineteenth century are derived mainly from opinions expressed by contemporary journalists and politicians. These opinions are at best imprecise; often they are utterly contradictory. Better evidence is available, of course, for more recent times. During the twentieth century the governments of most modern countries have regularly collected detailed statistics regarding the performance of a great many industries. But while these statistics are exact, they are by no means unambiguous; they lend themselves to alternative groupings and to alternative interpretations.

Two of the most widely held views as to the duration of business cycles have been advanced by J. A. Schumpeter[2] and the National Bureau of Economic Resarch with which some of America's foremost economists are associated. Schumpeter devised a three-cycle schema to represent the business fluctuations experienced in the Western World in the past two centuries. His theory was that there had occurred a series of "long cycles" of 50 to 60 years' duration, whose expansion phase had in each case arisen out of a group of major technological advances. These advances were introduced into one or a few sectors of the economy by pioneering businessmen; the pioneers were soon followed by a host of imitators. The new goods and techniques, developed by the innovators and copied by their imitators, ramified through the entire economy; firms in a great many industries incorporated the new products and methods into their own operations, so that a general acceleration of economic activity ensued.

The first long wave upward occurred in the period between the 1780s and the 1810s, when revolutionary advances were made in the spinning and weaving of cotton, when canals and modern roads were first built, and when the steam engine was first introduced as a source of power. The second long wave came in the period between the 1840s and the 1870s, being produced by the world-wide construction of railways and the development of revolutionary steel-making processes which drastically reduced costs, so that steel became a feasible construction material for machinery and buildings. The third great wave began in the early 1900s and carried forward till the 1920s; it was generated by the widespread introduction of electrical power and electrical equipment, by the development of the automobile, and by the emergence of the modern chemical industries.[3]

Following each of these long waves there had occurred, according to Schumpeter's theory, a period of slacker business activity when the economy "digested" the technological advances introduced during the expansion period. Upon these long upward waves and periods of "gestation" there were superimposed shorter cycles of 9-10 years' duration; these in turn contained even shorter cycles, of 3-4 years' duration.[4]

The National Bureau of Economic Research, on the other hand, takes the view

---

[2]One of America's outstanding economists, who was for many years a professor at Harvard.

[3]It might be noted that other students have stressed the importance of wars and gold discoveries in causing business fluctuations. Heavy government expenditures in wartime (and in preparation for war) have tended to promote prosperity. The discovery of major gold deposits has induced feverish activity on the part of gold-seekers and has resulted in large accretions to the world's supply of gold, enabling expansion of money stocks and credit. Major wars and gold discoveries did occur during all three of the long waves upward. The Napoleonic Wars extended over a good part of the first; the Crimean and American Civil Wars occurred during the second, as did the great California and Australian gold rushes. Dramatic gold discoveries were made in the Yukon and Klondyke and in South Africa at the beginning of the third. Preparation for World War I began near the beginning of the third wave and the war itself took place in about the middle.

[4]Each of the three types of cycle was named after the person credited by Schumpeter with having first observed it; thus the long cycles were Kondratieffs; the intermediate cycles were Juglars; the short ones were Kitchins.

that the business cycle is a phenomenon which characteristically has a duration of 40 to 50 months.[5] After painstaking analysis of all relevant data it has established the dates when the business cycles experienced in the U.S. since the mid-nineteenth century attained their peaks and their troughs. According to the Bureau there occurred in the U.S., between 1854 and 1938, 22 different business cycles whose length varied from 27 to 99 months.

These historical benchmarks established by the Bureau have furnished the basis of a great deal of economic inquiry. The cyclical experience of a very large number of industries has been investigated, to compare the timing of their peaks and troughs with those of business activity in general. The object has been to ascertain whether in these industries cyclical peaks were generally reached before, during, or after the peak period of general business activity and similarly, whether their cyclical troughs typically came before, during or after the troughs in general business activity. It has been hoped that such studies would yield valuable information in respect to what happens during business cycles in the various sectors of the economy, and would suggest what developments exercise causative influences.

THE BUSINESS CYCLE: GENERAL CHARACTERISTICS

In the following pages we shall describe the course of a "typical" business cycle. The cycle we describe is "typical" in the sense that its features have been present in most of the business cycles which so far have been experienced. The relative importance of its various features has been substantially different in different cycles, however. Our cycle is comprised of four broad phases: depression, revival, prosperity and recession, and should be considered as being one in an endless series of similar cycles, each of which follows immediately after the one before, with its phases in the same sequence.

The Depression Phase

With the economy in a state of depression a great many people are out of work, and are therefore unable to spend as much as they normally do. People who still have their jobs tend to spend their money cautiously. The prevalence of unemployment causes them to fear for their own jobs; if they lose their means of livelihood, every dollar of savings will be important. People make do with their present wardrobes, automobiles, and appliances, even though replacements would be welcome. Spending on luxuries is severely limited.

With the public's spending down, sales and production are at low levels. Production may be at an even lower level than sales, since a good many merchants will try to reduce their inventories; with sales down they do not need as large

[5]The definition given earlier in this chapter is that of the National Bureau.

inventories as they did when sales were high. Many businessmen will be using the money they take in from sales to pay off debts or to build up their cash reserves. A considerable number of firms will have recently gone bankrupt because they had too much stock, too much debt, and too little cash; the wary businessman tries to secure himself against a similar fate.

There is very little construction going on, whether residential or commercial. Most of the people who would like to live in better housing cannot afford it; those who can afford to build a new house or to occupy a better apartment are unwilling to incur a big mortgage debt or to increase their living expenses. Businessmen are not investing in new buildings, machinery and equipment. They cannot sell as much as their existing plant can produce; the construction of additional capacity would be pointless. To reduce their cash outlays they even defer necessary repairs or replacements of plant and equipment. With construction activity at a very low ebb, unemployment is particularly heavy among construction workers and workers in establishments which produce materials for construction: logging camps, iron mines, lumber mills and steel plants, cement and paint factories, plants which produce electrical and plumbing fixtures.

The unemployment, the low level of production and sales, the slackness of building, all contribute to a marked pessimism. The banks have large excess reserves, but are reluctant to make loans except on the very best of security. Businessmen in any case have little desire to borrow since there appear to be few opportunities for profitable investment. On the stock markets the prices of securities are low, reflecting the low level of current profits and the gloomy outlook.

The Revival

This unhappy situation does not last forever. Some of those very factors which are responsible for the low level of activity during the depression contain the seeds of a subsequent revival. People who have been deferring the purchase of new clothes, of new cars and other durable goods, eventually cannot make the old ones last any longer and must buy replacements. Businessmen who have been steadily reducing their inventories, reducing their debts, and building up their cash, eventually find that their inventories are too low even for their current level of sales. They must increase their orders from suppliers; thanks to their reduced debt and larger cash balances they are better prepared to commit themselves in this way. Old equipment which had been kept in use as long as possible must eventually be replaced. Pessimism weakens its grip. The number of bankruptcies tends to decline: weak firms were the first to go under; once they have disappeared the bankruptcy rate among the remaining stronger firms becomes a good deal lower. The very fact that the depression has lasted so long engenders the optimistic view that it cannot last much longer, that "prosperity is just around the corner."

There is more solid support for revival. Despite the depression, the country has not been standing still. The population has been growing; new products and new methods of production have been invented; new natural resources have been discovered. All these developments furnish new investment opportunity; the population increase furthermore brings an increase in sales which causes existing productive capacity to appear less excessive. To some businessmen the new investment opportunities appear so promising that, despite the depression, they feel that they ought to take them up. And from the point of view of building new housing or new business buildings the times could hardly be more favourable. Money can be borrowed from the banks at low interest; labour and materials are abundant and cheap.

Purely fortuitous developments may give the economy an upward boost. An unusually good crop may bring a substantial increase in farm incomes, together with greatly increased employment both in the industries which handle the movement of the crop to market, and those which process it into finished goods. A foreign market may materially improve, bringing a considerable increase in income and employment in the country's export industries. The international situation may deteriorate; a number of industries will be favourably affected by the armament building programme which becomes necessary. The government may raise tariffs, thereby improving the market prospects of some domestic firms (although this favourable effect, as we have seen in Chapter 17, is likely to be more than offset by unfavourable repercussions elsewhere in the economy).

Prosperity and Expansion

Once begun, the advance gains momentum. Favourable developments in one sector produce favourable repercussions in other sectors. People who previously were unemployed now get jobs, and are able to increase their expenditures. Many avail themselves of the opportunity to buy on the instalment plan, and increase their expenditures very greatly. Consumption standards rise; people tend to buy better quality goods and more luxuries. Through the action of the multiplier any initial increase in expenditures gives rise to a multiple increase in incomes and expenditures throughout the economy.

Confidence grows; adverse developments which earlier might have cut short the revival are now taken in stride. People become prepared to enter into undertakings of a long term character; ordinary persons buy houses on the basis of long mortgages; businessmen undertake long range investments. A great deal of housing has in fact become necessary as a result of the population growth which had occurred during the depression and the very limited house building carried on during that period. There is now a real need for business investment too. The expansion in demand for some goods has reached such a degree that existing productive capacity has become inadequate. The acceleration principle comes into operation. Businessmen enlarge and modernize their plants in order to cope with the increased demand. A great many new enterprises are launched, to produce the new goods and services which have been developed in recent years; in the increasingly confident atmosphere, businessmen are more willing to take the gambles involved in producing novelties.

The capital required to finance investment is readily available. Rising business profits furnish a growing volume of funds for investment. Out of their larger incomes private individuals are saving more, and apply their savings to the purchase of stocks and bonds. The banks, still possessed of ample reserves, and sharing in the generally buoyant mood, loan money readily.

Full employment is approached, or actually reached. The high level of demand for consumer goods supports a correspondingly high level of activity and employment in the consumer goods industries. Similarly, the rapid pace of residential and industrial construction supports a high level of employment in the construction industry and in the industries which produce construction materials.

Production costs rise, even before full employment is reached. With comfortable profits being earned, management relaxes its vigilance. Trade unions press successfully for wage increases. To achieve increases in output, overtime rates must be paid; inferior workers must be taken on. Some workers put less effort into the job; they know that, because they cannot be easily replaced, they are not likely to be fired; and if they are fired, there are plenty of other jobs available. For one reason or another, employers must spend more money to get the same amount of work done. Once full employment is reached the rise in costs becomes accelerated. Any firm which wishes to take on more workers can get them only by luring them away from their present jobs. Generally the lure will take the form of an offer of higher pay. Firms threatened with loss of staff must raise wages to keep them. Competition among firms will similarly drive up the prices of materials, industrial and commercial land, thereby increasing also these other elements in costs.

Rising prices induce speculative activities. People buy securities, materials, real estate, in anticipation of further price increases which will yield them capital gains. This speculative buying contributes in turn to the upward movement of prices. Speculative profits constitute the source of some of the funds spent on consumption and investment.

Recession

Unfortunately the good times cannot last forever. Sooner or later the level of business activity turns decisively downward, and the period of prosperity comes to an end. The downturn may be initiated by a purely chance development such as a bad harvest or the loss of an important foreign market. More probably, it will be attributable to the stresses and weaknesses that have been developing during the period of expansion and prosperity. Just as developments during the depression paved the way for a revival, so do developments of a different kind which occur during prosperity render the economy susceptible to a damaging reversal. Purely fortuitous events may bring on the downturn which ends a period of prosperity, but very likely it will be found that, at the time those events occurred, the economy had reached a state of high susceptibility to reversal. An economy going through a period of prosperity has been likened to a horse running a long and difficult steeplechase; the obstacles are so many, and it becomes so weary, that it is bound eventually to be brought down by one of them.

Strains are likely to have developed in both the consumer goods industries and in the capital goods industries. Some of the former, after enjoying good markets for some time, ultimately suffer a decline in sales, because public demand for their products has become sated. In other consumer goods industries, even though sales are continuing at a high level, businessmen reduce their orders from suppliers. Till now they have been ordering extra quantities in order to build up their inventories; but once inventories are at an adequate level they reduce their orders to suppliers to a rate which just matches their own sales to the public. It may turn out that some industries have over-expanded, expansion programmes having been based on excessively optimistic estimates of what the market would absorb. Such over-expansion would be particularly likely to occur in the case of industries which are comprised of many separate firms, each of which independently decides to increase its output in response to a favourable market situation. Because there is no coordination or control, too many firms expand, and the market becomes overloaded. Even if expansion programmes were based on correct estimates, the economy receives a deflationary jolt when new plant is completed and goes into production. While the plant was being built it furnished a large demand for labour and goods of all kinds. When it is completed, it may demand less labour and materials; in addition, it now pours its own output into the market, with depressive effects on the prices of competing and substitute products.

Powerful downward pressures develop in the capital goods sector of the economy. Some firms, once the prosperity period got under way, had determined upon programmes of expansion, but these called for the construction of only one or two specific projects. Once these are completed they build no more. If, at that time, other firms do not launch new programmes for expansion, the total volume of construction activity will decline.

There is a strong likelihood that the productive capacity of the economy will increase, during the expansion phase, more rapidly than does its readiness to consume. During the period of prosperity, investment in new plant is carried on at a high and rising rate, financed by the ever growing volume of savings which people are able to set aside out of their growing incomes. The large profits being earned constitute a particularly important source of funds which finance investment. Because a great deal of additional plant is being constructed, the productive capacity of the economy is becoming greatly enlarged; but the public demand for goods, while growing, does not grow at so rapid a rate. Eventually the economy is expanded to such a degree that it can produce more goods than the public is prepared to consume. The rate of investment must then turn down; there is no point in further expanding productive capacity when avaliable plant can more than satisfy the existing demand for goods.

Furthermore, because of the acceleration principle, a great deal of investment carried out during the period of prosperity has been induced by the current expansion of demand. *If ever this rate of expansion slows down, less investment will be required*, and a slowing down of the rate of expansion is *inevitable* following a period of prosperity. When that period began there were a great many unemployed people about, and a great deal of unused capacity. The economy was able for a while to achieve a high rate of expansion, by bringing idle productive capacity into action. But once full employment is reached, the same high *rate of increase* can no longer be maintained. An economy in which 10 per cent of the productive capacity is unemployed can readily achieve a 10 per cent increase in output; it simply puts the unemployed to work. But once it is using its capacity fully, it can achieve only the limited further increases in output which come from natural increase of the labour force, the use of more and better equipment, and the like. If investment depends upon the *rate* at which the economy grows, then a decline in investment becomes inevitable.[6]

Once a state of prosperity has prevailed for some time, therefore, a downturn is practically inevitable; too many possibilities of difficulty have come into existence during the course of the expansion, and some of these possibilities are bound to materialize. If the difficulties are insufficient in themselves to cause a decisive reversal, they at least weaken the economy and render it more susceptible to shocks from the outside. Unfavourable external developments such as a bad harvest, which earlier could have been taken in stride, now become seriously damaging jolts; the economy has become too weakened to absorb blows easily.

While the expansion is bound to die, it may be "killed prematurely." The banks, their reserves stretched to the limit, may be unable to provide the funds for a continuation of the expansion. Alarmed by the inflationary tendencies which have developed during the course of the prosperity, they may deliberately adopt restrictive policies. For lack of the necessary funds, the expansion inevitably slows down, and perhaps is halted altogether.

[6]The following example, while highly artificial, illustrates the principle involved. Suppose that an average bath-tub factory can produce annually the bath-tubs required for 5,000 new houses. Suppose now that in 1980, a year of considerable unemployment, there exist 20 such factories in the country, and exactly 100,000 houses are built. Suppose now that times improve in 1981 and 125,000 houses are constructed. Obviously, 5 new bath-tub factories will have to be built to produce the additional bath-tubs required that year. Suppose that times continue to improve and that 150,000 houses are constructed in 1982. Another 5 bath-tub factories will have to be built that year. Now suppose that with 150,000 houses being built the construction industry has achieved full employment. Henceforth it can build more houses only by using better methods, and by drawing additional people into the industry, away from other occupations. It might turn out accordingly that the maximum number of houses which could be built in 1983 would be 160,000. In this case only 2 new bath-tub factories will be required in 1983. The fact that house building *increased by less than previously,* and this was inevitable, will cause annual investment in new bath-tub factories *actually to decline.*

Some people, anticipating the end of the boom, may quietly sell out while prices are still high. Investors may sell their securities; businessmen with heavy stocks may clear them even before they are under any real pressure to do so. The effects of such anticipatory actions is to hasten the event which is anticipated; the boom is killed by those who expect that it will soon die.

Depression Again

Once a downturn begins, it gains momentum. Merchants, their sales having fallen, reduce their orders from suppliers. Because they are likely to be cutting their inventories,[7] they will probably reduce their orders from suppliers by more than the reduction in their own sales. Some firms sharply cut prices in order to clear their heavy stocks; competing firms become forced to match these price reductions, so that sales generally are made on an unprofitable basis. Workers who lose their jobs are obliged to cut their spending. The multiplier, now working in reverse, causes a multiple reduction in spending throughout the economy, and the unemployment spreads. Some businessmen become unable to repay their bank loans; the banks consequently adopt tighter lending policies. With credit less freely available, business generally experiences further constriction.

Construction Greatly Reduced

The volume of construction activity declines heavily. With public demand sharply reduced, the full output of existing plant cannot be profitably disposed of, and the construction of more plants would be utterly pointless at this time. The funds required to finance the former scale of investment are no longer available in any case. Profits, out of which a large proportion of these funds came, are much reduced. Because of the general reduction in incomes, personal savings are down. The banks are much less willing to lend. Investment activity may be cut to replacement and repairs only, and even these forms of investment may be drastically reduced. Replacements and repairs can generally be deferred, and businessmen, anxious to cut their cash outlays, may defer them as long as possible. With no new building going on, and plant replacement or repair at a minimum, the total volume of construction work may be only a small fraction of what it had been during the previous period of expansion. Such a cataclysmic decline in investment did occur in fact in the opening stage of the Great Depression of the 1930s.

The outstanding features of the depression are the very low level of construction activity, and the heavy unemployment among workers in the construction trades and in the industries which produce construction materials. Declines will have occurred in the consumption goods sector of the economy, but these are likely to be of smaller proportions. People must still buy food regularly, must occupy housing,

[7]With sales running at lower levels, smaller inventories are sufficient.

and must periodically buy new clothes. The decline in activity in the consumption goods sector reflects primarily the drop which has occurred in standards of living. In contrast, activity in the capital goods sector may fall practically to zero. The current public demand for goods could be served by the plant already in existence, and few businessmen are in a mood to make expenditures beyond those which are strictly necessary.

Business Cycles since 1945

The description of a "typical" business cycle given in the foregoing pages has referred to the cycles experienced in the Western World during the past two centuries. Since World War II a number of highly significant developments have occurred which have served to change the character and intensity of business fluctuations. Powerful stabilizing elements have become incorporated into our economy. Old age pension plans, family allowances, the unemployment insurance plan, now guarantee, for a great many people, higher and steadier incomes than they otherwise would have had. Governments have greatly enlarged the scope and scale of their activities; the consequent large and steady flow of government expenditures has had a powerful stabilizing influence on the national economy. Governments, in addition, have accepted responsibility for preventing both booms and depressions; we shall examine in Chapter 27 the various measures they can employ. We have experienced business cycles since World War II, but their intensity has been small and the duration of the depression phase was relatively short in each case. It may well be that the phenomenon of the severe business cycle in the course of which a very large proportion of a nation's work force remains unemployed over a protracted period—as during the 1930s—has passed into the limbo of history.

CANADA'S CYCLICAL EXPERIENCE

External Sources of Instability

Reflecting the specialized nature of her natural resources, Canada's economic history has been characterized by intensive concentration on a limited number of staple products, the bulk of which have been exported. Efficient exploitation of her resources required a huge and costly array of capital equipment, including canals, railways, handling and distributing equipment of all types. Furthermore, the people who came to live in the country needed all kinds of buildings and facilities: houses, stores, schools, hospitals, water and sewer and electrical services and the like. Much of the capital required to finance construction, both of equipment needed for resource development and of buildings and facilities required to serve the people, necessarily came from abroad; the Canadian economy was too limited to generate the savings required to finance the scale of investment involved.

In the Canadian economy there have always been these two large and important types of activity which depended upon circumstances prevailing in other countries: production for export, and externally financed investment. The origins of a good many of the cyclical expansions and contractions which Canada has experienced can be traced to fluctuations in the volume of these two types of activity.

Our external relations have been mainly with Great Britain and the United States; these two countries have absorbed the great bulk of our exports and have furnished practically the whole of our capital imports. Broadly speaking, our external dependence has been centred on only one of these countries at a time, however. Prior to World War I, Great Britain was the main market for our exports and virtually the sole source of our capital imports. Following the War, the United States became our main export market, and our main source of capital imports. As we have seen in earlier chapters, during the latter 1960s a distinct tendency developed toward greater diversification of our external relationships: we traded relatively more with such countries as Japan, France and Germany, and began to obtain capital from them on a significant scale.

Business Fluctuations in Canada

Following Confederation, Canada enjoyed a half-dozen years of prosperity, due largely to the buoyancy of the British and American markets for her chief exports, in those days lumber and agricultural produce. Between 1873 and 1896, however, commodity prices throughout the world were generally drifting downward, and the tempo of economic activity in Canada was for the most part slow.

A powerful boom got under way in the middle 1890s, based largely upon the settlement of Western Canada and the construction of the immense physical plant of the "Wheat Economy." Great Britain primarily, and other European countries in much lesser degree, furnished growing markets for our wheat and supplied the bulk of the capital required to finance the construction of railways and the Western towns and cities which served as receiving centres for grain and distributing centres for merchandise. The massive expansion proceeding on the Prairies supported prosperity in the other major regions of the country. British Columbia lumber companies found in the Prairies a booming market, as did the wholesale houses, the manufacturing plants and the financial firms of central Canada. The construction of two new transcontinental railways, together with a great deal of branch line mileage, furnished strong demand for the products of plants in the Maritimes which fabricated railway equipment. For two decades virtually the entire Canadian economy was characterized by high prosperity and rapid expansion. The times were not consistently good, however. Difficulties experienced by the London money market in 1907 and again in 1913-14, led to drastic reductions in the flow of capital to Canada; on both occasions investment activity was sharply curtailed, giving rise to general recessions. (Quite possibly a recession would have occurred around 1914 in any case: a number of major construction projects, notably the two new transcontinental railways, were approaching completion, and a decline in the rate of investment appeared imminent.)

The outbreak of World War I in August, 1914, brought a further curtailment of construction and other activities, and for a while caused the depression to become even more severe. War orders, high wartime prices for agricultural products, and an unprecedentedly large crop in 1915 brought about a revival, and prosperity continued throughout the war and immediate postwar years. A sharp reversal was experienced in the fall of 1920, following the world-wide collapse of commodity prices. Prosperity returned by the middle 1920s, featured by improved wheat prices and good crops, by large scale investment in the automobile industry and road construction, and by heavy American investment in the development of Canadian pulpwood and mineral resources.

A massive reversal commenced around 1930, following the Wall Street crash of 1929, the world-wide collapse of commodity prices, the succession of crop disasters, and the virtual cessation of investment activity. Revival got under way in 1933, but was interrupted in 1938 by local repercussions of the current American recession; full employment was only achieved during World War II.

Prosperity continued after the War, supported by strong foreign demand for Canada's exports and large scale investment in housing, in business plant and equipment, and in resource development (much of the latter financed by American capital). On two occasions the pace of activity accelerated sharply. Heavy defence expenditures following the outbreak of the Korean War in mid-1950 brought a spurt forward; in 1955-56, unusually large American investment in the development of Canadian resources produced something of a "boom." On the other hand, on three occasions, in 1949, 1954, and 1957-58, recessions in the U.S. had milder counterparts in Canada. As a matter of fact the performance of the Canadian economy for several years after 1958 was sluggish, characterized by the highest rates of unemployment experienced since the war and a negligible rate of economic growth. While most Canadians continued to enjoy a high standard of living, there was widespread disappointment with the unfavourable contrast between the country's lagging pace of development and the dynamic expansion proceeding in Europe. More buoyant conditions came to prevail after 1962, reflecting such favourable developments as the large wheat sales to the Soviet Union and China, the accelerating pace of economic activity in the U.S.—attributable partly to that country's expanded war effort in Vietnam—and the stimulus of the massive Expo 67 construction programme.

Inflation became a matter of urgent concern in 1967, prompting Parliament to appoint a special committee to investigate rising food prices. During the next two years the government applied a number of measures to curb inflationary pressure; the consequent slowing down of economic activity was in turn responsible for high levels of unemployment. Concern about unemployment replaced concern about inflation and in December, 1970, the Minister of Finance introduced a special budget designed to stimulate the national economy, particularly those sectors where un-employment was most severe; the rate of unemployment remained relatively high however; with the prospect of especially severe unemployment in the following winter, the Minister of Finance announced, in October 1971, a large scale programme calculated to stimulate the economy sharply and generate large numbers of additional jobs.

SUMMARY

A business cycle consists of simultaneous expansion in many fields of business activity, together with a following widespread contraction. Business cycles are characteristic of societies in which goods are produced primarily for sale in markets.

Each phase of the cycle brings its particular difficulties: the depression phase is characterized by unemployment; the prosperity phase is likely to be marked by inflation.

A modern economy possesses a number of features which tend to accelerate both upward and downward movements in business activity. The banking system, the multiplier, psychological tendencies and the acceleration principle all contribute to this "cumulative process."

According to the National Bureau of Economic Research, business cycles are all of one general type, though their duration may be from one to a dozen years. According to J. A. Schumpeter there are three distinct types of cycle, the shortest lasting about 40 months and the longest about 60 years. The expansion phase of these long cycles he considered to be initiated by major technological advances.

The prosperity phase of a business cycle tends to be characterized by a high level of investment activity, the depression phase by a low level of investment activity. The phases of the business cycle are linked together, in that each develops characteristics which help to bring on the next phase. The actual shift from one phase to the next may occur under the impact of some external development.

Because of Canada's heavy dependence upon foreign markets and foreign capital, she has experienced business cycles which closely paralleled those taking place in other countries, notably those which occurred in the United States.

FOR REVIEW AND DISCUSSION

1. Economic progress is incompatible with economic stability. Do you agree? Justify your answer.
2. Which phase of the business cycle would you say that Canada is currently in? What developments are going on which lead you to believe that the next phase will soon materialize?

3. There is one infallible maxim in business cycle analysis—"The bigger the boom, the bigger the bust." Do you agree that this is an "infallible maxim"? Justify your answer.
4. "We should all be alarmed by the growing volume of consumer credit." Do you agree?
5. The percentage of the National Income which goes to labour generally tends to increase during a depression. Why should this be so?
6. Make up your own example to illustrate the working of the "acceleration principle."
7. An individual industry might conceivably experience cyclical fluctuations which were quite unconnected with changes in the level of general business activity. Explain and illustrate.
8. Each phase of the business cycle contains within itself buds which will blossom in the next phase. Explain.
9. Whether a depression is mild or severe will depend primarily upon what happens to the construction industry. Comment.
10. Contrast the view of J. A. Schumpeter with that of the National Bureau of Economic Research, in respect to the duration of business cycles.

27 Economic Stabilization by Government Action

INHERENT TENDENCIES TO INSTABILITY

We saw in Chapter 24 that economic activity is carried out in response to the spending of money. The total amount of activity carried out in a country in any given year depends upon the aggregate of money spent. This aggregate of national expenditure is made, we noted, upon four broad categories of goods and services: consumption goods and services, capital goods, government goods and services, and exports. Not all of this expenditure, we observed, is paid out to factors of production within the country. Some of this expenditure goes to foreigners for goods and services which they provide; some is taken by the government in indirect taxes; some is set aside by businessmen in depreciation allowances. The balance left after these three deductions represents the amount paid to domestic factors of production, in return for which they perform their services.

Each of the categories of expenditure and each of the deductions, varies with its own particular set of determinants. The public's total expenditure on consumption goods and services reflects the decisions of millions of individuals, each concerned to satisfy wants and needs in the manner which appears most advantageous; these decisions vary from one time to another in accordance with changing incomes, needs and tastes. The total of spending on capital goods reflects the decisions made by countless businessmen, each of whom invests his own or borrowed money in ventures which promise a profitable return; in some years numerous profitable opportunities appear, in other years, very few. Government spending reflects the people's demand for public services, and their willingness to pay for them, both of which vary from one time to another. Foreign spending in any one country varies with the financial capacity of foreign nations and their desire to buy its exports; that country's spending on imports varies, conversely, with its own financial capacity, and its people's desire to purchase foreign goods.

With each of its elements determined by a host of ever changing variables, the aggregate of national expenditure may vary greatly from one period to another. In one year the influences upon each of the categories of spending may be expansive, so that the aggregate is large: in another year all the influences may be restrictive, so that the aggregate is small. But in any one year there is only one figure for aggregate national expenditure which would be "ideal." That would be the amount which induces full employment, without inflation. Because of the number and variability of its determining factors, the aggregate is unlikely ever to amount exactly to the "ideal" figure. It may, in fact, turn out to be considerably greater or considerably less. What is more, as we saw in Chapter 26, two of the main categories of expenditure in a country are liable to pronounced cyclical fluctuations. Because of the inherent characteristics of a modern industrial economy, expenditures on consumption and investment tend to spiral upward and downward in an ever-recurring sequence of phases.

THE "KEYNESIAN REVOLUTION"

Until about a generation ago it was generally agreed that there was little that need be done, or could be done, to achieve the optimum aggregate of expenditure. Adherence to the gold standard provided assurance against inflation. Everyone assumed that a depression was bound to be limited and liquidated in fairly short order by the "natural forces of recovery." No special governmental measures were called for to deal with a depression, aside from the provision of emergency assistance to the unfortunate individuals who had lost their means of livelihood. Prevailing economic orthodoxy instead called for government policies which, as we know today, had the effect of intensifying depression.

A major intellectual break-through occurred in 1936, in the middle of the Great Depression. In that year England's John Maynard Keynes published the *General Theory of Employment, Interest and Money*, a volume in which he outlined a brilliantly reasoned theory of how the aggregate level of economic activity is determined and how it can be influenced by government action.[1] Economists in other countries explored further along the path he opened up: the outpouring of new ideas on the subject became referred to as the "Keynesian Revolution." While not all economists agree wholeheartedly with Keynes or his disciples, all have been influenced; all are "Post-Keynesians." A new orthodoxy has developed: economists now generally agree that the government of a country can and should take action to maintain a high and stable level of employment. Governments have in turn acknowledged the responsibility. In 1944 the government of Great Britain issued a White Paper to that effect: in 1945 the Canadian government issued a White Paper along similar lines; a year later the American Congress passed the Employment Act which required the government to take appropriate action to ensure the maintenance of prosperous economic conditions.

[1]The analysis in Chapter 25 of the equilibrium level of National Income is derived from the work of Keynes.

STABILIZATION TECHNIQUES

If a government fulfils to perfection its role as stabilizer, it will arrange that total spending in the country amounts each year to the figure which will induce full employment without inflation. That figure will be higher in each successive year, since each year the economy's productive capacity becomes larger, thanks to increase in the labour force, the utilization of improved techniques, more and better plant and equipment. The government can affect the total spending carried out in a country by varying its own spending, and by causing private people to vary theirs. If the aggregate of spending is excessive, the government can reduce its own spending, and adopt measures which will reduce spending by private persons and firms. If the aggregate of spending is too small, the government can increase its own spending, and introduce measures which will cause private persons and firms to increase their spending.

The Automatic Stabilizers

In a modern country like Canada, the task of keeping the economy stable is, in part, performed automatically. There exist a number of "automatic stabilizers" which serve to offset, to some extent, any change in total spending in the country. Whenever an increase in spending occurs, the stabilizers automatically siphon off some of the extra money in circulation; when a decrease in spending occurs, the stabilizers automatically restore part of the reduction. The main stabilizers are the following three: *unemployment insurance, tax collections,* and *savings.* Let's see how they work to counteract tendencies to inflation and depression.

Against Inflation

When inflation threatens, or actually exists, full employment is likely to prevail, with wage levels high. Very few insured workers will be drawing benefits from the Unemployment Insurance Fund; practically all will be paying into it. The money they pay into the Fund is taken out of circulation. It cannot be spent by the people who earned it; inflationary pressure is reduced correspondingly. Similarly, when inflation threatens, tax collections by the government will rise, even without any change in the *rate* of taxation. The higher incomes which people are earning and the larger profits which firms are achieving, oblige them to hand over more money to the government in personal income taxes and corporation profit taxes. The public's heavy spending will result in larger government collections on the various sales taxes, excise taxes, and the like. These increased tax collections will reduce, desirably at the time, the public's spending power. Finally, during good times, individuals tend to save a considerable proportion of their incomes, while corporations accumulate profits which they do not distribute. The fact that these funds are saved rather than spent also eases the inflationary pressure.

Against Depression

During a depression the three stabilizers all operate in reverse. At such a time it would be desirable to have additional money put into circulation. Our stabilizers do just that. Large payments are made out of the Unemployment Insurance Fund to the many workers who have lost their jobs. Because personal incomes, corporate profits, and the public's spending are all lower, less money is drained out of circulation *via* taxation. Finally, a good many individuals whose incomes are down draw on their savings to tide them over; firms draw on previously accumulated surpluses to pay dividends or to pay for purchases. The total effect is to increase the money in circulation above the level at which it would have stood had the stabilizers not been in action.

Farm Price Supports

A price support programme for farm products *may* serve as a stabilizer. If farm prices tend to decline during a general business depression, then government payments to farmers desirably increase the money in circulation. If, however, farm prices tend to fall below support levels when business generally is booming, the government payments are de-stabilizing; they increase the money in circulation at a time when it is already adequate or more than adequate.

Automatic Stabilizers Do Only Part of the Job

The automatic stabilizers are helpful, but their effect is limited. They reduce inflationary and deflationary pressures, but only partially. It was estimated in 1948, that a $10 billion drop in the U.S. National Income would have had only one-third of its depressive effects offset by the automatic stabilizers which then existed. Their power has not greatly increased since that time. The situation in Canada is unlikely to be very different.

GOVERNMENT ANTI-CYCLICAL POLICY

If tendencies to inflation and depression are to be checked completely, the government must supplement the automatic stabilizers. When a danger of inflation develops, the government must take action to reduce the aggregate of spending in the country. When depression threatens, the government must take action to increase that aggregate. There are three distinct types of policy which the government may adopt in order to help stabilize the country: _monetary policy_, _fiscal policy_, and _trade policy_. They are not mutually exclusive; the government may adopt elements of all three in order to have a balanced programme. Let's see what each involves.

Monetary Policy

A good deal of the money spent by consumers and businessmen is borrowed from banks. All sorts of people are anxious to buy goods for which they do not have the ready cash. They borrow money from banks or from finance companies or they buy on the instalment plan. Whichever of these procedures they follow, bank lending is likely to be involved. Finance companies borrow from banks much of the money which they lend to their customers. Goods sold on the instalment plan are generally financed by bank credit. The merchant who sells on "terms" must himself pay his suppliers at once for the merchandise; he borrows the money from a bank, repaying the loan as his customers pay their instalments.

A great many business firms borrow from the banks in order to buy materials and equipment, to pay wages, to acquire inventory. Some firms finance such expenditures out of their own cash resources, but many need, and can use profitably, more cash than they themselves possess. They must borrow, and for many firms a bank is *the* source of borrowed funds.

To Counteract Inflation

As we saw in Chapter 22, the central bank of a country can affect the lending power of the commercial banks. To restrict bank lending it can sell bonds on the open market, thereby reducing bank reserves and bringing about an increase in the rate of interest. The reduction in commercial bank reserves reduces their capacity to lend; the rise in the rate of interest reduces the public's desire to borrow. The central bank may require the commercial banks to keep higher cash reserve ratios, thereby preventing them from lending out some of their funds. It may raise Bank Rate and so deter banks from increasing their lending. It may simply request the banks to restrict their loans, without actually adopting measures which would force them to do so.

To Counteract Depression

To bring about an increase in the spending of consumers and businessmen, these procedures would be exactly reversed. The central bank would buy bonds, thereby increasing commercial bank reserves and lowering the rate of interest. With larger reserves the banks would have increased capacity to lend; with the interest rate lower, the public would have greater incentive to borrow. The central bank might lower the cash reserve ratio which commercial banks were required to keep; more of their funds would thereby become available for lending. It might lower Bank Rate, thereby encouraging banks to lend more freely. Finally, it might urge the banks to adopt more liberal lending policies.

Government Responsibility for Monetary Policy

When any of the above measures are adopted to combat an undesired change in the amount of spending in a country, we say that *monetary policy* is employed. These measures will actually be applied by the country's central bank, rather than by the government itself. However, while the head of the central bank enjoys a considerable measure of independence, the bank's policies are likely to be in accordance with the government's wishes. There is, normally, close consultation with the government; if the government disapproves of the actions of the central bank, it can replace the persons in charge.[2] In the long run, therefore, the policies followed by the central bank must be the kind which the government wishes to be followed.

Fiscal Policy

In the category of fiscal policy we include three distinct measures which the government may adopt. It may vary its rates of taxation, increase its own spending, vary the scale of the various welfare payments it makes to its citizens. Let us see how each of these measures may be applied, in order to offset the total of spending in the country.

Varying the Rates of Taxation

A modern government takes away from its citizens an enormous sum of money each year, through its personal income tax, its sales and excise taxes, its tax on the profits of corporations. By varying the rates of taxation which it imposes, the government can affect the spending power of private persons and business firms. An increase in the sales tax or in the personal income tax will leave less money in the ordinary person's wallet and therefore compel a reduction in his spending. A reduction in these taxes will leave him with more money, and thereby enable an increase in his spending.

An increase in the corporation profit tax will reduce the sum which can be paid out in dividends to stockholders and which they might spend. Furthermore, it will tend to reduce investment in new plant and equipment, for two distinct reasons. With profits taxed at a higher rate, the investor will receive a smaller return and will therefore have less incentive to invest. Secondly, a great deal of investment is nowadays financed out of previously earned profit. The more of this profit the government takes away in tax, the less money will firms have available for investment. Conversely, a reduction in the tax on profits will have expansive effects. It will enable larger dividends to be paid to stockholders, increasing their spending power. It would, as well, increase the incentive to invest and enlarge the amount of money available for investment.

Government Spending

As we saw in Chapter 24, there is, realistically, only one type of government spending which can be substantially increased or reduced, as the government thinks fit. That

[2]Revelations made in June, 1961, indicate that there was very little consultation between the current Canadian government and the current Governor of the Bank of Canada. The federal Minister of Finance publicly accused the Governor of acting contrary to the government's wishes; in presenting his budget for the forthcoming year, the Minister emphatically declared that the Governor had not been consulted when it was being prepared.

is expenditure on public works, on the construction of roads, bridges, public buildings and the like. While such projects may be desirable, it may not be urgent to have them immediately. The government can build them at whatever time is most appropriate in respect to stabilizing the nation's economy. A certain highway might be useful at the present time, for instance, but the need for it will be really pressing only in ten years. The government would be able to exercise discretion in regard to the timing of construction. If the government wished to increase its current spending, it could safely defer construction to a later date.

During a business recession the government can increase its spending by undertaking a large public works programme. Projects which will be needed in the future can be built right away. The additional money is likely to go to people who need it badly. During a depression there is likely to be little building going on; there will therefore be large scale unemployment among construction workers and workers employed in the industries which produce construction materials. The government's building programme will provide work to people who would otherwise have been jobless. If, during an inflationary period, the government curtails its spending on public works, no one is likely to lose his job. At such a time the construction industry is likely to be fully occupied in building houses and business buildings, and there is no need for government work to provide jobs.

Varying the Scale of Welfare Payments

A modern government gives as well as takes. Each year it distributes very large sums to its citizens in the form of pensions, children's allowances and the like. The government-operated Unemployment Insurance scheme makes substantial payments each year to persons who have lost their jobs and are qualified for benefits. Since the bulk of these payments are made to people with low incomes, it can be relied upon that practically all the money paid out will be spent by the people who receive it. Accordingly, if the government wishes to increase spending, it can increase the scale of these various "transfer payments." A reduction in these payments would help to reduce spending in the country at a time when it was too great. (No government is likely to reduce welfare payments as an anti-inflationary measure, however, for reasons given later in this chapter.)

TRADE POLICY

Exports, Imports and Employment

We saw in Chapter 16 that the total of spending in Canada includes the spending of foreigners who buy our exports. We noted, too, that not all of the money spent by Canadians gives employment to Canadians; some of our spending is on imports which are produced by workers in other countries. If we increased our exports or reduced our imports, we would increase the spending which provides employment to Canadians. If we increased our exports, foreigners would be spending more money in Canada, providing additional jobs for workers in our export industries. If we reduced our imports, money hitherto spent by Canadians on foreign goods and services might be spent in Canada instead, and give employment to Canadians rather than to foreign workers.

How to Vary the Scale of Exports and Imports

A variety of means may be used to achieve these objectives. To stimulate an increase in exports, the government might depreciate the national currency; all goods produced in the country would thereupon become cheaper so far as foreigners were concerned, and presumably they would want to buy more. (Imports would likely be reduced; foreign goods would become dearer as far as Canadians were concerned, and presumably they would want to buy less of them.)[3] Or, to increase exports, the government might offer subsidies and tax concessions to exporters, so that they could offer their goods to foreigners at lower prices. Or the government could lend or give money to foreign countries, thereby furnishing them with means of payment which they otherwise would not have. To reduce imports the government might raise tariffs, reduce import quotas, and restrict the purchase by Canadians of the foreign currency they need to pay for imports. Money which otherwise would have been spent in foreign countries might be spent at home instead.

The foregoing measures would increase the amount of money spent in Canada. They would be appropriate, therefore, during a period of depression, when many people were unemployed and additional spending in the country would provide additional jobs (though, as we shall see, some of these measures have such severe drawbacks that it might be better not to use them). During a period of inflationary pressure these measures would be discontinued, and perhaps completely reversed. All forms of assistance to exporters would be withdrawn; restrictions might even be imposed on exports. Imports, on the other hand, might be encouraged.

LIMITATIONS AND DRAWBACKS OF STABILIZATION TECHNIQUES

Our argument is pat. Absolute economic stability seems readily attainable. The automatic stabilizers reduce considerably any tendencies to deviation. The government supplements the automatic stabilizers by *ad hoc* measures, and so prevents deviation altogether. When inflation threatens, the central bank takes action to check

---

[3] A change in monetary policy might serve to bring about the desired depreciation of the Canadian dollar. If the Bank of Canada were to increase the country's money supply, one likely result would be a fall in the dollar's foreign exchange rate.

the lending powers of the commercial banks; the government raises taxes, and reduces its spending as much as possible. Exports may be restricted and imports encouraged. When depression threatens, the policies are reversed. However, the argument is too pat. It ignores the very great difficulties which are encountered in the real world when stabilization measures are attempted, difficulties which cause these measures to work only imperfectly, or to give rise to problems of their own.

Monetary Measures

(a) **Ineffective Against Depression.** Monetary policies designed to bring about an expansion of bank lending may prove to be ineffective. The central bank may, by open-market bond purchases, increase the cash holdings of the commercial banks well beyond the amount they require for reserves. But the banks may not lend out the additional cash; they may simply hold larger reserves than necessary. The fact that they have more money to lend will prove significant only if businessmen want to borrow more. In the depths of a depression, with the outlook bleak, they may have no such desire. The same negative consequences may follow from a reduction in the cash reserve ratio which commercial banks are required to maintain. The decline in the rate of interest which accompanies bond purchases by the central bank may not induce any increase in borrowing. Most of the people who borrow for consumption purposes are probably unaware of the rate of interest they are being charged; for most business borrowers, interest charges constitute a very small item in their total costs, and changes in that item are unlikely to exert a significant influence upon their investment decisions. What is more, if the rate of interest is already very low, there is little room for a substantial reduction.

(b) **Obstacles to Use During Inflation.** Monetary policy is likely to be more effective in curbing inflation: while the authorities cannot force people to borrow when they do not want to, they can prevent them from borrowing when they do want to. But even in dealing with inflation monetary policies suffer from grave deficiencies. If applied too vigorously, restrictions on lending may convert an inflation into a depression: the economy is shifted from the frying pan into the fire. Also, open-market bond sales by the central bank cannot be pushed very far. As a result of the government's heavy borrowing in the past, a very large volume of bonds is now outstanding.[4] A great many individuals hold bonds as savings; banks and other business firms hold large quantities as liquid assets. If the central bank were to sell bonds to such a degree that their price fell greatly there would be a furious outcry from the numerous people who held them. What is more, these bonds can be readily sold at any time, so that banks which wish to increase their loans to businessmen can always sell some of their ample supply of bonds and lend out the cash received

---

[4]In the case of Canada (and the U.S.) the great bulk of the federal government's present debt was incurred to finance its expenditures during World War II, and most of the remainder was incurred in the course of World War I.

for them. Similarly, business firms which hold bonds need not borrow from the bank; they can raise money by cashing their bonds.[5]

(c) **Higher Interest Rates Ineffective.** With the central bank following a restrictive "tight money" policy, interest rates would rise; but higher interest rates might not provide the hoped-for deterrence against borrowing. As we have already noted, interest charges generally constitute a small proportion of operating costs: few businessmen would refrain from a contemplated investment merely because they had to pay more interest on borrowed funds. In the case of borrowing by consumers a rise in the interest rate can be effectively concealed by a lengthening of the amortization period. Instalment buyers might be required to make a longer series of payments, but the size of each payment—which is their chief concern—would be kept unchanged. But while a rise in the interest rate might not deter borrowing, it would make things awkward for the government. The federal government is a very large and frequent borrower, to raise the money it needs to pay off old loans which have fallen due and to finance projects for which tax revenues are not adequate. Like everyone else the government will have to pay the higher rate of interest; in view of the large scale of its borrowings the extra cost will be substantial, and will likely oblige the government to increase significantly its tax levies. Provincial and municipal governments will encounter the same difficulties.

(d) **Uneven Incidence of Credit Restrictions.** When, to curb inflation, the central bank adopts a "tight money" policy, it is intended that the credit restraints apply impersonally and evenly over the whole economy. Unfortunately, their incidence is not completely general and uniform. Some types of enterprise bear the full brunt of the restrictions while others are completely unaffected. For not all firms depend for their finances upon bank loans. Large corporations may be able to finance new investment out of their accumulated profits and reserves; when they do require outside capital they may be able to raise it by selling stocks or bonds to the general public. Furthermore, the banks are not the only institutions from which money can be borrowed. The life insurance companies, trust companies, pension funds, investment mutuals, and similar organizations, receive and lend out a large proportion of the nation's savings. In effect these financial houses constitute a separate banking system in the country, one which is unresponsive to restrictive measures adopted by the central bank.[6] Borrowers from these institutions may,

---

[5]The price received by sellers of bonds will depend upon market conditions prevailing at the time of sale. If a great many people are simultaneously trying to sell bonds, the price is likely to be driven sharply down. Anyone who sells bonds at such a time will suffer a substantial capital loss. The prospect of a large capital loss may deter the banks and other firms from selling bonds in order to raise cash. On the other hand, the use to which the cash can be put may be so profitable as to warrant the capital loss involved in selling bonds to acquire the cash.

[6]This view, recently put forward by some distinguished American economists, is not universally accepted. Speaking to the Royal Commission on Banking and Finance in January 1963, the Governor of the Bank of Canada expressed the opinion that in fact pressures applied by the central bank did affect all financial institutions and not just the chartered banks.

therefore, be little affected by those measures. Finally, as Canadian experience amply indicates, some firms, and provincial and municipal governments as well, may borrow money in foreign countries, thereby circumventing the restraints imposed by the central bank of their own country. Foreign owned firms may spend in one country money which they have obtained in their country of origin.

The burden of credit restrictions may not be evenly distributed even among those people who do borrow from the banks. There is evidence that when, because of the central bank's repressive measures, the commercial banks' lending powers are restricted, they show a preference for large borrowers as opposed to small. It is not difficult to see why such discrimination might occur. At a time when it could not satisfy all demands for loans, a bank might understandably lend out its available funds only to large and valued customers whose patronage it was most anxious to retain. Small borrowers who in ordinary times had equal access to bank loans would find themselves at a relative disadvantage during a period of "tight money." Money might be "tightened" primarily against them.[7]

(e) **Self-defeating possibilities.** The high rates of interest and the shortage of credit produced by anti-inflationary monetary policy may, ironically, aggravate the inflation it seeks to repress. High interest rates and limitation of credit are supposed to curtail the spending of borrowed funds: inflationary pressure will be eased, supposedly, because less money will be available with which to bid prices upward. But interest is a cost of production, a very important cost indeed in the construction industry; higher interest rates therefore require increases in building prices and rents and in the prices of all goods whose production involves the use of borrowed funds. What is more, high interest rates or limitations of credit may prevent investment in additional, perhaps more efficient productive capacity whose output, to be achieved in the future, would help keep future prices down. Hence, both in the immediate present and in the long run, restrictive monetary measures may prove to be self-defeating.

Public Works: The Problem of Timing

The appropriate variation in public works construction is by no means easy to arrange. Large projects must be planned and prepared for well in advance. It may take a year or more to draw up the plans for a bridge or building, or to acquire the right-of-way for a new road. Unless the government has previously made such preparations, actual construction can be begun only after a considerable delay. Where the anti-depression public works programme involves the construction of major projects which take a long time to complete, another kind of timing problem may develop: prosperity may return before the projects are completed. Since bridges, highways

---

[7]The federal government charged the banks with such discrimination in 1959. The banks denied the charge, however, and produced statistics to prove that small borrowers were getting their fair share and more of available funds.

and buildings cannot be left half-built, they must be completed at a time when their construction does not help stabilize the economy but actually increases inflationary pressures.

The Timing of Locally Financed Public Works

While the federal government phases its public works construction anticyclically, provincial and municipal governments are likely to do the opposite. During a period of depression these governments are likely to curtail their expenditures on public works. Their revenues are likely to be reduced, and they may experience difficulty in borrowing money. Because of the generally slack activity, there may be no real need for new public works; even if money could be borrowed it would be pointless to undertake the onerous debt charges involved in order to carry out new projects. During a period of inflation, on the other hand, provincial and municipal governments are likely to increase greatly their expenditures on public works. Revenues are buoyant and money can readily be borrowed. With large scale private construction going on, these governments become obligated to build new schools and hospitals, to lay down new roads, streets, sewers and water mains. The public's demand for these new facilities is insistent and must be met. Reductions in spending on public works by the federal government at this time may be offset by increases in spending on public works by local governments.

Public Works May Not Be Helpful

Public works projects may badly fit the need during some recessions. A business downturn may be due primarily to a slackening of demand for consumer goods or to a reduction in inventory accumulation by business firms. Construction activity may be continuing at a high level. In such a case the launching of a great public works programme will fail to provide help where it is most needed. It will produce competition for labour and materials—and therefore inflationary pressure—in the construction industry, without providing much assistance to the sectors of the economy which are worst hit by the recession.

Fiscal Policy and the Public Accounts

The fiscal measures which the government applies to counter the business cycle will affect the public accounts. As we have seen, the government, to deal with inflation, should raise its rates of taxation. What with the high incomes being earned at the time, its tax receipts would become very much larger than before. At the same time the government would be keeping its spending to a minimum. With receipts large and expenditures small, the government would likely achieve a considerable budget surplus.

Precisely the opposite result would occur when the government applied fiscal measures against a recession. Tax rates would be reduced; what with lower incomes and lower rates of taxation, the government's revenue would be considerably lower than before. At the same time it would be increasing its spending; the combination of smaller revenue and larger expenditure would produce a budget deficit.

Public Hostility to Anti-Inflation Fiscal Measures

Nobody likes to pay high taxes; except during emergencies such as in wartime, a government simply dare not introduce sharp increases in its rates of taxation, even if these would help keep the economy stable. As a matter of fact, the government may be under strong pressure to reduce taxes during a period of inflation. If its tax receipts exceeded its expenditures, political opponents would likely accuse the government of "over-taxation," charging that it was taking away from the people more money than it really needed. The general public might be impressed by such a charge. Every individual would naturally welcome a reduction in his taxes; many would fail to consider that a nation-wide tax reduction would leave more money in circulation, and would therefore aggravate the prevailing inflation.

Reductions in transfer payments, in old age pensions, family allowances, and the like, would help to curb inflation, but these are simply out of the question. Such payments go mostly to the poorer people of the country. Even if unchanged in size their purchasing power will have been reduced by the inflation. It would be unthinkable that the government reduce their size, and so impose further hardship upon its poorer citizens. In fact, on the grounds of social justice and political advantage, the government is likely to increase the scale of transfer payments during a period of inflation, and thereby to increase the inflationary pressure.

Worst of all, spending restraints are likely to give rise to unemployment. Ideally, reductions in spending in the country should be applied only to that portion of national spending which serves to bid up prices. In fact, reductions in the national aggregate of spending are likely to include complete cessation of demand for the services of a good many workers; the spending restraints cost them their jobs.

Ironically, the unemployment caused by spending restraints itself has inflationary effect. Unemployed persons, contributing nothing to national output, will be spending money drawn from savings or received as welfare allowances and as unemployment insurance benefits. The effect of their spending, without any corresponding output on their part, is inevitably inflationary.

Increasing the National Debt: Misgivings

Anti-depression fiscal measures are likely to be welcome. Few people will object to having their taxes reduced, or to receiving larger pensions and allowances from the government. Those persons who are employed on public works projects such as highways and schools, will be grateful for their jobs; the communities in which these projects are built, will be pleased to acquire them.

Nevertheless, a great many people are likely to have misgivings. The government, taxing less and spending more, will be incurring a budget deficit. The amount of this deficit will have to be borrowed, and this borrowing will be added to the national debt. Concern will be felt at the fact that the debt is being increased. Some people will take the stand that such increases endanger the whole financial structure of the country, and that any policies which involve large scale government borrowing are reckless and irresponsible.

We Owe the Money to Ourselves

These fears are unwarranted; the national debt is not the fearful burden that it is widely supposed to be. The overwhelming majority of the federal government bonds which constitute Canada's national debt, are owned by Canadian citizens and Canadian firms. This debt of the Canadian nation is owed to its own people. To pay interest and principal on this debt, the federal government takes money away from its citizens in their capacity of taxpayers; it pays back this same money to Canadian citizens in their capacity of bondholders. The country as a whole is neither richer nor poorer because that debt exists. The existence of the debt is merely responsible for some transfer of income within the country, from taxpayers to bondholders. To the extent that taxpayers are also bondholders there is not even such a transfer; people get back their own money.

The well-intentioned people who are concerned about the national debt are in error because they make a false assumption. They know that the debt of a family or a firm is burdensome, and that increases in such debts can be dangerous. They assume that the same must hold true for the national debt of a country. The debt of a family or a firm is owed to other people; interest and principal must be paid to outsiders. The national debt of a country, on the other hand, consists of money which the people of the country owe to themselves; the interest and principal which is paid by the nation, is received by people of that nation. "Debt" which we owe to ourselves is not really debt at all; some other word should be used to describe it.

Our Past Experience with the National Debt

Our historical experience confirms this view. In 1939, just before World War II began, Canada had a national debt of about $3 billion; as a result of heavy borrowing to pay for the national war effort, the debt rose to $13 billion in 1945. This gigantic increase did not damage the Canadian economy in any way. In fact, since 1945, the Canadian economy, with a national debt of over $13 billion, has been far more sound, healthy and prosperous than it was during the depressed 1930s, when the debt was only $3 billion. The experience of the United States, Great Britain and other countries, has been similar. Debt increases of utterly fantastic proportions would no doubt be harmful; our past experience suggests that we would not be harmed by increases of the proportions that would be required to offset a business recession.

While the national debt is not a burden in the generally understood sense, it does give rise to problems. In order to raise the money it needs to pay interest, the government is obliged to impose higher taxes than would otherwise be necessary. All taxes, however, have a deterrent effect on effort and enterprise; the higher the taxes, the greater the deterrence. An increase in the national debt, incurred for whatever reason, tends indirectly to interfere with the nation's production by enlarging one of the deterrents to effort and enterprise. Furthermore, as we have just seen, the debt gives rise to a transfer of income by the government, from the country's tax payers to its bondholders; this proceeding is not universally favoured.[8] Finally, the existence of a large national debt, as we saw earlier in the chapter, limits the degree to which monetary policy may be used to curb inflation. Each increase in the debt, even if incurred in the course of fighting a depression, aggravates the difficulty of dealing with a subsequent inflation.

There is legitimate cause for concern, therefore, about policies which result in increases in the national debt; some disadvantages and dangers are involved. However, where such policies are the only means of providing useful employment for people who would otherwise have been jobless, the benefits are likely to outweigh the drawbacks, and by a considerable margin.

Adverse Reactions to Trade Policies

If, to increase employment during a depression, the government artificially stimulates exports and reduces imports, its measures may backfire. Its assistance to exporters, whether in the form of exchange depreciation or subsidies, will give them a competitive advantage over the exporters of the same products in other countries. But the governments of those countries may adopt counter-measures; they may also depreciate their currencies or grant subsidies to their exporters. In that event no country would increase its exports substantially while all would realize lower returns.

Restrictions on imports, introduced to create jobs at home, in effect "export unemployment"; foreign firms lose some of their sales and are obliged to discharge some of their workers. The matter does not end here. Because these firms are earning less foreign currency for their countries, their governments will likely be obliged to reduce imports. Very likely among the imports which are cut, will be those from

---

[8] A word of caution is in order. Many people seem to think that the interest payments which the government makes to its bondholders represent money which they have not "earned," and which they otherwise would not have received. The fact is that bondholders paid for their bonds with their savings. Had they not bought the bonds, they could have used the money in other ways. They could have bought consumer goods for themselves, or they could have bought other securities on which they would also have received interest or dividends. In the case of wealthy people who own large amounts of government bonds, it should be recognized that it is not their ownership of the bonds which has made them wealthy; rather, it is because they were wealthy already that they were able to buy a great many bonds. If the government had never sold bonds, these people would presumably have invested their wealth in other ways, and would have received large annual returns in any case.

the country which introduced trade restrictions in order to increase employment. That nation will thereupon experience unemployment in its export industries. The ultimate result of the government's attempt to increase employment by reducing imports might therefore be harmful rather than helpful. Some jobs may indeed be created in industries for which the country is not naturally well adapted; in the process, jobs are likely to be eliminated in export industries for which the country is well adapted. If many countries introduce import restrictions, as was the case during the 1930s, a general reduction in international trade will occur, producing a general impoverishment and a general decline rather than increase in employment.

Stabilization Measures Always Lag

Government measures to offset the business cycle are virtually bound to be delayed, undertaken long after the need for them has first materialized. The reason is twofold. Neither inflation nor depression is likely to be clearly recognizable in its early stages. In a complex situation where some elements are rising, some standing still, and others falling, the beginning of a general tendency in one direction or another is not easily detected. The statistical figures which outline the situation and upon which final assessment must be based, may appear only weeks or months after the events to which they refer. Even if a general tendency is detected, there can be no certainty that it is actually the beginning of a major trend; it may turn out to be only a temporary movement in one direction which reverses itself before reaching really significant proportions. Like a doctor who can only diagnose with confidence once his patient's symptoms have become severe, so the economist may be able to diagnose an inflation or depression with assurance only after it has attained troublesome proportions.

Remedial action can safely be undertaken only once the nature of the problem has become clear; action undertaken on the basis of a wrong diagnosis would prove harmful. For example, unemployment may develop in some industries, leading the authorities to believe that a major depression was imminent. They might embark upon a massive anti-depression programme, reducing taxes, liberalizing credit, and launching large public works projects. The symptoms may have been misleading, however. Business may recover of its own accord. The government's anti-depression programme then turns out to be positively harmful because, under the circumstances, it contributes to inflation.

As we have just seen, some time is likely to elapse before an inflation or depression is confidently diagnosed and the need for remedial action conclusively established. Even when this need is fully acknowledged, there may be a considerable time lag before action is actually taken. In a democratic country special anti-cyclical measures must be approved by the parliamentary authority. The pros and cons may have to be debated lengthily before a particular course of action is decided upon and, once a decision is reached, there may be a considerable lapse of time before it is implemented. Lengthy communications may have to be passed through labyrinthine bureaucratic channels; it may take a long while before the slow and ponderous machinery of government translates parliamentary decisions into concrete actions.

Despite Limitations, Stabilization Attempts Justified

As we have noted in the last few pages, government attempts at stabilization are beset with formidable difficulties. Each line of action can only be pursued to a limited extent; a good many measures give rise to new problems. While the difficulties should not be overlooked they should not be over-emphasized either. Stabilization policies which are soundly conceived, and are applied with care and judgment, can be enormously worthwhile.

Where anti-cyclical measures give rise to new problems, these may prove to be less serious than the ones they liquidate. What is more, effective solutions may be found for these new problems. Where monetary restraints give rise to discrimination against small firms, the government may counter by providing special assistance to such firms. Remedial action which is taken only after a time lag is better than no remedial action at all. Furthermore, effective measures may be taken to reduce the delay. The government may maintain a "shelf" full of blueprints for specific public works projects. Construction contracts can be issued immediately the authorities feel that an increase in public works spending is warranted. There need be no wait while plans for projects are being drawn; the contractor is simply given a set of blueprints taken from the "shelf."

"Formula flexibility" may be introduced to short-circuit the lengthy interval between the emergence of a problem and the implementation of remedial measures. The government may legislate that whenever designated statistical indicators reach certain levels, then remedial action is to be carried out automatically. For instance, it may be laid down that for each percentage increase in unemployment, taxes are automatically to be cut by a certain amount, public works spending to be increased by a certain amount, and so on. For each percentage rise in the price level, taxes may automatically be raised and public works spending reduced, both by amounts designated beforehand. Like most anti-cyclical measures "formula flexibility" cannot be pressed too far, of course. Each situation has its own unique elements which must be appreciated and appropriately dealt with. While a single formula cannot deal adequately with all cyclical problems, it can, if carefully designed, strengthen the effectiveness of the "automatic stabilizers" which we now have; less difficulty would be experienced because of governmental delays in applying discretionary remedial measures.

Another method of ensuring speedier government action to deal with economic fluctuations would be to confer appropriate stand-by powers on the executive. In Great Britain today, for instance, the Chancellor of the Exchequer has the power to vary sales and excise taxes by as much as ten per cent in order to counter tendencies to inflation or depression. President Kennedy in 1962 sought, unsuccessfully, the authority to spend large sums on public works projects without waiting for Congressional approval.

NEED FOR NUMEROUS, SELECTIVE PROGRAMMES

The fact that any individual measure produces only limited benefits should not be allowed to obscure the fact that its results are beneficial, and that the country is better off because the measure has been applied. While the benefit yielded by any individual measure may be limited, a diversified programme which includes a number of different measures may produce great benefit. Each element in the programme may contribute its part to the solution of the problem, so that the total effect is substantial.

Like some of the artillery barrages of wartime, broad anti-cyclical measures may do a great deal of unnecessary damage, while touching their real targets only lightly. Highly specific measures may be needed, each aimed explicitly at a particular problem, as opposed to sweeping policies that will produce widespread, generalized effects. Thus if particular types of worker are unemployed, what may be needed are projects to stimulate selectively the particular sectors of the economy in which they can be employed, rather than generalized measures—such as reduction in taxation—which would generate widely diffused tendencies to expansion. Unless this is done serious unemployment may continue because very little of the expansive effort is applied to the real problem area, while inflation develops in other sectors because of expansive pressure that is being applied there quite unnecessarily.

ADDITIONAL GOALS OF PUBLIC POLICY

Appropriate Composition of the National Product

As if the task of ensuring full employment without inflation were not sufficiently complicated and difficult, we expect the government to achieve even more. We want the national aggregate of expenditure to be ideal not only in its size but also in its composition. The way money is spent determines the kind of goods and services which are produced. We desire that the various categories of spending which together compose the national aggregate should always be in proper proportion; if they are, then our productive capacity will be used to produce each kind of good and service in appropriate quantity. Government policies designed to achieve economic stability should have this additional objective in view.

In dealing with a depression the government should arrange for an increase in those expenditures which would bring about increased production of the goods and services which the country needed most. If standards of consumption were unduly low then the government, in countering the depression, should emphasize measures which would result in increased consumption by the public. If the buildings and equipment owned by private firms were outmoded and inadequate, the government should counter the depression by stimulating private investment. If the country were sadly deficient in public facilities such as schools, hospitals and highways, then the government should employ a public works programme as its main weapon against depression.

A corresponding issue arises in the combating of inflation. When the aggregate of expenditure threatens to be excessive, it is the government's responsibility to apply restraints. There is the same need to arrange that the resultant aggregate of expenditure be appropriately composed. Restraints should be applied particularly against those types of expenditure which result in the production of little-needed goods. Probably there should be no restrictions at all on the production of some goods which are vital to the national interest.

A good many people attribute little value to the goods and services provided by the government itself. When the total expenditure in the country threatens to be excessive they urge that government spending should be reduced first and foremost because of its low priority. Their judgment is an arbitrary one. The fact is that some public services are more necessary and desirable than are a good many privately produced goods and services. It should not be considered axiomatic that expenditure on all public services be reduced in a period of inflationary pressure, while expenditure on privately produced goods is permitted to increase, thereby creating the inflationary pressure. It would be intolerable if, because businessmen were contributing to inflation by heavy investment in luxury hotels and in factories to produce trinkets, the government, to reduce inflationary pressure, were to curtail its spending on the nation's defences or on its schools. Stabilization measures adopted during inflation should emphasize reduction in those categories of expenditure, whether private or public, which were least helpful to the national interest.

Appropriate Distribution of the National Income

Anti-cyclical measures are likely to affect the distribution of income in the country, as well as the proportions in which different goods and services are produced. If the government, in fighting a depression, lowers the tax on corporate profits the effect is to stimulate investment and also increase shareholders' incomes. If the government wishes to lower the personal income tax it can choose from a variety of formulas; some will confer practically the entire benefit of the tax reductions on low income groups, while others will confer substantial benefit on middle or higher income groups. Changes in the scale of transfer payments such as unemployment insurance benefits and pensions, will similarly affect the distribution of income as well as the aggregate of expenditure within the country.

Redistribution of income may have adverse consequences. If unemployment insurance benefits are raised too high, some people may prefer to be idle and artfully manage to evade work. Both government taxes and transfer payments discriminate in favour of the people who earn low incomes. Because of this discrimination people who earn much more than others may not have significantly larger disposable incomes (incomes left after payment of taxes and receipt of transfer payments). Accordingly, there may be little material incentive to individuals to work hard and to acquire the training and skills which will qualify them for superior occupations in which they would be more productive. If taxes were indeed very heavy on higher incomes and transfer payments to lower income groups were very large, the progress of the country might be badly retarded. With many of its citizens quite deliberately refraining from increasing their productive capacity, the production of the nation as a whole would be a good deal less than it might have been.

Absolute Stability Unlikely

We must not expect the government's attempts at stabilization to produce absolutely perfect results. As we have already seen, delays are virtually bound to occur before remedial measures are actually applied, both against inflation and depression. Furthermore, the authorities responsible for administering anti-cyclical policies are only human. They are liable to err, both in their judgment of the problems to be dealt with and in their application of remedial measures. What is more, because other important social objectives must also be served, the objective of perfect stabilization may at times be deliberately sacrificed.

"Frictional" Unemployment

We simply cannot expect that in a modern, free enterprise, progressive economy, every worker will be employed all the time. At any particular time there are bound to be some firms which have just been forced to contract or suspend their operations, because competitors have developed superior products or because consumer tastes have changed. Inevitably the workers involved will be unemployed for some time until they can find new jobs for which they are suited. Some workers, at any given time, will have deliberately given up their jobs or will refuse to take available jobs in the hope of getting something better. Some degree of such "frictional" unemployment is bound to exist, so long as businessmen are free to introduce new products, consumers are free to vary their consumption patterns, and workers are free to choose their jobs. We all want these freedoms of course; a certain degree of unemployment is the price which we must pay for them. U.S. experts have estimated that even under the most prosperous conditions, about three per cent of the national labour force is likely to be unemployed.[9] Probably something like the same degree of "frictional unemployment" is inevitable in Canada.

---

[9]Few workers would be unemployed for long periods however. The composition of the unemployed group would change from day to day. Each day some workers who had been unemployed would get jobs; others who had been working would lose their jobs, to join temporarily the ranks of the unemployed.

Seasonal Unemployment

In this country the unemployment rates also tend to show a pronounced seasonal variation. Several of our leading industries, notably construction and agriculture, characteristically are more active in the summer and fall, and slacken off very greatly during the winter and early spring. In Canada, even in the best of times we may find that because of the "frictional" factor unemployment does not fall much below three per cent in the summer and that in the winter, with the seasonal factor superimposed, the unemployment rate rises to five or six per cent.[10]

LONG TERM TRENDS

"Secular Stagnation"

During the Great Depression of the 1930s, the distinguished American economist, A. H. Hansen, referred to the possibility of a "secular stagnation" of the American economy. The aggregate of private investment was likely to be relatively small in the future, he argued, because there would no longer exist the powerful incentives for investment which had existed in the past. During the preceding century private investment had been based upon three mighty supports: rapid population growth, momentous technological advance, and the development of new and hitherto unoccupied land areas. All these supports were now weakening.

There was scant prospect that the American population would increase as rapidly in the future as in the past, when it had been swelled by heavy immigration and high birth rates. Never again would there be a need to carry out massive expansion of housing, public facilities and private productive capacity to meet the needs of a rapidly growing population.

The era of epoch-making inventions was over. The railway, the automobile, electrical power, had given rise to enormous amounts of investment in the industries they created and in associated industries. Vast sums had been expended in the construction of railways, and later, of automobile plants and electric power generating stations. Enormous investment had been required in plants to produce necessary materials and parts and to build roads and streets, garages and service stations. The availability of railroad and automotive transportation, and of electrical power, had given rise to a host of completely new industries in which the total investment had been immense. There was no prospect of future innovations which would give rise to investment on the same massive scales. It was likely that future technological advances would be *capital saving* in many cases. Recent trends suggested that new

---

[10]Actually, seasonal unemployment has been significantly reduced in recent years and further reductions may be possible. Modern equipment and materials enable many types of construction to be carried on nowadays during the most severe weather. By offering special bonuses on work done during the winter the authorities may induce contractors to carry out projects during this season. Thus several years ago the federal government made special contributions toward the cost of municipal public works undertaken during the winter months and also contributed $500 toward the cost of houses built during the winter. Both programmes evoked a substantial response.

machines and equipment would be devised which would enable the same amount of goods to be produced with a *smaller* capital investment than had heretofore been required.

The historic task of opening up the world's unoccupied land areas had been largely completed. The American West, whose development had absorbed untold amounts of investment, was now fully occupied. Throughout the entire world there were by now few unoccupied land areas in which large scale settlement and investment activity were feasible.

Lacking the components which had hugely swelled it in the past, the aggregate of investment was bound to be deficient in the future. Hansen accordingly saw the prospect of the American economy being characterized by a state of permanent under-employment. To prevent such economic stagnation, vigorous action would be required on the part of the government; there could be no reliance that the private economy would, of its own accord as in the past, generate and maintain a state of full employment.

Postwar Inflation

Wartime government expenditures of astronomical proportions liquidated the Great Depression of the 1930s. The enormous increases in incomes and in the money supply generated powerful inflationary pressures. These were suppressed, for the most part, by price and wage controls. A great many people who would have liked to spend more money were obliged, willy-nilly, to save their money instead; the amount of goods and services they could buy was limited by rationing or other means, and their prices were controlled.

Prices surged upward in the years immediately after the war. Wartime price controls were relaxed, while the demand for goods intensified. Consumers eagerly sought to satisfy their needs, pent-up during the war. War-devastated countries, plentifully supplied with American funds, anxiously purchased vitally needed food, materials and equipment. Businessmen invested on a massive scale to make up for wartime depreciation and to build up productive capacity to the level of demand.

Inflationary pressure persisted beyond the immediate postwar years. Government expenditures continued on a grand scale. Defence outlays were of a magnitude hitherto unknown in peacetime; expenditures were unprecedentedly large on public works, on health services, on government pensions and allowances.[11] Unexpectedly

[11]Since the government finances most of its expenditures by taxation, its heavy spending restricts private spending. Because they pay high taxes people have less money to spend. *However, many people would not have spent all of the money which the government takes away from them in taxation; some they would have saved.* Wealthy people in particular would likely have saved a very large proportion. Part of these savings would have been loaned to businessmen, to be spent by them on new buildings, machinery, and the like. But probably not all; some savings, very likely, would simply have been held in idle balances. Even when government expenditures are financed entirely by taxation, therefore, the effect of heavy government spending is to increase greatly the total spending of the country. The government is taking from people very large sums which in part would not have been spent; it spends the full amount.

rapid population growth required large scale housing construction. Higher living standards as well as population growth required an expansion of productive capacity and therefore heavy investment to provide that additional capacity. Rapid technological advance gave rise to large scale investment in plants designed to turn out new products, and in superior equipment capable of producing accustomed goods more effectively. The effect of all these vast outlays was to bring about so-called "demand-pull inflation," i.e. rising prices attributable to the fact that the aggregate demand for goods and services rose faster than the physical quantities being produced. As well, sellers of goods and services took advantage of their market power to raise their prices, giving rise to "cost-push inflation." In particular, trade unions employed their mighty bargaining power to achieve wage increases well in excess of productivity gains, thereby raising production costs.

"Built-in" Inflationary Pressures

In the view of a great many economists, inflation rather than stagnation has become our long-term threat. The very fact that governments have committed themselves to maintaining permanent "full employment" is itself a contributory cause to inflation. With the government guaranteeing that there will always be prosperity, members of the public no longer feel the same need to accumulate reserves in the form of savings as a precaution against unemployment. They become inclined to spend their current incomes more freely and, through instalment buying, to spend future income as well on current purchases. Businessmen respond to the guarantee of permanent prosperity by investing more freely in plant and equipment. Powerful economic groups, workers, farmers, businessmen, may irresponsibly seize opportunities to obtain higher rewards for themselves, since the government's guarantee of full employment ensures them against adverse consequences. The power of these groups is so great that they have become capable of pushing up their prices and therefore the general price level, even during a period of economic recession.

Severe Inflation a Real Peril

Permanent inflation would constitute a major hazard for our society. Admittedly a "creeping inflation" of the order of one or two per cent per year would in itself probably not be seriously damaging. We have experienced such inflation since the end of the war, and the harm has not been really severe. While it caused a loss of real wealth and income to a great many people, those whose wealth or income consisted of a specific sum of money, the postwar inflation did not interfere seriously with production. But there is danger that the creep will develop into a gallop. Once people become convinced that the value of money is bound to drop a little each year they may adopt spending habits which will accelerate the decline in the value of money: the prospect of continuously rising prices would induce speculative buying which would speed the rise in prices. Union leaders, anticipating continuing inflation, would demand very large wage increases to offset the expected decline in the value of money. Sharply increased wage rates would correspondingly raise costs and prices —and justify demands for even larger wage increases. Such escalating inflation could disrupt our economic system even more seriously than would a severe depression.

It has been urged, with a good deal of reason, that the democratic temper of our times is a major factor in contemporary cost-push inflation. Members of the "working-class" are well educated people nowadays, and perhaps equally important, are persuaded by all manner of influences to want and feel entitled to the material accoutrements of the good life. The gross disparities of income between different social classes which characterized former eras, are no longer tolerable. "Ordinary working men" demand a standard of living corresponding to that of the middle class. Some categories of skilled tradesmen, enjoying very great market power, are demanding and receiving incomes comparable to those received by members of the executive-professional class.

Insistent demands by workers for a larger share of the national income are likely to be an inflationary force. Simple arithmetic makes it clear that the attempt by one group to increase its share is implicitly an attempt to reduce the share of the rest of the community. If the others are able to resist reduction of their shares—by raising the price of their services as fast as workers raise the price of their labour— the original distribution will remain unchanged, albeit on the basis of a higher price level. With the real amount of output unchanged but incomes generally higher, prices will be correspondingly higher; everyone finds, to his chagrin, that with his larger income he can buy only the same amount of goods as before.

How Should We Deal with Inflation?

Wide division of opinion exists among economists as to what measures are the most appropriate for dealing with the inflationary pressures of our times. One broadly held view begins with the assumption that inflation can only be countered by policies which slow the pace of economic activity, generating unemployment: the more determined the battle against inflation the higher the rate of unemployment that will have to be endured.[12] What is advocated is that the government opt for an optimum "trade-off," i.e. adopt restrictive policies which keep inflation down to an acceptable level and be resigned to the inevitable accompanying unemployment that, hopefully, would be of tolerable magnitude.

Some economists have advocated voluntary "guidelines," i.e. that the authorities urge unions to exercise restraint in their wage demands and urge management to exercise corresponding restraint in determining selling prices. At one time or another during the 1960s the governments of the U.K., the U.S. and Canada did in fact exhort such voluntary self-restraint. President Johnson urged American trade unions, in

[12]Analyzing British statistics over the period 1861-1957, A. W. Phillips discerned a close inverse correlation between the rate of unemployment and the rate at which prices rose: the lower the rate of unemployment during any given period the faster was the rate of price increase; the price level tended to remain stable only when a significant fraction of the labour force was unemployed. American and Canadian statistics, examined by other economists, exhibited the same general tendency.

negotiating wage increases, to observe a "guideline" of 3.2 per cent, the current annual rate of productivity increases in the U.S. In the United Kingdom the government established the Prices and Incomes Board to review proposed price or wage increases (though it had no power to prevent them). In midsummer of 1966 the government announced a "wage freeze" for the next six months, to be followed by a period of voluntary "severe restraint." Canada in 1969-70 briefly instituted a guideline policy, described later in this chapter.

A considerable number of economists—and other people as well—have been advocating price and wage controls to prevent inflation. Proponents generally feel that it would be unnecessary to have total and comprehensive control over all prices and wages: it would be sufficient to control the prices of a few strategic products and services and to limit the wage increases of a few key categories of labour. If prices of key products were indeed prevented from rising then all those industries which used these products in their own production processes would be protected against increases in the cost of their inputs. If the wage rates of key labour groups were kept from rising not only would the production cost of their output remain stable but the example might be generally followed; till now large increases achieved by major unions have had the effect of triggering demands for similar increases throughout the entire economy. This view has been expressed in official U.S. policy. On August 15th, 1971, President Nixon suddenly announced a 90-day wage and price freeze for the U.S. and, before the expiry of the 90-day period, instituted a program for wage and price control that would be maintained until the danger of inflation had subsided.

Yet another line of action against inflation has recently been suggested: impose a tax on all year-to-year *increases* in income, levied at such rates as to collect a sum equal to the excess of national purchasing power. The rate of taxation could be graduated according to base income so that poor persons would retain most of their increases in income while well-to-do persons would retain only a small proportion of any increases that they received. By such a tax the aggregate of national spending power could be held down to a non-inflationary figure; at the same time inequality of incomes could be reduced without making anyone worse off than he had been in the previous year. The total amount collected through this tax would be paid out in subsidies to all employers in the country. Since this amount would correspond exactly to the inflationary excess in aggregate production costs, the total selling price of the national output could be held to a non-inflationary figure.[13]

[13]The following is an arithmetical illustration of the proposal. Suppose that the Canadian national income this year is $70 billions. Suppose that next year we could achieve an increase in real output of the order of 5 per cent but at the same time are threatened with inflation at the rate of 4%. Our object would be to limit the aggregate of national purchasing power and the aggregate of national production costs to $73.5 billion each. We could achieve this result by imposing a tax, to produce a total of $2.8 billions, upon those persons who collectively had obtained the $6.3 billions of additional income. This $2.8 billions could then be paid out as wage subsidies to all employers of labour in Canada so that, despite costs that totalled $76.3 billions, they could afford to sell their collective output for $73.5 billions. Those firms whose costs had been pushed up would have to charge more for their products; those firms whose costs had not been pushed up would be able to charge less. The reductions would exactly offset the increases so that the price level as a whole remained unchanged.

Each of these remedies for inflation has weaknesses and shortcomings. Deliberate slowdown of the pace of economic activity through restrictive fiscal-monetary measures may give rise to a rate of unemployment that is intolerably high. The burden of unemployment might be unfairly distributed, being borne chiefly by the most vulnerable members of the labour force—low-paid, unorganized workers, young people seeking their first job, older persons of limited employability. Skilled tradesmen, members of strong trade unions, might be quite unaffected by the overall decline in job opportunity and, despite the severe unemployment prevailing among others, press for large wage increases for themselves. Perhaps worst of all, it may turn out that restrictive policies hurt without being of any help: they may cause unemployment but not prevent inflation. Earlier in this chapter we saw in fact that tight credit and restrictive fiscal measures are in fact likely to cause prices to rise.

Voluntary guidelines are likely to prove a weak reed. Trade union leaders have scorned them wherever they have been instituted. Their scorn is understandable. They themselves would be unfavourably affected: if the size of wage increases is universally to be one simple figure then obviously there is no need for union agents in their role of bargainers. Probably much more important, union leaders are opposed on account of their responsibility to the men they lead. Any person who exercises voluntary restraint has to hope that everyone else will show corresponding restraint. Otherwise, he will lose out because of his forbearance: the greedy ones who grab as much as they can will wind up with part of his fair share. Union leaders have no confidence that any restraint they displayed at bargaining tables would be universally matched.

Price and wage controls would constitute a kind of strait jacket on the national economy. We have seen in earlier chapters that price movements reflect shifts in consumer preferences and changes in production costs. The ceaseless rise and fall of individual prices and wage rates bring about the continuing redeployment of productive capacity that is called for by ever changing consumer demands, technological advance, Nature's varying moods of niggardliness and generosity. Besides requiring an elaborate bureaucratic organization that exercised a stifling effect on the economy, controls probably could not be effectively enforced. Price and wage controls were accepted in wartime when the whole nation had the winning of the war as its overriding objective; controls would not be equally tolerated in peacetime when there was no great national goal which justified the suppression of legitimate private claims and interests.

Whether comprehensive or selective controls were instituted the effect would in all likelihood be highly discriminatory. If selective controls were applied the discrimination would be obvious and immediate: only persons in the designated categories would be subject to restraint; everyone else would be free to grab as much as possible. If comprehensive controls were instituted discrimination would develop because of the difference in "controllability" of different wages and prices. Some could be controlled fairly readily; the wages of government employees, for instance, would be relatively easy for governments—their employers—to control. The wage rates of powerful unions in strategic sectors of the economy would be very difficult to control: such unions might be able to insist on wage increases despite the government's decrees to the contrary. As well, purely because of administrative complexities, some wages and prices could not be firmly controlled. The incomes that different persons earned would vary, not in accordance with their deserts or any rational principle, but simply according to the ease or difficulty with which their wage rates could be controlled.

A policy of taxing increases in income and using the proceeds to subsidize all producers, never tried anywhere so far, offers good promise of controlling inflation without giving rise to large scale unemployment. But it would have its difficulties too. Administrators of the programme would encounter a good many complications. The decision as to how progressive to make the rates of taxation would be a sharply divisive political issue. Heavy taxation of increases in income might exercise a serious disincentive effect: if most of the additional earnings were going to be taken away by taxation individuals might be deterred from working longer and harder than before or from accepting positions of higher responsibility.

This is an imperfect world. For few problems are there perfect solutions which completely eliminate the problem without giving rise to new difficulties. To deal with inflation we must, realistically, adopt that policy or combination of policies which involves the least number of evils; comparison of the foregoing alternatives must be in these non-utopian terms.

"We Will Bury You"

The free enterprise system has been continuously exposed to the threat of being supplanted by alternative economic systems. In the Communist Manifesto, published in 1848, Karl Marx and Friedrich Engels predicted the doom of free enterprise and its replacement by a classless socialist society. The inept performance of the free enterprise system in Italy and Germany during the inter-war years was probably the main factor in bringing Fascism and Nazism into being in those countries. In the 1950s the Premier of Soviet Russia brusquely predicted to an American visitor that "We will bury you."

The free enterprise system possesses enormous advantages over socialism. It provides to individuals a maximum of liberty to order their own affairs as they choose, to spend their money as they see fit, to select the occupation they prefer, to set up their own business if they so desire. It is conducive to material progress for it enables, and provides inducement for, individuals to exercise their ingenuity in the devising of new products and in the developing of new and superior methods of production.

A free enterprise system contains powerful safeguards against oppression. Socialism provides for the concentration of economic authority in the hands of a limited group. And while this group may be chosen by democratic means, it may be inadequately kept in check by the democratic process; conceivably it may acquire control over that process. A free enterprise system, on the other hand, provides for a broad dispersion of economic power. For the public which is subject to that power there is safety in the number of those who wield it. No individual or group which possesses economic power is so powerful as to defy public opinion or ignore public wants; to retain his power each person who possesses it must employ it in a manner consistent with the public advantage, or at minimum, consistently with what the public conceives to be its advantage.

However, the free enterprise system has exhibited disheartening defeats. It has shown itself to be liable to severe depressions in the course of which great numbers of people were reduced to penury, and to bouts of inflation in the course of which the real wealth and income of the country was suddenly and inequitably redistributed. To a great many people these defects of the system outweigh its advantages. It is probably no exaggeration to say that the capacity of the free enterprise system to survive the current challenge of socialism will hinge upon the success it achieves in attempts to rid itself of these weaknesses. Failure in these attempts will cost it adherents in the countries in which the system now prevails, and will deter people in the world's uncommitted countries from adopting free enterprise when they choose the system under which their economies will operate.

Earlier editions of this book defended government stabilization policies against the charge that they constituted "creeping socialism." A great many people objected to government attempts to regulate the pace of the nation's economic activity: they saw here a serious diminution of the importance of the private business community that would eventually lead to full-blown state control over the entire economy. Such criticism is little heard today. There is a fairly general concensus that the government ought to stabilize the national economy; the quarreling is about what measures are most appropriate. The critical problem confronting free enterprise societies in the years ahead will be to maintain economic stability, to avoid both unemployment and inflation, by methods that are effective, acceptable, and reasonably consistent with the principle of free enterprise.

ECONOMIC STABILIZATION IN CANADA

Pre-1930 Views and Practices

In Canada, as in other countries, the belief is only recent that the government has the power and the responsibility to control the national level of economic activity. Prior to 1930 it was generally taken for granted that the responsibility of government was merely to provide needed public works and services, paying for them with funds raised by taxation. The normal objective of fiscal policy was a balanced budget. Borrowing by the government was condoned only during emergencies such as wartime, or for the financing of major public works. A budget deficit deliberately incurred as a means of combatting a depression was unthinkable.

In accordance with centuries-old Anglo-Saxon tradition, local governments were expected to handle the problems of unemployment which developed in their communities. Under the B.N.A. Act provincial governments were made responsible for the care of the indigent; they in turn delegated this responsibility to their respective municipalities. Provincial governments usually contributed in some measure toward municipal relief costs: during the 1920s, when on one or two occasions the burden became unusually severe, the federal government also contributed.

No real safeguard existed against inflation, at least after 1914. As we noted in Chapter 21, the chartered banks were able to increase their reserves as much as they pleased, by taking advantage of the provisions of the Finance Act. A degree of inflation did in fact occur in the later 1920s, partly as a result of an uncontrolled expansion of bank lending.

Stabilization Attempts During the Great Depression

Two sectors of the Canadian economy bore the brunt of the Great Depression of the 1930s. The prices of staple products virtually collapsed, the effect being aggravated by a series of disastrous crop failures in Western Canada. Secondly, private investment dwindled to a small fraction of its previous figure. The government of the day attempted, vainly, to hold back the avalanche by embarking upon a small-scale public works programme, raising the tariff, and introducing measures designed to support the price of Western wheat.

Meanwhile, the catastrophic decline in economic activity became reflected in public revenues. Despite sharply increased rates of taxation, government revenue declined drastically. Government expenditures were cut to the bone, but large budget deficits could not be avoided. In the absence of a central bank these were financed with some difficulty; they were, furthermore, offensive to the prevailing financial orthodoxy. Finally, in 1932, the federal government gave up its costly attempts to fight the depression. For the next two years it merely contributed to the unemployment relief costs of provincial and municipal governments.

The improvement in Canadian economic conditions which occurred after 1933 was attributable primarily to the economic recovery which commenced that year in the United States and throughout the world. Federal economic policies did contribute in some degree, however, to the subsequent betterment of conditions in Canada. The price of wheat was supported after 1935 at a fairly generous level. Substantial public works programmes were carried out and programmes were introduced whereby the federal government gave financial assistance toward housing construction and repair.

While these measures were helpful they did not by any means restore prosperity; the economy remained in a depressed state throughout the remainder of the decade. Full employment was achieved only in World War II once the war effort swung into high gear. During the war years inflation became the pressing danger, requiring an elaborate system of price and wage controls.

Postwar Application of Modern Techniques

Apprehension was widespread that when the war ended, the depression would be resumed. The closing down of war factories and the demobilization of the armed forces would, it was feared, produce large-scale unemployment. The chaotic conditions prevailing in foreign countries indicated that foreign markets for Canada's products were likely to be disorganized or non-existent.

If a severe postwar depression was to be avoided, vigorous government action was called for. Accordingly, the government, in the latter part of the war, created a number of federal agencies which would foster and support private economic activity.[14] The Bank of Canada made clear its intention to maintain an expansionary monetary policy into the postwar period. In April, 1945, the federal government, following the British example of the previous year, issued a White Paper in which it declared the achievement of a high and stable level of employment to be an objective of government policy. The old fiscal orthodoxy was renounced. "The government will be prepared, in periods when unemployment threatens, to incur the deficits and increases in the national debt resulting from its employment and income policy. . . . In periods of buoyant employment and income, budget plans will call for surpluses".[15]

The government has indeed attempted to fulfil the undertaking given in the White Paper. Since 1945 fiscal and monetary measures have been applied, in the manner prescribed by the new economic orthodoxy, to counter recessions and inflationary trends. Taxes have been lowered and credit eased during periods of recession; taxes have been raised and money tightened during periods of inflation.

A variety of additional measures were adopted at various times to contain inflationary pressures. During the Korean War controls were imposed on instalment buying. From 1968 to 1970 the federal government made a determined effort to curtail its spending and urged similar restraint upon other government bodies and upon private business firms. It established a Prices and Incomes Commission in 1969 to maintain surveillance over the economy, investigating inflationary trends and seeking to dissuade actions by anyone that would have inflationary consequences. The Commission urged in the summer of 1970 that a six per cent guideline be followed in wage negotiations, i.e. that increases in the wage rates provided for in new contracts should not exceed six per cent per annum. However, this plea was widely ignored and the guideline was formally renunciated before the year ended.

---

[14]Notably the Central Mortgage and Housing Corporation which would lend money for housing construction; the Industrial Development Bank which would lend money to small business firms; the Exports Credits Insurance Corporation which would insure Canadian exporters who sold on credit to foreign purchasers. Provision was made as well for increased loans to farmers and price supports for a number of agricultural poducts.

[15]*White Paper on Employment and Income*, King's Printer (Ottawa, 1945).

(Because of the severe unemployment caused by the spending restraints the government reversed itself in December, 1970, in a special budget providing for large increases in its expenditures.)

The Canadian Economy Especially Liable to Instability

Despite the application of modern fiscal and monetary techniques, the stability of the Canadian economy has been a good deal less than perfect. Between 1945 and 1970 consumer prices approximately doubled; the unemployment rate at one time exceeded eleven per cent. Nevertheless the performance of the economy in the postwar era, when these measures were vigorously applied, compares favourably with its previous performance. There seems little reason to doubt that in the absence of attempts at stabilization, the postwar fluctuations would have been a good deal more severe than they actually were.

Earlier in this chapter we catalogued a formidable list of difficulties which hamper the application of the various stabilization techniques. In Canada the list is even longer, and some of the difficulties are particularly severe. Our heavy dependence upon foreign trade exposes our economy to instabilities which cannot readily be countered by our own fiscal and monetary measures. A sharp increase in foreign demand for our exports or a sharp increase in the price of our imports, such as occurred in the immediate postwar years, is bound to produce a rise in the Canadian price level. A major decline in foreign demand for our exports, such as occurred in 1957, is bound to result in a significant volume of unemployment in Canada. The scope of monetary policy is restricted by the fact that a good deal of the investment carried out in Canada is financed from foreign (chiefly American) sources. The inflationary pressures of 1955-56 stemmed largely from heavy spending by American firms on resource development in Canada and heavy spending on capital projects by Canadian firms, provinces and municipalities; a considerable part of the money spent on these projects was borrowed in the United States. Such investment activity financed from foreign sources was virtually immune to credit restraints imposed by the Bank of Canada.

In Canada, as elsewhere, a tendency to inflation may prove more intractable than a tendency to stagnation. The governmental measures required to cope with inflationary pressure would encounter greater public resistance and would be more difficult to apply. The measures which a government adopts to deal with a depression are expansionary and helpful to most individuals. Taxes are lowered; jobs are created by public works programmes; the monetary policy adopted leads to increase in the value of bonds which people own. The measures which must be applied to counter inflation, on the other hand, are repressive and harmful to individuals. Taxes are increased. Trade unions are exhorted not to ask for wage increases or actually prohibited by law from doing so. Monetary policy depresses the value of bonds which people own, and prevents business men from borrowing the money they need to take advantage of profitable opportunities.

Clearly, if as seems likely, inflation continues as a major threat to the Canadian economy, we will need very able helmsmanship on the part of our government authorities. And, hopefully, no powerful private groups will dangerously rock the boat by pressing their claims with no regard for their effects on the economy as a whole.

SUMMARY

Thanks in considerable measure to the path-breaking work of John Maynard Keynes, modern governments have come to realize that they can substantially reduce economic fluctuations, and have accepted responsibility for maintaining stable and prosperous economic conditions.

Monetary and fiscal policy are now both employed to stablize an economy. The central bank applies its various measures of control to maintain the national money supply at the appropriate level. The government adopts taxation and spending policies designed to help maintain the aggregate of national spending at the optimum level.

"Built-in stabilizers" exist which automatically repress upward and downward tendencies in general business activity. These are incapable of maintaining complete stability, however, and must be supplemented by *ad hoc* measures.

All of the measures which may be used to counter undesirable tendencies have their limitations or drawbacks. Monetary policy is unlikely to be effective in combatting a depression, while anti-depression fiscal measures may give rise to problems at a later date. Both monetary and fiscal anti-inflationary measures are likely to meet with strong objections from the public. Almost inevitably, most remedial measures are likely to be applied belatedly; because of their faulty timing, some well intentioned measures may do more harm than good.

Stability is not the only goal of public policy; an appropriate composition of the GNP, and appropriate distribution of the National Income, are also desired.

During the 1930s we were faced with the prospect of long run stagnation; currently we face the prospect of continuous inflationary pressure.

Since the end of World War II the Canadian government has employed both fiscal and monetary policies to maintain economic stability; a variety of supplementary measures has been attempted to deal with inflation.

FOR REVIEW AND DISCUSSION

1. Suppose that, at a time when full employment prevailed, it became necessary for Canada to increase its expenditure on armaments by $1 billion. What fiscal and other measures should the government adopt?

2. If we committed ourselves to giving $1 billion a year to underdeveloped countries, we would be assured of continuous full employment. Comment.
3. We will never again experience a really severe depression such as occurred during the 1930s. Do you believe this? Justify your answer.
4. A snowstorm increases a city's welfare because it provides jobs for the unemployed. Comment.
5. The Tax Rental Agreements did absolutely nothing to ensure that provincial governments arrange their expenditures in anti-cyclical fashion. Do you agree?
6. "We should strengthen our automatic stabilizers to such a degree that they alone would ensure absolute economic stability." Do you agree? Justify your answer.
7. The size of its national debt is unimportant to a country. Comment.
8. If a depression occurs, all the government has to do is pump more money into circulation. Do you agree?
9. "The Keynesian prescription for maintaining economic stability is straight socialism." Do you agree?
10. A British Chancellor of the Exchequer once declared that anyone who advocates a "pool of unemployment" should be thrown into it. Comment.
11. Wage, price and credit controls would be the most effective—and the most equitable—means of preventing inflation. Comment.
12. "Human nature being what it is, a policy of voluntary wage guidelines is quite unrealistic." Discuss.

28

The Location of Economic Activity*

The industrial revolution which has been proceeding for the last two centuries has produced drastic changes in the location as well as the character of economic activity. Previously, the overwhelming proportion of the world's population were farmers or herdsmen living on the land; towns and cities were few, scattered, and limited in function. Aside from a handful of great cities such as London, Paris, Amsterdam and Venice, which were seats of government or centres of international trade, towns were generally small affairs in which a few craftsmen using simple tools and a few merchants tending small shops served a surrounding countryside of short radius. Significant changes, it is true, had begun to occur in industrial organization even prior to the industrial revolution. The so-called "putting-out" system had been introduced in England, chiefly in the clothing industry, in which merchants supplied raw material to farm families to be worked up at home. However, this system did not disturb the prevailing pattern of population distribution; if anything it supported it by enabling farm families to earn auxiliary income while living on the land.

It was the introduction of equipment powered by inanimate sources of energy that shifted manufacturing activity out of the shop and home. Waterfalls were the first of the new energy sources to be tapped and they imposed their own unique locational requirements: the prime mover being a wheel spun round by the falling water, manufacturing had to be carried on immediately beside a waterfall. The steam engine, developed in effective form around the end of the eighteenth century, freed manufacturers from the necessity of locating near remote waterfalls but imposed its own locational constraints. The coal it burned was heavy and bulky and the earliest engines consumed a great deal in relation to the power they generated,[1] means of transportation were crude and inefficient and transport costs heavy. Accordingly, steam engines could be operated economically only in or near coalfields; further away the cost of fuel became impossibly high. Industrial cities arose near

*The author is grateful to the editor of the *Town Planning Review* for kind permission to use in this chapter portions of his article on the future growth of British cities, published in the October 1966 issue.

[1]The Newcomen engine required 20 pounds of coal per horsepower generated and the Watt engine, a great improvement, required 6-8 pounds; less than one pound of coal is used today per horsepower generated.

the coalfields, containing scores of factories and thousands of operatives and these became the chief centres of production of manufactured goods; neither the craftsman in his shop nor the worker in his farm cottage could compete against the untiring efficiency of the machine.

With improvements in transportation, notably the construction of canals and railways, the cost of moving coal declined substantially. Businessmen now had the option of locating industrial plants near a coal source or—without incurring prohibitively high fuel costs—in a large centre of population where they would gain the advantages of proximity to market. Each alternative had its pros and cons which had to be weighed and assessed before a choice might be made, and this kind of judgement has had to be made ever since. Let us examine the considerations involved in choosing between a resource-oriented and a market-oriented site for a production process.

LOCATION NEAR NATURAL RESOURCES

Many raw materials are "weight-losing": they contain waste material that is eliminated and discarded in the production process or, as in the case of coal used for cumbustion, they are altogether consumed. Where large quantities of such materials are used there is a strong case for carrying on production as near as possible to the source from which they are obtained. The finished product will weigh a good deal less than the materials used to make it, and the cost of transporting it to market will be less than the cost of transporting the materials to a plant located in the market.

Geographical or climatic considerations may be significant in some industrial processes and exercise strong influence in site selection. Thus Lancashire became the centre of the British cotton industry, partly because the typically damp weather caused fibres to adhere closely in the spinning process, producing a tight, strong thread. California is a favourable locale for the airplane building industry because of its climate: consistently warm dry weather allows parts to be safely stored out of doors; the huge hangars where planes are assembled require no heating; weather conditions are generally ideal for test flights. Firms that require large volumes of water for cooling purposes will prefer sites near a lake, river or the sea; firms whose production process gives rise to large quantities of liquid wastes will want sites near bodies of water into which effluents can be poured.

Once a significant number of firms in an industry establish themselves in a particular district, attracted by some local advantage, it becomes a recognized centre for the industry with important locational consequences. Firms that supply materials and services to the industry will find it advantageous to establish themselves in the area in order to be near an important group of customers. Firms that use the industry's products on a large scale in their own production may set up plants here to take advantage of the immediate availability of supplies. Large numbers of local people will acquire skill and experience in the industry; young people who grow up here will have a strong tendency to seek jobs with local firms and will likely prove to be desirable workers. Such developments will strongly enhance the original attraction of the locality for firms in the industry; if the industry expands the additional plant will probably be located here to take advantage of the availability of necessary goods and services, of the immediate market, of a population that contains many people having relevant skill and experience as well as young people predisposed to seek employment in the industry. These man-made advantages may assume such importance that the district continues to be the main centre of the industry, long after the natural advantage which originally attracted firms has ceased to be of any significance.

LOCATION AT THE MARKET

In some industries the main ingredients used are heavy and bulky natural materials that are found practically everywhere; such industries tend to locate themselves in their markets, thereby avoiding needless freight charges on materials or products. Brewers and soft drink manufacturers, for instance, who use large amounts of drinkable water, generally locate plants in their markets, using local water supplies; any other location would involve heavy and needless costs. Where a firm's products, while light, are bulky and awkward to handle, a market-oriented location is preferable. Freight charges on such goods are high whereas freight charges on the materials out of which they are made—very probably supplied in compact shapes and easily handled—are likely to be much less. A plant located in the market incurs the relatively low cost of transporting the materials instead of the high cost of moving the finished product. Where a product is fragile or perishable and therefore liable to breakage or spoilage in transit, production is obviously best carried on as near as possible to the market. If a product is complicated and purchasers' requirements are exacting, the maker needs to be in frequent consultation with the buyer and therefore as near as possible to him. Thus the dress making establishments which sew the articles of clothing designed by the leading couturiers of Paris, New York and London, are mostly located within a few blocks of the designers' salons.

SHIFTS IN LOCATIONAL ADVANTAGE

Technological advance has greatly altered the relative attractiveness of different locations as sites for industry. New sources of energy, in the highly transportable forms of oil, gas and electric current, have replaced coal in a great many uses; coal itself is transformed into mobile electric power in thermal generating stations. Industry is no longer virtually compelled to locate near coalfields; it can choose other localities which offer important advantages that hitherto had to be sacrificed because of the paramount necessity of being near a source of coal.

Improvements in transportation and communication have shattered a good many time-honoured locational constraints. So long as transportation was by packhorse, wagon and sailing vessel, manufacturing was typically carried on in small plants serving local markets. The railway and the steamship, by sharply reducing transport costs over long distances, vastly increased the effective market area available to manufacturing plants; giant firms came into existence that achieved enormous economies of scale and distributed their products over vast distances. The automobile and the truck freed manufacturing firms from the obligation to locate beside railway trackage; the cargo-carrying airplane has rendered it unnecessary to produce in the market those goods that required immediate delivery. The passenger plane, the telephone and teletype, by enabling quick and easy interpersonal communication, have reduced the need to fabricate complex goods in close proximity to the market. Even in so recently arrived a newcomer as the petroleum industry technological advance has given rise to major shifts in the location of plants. Until the postwar period a very substantial proportion of a refinery's output consisted of waste material which was eliminated as early in the production process as possible to avoid needless transportation charges. Refineries were therefore located at the oilfields. Now, however, these former wastes are being put to use, providing the basic materials for the burgeoning petro-chemical industry, and refineries are being built close to the markets for petroleum products; since there is virtually no waste to be discarded there is no longer any transportation economy to be achieved by refining at the oilfields.

Climate and special skills have lost a good deal of their locational significance in recent years. Ventilation engineers can create within building interiors whatever atmospheric conditions are desired and people can now live comfortably and work effectively in areas where climate formerly constituted an effective deterrent. Centres of specialized skill have lost a good deal of their attractive power since, with machines increasingly replacing craftsmen, manual skills have lost much of their former essentiality. Highly mechanized plants can be built practically anywhere; their operation requires primarily intelligence and alertness rather than manual skills that were acquired by long training or were somehow absorbed from the local atmosphere. It is true, of course, that such plants can be designed and built only by highly qualified architects and engineers, but such men are quite mobile nowadays and their services are available practically anywhere.

Transport Charges

In drawing up their schedules of freight charges for different types of goods, railway companies take a great many considerations into account: the labour and material that must be directly used to transport any particular load; the need to obtain revenue which would help pay the company's heavy fixed costs; the degree of road, water and air competition; the desirability of encouraging some types of traffic in order to develop large future volume; the regulations laid down by government authorities. The actual schedules of freight rates, framed with all these considerations in mind, constitute important determinants of industrial location. The tendency of ratemakers to charge lower freight rates on raw materials than on finished goods has favoured production in market centres; the low competitive rates charged to points served by water carriers has helped channel economic activity into ports. The favouritism that was shown to established distributing centres tended to bring about the concentration of wholesaling activity in a few key cities. Winnipeg, for instance, becames the overwhelmingly dominant distributing centre of Western Canada in the early years of the twentieth century, not just because of its strategic location but partly also because of freight rate privileges accorded by the railways. When these privileges were withdrawn in the 1920s by order of the Board of Railway Commissioners, a decided shift occurred of wholesale trade from Winnipeg to other Western cities. (At the same time, Vancouver, supported by the newly-completed Panama Canal, also pressed deeply into territory that had formerly been Winnipeg's virtually exclusive preserve.) Change in the relative costs of different transport operations, and consequent shifts in relative freight rates, may have significant locational effects. Years ago, for example, Canadian freight rate schedules favoured the shipment of Western live cattle to abattoirs in Winnipeg and Eastern Canada; today's schedules favour the shipment eastward of carcasses, and abattoirs are built near the cattle raising centres.

The Regional Multiplier

We saw in Chapter 25 that a person's decision to increase his spending will bring about a multiple increase in spending, and therefore of employment and income, throughout the country. The multiplier effect commences of course in the locality where he resides and spends the money; the first effect of his additional spending will be to increase the income of other local persons; those people will thereupon spend more, thereby increasing the incomes of others, and so on. The local people who receive additions to their income will no doubt save part of the increase, and part of their spending will be on goods and services sold elsewhere. The size of the local multiplier will reflect their savings ratio and the speed with which money is drained out of the community in payment for "outside" goods and services. In a small community where very few goods and services are locally available the great bulk of any increase in income will quickly be spent elsewhere, so that the local multiplier effect is small; in a large community where a great variety of goods and services can be obtained, most of the spending and respending of any addition to income will be local so that the local multiplier will be large.

Probably the most significant effect of this multiplier is its effect on local employment opportunity. If a new enterprise is established in any town or city the number of additional jobs generated in the community will substantially exceed the number of jobs in the enterprise itself. The firm's employees will shop in local stores;

they will need housing; their children will attend local schools. More store clerks will therefore be needed, more building tradesmen, more school teachers. The enterprise is likely to require local services, of trucking firms, of lawyers, accountants and so on. It has been calculated that in North American cities with population of about a million the employment multiplier is two; i.e. for every thousand jobs created in new local enterprises serving outside markets another thousand jobs are indirectly generated in trades and services required by the new firms and their employees.

What is more, the entry of a new business establishment may trigger off expansion in other directions. As we have already seen, firms that supply it with goods or services may decide to locate plants here in order to be conveniently near to an important customer; firms which use its products may locate here because of the conveniently available supply. Firms that employ mostly female workers may establish plants here in the expectation of recruiting wives and grown-up daughters.

It is because of considerations such as these that local authorities are anxious to have new firms establish in their community. The newcomers contribute to local public revenues, and, directly and indirectly, generate new employment opportunity for local people. The scale and tempo of local business activity is enhanced and local property values rise, reflecting the increased demand for business premises and housing space. To promote such development local authorities frequently go to considerable lengths to attract new firms, offering tax concessions, low rents in publicly owned buildings, and sometimes even cash grants and loans.

The Drift from the Land

We are all familiar with tales of amazing new machinery which reduces practically to nil the manpower required in certain industrial processes. Less spectacular, but thus far of greater overall significance has been the revolution in agricultural technology that began about half a century ago. The tractor, introduced in the 1920s, enormously increased the physical power that could be controlled by one man, enabling him to operate far bigger, heavier equipment and at faster speeds than could be managed by a man driving a team of horses. The milking machine virtually eliminated a daily chore of enormous aggregate dimension; the combine ended the need for the traditional harvest gangs. Improvement has been proceeding continuously; each year more effective equipment has appeared on the market, togther with altogether new machines to do jobs hitherto done by hand. The use of weed-killers and insecticides, the application of modern accounting methods and management techniques, have further improved the efficiency of agricultural operations; the farm worker of today produces many times as much as his counterpart of fifty years ago was able to do.

In some industries that have experienced spectacular technological advance employment has remained steady or even increased because the quantity demanded ballooned to enormous dimensions following the reduction of price or the improvement of quality. Not so in agriculture. Despite population growth and increasing opulence the demand for food did not grow nearly as rapidly as did agricultural productivity. People can eat only so much; as their incomes increase they do not usually eat more (some acquire ulcers in the course of achieving their higher incomes and eat much less); typically they substitute more expensive for cheaper foods and demand foods which are more attractively packaged and more conveniently prepared; the total amount of food they consume changes little.

With the individual farm worker able to produce much more food, but the public wanting to buy relatively little more, far fewer people were needed on the land. Small farms, each of which had been a separate family enterprise, were amalgamated into large holdings each worked by a very few hands using heavy modern equipment. Most of the redundant farm personnel moved into the cities, but some remained on their small farms, being unwilling to accept so drastic a change in their way of life or unable to sell their properties at reasonable prices. Their number keeps diminishing as young farm-born people, better educated and more adaptable than their parents, refuse to accept the narrow and cramped existence of a small, under-equipped farmer.

The modern agricultural revolution has occurred at the same time as the modern transportation revolution. The timing is not coincidental, of course; these two revolutions have a common origin in the development of the gasoline engine. Together they have profoundly altered the shape of the countryside. The decline in rural population has been accompanied by a spectacular increase in the mobility of those who remain, travelling as they do in automotive vehicles on good roads. The economic base has seriously eroded of the numerous hamlets and villages which sprang up in the initial settlement of the Canadian West, each serving a small surrounding population, with radius limited to the distance that could be traversed in a few hours by ox-drawn or horse-drawn wagon. Many of these small centres have altogether disappeared as the size of their surrounding population has dwindled and the people who remain are able easily to travel long distances to cities which offer a broader and more attractive range of goods and services. Many of the little centres which still exist are seriously threatened: the railway companies, finding traffic to them and from them greatly reduced, have been eliminating services to them and propose to eliminate more. Educational authorities have been building large centralized schools to achieve the advantages of scale and a good many small centres have lost the little schools which constituted important props to the local economy. The former urban pattern of a multitude of small centres densely scattered throughout the agricultural countryside is giving way to a new pattern characterized by a relatively small number of larger centres each serving a very large surrounding area that is inhabited by relatively few people.

Regional Depression

A few large industries may constitute the economic base of an extensive region with a substantial population. If ever one or more of these industries declines, whether because of exhaustion of a key natural resource or decline in demand for it, the whole region becomes depressed. Through the action of the multiplier the unemployment and underemployment experienced by the employees of these industries spread to local trades and services. The widespread reduction in living standards and the bleak prospects cause many people to leave, with the exodus being selective and its effects especially adverse. It is the younger, more vigorous and more enterprising who typically decide to move away; their departure leaves a residual population which does not have the energy and initiative to make the fullest use of local opportunities that still exist. The prevailing atmosphere of gloom and despair instils a general defeatism that aggravates the effects of the loss of many of the community's brighter elements. Because public revenues are limited, schools are inadequately supported and children emerge from them with substandard education and limited horizons; thus stagnation may continue indefinitely, with a new generation handicapped by its legacy from the old.

Such indeed has been the state of affairs in the United Kingdom, in the shipbuilding centres of Newcastle, Clydeside and Jarrow, in the coal-mining districts of Wales, in the cotton towns of Lancashire. In the United States the coal mining districts of Appalachia have been characterized by decades of depression, following the shift from coal as an energy source to gas and oil and the introduction of highly automated equipment to mine such coal as is still demanded. In Canada the Maritime Provinces have failed to share in the general prosperity and expansion of the Canadian economy in the twentieth century as demand declined or disappeared for the fish and wooden ships which in the nineteenth century had furnished a broad and sturdy economic base for the Maritime economy.

The problem of the depressed region is not that of the "ghost town." The latter has typically been a small community which hastily sprang into being on the basis of some local natural resource; with the exhaustion of the resource the community had to be abandoned for lack of an economic base. This was no catastrophe; the community invariably was small, its buildings flimsy and cheap, and no one had deep local roots or strong local attachments; abandonment involved little material or psychic loss. The case is very different in the regions of the U.S., U.K. and Canada that have been characterized by long term depression. A great many people are involved; their local roots are deep and their attachments strong; the local investment is very large in private buildings and in public buildings and facilities. There can be no question of abandonment; solution must be sought along other lines.

Big Cities and Small

The drift to the cities has not been an equal drift to all cities; in many countries the largest cities have tended to grow most so that an ever increasing proportion of the national population is becoming concentrated in a few great urban centres. The percentage of Canada's population living in the three largest metropolitan areas,

Montreal, Toronto and Vancouver, rose from twenty-three per cent in 1951 to twenty-six per cent in 1961; and the trend appears to be continuing.

The attractive power of the giant city reflects the advantages it offers to businessmen, workers and consumers. Large scale manufacturing enterprises can here achieve economies of scale and at the same time low delivery costs to consumers. Every kind of supporting service is readily available—a particularly valuable feature for small specialist firms that must rely on outside organizations for all sorts of necessary services. Information required for decision-making is immediately at hand; the latest news on all matters routinely flows into the great metropolitan centres. What is more, the large number of well-informed individuals offers the possibility of frequent chance encounters that will yield valuable information for which the businessman would not have even known to seek.

Employers and employees both benefit from the scale and diversity of the local labour market: firms have better prospect of obtaining the numbers and type of workers they need; workers have a better chance of obtaining jobs for which they are qualified. Each individual has reasonable assurance that if he loses his job he will be able quite easily to obtain an acceptable alternative. The leading practitioners in practically every field of endeavour—the arts, entertainment, the professions —will find here the largest and most lucrative markets for their services and will be central as well to the additional markets of the surrounding hinterland. Because every kind of supporting service is immediately at hand they will be able to do their work with maximum effectiveness.

The great metropolis has much to offer to the consumer as well. The economies of scale and of transportation achieved by large local firms are generally passed on to consumers. The size of the local market makes it feasible to have available a great variety of goods and services—a far more diversified selection than could be had in smaller centres. The reason is of course that many private and public services can be provided economically only at or above some minimum volume of output; the larger the city the more such thresholds can be crossed. Because the big city is a convenient proving ground new products are likely to be introduced here first; its residents are agreeably aware that they are the first to have the latest. The sheer size and diversity of the metropolitan mass exercises upon many people a perpetual fascination. And since so many people want to live in the metropolis because of the interest and excitement it affords, businessmen find it easier to recruit here workers at every level.

These advantages are purchased at heavy cost. Great metropolitan concentrations give rise to severe economic and social problems: lengthy and tiring journeys to work and to amenities in the countryside; limitations of household living space; the frequent incidence of behavioural extremes; absolute dependence of multitudes of people on facilities that might break down and on strategic workers' services that might be withheld. Presumably these costs are not excessive since a large and growing number of persons are evidently prepared to pay them. Furthermore, some of the most trying problems of living in a great metropolis can be ameliorated by capital investment and general economic progress. Rapid transit systems, arterial thorough-fares and improved traffic controls enable the population of even the largest cities to move about quickly, while slum clearance and urban renewal projects are markedly improving the quality of the urban environment.

No doubt cities will continue to come in different sizes. There will always be people who prefer the quieter life of a smaller centre and such cities will have important advantages in the future, as many do now, which will enable them to maintain sturdy and viable economies. Local natural resources will continue to provide a sound economic base for many, as will special geographical features, strong local attachments and a heavy investment in private plant and public facilities. If recent trends are any guide, however, future population increase will be channelled primarily to the already large metropolitan centres; the biggest will grow most.

The Pattern of Urban Growth

Unplanned though it generally has been, the layout of cities has not been as random and haphazard as superficially appears. Certain types of firm, department stores for instance, seek a central location in order to be most conveniently accessible to the largest possible number of people. Other firms whose customers are relatively few but scattered throughout the community—such as specialty shops and leading medical practitioners—also seek central locations. Firms which employ large num-bers of female workers tend to prefer a central location that is readily accessible by public transit. Firms in industries liable to quick and sudden changes will want to be near the sources of the information required to make the necessary adjustments; in all likelihood these will be centrally located for the convenience of staff and clients. Firms providing auxiliary services, such as lawyers, accountants and advertising agencies, will seek downtown locations in order to be near customers and clients. Business firms in the central area tend to be mutually supporting and mutually attractive; each firm finds it advantageous to be in the central business district because all the other firms are there, providing necessary services and convenient markets, and by their presence helping to attract crowds to the area.

The process of urban growth generates a characteristic set of market pressures that shape the course of expansion. As the local population grows corresponding increase occurs in the volume of services that are best provided in a central location. The demand for central locations drives up the price to levels that compel the removal of relatively low order functions occupying sites in or near the centre. Houses are torn down to be replaced by business buildings; warehouses and factories are replaced by office buildings.

The technological progress of recent decades and the mobility conferred by the automobile and the truck have given rise to major alterations in the traditional distribution pattern of enterprises throughout a large urban centre. The most effi-cient methods of goods handling, by fork-lift truck and conveyor belt, can be effectively employed only in the horizontal, so that single storey plants are preferred to multi-storey. Much more land space is consequently required nowadays for ware-houses and factory premises, augmented by the need for ample parking space. Whole-sale and manufacturing firms that had to be centrally located when goods were carried about within a building by hand and distributed in town by horsedrawn wagon, have moved to large sites on the city's perimeter that are strategically located in relation to arterial thoroughfares. Other types of firm which formerly required central locations conveniently accessible to customers and employees travelling on foot or by public transit, can now locate practically anywhere and choose sites distant from the centre where land can be got cheaply. There has been a rough balance between the additions to central business districts attributable to the overall growth of metropolitan centres and the exodus of firms to suburban localities which better serve their interests; a recent U.S. survey indicates that the number of persons employed in the central areas of a large number of U.S. metropolitan centres has remained virtually constant over the last thirty years.

GOVERNMENT POLICY

Governments have always played an important role in the location of economic activity: government decisions in relation to the routes followed by railways and highways, by oil and gas pipelines, have determined the position and shape of the national infrastructure and therefore the geographical distribution of economic opportunity. Governments have as well used their fiscal powers to aid distressed regions and, in response to political pressure, have given special support to favoured localities. The role of government in the spatial disposition of economic activity has become even more significant in recent years: the government operates large com-mercial enterprise, maintains substantial research and military establishments and employs great numbers of people in all sorts of regulatory functions; accordingly, it has under its immediate control the spatial disposition of a significant proportion of the national labour force.

Governments have as well commenced to use their power and authority to achieve a preferred regional distribution of private economic activity. Since 1945 the United Kingdom has built up a comprehensive system of controls over the location of industry, designed both to prevent further expansion in already con-gested localities and to induce the location of new plant in depressed areas where employment opportunity was inadequate. Industrial firms are required to obtain special permits from the Board of Trade for the construction of new plants (unless their size is trifling) and these permits are issued only if the Board approves the location. An order issued in 1965 forbade the construction of additional office buildings in central London, to forestall worsening congestion. In addition to these negative controls, the government offers a variety of inducements, including cash grants, tax concessions and cheap factory space, to firms which locate in areas where the rate of unemployment is above the national average. The distribution of population is also subject to centralized control; each local authority is required to draw up a town plan indicating how it proposes to develop the area under its jurisdiction, and all plans must be approved by the Minister of Housing and Local Government. A number of cities have set up "Green Belts," i.e. they have decreed that a broad belt of underdeveloped land around their perimeter must not be built upon, thereby setting a limit to their possibilities of expansion.

In the United States, the federal government in 1965 launched a massive attack on poverty in Appalachia. Here in an area of some 80,000 square miles, reaching into seven states, some six million people lived in a generalized poverty following decline of the coal mining base. The federal strategy was to promote the development of a relatively small number of urban centres and build a network of roads throughout the region that would enable the jobless and impoverished to emerge from their isolated hollows and avail themselves of the opportunities in the centres of expansion. The Public Works and Economic Development Act, passed in 1965, in effect provided for the application generally of the approach adopted in Appalachia: growth centres would be fostered in regions of economic decline and residents in the surrounding areas would be encouraged to commute to them or move into them.

In Canada a number of special programmes have been instituted in recent years to provide assistance to lagging regions. Under the Agricultural Rehabilitation and Development Act (ARDA) the federal government signed an agreement in 1962 with each province under which both federal and provincial authorities subsequently selected and carried out projects designed to bring improvement to poor and stagnant rural areas. A wide variety of individual projects was undertaken, including the construction of drainage channels, subsidization of farmers to clear bush land and to plant grass, acquisition of sub-marginal farms to be consolidated into larger holdings or to be reverted to wildlife, training courses for farmers and fishermen. The cost of each project was shared equally between the federal government and the provincial government concerned.

The ARDA programme suffered from two critical deficiencies. Firstly, the requirement that the provincial government contribute half the cost of any project undertaken within its boundaries limited participation by poorer provinces. Secondly, within each province ARDA projects were widely scattered geographically, with only one or two carried out in any particular locality; as a consequence no locality was significantly helped. To overcome both deficiencies the Fund for Rural Economic Development (FRED) was established in 1966. With an initial capital of $50 million (increased in 1967 to $300 millions) the Fund was designed to achieve the total rehabilitation of designated rural areas by attacking simultaneously *all* the causes of their poverty. It was anticipated that only one such region would be designated in each province; the federal government would contribute money in each case out of the capital of FRED, without requiring the provincial government to make a matching contribution.

The Atlantic Development Board was formed in 1962 to plan and promote improvement of the economy of the Maritime provinces; to finance its various projects the Board was provided with a fund of $100 million, subsequently increased to $150 million.

The Area Development Agency, formed in 1963, sought to assist those urban areas of Canada that were characterized by heavy unemployment and low incomes; incentives were offered to manufacturing firms that located plants within these areas, at first in the form of tax concessions and subsequently in the form of contributions to capital costs.

Powerful impetus was given to regional policy in 1969 with the formation of the Department of Regional Economic Expansion (DREE). Under the Regional Development Incentives Act, passed in the same year, the new Department was authorized not only to make contributions to the capital costs of firms locating in designated slow growth areas but also to make grants of up to $30,000 for each new job created; an individual firm might receive as much as $12 million in grants. With the establishment of DREE, the Area Development Agency and the Atlantic Development Board were dissolved, the latter being replaced by a purely advisory council.

SUMMARY

Established population centres and the sites of natural resources are rival magnets for the location of economic activity, with each especially attractive in relation to particular products and services. The technological advances of recent decades have tended on the whole to shift the balance of advantage in favour of large, well-established population centres. Through the operation of the local multiplier the addition of any new enterprise has given rise to further growth; on the other hand decline in any region has tended to have cumulative effects and in some areas has led to long term stagnation. Population and economic activity have tended to become concentrated, to an ever increasing degree, in the very largest urban centres; within these centres there has occurred a major redeployment of population and business enterprises, based on new means of transportation and new techniques of production and goods handling. Primarily to deal with the problem of regional depression governments have introduced a variety of measures designed to influence the location of economic activity.

FOR REVIEW AND DISCUSSION

1. Explain why steel makers have tended to locate near coal fields, brewers in large urban centres, wine makers near vineyards.

2. Suggest how the introduction of television, of the modern computer, of the jet airplane, affected the location of population and economic activity.
3. A certain city has a population of about half a million. What advantages and disadvantages would it experience, in your opinion, if its population were to increase at the rate of ten per cent a year?
4. National populations are becoming, at one and the same time, more concentrated and more dispersed: people formerly living in the countryside have been moving into the cities, but the cities have been spreading out extensively. Discuss.
5. On what grounds would you justify government attempts to influence the location of population and business enterprises?
6. Compare the British, American and Canadian programmes for dealing with regional depression.
7. Give a reasoned argument in favour of a particular distribution of the Canadian population, in terms both of the size of the communities that would be most desirable and the region of the country in which they should be concentrated.

29   Economic Progress

THE CONDITIONS OF PROGRESS

In any country, the material welfare of the typical person will depend primarily on three considerations: how much the nation produces; among how many people the national product must be shared; how equally or unequally this product is divided up. In many countries where widespread poverty prevails, all three of these factors are adverse. The country's output of goods and services is very small. Because the population is large, that output must be shared among a great many people. The sharing is very unequal; a small minority obtains a very large proportion of what is produced, leaving very little to be shared out among the majority of the people. If the typical inhabitant of such a country is to become substantially better off, these factors must become more favourable. The nation's output must increase; population must not increase at all, or only very little; output must be shared more equally.

Economic and Non-Economic Factors

In examining the prospects for economic progress, we shall concern ourselves primarily with the possibilities of increasing national output. The rate of population growth, and the equality or inequality of income distribution, are, for the most part, determined by non-economic considerations. Religious faiths, deep-rooted customs and beliefs, knowledge or ignorance of contraceptive methods—all these will markedly affect the rate of population growth. How the nation's product is shared among the people of a country will depend, in great degree, upon the distribution of political power. In a democracy, where the administration of the country responds to the will of the majority of the people, the distribution of income is likely to be reasonably equal. In a dictatorship or oligarchy, where one person or a small group completely controls the country, the distribution of income may be extremely unequal.

Increase in Output

As we saw in Chapter 24, the output of a country will depend upon its productive capacity and the degree to which that capacity is actually used. An increase in either of these will bring an increase in output. The first can be increased in unlimited degree; a nation can increase its capacity year after year, and so keep on increasing its output. The second can only be increased up to a point. If we have unemployed people or resources, we can increase output by putting them to work. But once they are all at work, output cannot further be increased by putting unemployed people to work; there are no more unemployed. To achieve continuing increases in national output, a nation must continuously increase its productive capacity.[1]

Expansion of Productive Capacity

Our discussion in Chapter 24 suggests how a nation can increase its productive capacity. We saw there that a country's productive power will depend, at any given time, upon these four main factors:

The number, skill and energy of its workers.

The quality and abundance of its capital equipment.

The quality and abundance of its natural resources.

The mode of its industrial organization.

Expansion of productive capacity can be achieved only if gains are made in respect to one or more of these factors. The work force must be enlarged, rendered more skilled, more vigorous; additional capital equipment must be acquired; additional natural resources must be discovered and developed; the mode of industrial organization must be improved. Only by such means can national output be continuously enlarged. If the increases in output are to bring increases in welfare, the gains in output must outstrip the growth of population and the benefits of increased output must be widely distributed.

THE PAST TWO CENTURIES

A Roman Rip Van Winkle who fell asleep in A.D. 250 and only woke up 1500 years later, would have been little impressed by the world he saw about him. In only a few respects would it have surpassed the world he knew. Ships would be a good deal larger; armies would be equipped with cannon and small arms the like of which he had never seen. The printed books and the paper of which they were made would excite his interest. But the implements used to till the soil would be hardly different from those which he had known, as would be the tools used in manufacturing goods

---

[1]Taking wealth from the rich and giving it to the poor may also improve the lot of the typical person. But this, too, is the kind of gain which can be achieved once only. Once the rich have been completely despoiled, nothing can be taken from them again. Poor people can further improve their welfare only if they produce more for themselves.

and the conveyances used for transportation. The roads and highways would be very much inferior. Material comforts would be fewer and cruder. There would be none of the gigantic public baths to which he had been accustomed, the superbly engineered aqueducts and sewers, the magnificent public buildings.

If our man slumbered on for another two hundred years, waking up in the middle of the twentieth century, then he would be impressed by what he saw. For while the world had not managed by 1750 to equal many of the achievements of ancient Rome, during the next two hundred years it advanced spectacularly to unprecedented levels of human achievement. During these two centuries men gained an enormous fund of new knowledge about the characteristics and the working of the human body, enabling the subjugation of age-old diseases and the lengthening of the typical span of human life. They devised new implements and new methods whereby to win far more food from the earth. They accomplished prodigious feats of engineering which involved the production of an outstanding quantity and variety of amenities for human gratification; they devised, perhaps most fantastic of all, vehicles capable of voyaging into space to explore the universe.

The "Dismal Science"

These spectacular advances were not envisaged, even after the great advance had got under way. In a pamphlet published in 1798, Thomas Robert Malthus, an English clergyman, made the cheerless observation that the population of Europe was tending to increase more rapidly than was the food supply available for its sustenance. In his "Essay on the Principle of Population as It Affects the Future of Society" Malthus suggested that population tended to increase by a geometric ratio, the tendency being to double itself every 25 years; the food supply, on the other hand, tended to increase in only an arithmetical ratio.[2] Inevitably, the population would tend to outrun its supply of food. Inevitably, the excess population would have to be cut down by what he called the "positive checks": famine, disease, pestilence, and war. If mankind were to avoid this fate, it would have to adopt "preventive checks": to practise sexual abstinence, marry at later ages, and only marry when assured of ample means for supporting offspring. The practice of such measures would restrict the rate of population growth, and therefore render unnecessary the "positive checks." Not having been born, it would not be necessary for excess population to die, through one calamity or another.

David Ricardo, in his "On the Principles of Political Economy and Taxation" published in 1817, issued another sombre forecast. He enunciated the doctrine, subsequently dubbed "The Iron Law of Wages", that wages could never remain for long above the subsistence level of workers. Whenever wages rose, workers' families

---

[2]"Taking the whole earth—and supposing the present population to be equal to a thousand millions, the human species would increase as the members 1, 2, 4, 8, 16, 32, 64, 128, 256, and subsistence as 1, 2, 3, 4, 5, 6, 7, 8, 9,—."

would increase. The larger sum available for payment to workers would become divided up among a larger number; in the long run the amount available for each would be restored to the subsistence level.[3]

Small wonder that, following the publication of Malthus' *Essay* and Ricardo's *Principles*, Economics became known as "The Dismal Science."

THE ADVANCED COUNTRIES

Population Growth

The march of events in Europe and America confounded the gloomy prophecies. Population growth occurred at an unprecedented rate, as one after another of the restraints was shattered. Brilliant medical discoveries enabled the conquest of diseases which had hitherto claimed the lives of untold numbers of people, and so had inhibited as well the birth of even more. In Vienna, Ludwig Semmelweiss learned the cause of puerperal fever which had carried off countless women in childbirth. In England Joseph Lister drastically reduced the morality rate in surgery by introducing the practice of antisepsis. In France, Louis Pasteur discovered the nature of bacterial infection and methods for its cure.

Hardly less important than these epochal victories over disease were the successes achieved in preventing the conditions which produced disease: filth, squalor, congestion, contamination. Engineers finally managed to build water works and sewage disposal systems which surpassed those of the Romans. Municipal authorities began to take active measures to safeguard the health of their communities. They adopted quarantine regulations to prevent the spread of disease, and insisted upon adequate measures for refuse disposal. New housing was required to have proper sanitary facilities and adequate ventilation; overcrowding was prohibited. Cities became more healthful, and mortality rates in them dramatically declined.

It was the sharp fall in mortality rates which was primarily responsible for the upsurge of population during the nineteenth century. More children survived to adulthood, to beget children in their turn. The birth rate rose slightly in some countries, due in part to the increased number of children who reached adulthood, and in part to the increase in employment opportunity and prosperity which enabled people to marry at earlier ages. During the first half of the nineteenth century the average annual rate of population increase in Europe was .707 per cent; during the second half it was .823 per cent, over one-sixth greater. The combined population of Europe and North America rose from just under 200 million in 1800 to 480 million in 1900, and to 750 million in 1950.

In Western countries the birth rate declined substantially during the twentieth

---

[3]Ricardo suggested however that the subsistence level could rise, as workers became accustomed to, and absolutely insisted upon, additional amenities and comforts.

century, following the widespread adoption of modern methods of birth control. The decline was particularly marked during the 1930s, when depressed economic conditions forced young persons to postpone marriage and obliged married couples to limit closely the number of their children, in order to maintain their standard of living. Following the end of World War II, the birth rate rose spectacularly, reflecting a number of favourable developments. Prosperous economic conditions encouraged marriage at earlier ages; a great many marriages, postponed because of depression and then war, were now contracted; facilities and conveniences became generally available which drastically reduced the labour involved in bringing up children.

Expansion of the Food Supply

Contrary to Malthus' prediction, the food supply offered little restraint to population growth. New methods, superior equipment, and the liberal application of fertilizers, made possible an enormous increase in the size of the crops harvested in Europe. Modern means of transportation rendered accessible vast new areas of land suitable for agriculture, in North and South America, in Russia, Australia, and India. Europeans streamed across the seas in millions to settle on the rich lands of the New World, there producing immense surpluses of food which, shipped to Europe, helped to feed those who remained. World gluts of wheat became more common than scarcities, so far as Western Europe and America were concerned.

The Industrial Revolution

The nineteenth century was the era of the Industrial Revolution. Practically all fabricated goods had been manufactured, hitherto, by craftsmen using simple tools and equipment, and applying only the power of their own bodies. Now machines were devised, driven by steam power, to perform operations previously performed by human beings. At first applied to Great Britain's textile industries, the new mechanical methods were adopted in a host of other industries, and in other countries as well. The output of manufactured goods of every description grew by leaps and bounds as more machines were built and installed, to swell the numbers of those already at work.

"Every morning when the world woke up, some new machinery had started running. Every night, while the world had supper, it was running still."[4]

The Favourable Political and Social Conditions of the Nineteenth Century

The political and social climate was hospitable to economic progress. For a hundred years, from the end of the Napoleonic Wars in 1815 to the outbreak of World War I in 1914, Europe enjoyed freedom from major wars. International conflicts there

[4]Winston Churchill, quoted in J. H. Clapham, *An Economic History of Modern Britain*, Book IV. (Cambridge, 1938), p. XV.

were,[5] but there was none of the prolonged devastation and bloodletting which had characterized earlier centuries. In an era of almost permanent peace, men could safely undertake long range developmental enterprises; productive capacity could be used for the expansion of productive capacity rather than the support of armies and the output of munitions.

Current social attitudes and the prevailing distribution of political power enabled and encouraged rapid economic change, in Great Britain particularly. Enterprising individuals were free to devise new products and new methods of production; few legal or customary obstacles barred the implementation of ingenious new ideas. Few restraints hindered the flow of labour into new enterprises; labour became in effect a purchasable commodity which could be bought by whoever needed it, and discarded by him whenever he no longer needed it. In an unrestrained and unregulated market economy there could be carried out the intensive mobilization of productive capacity for any purpose whatsoever; entrepreneurial decisions to expand productive capacity could be implemented fully, regardless of their effects on human beings.

Great Britain: The First Industrial Nation

In the general advance to modern industrial society Great Britain led the way. The favourable political and social atmosphere prevailing in the country reflected the existence of a powerful, well-established entrepreneurial class, together with economic institutions and market connections which provided a solid base for expansion. Britain had already established herself as the world's foremost trading nation; her merchants, numerous and able, were accustomed to doing business throughout the world; her mercantile marine, the world's largest, reached out to every corner of the globe. Ingenious mechanics devised machines to do jobs hitherto done by hand. The introduction of machine methods and the factory system enabled the country's production of manufactured goods to be enormously increased; much of the expanded output was exported in British ships to overseas markets built up in the previous era of commercial domination.

The Later Industrial Nations

For half a century Britain enjoyed a virtual monopoly of the new manufacturing methods; she was the "workshop of the world." Toward the close of the nineteenth century, however, other nations embarked upon programmes of intensive industrialization. In the United States industrialization proceeded at a headlong pace until, early in the twentieth century, the country had become, by a great margin, the world's foremost industrial power. In Europe, Germany overtook and surpassed Great Britain in many branches of industrial production; the other nations of Western

---

[5]The Crimean War of 1853-55, the Franco-Prussian War of 1870-71.

Europe also became major industrial powers. Russia, after achieving a limited degree of industrialization under a Czarist regime, advanced industrially, under a ruthless communist dictatorship, at a rate which apparently exceeded even that recorded in the United States. In the Far East, Japan, a feudal country until the 1870s, transformed herself into a modern industrial nation within three or four decades. In our own time, China, ruled since 1949 by a communist regime, has been expanding her productive capacity at a rate which, if reports are true, exceeds even that achieved by Russia.

In this world-wide spread of industrialization, those nations which became industrial powers early, contributed to the development of those which industrialized later. Machinery, equipment, capital, technical skill, and the lessons of their experience, supplied by nations which had already advanced, enabled others to advance. Great Britain contributed powerfully to the industrial development of the United States and Germany; these three countries together with France contributed importantly to the industrial development of Russia; Russia gave valuable assistance to China. A late start in the race to industrialization had its advantages. Mistakes made by earlier entrants might be avoided by late starters through profitable study of the experience of others. Furthermore, while an older industrial power was likely to have a good deal of equipment that was outdated and inefficient, a newly industrializing nation would adopt only the latest and the best.

The Different Paths to Economic Progress

In achieving industrial advance, each nation followed its own particular path. In Anglo-Saxon countries the advance was achieved primarily through the efforts of private enterprise, operating in an unregulated market economy where the individual had a maximum of economic freedom, in accordance with the doctrine of laissez-faire. In Japan, on the other hand, the transformation of the economy was directed by a powerful bureaucracy which retained many feudal vestiges, and by massive private economic dynasties such as the Mitsui and the Mitsubishi. In the case of both Russia and China the country was thrust upon the road to industrialization by a communist dictatorship which had acquired its power through political revolution.

The Human Costs of Rapid Progress

Nowhere was rapid economic progress achieved without enormous sacrifice in human terms. England's early and impressive industrial gains involved the crowding of thousands of workers into dirty, squalid industrial towns, where their lives were characterized by racking toil, poverty and social degradation.[6] Distinguished authori-

---

[6]c.f., the following comment. "At the heart of the Industrial Revolution of the eighteenth century there was an almost miraculous improvement in the tools of production, which was accompanied by a catastrophic dislocation of the lives of the common people." K. Polanyi, *The Great Transformation* (New York, 1944), p. 33.

ties have suggested that only in the twentieth century did the English working man regain the level of well-being he had known in the eighteenth, before the Industrial Revolution began.[7] A leading British politician expressed the view that had British working people possessed in the eighteenth century the political power which they came to possess in the twentieth they would have used it to prevent the Industrial Revolution from happening.[8] In the United States too, the era of rapid industrialization was for many people a period of long, hard hours of work for miserably low pay. In Russia the forced pace of economic advance involved the death of millions of people and, for most of those who lived, a bare subsistence; productive capacity was used to build armaments and more productive capacity and only a minimum of consumer goods. China's frantic attempt to industrialize at a breakneck pace was responsible for hunger and misery on a scale so great as to compel a drastic slowdown in the pace of industrialization.

"Automatic Progress"

Available evidence suggests that throughout the more advanced countries of the world, there has occurred in recent years a general increase in well-being. Fewer hours per week are being worked; a good many dirty, disagreeable, and dangerous jobs are now done by machines; more material comforts and amenities are generally available. The fruits of past investment are being realized. Progress continues everywhere at a rapid pace, but no longer imposes the need for sacrifice. Whereas in a poor country progress is difficult because the country is poor, in a rich country progress is easy because the country is rich.

In fact, in a rich country, progress is virtually inevitable. With high personal incomes, a large volume of savings is bound to accumulate each year; this in turn will finance massive investment in additional capital goods, which will further augment the productive capacity of the country. High personal incomes involve correspondingly high taxable capacity. Governments are able to raise large sums for investment in social capital such as highways and power generating plants, which further strengthen the national economy. Governments are able to maintain elaborate educational systems in which young people acquire the knowledge and the skills which will enable them to devise new and superior products, new and superior methods of production. Ample private and public funds are available to support research activities which ensure progress. The concern of a modern "affluent society,"

---

[7]Jacob Viner, *Stability and Progress: the Poorer Countries' Problem*, paper presented at the First Congress of the International Economic Association, published in *Stability and Progress in the World Economy* (London, 1958), p. 62.

[8]"It is doubtful whether the achievements of the Industrial Revolution would have been permitted if the Franchise had been universal. It is very doubtful because a great deal of the capital aggregations that we are at present enjoying are the results of wages that our fathers went without." Aneurin Bevan, in "Democratic Values", Fabian Tract No. 282, London, 1950. Quoted in Gunnar Myrdal, *Rich Lands and Poor* (New York, 1957), p. 46.

as J. K. Galbraith has pointed out,[9] is not so much to increase its total output as to ensure that the various kinds of goods are produced in the right proportion and properly distributed.

ECONOMIC PLANNING

Following the Keynesian Revolution it has become a commonplace that the governments of free enterprise countries should apply broad fiscal and monetary policies to control the tempo of economic activity. In recent years the view has gained ground that governments should intervene more actively to ensure the achievement not only of full employment without inflation but also a rapid rate of economic growth and an appropriate composition of the national output. In many countries leading businessmen, trade union leaders and government officials have joined to express a demand for economic planning meaning thereby, in the words of one definition:

> . . . the whole process by which national economic goals are specified and ranked, by which an estimation is made of how closely the economic system is expected to meet these goals, and by which economic measures are used to alter the behaviour of the economic system in the direction of the goals.[10]

It has become fashionable in Western European countries to draw up national economic plans, though their significance is not always clear; in a number of instances, notably the U.K. and Sweden, the Plan is a compromise between a forecast and a pious wish, with the government quite unprepared to intervene in the economy to ensure the realization of goals set forth. (It is hoped, however, that the business community will entertain a common set of expectations—those set forth in the Plan —and will act in conformity with its objectives.) Only in France has the national plan been a genuine guide to action, with the administrative authorities using their powers negatively to deter firms from contravening the Plan and positively to reward compliance. One observer has suggested as explanation for the French planning style that:

> The essential French view, which goes back to well before the Revolution of 1789, is that the operative conduct of a nation's economic life must depend on the concentration of power in the hands of a small number of exceptionally able people, exercising foresight and judgement of a kind not possessed by the average successful man of business.[11]

[9]In J. K. Galbraith, *The Affluent Society* (Boston, 1958).
[10]L. A. Skeoch and D. C. Smith, "Does Canada Need Economic Planning: the Relevance of West European Experience for Canada," in *The Canadian Economy, Selected Readings* (Toronto, 1965) p. 131.
[11]A. Shonfield, *Modern Capitalism.* (Oxford, 1965) p. 71-2.

Canada moved a step in the direction of economic planning with the setting up of the Economic Council of Canada in 1964, a 28 member body broadly representative of the nation's economic community and given the responsibility of advising the government how Canada could achieve: "The highest possible levels of employment and efficient production in order that the country may enjoy a high and consistent rate of economic growth and that all Canadians may share in rising living standards."

The Council has no coercive power: its responsibility is to obtain and disseminate information on the Canadian economy, thereby promoting widespread public understanding of our economic problems and the possible courses of action available, and helping to produce a broad national concensus on basic economic issues.

More Equalitarian Income Distribution

Enormously increased economic and political power of formerly subservient majorities has brought about a more equalitarian distribution of income and welfare. Through trade union organization, workers have been able to make effective demands for higher wages and improved working conditions. Where democracy has prevailed, the economically inferior members of the community have been able, because their number is large, to influence legislation to their own advantage. Heeding the desires of the politically powerful lower income groups, governments have introduced policies and measures which favour their interests; the cost is borne by the community's higher income groups, who are politically weaker because of their smaller numbers. Welfare measures, such as Canada's pension programmes, family allowance plans, and free hospital and medical services, involve in effect a transfer of income from higher to lower income groups and therefore a more equal distribution of material welfare. The configuration of the country's economy reflects the equalitarian distribution of income; to an ever increasing degree our economy stresses the production, not of limited quantities of extravagant luxuries for a tiny minority, but the mass production of amenities and comforts for the great majority.

It has been suggested, not unreasonably, that equalitarian redistribution of income slows down a country's rate of progress, because it causes a reduction in the rate of capital accumulation. A good part of the money paid out in higher wages and in transfer payments would have been saved and invested, and the country's productive capacity would have been increased. Despite these adverse effects, however, the scale of capital accumulation is still very large, assuring an ample rate of progress. Furthermore, it may be argued that a good deal of the money spent by governments on welfare measures represents a form of social investment; expenditures for education and health which improve the well-being of the people also increase human productivity and so contribute to the material progress of the nation. On the other hand, it must be recognized that measures of income redistribution undertaken by the government, may reduce individual incentives. Those from whom income is taken away may be discouraged from putting forth their best efforts; those to whom income is freely given may decide that work on their part is unnecessary.

THE UNDERDEVELOPED AREAS

The spectacular economic progress recorded in the past two centuries has been achieved by only a few fortunate countries, notably the United States, Canada, Australia, New Zealand, and countries of Western Europe. In the remaining countries of the world, the amenities and comforts common to the advanced countries are scarce or altogether lacking. In a large number of countries, particularly in Africa and Asia, the majority of people live in abysmal poverty, exposed to premature death through disease or malnutrition.

The "Revolution of Rising Expectations"

The people who live in the underdeveloped countries, comprising some two-thirds of the world's population, are now refusing to accept submissively their hard lot. Observers report that there is now proceeding throughout the world's poorer lands a "Revolution of Rising Expectations." These people have become very much aware of the superior living standards achieved in the advanced countries, and eager to emulate them. They want to be freed of the prospect of early death through disease or hunger; they want to obtain for themselves comforts and amenities of the sort common in advanced countries. And they do not want to wait very long.

The Prospects for Progress

Will the world's underdeveloped countries be able to achieve the rapid economic progress to which they aspire? There are ample grounds for both doubt and confidence. The prospects vary from one country to another, according to the character of local problems and local possibilities. In most of the presently underdeveloped countries natural resources are poor, and population density is greater than was the case in Europe two centuries ago, when that continent launched its great forward drive. There are not today, as there were then, vast and empty continents whose fertile lands and rich resources are available to support population growth and economic expansion. Probably in none of today's underdeveloped lands does their exist a strong entrepreneurial class, well-established trade connections, effective arrangements for public administration, education, law and order, such as existed in Great Britain and the United States in the eighteenth century.[12]

[12]The countries which have achieved modern industrial status only in recent years also launched their advance, in each case, from a strong and well developed base. Thus Communist Russia and China, for instance, had the benefit of distinguished cultural heritages which indispensably contributed to their rapid material advance. Viz. the following observation regarding the U.S.S.R. "Yet one should not minimize the fact that by the end of the empire Russia had a relatively recent but nevertheless a firmly rooted cultural tradition of the western type which, contrary to what is often alleged, put her into an entirely different class from the undeveloped countries of the post-World War II era.

In its upper levels Russian scientific and technical work was as expert as any and there was a sizeable body of men and women trained in various fields of endeavour. Although much of this precious heritage of knowledge and experience was destroyed in the Revolution, it provided a solid, albeit narrow, base without which the advance of Soviet science and technology would have been far more difficult, if not actually impossible, than it proved to be." Michael T. Florinsky, *Education in Imperial Russia*, Current History, July 1958, p. 5.

In some countries today political instability discourages long range investment, domestic as well as foreign, and so constitutes a handicap to progress. In some countries nepotism, corruption, or a rigid caste system, enable poorly qualified persons to occupy positions of responsibility, while abler individuals must accept inferior positions. In many countries powerful bonds of custom and tradition bind people to ancient ways, preventing the adoption of those new patterns of living which must be adopted if economic progress is to be achieved. In a good many countries the high mortality rate of young people implies a unique and heavy burden; large numbers of persons must be supported who never attain the age when they can be economically productive. In most underdeveloped countries educational facilities are grossly inadequate; few young people are able to acquire the skills and the knowledge which they must possess in order to achieve any degree of economic advance. The people of many countries cannot, through their own effort, accumulate capital in the form of roads, buildings, equipment, and so enlarge their productivity. Such capital accumulation can be acquired only through saving, but people who are desperately poor cannot save. There does exist, in some underdeveloped countries, a class of wealthy persons, but these do not invest their wealth in productive enterprises: they squander it instead in wild extravagances, or pile it up in fruitless hoards. In a great many of these countries large numbers of people are wholly unemployed for much of the time. Many are employed at unproductive tasks; the nation's output would fall only negligibly or not at all if they stopped doing their "work." Viewed realistically such people should also be considered as being unemployed; theirs is simply a "disguised unemployment."

INTERNATIONAL ASSISTANCE

The underdeveloped countries enjoy one priceless advantage, however; other nations have already blazed the trail which they hope to follow. The experience of the advanced countries during the past two centuries offers invaluable guidance, suggesting what paths should be followed and what paths should be avoided. The knowledge and skills which these nations have acquired, together with some of the capital which they have accumulated, is available to assist the progress of the underdeveloped countries. For both humanitarian and political reasons, the world's more advanced countries have been extending technical assistance, free training, loans and gifts to underdeveloped countries. It is no easy matter to adapt the technology and the equipment of advanced countries to the primitive circumstances of backward countries. Furthermore, in relation to the needs of the latter, the amount rendered of such assistance has been small. Nevertheless, the example and the assistance rendered by the advanced countries is likely to prove a decisive factor in the progress achieved by the underdeveloped countries. Their progress will depend very largely upon the scale and character of the assistance they receive and upon their success in adopting the superior technology demonstrated to them by the world's advanced countries.

Point Four

In 1949 the Americans launched a new programme against an age-old problem. In his Inaugural Address delivered in January of that year, President Truman announced a broad programme for peace and freedom which would emphasize four major courses of action. The one he mentioned last, "Point Four," acquired historic significance.

> "Fourth we must embark upon a bold new programme for making the benefits of our scientific advances and industrial progress available for the improvement and growth of underdeveloped areas.
>
> More than half the people of the world are living in conditions approaching misery. Their food is inadequate. They are victims of disease. Their economic life is primitive and stagnant. Their poverty is a handicap and a threat both to them and to more prosperous areas.
>
> For the first time in history, humanity possesses the knowledge and the skill to relieve the suffering of these people.
>
> The United States is pre-eminent among nations in the development of industrial and scientific techniques. The material resources which we can afford to use for this assistance of other peoples are limited. But our imponderable resources of technical knowledge are constantly growing and are inexhaustible.
>
> I believe that we should make available to peace-loving peoples the benefits of our store of technical knowledge in order to help them realize their aspirations for a better life. And, in cooperation with other nations, we should foster capital development in areas needing development.
>
> Our aim should be to help the free people of the world, through their own efforts, to produce more food, more clothing, more materials for housing, and more mechanical power to lighten their burdens.
>
> We invite other countries to pool their technological resources in this undertaking. Their contributions will be warmly welcomed. This should be a cooperative enterprise in which all nations work together through the United Nations and the specialized agencies wherever practicable. It must be a world-wide effort for the achievement of peace, plenty, and freedom."

A Technical Cooperation Administration was established in 1950 to implement the President's proposal. Its functions included the granting of American technical assistance toward the formulation of basic programmes in relation to health, sanitation and food supplies in underdeveloped countries, and the training of selected personnel from these countries in American educational institutions and training establishments.

Private Aid

Not all of the American aid to underdeveloped countries is given by the U.S. government. Approximately fifty religious and secular agencies carry on welfare work in these countries; other private organizations make large contributions toward relief, education, and economic development. While the total of such private aid is only a small fraction of that extended by the U.S. government, it is nevertheless substantial, and amounts to far more than is contributed by the governments of most countries.

United Nations Technical Assistance Programme

Beginning in 1946 a number of the specialized agencies affiliated with the United Nations provided the services of experts to economically backward countries, at no charge, to help them deal more effectively with their problems. Each agency was concerned only with problems in its own particular field, and met the cost of providing these services out of its regular budget. In 1948, the United Nations set aside a relatively small sum, just over a quarter of a million dollars, to initiate a programme of technical assistance in fields not covered by the specialized agencies. In response to President Truman's suggestion that nations cooperate to provide technical assistance on a greatly enlarged scale, the U.N. introduced in 1949 an "Expanded Programme of Technical Assistance," financed by voluntary contributions of the member nations. The funds subscribed have been used to support greatly enlarged technical assistance programmes by the specialized agencies[13] and by the U.N. itself. (The Technical Assistance Administration, created by the U.N. in 1950, acts as the directing and coordinating agency.)

The "Expanded" programme proceeds along three main lines. Technically qualified experts are sent out, upon request, to advise governments and to train local staffs. Fellowships and scholarships are granted to nationals of underdeveloped countries to enable them to pursue courses of study in more advanced countries. Training centres and regional centres are organized, where experts from different countries can meet to exchange ideas and compare experiences.[14]

The experts are recruited from all over the world and dispatched all over the world. Thus in 1967, a total of 5,289 experts, who came from 44 different countries, were sent to 60 different countries and territories. In a good many cases a country which sought the services of experts in one field was able to supply the services of experts in another field.

The Colombo Plan

In the Far East, throughout Asia and the South Pacific, World War II hastened the end of the era of colonialism. Countries which for generations had been the colonies

---

[13]Currently the specialized agencies participating in the technical assistance programme are the following seven: Food and Agricultural Organization (FAO); United Nations Educational, Scientific and Cultural Organization (UNESCO); World Health Organization (WHO); International Labour Organization (ILO); International Civil Aviation Organization (ICAO); International Telecommunications Union (ITU); World Meteorological Organization (WMO).

[14]The scale of operations has been substantial; up till 1958 more than ten thousand experts had been sent out on missions; over eighteen thousand persons had received fellowships enabling them to study in foreign lands.

or dependencies of Western powers, through force or political pressure gained their independence within a few years of the war's end. Once free to direct their own destinies, they launched ambitious programmes of development designed to expand their economic productivity and raise the living standards of their people. The obstacles were immense. Large-scale programmes of economic development require modern machinery and equipment, expert knowledge and skills; in the poor and backward countries of Asia and the South Pacific these were in critically short supply. In countries where the population was already enormous, and each year swelled by additional millions, a substantial increase in productive capacity was regularly required merely to maintain even the existing low standards.

The foreign ministers of the British Commonwealth, meeting in January, 1950, in Colombo, capital of Ceylon, took note of these problems. A resolution passed at the conference urged that Commonwealth governments join together in a programme to further the economic development of South and South-East Asia. The improvement of economic conditions in these areas, the Resolution declared, would powerfully support peace and prosperity throughout the world. Accordingly, a Committee representing Commonwealth governments met in London in September, 1950, to blue-print the "Colombo Plan."[15]

As originally drawn up, the Plan called for the more advanced countries of the Commonwealth to give aid to the less advanced member countries in Asia. An invitation was extended to non-Commonwealth countries to join the Plan, both as recipients and donors. Half a dozen additional countries in Asia and the South Pacific joined the Plan to receive aid, while Japan and the United States undertook to contribute. The Plan called for assistance to be given over a six-year period, ending in June, 1957; the terminal date has since been set back to 1976 however, and it is quite possible that the Plan will be continued even beyond this date.

Under the plan each donor country determines the size of its annual contribution, and, in bilateral negotiation with recipient countries, arranges the form which its assistance will take. Thus Canada undertook to contribute $25 million per year toward the Plan, the money being used to provide equipment, materials and expert services for such projects as a cement plant in Pakistan, a Technical High School in Burma, a hydro-electric power project in India. Portions of our Colombo Plan contribution have also been used to purchase our wheat, and to purchase railway engines built in Canada, for use in Asian countries.[16] Recipient countries may also be donors; thus India, the major recipient country, has also extended assistance under the Plan to other Asian countries.

[15]Officially described as the "Plan for Cooperative Economic Development of South and South-East Asia."

[16]Canada has since substantially increased her contribution, the 1968-69 allocation being $126 millions. During the 18-year period from the inception of the Plan to March, 1968, Canada made available a total of $982 millions, sent more than 500 Canadian experts to recipient countries to act as teachers and advisers and provided instruction in Canada to over 4,400 trainees from these countries.

The total value of all assistance contributed to Colombo Plan countries amounted to well over $20 billion by 1965, with the United States supplying over three-quarters of the total.[17] Under the Plan itself, assistance took the form of materials, equipment, supplies, and expert help in the construction of specific projects. Additional provision was made for technical assistance such as provided by the United Nations and its affiliated agencies. Under the Technical Cooperation Scheme operated in conjunction with the Plan, experts are sent to recipient countries to give technical advice in agriculture, engineering, welfare and other fields; students from South-East Asian countries are given training in other Colombo Plan countries; special equipment for training purposes is provided.

The World Bank[18]

The assistance provided to war-ravaged and underdeveloped countries under the various American and U.N programmes and the Colombo Plan, has been primarily in the nature of free gifts. Another type of aid has been available as well—loans from the World Bank. This institution was designed at an Economic Conference held at Bretton Woods in the United States in 1944 where experts from Allied and friendly countries drew up plans for international economic institutions which would be established following the end of the war. The experts anticipated that war-damaged countries would require a great deal of foreign aid for their reconstruction; they anticipated, too, the need for large scale assistance to underdeveloped countries if they were to enlarge their productive capacities. Blueprints were accordingly drawn up for an international bank whose capital would be subscribed by the nations of the world, and which would make loans for the reconstruction of war-damaged countries, together with loans for basic development projects in underdeveloped countries.

The Bank actually commenced operations in 1946, with a subscribed capital of $9.4 billion (by 1970 it had been increased to $23 billion). Its first loans were made to war-damaged European countries, but, with the inauguration of the Marshall Plan in 1948, such loans became unnecessary. Henceforth the Bank concentrated on making loans to underdeveloped countries, which would enable them to build the foundations of economic advance. Approximately one-third of the Bank's development loans have been made toward transportation improvements—the construction of roads, railways, airfields, and port facilities; another third has been made toward the construction of electric power generating plants; the remainder have been made for such projects as irrigation works, steel plants and other major facilities which would materially strengthen the economic base of the borrowing countries. The Bank's loans are made to governments, with each loan advanced to finance a specific

---

[17]The American contribution has been made in the form of grants under a variety of American programmes, including the Mutual Security Program, the Agricultural Trade Development and Assistance Program, the Atoms for Peace Program. In addition to grants, loans were made by the Export-Import Bank and the Development Loan Fund.

[18]Formally known as the International Bank for Reconstruction and Development.

project. Before a loan is made, the Bank sends out experts to investigate the project in detail, in order to ensure that it is economically sound, that it will strengthen the economy of the borrowing country, and that the loan is likely to be repaid.

The average term of loans has been 20-25 years with the rate of interest charged depending upon the level of rates prevailing in major capital markets at the time the loan was made. The Bank lends not only money which has been subscribed by member countries, but also part of its accumulated reserves and money which it raises through the sale of its own bonds. In addition, having made a loan, the Bank may "sell" a part of the loan to private investors. By this procedure, the Bank uses its money just to start a loan; once the loan has proven to be safe and sound, the Bank gets its money back by selling it to private investors, and is then able to lend that money to someone else. The scale of its operations has been substantial: by 1970 the total of loans it had made was nearly $9 billions. Operations have been financially successful as well as large in scale: in fiscal 1970 net income amounted to $213 millions and accumulated reserves stood at $1,442 millions.

The International Finance Corporation

While the World Bank is authorized to make loans to private corporations, the number of such loans has been negligible. A loan may be made to a private firm only if the government of the country concerned guarantees it; few governments are prepared to commit themselves in this way. The fact that, in practice, the Bank could not lend to private firms, was reckoned to be a serious deficiency. Accordingly, in 1956, the International Finance Corporation was established with a capital of $100 million, to lend money to private firms without requiring government guarantees. The Corporation obtains its funds on loan from the World Bank and is administered by the Bank. The scale of its lending is far smaller than that of its parent institution; in fiscal 1970, when the Bank made loans to governments totalling $1,680 millions, I.F.C. loans, to private enterprises, totalled $112 millions.

The Special Fund

While grateful for such assistance as they have received, the underdeveloped countries have made it clear that they could use a great deal more. Their prime need, they point out, is for "social capital"—for roads, railways, water works, sewage systems, and the like. Without such basic facilities they can register very little advance, in any direction. Such projects are generally not self-liquidating, for, while they are essential to the progress of a country, they do not directly produce revenues, foreign exchange particularly, out of which their cost can be paid. The benefits which they yield are for the most part indirect, and may materialize only in the distant future. Accordingly, it would not be feasible to construct such projects with funds borrowed from the World Bank; the Bank insists that loans be repaid within a specified period, and it charges a commercial rate of interest.

What the underdeveloped countries need is large scale free grants, or loans at very low interest and repayable over a very long period of time. At the instigation of these countries, serious consideration was given in the U.N. in 1956 to the establishment of a new fund, the Special United Nations Fund for Economic Development (SUNFED). It was proposed that nations contribute to the fund on a voluntary basis; the hope was expressed that an easing of international tensions would enable nations to reduce their expenditures on armaments, and that they would finance the construction of needed projects in underdeveloped countries through either an outright grant or a very long term loan at a very low rate of interest. However, the United States, which was expected to contribute the lion's share of the funds, was lukewarm to the proposal, American representatives arguing that the tense international situation did not warrant large scale reductions in armament expenditures.

Nevertheless, in December, 1957, the U.N. General Assembly voted to set up the SUNFED, and the new agency came into existence on January 1, 1959. Its finances and its functions were a good deal more modest than had been originally contemplated. Its funds for the first year, subscribed voluntarily by member countries, totalled only about $27 million, instead of the $100 million which had been hoped for. Instead of lending money to underdeveloped countries, the new organization was to provide special forms of technical assistance. It was to establish major research institutes, and to support large scale engineering surveys in underdeveloped countries such as of river basins and geological formations. These surveys would indicate the feasibility of hydro-electric power plants, mining ventures and other developmental projects.

The International Development Association (IDA)

As a modified version of the original SUNFED proposal, the United States advocated the establishment of an International Development Association which would make loans on very easy terms to the world's badly underdeveloped countries. The IDA came into being with an initial subscribed capital of $765 millions which it used to make 50-year loans at no interest to countries whose per capita income amounted to less than $250. By 1964 its initial capital was fully committed and member countries subscribed additional funds; further replenishments were made subsequently. The World Bank transferred a total of $385 millions to IDA between 1964 and 1970, as grants out of net income earned in those years. During the decade of the 1960s the Association made a total of 221 loan commitments to 55 countries, amounting to $2,773 millions, for such basic developmental purposes as irrigation, drainage, education, power and water supply.

The "Politics" of International Assistance

The United States has contributed the great bulk of the total assistance extended to underdeveloped countries. Its own programmes have been large in scale; it has been the major contributor to the technical assistance programme carried out by the United Nations; it is the major source of funds loaned out by the World Bank. In the 23-year period 1945-68 the U.S. made grants to foreign countries aggregating more than $53 billions and extended credits totalling more than $21 billions; grants for military purposes amounted to an additional $39 billions. American motivation has been humanitarian, reflecting her traditional generosity, and self-interested, reflecting the realities of the prevailing international situation. In the "cold war" now being waged between the Union of Soviet Socialist Republics and the United States, each with its supporters and allies ranged alongside, the friendship of the world's underdeveloped countries is a prized objective. These nations possess rich natural resources and enormous numbers of people. The side which they support is likely to gain preferential access to their resources and their markets, and the military and political advantage of many millions of converts to their cause.

To counter American efforts, the Union of Soviet Socialist Republics has embarked upon an aid programme of her own. Although still a good deal less than the American, this assistance to underdeveloped areas has assumed significant proportions, particularly in some countries. Soviet aid is given direct; the U.S.S.R. is not a member of the World Bank and contributes little toward the cost of the U.N. Technical Assistance Programme. Again in contrast to American procedure, the U.S.S.R. has extended very little assistance in the form of outright gifts; her aid has consisted to a very large extent of machinery, equipment, supplies, and the services of technical experts, furnished under long term credit arrangements at low rates of interest.[19]

Limitations of International Aid Programmes

The assistance rendered to underdeveloped countries, by gift and loan, has been of great help, but has wrought no miraculous transformation of their productivity and living standards. The plain fact is that the great bulk of any nation's output must always be produced through that nation's own efforts. Foreign experts can constitute only a minute fraction of the labour force; the overwhelming proportion of work done will be by native people and its effectiveness will depend upon *their* education, *their* skill, *their* energy. Funds supplied by foreigners can seldom provide more than a fraction of the total capital required for comprehensive national development. The size of a nation's outlays on development will depend primarily upon the amount of income which its own nationals are prepared to save and invest. The main contribu-

---

[19]Some observers question the value of economic aid as a means of winning the friendship of underdeveloped countries. For all sorts of reasons, they suggest, the reaction of the recipient country may turn out to be perverse. The administrative procedure of the donor country may be ill-considered; its administrative personnel may be inept or their behaviour exasperating. Real or imagined strings attached to the aid may be intensely resented. Unfavourable comparisons may be drawn with the aid granted to other countries. When the aid programme is ended, the final attitude of the people of the recipient country may be hostile because it was ended, rather than grateful because it was begun.

tion which foreign assistance can render to underdeveloped countries is to show their people how to help themselves.

The road to development, it has been observed, is paved with vicious circles. Because of the general backwardness a potentially valuable new element introduced into a backward country may be ignorantly applied, improperly and inadequately used. The farm machinery that contributes to high agricultural productivity in Canada, in a backward country may be speedily wrecked by careless operators, left unrepaired for lack of skilled mechanics, do harm because it is used in wrong ways or for unintended purposes. A supply of good steel spades, hoes and scythes is likely to prove of greater value in some countries than would tractors and combines. Foreign experts may give advice that is related to the advanced technology of their own countries, and is quite irrelevant to the circumstances of a primitive country struggling to achieve the very beginnings of progress.[20]

Defects of the U.S. Aid Programme

While the U.S. aid programme to underdeveloped countries has been very large in scale, most observers agree that its results have been disappointing. The different forms of aid are each given by different agencies and departments, so that the administration is confused and often overlapping. Aid has not been given in accordance with long range plans which aimed ultimately to have these countries advancing under their own steam. Instead, aid has been given on a year to year basis; in many cases it has been designed simply to meet crisis situations and to achieve short range political objectives. Receiving countries have tended, furthermore, to be highly suspicious of American motives in offering aid, and therefore wary about accepting.

Possible Misdirection of Effort

To achieve rapid and continuing progress a nation should not merely expand its output, but expand the kind of output which enables further progress to be made. It should emphasize the production of machinery and equipment and the construction of buildings and facilities which will enlarge productive capacity. There is a considerable danger, however, that in some countries output will not be increased in the optimum way. Because of impatience to achieve living standards closer to those of advanced countries, income which should really be saved and invested may be devoted instead to raising current levels of consumption. Because of eagerness to impress, investment may be carried out in showpieces, dramatic symbols of achievement such as steel factories, rather than in projects which would prove more

---

[20]Unfortunately, just as the people of a primitive country may find it very difficult to acquire complex modern skills, the expert who is sent to their country may find it very difficult to realize how inappropriate is the equipment and technology with which he is familiar. All too often experts, who were sent out on missions to underdeveloped countries, followed the maxim "When in Rome, do as at home."

fundamentally useful such as the improvement of educational facilities. Because of failure to realize the priorities involved the resources available for development may be devoted to low priority projects that should really have been postponed; far more would have been achieved if available capacity had been concentrated on strategic developments that would provide the basis for broad and massive advance. Thus labour, materials and foreign exchange that might have been used to build a hydro-electric power plant might be used instead to build government office buildings.

Students sent abroad to learn modern technology may not return; because their personal circumstances would be much more agreeable they may elect to live in an advanced country rather than in their poor and backward homeland. In such cases training abroad serves to cream off bright young natives of underdeveloped countries for the benefit of advanced countries; the effect of such a "brain drain" is to retard rather than advance the progress of those countries which need it most badly. Some of the people sent abroad to learn have returned to their homelands replete with irrelevant knowledge and cherishing inflated notions of their worth and deserts; their contribution to national progress has been slight or negative.

Gains achieved in one direction may prove to be of little benefit unless, simultaneously, gains are made in other directions as well. Thus an improvement in medical practices and sanitation methods, if unaccompanied by increases in the output of food, may simply mean that more people will starve. The construction of a modern industrial plant which is capable of efficiently producing a very large output, is of limited value if there are no roads or railways over which its products can be widely distributed, or if there are no merchandising facilities capable of marketing them properly.

The Role of Government

In a good many underdeveloped countries, notably those of South America and Asia, there exist tiny, wealthy elites able to exercise comprehensive political as well as economic domination; the mass of population barely scratches out a subsistence. Economic progress in such countries does not mean that their elites should acquire additional luxuries; it means rather that the mass who live in abysmal poverty should acquire some modicum of material well-being. The present distribution of power implies massive obstacles in the way of such progress. Solidly entrenched oligarchies may use their power to obtain for themselves or for their friends all of, or virtually all of, any increases in national output; little or nothing of the additional goods available find their way to the struggling poor.

If indeed the fruits of progress are thus divided it is likely that the actual amount of progress will be slight. Oppressed and exploited workers will not put forward their best efforts if the result will be primarily to enrich the already rich. Substantial and meaningful advance will only be achieved when additional output serves to improve the lot of the common man; what is needed is not a few more

Cadillacs but a great many more bicycles. If progress takes this form it is likely to elicit the effort needed to achieve that progress; the humble man who has always journeyed afoot will be prepared to work hard for his bicycle.

Progress may demand not merely that ruling oligarchies refrain from claiming additional national output for themselves; it may demand that they yield up some of their present wealth and income. To achieve additional output the nation will need to enlarge its stock of capital goods. Larger national savings will therefore be needed, for foreign gifts and lending can provide only a small portion of what is required. But very little of these savings can come from poor people whose incomes barely suffice for existence; by one means or another the present wealth and income of rich persons will have to be diverted toward the acquisition of capital goods needed to enlarge national output.

Militant socialists insist that existing power structures will inevitably thwart attempts at national progress; they proclaim that advance can be achieved only when an all-powerful government harnesses and controls the nation's total productive capacity, ruthlessly seizing private wealth that may be required for the purpose. Since there is a paramount need for rapid progress the present obstructive social systems must be replaced, they aver. Exponents of economic liberalism contend that the preservation of individual liberties is more important than rapid economic progress and that, in any case, progress can equally be achieved under free enterprise arrangements. Revolution is not necessary; reform will suffice, particularly if assistance is provided on a generous scale by other countries in a position to give it. They urge that in fact private enterprise offers surer promise of economic development: libertarian arrangements assure the possibility of the numerous individual initiatives that are indispensable to national progress. Socialism, on the other hand, inevitably establishes a rigid, stultifying bureaucracy and launches grandiose, unrealistic plans that involve drastic misdirection of productive capacity and impose heavy burdens and sacrifices on the population at large.

It is clear that even in countries which eschew full-blown socialism the government will be called on to play a large role in national economic development. As a matter of course governments will be responsible for construction of the extensive infrastructure required—roads, railways, water supplies, electricity systems, telephone networks and so on. Governments will have to institute comprehensive school systems; they will have to institute effective arrangements for the protection of life and property, the preservation of law and order. These are now routine government responsibilities in advanced countries; they will be as a matter of course public responsibilities in underdeveloped countries.

It is likely that governments of some of these countries will find themselves obliged to initiate and administer economic activities of types commonly handled by private enterprise elsewhere. A good many countries, especially in Africa, simply do not have people capable of performing the role of large scale entrepreneur and administrator; nor can their citizens raise substantial amounts of capital. Only in the service of the government are there likely to be found persons with the will, the ability and the experience required to establish and administer large undertakings, and only the government would be able to raise the necessary capital either at home or abroad. The government, of course, may not have in its service the required types of persons either; in that case large enterprises must be established and run by qualified foreigners or not at all.

Large international corporations may serve as the channels through which modern technology is introduced into a primitive country. If valuable natural resources exist in such a country foreign firms will be anxious to exploit them, introducing whatever capital and administrative skills may be required. Their operations may constitute a springboard for broad national development: royalties paid to governments may enable the purchase abroad of all manner of capital goods; native persons whom they employ may acquire skills and experience that can be of immense value in the drive for national development. (On the other hand there is the possibility, as ample experience has indicated, that foreign owned firms may continue indefinitely as enclaves of modernity in primitive subsistence economies, contributing virtually nothing to their advancement, and exploiting for their private profit resources which could have been used as a basis for broad national development.)

On the Road to Progress

Once an underdeveloped nation has achieved "take-off speed," once it has cracked the restraining shell of apathy, ignorance and poverty, and has achieved a significant increase in output, then further progress becomes assured. Age-old stagnation gives way to steady progress. Progress makes possible an acceleration of progress. The increase in productive capacity make it possible to devote more effort to activities which will further increase productive capacity. Additional capital facilities can be constructed, educational facilities can be improved and extended. The nation becomes better off, and at the same time increases its productive capacity, thereby ensuring that it will become even better off in the future. Having improved its educational system and acquired additional elements in its economy, the nation is able to utilize more advanced methods and equipment, and thereby to speed its further progress.

There is a strong possibility that the people of advanced countries will underestimate the progress achieved in underdeveloped countries. In the early stages of their development, much of the economic effort expended in these latter countries must be devoted to the building of foundations, a tedious task whose results are seldom dramatically evident to the observer. Furthermore, despite gains which they may achieve, living standards in the presently underdeveloped countries are likely to remain far behind those of advanced countries. If anything, the gap is likely to widen, since the advanced countries are maintaining a rapid rate of progress themselves. If the progress of the underdeveloped countries is to be judged realistically, the criterion ought not to be how their present living standards compare with those of advanced countries, but how their present standards compare with their lot in past ages.

Implications for the Rest of the World

How many presently underdeveloped countries will achieve a "take-off," it is now impossible to foresee. The success of those which do manage to thrust themselves on to the path of progress will pose problems and create opportunities for the rest of the world. The emergence of strong new industrial powers will no doubt require adjustments on the part of other nations. Competition will be keener for raw materials; some of the newcomers will likely prove to be superior producers of some goods now provided by presently advanced countries and take away part of their markets. But by increasing their productive power, the newly developed countries will themselves become more profitable markets and more advantageous sources of supply, so far as other nations are concerned. The principle of comparative advantage, described in Chapter 15, suggests that once the appropriate adjustments are made, the total productive capacity of the world will become enlarged, and that it will become possible for all nations to be better off. The nation which achieves economic progress enriches the world as well as itself.

Space Exploration

We stand today at the threshold of the era of space exploration. How this great adventure will affect the world, no man can now tell. A reasonable presumption is that its impact will be at least as great as the impact which the discovery of America had upon Europe. The prospective enlargement of the world's economy, by the advance of both developed and underdeveloped countries, may prove to be highly opportune. Expansion of productive capacity will mean not merely that people will be able to eat more and better food, enjoy more material comforts, achieve increased leisure time, but also that programmes of space exploration will be broadened and accelerated. And it may well be that achievement in the realm of space will become the most prized form of national progress.

SUMMARY

In order to achieve long-run economic progress, a nation must increase its productive capacity. Such an increase can be achieved by improving the size and quality of its work force, by acquiring more capital equipment, by developing its natural resources, by improving the mode of its industrial organization. Population must not grow as rapidly as does productive capacity.

The world's advanced countries achieved most of their progress during the past two centuries, thanks to revolutionary technological advances. Their populations grew rapidly, during the past century particularly, largely as a result of a sharp reduction in the death rate; this reduction in turn was largely attributable to medical advances and improvements in urban sanitation. Rapidly increasing productive capacity, however, enabled growing populations to enjoy rising standards of living.

Different nations advanced along different paths. In Great Britain and the United States, rapid progress was achieved through the virtually unrestricted application of the principles of laissez-faire. In Russia, rapid industrial progress was achieved through the imposition of ruthless authoritarian controls. In all countries rapid progress was achieved at great cost in human terms, with large numbers of people obliged to suffer hardship and sacrifice.

Once a country achieved considerable progress, further gains became easy and almost automatic. In democratic countries a more equalitarian distribution of income has generally come to prevail, distributing more broadly the fruits of progress.

The world's underdeveloped countries are anxious to raise sharply their productivity and living standards. They suffer from severe handicaps, whose nature varies from one country to another. They have, however, the enormous advantage of assistance and guidance from the advanced countries.

Private enterprise arrangements, foreign if need be, may prove more generally desirable than government ownership and control; foreign ownership and control need not endure forever.

The achievement of modern industrial status by additional countries will pose some problems for the older industrial powers. The ultimate results should be beneficial rather than harmful, however, if the latter nations appropriately reorganize their economies. Greater well-being should become possible throughout the world; achievement in the realm of space exploration should be accelerated.

FOR REVIEW AND DISCUSSION

1. Which of the world's underdeveloped countries do you feel are likely to achieve rapid material advance in the near future? Justify your answer.
2. Some people claim that in order to advance rapidly, underdeveloped countries must become wholly socialistic. Do you agree? Justify your answer.
3. Should advanced countries extend large-scale assistance to underdeveloped countries? Why or why not?
4. "If, in order for a country to achieve economic progress, it is necessary to sacrifice a whole generation of its people, then that progress is not worth while." Discuss.
5. "The present rapid rate of population growth, in both advanced and underdeveloped countries, is likely to continue indefinitely." Do you agree? Justify your answer.
6. Do you believe that the American government would be justified in raising

taxes in order to finance a greatly expanded space exploration programme? Why or why not?

7. Should Canada reduce her armament expenditures, and use the saving to increase her assistance to underdeveloped countries? Why or why not?

8. If we take into account such considerations as strain, congestion and pollution, we must conclude that we are probably worse off than our fathers and grandfathers. Discuss.

9. While economics might have been deservedly called "the Dismal Science" in the past, the epithet is no longer appropriate. Comment.

10. "Only rich countries can make progress." What truth is there in this observation?

11. "There is every reason to expect that, within a generation or two, the presently underdeveloped countries will catch up with the presently advanced countries." Do you agree? Justify your answer.

30

Capitalism and its Critics

The Capitalist System

By the phrase "capitalist system" we generally mean the kind of economic organization that has characterized the advanced nations of the Western world during the nineteenth and twentieth centuries. Its salient features are the following: the production of goods by hired staffs working in factories with mechanical equipment; the ownership and control by private individuals of the physical properties used in production; the freedom accorded to any individual to set up his own business enterprise; the rational management of business enterprises with a view to earning maximum profit; the existence of markets in which goods and services, including the labour upon which human beings depend for their livelihood, are bought and sold on a completely impersonal basis. The system is by no means standard or uniform; different features are emphasized in different countries. What is more, its character has changed in the course of time. During the twentieth century, rapid technological progress has spawned a host of new products and services; more powerful machinery has increased productive capacity and has brought into existence huge industrial plants; small groups of individuals have achieved control over great aggregations of productive property. Giant corporations operate on a world-wide basis. The economic principles that were outlined in previous chapters of this book, and the economic institutions that were described, are those of a modern, capitalist, free enterprise society such as that of contemporary Canada.

The capitalist system did not come into being all at once during the nineteenth century. Even during the feudalistic Middle Ages there had been stirrings of capitalistic-type enterprise, and such enterprise became progressively more common. The great leap forward of the Industrial Revolution was made from a base that had been building up for centuries.

Wealth and Poverty

There was one characteristic common to all centuries: a few people were rich and a great many were poor. Under feudalism the manorial lord and his attendants enjoyed abundance and luxury. Serfs and freemen were obliged to labour, without pay, in the lord's fields; out of the meagre produce of their own scanty plots they had to deliver to him a substantial portion. When feudalism declined and money rents replaced feudal obligations, the rent paid by the yeoman to his lord in many cases sorely reduced an already low income; the lord used the money to live sumptuously and extravagantly. Following the enclosure movements of the sixteenth and eighteenth centuries, a great many small farmers were deprived of land altogther. The expansion of commerce and the development of modern industry brought into being new forms of both wealth and poverty. Resourceful and aggressive merchants and industrialists amassed huge fortunes that enabled them to live in the style of the landed nobility; hitherto, ownership of land had been virtually the sole basis of wealth. The factory system of the nineteenth century brought into being a new class of poor: the urban workers employed for exhaustingly long hours, at miserably low pay, in grimy and evil-smelling factories, living in wretched hovels and tenements, fearful of losing the jobs upon which their scant livelihood depended.

Social Critics—The Utopians

Throughout the centuries, high-minded idealists and reformers denounced the gross inequalities they saw about them, and urged the establishment of a new social order in which all men would live happily and harmoniously together. Their proposals were generally fanciful and visionary, but some opened men's eyes to new ideas and new aspirations and thereby affected the subsequent course of history.

Writing in the early sixteenth century, Sir Thomas More described the island of "Utopia" where every person performed useful work, where none were rich and none poor, and where each family took what it needed from the common store. During the nineteenth century, four Frenchmen, dubbed the Utopians, contributed their own visions of a new society in which all men would live agreeably and harmoniously. Count Henri de St. Simon urged the creation of a new society in which the state ensured equality of opportunity for all. His followers, though not he himself, advocated the abolition of inheritance to ensure such equality. Charles Fourier advocated the reorganization of society into new units, "phalanxes," each to be composed of about eighteen hundred persons. The members would live in a large central building, a "phalanstère"; they would be engaged primarily in agriculture, with each task being performed by a small group of persons who had voluntarily associated themselves.[1] Louis Blanc urged that the government set up "social workshops" where employment would be assured for anyone who desired it. Each worker would perform according to his capacity, but would be paid according to his need. While the government would have to operate the workshops in the first instance, eventually they would be administered by the workers themselves. Pierre Joseph Proudhon condemned the institution of private property which enabled some

[1]Robert Owen advocated the establishment of cooperative agricultural-industrial villages along the lines of Fourier's phalanxes.

people to receive income without work. "La propriété, c'est le vol," he declared—Property is theft. Accordingly he advocated the establishment of a national bank from which workers would be able to obtain the instruments of production without payment of rent or interest. Each man would earn exactly what he had produced with his own labour and all men would associate on terms of equality.

Karl Marx

Amid the nineteenth-century critics of the social order one towering figure emerged, in the unlikely form of a German exile who spent the last three decades of his life studying and writing in the British Museum in London. Karl Marx left his imprint on history. His analysis of historical development gave rise to major new currents of thought; his call for the overthrow of the capitalist system by force gave rise to epoch-making upheavals.

Adapting the Hegelian dialectic[2] to economic development, Marx advanced the doctrine that the capitalist system had the historic role of expanding the productive capacity of mankind; its inner contradictions, however, prevented this capacity from being fully used. Under the capitalist system, workers were bound to be exploited by the owners of property, never receiving the full value of their labour. Inevitably, too, there would occur a series of progressively worsening economic crises; the lot of the worker would become ever more miserable. Eventually, the oppressed proletariat would rise up against the bourgeoisie who controlled the state and administered the system, forcibly overthrow their regime and establish a "dictatorship of the proletariat." A new, classless, communistic society would come into existence in which each individual would work to his full capacity; out of the abundance of goods produced, each would take whatever he needed. The state, an instrument whereby one class oppressed another, would "wither away"; the communist panacea would be stateless as well as classless.

Marxism in Europe

Followers of Marx in European countries organized workingmen into political parties whose platform was the achievement of a socialist society. The Social Democratic party which emerged in Germany during the 1860s become a major political force in that country; partly in response to pressure which it exerted, major reforms were instituted.[3] In France the trade union movement became imbued with the militant philosophy of *syndicalism*: through a unique revolutionary weapon—the general strike—workers, it was urged, could overthrow the regime. Simply by folding their arms the workmen of France could completely paralyze the country's economy, force

[2]The German philosopher Hegel (1770-1831) developed the thesis that each thing or state gives rise to its opposite; the opposites clash, thereby producing a new thing or state and a recurrence of the same process. The doctrine has been aptly summed up in the phrase "thesis, antithesis, synthesis".

[3]Influenced by the party's views and anxious also to weaken its appeal to German workingmen, Bismarck, the "Iron Chancellor", introduced legislation providing for sickness and accident insurance and old age pensions.

its rulers to capitulate, and institute a socialist society. Socialistically-oriented political parties and workingmen's associations came into being in every other country in Europe; in several countries, notably Belgium, Austria, Denmark, Norway and Sweden, socialist parties held political office and introduced socialist legislation.

Socialism in Great Britain

In England, the Fabian Society,[4] formally organized in 1884, worked for the establishment of socialism by piecemeal measures and constitutional means. Members of the Society devoted themselves to the investigation of particular social problems, pointed out remedies that were socialistic in character, and urged the adoption of their remedies by the authorities. Thus, by one small step at a time, the country would proceed toward socialism. The working classes, thanks to their numerical superiority, could achieve political power in a democracy through perfectly constitutional means, and create a socialist society by legislation. In part this goal was realized. The British Labour Party, influenced by Fabian thought, adopted as one of its planks the nationalization of major industries. The party won the general election of 1945 and, during the next six years when it controlled the government, nationalized the Bank of England, the coal mines, inland transport, electricity, gas, civil aviation, cable and wireless communications and the steel industry. (The Conservative administration which took over in 1951 "de-nationalized" the steel industry, returning it to private ownership; following its return to office in 1964 the Labour Party "re-nationalized" the industry.)

A significant division of opinion developed in the Labour Party in the late 1950s when it became evident that nationalization was far from being a panacea. Leading figures in the party now declared that the government ought to leave alone those private firms that were serving the country well and take over only those which were failing to operate in the public interest. They urged, what was more, that adequate control over firms could be achieved without outright nationalization: the government could become a major part owner through the purchase of a substantial block of shares and thus be in a position to influence company policy.

THE COMMUNIST ECONOMIES

The Russian Revolution

While the ideology of socialism affected in varying degree the course of events in all European countries, its most powerful impact occurred in Russia; a Marxist party seized power in 1917 and set about to transform the nation into a socialist society.

---

[4]Named after the Roman general Quintus Fabius, whose cautious tactics proved successful against Hannibal when the latter invaded Italy. Fabius refused to engage in a major battle; over a period of years he gradually weakened his enemy through harassment and victories in minor engagements until eventually Hannibal was forced to withdraw. The Society attracted some of the most brilliant men of the country; among its members were George Bernard Shaw, H. G. Wells, Sidney Webb.

The locale of the experiment belied a Marxian forecast; according to his historical analysis, the proletarian revolution would occur only in advanced industrial countries where a large, urban working class had come into being. Some eighty per cent of the population of Russia was still living on the land in 1917, and industrial development was far behind that of the nations of Western Europe.

The country was ripe for insurrection, however. Throughout the nineteenth century there had been revolutionary rumblings against the despotism of the czars and the feudal structure of society. The emancipation of the serfs, ordered by the czar in 1861 to prevent a "revolution from below," broke the fetters which bound the peasantry to the land. Industrialization, strongly supported by the state and financed to a considerable extent by foreign capital, furnished increasing employment opportunity in the cities. Peasants accustomed to poverty and oppression in their villages, now experienced poverty and oppression in cities. An urban proletariat emerged, subject to harsh and ruthless factory discipline and nourishing a bitter class hatred.

The smouldering fury broke out in open revolt in 1905 following Russia's defeat in the war against Japan and the revelation of gross corruption and inefficiency in the czarist regime. The uprisings were bloodily suppressed, but the alarmed czar, as a gesture toward satisfying the widespread demands for democratic government, established the Duma, an elected assembly with limited powers. At about the same time a new form of organization spontaneously arose to reflect the popular will —the "soviets"—these being councils of elected representatives of working men, soldiers, peasants, professional persons.

Czarist Russia was an ally of Britain and France in World War I. In February, 1917, after more than two years of war in which the Russian army had suffered massive defeats and the nation's economy was in a state of near chaos, a strike in St. Petersburg led to a nation-wide uprising. The czar abdicated and a provisional government was formed, consisting of moderate reformist elements committed to continuing the war against Germany. The Russian army suffered further heavy defeats during the summer of 1917; the economy became ever more chaotic. The soviets, now leagued together in a nation-wide federation, expressed increasing dissatisfaction with the economic and political policies of the new regime. By the fall of 1917 revolution was again in the air, this time against the democratic government that had been installed only months before, following the February uprising.

Lenin and Bolsheviks

Just before 1900, Russian Marxists had established the Social Democratic Labour party. At its congresses of 1903 and 1904 the party proved itself to be irreconcilably divided on a number of major issues. One faction, the Mensheviks,[5] held the

---

[5]When a vote was taken, one faction proved to be slightly larger. Its members were thereupon referred to as Bolsheviks, derived from the Russian word "bolshe", meaning "more"; members of the other group were called Mensheviks, derived from "menshe", meaning "less".

orthodox Marxian view that a proletarian revolution could be carried out in Russia only after the country had achieved advanced economic status with a major portion of the population employed in industry. The task of advancing the Russian economy would have to be carried out by the bourgeoisie; while this task was being accomplished the Marxists would simply act as a kind of extreme opposition party. The Bolshevik group, led by Vladimir I. Lenin, maintained on the other hand that it would be possible to proceed from Russia's primitive state directly to socialism, without passing through the intermediate state of bourgeois capitalist development. The two factions differed on the issue of organization and tactics as well. The Mensheviks held that the party should be genuinely democratic, with the leadership exercising relatively loose control and local groups permitted considerable freedom of action. Lenin, however, adamantly insisted that all party organizations submit absolutely to one central group which alone would decide and act. This central group would be composed of a virtual caste of professional revolutionaries to whom all means would be justified if they helped secure the end.

Following a period of exile in Siberia, Lenin fled Russia in 1900 to live as a refugee in several Western European centres and plan for revolution in Russia. Other Russian refugees joined him, notably Leon Trotsky who had played a leading role in the St. Petersburg uprising of 1905; Trotsky had been sentenced to life imprisonment but had managed to escape and flee the country. Lenin returned to Russia shortly after the revolution of February, 1917, to lead the Bolshevik group, and Trotsky soon arrived to assist. While the provisional government installed in February attempted relatively minor economic reforms and continued the war against Germany, the Bolsheviks demanded that the land be confiscated and distributed among the peasants, that industry be nationalized, and that peace be sought with Germany. With the economy becoming ever more chaotic and the army becoming increasingly demoralized, the country's mood became desperate. In October the Bolsheviks seized their opportunity; winning over to their side the Petrograd garrison and another regiment, they were able to seize all strategic points in the city and depose the government. Thus did the present communist regime come to power in Russia.

Soviet Russia

For nearly half a century now the rulers of Soviet Russia have been pursuing the goal of transforming the country into a socialist state with high living standards. They contrived an economic system radically different from our own; its operation has been characterized by upheaval, oppression and tragedy. The country suffered colossal disasters, through civil war, through invasion and wartime devastation, through natural calamities such as drought, through the monumental blunders committed by its leaders. To achieve their purposes the Soviet rulers adopted drastic and sweeping measures which imposed intense privation upon the Russian people;

they imprisoned millions and were responsible for the death of millions. The country achieved magnificent victories in the war against Germany; in peacetime it performed technological feats unmatched elsewhere in the world—while large sectors of the economy were primitive and the standard of living of its people was far below that of many other countries. Living conditions have markedly improved in Russia in recent years and there are indications that oppression and terror have ceased to be the normal instrument of government administration. Nevertheless, the Russian standard of living is still far below our own, and liberties that we take for granted are totally lacking.

What is this economic system of theirs and how does it work?

State Ownership of the Means of Production

On the day following the Revolution, Lenin signed a decree which abolished private ownership of land, without compensation to the owners. All land was declared to be the property of the state, with farm land to be allocated to individuals who would cultivate it themselves, the allocation to be carried out by local committees. A number of large estates were reserved, to be operated as state farms. Actually in many areas the peasants had already seized the property of landowners and divided it up among themselves, without waiting for government decrees.

The banks and other key organizations were nationalized at once, as were those enterprises whose owners had fled the country or had abandoned their properties. In a good many factories the workers simply took control, ousting the owner or manager, and ran the plant to suit themselves. To halt the spreading anarchy and to maintain production of goods desperately needed to fight the counter-revolution, the government nationalized all small enterprises as well. During the "War Communism" period of 1918-21, money virtually ceased to have value. The government seized food from the peasants; industrial production was directed by government decrees; workers were given food and goods.

When the civil war ended Lenin introduced the New Economic Policy (NEP) under which free enterprise was permitted in several sectors of the economy. Private individuals were permitted to engage in retail and wholesale trade; small industrial plants were leased to private operators or restored to their former owners. The government retained tight control only of the "commanding heights" of the economy: large industry, transport, banking, foreign trade. The highly successful operations of free enterprise alarmed the communist rulers; very soon after permitting it they took steps to repress it. Heavy taxes were imposed on privately operated firms; restrictions were imposed on their purchases from state-owned enterprises; new regulations made it difficult or impossible for them to transport goods by rail. By 1931, just ten years after it had been introduced by the NEP, private enterprise in trade and industry virtually ceased to exist. In 1932 the buying and selling of goods for private profit was made illegal. Cooperatives were tolerated, in both industry and trade, these being considered socialistic and therefore compatible with the goals of the regime. The relative importance of cooperatives has been small, however; the overwhelming proportion of goods is produced by state enterprises and is distributed by state agencies.

The Collective Farms

In 1928 the government embarked upon a campaign to amalgamate small peasant holdings into large farms which would be collectively owned and operated. Two major objectives were involved. Larger farm units would be more efficient, it was believed, and would be easier to deal with and control; the government would experience less difficulty in obtaining from the countryside the food it needed to supply urban populations. Secondly, individualistic agriculture enabled the more able, energetic and ambitious peasants to acquire substantial land holdings together with considerable numbers of cattle and a good deal of equipment; these "kulaks" were generally hostile to the regime, and in any case their very existence was intolerable to Communists opposed in principle to private ownership of the means of production. Using a combination of persuasion, inducement, confiscation, force and terror, the government carried through the collectivization programme. By 1936 individual land holdings virtually ceased to exist, having been amalgamated into some 246,000 collective farms, on which lived more than 20 million farm families. Following the War, groups of collective farms were amalgamated to form larger operating units, reducing their number to about 50,000.

The collective farms currently occupy some 66 per cent of the sown area of the Soviet Union. The state farms account for another 30 per cent, the remainder being composed of small private holdings operated by individual farmers and urban workers. Private plots exists on the collectives as well: each family is allotted a small area—no more than an acre or two—for its own use. In outward form each collective farm is

> ". . . a democratic, cooperative association of farmers who have pooled their land and capital to form a large enterprise, which they operate in common, sharing its net proceeds in proportion to the quantity and quality of the work they do."[6]

While, theoretically, the farm is run by elected officers, with ultimate authority residing in the general meeting of all members, in fact farm officials are often appointed and removed by the government or the local Communist Party.

Soviet Economic Planning

Production is carried out in Russia according to plans drawn up by specialized planning agencies. The central planning authority (GOSPLAN) draws up the master plan for the country as a whole, which sets forth the amounts to be produced of all goods and services during the period of the plan. Before announcing the plan,

[6]H. Schwartz, *Russia's Soviet Economy* (Englewood Cliffs, 1950), p. 259.

GOSPLAN would first have ascertained what productive capacity there actually existed in each industry. The government would indicate what kinds of goods ought to be emphasized; GOSPLAN would then draw up a plan which reflected the priorities laid down by the government and which, to be fulfilled, would require the fullest possible use of the country's productive capacity.

Each individual enterprise in the country would ultimately be assigned an output quota for the period of the plan (usually five years). The planned output of each industry would be the amount of its product required to carry out some other part of the overall plan. For example, suppose that the country had four steel-producing firms and three implement-manufacturing firms. Plans might be drawn up as follows:

Steel Industry			*Implement Industry*		
Planned Output of Steel			Planned Consumption of Steel		
By Firm A	10,000	tons	By Firm X	10,000	tons
By Firm B	15,000	"	By Firm Y	25,000	"
By Firm C	20,000	"	By Firm Z	35,000	"
By Firm D	25,000	"			
Total Planned			Total Planned		
Output	70,000	"	Consumption	70,000	"

Obviously if each steel firm produces its planned output, each implement firm will be able to obtain all the steel it requires to fulfil its plan. Similar plans would be drawn up for the industries producing the other materials needed by implement firms, to ensure that they were all produced in the appropriate amounts. The overall national plan would provide for the production of specific amounts of consumer goods and services, government goods and services, machinery and equipment, and the construction of buildings. Exact production plans would be made only for highly important items which were of strategic importance in the economy and whose output could be effectively controlled. In the case of less important goods and agricultural products of which the output would inevitably be affected by weather and the like, the planners would merely indicate targets rather than assign precise production quotas.

Each enterprise is continuously supervised to ensure that it is fulfilling its quota; such supervision is exercised by agents of the planning authority, by banks from which the firm obtains credit, by the local branch of the Communist Party, by its own workers. Changes may be made in plans, as a result of developments that were not foreseen when the plans were drawn up.

The Use of Money

While production in Russia is planned, goods are bought and sold, and money is required as a medium of exchange. All goods and services have prices fixed by the state, and the price must be paid by whoever wishes to obtain any good or service.

Firms must pay wages to their workers and must pay for the materials they receive from other firms; each firm has a money income amounting to the value of the goods it sells. Along with the production plan drawn up for each enterprise, a financial plan is prepared which sets forth planned receipts from sales and planned expenditures on labour, materials and other items. To make necessary payments the firm has a certain amount of capital of its own and its receipts from sales; in addition it can borrow from the state bank. Consumer goods are sold in retail stores; members of the public buy them with the income they have earned. Prices are set so as to achieve equality between the aggregate value of all consumer goods and the total spendable income of the general public.

The Managers of Firms

Every enterprise has a manager who will have been chosen by the local Communist Party; very likely he will be a member of the party himself. His primary responsibility is to ensure that the plant produces the amount specified by the planners. Although bound by numerous regulations and provided with a limited budget, the manager of a firm possesses considerable freedom of action; according to informed observers of the Russian scene, managers frequently break the rules in order to operate successfully. What is more, the manager who gets results is not chastised for his rule-breaking.

The manager is free to make his own arrangements with suppliers of materials and the buyers of his plant's products. (To obtain high priority materials he will require an allocation order from the authority which is responsible for their distribution.) He can make his own arrangements for advances from the state bank. He can hire staff as he sees fit and can dismiss employees whose work is unsatisfactory. He is subject to constant supervision, however, from above and below: from the local Communist Party, the local press, the banks from which he obtains credit and the workers' organization in the plant. But while he may be criticized by these agencies, he cannot be controlled by them; so long as he is the manager he can do as he sees fit, regardless of their criticism.

The manager has no power to set the price of his firm's products, or the wages of its workers, or the prices of the material he buys; these are all fixed by the state. Characteristically, the selling price of his product will be fixed so as to cover costs and yield a small profit. If the plant produces more than its quota, or produces at less than the planned cost, it will earn more than the planned profit.

Profit is used in three ways: one part is taken in tax by the government; another part is kept by the firm either to increase its financial resources or to be invested in additional plant or equipment; four per cent of planned profit and fifty per cent of the profit realized above the planned figure is allotted to the "manager's fund."[7] Out of this fund the manager may pay bonuses, build or repair workers' housing, provide cultural and recreational facilities for the use of plant personnel.

[7]These were the pre-war figures; it is not known whether they apply currently.

Managers are understandably keen to earn profits, and the state welcomes them in so far as they reflect productive efficiency. However, the primary responsibility of the plant is to produce its assigned quota; if ever the earning of profit conflicts with fulfilment of the quota then it takes second place. Firms are required to suffer losses, if necessary, to produce the planned output.

The Earnings of Individuals

"Work in the U.S.S.R. is a duty and a matter of honour for every able-bodied citizen, in accordance with the principle: 'He who does not work, neither shall he eat.' " So runs Article 12 of the Soviet Constitution. But how much should people receive for their work? From the very beginning the regime sought to apply the principle of piece rates, i.e. that people should be paid according to the amount of work they did. Policy varied from time to time on the issue of whether higher rates should be paid for work that was more skilled. During the period of War Communism there was very little difference between the wage rates of skilled and unskilled workers, reflecting in part the widespread belief that under a communist regime there should be no great inequalities of income. Policy was reversed in 1920-21, after it became evident that without a financial incentive to acquire skill many workers would remain unskilled and production would be correspondingly smaller than might be achieved. In 1927 policy was again reversed; new wage scales provided for a substantial reduction in the differential between skilled and unskilled pay. Again the effects on production were unfavourable and in 1931 the principle was laid down that skilled men should be paid at higher rates than unskilled; it has been in effect ever since. Pay differentials based on skill are in fact greater in Russia than in Canada or the United States; whereas in the latter two countries the rate of pay of the most highly skilled operative in any plant is unlikely to be more than double that of an unskilled labourer, in a good many Russian firms the rate of pay of the most highly skilled men is over four times as great as that of unskilled labourers.

Scales of pay are set by the government, and occasionally altered in order to achieve particular objectives. To attract additional workers to a certain trade or to a certain region of the country, new, higher rates of pay might be introduced. Dangerous and disagreeable work would also be paid at higher rates.

The great majority of Russian workers are paid on a piece rate basis. For each job an hourly or daily "norm" of output is established, and workers who produce this quantity are paid at the standard rate; for output above the norm the worker is paid at a higher rate. In a good many cases "progressive piece rates" are paid: for each additional unit above the norm the worker is paid at a progressively higher rate. Where a number of men form a single production team, piece work rates and a norm would be set for the team as a whole.

There is keen competition in Russia for executive and professional jobs, partly because of the superior rewards attached. Persons in these employments are likely to receive from seven to twenty times the average earned by ordinary work people. Eminent professors, for instance, may have total incomes, comprised of salary, royalties, consultants' fees and prizes, amounting to about twenty times what is earned by an average worker. Plant managers receive substantial salaries; in addition, for fulfilling and over-fulfilling their production quotas, they receive bonuses which may be nearly as great as the salaries themselves.

In addition to earning higher pay, outstanding workers and professional persons are likely to receive special privileges such as better-than-ordinary housing and free vacations at attractive resorts. Workers may receive honours and awards such as the "Order of Lenin," "Order of the Red Banner," or be made a "Hero of Labour"; outstanding writers and scientists may be awarded prizes, and so on.

Soviet Public Finance

Like the government of any other country, the Soviet government needs money to maintain the nation's armed forces, to maintain its educational establishments and civil administration, to make welfare payments to individuals. Because the state in Russia owns virtually all industrial enterprises in the country, the Soviet government needs money as well to finance investment in new plant capacity. In Canada, of course, funds for this purpose are obtained from private investors by privately owned firms. The Soviet government budget is drawn up as part of the nation's overall economic plan, and constitutes a very large and important sector of the plan.

The government's annual revenues are derived primarily from five sources: the "turnover tax," the tax on profits, the tax on personal incomes, social payments, and the sale of government bonds.

The turnover tax, which provides about two-thirds of the government's total revenue, is essentially a sales tax levied at the producer's level. On industrial goods it is paid by the manufacturing firm; on agricultural products it is paid by the agency which acquires them from the farm. The rate of tax is not uniform; military equipment and capital goods are taxed only lightly or not at all; consumer goods are taxed very heavily, with the rate varying as between different goods. Generally speaking, the tax imposed on each good is the difference between its cost of production and the price at which the planned output can be sold in the market.[8]

[8]Figure 1 illustrates. D represents the market demand for the product; OQ represents the planned output; OR represents the cost of production per unit. With output amounting to only OQ, a price of OP could be charged; the tax rate would be set at RP per unit.

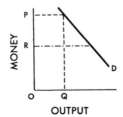

Figure 1.

The rate of tax levied on the profits of firms varies from industry to industry, from year to year, and from region to region. A low rate is imposed on industries whose expansion is considered desirable, so as to leave them with ample funds for investment. The amount of tax levied on any individual firm would depend upon how much investment capital it was considered desirable for that firm to have.

Soviet citizens are liable to a progressive income tax, the rates being very much lower than those levied in Canada or the United States. Different schedules are applied to workers, to members of collective farms, to writers and artists, with the most favourable schedule applied to workers. Members of collective farms pay income tax on a slightly higher schedule; writers and artists who receive very high incomes are liable to very much higher rates. The relatively low rates imposed on workers and farmers reflects the Soviet view that people who have superior skills and work harder should receive correspondingly higher pay; steep income tax rates which reduced income differentials would reduce the incentive to acquire skill and to work hard.

While individual decisions to buy bonds are "voluntary", people are expected to spend from five to eight per cent of their income on bond purchases.

Soviet Economic Problems

Despite spectacular achievements in some fields, per capita output in Russia is far below the Canadian and U.S. figures and the general standard of living is correspondingly lower. In part the Russian inferiority is attributable to handicaps for which the Communist regime cannot be blamed, including the backwardness of the country in 1917 and the devastation wrought by war. It is clear, however, that the economic system is also to blame for some of the country's difficulties, and many of its achievements are due not to the economic system but rather to the prodigious efforts put forth by the people and the monumental sacrifices they bore.

The phrase "planned economy" sounds well but in practice gives rise to endless problems. It is administered by a vast bureaucracy, necessarily according to rigid rules. When unexpected developments occur which require decisions, people on the spot may refuse to make them because of regulations or may be fearful of making them because of possible repercussions. The necessary decisions are made after long delays by distant bureaucrats who know nothing of the local situation. All elements in a plan are interdependent. Failure to produce the planned output of spark plugs may render useless the supplies of all the other components required to produce automobiles.[9]

All too often plant managers find it expedient to conceal information from the planning authorities and to operate in a fashion contrary to the national inter-

[9]To obtain critically required supplies of needed components or materials plant managers may depend on "blat"—influence—or may employ "tolkachi"—salesmen in reverse who call on suppliers, and, by judicious gift-giving and smooth public relations, wheedle out the wanted goods.

est. Managers understate the capacity of their plants in order to have low quotas which can easily be fulfilled. Since his quota is set in terms of quantity only, a plant manager may skimp on quality in order to produce quantity; complaints are frequent of the shoddiness of consumer goods. Because, understandably, he lacks confidence that he will obtain materials and equipment when he needs them in the future, a manager will seize any opportunity to obtain them, even when he has no immediate use for them. Many managers, to play safe, order far more than they actually need; sometimes they get all they ordered. While some firms are short, unneeded materials and equipment are hoarded by others. Some managers pad their reports, claiming credit for non-existent output, so that they can appear to have fulfilled their quotas or to have qualified for bonuses.

Whereas Canada and the United States must deal with the awkward dilemma of farm surpluses, the Russians have experienced the explosive problem of farm shortages. Adverse weather has been a factor, but weaknesses in the Communist administration of agriculture have been major contributory causes. Elaborate bureaucracies have been created on the collective farms, staffed by persons who would contribute far more to output by working in the fields. The methods of payment have failed to elicit from workers the full effort of which they are capable. Many families stint the amount of work they perform for the collective, preferring to apply themselves to their private plots. Output from these plots has been more than proportionate to the acreage cultivated.

Recognizing the enormous drawbacks involved in rigid adherence to the dogmas of "planning" and "collectivism," the regime in the early 1960s, significantly modified its economic policies. In accordance with the proposals of the economist Evsei Liberman, a considerable number of industries were freed of control by the planners; the managers were allowed to make their own output decisions, with a view to earning maximum profit. Collective farm workers were paid wages rather than given a share of the farm's output. Russian authorities reported that economic performance improved appreciably wherever these reforms were introduced.[10]

Communism in China

Chinese Communists overthrew the government of Chiang Kai Shek in 1949 and established themselves as the country's rulers. Having studied the experience of Soviet Russia, and aided by material and technical aid from that country, they set about to create a socialist society. A programme of land redistribution was introduced: land was confiscated from landlords and rich peasants and distributed among poor peasants and agricultural labourers. Key industries were nationalized and comprehensive economic planning was adopted. The nationalization measures were

---

[10]The liberalization was apparently limited in both scale and duration. By the later 1960s party leaders were decrying profit as a production guide and emphasizing the need for centrally controlled planning.

not so sweeping as one might imagine: a good deal of the country's industry was already state-owned when the Communists seized power, and a considerable number of the firms that were still in private hands were left with their owners. It was expected, however, that these firms would ultimately be nationalized; in the meantime they were required to comform absolutely to the government's economic plans.

Sweeping measures were introduced during the 1950s to speed the country's progress. As the rulers of Russia had done twenty years before, the new rulers of China embarked upon a massive programme of agricultural collectivization. Vigorous and dramatic measures were adopted to achieve rapid industrial advance, to make a "great leap forward." However, it became evident after a relatively short period that many ambitious industrial projects were ill-considered and unrealistic, harmful rather than helpful. The agricultural communes into which people were forced failed to fulfil the high hopes; they were, it is true, afflicted by natural calamity such as drought, but by the Communists' own admission, mismanagement, errors in judgment and peasant hostility contributed to the difficulties. It became necessary to modify the collectivization programme and to plan for a slower rate of industrial advance. The scanty reports reaching the outside world suggest that after a period of political turmoil in the late 1960s the country began to achieve substantial progress on a number of major economic fronts.

COMMUNISM AND FREE ENTERPRISE: A COMPARISON

An economic system is a many-splendoured thing; it performs a great number of functions and has many attributes. In comparing the merits of different systems multiple criteria must be employed; the following, it is suggested, are the most important in a comparison of free enterprise and communism.

1. Production in accordance with the people's wishes. Here the free enterprise system is unquestionably superior. The goods produced are those the public wishes to buy; production responds sensitively to changes in buyers' preferences. Errors in judgment are made from time to time, of course, but when it becomes apparent that the public does not want a particular good, its production is speedily discontinued. It is true that buyers are influenced by advertising, but the effect of advertising is primarily to influence the distribution among competing firms of a customer demand which already exists. People buy electrical appliances and automobiles because they are pleasant things to have; the main consequence of the advertising effort devoted to these products is to decide how purchases are distributed between General Electric and Westinghouse and among Ford, Chrysler and General Motors.

In a planned economy, on the other hand, a small group of bureaucrats decides what shall be produced. They are unlikely to know all the enormous diversity of tastes which exists among the public at large; they will inevitably tend to order the production of standardized products which, in a great many cases, fail to satisfy individual preferences. Because of the rigidity of bureaucratic arrangements, production will not be readily adjusted to meet shifts in public demand. Where the planners are responsible not to the public at large but to a self-perpetuating power group like the communist party, they may deliberately impose a production plan which is contrary to the public's wishes. They may emphasize the production of capital goods, so that the current generation is forced to endure privation in order that future generations enjoy abundance. They may emphasize the production of space vehicles rather than consumer goods, partly for political reasons, and partly because a space programme is relatively simple to administer; production and distribution of the kind of consumer goods people would like to have are difficult and complex operations and cruelly reveal the inadequacies of bureaucratic planning.

2. Full employment of productive capacity. It is obviously desirable that the productive resources of a country should be fully utilized, that there should be no waste due to unemployment and aggravated by the psychic costs which unemployment imposes. In free enterprise countries, financial obstacles have been responsible for a great deal of unemployment in the past. We have devised techniques for preventing unemployment, but they are as yet not wholly effective. In this respect it must be admitted that Soviet Russia has proven superior; there has been no really significant unemployment in that country since 1930. Communist economic arrangements ensure that the country's firms will always want to hire more workers than are actually available, so that any person who wants to work can always find a job. Such unemployment as has occurred has been attributable primarily to errors and breakdowns in planning: workers have been idle for lack of materials that were not arranged for in drawing up plans or were not produced because some firms failed to fulfil their quotas.

3. Equitable distribution of the goods produced. What is equitable? Should people receive incomes corresponding to the contribution they make to output? Should all people receive the same income? Should people receive incomes according to their needs?

In fact each of these criteria can be applied under both free enterprise and communism, and inequities can develop under both systems. A communist regime may determine the incomes that people receive through its power to set wage scales. In a free enterprise economy, the government, through taxation, transfer payments and free government services, can also achieve practically whatever income distribution it cares to. Under both systems equalitarian distribution of income may harm production by removing incentives to work hard and to acquire additional skill. Under both systems some people may get far more than they genuinely deserve: under free enterprise some individuals receive incomes which are far greater than the value of their contribution to production; under communism some individuals who occupy strategic positions in the hierarchy are able to grab a great deal for themselves.

4. Procedure for selecting managers. Good managers are needed in any modern industrial society. Whether it be communist or capitalist there will be enterprises in which staff and equipment are employed and which should be run by the most competent people available. One criterion whereby to judge the relative merit of different economic systems is the efficacy of their methods for recruiting managerial personnel.

In Soviet Russia, as we have seen, managers are nominated by the communist party; the possibility exists, accordingly, that a person will be chosen on the basis of party loyalty and connections rather than managerial competence. However, it must be admitted that all is not perfect in free enterprise societies: inherited wealth, nepotism and "influence" are the reasons for the appointment of a good many people to administrative positions.

A free enterprise society does possess one very great advantage: individuals can select themselves as managers by setting up their own enterprise. This possibility can be supremely valuable. In any society the groups which have the power to select managers may assess candidates on the basis of irrelevant or outmoded criteria; a person who is fresh and different may be rejected. In a communist society such a person would have no recourse; in a free enterprise society he can set up his own firm, with benefit to himself and to the country as a whole.

5. The rate of economic progress. Soviet Russia, it is acknowledged, has been achieving a more rapid rate of growth than have Canada and the United States. But while they are impressive, the statistics indicate nothing about the relative merits of communism and free enterprise as economic systems. There are countries with free enterprise systems, notably Japan and West Germany, whose rate of economic growth surpasses that of Russia. The slower rate of economic growth of Canada and the U.S. reflects in part the fact that their standard of living is already very high, and they do not really need great quantities of additional material goods. As J. K. Galbraith has pointed out, a change in the composition of their output would probably be more desirable than simply increase in its size. Finally, Russia's rapid economic growth has been achieved, in large part, through concentration of productive capacity on the output of capital goods rather than housing and consumer goods; intense privation has been imposed on the Russian people. It is a moot point whether rapid economic growth is worth such a price; available evidence suggests that if the Russian people had had any choice in the matter they would not have paid it.

6. The concentration of power. Under communism both political and economic power are concentrated in the hands of the small number of persons who control the government. These people are chosen by the communist party rather than by the public at large. But even if they had been elected through a genuinely democratic process, the complete concentration of power in their hands would involve serious drawbacks and dangers. Power corrupts, it has been shrewdly observed, and absolute power corrupts absolutely. The broad dispersion of economic power which characterizes a free enterprise society limits the harm which can be done through the abuse of power by individuals who possess it. Every powerful individual is held in check by the countervailing power of others. Where one group exercises complete political and economic control, the restraint of countervailing power is lacking. While it is true that great abuse has occurred under free enterprise systems, complete economic control by the state creates the possibility of greater abuses of its own.

7. The preferred way of life. In our society a great many persons keenly desire to be their own masters. They would be dissatisfied if they had to be employees, carrying out orders issued by others; they prize the freedom to make their own decisions, with all its possibilities and risks. They wish to have their abilities assessed impersonally by the public in the market-place rather than by one individual or a small group of individuals who stand immediately above in a hierarchy. Under communism such persons must necessarily suffer frustration. If they are unfairly dealt with by their superiors they have no recourse, no alternative to turn to. What is more, a society which includes a large number of persons who are their own masters is likely to be characterized by a great degree of vigour and independence. The free enterprise system, in short, makes possible a way of life which appeals to individuals and buttresses the society in which they live.

As we have seen in earlier chapters, a modern free enterprise community requires a sense of social responsibility on the part of its members. If private power groups contend, unrestrainedly and irresponsibly, for larger shares of the national income, they may bring on inflations which will spawn a whole host of evils and threaten the very viability of the economic system. Governments very likely will have to play larger roles than heretofore to ensure that free enterprise systems perform acceptably.

SUMMARY

Modern capitalist free enterprise society emerged out of the feudalism of the Middle Ages, developing to its present form over a period of centuries. The inequality of wealth and income which characterized each generation stirred numerous critics and reformers who put forward various panaceas. The most influential was Karl Marx who in the mid-nineteenth century advocated the overthrow of the capitalist system by force and the establishment of a new classless communistic society. Successful revolutions were in fact carried out in Russia and China during the twentieth century by adherents of Marxism. In both countries the new regimes set about to create a communistic society.

In Russia today the state owns virtually all the means of production and the economic activities of the country are planned by a central agency. Money is used as a medium of exchange, and substantial differences in income exist, these being considered necessary to provide incentive for self-betterment through education and hard work. Established three decades later, the Communist regime of China has followed Russia's example, albeit with some highly significant deviations.

While Soviet Russia has recorded some striking achievements it has also suffered colossal setbacks and the general standard of living is low. Unavoidable calamities have been partly responsible but weaknesses implicit in the economic system have also contributed.

A careful comparison of the features of the socialist and free enterprise systems indicates that in most significant respects the free enterprise system is likely to prove more effective and desirable.

FOR REVIEW AND DISCUSSION

1. In your opinion, what are the most significant merits of the free enterprise system and of the socialist system?
2. Evaluate the contributions to economic thought made by the French Utopian writers of the nineteenth century. To what extent, if any, have their ideas been adopted in North America?
3. Explain Marx's "Labour Theory of Value." Does it provide an adequate explanation of market prices? Explain.
4. According to Marx the proletarian revolution could occur successfully only in a country which had attained advanced industrial status; in fact the first such revolution occurred in a country that was agricultural and primitive. Explain.
5. Contrast the Soviet economic system with that of Canada.
6. Contrast Syndicalism with Fabianism.
7. It has been said that the communist and free enterprise economic systems have been moving toward each other, diminishing the contrast between them. Do you agree? Justify your answer.
8. "As the Russians have discovered, agriculture does not lend itself to central planning." Discuss.

INDEX